THE AMERICAN PLANNER

THE AMERICAN PLANNER
BIOGRAPHIES AND RECOLLECTIONS

SECOND EDITION

EDITED BY
DONALD A. KRUECKEBERG

CENTER
FOR URBAN
POLICY RESEARCH

First published in 1983 by Methuen, Inc., New York
Published in Great Britain by Methuen & Co., Ltd., London

Second edition © 1994 by Donald A. Krueckeberg

Published by the Center for Urban Policy Research
New Brunswick, New Jersey 08903

Printed in the United States of America on recycled paper

Interior designed by Judith Martin Waterman
Martin-Waterman Associates, Ltd.

Cover designed by Leslie Mullen Graphic Art

Library of Congress Cataloging-in-Publication Data

The American planner : biographies and recollections / edited by
    Donald A. Krueckeberg. — 2nd ed.
        p.   cm.
    Includes bibliographical references and index.
    ISBN 0-88285-148-9
        1. City planners—United States.   2. City planners—United States—
Biography.   3. Regional planning—United States.   I. Krueckeberg,
Donald A.   II. Rutgers University.   Center for Urban Policy
Research.
HT167.A5767   1994
307.1'2'092273—dc20
[B]
                                                        94-6087
                                                          CIP

CONTENTS

LIST OF FIGURES

ACKNOWLEDGMENTS

IT IS EASY TO SAY, because it is true, that the old debts from the first edition carry over to this one, for without the first there would be no second. However, it is difficult to know where the new debts begin. In part, as I admit in chapter 1, the new introduction, they begin with the critics of the earlier work.

I know that thanks are long overdue to Stephen Kalish, professor of law, and Robert Audi, professor of philosophy, both at the University of Nebraska at Lincoln. They led an interdisciplinary seminar, "Ethics in the Professions: Moral Theories and Contemporary Problems," in the summer of 1990, in which I eagerly participated. I am thankful also for the stimulation and encouragement of the other eleven participants, especially Sue Hendler of Queen's University at Kingston in Ontario, Canada, the other planner in the group. Preparation for that seminar, as well as time to follow its leads, was made possible by a Faculty Academic Study Program leave from Rutgers—The State University of New Jersey for the calendar year 1990, which I gratefully acknowledge.

Those weeks in Nebraska sparked an interest in Alasdair MacIntyre's 1984 book, *After Virtue* (Notre Dame, Indiana, University of Notre Dame Press) that was shared by several colleagues here in New Brunswick for a semester the following year. They were George Carey, Mark Lapping, and Dona Schneider, all of Rutgers, and my good friend Jeffrey Eaton, pastor of Emanual Evangelical Lutheran Church in New Brunswick and formerly of the faculty of philosophy at Hamilton College in Clinton, New York.

Some of the motivation emanates from deceased friends and colleagues, whose passing steps each year increase their pace and number: I think especially of Donald Sullivan at Hunter College in

New York, Stewart Marquis at the University of Michigan in Ann Arbor, and David Hill at the University of Colorado in Denver.

Two young scholars subjected several drafts of the new introduction to intense but patient correction of my history and English; many thanks to my son, John Krueckeberg, at the University of Arizona in Tucson and to Adam Rabiner at Rutgers. Thanks also go to John Forester of Cornell University in Ithaca, New York, who, after hours of argument and years of prodding, finally got me to read the work of Martha C. Nussbaum on the relationship between literature and moral philosophy—*Love's Knowledge* (New York: Oxford University Press, 1990)—that shed new light for me on the nature of biography.

I am especially pleased with the authors whose work newly appears in this edition and I am very grateful for their contributions: Irving D. Fisher, Susan Marie Wirka, John L. Thomas, Eugenie Ladner Birch, George C. Hemmens, Tridib Banerjee, and Michael Southworth.

I am also grateful to H. John von Knorring, president of Routledge, Chapman and Hall, for graciously cooperating in the transfer of rights from the first edition, published in 1983 by Methuen, a division of Routledge, Chapman and Hall. Thanks also to George Thompson of the Center for American Places in Harrisonburg, Virginia, John Reps of Cornell, and Richard Foglesong of Rollins College in Winter Park, Florida; each gave me encouragement over the years to find some way of getting this book into a paperback edition. Robert W. Lake, editor in chief of the Center for Urban Policy Research Press, was there when it finally came together, and his enthusiasm and support have been important. Thanks also go to Arlene H. Pashman, senior editor; to Denice Anderson, copy editor; to Leslie Mullen of Leslie Mullen Graphic Art, Kendall Park, New Jersey, for the cover design; and to Judith Martin Waterman of Martin-Waterman Associates, Ltd., Highland Park, New Jersey, for interior design and production.

Donald A. Krueckeberg
New Brunswick, New Jersey
Easter 1993

ABOUT THE EDITOR

Donald A. Krueckeberg is a professor of urban planning and policy development at the Edward J. Bloustein School of Planning and Public Policy, Rutgers University, New Brunswick, New Jersey. His other books are *Introduction to Planning History in the United States* (1983), *Local Population and Employment Projection Techniques* with Michael R. Greenberg and Connie O. Hughes (1978), and *Urban Planning Analysis: Methods and Models* with Arthur L. Silvers (1974). He was president of the Association of Collegiate Schools of Planning from 1987 to 1989 and editor of the *Journal of the American Planning Association* from 1976 through 1978. His Ph.D. in City Planning (1966) and M.C.P. (1962) are from the University of Pennsylvania, and his B.S. in Urban Planning (1960) is from Michigan State University. He was born in Fort Wayne and grew up in Mishawaka, Indiana. His current research focuses on planning history and Africa.

ABOUT THE CONTRIBUTORS

TRIDIB BANERJEE is a professor of urban and regional planning at the University of Southern California, Los Angeles, California.

EUGENIE LADNER BIRCH is a professor of urban planning at Hunter College of the City University of New York, New York.

HENRY CHURCHILL (deceased) was the author of *The City Is the People* (New York: Harcourt, Brace and World, 1945) and practiced architecture and planning in New York City and Philadelphia.

IRVING D. FISHER is a professor of political and social thought at the University of Southern Maine, Portland, Maine.

LAURENCE C. GERCKENS is a professor and the president of the On-call Faculty Program of Hilliard, Ohio, and is an emeritus professor of city and regional planning at Ohio State University, Columbus, Ohio.

JOHN HANCOCK is a professor of urban planning at the University of Washington, Seattle, Washington.

GEORGE C. HEMMENS is a professor of urban planning and policy at the University of Illinois at Chicago, Illinois.

NORMAN J. JOHNSTON is an emeritus professor of urban planning at the University of Washington, Seattle, Washington.

HARVEY A. KANTOR (deceased) was an assistant professor of American urban history at the University of Rhode Island, Kingston, Rhode Island.

DONALD A. KRUECKEBERG is a professor of urban planning and policy development at Rutgers—The State University of New Jersey, New Brunswick, New Jersey.

THOMAS J. SCHLERETH is a professor of American studies at the University of Notre Dame, Notre Dame, Indiana.

MICHAEL SOUTHWORTH is an associate professor of city and regional planning at the University of California at Berkeley, California.

BERNARD TAPER is a professor of journalism at the University of California at Berkeley, California.

JOHN L. THOMAS is George L. Littlefield Professor of American history at Brown University, Providence, Rhode Island.

SUSAN MARIE WIRKA is a doctoral student in the graduate program in women's history at the University of Wisconsin-Madison, Wisconsin.

THE AMERICAN PLANNER

I

THE AMERICAN PLANNER
A NEW INTRODUCTION

DONALD A. KRUECKEBERG

WHY PLANNING BIOGRAPHY?

THIS IS A BOOK ABOUT the urban and regional planners who have shaped the American landscape over the last one hundred years. It is a book about people whose heads were filled with theories and whose hearts were filled with aspirations, who strove to make a better world. They are only a few of many such planners. They found their roles by accident of birth and fate as well as strength and conviction. Like you and I, they also made mistakes, experienced failure, and were not always the good guys they set out to be—but in the resonance of their lives is a collective richness of ideas and experience. They overcame their fears and discouragements, handicaps and inhibitions long enough to make an indelible mark on the design of modern America.

I edited the first edition of this collection ten years ago (D. Krueckeberg, 1983). When I conceived of the project, I thought of it as something that would be fun to read—no numbers, no equations, no jargon—a sort of beach book for planners. While it did not sell a lot of copies, those who read it seemed to like it. The reviews were all pretty good except for two that really got under my skin. One of these said the book contained too much hagiography. While the dictionary told me that this might mean it was too biblical, the

I

real meaning was that it treated its subjects too much like saints. Their true characters, as one scholar put it, were camouflaged by the writers' motives. The other criticism was that the book was not very good social history. This was especially irritating because I thought biography was not social history.[1]

For years I have been telling my doctoral students that only after they have finished writing their dissertations will they discover what their research problem *really* was about. About a year ago I picked up *The American Planner* again—having in mind those nagging criticisms of it—and reread my "Introduction." I discovered what the book was really meant to be about. I had begun by quoting Dick Bolan (1981) and Allan Jacobs (1981), each having recently published reviews in which they expressed a deep emotional response to the books they were reviewing, calling up the humanistic vision that had drawn them into the field of planning in the first place. The "Introduction" concluded with the moral code of the great sociologist/planner Louis Wirth from a speech he made in 1947 entitled "Planning Means Freedom," later called "A Planner's Creed." I realized then what was important. The biographies and recollections were about visions, emotions, and what I thought planners should believe in.

Is it obvious that the telling of life stories is the study of life's meanings? It took me eight years to figure it out. The real value of contemplating people's lives is in discerning how their moral nature was created, tested, changed, and ultimately endured. So there is more to biography than just providing role models or molding heroes out of hacks wearing hair shirts. Biography done well is not just the collection of a person's facts—"facts-shoveled-on-facts," as Marc Pachter calls it, "in which the biographer buries alive both his hero and his reader" (Pachter, 1979, p. 3). What really sets it off is the revealing of the hidden self, of the underlying myth, of the shared experience and meaning that links the subject's and the reader's inner lives. Not all biography achieves this—and certainly not in the same way for everyone—but when it works, it is powerful. "There is some one Myth for every man," said William Butler Yeats, "which, if we but knew it, would make us understand all that he did and thought" (Kaplan, 1979, p. 46).

Empathy is essential to that kind of understanding. We want to feel Frederick Law Olmsted's frustration with constant financial failure; Mary Kingsbury Simkhovitch's heartache for the helpless old woman alone in her icy tenement; the loneliness of John Nolen's fatherless childhood; the love of Lewis Mumford and Catherine Bauer; and Rexford Tugwell's unspeakable anger with Robert Moses. We are not necessarily "edified" by the knowledge of these conditions, says Pachter, "but we are warmed to the presence of a living being" (Pachter, 1979, p. 5).

The reader's empathy for the subject travels through the author. Thus, every biography presents two selves—that of the subject and that of the biographer. "Never does a man portray his own character more vividly than in his manner of portraying another," said John Paul Richter (Vandiver, 1983, p. 20). The same applies in the ultimate sense in the case of autobiography. Hans Blumenfeld admitted up front that his autobiography probably omitted things he had conveniently forgotten, and he reminds us that "Goethe entitled his memoirs *Dichtung und Wahrheit*—putting poetry ahead of truth" (Blumenfeld, 1987, p. 9). There is no such thing as definitive biography.

Biography and autobiography are not so different from fiction, in that each is trying to understand life. The author and critic Wallace Stegner overheard novelist John Cheever at a literary meeting respond to the question of why he wrote fiction; Cheever replied, "To make sense out of my life." Stegner elaborates:

> The life we all live is amateurish and accidental; it begins in accident and proceeds by trial and error toward dubious ends. . . . But the dream of man will not accept what nature hands us. We have to tinker with it, trying to give it purpose, direction and meaning—or, if we are of another turn of mind, trying to demonstrate that it *has* no purpose, direction, or meaning. Either way we can't let it alone (Stegner, 1992, p. 219).

"Personal history," in Alfred Kazin's interpretation, "is directly an effort to find salvation, to make one's own experience come out right" (Kazin, 1979, p. 79).

Our Western notion of self, history tells us, is a construct of culture and hence has certain limits. Its origins are in the mid-twelfth to thirteenth-century Europe, along with notions of romantic love, friendship, faith, and autobiography (Morris, 1972). We learn that the myths of culture produce the self as well as that the myths of self form the culture. This notion of the symbiotic relationship between self and culture leads to the view "that cultures are simply a collective version of the psyches that comprise it, and so the culture will possess the same traits as its members" (Erchak, 1992, p. 92). The danger of this view is to be overimpressed with the capacity of the individual to internalize and integrate the culture, as well as to exaggerate the ability of cultures to tolerate and support differences among individuals and nondominant groups. The notion of tranquil mutuality—of culture and personality in perfect balance and mutual determination—belies the conflicts of the unconscious, of wish, of emotion and fantasy, and of life that doesn't make sense. Historian Peter Gay, the interpreter of Sigmund Freud, calls these the stuff of the stubborn self—stubborn because culture is, for the individual, both "indispensable and stifling at the same time. . . . 'Somewhere in the child, somewhere in the adult,' Lionel Trilling tells us, 'there is a hard, irreducible, stubborn core of biological reason, which culture cannot reach and which reserves the right, which sooner or later it will exercise, to judge the culture and resist and revise it'" (Gay, 1985, p. 175).

Lewis Mumford, in his intellectual life and work, struggled with these questions of personality and American culture. Mumford's position, developed in the 1930s and 1940s, "rested on the simple proposition—taken for granted by the democratic theorists of the nineteenth century but forgotten by the twentieth century progressives—that a self-governing, self-acting and self-respecting person is the very foundation of democracy" (Lasch, 1980, p. 15). Herein, perhaps, lies the error of social ethics today that see the choices to be either selfishness or conformity. Mumford saw more clearly than most that these are not the choices. Located somewhere between the stubborn self and the stifling culture lay a possible community of self-control, self-esteem, and common purpose. "The real problem of life," he wrote, "both for men and for societies, is to keep the organism and the environment, the inner and the outer, the personality and its creative sources, in a state of tension wherein growth and renewal may continually take place" (Blake, 1990, p. 291; Mumford, 1930, p. 268).

We may go back now and ask again, must biography be social history? The answer, I believe, is yes—but it must also be something different. Insofar as it reveals the myths that people share, it is social history, and insofar as it reveals the hidden, stubborn self—that part that Trilling claims culture cannot reach—it is something different than social history. It is purely personal.

The role of good planning biography, then, is to show how particular planners acquired their own personality from the conflicting demands of self and culture and how that solution was reflected in these planners' social actions—actions that altered the connections between self and culture that made community both possible and impossible in American society. This is why good biography in planning is important—to reveal the myths and virtues of our profession in human terms, the wildest hopes, the darkest fears, the sweetest dreams, the worst offenses, the dullest foolishness we hide. In the sharing of these secrets, we form a culture, a community of ideas and contentions that define and redefine our salvation in our practices.

The planners whose lives and recollections are presented in this collection played no singular role in American culture: they strove to build, promote, resist, revise, and save it from its various corruptions. As planning educator Paul Niebanck has said, it is a wrenching experience to realize that we are part of the culture we seek to change and thus to find ourselves the object of our reformations. Still, we often wonder and doubt that we can do anything about anything at all. We can be lost, so much of the time, in the details of our daily lives that they occupy our entire vision. The present pretends it is not just the present but also the past and the future. These histories remind us that the past was often different from our daily lives—not so routine. The importance of recollection is that it reopens the imagination to thinking differently about the present and the future. Biographies personalize this experience. Through them, perhaps, we build a better understanding of ourselves and of our world.

ABOUT THIS NEW EDITION

I must at once admit that the biographies and recollections that follow often fall short of the lofty aims I have expressed for them—but would anyone have us aim lower? These chapters, with two major exceptions, are an edited collection of pieces that were not written for this presentation, so certainly the authors cannot be held responsible for a measure of good biography that may not be theirs. Even those two exceptions—chapter 8 on Alfred Bettman by Laurence C. Gerckens and chapter 17 on women in planning by Eugenie Ladner Birch—were written for the first edition and certainly without any exposure to the editor's present thoughts. Nonetheless, I have chosen in every case to include the following particular sixteen chapters because, of the many pieces that are available in the literature, these do their jobs best in my view. They were chosen partly for the extent to which they fit my ideal of good biography. In some cases, I would admit that they do not fit very well, but there were other objectives, too. Balance was important, between the number of early figures and later figures, between those with a narrower view of the field and those with a wider view, between those whose interests were in the law versus housing versus the environment versus design, and so on.

Four chapters in the first edition have been replaced by what I feel is more appropriate material on the same people. The former chapter called "Woman-made America" (Birch, 1978), which dealt with Edith Elmer Wood and Catherine Bauer and the battle for federal public housing policy, has been replaced by another chapter by Eugenie Ladner Birch, this one exclusively on Bauer, and one that treats her much more personably and comprehensively. The formerly separate chapters on Lewis Mumford (Goist, 1972) and Benton MacKaye (Ross, 1975) have been replaced by a single long chapter on the two of them. The former chapter on Rexford Tugwell and the New Deal's new towns (Myhra, 1973) has been supplanted by a paper on Tugwell's conflicts with Robert Moses over the New York City Planning Commission, one that focuses more on Tugwell's character and personal integrity and on the nature of planning in a democracy.

New chapters also include one on Frederick Law Olmsted's theories of design, which, while highly specialized in one aspect of Olmsted's life, really gets to the core of what Olmsted believed about his work. Olmsted, like Mumford, is an important historical figure in American intellectual history; hence, there is much more material to choose from than there is for more obscure planners. However, the choice is harder because papers are highly specialized, whereas in the case of less famous figures, say Henry Wright, the available materials are few and tend to be more comprehensive.

Other new material includes a chapter from Mary Kingsbury Simkhovitch's autobiographical *Here Is God's Plenty,* introduced by Susan Marie Wirka, whose master's thesis at the University of California at Los Angeles won a National Certificate of Merit from the Society for American City and Regional Planning History in 1991. Also added are excerpts from Hans Blumenfeld's autobiography and a chapter on Kevin Lynch by two of his former students.

Several old pieces had to be removed to make room for the new, including the excerpts from Edward Bassett's autobiography and the edited recollections of Ladislas Segoe, Coleman Woodbury, and Charles W. Eliot, 2nd. The true enthusiast may still find these in library copies of the first edition and, in the case of Bassett and Eliot, in prior publications.

One other improvement to this edition has been achieved by restructuring its organization. The first edition was divided into three parts or periods: the pioneers, the regionalists, and the professionals (or the progress of the profession!). I now find these individuals much more difficult to classify into simple boxes and the engine of progress harder to identify. So the best I have been able to do is to pair some of them on their similarities and to present them in roughly chronological order.. Hence, we begin with Frederick Law Olmsted and John Nolen from the City Beautiful movement; then Mary Kingsbury Simkhovitch and Benjamin C. Marsh from the City Social movement; then Walter D. Moody and Charles Dyer Norton from the early City Practical movement; and then Alfred Bettman and Harland Bartholomew, who might represent the later City Practical phase of the institutionalization of planning into government. At this point, we seem to cross a divide, to find Henry Wright, Lewis Mumford, and Benton MacKaye, who represent a more critical practice of planning conventions in their day, as do Catherine Bauer and Rexford G. Tugwell, who carry their critique into the national political arena. Hans Blumenfeld, Charles Abrams, and Kevin Lynch—all one of a kind, along with Bauer and Tugwell— also represent the rise of modern scholarship in the field. The final chapter, Eugenie Ladner Birch's superb survey of women's contributions and struggles with the planning profession between 1880 and 1980, remains in place as it continues to fill a void in the literature. Surely, someday soon, with more young scholars like Susan Marie Wirka on the scene, this chapter will become obsolete.

So for those who somewhat know the history and literature of the field, I thus explain the not very logical presentation of these individuals and their acts. However, the more important point, perhaps, is to understand that these simple categories of "City Beautiful" or "City Practical" usually do justice neither to those who are awarded the label nor to those excluded from it. Planning history, like life itself, is complex; the motives and values of planners were almost never so single-minded as these or any labels imply.

Perhaps my case is best made, especially for those who are already initiated into planning, in the biographies and recollections themselves. For some, I've said enough, and you should now pass over any further introductory comments and form your own judgment in these matters. For those other readers who are either venturing into planning history for the first time or who may feel the need of more context, I will offer in the balance of this introductory chapter a brief history of the rise of planning in the United States and the role of these people in it.

THE CONTEXT OF AMERICAN PLANNING HISTORY

Modern American planning began in the Progressive era of American history, the closing decades of the 1800s and the first two decades of the 1900s. It was an era in which widespread political corruption in cities was routed by reform governments promoting professionalism, efficiency, and social improvement: hence, "progress." Many planning historians mark 1893, the year of the Chicago Columbian Exposition and World's Fair and the building of a great white model city on the shores of Lake Michigan to house it, as the beginning of modern planning in America. Others suggest 1909 as the year of really serious beginnings, with the publication of Daniel Burnham and Edward Bennett's amazing *Plan of Chicago,* the First National Conference on City Planning, and the introduction at Harvard of the first course in an American university on city planning. Perhaps, though, it is easier to understand why this field of endeavor arose, and why its practitioners struggled (and continue to wrestle) with their particular problems in the ways they do, if we begin the story a bit earlier.

In the early English colonies, the towns were certainly planned, but the plans were based upon English models. The process of making the plans was not democratic, yet historians tell us somehow the result was. In particular, the land was owned, at least initially, by the persons who lived on it, except for the case of indentured servants and slaves, and while not all portions handed out were of equal value, the idea was that each household had a private plot on which to build a house and on which to garden and to farm. In addition, all residents shared ownership in common lands for public use. This model of a town was applied not just in the colonies of New England but in variations in other portions of the continent. Yet "In

New England where our modern land law developed," Foglesong (1986, p. 29) says, "private landholding was based upon a more equitable distribution of land than has existed at any time since." House lots were arranged around central common spaces and were surrounded by individually owned and worked farmlands. Town size was strictly limited, and the religious culture and theocratic governance restrained individual motives toward profit-making from land speculation.

It is important not to overidealize these towns. The southern seaboard communities of Savannah, Georgia, and Charleston, South Carolina, are often praised for their likewise democratic, if not utopian, structures (Holmes, 1992), but these town pictures often belie a darker past. These urban spaces, like those in New England, witnessed devastation wrought by the inadvertent introduction of infectious diseases, the massacre of native populations (as well as the destruction of their means of livelihood), and the propagation of slavery by European planners (J. Krueckeberg, 1992).

With the ending of nearly forty years of French–English wars fought in the colonies in the late seventeenth century and the standardization of English paper money in the early eighteenth century, the system of controlling land speculation that had been maintained began to break down. Land speculation was not new in the New World, but now speculation flooded the land as English colonists looked west of the Appalachians. The democracy of the town developed what is called "the property contradiction." Foglesong (1986, p. 40–41) describes it like this:

> Throughout most of the seventeenth century the "town" was the "propriety" and, in its original conception, the town meeting was nothing but a proprietors' meeting. With the arrival of new settlers and the division of the common lands, however, the proprietors as an organized body passed out of existence and the town no longer exercised control over individual property. . . . With this separation, a conflict emerged between the needs of the inhabitants of the town and the interests of the proprietors who, by virtue of their land ownership, controlled the town's development. It is this contradiction between the social character of the land and its private use and control that provided the impulse for modern town planning.

The notions of democracy and equity that had been joined in

the distribution and sharing of lands that made proprietors of town residents now came apart as the power to control the land became separated from the responsibilities of residency. We cannot pretend that the original system was without conflicts between neighbors, but their rights of property were at least relatively equitably balanced and the maintenance of the common was shared by every family, for every household had a recognized stake in the government, the economy, and, of course, the common church and culture. The concept of private property rights that subsequently evolved in the speculative markets that flourished in the development of the new postrevolutionary nation embodies this property contradiction, which really involved two problems. First is the "Tragedy of the Commons" (Hardin, 1968); as care for the common good weakens and motives for private gain take a larger role, the incentive to exploit the common or free goods is unavoidable. Thus, I want to ignore the impacts of my using more than my share of common pasture land; I want to ignore the physical proximity of my personal land to your land, despite the fact of the water table under my land being connected to the water table under yours, the air flowing over mine being the same as over yours, and the pollution I generate being the degradation you suffer. All these interdependencies between neighbors are contradicted by the claims of American property rights. My home is my castle. To develop it to its highest and best use is my civil right. I am not responsible to you.

Second, the problem is that those rights are transferable; they can be bought and sold and controlled for gain and exploitation by enterprising people who do not suffer the local impacts, diseconomies, and spillovers of their actions. Hence, local democracy is no longer adequate to control local social, economic, and environmental impacts of the actions of ownership of land, the traditional source of community rights. Into this property contradiction, made worse over time by the mounting pressure of population growth and technological change, stepped the planner to shape order from chaos in the service of common values, good government, and equity.

In addition to the changing concepts of law, rights, and ownership came the industrial revolution. By the nineteenth century, urban and rural landscapes had been transformed through massive technological change. "To see the nineteenth century pure and undefiled," Catherine Bauer (1934, p. 5) advises us, "we must go to the railroad station." The rise of the railroad is a powerful and

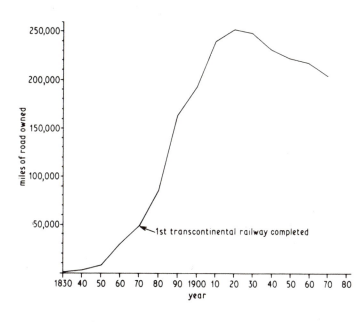

FIGURE I.I   *Railway mileage in the United States.*

dramatic barometer of the expansion of and access to new lands. There were fewer than forty miles of railroad owned in the United States prior to 1830. By 1840, there were three thousand miles. This tripled in the following decade, tripled again in the next, and increased on the average more than 75 percent in each of the next three decades. The growth of the railroad mileage is shown in Figure I.I.[2]

Railroads, of course, were only one of many technical innovations that altered the structure of American cities. In the field of transportation we also had turnpikes, steamboats, canals, steel bridges, subways, and electric trolleys. In industry came large water- and steam-powered mills, gas lights, electric lights, telegraphs, telephones, and business machines. In the building industry came the balloon-frame, tenements, department stores, cast-iron and steel construction, elevators, skyscrapers, and the consolidated railroad terminal: all of the building blocks of the modern city but one—the people.

The people came in masses. The eastern shores were awash, like a flooded beach in a storm, as wave upon wave of immigrants

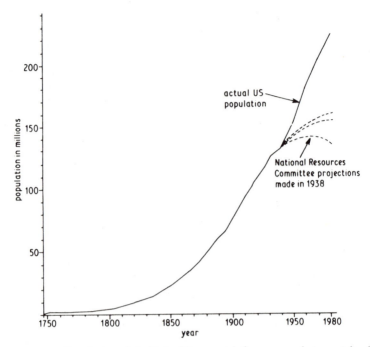

FIGURE 1.2   *Population of the United States with forecasts made in 1938 by the National Resources Committee.*

landed. Their annual number did not surpass 50,000 until after 1830, reached 100,000 before 1850, and then in a pattern of pulsating crests rose to 400,000 in the 1850s and again in the 1870s, to nearly 800,000 in the 1880s and to its apogee in 1908 of more than one-quarter million in one year. The resultant curve of population growth in the United States is shown in Figure 1.2.[3] (The forecasts shown in Figure 1.2 will be discussed later.)

The efforts to accommodate this abundance of people resulted in terrible congestion. Catherine Bauer (1934, p. 5) goes on to describe the view from her railroad station:

The foreground of noise, dirt, beggars, souvenirs and shrill competitive advertising, of tangled street-car lines and tortuous traffic. A middle-ground of warehouses, gilded theaters, competing shop-fronts and commercial hotels with gruesome ornament and unconvincing marble entrances. A background of smokestacks and tall crowded tenements. "Down by the railroad tracks" or "Back of the station" means "slum" in any language.

The sheer magnitude of urban growth in the United States between 1790 and 1930 is difficult to grasp. In 1790 there were *twenty-eight* cities in the United States between 2,500 and 10,000 in population. By 1930, there were *2,183!* There were *five* between 10,000 and 100,000 in population in the year 1790; in 1930, there were *889!* There were *none* over 100,000 in 1790; by 1930, there were *ninety-three!* Ponder, for the sake of comparison, a nation today that might consider a national building program for new towns that would require it to commit resources to the building of twenty-two new towns *in one year* and then sustain this rate of building every year for the next *140 years,* further stipulating that in two out of three years, one of the twenty-two cities built would exceed a population of 100,000 people. We would consider such a proposal preposterous, if not completely insane. Yet that, in effect, is exactly what happened. How many planners would you need to build that many new towns? The planning for all this growth was not "planning" in the sense of the public, democratic deliberation and governmental regulation we have today. The planning was private, entrepreneurial, and atomistic, the work of land surveyors, real estate developers, industrial managers, and transport companies. As to physical city planning, it usually consisted of the layout of a grid of streets, the subdivision of blocks into lots, and the location of a few key public buildings (Reps, 1965, 1979). Later, in the twentieth century, professional planners would develop a formula for a comprehensive city plan that was qualitatively different, the result of a process of research and study and the rational differentiation between ends and means.

Amid these plans of private capitalists, the nineteenth century had no shortage of utopian ideas and experiments that were also an early form of the planning impulse. They took on a great variety of political, religious, industrial, and philanthropic forms. For example, in America, Edward Bellamy's utopian novel *Looking Backward: 2000–1887,* published in 1887, presented a complex urban commercial-industrial city, imagined in the year 2000, that captured the imagination of a very large public. Bellamy's work, as well as others, influenced the thought of a London clerk, Ebenezer Howard, whose short treatise *Tomorrow: A Peaceful Path to Real Reform* (1898) sparked the British garden city movement. Howard's work and that of his followers, including Sir Raymond Unwin and Barry Parker, evolved into the British New Towns program. Never achieving the political success of their British counterparts, American new town efforts remained often philanthropic and piecemeal. Nonetheless, utopian philosophy remains a basic underpinning of American planning thought today.

THE PATHFINDERS OF MODERN PLANNING

In addition to the entrepreneurial efforts of industrial and real estate developers and the examples of utopian community schemes, the roots of American planning in the nineteenth century include the contributions of architects, landscape architects, philanthropists, settlement house workers, journalists, reform politicians, engineers, lawyers, and a host of local organizers for civic improvement. In landscape architecture, we see the development of major city parks—New York's Central Park being the forerunner of these—the college campus, and the modern garden suburb. In architecture, we find the development of planned groups of civic buildings—the "White City" of the 1893 Chicago World's Fair and Columbian Exposition being the flagship of these—and the rise of the downtown skyscraper. The movement for civic improvement fostered the organization of hundreds of local reform groups and clubs devoted to civic arts, public health, housing laws, better working conditions, sanitation, and eventually to comprehensive city plans.

Frederick Law Olmsted, John Nolen, Mary Kingsbury Simkhovitch, Benjamin C. Marsh, Walter D. Moody, Charles Dyer Norton, Alfred Bettman, and Harland Bartholomew were all pathfinders in this exploration to avert the tragedy of the commons and to mediate the contradictions of property that proliferated in the explosions of population and technological change that transformed life and livelihood.

FREDERICK LAW OLMSTED (1822–1903) was born in Hartford, Connecticut, a city founded by his Puritan ancestors from the Massachusetts colony. His childhood, largely spent under the tutelage of several Congregational ministers, concluded with three years of study with a civil engineer. This out-of-door occupation fitted Olmsted's love of the natural countryside, but he moved on to try life at sea, sailing to China and back, and then settled on a career of scientific farming. His appreciation of scenic beauty was heightened on a walking tour of England with his brother and a friend, recounted in his first book, *Walks and Talks of an American Farmer in England;* this revealed his first exposure to English parks. Returning to his farm on Staten Island, Olmsted's literary reputation got him a commission to travel throughout the South for the *New York (Daily) Times* to investigate, firsthand, the slavery question, resulting in his publication of articles and journals on the seaboard slave states and Texas.

In 1857, he achieved appointment as supervisor of construction of Central Park in New York City and collaborated with the young English architect Calvert Vaux on its design. It is considered today to be one of the world's greatest achievements in civic design. Olmsted's extraordinary administrative skills, demonstrated in the supervision of the Central Park construction, led to his appointment during the Civil War as General Secretary of the U.S. Sanitary Commission, precursor of the American Red Cross. Shortly after the war, he began his career in landscape architecture. Rejoining Vaux in New York in 1865, they produced numerous park designs throughout the country. Olmsted's suburban design for Riverside, Illinois, in 1869 is among the earliest of the curvilinear street pattern suburbs that comprise the modern subdivision. Other important design projects include Stanford University's campus in California, the National Capital site in Washington, D.C., the Boston park system, and the Chicago site of the 1893 World's Fair, in collaboration with Daniel Burnham. The Olmsted firm was continued by his stepson, John Olmsted, his son, Frederick Law Olmsted, Jr., and Charles Eliot. The younger FLO went on to become chairman of the National Conference on City Planning in 1911 and was the first president of the American City Planning Institute in 1917. The interested reader may wish to look at Fisher's 1986 larger work on Olmsted, *Frederick Law Olmsted and the City Planning Movement in the United States.* See also the beautifully written 1973 book, *FLO: A Biography of Frederick Law Olmsted* by Laura Wood Roper.

JOHN NOLEN (1869–1937) was the most productive city planner of his time. He was born in Philadelphia and educated at the high school level at Girard College, a school for poor, fatherless boys. In 1891, Nolen entered the University of Pennsylvania. His senior thesis was a study of the Philadelphia Gas Works, in which he applied his interests in law, economics, and management to municipal corruption. After ten years with the university's extension teaching programs in adult education and after three visits to Europe, he decided that a career in landscape architecture would best fit his goals, which included a commitment to art, to being out-of-doors, and to working for the public good. Hence, at the age of thirty-four, Nolen went to Harvard University to study this new profession and to begin a new career of awakening civic consciousness and civic spirit. An eternal optimist, his intellect, voluminous writings, and personal leadership were enormously important in shaping the growth of the planning field.

MARY KINGSBURY SIMKHOVITCH (1867–1951) represents the development of another major impulse, the City Social, paralleling the City Beautiful, with the two forming the foundation for the City Practical, which came soon after. She opens her largely autobiographical 1949 book *Here Is God's Plenty: Reflections on American Social Advance,* a portion of which is reproduced here in chapter 4, by claiming that it is not really autobiography but "our lives lead us to certain conclusions . . . there is a relatedness between our personal histories and our thoughts about life that is undeniable" (preface). Her chapter on housing is reproduced here. To Simkhovitch, housing was more than just shelter, it was a metaphor for "the social situation as a whole." The metaphor persists to the closing lines of the book, where she states, hopefully, that "This planet as it whirls on to an unknown future is still full of families who live in neighborhoods, in nations and in a slowly developing one world. . . . It is only as we begin to understand the relationships in which personality is enmeshed that we can with faith continue our journey" (p. 180).

BENJAMIN C. MARSH (1879–1953) was hired in 1907 as Executive Secretary to the Committee on Congestion of Population in New York City, a coalition of leadership in settlement houses chaired by Mary Kingsbury Simkhovitch. The son of New England Congregational missionaries, he spent much of his youth with them in Bulgaria. From Grinnell College in Iowa, he went to the University of Pennsylvania in 1902 to study social philosophy, heavily under the influence of institutional economist Simon Patton, who had also strongly directed the thinking of John Nolen. Also, like Nolen, Marsh traveled extensively in Europe, studying housing problems and solutions to congestion as part of his new job with the Committee on Congestion.

Marsh had a strong personality, to put it mildly. His biographer here, Harvey A. Kantor, describes him as iconoclastic, brash, feisty, a "bantam rooster," an infighter, a zealot, and wiry while his enemies called him a charlatan radical. Kantor, who may exaggerate a bit in his enthusiasm for us to know the importance of Marsh, suggests that Marsh was "the founder" of the first National Conference on City Planning. He was one of them, certainly, and an active organizer of the event, but the record suggests that he was one of many heavy hitters on the team. Kantor also claims for his hero the authorship of the first book "devoted entirely to city planning" published in 1909. This may be a question of definitions, but I would argue the point, simply by pointing to Charles Mulford Robinson's probably more influential *The Improvement of Towns and Cities* (1901) or his *Modern Civic Art* (1903), which even contains a chapter devoted to the "Comprehensive City Plan." In addition, I would be hard pressed to argue that even Robinson was first. Regardless, the book by Marsh was important and of perhaps a new style, marking the beginning of the City Practical phase of city planning.

We have looked at two people who are traditionally associated with the City Beautiful phase of planning, Olmsted and Nolen. Their focus on beauty and art is clear, not as ends in themselves but as means of transforming the unconscious deleterious effects of urbanism into a spirit of democracy. We have also looked at two representatives of the City Social phase through the housing and planning work of Simkhovitch and Marsh. We now turn to Walter D. Moody and Charles Dyer Norton, two people involved in the early City Practical, and then to two figures who represent the City Practical in full bloom, Alfred Bettman and Harland Bartholomew. Some readers may feel that Moody and Norton are strange introductions to this phase, associating them with *The Chicago Plan* of 1909, often considered the epitome of the City Beautiful plans. Beauty was certainly a key element in the Chicago Plan, with its emphasis on civic architecture and classic revival style. Daniel Burnham's famous credo captures the spirit:

> Make no little plans, they have no magic to stir men's blood, and probably themselves will not be realized. Make big plans; aim high in hope and work, remembering that a noble logical diagram once recorded will never die, but long after we are gone will be a living thing, asserting itself with ever growing

insistency. Remember that our sons and grandsons are going to do things that would stagger us. Let your watchword be order and your beacon beauty (Hasbrouck, 1970, p. v).

Beauty was the beacon, the means to order, but in the Chicago Plan that order was first and foremost an economic order. The plan reminds the reader that Paris taxes the world with its beauty, drawing sightseers and consumers to its doorstep—and so could Chicago. That growth in commerce was the plan's primary objective. It was, after all, the Commercial Club of Chicago that paid for the plan and hired Moody to sell it to the city, and it was Norton, a banker, who was a prime mover in the Commercial Club's support for planning. So while the style of the design for Chicago was City Beautiful, the objective was not Olmsted's liberation of the individual spirit and promotion of democracy but to make the city of Chicago the commercial capital of the world.

WALTER D. MOODY (1874–1948) was a very modern man. With his more than twenty years experience as a salesman, his evangelistic style, and his confidence in the future and in experts, his skills as a promoter of visions are truly impressive. He wrote a textbook for eighth graders, the *Wacker's Manual* of the chapter's title, that sold more than fifty thousand copies (about five times the number of copies that a professional best-seller in planning sells in today's world). Among its many messages, the manual introduced eighth graders to civic art and public architecture, areas of fine arts that were sorely neglected in most American classrooms then—and still today. Moody believed, as his biographer Thomas J. Schlereth points out, in John Dewey's educational philosophy, new in those days—change children and you change the future of the world. A strong supporter of capitalistic individualism, still Moody worried that such tendencies might go too far in society, and he attempted to use the *Plan* and the *Manual* to create patriotism and community virtues as well.

CHARLES DYER NORTON (1871–1923) was the son of an Illinois clergyman who became well established as a Chicago banker and who was instrumental in hiring Daniel Burnham and Edward Bennett to do the *Plan of Chicago*. After a stint in Washington, D.C., as Assistant Secretary of Treasury, he moved to New York City and promoted a vision of planning there that begot the seminal *Regional Plan of New York and Its Environs*. While the chapter presented here

gives you little, if any, insight into the personality and inner character of Norton and his cohorts, it does reveal many of the personal
and professional associations that link individuals in other chapters,
especially Wright, MacKaye, Mumford, Tugwell, and Bauer.

ALFRED BETTMAN (1873–1945) is the shining knight of the
reform movement and the City Practical era at its best and brightest.
The son of a German clothing manufacturer in Cincinnati, Bettman
grew up at the center of progressive reform Judaism in a city
incontestably the most corruptly governed in America. After law
school at Harvard, his local leadership in the movement to reform
Cincinnati government spread to the state of Ohio and to national
proportions. He is most famous for his winning brief before the U.S.
Supreme Court in the classic test of the validity of zoning, *Village of
Euclid v. Ambler Realty Co.* in 1926. It is amazing that many of
Bettman's other accomplishments in planning, documented here by
Laurence C. Gerckens, including important legal contributions in
housing, civil liberties, and state enabling legislation, were all done
as a sideline, in the public interest, apart from his principal law practice.

HARLAND BARTHOLOMEW (1889–1989) was born near Boston,
attended high school in Brooklyn, New York, and studied civil
engineering at Rutgers University in New Jersey for two years. He
left college to go to work for E. P. Goodrich, a civil engineer in New
York City, where he was put in charge of the Technical Advisory
Corporation's plan for Newark. In 1914, Bartholomew left the firm
to work full-time for the city, making him, it is claimed, the nation's
first full-time employee of a city planning commission. In 1916, he
moved to St. Louis, Missouri, where he established the home base of
his consulting firm and colonized the nation with his plans and his
planners. In more than fifty years of practice, Bartholomew also
published research, taught planning at the University of Illinois for
thirty-seven years, and provided national leadership in the profession. His greatest contribution was probably also his least enviable,
for he perfected the development of the comprehensive city plan to
the point that one plan came to look like every other, leading to the
suggestion that the only thing consultants were good for was to take
the last plan they sold, change the name of the city throughout, and
sell it to the next city. These "off-the-rack" plans often met their just
deserts in city halls by going "on the shelf" and staying there.

From the City Practical through Regionalism to the Liberal/Rational Model

The ideas of the City Practical were fully in place by the end of the first decade of the twentieth century. The professional vehicle was still the idea of a plan, but where beauty and health had been the chief concerns now were added engineering, economy, sociology, and law. "City planning is not tying pink ribbons to the lamp posts!" was the epithet. Clearly, concerted action and tough implementation were required to deal with the great evils of municipal congestion and corruption.

The spread of the planning movement across American cities took place rapidly over those first few decades. This growth was simultaneous with the technical expansion of the scope of planning concerns, encompassing increasingly sophisticated attention to matters of transportation, housing, sanitary conditions, land use law, and governmental organization, in addition to continued attention to matters of aesthetics and civic design.

Data on the growth of planning in the early decades of the movement were meticulously documented by John Nolen in his presidential address to the National Conference on City Planning in 1925 (Nolen, 1927). There were, according to Nolen, 176 comprehensive planning reports produced for U.S. cities between 1905 and 1926. Of these 176 reports, 93 percent were done by forty-three different outside consultants (not by regular city employees). Since a few of these consultants occasionally formed temporary partnerships for some projects, the number of distinct firms is difficult to enumerate exactly. Nonetheless, a few leaders were clearly prominent in these early years: the firms of Charles Mulford Robinson, John Nolen, F. L. Olmsted, Jr., George B. Ford, and E. P. Goodrich (who were the Technical Advisory Corporation—TAC), M. H. West, and H. Bartholomew accounted for 70 percent of the plans. The distribution of work among firms, for the period, is illustrated in Figure 1.3.[4]

The comprehensive plan, however, was only one manifestation of the movement. Nolen's 1927 data have been combined with other sources in Figure 1.4 to show the cumulative number of places with comprehensive plans, official planning commissions, zoning ordinances, and, later, regional and county planning agencies. Four distinct phases of development can be seen in this graph.[5] The first

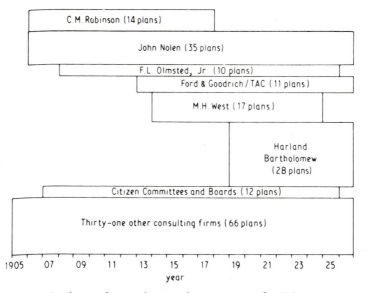

FIGURE I.3   *Producers of comprehensive planning reports for U.S. cities, 1905-26.*

phase runs from 1905 to 1915, when the dominant instrument of planning was the comprehensive plan. Sixty-six plans were produced in this period. In the second phase, from 1915 to 1922, the establishment of official city planning commissions dominated the cities, institutionalizing the planning process in local government and converting it from a political movement to a governmental practice. While the production of comprehensive plan reports continued to rise steadily, the infant zoning law began its takeoff about 1918. After 1922, zoning ordinances led the third phase, stimulated, at least in part, by the national model state enabling act of 1924. Later we see the emerging organization of regional planning agencies take off between 1930 and 1936.

The planning literature parallels these shifts in planning practice. The American City Planning Institute began publishing its first journal in 1915 under the title, *The City Plan,* precisely at the end of the period during which "the city plan" dominated practice. They changed its name to *City Planning* in 1925, putting greater emphasis on the process of planning, and immediately after the official city planning commission's period of domination. The name was changed again, in 1935, to *The Planners' Journal,* recognizing an expanded constituency of regional and national planners.

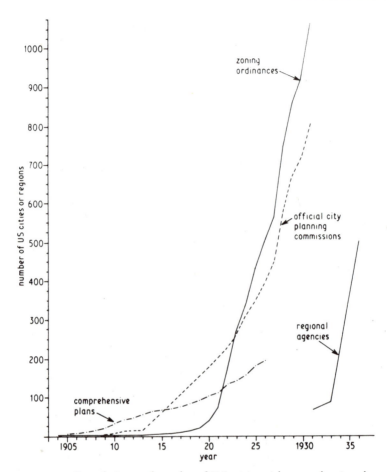

FIGURE I.4   *Cumulative total number of U.S. cities with comprehensive plans, official planning commissions, and zoning ordinances; and cumulative total number of regional planning agencies.*

The idea of regional planning grew as a response to needs and had different meanings for different people. One view of the region was from the metropolis. Its archetype and epitome was the *Regional Plan of New York and Its Environs* prepared under the general direction of the British town planner Thomas Adams. Sponsored by the Russell Sage Foundation, the greatest assemblage of planning studies ever focused on an American city filled more than ten volumes of research and recommendations published between 1929 and 1931. The work was begun in 1921 under the Sage Foundation's Committee on the Regional Plan of New York and Its Environs, chaired by Charles Dyer Norton. At about the same time, regional planning organizations were also formed in Chicago, under private auspices also, and as a public office in the Los Angeles County Regional Planning Commission.

A second view of the region was established at the other extreme position—from the mountaintop. The view of the decentralists was not to abandon the city but to achieve a more balanced form of development in harmony with the natural resources of the region. This view was most eloquently articulated by a group of influential intellectuals in and around New York City who formed the Regional Planning Association of America (RPAA). The core group included Clarence Stein and Henry Wright, the architects and planners of the famous Radburn, New Jersey, suburb; Lewis Mumford, the brilliant young social critic; Catherine Bauer and Edith Elmer Wood, housing reformers; Benton MacKaye, the naturalist; Stuart Chase, the economist; and Charles Harris Whitaker, editor of the *Journal of the American Institute of Architects.*

Of the several causes advocated by the members of the RPAA, a new towns program for America and urban deconcentration, in the spirit of the British movement, were high on the list. Their reputation was equally well earned as critics of the establishment, no better demonstrated than in their blistering public debate with Thomas Adams and the Regional Plan of New York over issues of housing and centralization. They argued that housing for the poor had been ignored and that there was too much concentration. Adams considered their arguments impractical.

A third strain of regional planning emerged between the world wars from Franklin Delano Roosevelt's New Deal and its National Planning Board, established in 1933 and subsequently renamed the National Resources Board, the National Resources Committee, and, finally, the National Resources Planning Board. While city planning agencies generally atrophied during this period, as a result of the Great Depression and the building slump that followed, the New Deal expanded the horizons of the planning vision through the vigorous promotion of state planning activities, regional development projects, such as the Tennessee Valley Authority, and a program of Greenbelt New Towns under the direction of Rexford G. Tugwell.

If the planners at the National Resources Board (NRB) had correctly forecast national growth, the story of the development of city and regional planning might have ended fifty years ago. You will recall from our graph of U.S. population growth in Figure 1.3 that the several forecasts made by the NRB in 1938 assumed that the great age of expansion was over. There were several events in the succeeding few years that encouraged this view.

The most monstrous surprise, of course, was World War II. Many of the younger planners entered the armed services, decimating the ranks of the profession. Those who were not sent to fight abroad found themselves fighting different battles at home. The great domestic issue was planning for postwar recovery and the expansion and redevelopment of cities after the war. Britain had taken bold and decisive steps toward centralized national control of these matters. The debate over centralization versus decentralization in America was bitter, with many planners caught in the middle. The left was critical because America did not think boldly enough, along the lines of the British. The right considered all planning as fundamentally communistic and inherently un-American. The middle ground was found in a postwar agenda for urban redevelopment and public works that would bridge the anticipated valleys of unemployment and housing shortage immediately after the war. The big political question was who was going to control these jobs and expenditures. It was the classic struggle between home rule and nationally centralized power. Robert Moses of New York, who probably controlled more local public works than any other single individual in America, led a vulgar campaign against his enemies, the "long-haired planners."

After the war, these issues of ideology were slowly buried in the flood of new realities. Home building mushroomed. From 1930 to 1945, the number of housing starts in the nation had averaged less than one-half million per year. After the war, this figure jumped to two million units per year. The other powerful force in urbanization was the ubiquitous automobile. The growth of suburban housing and its complement in private automobile consumption are shown in Figure 1.5.[6]

The expenditure of public dollars on domestic development programs also exhibited a takeoff after the war. Direct federal expenditures plus state and local expenditures on highways, housing, and urban renewal are shown in Figure 1.6.[7] The planning profession flourished in the successive waves of federal programs. The various housing construction, loan, and mortgage insurance programs, the urban renewal program, the comprehensive planning

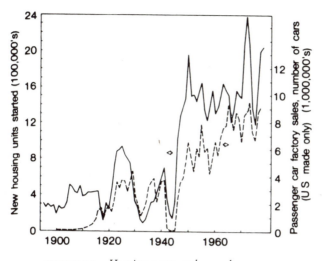

FIGURE I.5   *Housing starts and car sales, 1900-70+.*

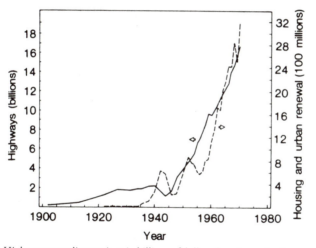

NOTE: Highway expenditures given in billions of dollars; housing and urban renewal given in 100 millions of dollars.

FIGURE I.6   *Federal, direct, plus state and local expenditures on highways, housing, and urban renewal, 1902-70.*

assistance program, and the 42,500-mile interstate highway pro-gram—these filled the agenda of the 1950s.

The early 1960s brought harsh reactions to the postwar building boom. There were unintended side effects of urban renewal—at least unintended by some—that aggravated racial and class inequities and destroyed the social fabric of neighborhoods. The highway program that drove people to the suburbs fostered suburban shopping malls and industrial parks that undermined the economies of the older downtowns and further reduced both the quantity and quality of inner-city living space. In the face of this, inner-city residents lost confidence in local government in general, which was too often of little protective or directive assistance to less powerful constituencies.

The ranks of the planning profession grew by leaps and bounds. The late 1960s brought the programs of "the great society," "model cities," and the "war on poverty" that tended to displace the long-range comprehensive plan and focus instead on shorter-range policy formation and program implementation. Integral to these new programs was the extension of community participation in control over public expenditures. The federal grants economy developed. The 1960s brought greater involvement of the federal government in providing local revenues. In the 1970s, block grants and revenue sharing attempted to reallocate control over these federal expenditures. New national priorities arose again, first in environmental protection and then in energy development and conservation. As each of these initiatives grew, more diverse planners joined the pool of sociologists, geographers, engineers, economists, political scientists, and lawyers assembled to tackle these problems.

The postwar era was also a period of great intellectual ferment and change within planning and allied disciplines. The social sciences were slow to shift their traditional priorities toward the applied problems of urban affairs. Sociology and geography were among the first and more successful to develop recognized urban subdisciplines. Regional science, established as a new field about 1955, attempted to reform geographic theories, economic analysis, and urban and regional planning problems in models of mathematics and statistics. It fueled the hopes for a science of planning and transformed permanently the analytic capacity of the field. It also generated a lot of skepticism among some who ill understood it and were impatient for its proofs of practicality. The broader interests of mainstream economists and historians were more slowly attracted to urban categories of problems, stimulated by conflicts among economic growth, environmental quality, and social equity. The pre–World War II dominance of the design professions—architecture and landscape architecture—diminished. While imaginative university programs in urban design, regional land use planning, and behavioral aspects of environmental design have newly developed, the limelight of planning has been dominated by the greater interest in so-called nonphysical solutions and the impacts of global economic and political restructuring. Of course, these tendencies in the expansion of the field were felt long ago and noted, disapprovingly, as early as 1922 by Hegemann and Peets (p. 4).

> The young profession of city planning is drifting too strongly in the directions of engineering and applied sociology. This is perhaps natural, for there are problems of such tremendous importance in these fields, problems of a practical importance which newspapers and public officials can appreciate and even property rights can be induced to recognize, that men in the profession are attracted in that direction. Besides, it is much easier and more respectable to be an engineer, an "uplifter," or a business man, than it is to be an artist.

The seeds of this change have already been seen in people like Benjamin C. Marsh, Walter D. Moody, and Alfred Bettman and are easily apparent in Henry Wright and those who follow.

HENRY WRIGHT (1878–1936) was an artist and "a nice man to know." Thus Henry Churchill begins the story of his friend. Wright created with Clarence Stein what is possibly today the most famous suburban design in the world—Radburn, New Jersey. He also pioneered work in the economic analysis of housing development and served on the design team for Greenbrook, New Jersey, one of the new towns of Roosevelt's Greenbelt New Towns program, for which Rexford G. Tugwell was the administrator. Wright was an integral part of the inner circle of the Regional Planning Association of America and hence among the severest critics of Thomas Adams and the *Regional Plan of New York and Its Environs*. That Wright was a very "nice" person is uniquely illustrated in the following recollection of Frederick J. Adams, Thomas Adams's son[8]:

> Henry took me over into his office and I worked laying out sidewalks and superblocks. The thing was I had ten months of association with him which was absolutely remarkable. I mean, he was really a wonderful person—very introverted and very aggressive at times, but intellectually very stimulating. He took me over to Sunnyside the first time I met Lewis Mumford.

I think the same day he took me up to somewhere on Central Park to meet Catherine Bauer who was working there. I had no intention of going into planning until then. Everybody would assume that I did it because of my father. If I'd gone back to England and worked (as an architect) in his office I probably wouldn't have. But I stuck.

Adams eventually served for many years as head of the program in planning at the Massachusetts Institute of Technology (MIT) and contributed a distinguished scholarly and professional career.

BENTON MACKAYE (1879–1975) was the founder of the Appalachian Trail. Born in Shirley, Massachusetts, he was a lover of the wilderness. As some men yearn "to run away to sea," he confessed, his great desire was "to run away to land." He was educated at Harvard. After thirteen years with the National Forest Service, he went into the U.S. Department of Labor. MacKaye was a rare individual—a utopian in government. His idea for the Appalachian Trail gained the support of Charles Harris Whitaker, editor of the *Journal of the American Institute of Architects*, through whom MacKaye entered the fold of the RPAA, where his philosophy of regional planning was nourished and grew into a concept of the environment as "common mind." He was far ahead of his time but lived to see the environmental movement reemerge in the 1970s and his book, *The New Exploration,* revived.

LEWIS MUMFORD (1895–1990) never formally studied planning, but it is probably safe to say that no one who has, in the last forty years, has done so without studying Lewis Mumford. He grew up in New York City's upper West Side. While still attending college, he read and then established a correspondence with Patrick Geddes, the great Scottish biologist, social theorist, and regional planner. Mumford's own career is phenomenally broad, employing a historical mode of understanding to bridge the gap between science and humanism. He was proud that Frank Lloyd Wright, the great American architect, once saluted him as "the real successor to Emerson." Mumford was a central actor in the RPAA and a passionate critic in modern planning, architecture, and city building. Regionalism, decentralism, and city form at a human scale for human needs—these were central to his creed and the themes of more than twenty passionate books. The most influential in planning is probably *The Culture of Cities* (1938).

CATHERINE BAUER (1905–1964) was the daughter of New Jersey's chief highway engineer. A graduate of Vassar, with strong interests in architecture and literature, she too was a central figure in the RPAA and went on to national prominence for her skill in political strategy and organization, expressed in a fiery moral passion that leaps from the pages of her famous book, *Modern Housing* (1934). Eugenie Ladner Birch's thorough review of Bauer's ideas and positions on issues reveals, as such an assessment might for anyone, contradictions that seem inherent in American society. Bauer defended the promotion of "exclusive communities (meaning homogeneity in population)" and, in what seems like the same breath, advocated "suburbs with residential choice open to all economic and racial groups." Birch credits Bauer with articulating several other enduring professional dilemmas as well. It was, no doubt, the recognition of these contradictions that led Birch to characterize Bauer's work as "a vision of balance."

REXFORD GUY TUGWELL (1891–1979) had been an agricultural economist at Columbia University until President Roosevelt put him in charge of the Resettlement Administration in 1935. Hailing from Sinclairsville, New York, the son of a farmer and cannery owner, he went to college at the University of Pennsylvania. There he earned a doctorate from the Wharton School of Finance and Commerce and developed a passion for what he called "the magnificence of planning" as a route to social betterment. After managing the Greenbelt New Towns program for Roosevelt, Tugwell became the first chairman of the New York City Planning Commission in 1938. What happened next is the story told by George C. Hemmens in this volume. Later Roosevelt appointed Tugwell chancellor of the University of Puerto Rico and in 1941 governor of the island. In 1945, he went to the University of Chicago, one of the most influential places in the development of modern planning ideas at that time, to head its graduate program in planning. Through that program's faculty and student body passed a cadre of thinkers whose works very largely determined the direction of the field for the next forty years: Edward C. Banfield, Melville C. Branch, John Dyckman, John Friedmann, Britton Harris, Melvin Levin, Julius Margolis, Stewart Marquis, Richard L. Meier, Martin Meyerson, Harvey S. Perloff, and others, not to forget Tugwell himself.

HANS BLUMENFELD (1892–1988) lived a very long and active life. If you had met him in his later years, you might have been tempted to tease him with, "How could anyone so short live so long?"—and he would take it in good humor and doubtless get you back. His wit and intellect were gargantuan. Blumenfeld admitted that the title to his 1987 autobiography, *Life Begins at 65: The Not Entirely Candid Autobiography of a Drifter,* was tongue in cheek. European born, trained as an architect, a devoted and active member of the Communist party for many years, he worked professionally in Russia before coming to the United States and eventually settling in Canada. The portions of his story that cover his work in the United States are included in this collection, revealing primarily his time in Philadelphia and his wonderful independent spirit. Blumenfeld's major writings, collected in two volumes, contain seminal contributions to quantitative urban demography, urban economics, history, and civic design.

CHARLES ABRAMS (1902–1970), lawyer, educator, and author, is the storybook New Yorker. His father sold herrings and pickles from a sidewalk stand across the street from their tenement in the Williamsburg district of Brooklyn. Not of the stream of progressive New York and Cincinnati Jews who could look forward to sending their sons to Harvard, the Orthodox community of Poland and Eastern Europe lived for the most part in six-story walk-ups and three-room flats. For Abrams, it was evening classes at Brooklyn Law School. After a short and profitable career in law and real estate speculation, his earnings and holdings of Greenwich Village properties and the lessons learned in the marketplace supported his subsequent career in planning and housing law. Abrams was a distinguished author and teacher and a model of intellect, wit, and charm.

KEVIN LYNCH (1918–1984) was, without a doubt, "the leading environmental design theorist of our time," as Tridib Banerjee and Michael Southworth suggest. Their chapter on Lynch, who was also their professor at MIT, where he taught for many years, is adapted from their 1990 introduction to his collected writings and projects, *City Sense and City Design.* Lynch is one of a very small number of theoreticians whose work was immensely practical, as it was created in the midst of practice, and whose work also had a major impact on the development of numerous other academic disciplines outside of planning. So seminal was his work; so grounded was his life.

There are a lot of men in this book. Women have contributed greatly to American planning, but published material on their lives is very slow in catching up to those accomplishments. In the first half of the century, their roles were largely confined to grass-roots organizations and community work, which Mary Kingsbury Simkhovitch exemplifies. In the latter half of the century, women have achieved key leadership roles, of which Catherine Bauer is one exemplary model. In the final chapter, Eugenie Ladner Birch reviews these and other women's lives in planning through several prominent figures: THEODORA KIMBALL HUBBARD (1897–1935), Harvard planning librarian, researcher, and author; CHARLOTTE RUMBOLD (1865–1960), planning leader in Cleveland, Ohio; ELISABETH HERLIHY (1880–1953), prominent Massachusetts planning official; HARLEAN JAMES (1877–1969), author and executive secretary to the American Civic Association for thirty-seven years; and many others. The first women to receive planning degrees from American universities earned them during the New Deal era. By 1976, 28 percent of the planning degrees being awarded were earned by women. In 1978, Constance Lieder, who held the position of cabinet-level officer for planning for the state of Maryland, became the first woman president of the American Institute of Planners, now the American Institute of Certified Planners.

PLANNING LIVES

Today most people enter the field of planning through schools of planning. There are a small number of undergraduate degree programs (eleven accredited) that graduate about 150 planners per year; sixty-three accredited graduate programs that produce about a thousand graduates per year; and about twenty-seven Ph.D. programs that award about forty degrees per year. Women comprise about 25 percent of these degrees and minorities about 10 percent.

There are somewhere in the neighborhood of 35,000 to 40,000 planners in the United States today; no one knows the exact number. They work in local governments for city planning commissions, county planning commissions, local economic development authorities, transportation departments, health departments, and so on. They work in regional agencies, like the Pinelands Commission in New Jersey or The Port Authority of New York and New Jersey. They work in state governments in departments of community affairs, environmental protection, transportation, labor, and health, and in governors' policy planning offices. They work for private consulting firms doing everything from local zoning ordinances and environmental impact statements to planning postwar reconstruction in Iran. They work in the federal government in the departments of

Housing and Urban Development and Transportation, and in the Environmental Protection Agency and the Office of Management and Budget. They work for the U.S. Agency for International Development, for the World Bank, and for the United Nations' Development Program. They work almost everywhere.

Newly elected President Bill Clinton appointed in 1993 two planners to his cabinet: Henry Cisneros received a master's degree in urban planning from Texas A&M in 1970, is a former mayor of San Antonio, Texas, and is now U.S. Secretary for Housing and Urban Development (HUD). Donna Shalala, who graduated from the Maxwell School of Syracuse University, who served as Assistant Secretary for Policy Development and Research at HUD during the Carter administration, and who taught in the graduate program in urban planning at Hunter College in New York City while serving as its president, is now U.S. Secretary for Health and Human Services. Do these high appointments to power signal a new level of social maturity for the profession of planning? Perhaps—but that is precisely not the point of this book. The point of these biographies and recollections is not only our social history but something more, namely, that the source of power and the measure of maturity are not in giants and geniuses, royalty and gods. As he so often did, Lewis Mumford said it best:

> The test of maturity, for nations as well as individuals, is not the increase of power, but the increase of self-understanding, self-control, self-direction and self-transcendence. For in a mature society, man himself, and not his machines or his organizations, is the chief work of art.[9]

I once proposed *Planning Lives* for the title of this book but was persuaded not to use it. It was too ambiguous: did I mean planning is alive?; or is this a how-to-plan-a-life book?; or was it, like *Plutarch's Lives*, a collection of worthy stories? I wish I had used it because it is all of these. The life, the text, and the tale; all remain unfinished—a chronicle of good intentions and some successes that often seem too small amidst the problems of this world. Yet, as I look over these individuals once again, I try to cull their virtues: artistic, spirited, determined, wise, zealous, sympathetic, passionate, committed, courageous, brilliant, sweet, open, intellectual, witty, wily, authentic, free, active, imaginative, independent, caring, efficient, tenacious, strong, orderly, balanced, loving.

That's alive; that's how to do it; and that's a story worth telling.

NOTES

1. The first section of this chapter, "Why Planning Biography?," relies heavily on my recently published essay in the *Journal of the American Planning Association*, "Between self and culture: or what are biographies of planners about?" (D. Krueckeberg, 1993), with the kind consent of the *Journal* editors.
2. Compiled from data in the U.S. Bureau of the Census (1975), part 1, series Q 284–312, pp. 727–30.
3. Compiled from data in U.S. Bureau of the Census (1975), part 1, series C 89–119, pp. 105–9; National Resources Committee (1938), p. 24; and U.S. Bureau of the Census (1977).
4. Composed from data in Nolen (1927).
5. Compiled from data in Nolen (1927); the annual surveys of city and regional planning in the United States, published in the journal *City Planning* by Theodora Kimball Hubbard from 1926 to 1930, and by Harold S. Buttenheim in 1931 and 1932; and Perloff (1957).
6. Compiled from data in U.S. Bureau of the Census (1975), part 2, series N 156–69 and Q 148–62; U.S. Bureau of the Census (1978, 1979); and Motor Vehicle Manufacturers Association (1978), p. 9.
7. Compiled from data in U.S. Bureau of the Census (1975), series Y 605–37 and Y 682–709.
8. Unpublished interview of Frederick J. Adams, January 4, 1979.
9. Quoted in Mumford's obituary, the *New York Times,* Sunday, January 28, 1990, p. L30.

REFERENCES

Banerjee, Tridib, and Southworth, Michael, eds. (1990) *City Sense and City Design: Writings and Projects of Kevin Lynch,* Cambridge, MIT Press.

Bauer, Catherine (1934) *Modern Housing,* Boston, Houghton Mifflin.

Bellamy, Edward (1887) *Looking Backward: 2000–1887,* New York: Ticknor.

Birch, Eugenie Ladner (1978) "Woman-made America: the case of early public housing policy," *Journal of the American Institute of Planners,* 44, 2, 130–44.

Blake, Casey (1990) "The perils of personality: Lewis Mumford and politics after liberalism," in *Lewis Mumford: Public Intellectual* edited by Thomas P. and Agatha C. Hughes, New York, Oxford University Press.

Blumenfeld, Hans (1987) *Life Begins at 65: The Not Entirely Candid Autobiography of a Drifter,* Montreal, Harvest House.

Bolan, Richard (1981) "Review of *History and Human Existence: from Marx to Merleau-Ponty*" by James Miller, in *Journal of the American Planning Association,* 47, 3 (July), 357–9.

Erchak, Gerald M. (1992) *The Anthropology of Self and Behavior,* New Brunswick, Rutgers University Press.

Fisher, Irving D. (1986) *Frederick Law Olmsted and the City Planning Movement in the United States,* Ann Arbor, UMI Research Press.

Foglesong, Richard (1986) *Planning the Capitalist City: the Colonial Era to the 1920s,* Princeton, Princeton University Press.

Gay, Peter (1985) *Freud for Historians,* New York, Oxford University Press.

Goist, Park Dixon (1972) "Seeing things whole: a consideration of Lewis Mumford," *Journal of the American Institute of Planners,* 38, 6, 379-91.

Harding, Garrett (1968) "The tragedy of the commons," *Science,* 162, 1243-48.

Hasbrouck, Wilbert R. (1970) "Introduction," in *Plan of Chicago* by Daniel H. Burnham and Edward H. Bennett, New York, DaCapo Press.

Hegemann, Werner, and Peets, Elbert (1922) *The American Vitruvius: An Architect's Handbook of Civic Art,* New York, Architectural Book Publishing.

Holmes, Michael D. (1992) "Planning method: the case of colonial South Carolina, *Planning Historian's Notebook,* no. 1 (Society for American City and Regional Planning History).

Howard, Ebenezer (1898) *Tomorrow: A Peaceful Path to Real Reform,* London, Swan Sonnenschein.

Jacobs, Allan (1981) "Review of *A Theory of Good City Form*" by Kevin Lynch, in *Journal of the American Planning Association,* 47, 3 (July), 356-7.

Kaplan, Justin (1979) "The naked self and other problems," in *Telling Lives: The Biographer's Art,*" edited by Marc Pachter, Washington, D.C., New Republic Books/National Portrait Gallery.

Kazin, Alfred (1979) "The self as history: reflections on autobiography," in *Telling Lives: The Biographer's Art,* edited by Marc Pachter, Washington, D.C., New Republic Books/National Portrait Gallery.

Krueckeberg, Donald, ed. (1983) *The American Planner: Biographies and Recollections,* New York, Methuen.

—— (1993) "Between self and culture: or what are biographies of planners about?," *Journal of the American Planning Association,* 59, 2 (Spring), 217-20.

Krueckeberg, John C. (1992) "Colonial South Carolina: the case against planning method—a brief response to M. Holmes," *Planning History Present* 6, 1, 4-5.

Lasch, Christopher (1980) "Mumford and 'The myth of the machine,'" *Salamagundi,* 49 (Summer), 4-28.

Morris, Colin (1987) *The Discovery of the Individual: 1050-1200,* Toronto, University of Toronto Press.

Motor Vehicle Manufacturers Association (1978) *Motor Vehicles Facts and Figures,* Detroit, Motor Vehicle Manufacturers Association.

Mumford, Lewis (1938) *The Culture of Cities,* New York, Harcourt Brace.

—— (1930) "What I believe," *The Forum,* 84 (November).

Myhra, David (1973) "Rexford Guy Tugwell: initiator of America's Greenbelt New Towns, 1935-1936," *Journal of the American Institute of Planners,* 40, 3, 176-88.

National Resources Committee (1938) *The Problems of a Changing Population,* Washington, D.C., U.S. Government Printing Office.

Nolen, John (1927) "Twenty years of city planning progress in the United States," in *Planning Problems of Town, City, and Region,* Philadelphia, National Conference on City Planning, 1–44.

Pachter, Marc (1979) "The biographer himself: an introduction," in *Telling Lives: The Biographer's Art,* edited by Marc Pachter, Washington, D.C., New Republic Books/National Portrait Gallery.

Perloff, Harvey S. (1957) *Education for Planning: City, State, and Region,* Baltimore, Johns Hopkins Press.

Reps, John (1965) *The Making of Urban America: A History of City Planning in the United States,* Princeton, Princeton University Press.

——— (1979) *Cities of the American West: A History of Frontier Urban Planning,* Princeton, Princeton University Press.

Robinson, Charles Mulford (1901) *The Improvement of Towns and Cities or the Practical Basis of Civic Aesthetics,* New York, G.P. Putnam's Sons.

——— (1903) *Modern Civic Art or the City Made Beautiful,* New York, G.P. Putnam's Sons.

Roper, Laura Wood (1973) *FLO: A Biography of Frederick Law Olmsted,* Baltimore, Johns Hopkins Press.

Ross, John R. (1975) "Benton MacKaye: the Appalachian Trail," *Journal of the American Institute of Planners,* 41, 2, 110–14.

Simkhovitch, Mary Kingsbury (1949) *Here is God's Plenty: Reflections on American Social Advance,* New York, Harper and Brothers.

Stegner, Wallace (1992) *Where the Bluebird Sings to the Lemonade Springs: Living and Writing in the West,* New York, Random House.

U.S. Bureau of the Census (1975) *Historical Statistics of the United States, Colonial Times to 1970,* Washington, D.C., U.S. Government Printing Office.

——— (1977) *Statistical Abstract of the United States: 1977,* 98th edition, Washington, D.C., U.S. Government Printing Office.

——— (1978) "Housing starts, C20-78-10," in *Department of Commerce Construction Reports,* Washington, D.C., U.S. Government Printing Office, December.

——— (1979) "Housing starts, C20-79-2," In *Department of Commerce Construction Reports,* Washington, D.C., U.S. Government Printing Office, February.

Vandiver, Frank E. (1983) "Biography as an agent of humanism," in *The Biographer's Gift: Life Histories and Humanism,* edited by J. Veninga, College Station, Texas A & M University Press.

FIGURE 2.1   *Frederick Law Olmsted, c. 1860.*

2

FREDERICK LAW OLMSTED
THE ARTIST AS SOCIAL AGENT

IRVING D. FISHER

IN RECENT YEARS, we have rediscovered an American artistic genius. Historians, especially historians of the antebellum South, have long known of Frederick Law Olmsted's reports of his travels in the pre–Civil War southern states. His accounts of the slave society were known to the Scottish philosopher, historian, and economist James Stuart Mill (the father of John Stuart Mill), and Karl Marx mentions Olmsted's accounts and description of southern slavery in his *Das Kapital* of 1867. We may ask: How does one who aspired first to be an enlightened farmer, a litterateur, and then a publisher become a landscape architect, indeed, the professed founder of the profession of landscape architecture? It was a matter of chance. While Olmsted was commiserating at a Connecticut seaside resort over the recent failure and bankruptcy of his publishing venture, a chance acquaintance suggested to him that he apply for an open position as the superintendent of the newly created Central Park in New York City. Aided by friends and acquaintances who spoke for him, Olmsted got the position.

Fortune benignly continued to grace Olmsted's life. In no small measure, the creation of the new Central Park was due to the efforts of the poet and newspaper editor, William Cullen Bryant, and the landscape gardener and horticulturist, Andrew Jackson Downing. With the creation of Central Park, it could be assumed that Downing, famous also as a nurseryman, as a writer on gardening and architecture, and as a proponent of the park, would have been chosen by the Park Commissioners as the park designer. However, in 1852 Downing lost his life in a tragic Hudson River accident. Thus it was that when the competition for the design for Central Park was announced in 1858, Calvert Vaux, Downing's former architectural assistant, sought out Olmsted, whom he had formerly met. Olmsted was now the park superintendent, and both collaborated on the winning design for the new park.

Given his training—or lack of it—Frederick Law Olmsted was hardly qualified in 1858 to call himself a landscape architect. His talents notwithstanding, he was acutely aware of his deficiencies, and he was most acutely aware of his inability to arrive at a literary statement of a cohesive theory of landscape architecture that satisfied him.

In a letter dated 1881, which Olmsted wrote to his friend, the art critic and Harvard professor, Charles Eliot Norton, he deplored his inability to develop a satisfactory aesthetic theory to define the art of landscape architecture. In his letter, Olmsted urgently requested Norton's aid in finding a "definition of art which will include" landscape architecture. He asked Norton to "advise" him on reading material "whereby I can better ground myself. . . . Of course," he continued, "I can't begin at 60 a University course" to get the proper grounding to distinguish the art of landscape architecture from gardening on one side and the art of engineer and bricklayer on the other. (This letter can be found in the Norton collection in the Houghton Library at Harvard.)

Another possible source that Olmsted might have utilized to define a theory for landscape architecture was the writings of the English gardeners William Gilpin, Uvedale Price, Humphrey Repton, and John Claudius Loudon, along with that of the respected American disciple, Downing. Their landscaping followed the so-called natural style of the English garden. However, in a most significant way, Olmsted's view of the nature and purpose of the art of landscaping differed radically from any previous ventures in landscaping art. The English and American landscape gardeners who preceded Olmsted implicitly or explicitly belonged to the classical school of aesthetics, which was based on associational psychology and empirical rationalism. The work of these gardeners was technical and gardenesque. For the most part, the English practitioners served the pleasures of rich landlords. As one of this school, Humphrey Repton, explained: "I hope never to lose sight of the great and essential object of my profession, the elegance, the magnificence, and the convenience of rural scenes, appropriated to the uses of a gentleman's habitation."[1]

Olmsted knew and respected the writings of these precedent-setting gardeners. He instructed students of the landscape art to read their works in order to learn the technical side of landscaping. Respected and popular as Downing was, though, I have not found in the Olmsted materials any reference that he thought Downing's writings on landscaping were worthy of study. In any case, Olmsted differentiated his conception of the art of landscaping from that of the earlier landscape gardeners. His theory for the design of large-scale natural landscape was based upon the aesthetics of romantic idealism.

While Olmsted did not provide us with a comprehensive statement regarding his aesthetic theory, it is possible to construct it from his life experiences and from fragments that appear in his reports and letters. There is no doubt that he carried in his mind an operational theory that controlled his creative efforts. There is evidence that his ideas regarding the creative process and his conception of the aesthetic experience derive from the philosophy of German idealism.

Olmsted came under this influence during the formative years of his youth. Of prime importance in this regard is his association with the Reverend Horace Bushnell of Hartford, the product of the Yale Divinity School—but a rebellious one who rejected the hard, orthodox Puritan faith of his rural upbringing. In his search for a new approach to religious experience more acceptable to a sophisticated, urban society, Bushnell turned to the writings of the English poet Samuel Taylor Coleridge and to romantic philosophy.[2] He turned away from the rationalism and individualism that characterized traditional Calvinism and instead followed the lead of such German theologians as Friedrich Schleiermacher and Johann Neander. From Coleridge and German idealism, Bushnell acquired the conception that all society—the church, the state, the school, the family, and, indeed, the universe—is permeated throughout by a spiritual unity. He carried over into his reinterpretation of Congregational theology the very analogies from the plant and vegetable world so profusely used by the German idealists and by Coleridge and the Scottish essayist and historian Thomas Carlyle to characterize the relationship of the creative artist to nature and the individual to the universe. To the doctrine that society is spiritually united in an organic whole, Bushnell related the notion, also developed by the German idealists and their English interpreters, that there exists among the members of society an involuntary communication and sympathy—an unconscious influence that determines character. He infused this into his religious doctrine. In so doing, Bushnell knowingly undermined the extreme individualism of the existing Congregationalist doctrine.

Olmsted's close association with Bushnell was important because, as his letters indicate, Olmsted and his young Yale friends were deeply steeped in religious discussions. In addition to Bushnell's guidance, he found reinforcement to romantic idealism through his reading of other transcendentalists. His study of the writings of Thomas Carlyle, John Ruskin, and Ralph Waldo Emerson had a particularly significant impact upon Olmsted's thinking. Each of these writers influenced him to evolve a worldview that, in turn, contributed to the development of his aesthetic theory. Indeed, according to Olmsted's wife, Carlyle's *Sartor Resartus* and Ruskin's *Modern Painters* were textbooks for Olmsted and his friends.[3]

With their introduction in the 1820s, Carlyle's writings enjoyed a growing distinction in the United States. He was the first to transmit to Americans the philosophic idealism of the German writers. Among American intellectuals Carlyle's papers were widely read. Olmsted found his enthusiastic reading of Carlyle's *Sartor Resartus* an illuminating experience. In a letter to his father, Olmsted wrote:

> I have been reading *Sartor Resartus*. It took me about three weeks, but I was intensely interested before I finished. And now if anybody wants to set me down for an insane cloud dwelling Transcendentalist, because I like Carlyle, I hope they'll gratify themselves. I do think Carlyle is the greatest genius in the world.[4]

In his letter, Olmsted described his reading of *Sartor Resartus* as experiencing a "Hurricane." He was sensitive to Carlyle's doctrine that man's moral duty consisted in working to the utmost in that specific work to which each is called by his special, innate capacities. It is in this manner that man, especially the artist or the seer, evidenced divinity and was bound, albeit unconsciously, into an organic unity with humanity and with the universe.

Another one of Olmsted's "prophets" was the Englishman John Ruskin. With the publication in the United States of his book, *Modern Painters,* Ruskin achieved a position of great influence and importance, first as the arbiter of aesthetic taste and art criticism and later as a social critic and reformer. In reading *Modern Painters* and *The Seven Lamps of Architecture,* Olmsted and his circle of friends were immediately captured by the didactic and moral aspects of Ruskin's writings. In these early volumes, Ruskin offered the aesthetic impulse as the mediator between nature and man to reveal the divinity and the spirituality within the physical manifestations of nature. His views were transcendental, deriving and holding in common many of the concepts held by Carlyle, Coleridge, and William Wordsworth. In Ruskin's writings, Olmsted found principles in landscape painting that were to guide him in his own artistic work. When he turned to planning urban parks, he invariably found the opportunity to invoke Ruskin to support his thesis that beauty—and particularly the beauty of natural landscape scenery—must be the means to improve the quality of life.

Long before Olmsted had any thought that he would find his vocation in planning parks and cities, he found Ruskin's descriptions of the natural beauty of Europe's landscapes a reminder of his own childhood travels with his parents throughout New York, New England, and Canada. Both Ruskin and Olmsted regarded beautiful landscape with reverence and passion.

Imbued as he was with the intellectual orientation of romantic idealism, Olmsted differentiated himself from the prevailing notions of landscape gardening. He gave to the natural school of landscape design an aesthetic theory based upon an organic conception of art. The German critic and poet August Wilhelm von Schlegel stated, "Organic form . . . is innate; it unfolds itself from within, and reaches its determination simultaneously with the fullest development of the seed. . . . In the fine arts, just as in the province of nature—the supreme artist—all genuine forms are organic."[5] This is the conception that controlled Olmsted's art of landscape design.

Because of the nature of the material with which he worked, Olmsted was able to embody the organic conception of art in the most direct manner. The unfolding world of live nature was, indeed, his realm. Olmsted made this clear when he said:

In gardening in the natural school our efforts should be to prepare a field for the operations of nature. We should depend upon nature, not simply as some teach, [or] appear to do so, but actually trust nature only offering certain encouragements by means of ground work. *The details must be left to shape itself* [*sic*].[6]

In stressing the organic unity of Central Park, as well as in each of the parks that he created, Olmsted subordinated the artificial and man-made objects to the vegetation. To the extent that roads, bridges, walls, seats, and buildings must be constructed for the convenience of a mass of people, they detract from the aesthetic element of the park. However, where they are required, they must be subordinate and harmonious with the natural features. They must not conspicuously obtrude. Whatever necessary construction is to be introduced must be "fitted to nature" so that it will blend naturally with the pastoral or picturesque vegetative environment.

In advising the architect preparing a public house for the convenience of visitors in Montreal's Mount Royal Park, Olmsted directed that the conspicuous parts were to be of ax-finished timber and unpainted. The building was to be fitted "to sit on a saddle of rock, so surrounded by natural low wood, growing on the ground declining from it, that while commanding from its upper parts a magnificent outlook the building will scarcely be seen except by those who have occasion to use it."[7] To maintain the integrity of this principle, Olmsted vehemently fought with every means available to him against politicians, park commissioners, recreational groups, unknowing do-gooders, patriotic groups, businessmen, real estate speculators, newspaper editors, and others who attempted—and in some cases succeeded—to destroy the wholeness of his artistic work. Were Olmsted to have had his way in Central Park, there would be no zoo, no statues, no buildings, no flower gardens, no swimming pool, no theater, and no cafés to destroy the organic unity of the design he and Vaux conceived and executed.

The organic principle was so imperative to Olmsted that it led him to consider the fitness of the artistic design in relation to the region and the locality. The result in a design had to be locally congruous and appropriate to the "original conditions of the locality."

In planning the Back Bay area in Boston, Olmsted undertook to solve three problems: to control flooding, to correct the unhealthy

FIGURE 2.2   *Plan for proposed improvement of Back Bay, Boston, 1879.*
COURTESY NATIONAL PARK SERVICE, FREDERICK LAW OLMSTED
NATIONAL HISTORIC SITE

conditions caused by brackish water, and to beautify an uninterest-
ing area. The first two problems were matters of engineering that
posed no difficulty of solution for Olmsted. It was the landscaping
problem that gave him momentary pause. The organic principle
required him to conceive of an artistic composition that would
utilize the vegetation, the meandering water, and the blooming islets
indigenous to the Back Bay. Olmsted intended his design to be a

> direct development of the original conditions of the locality in
> adaptation to the needs of a dense community. So regarded, it
> will be found to be, in the artistic sense of the word, natural
> and possible to suggest a modest poetic sentiment more grate-
> ful to town-weary minds than elaborate and elegant gardenlike
> work would have yielded.[8]

An aspect of the Back Bay project involved the construction of
the Fenway—a city–suburb parkway in which Olmsted creatively
attempted to incorporate the assets of natural beauty while providing the utility of a broad highway for the efficient flow of vehicular
traffic. To aid him in the construction of the parkway bridges,
Olmsted called upon his neighbor and long-intimate friend, Henry
Hobson Richardson, the outstanding American architectural pio-

neer, with whom Olmsted had maintained over the years a professional association.

The compatibility of Richardson's principles with Olmsted's can be seen in their joint endeavors. In the Fenway bridge, there is plainly visible the organic beauty–function aesthetic. Richardson had early established the practice of using local materials so that his buildings would be congruent with their surroundings.[9] Henry–Russell Hitchcock, Jr., describes the Fenway bridge as really two bridges— one of Roxbury, Massachusetts, pudding stone across the water and the other of metal over the railroad tracks and the street. The bridges are simple and without embellishment; the result, said Hitchcock, is inconspicuous. The pudding stone bridge is "harmonious with the curves of the landscape, quite as the metal bridge is appropriate to the straight lines of the railroad." Hitchcock describes Olmsted's Back Bay planning as a "remarkable example of a new and more intelligent attitude toward the problem of large-scale urban planning and landscape design."[10]

When called upon to plan the layout of Stanford University in California, Olmsted showed how architectural forms and landscape materials suitable to West Coast conditions could be properly used in a functional and aesthetic manner. In consideration of his organic conception, he took into account the characteristics of the California topography and climate and the use to which the grounds would be put. Given the prevailing conditions, Olmsted rejected the customary traditional approach of building and landscaping in imitation of the East Coast. He employed instead Richardson's Romanesque style of architecture—similar to the California Mission style.[11] In the landscaping aspect, too, Olmsted abjured the plants, trees, and turf of the East Coast for a vegetation common and natural to the climate of southern Spain and the Mediterranean lands. These, he held, were adaptable to the natural circumstances of the California climate and the site of the university.[12]

When Olmsted turned his attention to the planning of suburban towns, the organic principle acquired multiple applications. First, the town plan must be consonant with the topography; it must be a self-contained artistic whole. If the site of the town were to be artistically "true," then the planned town must develop in relation to the natural environment. There would be no arbitrary graphlike rectangularity, no forcing of straight streets where a glen or rock promontory would more naturally call for a curve. The regular and monotonous grid pattern would have no place where irregularity and picturesqueness were the more natural. The plans for the suburban towns of Riverside, Illinois, and Riverdale in New York City are examples of Olmsted's use of the organic, beauty–function aesthetic. He combined the organic conception of humanity with an organic aesthetic. He attempted to fuse these two in the hope that he would overcome the "unnatural" conditions of alienation fostered by antagonisms engendered by trade and commerce and the friendless, impersonal relations characteristic of mass society.

These principles led him to advocate the need for comprehensive city plans, especially for great rapidly growing cities, such as Boston, New York and London.[13]

As was earlier stated, Olmsted absorbed from Bushnell, Carlyle, and Coleridge the conceptions of the organic nature of the universe and the complementary notion of the unconscious. In the hands of the romantics, the role of the unconscious in epistemology and in the psychology of artistic creativity achieved great importance. For Olmsted, the conception of the unconscious and its use were of foremost importance. He viewed the unconscious as an active element in the human learning process. However, he extended the function of the unconscious into his aesthetic theory, considering it, first, as necessary in the creative process of the artist and, second, as the link by which the artist reaches the spectator. As will be explained presently, this will be the means by which Olmsted hoped to reform society.

In regard to artistic invention, he deliberately attempted to focus directly upon the psychological process by which he created the design that would determine his artistic product. For Olmsted, there were two general areas of operation in creative activity. First, there was the inductive process, which involved the rational, conscious effort to become empirically familiar with the topography of the ground with which he worked. This required a comprehensive study involving the relations of the parts to one another and to the whole, the character of the construction, and the emergence of a general plan or design incorporating some idea of the principles to be undertaken.

Once the awareness of the design was secured, then the planning could "go on in a deductive way, from comprehensive to the incomprehensive, larger to smaller, from the more controlling to the less controlling features."[14] What Olmsted meant by the "deductive"

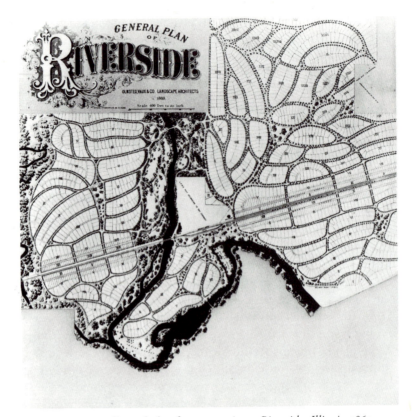

FIGURE 2.3   *General plan for community at Riverside, Illinois, 1869.*
COURTESY NATIONAL PARK SERVICE, FREDERICK LAW OLMSTED
NATIONAL HISTORIC SITE

in the creative process is the welling up of unconscious elements into consciousness to provide the detailed substance in which the general empirical design is filled in to complete the grand design. It is in this latter process that the genius of the artist emerges and manifests itself. Unlike "inductive reasoning" the "deductive" operation is "a natural, spontaneous, individual action of the imagination—of *creative fancy*," Olmsted said. "It is a matter of *growth;* involuntary and unconscious growth. I cannot come to a designing conclusion just when I want to. I must muse upon the conditions to be dealt with, have them upon my mind, and, after a time, I find a conclusion. I do not make it. It has to come to be in my mind without my knowing it. . . . A well considered plan," Olmsted wrote, "cannot be had by any forced mental process. It must be reached by a natural and fluent, deliberately contemplative action of the imagination."[15]

In his all-too-brief accounts of the psychology of his own creative activity, Olmsted described the process by which the artist arrives at a synthesis. It is apparent that he was careful to explain that a necessary awareness of empirical factors of area, topography, climate, and function consciously gave form to his creative effort. For Olmsted, the artistic invention was a reciprocating activity between the conscious and the unconscious. A work of art achieves completion in this intimate union.

On first reading John Ruskin's writings, he was intrigued by the essayist's identification of beauty in art and nature with morality and religion. When Olmsted turned to designing landscapes, he found a use for Ruskin that he had not at first anticipated in his earlier study. The reformer's critical analysis of landscape paintings gave Olmsted guidelines for the development of his own art of landscape architecture. Ruskin's writings became part of the intellectual corpus with which Olmsted approached landscape design. He averred that "as to general principles and spirit of design, all of Ruskin's art works are helpful."[16] However, Olmsted differed from the Englishman's views in a number of respects. He was aesthetically more progressive than was Ruskin. Unlike him, Olmsted did not accept the Gothic as the ultimate form in architecture. While Ruskin rejected the picturesque as a degraded form of artistic expression—except in the very special character given to it in the English landscape paintings of Joseph Mallord William Turner—Olmsted always included elements of the picturesque—roughness and ruggedness—in his park designs. Further, Olmsted rejected Ruskin's view that "Man never touches nature but to spoil; he operates on her as a barber would on the Apollo."[17]

Had Olmsted unreservedly followed Ruskin, he could never have claimed that Central Park in Manhattan, Prospect Park in Brooklyn, Franklin Park in Boston, and all the other great public grounds he designed were re-creations of nature. He said that man can rationally give to nature a better aspect than nature itself could produce unaided.[18] In his plan for Mount Royal in Montreal, he asked, "Why is it more irrational to . . . sympathetically cooperate with nature for the end which you have in view?" The artistic function of the landscape architect is "to so select the material of planting, or the native material to be left growing, that, within reasonable limits, the principle upon which nature, unassisted, proceeds in her selection (though often very imperfectly) shall be emphasized, idealized, or made more apparent in landscape quality."[19] By this method, Olmsted held, the artist rationally and sympathetically cooperates with nature to produce a new perception of nature "which will in truth be equally natural in aspect . . . and far more charming than the best that nature, *unencouraged,* would much more slowly give you."[20]

In contradistinction to Ruskin's view, Olmsted claimed that the landscape architect creates beauty in nature by epitomizing and idealizing it through his genius. He reformulates nature as a landscape painter would by selecting, leaving out, and including. This way, the artist removes the blots of ugliness, decay, and enfeebled forms and progresses toward a harmonized conception of natural beauty.

Olmsted, the creative artist, differed from Ruskin, the aesthetic critic, at various points. Nonetheless, Olmsted respected Ruskin and turned to his writing for support. It is likely that the reason for Olmsted's copious use of Ruskin lay not only in Olmsted's affinity for Ruskin's moral and aesthetic position but also in his tactical purposes. Much of Olmsted's writings, including his reports, surveys, and planning projects, was, like Ruskin's, didactic. To gain support for his plans, he was wont to use Ruskin's popularity as an arbiter of aesthetic taste.

In the second volume of *Modern Painters,* Ruskin stated the elements that he believed to be the roots of beauty: typical beauty and vital beauty. The first consists of that "external quality of bodies . . . which, whether it occur in a stone, flower, beast, or in man, is absolutely identical, [and] which . . . may be shown to be in some sort typical of the Divine attributes." Ruskin invested his idealized world of nature with divine or spiritual qualities. The second consists of "the appearance of felicitous fulfillment of function in living things, more especially of the joyful and right exertion of perfect life in man."[21] According to Ruskin, the moral qualities comprising typical beauty that may be reflected in natural objects are repose, unity, infinity, symmetry, purity, and moderation. Olmsted received these qualities of beauty as principles of artistic composition, as well as the means to achieve a functional realization of social purpose through art. The qualities that he emphasized in his designs are those of repose, unity, and infinity.

In designing his great urban parks, Olmsted considered the quality of repose of foremost significance. To provide relief from the anxieties provoked by the discrepant conditions of the nineteenth-century commercial–industrial city, he urged the creation of large municipal parks, believing that the natural scenery of the park would offer a "suggestion of freedom and repose which must in itself be refreshing and tranquilizing to the visitor coming from the confinement and bustle of crowded streets."[22] Olmsted attempted to achieve the sense of repose in his park designs by creating scenes of landscape beauty that would soothe and refresh. In the heart of the city, he created compositions of open, pastoral landscapes and sylvan scenes that emulated the rural quiet and tranquillity of his native Connecticut countryside.

Although John Ruskin's aesthetics reinforced Olmsted's conclusion that the quality of repose is an essential feature of great art, he had already arrived at the notion from his early reading of Uvedale Price's *On the Picturesque* and also from his study of *Solitude,* the work of the Swiss physician, Johann Georg von Zimmermann (1728–1795).

Price distinguished between that which is characteristically beautiful and that which is picturesque in painting and landscape scenery. The beautiful, he averred, consists of "the quality of smoothness, and consequently of ease and repose"[23] to the viewer. He claimed that the effect of repose can be attained with a gently sloping bank of soft and smooth turf, the flowing lines and breadth of a grassy meadow, the gently swelling hillocks of soft and undulating form, and the tranquil surfaces of a lake. In contrast, Price said the picturesque consists of rough, rugged, and abrupt surfaces, such as forests, tangled thickets, rocky projections, and fragments of rock and large stones lying in irregular masses. He associated the ideas that these elements convey with the sensibilities of irritation, animation, variety, and curiosity. Price felt that the qualities of both, the beautiful and the picturesque, are found blended in great works of art.[24] In designing his parks, Olmsted viewed beauty in the collective or blended sense suggested by Price.

Olmsted's concern to establish a haven of repose within the city came also from his study of Zimmermann's *Solitude,* a book widely read in America. Emerson and the Concord group, especially the writer Henry David Thoreau, acknowledged its influence. Zimmermann's purpose was "to exhibit the necessity of combining the uses of Solitude with those of Society."[25] He recognized that civilization can be attained only in society. Society, he stated, unites men with a community of pursuits and interests by which the means of human knowledge are advanced; but, said Zimmermann, metropolitan society is an arena of vice, avarice, antagonisms, tensions, and anxieties. These weaken or destroy virtuous conduct and dignity of character.

To surmount the disadvantages of society, Zimmermann advised occasional solitude, primarily in an environment of unembellished nature. Amid the repose and tranquillity of rural scenery or natural landscape, solitude, he affirmed, "induces a habit of contemplation which invigorates the faculties of the soul . . . [and] raises them to the highest energies."[26] The repose and serenity of green pastures and still waters free the imagination so that it may turn the mind to the development of worthy and virtuous sentiments. In the solitude of rural repose, man may re-create himself and return to society to carry out the inevitable duties that everyone—whatever his station in society—must perform.

The idea of repose was never far from the idea of duty in Zimmermann, Ruskin, or Olmsted. They did not consider repose to be a state of indolence or intellectual torpidity. Rather, it was a stage of freedom is which the mind, unconsciously, sharpens its faculties and perceptions; fosters reflection and re-creation; encourages the mind to find inspiration.

For Olmsted, the quality of repose fulfilled a social function for which the park was created. He said, "the most essential element of park scenery is turf in broad unbroken fields, because in this the antithesis of the confined spaces of the town is most marked."[27]

In interpreting the features of his first venture in park planning, Central Park in New York City, Olmsted asserted: "The Park throughout is a single work of art, and as such subject to the primary law of every work of art, namely, that it shall be framed upon a single, noble motive, to which the design of all its parts, in some more or less subtle way, shall be confluent and helpful."[28] He explained that in the original plan, Central Park was invisibly subdivided into five distinct sections that would, nevertheless, have unity of effect as a whole.

As Olmsted progressed from one project to another, he attempted to refine his theory. He was self-consciously endeavoring to establish and define an area of art that incorporated the techniques of the painter, the gardener, the botanist, the engineer, and the architect. He denominated the result as the art of landscape archi-

FIGURE 2.4   *Landscaped site in Central Park, New York City.*
COURTESY NATIONAL PARK SERVICE, FREDERICK LAW OLMSTED
NATIONAL HISTORIC SITE

tecture. In the process of refining and defining, he purified his conceptions of what his art should be. In the projected development of Prospect Park in Brooklyn in 1866, he pointed out that in the formation of park scenery in the natural style, it was not his intention merely to imitate nature. This, he said, is not art, no matter how successful he might be in providing a mirror of nature. The concern of the artist in re-creating scenes of nature's beauty is to realize that a

> scene in nature is made up of various parts; each part has its individual character and its possible ideal. It is unlikely that accident should bring together the best possible ideals of each separate part, merely considering them as isolated facts, and it is still more unlikely that accident should group a number of these possible ideals in such a way that not only one or two but that all should be harmoniously related one to the other.[29]

Only the genius of the artist can discover the law of harmonious relation between multitudinous discrete details and bring them together into an organic whole. In his Mount Royal plan, Olmsted restated this point:

In works of art which the experience of the world has stamped of a high grade of value, there is found a strong single purpose, with a variety of subordinate purposes so worked out and working together that the main purpose is better served because of the diversity of these subordinate purposes. The first secures the quality of unity and harmony; the others, that of a controlled harmony.[30]

To the residents of the agglomerated city, confined by the blank walls of city buildings and restricted by the grid patterns of the city streets, Olmsted offered in his parks the suggestion of great open spaces—a sense of vast distance. His object in creating this impression was not mere contrast, a mere change of view for the sake of change. He believed that the buildings and the street patterns must have a psychological effect upon the mind that limits man's conception of the universe and his role in it. The impulse to imaginative thought and the sense of freedom are curtailed by the physical and psychological block to the spirit of the city dweller. To counteract the sense of confinement, Olmsted instilled the quality of infinity in his landscape theory as a necessary antithesis to the city pattern. The sense of infinite space that he sought to provoke in the mind of the park spectator is deliberately implanted in his landscaping art. He regarded spaciousness as "the essence of the park"[31] and created the illusion of infinite space by inducing the vision of the spectator to focus on the curve of the horizon. For Olmsted, the artist's ability to impart the sense of infinity was central because "this character is the highest ideal that can be aimed at for a park under any circumstances, and . . . it is in most decided contrast to the confined and formal lines of the city."[32] Olmsted illustrated this motive in his explanation of an aspect of his design of Central Park.

Vista Rock, at the southwest corner of the reservoir in Central Park, is the most distant natural eminence that can be seen from any point in the southern part of the park. If the observer enters the park from the southernmost entrance at Columbus Circle, the visitor's eye falls upon an unbroken meadow that extends nearly a thousand feet. The artistic purpose of the meadow is meant to give the suggestion of freedom and repose, a refreshing and tranquilizing effect in contrast to the confinement and bustle of crowded streets. However, Olmsted explained, there is more to the scene:

The observer, resting for a moment to enjoy the scene, which he is induced to do by the arrangement of the planting, cannot but hope for still greater space than is obvious before him, and this hope is encouraged first, by the fact that, though bodies of rock and foliage to the right and left obstruct his direct vision, no limit is seen to the extension of the meadow in a lateral direction; while beyond the low shrubs, which form an undefined border to it in front, there are not trees or other impediments to vision for half a mile or more, and the only distinct object is the wooded knoll of Vista Rock, nearly a mile away, upon the summit of which it is an important point in the design . . . to erect a slight artificial structure, for the purpose of catching the eye and the better to hold it in this direction. The imagination of the visitor is thus led instinctively to form the idea that a broad expanse is opening before him.[33]

Inducing the eye to a distant point where the green of the field meets the light of the horizon was one of the three artistic techniques that Olmsted employed to implant a sense of infinity in the observer.

Another technique that Olmsted used to give the semblance of infinity was to impart a sense of gradation through chiaroscuro. By the imaginative clustering of trees, shrubbery, mosses, and rocks, he contrived intricate scenes of nature in which the dispersion of lights and shadows "would create a degree of obscurity not absolutely impenetrable, but sufficient to affect the imagination with a sense of mystery." Just as a painter uses the colors of his palette, Olmsted used the natural colors of vegetation and the sunlight to show gradations of light and color. This subtle combination and interplay of the "soft commingling lights and shadows and fading tints of color" in the varicolored context of undergrowth encourage the possibility of infinite space.[34]

The third device that Olmsted used to obtain the sense of infinity was the curve. He thought that by its changes of direction, the curve divides itself infinitely. He believed with Ruskin that "there are no lines nor surfaces of nature without curvature" and that all curves are more beautiful than right lines.[35]

Olmsted utilized these conceptions in every aspect of his planning of parks. The whole panorama of the park consists of groupings of trees and shrubs, hills and outcroppings of rock, meadows and bodies of water that he looked upon as visual stanzas in a consistent landscape poem. Each part is united with every other by means of curved roadways and walkways that permit the spectator to gain the maximum visual poetic effect—"the bracing, soothing, tranquilizing medication of poetical scenery."[36]

It would be a mistake to disregard the effect of Olmsted's Calvinist upbringing upon his landscaping art. The religious orientation and training of young Olmsted were intense and pervasive. He described his parents as typically Puritan. Both at home and at school he experienced the inculcation of the Protestant ethic. Religion, as a motivating factor in his life, had become deep-seated for Olmsted by the time he was twenty-four years old. Although his religiosity declined in his later life, the psychological sanctions that gave direction to practical conduct in the form of an ethic remained with him. In all his endeavors—whether as a farmer, as a writer, as a city planner, or as a landscape architect—there was the sense of duty to perform his calling for the purpose of perfecting society. One must always understand Olmsted as a social reformer.

Earlier in this chapter, when I discussed Olmsted's conceptions of organic unity and the complementary notion, the unconscious, and their relationship to his aesthetic theory, I considered these in the context of the creative impulse of the artist. I mentioned, however, that for Olmsted the unconscious became the link by which the artist reached the spectator. It is in this link that Olmsted consummates his aesthetic theory. It is, ultimately, the means by which art achieves the reform of society.

In Olmsted's aesthetic, it is only in the mind of the spectator that the creative idea can achieve the purpose that the artist intended. It is not enough that the artist attain the highest synthesis in a work of art. The fact that in the creative process the artist discovers himself and his own idea in the materials with which he works is only part of the total aesthetic experience. The artist must identify with the spectator to cultivate and predispose the mind of the observer to see the world as the artist has organized it. Art and nature and art as nature attain significance through the aesthetic reason. The circle of aesthetic experience achieves closure when the spectator realizes the intent of the artist.

Olmsted's public was the heterogeneous mass of population who flooded into the cities of the United States during the latter half of the nineteenth century. He was fully aware that the commercial-industrial city produced effects that were detrimental to the physical and mental health of the inhabitants of cities. The failure of

FIGURE 2.5 *Frederick Law Olmsted, c. 1895.*

COURTESY NATIONAL PARK SERVICE, FREDERICK LAW OLMSTED
NATIONAL HISTORIC SITE

public and private agencies to provide adequate services and accommodations for the city dwellers had resulted in noxious conditions calling for reform. He intended that his parks represent something more than green oases in the teeming, fetid cities. Olmsted considered his urban parks to be a means of social reform. To achieve this, he joined the aesthetic experience with social use. With Emerson and the American sculptor Horatio Greenough, Olmsted held that beauty and function are essentially bound together; art must have social relevance. In order to provide his parks with a function, he imputed a social value to them.

Olmsted believed that his parks would exercise "an immediate and very striking educational influence" that would "soon manifest itself in certain changes to taste and of habits, consequently in the requirements of the people."[37] He held that the enjoyment of the park scenery would inspire the spectators to participate in the chain of aesthetic experience that is somewhat similar to the artist's path of creation. In this process, the observer identifies with the creator. The casual park stroller, exposed to the beauty and grandeur of nature, is invited to participate in the creative reason of the artist. The visible world of the park provides a mnemonic to the unconscious and activates dormant potentialities. In his assessment of the value of his parks, Olmsted insistently relied upon the unconscious. He asserted that if Central Park had any relevance,

> in the last analysis it will be found to be to produce certain influences on the imagination of those who visit it, influences which are received and which act, for the most part, unconsciously to those who benefit by them.[38]

For Olmsted, the unconscious was as significant in the artist-spectator relationship as in the creative activity of the artist.

Inspired by beauty, the spectator reaches the aesthetic condition—a condition in which the beauty of nature or a genuine work of art releases the spectator from sensuous and intellectual constraints. In appreciation and response to the beauty of the park, the mind is educated aesthetically, freeing it to unfold in disinterested contemplation. In this state, the compulsions that motivate man negate each other by their mutual opposition. However, the drives of sense and reason simultaneously remain active, achieving reconciliation in the perception and appreciation of beauty. Olmsted put it this way:

the enjoyment of the emotions caused by natural scenery . . . employs the mind without fatigue and yet exercises it; and thus, through the influence of the mind over the body, gives the effect of refreshing rest and reinvigoration to the whole system.[39]

While the aesthetic experience may be consciously perceived, Olmsted contended, most of the effect of the experience is of an unconscious nature. Consciously and unconsciously, the contemplation of scenes of beauty results, he said, in "a sense of enlarged freedom [which] is to all, at all times, the most certain and the most valuable gratification afforded by the park."[40] It is a freedom that is to be apprehended by the energized psyche in the state of active repose. In the dynamic reciprocity of the two drives—the intelligential and the sensuous—the constraints upon the psyche are annulled and man achieves the realization of a third nature—the aesthetic or poetic. At the same moment, he becomes aware of the potential power of the self—for, as Olmsted stated it, "The whole body of the susceptibilities of civilized men and with their susceptibilities their powers, are on the whole enlarged."[41]

Olmsted was convinced that aesthetic education would expand the understanding so that individuals would develop a better society. His intention was to enhance the quality of life for all by putting his art to social use. In his essay on "The Sociological Viewpoint in Art," Oscar Lovell Triggs recognized Olmsted's effort. Triggs wrote, "When art is considered as one of the processes of idealization by which all psychic forms and social institutions are shaped, its proper place appears in the circle of social agents."[42] Because he believed that Olmsted carried this principle into effect through the creative art of his urban parks, Triggs described Frederick Law Olmsted as the greatest American artist of the nineteenth century.

NOTES

1. Humphrey Repton (1907) *The Art of Landscape Gardening,* edited by John Nolen, Boston, Houghton Mifflin, p. 167.
2. Mary A. Cheney (1880) *Life and Letters of Horace Bushnell,* New York, Harper and Brothers, p. 499.
3. Frederick Law Olmsted (1922) *Forty Years of Landscape Architecture,* edited

by Frederick Law Olmsted, Jr., and Theodora Kimball, 2 volumes, New York, G. P. Putnam's Sons, 1:80.

4. Charles Capen McLaughlin (ed.) and Charles E. Beveridge (assoc. ed.) (1977) *The Papers of Frederick Law Olmsted: The Formative Years, 1822–1852*, Baltimore and London, Johns Hopkins University Press, vol. 1, p. 272.
5. Quoted in M. H. Abrams (1958) *The Mirror and the Lamp: Romantic Theory and the Critical Tradition*, New York, W.W. Norton, p. 213.
6. Frederick Law Olmsted, undated fragments, Olmsted Papers, Library of Congress. My italics.
7. Frederick Law Olmsted (1881) *Mount Royal, Montreal*, New York, G. P. Putnam's Sons, pp. 55n, 77.
8. Olmsted explained that he expected the improvement to be so natural that the Back Bay's "rushy glades and bushy islands will supply well-guarded seclusions" for all manner of wild water-fowl to breed but at the same time will have an educative effect for young, observing children as a kind of living museum of wildlife. *Annual Report*, Doc. No. 5, Boston, Board of Commissioners of the Department of Parks, 1880.
9. Henry–Russell Hitchcock, Jr. (1936) *The Architecture of H. H. Richardson and His Times*, New York, Museum of Modern Art, pp. 111, 119.
10. Ibid., pp. 214–15.
11. Diane K. McGuire (1957) "Early site planning on the West Coast: Frederick Law Olmsted's plan for Stanford University," *Landscape Architecture*, 47 (January), pp. 345, 346, 349.
12. Olmsted had made similar landscaping suggestions to the College of California at Berkeley; Olmsted, Vaux & Co. (1866), *Report upon a Projected Improvement of the Estate of the College of California at Berkeley, Near Oakland*, San Francisco, Towne and Bacon; reprinted in *Civilizing American Cities, A Selection of Frederick Law Olmsted's Writings on the City Landscape*, edited by S.B. Sutton, Cambridge, MIT Press, 1971, pp. 286–87.
13. Frederick Law Olmsted (1871), "Public parks and the enlargement of towns," *Journal of Social Science*, 3, pp. 13, 14, 21, 24.
14. Frederick Law Olmsted to Morris K. Jessup, January 31, 1889, Olmsted Papers, Library of Congress.
15. Frederick Law Olmsted to Board of Commissioners of the Central Park, January 22, 1861.
16. Quoted in Laura Wood Roper (1973) *FLO: A Biography of Frederick Law Olmsted*, Baltimore and London, Johns Hopkins University Press, p. 408.
17. John Ruskin (1904–1912) *The Works of John Ruskin*, edited by E. T. Cook and Alexander Wedderburn, Library Edition, 39 volumes, London, George Allen, 3: 627–28.
18. Olmsted, *Mount Royal*, pp. 33, 34.
19. Ibid., p. 43.
20. Ibid.
21. Ruskin, *The Works*, 4: 64.
22. Olmsted, Vaux & Co. (1866), "Sixth annual report, 1866" [Prospect Park], *Brooklyn Park Commissioners*, p. 101; Olmsted, *Forty Years*, 2: 239 and n.
23. Uvedale Price (1842) *On the Picturesque, with an Essay on the Origin of Taste*

by Thomas Dick Lauder, Edinburgh, Caldwell, Lloyd, pp. 112–13. Also see note 25 below.

24. Ibid., pp. 105, 115, 116.

25. Johann Georg von Zimmermann (1798), *Solitude,* 2 volumes, London, 2:308 9.

26. Ibid, 1:99.

27. *American Cyclopaedia,* Frederick Law Olmsted (1881) "Park."

28. Olmsted, *Forty Years,* 2:45.

29. Olmsted, Vaux, "Sixth annual report, 1866," p. 98.

30. Olmsted, *Mount Royal,* pp. 42, 43.

31. [Frederick Law Olmsted] (1886) *Notes on the Plan of Franklin Park and Related Matters,* Boston, City of Boston Park Department, p. 107.

32. Olmsted, *Forty Years,* 2:214.

33. Olmsted asserted that to achieve "this most important purpose in the scenery of Central Park" required "much more labor and a larger expenditure than any other landscape feature of the undertaking"; Olmsted, *Forty Years,* 2:239–40n, 495. Tunnard and Pushkarev claim that "human beings have some physiological needs which can be satisfied only by open space"; Christopher Tunnard and Boris Pushkarev (1963), *Man-Made America: Chaos or Control? An Inquiry into Selected Problems of Design in the Urbanized Landscape,* New Haven, Yale University Press, p. 359. The authors support Olmsted's aesthetic principles with their assertion: "Beyond the conceptual requirements, we know that a view of space in nature must give satisfaction in some of the basic ways in which any beautiful object satisfies"; ibid., p. 363. See their discussion on the aesthetics of open space; ibid., pp. 361–87.

34. Olmsted, *Forty Years,* 2:250.

35. Ruskin, *The Works,* 4:88, 106.

36. Olmsted, *Mount Royal,* p. 25.

37. [Frederick Law Olmsted] (1869) Buffalo Park Commission, *Preliminary Report Respecting a Public Park in Buffalo and a Copy of the Act of the Legislature Authorizing Its Establishment,* Buffalo, Matthews and Warren, p. 15.

38. Olmsted, *Forty Years,* 2:435–46.

39. Frederick Law Olmsted (1952) "The Yosemite Valley and the Mariposa big trees: a preliminary report (1865)," edited with an introductory note by Laura Wood Roper, *Landscape Architecture,* 43 (October), pp. 20–21.

40. Olmsted, Vaux, "Sixth annual report, 1866," p. 93.

41. Olmsted, "The Yosemite Valley," p. 20.

42. Oscar Lovell Triggs (1905) *The Changing Order: A Study of Democracy,* Chicago, Oscar L. Triggs Publishing, pp. 200–201.

FIGURE 3.1   *John Nolen, 1895.*

3

John Nolen
THE BACKGROUND OF A
PIONEER PLANNER

JOHN HANCOCK

IN THE FALL OF 1908 a group of prominent business and professional men formed the Civic Association of Reading, Pennsylvania, for the singular purpose of promoting their city's better physical development. Officially a nonpolitical body, their aim was to influence key local power groups by making an extended survey of Reading's problems and then to use its results in pressuring for improvements through concerted municipal action. Later the Association members were to indicate, individually, some strong ideas about the nature and solution of civic problems in Reading; but they did not specify any particular course of improvement during the period of organization. Instead their first act as an organized body was to seek the advice of an "expert" who, coming from outside the city, could analyze its physical problems, forecast future needs, and then "form a general programme of city making."[1]

The "expert" they selected was John Nolen of Cambridge, Massachusetts, a man whose professional title was "landscape architect," although he had been working extensively with the replanning of cities for three years and had been interested in municipal problems since his undergraduate days in the 1890s. The choice of

Reprinted with permission from John Hancock, "John Nolen: The Background of a Pioneer Planner," *Journal of the American Institute of Planners* 26, no. 4 (1960): 302–312.

the Association was a fortunate one for both parties. For the Association, Nolen was an unbiased specialist whose presence in Reading could not offend anyone. It was announced in the newspapers that Nolen, a man who "beautified cities," had come to Reading to advise its citizens on the means of making it a more attractive place, particularly to outside businessmen looking for new industrial locations.[2] To Nolen, the Association represented a body of intelligent leading citizens seriously interested in civic betterment who could be taught, should they not realize it already, that city planning meant not just beautification but also provision for environmental needs of all Reading's citizenry—that planning for the health and welfare of her people was sound business sense as well as the ultimate purpose of "city making."[3]

In interests and background, Nolen had much in common with these men. Born in Philadelphia in 1869, he remained an urban Easterner all his life. College educated, he was able and eager to give expression to his concerns. Although never a businessman in the limited sense, he was a professional in business for himself, whose work consisted of selling services—ideas and plans—to others. His office undertook the planning of large-scale municipal projects on a contract basis throughout the United States without ever being an official part of any government, as are so many planning services today. His success, like that of the commercial and civic organizations who first employed him, depended in large measure upon his persuasive abilities. At the same time, his early life was more thoroughly illustrative of mobility and success in the traditional American ideology than that of his sponsors and emphatically unlike that of his predecessors in the field of large-scale planning[4]: he was of obscure lower-middle-class parentage; he had to make his own way from early adolescence; he had not set out to be an artist, architect, or engineer as an undergraduate—he did not even become a landscape architect until he was thirty-five; his interests at college were in economics, history (especially near-contemporary American history), philosophy, and public administration; although widely traveled, he never studied in any of the European art schools; he had very few personal contacts with members of the social register or with the well-known late-nineteenth- and early-twentieth-century artists then admired, such as Charles McKim, Stanford White, the Hunts, Saint-Gaudens, the elder Olmsted, and D. H. Burnham, although he had met these men and soon acquired many prominent, powerful friends among the newly and the almost wealthy. In brief, his background equipped him with a point of view as a planner more characteristic of the young militant, middle-class reformers of the twentieth century than of the more established, paternalistic stewards of wealth and their retinue of the late nineteenth. From both groups, however, he inherited the common legacy of a sense of responsible leadership and an adherence to the main tenets of the American value system.

EARLY EDUCATION IN LAISSEZ-FAIRE AMERICA

Hard work, sympathetic awareness of man's needs at several levels, and continuous education were the main foundations of Nolen's development in professional planning. He came by these character-istics early and almost instinctively. His father, a carpenter, died when the boy was less than two years old; his mother, long an influence on his ambitions, cared for him until the age of nine when she was able to take him out of the Philadelphia public schools and enroll him in Girard College, where he graduated in 1884. The training young Nolen received at this school for fatherless, poor, white boys was to be recalled vividly in his later ideas and activities. In accordance with its founder's firm views on education, Girard College sought to develop, or redevelop if you will, every aspect of a boy's character. Nolen and others like him received closely super-vised training in academic, vocational, physical, and moral subjects. At Girard, Nolen, who graduated first in his class, acquired his lifelong love for literature, was exposed to European history and the modern romantic languages, demonstrated an unusual capacity for public speaking on contemporary issues, learned the Bible thor-oughly from a nonsectarian but basically Protestant point of view, and was trained unceasingly in the rudimentary duties of responsi-ble citizenship. In addition he learned to use industrial machinery, should the future require his employment as a workingman; and, finally, he was imbued with the concept of regular daily exercise in the out-of-doors and the need to be proficient in at least one sport throughout life.[5]

Girard College's rigorous curriculum was based upon the activ-ist, somewhat Calvinistic, notion that men succeeded in life only through individual hard work, self-discipline, clean living, and service to others. In fulfilling Stephen Girard's dictum that "No man shall be a gentleman on my money," idleness was never tolerated.[6] But the training was also extremely practical when one considers how closely it paralleled the ethic of success in New Testament America—if one did not become a Captain of Industry he would at least acquire skills enough to be satisfied with the existing system of mobility, just as he would understand he had been the one poor orphan Alger out of five or six fortunate enough to have been snatched away from a probable life of degradation and misery in the streets. Furthermore, the training had the real merit of being very progressive for its time, thanks to frequent reinterpretations of Girard's liberal, if nonpermissive, will. Cheesman A. Herrick, a Nolen classmate at the University of Pennsylvania and a later president of Girard, has summarized the school's close kinship to the changing world outside:

> In the last analysis, Girard College is a little world . . . [boys] are getting their equipment for the life they will later go to, and they are fitted for the real world just so far as the elements and features of this world are brought into their training . . . the school is more than preparation for life; it is life.[7]

Thus, Nolen finished his early education equipped with the basic tools for success in late-nineteenth-century America and supplied with a headful of moral rationalizations of the status quo in the very possible event that the tools were not enough.[8]

Most of Nolen's worldly experience before 1904 was acquired in administrative and educational positions. After Girard, he clerked in a grocery store for a year and then returned to the school at sixteen to serve as a minor secretary of the Girard Estate Trust Fund for the next five years. These jobs enabled him to accumulate money enough to enter the University of Pennsylvania's Wharton School as an economics and public administration major in 1891. Upon examination, he entered as a junior, and in 1893, at the age of twenty-four, he was graduated with a Bachelor of Philosophy degree. Thus, although he had come comparatively late to college, he already had accumulated five years of administrative experience and several more of constant employment. In three summers away from the University he also served as director of Onteora Park, a New York State resort; and before his graduation, he undertook a full-time job with the newly formed Society for the Extension of University Teaching.

Learning to Challenge the Older Order in a Changing Society

At Pennsylvania he combined several of his former interests with formal training in administrative work. He was a member of the Wharton Congress, a debating group; he won third prize in the University oratorical contest in his senior year; together with Franklin Spencer Edmunds, he founded and wrote for the Wharton *Bulletin;* continuing his progress as a distinguished student (he graduated "with distinction" in a class that included Thomas Soverign Gates, who became president of the University in 1930), Nolen was deemed certain to attain success and renown.[9]

His formal course work reflected his interests in contemporary affairs and it was also an index to the near-vocational fields then opening up on the edge of the traditional humanities. He took courses in "money management," "constitutional law and politics," the "sociology" of the state, "finance and administration." From liberal economist Simon N. Patten (who along with Richard Ely and others led the revolt against classical economic theories and spearheaded the modern interest in national economic planning), he learned the rudiments of "political economy." Patten was also the source for many of the concepts on national planning held by Rexford G. Tugwell, head of the Resettlement Administration during the New Deal; and Patten's ideas appear nearly unadulterated in the writings of Walter Weyl (*The New Democracy*), one of the theorists of the progressive movement.[10] Strikingly close as thinkers although not contemporaries as students, Nolen, Weyl, and Tugwell all studied under Patten at Pennsylvania.

In contrast, Nolen also had a course from Francis Moore on the new "science" of sociology; his handwritten notes reveal Moore's view that the function of the state was to govern as little as possible and that Socialist "theory" was based on obtaining control of industrial affairs. Professor Robert Ellis Thompson (who also taught Nolen's course in American church history) lectured optimistically on American industrial history but warned his students that, despite the general correctness of the stewardship doctrines of wealth, competition in some fields was insufficient protection to the public interests and in a few cases (he mentioned the railroads) even required government regulation. For pioneer social historian John MacMaster's course on the "political history of the United States,"

Nolen wrote a factual, historical essay on private acquisition of the public domain. He was also in James Harvey Robinson's first class on European history—Robinson later remembered Nolen as his most outstanding student at Pennsylvania. Nolen also wrote papers on the history of philosophy—on Descartes because he was, said Nolen, "the father of modern philosophy," and on John Stuart Mill, the political theorist.[11]

For his senior thesis and first real published work, Nolen characteristically wrote of a contemporary problem: municipal mishandling of the Philadelphia Gas Works and the steps which should be taken to correct the corruption. His conclusion was that the early mismanagement was "not chargeable to public ownership; it was inherent in the system adopted." He suggested that instead of granting a public lease to private corporations there should be outright public ownership, development, and maintenance of gas facilities. He also pointed out that *city* departmental "waste" of gas could be prevented by deducting the cost of gas used from their budget appropriations and that the price of gas to the consumer should be little more than the cost of its manufacture plus a small amount set aside for its future improvement: "Otherwise a portion of the gas rate becomes a tax upon the consumers of gas, and [since the 'wealthy classes' use, proportionally, less than the 'poorer classes'] . . . this tax is an unfair burden upon the latter."[12] This paper was written under the general supervision of Dean Edmund James, of the Wharton School, who, with Patten, Ely, and other rebels against the laissez-faire school, had formed the American Economic Association in 1885.[13]

A "Municipal Statesman" Foreshadowed

There is no doubt that Nolen considered the administrative problems of city government the most pressing domestic issues of the day. In the next few years, he would turn to them again and again—foreshadowing his later, immediate shift from landscape architecture to cooperative municipal action in planning. Addressing the Girard College Class of 1895, he spoke of the city's new role in American life and the need for a new type of local leader to cope with its problems.

The problems of the day . . . which demand our attention are not so much *national* as *municipal*. Life, in its most complex relations, is now in the cities, the vilest criminals, the purest saints are to be found in the great centres of population. Public spirit is not so much needed in Washington as in Philadelphia. On every side we hear the cry for *Municipal Statesmen.*

Who is the man, then, that we should honor? Who is it that deserves our praise? It is he, who lives the fullest civic life. It is he who works for his city with a confidence born of faith. . . . He keeps ever before him an ideal, and strives to make it a reality. Citizenship to him does not merely mean good government and politics, but includes all that effects the happiness, usefulness and virtue of any individual.[14]

Overtly he was leading up to a few words of praise for Stephen Girard, but in fact he was describing his own deepest beliefs, beliefs which in ten years were to make city planning almost a religion with him. His eventual move into that field occurred precisely because he visualized city planning as a profession which must consider "all that effects the happiness, usefulness and virtue" of men. Nolen aspired to be a "Municipal Statesman" himself because, in his eyes, it offered the chance for service, hard work, and self-sacrifice to community goals he had learned to believe in. Nolen was seeking for some kind of total commitment to his society's basic ideals. He did not stop to find it either in political or aesthetic reform but went beyond these to something that might include them and more—the challenge of "comprehensive" (his favorite word) city planning, the opportunity to redesign man's whole environment.

"THE PEOPLE'S UNIVERSITY"

But professional city planning in America had not yet developed, just as urban reform had not yet found the broad public support necessary for sustained action. So for the next ten years after college, Nolen's education continued as he accumulated administrative experience in Philadelphia as executive secretary of the Society for the Extension of University Teaching. He had been recommended for the post by Dean James, a founder of the Extension.

The Extension is an example of the rising popularity of adult education in late-nineteenth-century America and the attempt by men like James to devise a means for the further development of an informed citizenry in a rapidly concentrating democratic society. Somewhat like the old Lyceum, Chatauqua, and Redpath Bureau lectures, it brought a series of public lectures to Philadelphia and other eastern cities—usually to give a "course" consisting of six evening talks on a single subject. Like the winter Chatauqua correspondence program and the newly created night schools for workingmen and immigrants, papers were graded and certificates were awarded those who paid fees and completed the "course." Unlike all the others, it also offered the prestige of association with a university-level, adult educational movement which had its beginning at Oxford. And, most importantly, this early experiment in university extension schooling provided lecture discussion by outstanding figures on some of the most stimulating issues of the day. Besides the usual presentations on literature, art, and the sacred trinity of mother–home–God, the Extension (from 1890 to 1903) offered college credit in most of the humanities and sciences. It introduced lectures on unionism, socialism, social reform, psychology, evolution, heredity and environment, conservation, the American Negro, and Philadelphia municipal government—to name but a very few current topics and new intellectual interests of that day.[15]

These ten years of working for "The People's University," as it was sometimes called, were heady stimulus to Nolen's own intellectual development. He attended almost every lecture given in Philadelphia; he participated as moderator or devil's advocate in the open questioning which followed each talk; he edited most of the Extension's annual reports and campaigned throughout the mid-Atlantic area for the idea of education beyond the formal school years; and for a short time he helped found and edit the Society's short-lived bulletin, *The Citizen*.

Always a prolific reader, Nolen also began to develop his extensive personal library in this period, collecting books by men who remained favorites throughout his life—Emerson, Whitman (then considered a major writer by sociologists if not by English professors), Franklin, Veblen, Bellamy, Twain (whom he knew), Sir Thomas More, Dickens, Arnold, Ruskin, Mill, Goethe, Barrie, and Stevenson among many. All had been subjects of Extension lectures; all were representative of Nolen's general, non-professional reading habits. Self-made men, social critics and utopians, and writers of the whimsical world of children were the authors he preferred.[16]

Conspicuous by their absence in his library were the works of such important modern intellectual giants as Marx, Darwin, Freud, and other determinists who challenged, effectively if indirectly, his optimistic American belief in a society growing out of individual free will, hard work, and voluntary self-sacrifice to commonly agreed upon goals. For Nolen, never an angry man although often a zealous one in quest of his beliefs, anything was possible; the pursuit of the grandest schemes was preferable to patchwork adjustments of reality. In the height of the progressive era he had said: "we have given, heretofore, too much attention to caring for the mere wreckage of society, and too little toward establishing a better social order that would permanently reduce the amount of wreckage."[17] Not a utopian believer in overnight millenniums, he nevertheless sought a broader social order which, although achieved in the future, could be prepared by continuous replanning in the present. His own early mobility had only substantiated his beliefs, only reinforced what had been held up to him as true. His early reading choices confirmed them. Yet he was not a formalist either, in life values or in his art and behavior. To the end of his life he never stopped expanding his intellectual horizons, never ceased looking for new ways of solving both his own and his culture's larger problems. Ever the pragmatist and innovator, John Nolen's core values, derived largely from his early experiences, were quite sufficient to help direct him successfully through the changing dimensions of twentieth-century America. Later compromises, however necessary, would not dissuade him of their general validity.

LANDSCAPE ARCHITECTURE

In 1903 Nolen left the Extension service and entered the School of Landscape Architecture at Harvard University. From the available evidence, his decision seems a sudden one, but it is not surprising given his earlier orientation.

In the first place, there was the importance of his working background—more than fifteen years of administrative experience in service fields plus two more of formal training for such work—all of it in areas more idealistically than financially remunerative. In landscape architecture, his already practiced ability at popularizing and selling services would go far in determining his success. Skill at oratory and writing would underscore that ability. The friendship of many people associated with his work and early life gave him contacts throughout the United States and Europe. Among other things on his application for the degree in landscape architecture, he stated specifically that he wanted his work to "consist in writing and speaking upon the subject, as well as in professional practice."[18]

In the second place, there were the always-present influences of his beliefs in a well-managed, free society, in an environment which could provide opportunity for all people, and in the satisfaction of meeting new challenges, all combined, most importantly, with a love for life out-of-doors. Girard College's emphasis upon a healthy life as a happy one, three pleasant summers as superintendent in charge of landscape work at Onteora Park, a move (in 1896) away from the city's closeness to his own piece of wooded land in Ardmore, where he could, and did, practice the art of landscaping his property—all were forms of preparation for the apparently sudden move.[19]

In the third place, Nolen now had a wife and two children who required adequate means of support. He needed to find a professional or business field with a promising future. Realistic about family needs and idealistic about personal ones, he had too much of the creative instinct to be content with merely administering forever the ideas of other men. Having already worked seventeen years for the things he wanted, ready to sell his Ardmore house to obtain the money for a return to school, he surely believed that landscape architecture not only would challenge his ideals but also could offer reasonable opportunity for economic self-sufficiency.

THE LESSONS OF EUROPE

Finally, there is evidence to suggest that, after a yearlong visit to Europe in 1901–2, Nolen decided to study landscape architecture as a means of redesigning the city. During this visit, his third and most extensive in six years, he saw most of the great cities and architectural complexes of western Europe. The cities of Germany and Switzerland impressed him the most—Switzerland because of the beauty its natural environment gave its urban environment and Germany (which he always loved above all the foreign countries he visited) because of the forest conservation and urban relandscaping projects under way through the stimulus of state law and municipal planning commissions. He informally attended courses at the University of Munich on German law, economics, the history of Italian painting, German architecture and plastics, and the cultural history of the Renaissance, and while there he visited in the homes of his professors.[20]

His scrapbooks and notes on this period did not reveal his

attitude about such well-known examples of landscaping as England's formal gardens, Italy's terraced estates, the great boulevards of Baron Haussmann in Paris, and the vast expanse of gardens at Versailles. Apparently even during this first flirtation with the landscape arts, Nolen shied away from the sculptural monumentality and aesthetic impact of large design. From his later writing on the subject, one gathers that, instead, he sought landscaping techniques which were inclusive but adaptable to a more modest, more natural, above all less wasteful scale of human existence.[21]

He was probably one of the few Americans more overwhelmed by the industrial city of Düsseldorf than by the famed gardens of Versailles. The former represented what was possible in the campaign against human and natural waste so important to Nolen; without disparaging the latter, he merely said that in borrowing from Europe one took what one could use in his own country. He believed that Düsseldorf's parks, fountains, playgrounds, belt lines, and zoning system—in a city otherwise so comparable to Pittsburgh—were stimulating examples of what could be done inexpensively yet at great savings of human lives in America.[22] Thus Nolen stood some distance from the many American landscape architects at the century's end who were still concentrating upon grandiose appearance rather than everyday utility in the practice of their profession.

Probably there was no *exact* moment when he decided to study landscape architecture. In any case, this decision and his later use of that training come as no surprise. The earliest record of his decision that is available to me was in a letter to his wife, September 17, 1902, after the return from Europe and written just after a visit to Central Park to study the "effects of Landscape Architecture, in which my interest now is naturally very keen." And again in a letter to his wife the same week, he spoke at length of his decision:

> In the intervals of work, I have naturally thought some of the future possibility of "John Nolen: Landscape Architect." And I must say I have only satisfaction in the thought—in spite of obstacles ahead. In one respect my experience in selecting the profession is not unlike Charles Eliot's. Once the decision is made or even seriously considered, so many things in the past seem to point to it. For example, out of last year (European trip), when I was away from the things that ordinarily engross me, come three convictions: (1) that art had permanent inter-

est for me and that I must try to do something in it myself; (2) that I love to be out of doors, especially in the open country; (3) but in spite of that fact I doubted any high satisfaction in farming at this time of my life, because it would cut me off so from intellectual contact and afford no large and constant opportunity for public good. Now this new career fits in these [*sic*] like a ball in a socket.[23]

The "now" of that last sentence apparently stems directly from his reading of Charles William Eliot's book about his son, *Charles Eliot, Landscape Architect,* which had just been published. Although he did not always agree with the ideas of the younger Eliot, his later career shows how fundamentally he took to the idea "what must be fair, must be fit." Moreover, it was the Eliot book which confirmed Nolen in the beliefs that "I have a fundamental fitness for such a career" and "that it is a career that I would find congenial and useful."[24]

In these earliest days of defining what would later become his lifelong professional interests, Nolen knew of but apparently was not heavily influenced by the English garden city movement—a movement which vitally affected his work after 1909. But although the direct early evidence of cross-cultural influence is not yet known to me with any completeness, it seems clear that Nolen was but one of several men in the Western world, impelled by idealism and the press of modern, urban industrial life, to turn to the physical replanning of society. One of them, an English court stenographer named Ebenezer Howard, had already published a widely popular book, *Tomorrow: A Peaceful Path to Real Reform* (1898), better known later (1902) as *Garden Cities of Tomorrow,* which described, as one historian put it, his plan for the "healthy, natural and economic combination of town and country life."[25] Howard, who had lived in the United States and had participated in two earlier social experiments, states flatly that his book was born from an enthusiastic reading of the American Edward Bellamy's *Looking Backward* and from his subsequent decision to test the practicality of Bellamy's cooperative principles in action.[26]

Howard's first Garden City, Letchworth, was dedicated in October 1903, just as Nolen entered Harvard. The new town proved a landmark in city planning's professional development—much more indicative of the field's future directions in comprehensive community planning than the so-called "City Beautiful" movement associated with Burnham and Olmsted's plan for the Chicago World's Fair; and it remains today a living symbol of early-twentieth-century English social reform. By no means utopian, it attempted a workable combination of rural land ownership and diversified urban services through public control of land use, landscaping of individual homes, and the creation of green-belt barriers to separate the town's several functions. Nolen, who formed a close, lifelong friendship with Raymond Unwin after 1909 and who succeeded Howard in 1931 as president of the International Federation of Housing and Town Planning, incorporated many of the pioneering Englishman's ideas into his own distinct contributions to new town and other city design—including a stress upon public ownership and control of land, although the American economic system and cultural pattern would modify its application.[27]

Toward a Professional Point of View

Nolen hurried through his courses at Harvard's new school of landscape architecture. By virtue of his graduation "with distinction" from Pennsylvania, his long work and independent study period from 1893 to 1903, and his year of informal study in Europe, he was admitted to the second-year class in 1903 and immediately entered the summer school to pick up a course in architectural drawing, which he never had as an undergraduate.[28]

At Harvard the curriculum was dominated by an accent on nature's beauty and vicarious uses despite many deferences to the "utility" of open spaces. Nolen studied under several of the most important figures in the American field of landscape architecture, including the younger Olmsted, who were then teaching, as Charles Eliot once put it, a version of the fine arts:

> Landscape Architecture is primarily a fine art, and as such its most important function is to create beauty in the surroundings of human habitation . . . but it is also concerned with promoting the comfort, convenience, and health of urban populations, which have scanty access to natural scenery, and urgently need to have their work-a-day lives refreshed and calmed by the beautiful and reposeful sights and sounds of which Nature, aided by the landscape art, can abundantly provide.[29]

No one would deny landscape design the status of an art, of course, nor that it should help promote man's "comfort, convenience, and health." These indeed were Nolen's aims also. However, he did not agree they were achieved by merely tickling the "work-a-day" individual's sense of "sights and sounds," as he rushed by to and from the factory. Nature's beauty, said Nolen, was meant to be enjoyed physically, too, not just stared at as though it were only a highly valued pastoral painting:

> It is a grave mistake to look upon civic improvement as concerned mainly, or evenly primarily, with beauty; at least if by beauty is meant an agreeable and pleasing appearance. "What is fair must be fit." Serviceableness as well as charm, use as well as beauty, must always be secured. Without serviceableness city life is inefficient, without beauty, sordid and commonplace.[30]

As for the "uses" of nature, these should be in the form of large, free, out-of-the-city parks which "people of small means" and "worn out workers" could periodically vacation in.[31] The city had a further responsibility to provide for landscaped open spaces, playgrounds, and small parks within its confines sufficient to "guarantee" daily recreation, rest and fresh air "to every child and citizen of the town."[32]

EARLY WORK

Once in the field of landscape architecture as a professional, John Nolen moved quickly from landscaping private estates to planning complete park systems and other large-scale civic improvements—his original goal—and to city planning—its ultimate result. In 1904, almost a year before his graduation from Harvard, he opened an office on the Square in Cambridge and immediately began to practice, landscaping several private homes in Ardmore and a West Philadelphia factory grounds for Joseph Fels (the famed soap tycoon associated with the Progressive movement who, like Thomas Lawson and Tom Johnson, underwent a change of conscience about the manner in which his money had been accumulated). By 1905 and his graduation from Harvard with a Master of Arts degree, the thirty-six-year-old landscape architect had small projects under way in several states.

His first real breakthrough to civic work came that June when President Eliot and several of his instructors at Harvard recommended him for the job of advisor to the Park and Tree Commission of Charlotte, North Carolina.[33] Within two years, thanks to his ceaseless plugging for unified civic design, the scope of his work broadened from advising individual home owners about shrubs and grass to drafting a complete city plan and report. This report, and a park plan for Savannah, Georgia, about the same time, was as close as Nolen would ever get to the "City Beautiful" movement. Its recommendations included all the exterior trappings then in vogue among the civic-minded—a park, a public square with pseudoclassical buildings facing on it, and tree-lined streets. These things were not objectionable in and of themselves—Charlotte undoubtedly would have looked better had all of them been carried out—but compared with his later work, including that in the Myer's Park subdivision of Charlotte (1912), they were not enough. The recommendations lacked any real human relevance or scale; they appeared imposed from without and lacked a sure grasp of broad local needs.[34] They were almost certainly among the last vestiges of a purely textbook approach to local community needs, but at least he had made the big step, if cautiously, into city planning. Once there he never turned back to the comforts of smaller triumphs. His work now took him to planning cities and laying out large-scale park and street systems and residential areas throughout the United States, Cuba, and Canada.

As more work was obtained, Nolen increased the range of his recommendations and the intensity of his criticisms. The main recommendations still included the nature and disposition of parks, playgrounds, and civic squares. But now more space was devoted in his reports and surveys to recognizing and easing such urban irritants as traffic patterns, indiscriminate overlapping of industrial and residential areas, poor railroad and streetcar routings, the conflicting role of business and government in the community, the city's responsibility for the rights of children, and other ideas about government's share in promoting human welfare and, in advance of other planners, the need to eliminate submarginal housing.[35]

Although he did not always succeed in obtaining the city's follow-through on a plan, he generally had the enthusiastic support of his sponsors, many of whom were, like himself, advocating municipal reform. They included well-to-do private individuals

(novelist Zona Gale; paper manufacturer Charles S. Bird; department store merchant George S. Marston—extremely significant
social reformers in their own regions); civic, commercial, and art
associations—generally in cities with newly elected, liberal governments (San Diego, 1908; La Crosse, 1908; Montclair, 1908; Madison,
1909); and large business corporations (Pabst Brewing Company,
1910; American Brass Company, 1916; American Cast Iron Pipe
Company, 1915; General Electric Company, 1916).[36]

Growth of the Social Conscience

Thus working together, the city planner and civic reformer slowly
pushed long-range planning and physical development of the city to
the fore as an approach to solving America's rapidly multiplying
domestic problems. Playgrounds were urged as a means of fighting
vice and promoting teamwork, parks were offered as essential to the
requirements for fresh air and health of those who could not afford
their own piece of land, and so on. Planning was visualized as a way
of bringing "vitality" back to the public body; and vitality, as
everyone was told, was one-half of "efficiency and happiness."[37]
"What is needed in American city planning?" asked Nolen at the
first National Conference on City Planning in May 1909. "Everything," was his conclusion, paralleling Lincoln Steffens's assessment
of the corrupt municipal government situation uncovered by his
muckraking (e.g., *The Shame of the Cities*). More optimistic about
solutions than Steffens, Nolen, in the language of the progressives,
went on to suggest:

> We need (1) to make recreation more democratic; (2) to devel-
> op the individuality of our cities; (3) to stop waste. First, then,
> we need to make many improvements which are for the benefit
> and enjoyment of everybody, for the common good. . . . [Here
> he cites things that are free in Germany which are accessible
> only to the wealthiest in America.] We should no longer be
> content with mere increase in population and wealth. We
> should insist upon asking, How do the people live, where do
> they work, what do they play . . . there is a close relation
> between moral reform and material progress. A more honest,
> economical and wiser expenditure is indeed sorely needed,
> and, ultimately the change of (civic) policy would lead there.

. . . The main source of this new wealth . . . is in a wiser husbanding of our aesthetic and human as well as our national resources, in the promoting of physical health, legislation that meets more successfully the needs of twentieth century city life, in doing things at the right time . . . in the right way, using to our advantage science, art, skill, and experience. . . . By saving waste in these ways and by the timely investing (not spending) of public money in great enterprises. . . . [we shall obtain the improvements we want but thought we couldn't afford].[38]

The importance of this quote is its general philosophic position; Nolen was critical of the present yet not discouraged about the future. If the senses were open and clear, man *could* plan a better future using many of the basic stuffs of the present. There was no need for the fatalism or pessimism being prophesied by some men.

A case in point is the difference between the positions of Nolen and Steffens (1866–1936), contemporaries in their life spans and sharing a common concern for reform. In his understanding of the world and hence of its future, Nolen was much the more optimistic, essentially because he never really had learned to mistrust it or himself in it. With some small measure of outside assistance, he had helped himself steadily up from near the bottom of the socioeconomic ladder. Although not at the top nor particularly aspiring to many of the badges and awards of success, he was still the gainer as he moved on up; and, almost certainly, there was little opportunity in these early ambitious years to establish sufficient position from which to experience the steady and disillusioning falls from idealism that Steffens suffered. What had Nolen to fall from, coming out of nowhere and working in a field whose theoretical bases were barely outlined as yet? Never doubting the need for planning, he campaigned strenuously for broad planning's acceptance and sometimes found success.

But Steffens, the journalist from a comfortable, upper-middle-class home, suffered from the unsettling mixture of an overly romanticized but nevertheless workable childhood idealism diluted by his deeply sensitive awareness and gradual initiation into its opposite, the world of reality—which he found to be a greedy, rather ugly, entirely adult world. He found that

cities and states are jelly-fish now. They have a life of their own but no mind. The people in them have minds, but the people *as a community* have no conscious purpose as communities. Nothing but instinct guides them, or at best, a few bum politicians who live off the flabby, hog-selfish people.[39]

In Steffens's lifelong search for some hint of a better world he did not find conditions anywhere permanently otherwise, from reform capitalism to Russian communism, and thus he trusted finally to love alone, as shared by two people amid the world's growing, chaotic forces.[40] Nolen's equally sensitive but more realistic and (perforce) active idealism, on the other hand, developed, as we have already seen, out of early chaos and uncertainty into an enthusiasm for society's future. He understood Steffens but was incapable of sharing his pessimism, except as a warning of what *could* happen if man lost faith in working for the future. Although a cluster of divergent circumstances fell into a satisfactory pattern for Nolen's ambition and of course had much to do with his beliefs, he was still accurate in assuming from the evidence of his own life and of the lives of men he had learned to admire that the requisites for *his* better world were good fortune, an open society, hard work, and seriousness of purpose. Like the progressives, if not like Steffens, he intended to work at expanding the opportunities already existent in American culture. And unlike both the general run of progressives and Steffens, the circumstances of Nolen's beginnings continued to play a major role in his successful transition and growth through several periods of civic reform, planning, and change, until his death in 1937.[41]

Almost all his early life had been preparation for guiding the "civic spirit" he so much believed in. "The first and last need of a city, the one that outweighs all others," civic spirit, was to Nolen "the main end of reforms," the raison d'être of planning. In an era of reformers agitating for "good," "honest" government, for the elimination of "waste," and for restrictions on the "evils" of the competitive system, Nolen, like his peers in the political arena, rededicated himself to the highest aspirations offered by the existing culture. Thus Nolen went to the communities which sought his services to activate their civic ideals, believing that "comprehensive" city planning was "one of the best means for expressing this awakened consciousness, this stirred conscience" whose stimulus had in large part been a too sudden human and technological growth.[42]

NOTES

This essay originally was written as part of a case study of city planning as an agent for cultural change in Reading, Pennsylvania, 1908–16. It is *not* a definitive statement of Nolen's total life or works; instead, it seeks to define the societal and intellectual milieu of Nolen *up to* the eve of his first major planning efforts.

For their helpful reading of this text, I wish to express my appreciation to members of the City Planning Department at the University of Pennsylvania, to Wallace E. Davies of the History Department, for whom this was first written, and to Barbara Nolen Strong, Mr. Nolen's daughter. For their intellectual support and incisive critical perceptions, I am indebted above all to William L. C. Wheaton, of the University's Institute for Urban Studies, and to planning consultant John Nolen, Jr., who also has made his father's papers available to me. Judgments expressed in this paper are the sole responsibility of the author.

The unpublished "Nolen Papers" cited below at the University of Pennsylvania were acquired by Cornell University in 1969. For the published work and reports see John Hancock (1976) *John Nolen: Bibliographic Record of Achievement,* Cornell University, Program in Urban and Regional Studies. For an expanded version of this article see chapter 1 in John Hancock (1964) "John Nolen and the American city planning movement: a history of cultural change and community response, 1900–1940," Ph.D. dissertation in American Civilization, University of Pennsylvania.

1. H. J. Potts to John Nolen, January 13, 1909; Nolen to Potts, January 15, 1909, and January 21, 1909; all in office correspondence, Reading folder, Nolen Papers (hereafter cited as IV NP), Fine Arts Library of the University of Pennsylvania; and Nolen (1910) *Replanning Reading: An Industrial City of a Hundred Thousand,* Boston, George Ellis, p. iii. The roman numeral system used here to designate sources is arranged as follows: I or Box I is used to denote all primary material of an autobiographical or biographical nature and all articles on Mr. Nolen; II indicates citations from the library holdings of Nolen, both personal and professional, and all papers written or accumulated by him on nonplanning matters; III refers to all his unpublished essays, lectures, and speeches on planning; IV is the source of all project folders, plans, survey data, office records, and correspondence; and V contains his collection of photographs.

2. Announcement of a Nolen slide lecture, *Reading Eagle,* March 14, 1910.

3. Nolen, op. cit., pp. 87–90.

4. For recent historical treatment of municipal reform in this period see George E. Mowrey (1958) *The Era of Theodore Roosevelt,* New York, Harper Brothers, pp. 1–105; information on Nolen's sponsors in Reading was drawn from city directories, wills, and letters and is discussed at length in my unpublished paper (1958) "City planning in the progressive period: a case study of John Nolen's plans for Reading, Pennsylvania." This information correlates closely with that found in Mowrey's study (1952) of the

life histories of select individuals connected with municipal reform in one state, *The California Progressives,* Berkeley, University of California Press.

5. Autobiographical notes, Box II NP; Nolen's student notebooks, Box IV NP; both in temporary possession of the author. Unless otherwise noted all Nolen biographical information is taken from his private papers and published works. Girard College aims and values taken from Cheesman A. Herrick (1927) *History of Girard College,* Philadelphia, Girard College, pp. 201–47.

6. Quoted in Herrick, op. cit., pp. 228–9.

7. Ibid., p. 228. Nolen owned a copy of this book and underlined the sections stressing mental, moral, and physical development.

8. In his last several years as a student at Girard, Nolen had been the president's office boy. In two alumni addresses at Girard, forty years apart, Nolen characteristically stressed Stephen Girard's own personality development and expressed his belief that this personality above all was Girard's bequest to the future. See 1895 Alumni Address, II NP; and 1936 Anniversary Address (1936) reprinted in *Steel and Garnet* XXX, x, p. 70. It is hardly strange after such training that Nolen's earliest American heroes were the adaptable and supposedly "self-made" Benjamin Franklin, Stephen Girard, Samuel F. B. Morse, William Cullen Bryant, and Mark Twain. See his personal notebook of great men and events in history, compiled 1884, I NP.

9. University of Pennsylvania, *Class Record of '93* and additional *Records of the Class of '93* in 1898, 1903, and 1930.

10. Sidney Fine (1956) *Laissez Faire and the General-Welfare State,* Ann Arbor, University of Michigan Press, pp. 241–7. Patten's best early statements are found in *The Premises of Political Economy* (Philadelphia, 1885) and *The Theory of Dynamic Economics* (Philadelphia, 1892), both known to Nolen. For a recent perceptive treatment of Tugwell, Patten, and the national planning people see Paul K. Conkin (1959) *Tomorrow a New World: The New Deal Community Program,* Ithaca, Cornell University Press, pp. 73–92.

11. Information on Nolen's class work is taken from his class notebooks, inscribed texts, and essays. The Robinson reference is found in Robinson to Nolen, January 1, 1931, I and II NP.

12. This senior thesis was printed along with others by members of the senior class in *The City Government of Philadelphia: A Study in Municipal Administration* (1893), introduction by Edmund J. James, Philadelphia, Wharton School of Finance and Economy, pp. 99–110.

13. Fine, op. cit., pp. 216–19; Richard T. Ely (1886) "Report of the organization of the American Economic Association," *AEA Publications,* I, pp. 5–16; and Ely (1910) "The American Economic Association 1885–1909," *AEA Publications,* XI, pp. 47–92.

14. From the original notebook draft of his Alumni Address to the Girard College Class of 1895, Box IV NP.

15. The records of this Society are quite complete and an index of them in the Nolen Papers alone, as catalogued by the author, covers four pages. The Society's publication of "Syllabi" is a treasure of information for students of intellectual and cultural history of the period. They have not been

expanded upon here because of space limitations, but they include talks by
Charles Andrew, John Fiske, W. E. B. DuBois, MacMaster, Patten, Robinson,
Woodrow Wilson, Lyman Powell, Brander Matthews, Arthur T. Hadley,
Bliss Perry, Hilaire Belloc, Graham Wallas, W. Hudson Shaw, and Michael
Sadler—many of whom became longtime friends of and correspondents
with Nolen; *Syllabi of the ASEUT for the Academic Years 1901–1902, 1902–1903*,
Philadelphia, American Society for the Extension of University Teaching
(ASEUT) 1903, and *Records, Reports, Lecture Syllabi, 1890–1900*, Philadelphia, 1899, 5 vols. The Society grew out of the Oxford experiment and an
early series of University of Pennsylvania "afternoon" extension lectures
begun in 1887. From 1893 to 1903, the years of Nolen's association with it,
the Society brought in over a hundred lecturers per year for six talks each
before audiences of up to as many as two hundred interested townspeople,
many of whom took the courses for college credit at a small fee. Information in the text above is taken from the reports just noted and from the
Board of Directors (1901) *Ten Years' Report of the American Society for the
Extension of University Teaching, 1890–1900*, Philadelphia, ASEUT; Secretary of the Extension (Nolen), *Annual Reports*, 1890–1900; and annual
Syllabus, 1890–1900. Anonymous (1899) *Concerning University Extension:
Its Significance, Method and Results*, Philadelphia, ASEUT; a more recent,
brief account by Franklin Spencer Edmonds also sheds light on this group
(November 1943) "The beginnings of University Extension in Philadelphia," *Philadelphia Forum*, pp. 12–14. Nolen edited all the secretary's
reports after 1896.

16. Unpublished lists of "The personal library of John Nolen"; "Catalogue of
books (professional), library of John Nolen"; Box II NP. Many of the latter
are part of the John Nolen City Planning Collection, University of North
Carolina Library. Manuscripts of all unpublished reports and printed copy
of all published reports and books are on temporary loan to the Fine Arts
Library, University of Pennsylvania.

17. John Nolen (1912) *Replanning Small Cities*, New York, B. W. Huebsch, p.
2; for an early statement on the importance of constant and "comprehensive" replanning see Nolen (1908) *San Diego, A Comprehensive Plan for its
Improvement*, Boston, George H. Ellis, pp. iii, 10.

18. Nolen to the Administrative Board of the Graduate School, Harvard
University, March 14, 1904, Box I NP.

19. Description of the Ardmore property in "John Nolen, miscellaneous
papers," 1895–1903, Box I NP.

20. Unpublished "Scrapbook, record of European trip, 1901–1902"; Ex-Ma-
triculation certificate, "Universität München," October 19, 1901, to March
4, 1902 (winter semester), in "Miscellaneous papers"; record of courses
taken at Munich in Nolen to Administrative Board, ibid. (March 14, 1904);
all Box I NP.

21. See the following, all by Nolen: *San Diego*, 13, 29–40; *State Parks for
Wisconsin*, Madison, State Park Board, 1909; p. 41; *Re-Planning Reading*,
pp. 81–4; *Replanning Small Cities*, p. 13; offprint of Address to the First
National Conference on City Planning, "What is needed in American city

planning?" May 21, 1909; and unpublished report to the Boston Municipal Planning Commission, "Public hospitality in Europe," September 1911, III NP.

22. Interview, John S. Gregory (1913) "The coming city," *The World's Work*, pp. 82–4.

23. Nolen to Barbara S. Nolen, September 17, 1902; for long quote Nolen to Barbara S. Nolen, September 19, 1902; both extracted from letters in possession of John Nolen, Jr., forwarded to the author June 3, 1960.

24. Ibid., for reference to an inquiry made before the European trip in September 1901, about studying at the Lawrence School, see Nolen to J. L. Love, September 12, 1902, I NP.

25. Ebenezer Howard (1902) *Garden Cities of Tomorrow*, London, Faber & Faber. The quote is from Dugald Macfadyen (1933) *Sir Ebenezer Howard and Town Planning*, Manchester, England, Manchester University Press, p. 27.

26. Howard also rejected Bellamy's "most outstanding" contention that change of this scale could be effected "overnight," ibid., pp. 20–21.

27. John Nolen (1927) *New Towns for Old*, Boston, Marshall Jones Co. Although better known for his work in such new towns as Kingsport, Tennessee, and Mariemont, Ohio, Nolen's use of the garden city scheme as applied to a cooperative system of land ownership is seen as early as 1912–13 in his plan for Neponset Village, East Walpole, Massachusetts. The whole question of cultural modifications to Nolen's American planning schemes is the subject of a longer paper I now have in progress.

28. Nolen to the Lawrence Scientific School, September 11, 1902; Nolen to J. L. Love, May 3, 1903; Love to Nolen, May 19, 1903; Nolen to Administrative Board, March 14, 1904; John G. Hart to Nolen, May 3 and July 7, 1904 (receives Austin Scholarship for 1904–5); all in Box I NP.

29. Quoted in T. A. Mawson (1927) *The Life and Work of an English Landscape Architect: An Autobiography*, New York, Charles Scribner's Sons, p. xii. For further expressions of this point of view see Charles William Eliot's book about his son: (1902) *Charles Eliot, Landscape Architect*, Boston, Houghton Mifflin, pp. 551–5, 592–601, and other direct statements by the younger Eliot. It should be added here that no attempt is being made by the author to disparage the many contributions of men like Olmsted and Eliot to landscape architecture nor to underscore the importance of beauty to Nolen. The influence of both on Nolen's work is obvious, *but* so are his own innovations on accepted ideas in the fields of landscape architecture and large-scale planning which developed out of his personal orientation.

30. John Nolen (1907) *Roanoke: A Small City of the New South*, Roanoke, Roanoke Civic Improvement Association, p. 13. Despite this clear point of view, the report has been considered by one writer as an example of the strong "City Beautiful" bent of planners before the First World War (Robert A. Walker [1930] *The Planning Function in Urban Government*, revised edition, Chicago, University of Chicago Press, pp. 14–15). Actually no ongoing society switches so abruptly from one viewpoint to another in just a year or two. The Nolen quote above, for example, is merely an early

reference to the "City Efficient" point of view which the progressively inclined pioneer planner was expressing long before the First World War.

31. Nolen, *State Parks for Wisconsin,* p. 41.

32. John Nolen (1909) *Montclair: The Preservation of Its Natural Beauty and Its Improvements as a Residential Town,* Montclair, Municipal Art Commission, p. 63.

33. Conversation with John Nolen, Jr., May 28, 1959.

34. Unpublished report, project folder, "Charlotte, N.C.," Box V NP; for a published report of Meyer's Park see Alfred F. Muller (Spring 1915) "Meyer's Park, Charlotte, N.C.," *The Wildwood Magazine,* pp. 8ff.

35. Nolen, *San Diego,* pp. 58–61; (1911) *Madison: A Model City,* Boston and Madison, Madison Park and Pleasure Drive Association, pp. 35–150; *Montclair,* pp. 59–72; *Replanning Small Cities,* pp. 1–21; John Nolen (1910) "The parks and recreation facilities in the US," *Annals* of the American Academy of Political and Social Science, p. 217; anonymous (1937) "John Nolen," *Newsletter,* American Society of Planning Officials, III, p. 3.

36. See project folders indicated by name, as above, in Box V NP. See also project folders "Portage, Wisconsin"; "Erie, Penna."; and "Waterbury, Conn."; *San Diego,* p. iii; the *La Crosse Tribune* and *La Crosse Leader-Press,* both November 11, 1908; *Montclair,* pp. 9–12; *Madison,* "Explanatory"; this last report, in the city Nolen admired above all others before the First World War, also contains some early ideas on regional planning, see the Montclair–Glen Ridge reports for same. In the project folder "High Shoals Village, N.C.," Box V NP, is a preliminary plan for a new town, one of the earliest in America in this century and foreshadowing, like Neponset, Nolen's eventual great interest—creating a new town from the ground up—and that of his later associates Hale J. Walker (Greenbelt town planner) and Justin R. Hartzog (Greenhills town planner).

37. Nolen, "Parks and recreation facilities," *Annals,* pp. 217–18.

38. Offprint of Address to the First National Conference on City Planning (May 21, 1909), Box I NP.

39. Original source unknown, quoted in John Nolen (1915) unpublished "Address on the Boston Community Planning Project," Boston, A Program for 1911, III NP.

40. Consult the general divisions and especially the last section of Steffens (1931) *Autobiography,* New York, Harcourt, Brace, 1931.

41. The best study of class, mobility, and role of the progressives is Mowrey's discussion of forty-seven life histories in *The California Progressives,* pp. 86–104. With an occasional major exception like Harold Ickes, it is clear the progressives were definitely out of political favor by the period of the New Deal, which enacted so much of the legislation they had demanded twenty years earlier. While the reasons for their demise are not yet clear, it may be suggested that the answer lies partly in their strong individualistic beliefs, their emphasis on *restrictive* legislation and their refusals to admit, even privately, that there were *traditional* class divisions in America. See Mowrey, ibid., and his more recent summary, *Theodore Roosevelt and the Progressive Era,* pp. 1–105. In contrast, Nolen was never a dogmatist,

welcomed the passing of an older order, served as consultant to the Division of Subsistence Homesteads and the National Resources Board, and remained an enthusiastic New Dealer to his death.

42. Nolen, unpublished "Address on the Boston Community Planning Project," 1911, Box I NP.

4

HOUSING

MARY KINGSBURY SIMKHOVITCH

INTRODUCTION
BY SUSAN MARIE WIRKA

MARY KINGSBURY SIMKHOVITCH'S BOOK, *Here Is God's Plenty: Reflections on American Social Advance,* was published in 1949, two years before her death. While she emphatically states that it "is not an autobiography"[1] at the outset, the volume is autobiographical in nature, offering glimpses of a dedicated social welfare pioneer's understanding of the important issues of her time. When Simkhovitch sat down near the end of her life to write *Here Is God's Plenty,* she drew heavily on her five decades of experience in the New York settlement house movement, leaving us with a series of recollections about various urban and social reform issues. In addition to the chapter on housing, reproduced here in its entirety, *Here Is God's Plenty* also details her reflections on education, recreation, the arts, welfare, community organization, politics, and religion. These issues created a framework for Simkhovitch's life's work. Through its publication, she hoped to add "one drop more of understanding of the themes that have been the structure of my life—the building in which I have lived, if not my life itself" (HIGP, 1949, preface).

Fittingly, Simkhovitch begins her chapter on housing with a description of houses as more than just buildings in which people

Reprinted from Mary Kingsbury Simkhovitch, "Housing," in *Here Is God's Plenty: Reflections on American Social Advance* (New York, Harper and Brothers, 1949). Copyright © 1949 by Harper and Brothers. Reprinted by permission of HarperCollins Publishers.

FIGURE 4.1   *Simkhovitch standing in front of fireplace at Greenwich House.*
COURTESY TAMIMENT INSTITUTE LIBRARY, NEW YORK UNIVERSITY, GREENWICH HOUSE PAPERS

live. She asks her readers to think about "Housing with a capital H" (HIGP, 1949, p. 25), challenging us to consider housing as an issue rather than just a commodity. Simkhovitch's dedication to the housing issue grew directly out of her experience as a settlement house worker. She writes:

> In and out of the tenements day by day, one gradually got the feeling of the significance of these dwellings, their congestion, their inconveniences, their darkness, their noise, their smells, and their lack of privacy (HIGP, 1949, p. 27).

Observing uninhabitable housing conditions firsthand was a turning point for Simkhovitch. "And it was this [experience] rather than any academic consideration that led me to study economic history ... at Radcliffe," she explains (HIGP, 1949, p. 26). Born in Chestnut Hill, Massachusetts, in 1867, Simkhovitch spent her childhood in comfortable suburban homes. In 1886 she graduated from Newton High School, just outside of Boston. After receiving her Bachelor of Arts in economics from Boston University in 1890, Simkhovitch went on to complete a graduate program in economic history and political science at Radcliffe College.

During her college years, Simkhovitch was a member of the Church of Carpenter, led by the Reverend William D. P. Bliss, a Fabian socialist who held strong social reform convictions. Attracting a broad spectrum of workers, labor leaders, reformers, and academics, Bliss created an environment for the practice of a kind of Christian-reformist-socialism. Simkhovitch joined in the Sunday supper meetings where "practical labor problems of the day" (HIGP, 1949, p. 165) and other social issues were discussed. Through her association with the Church of Carpenter, she met several of the residents at Denison House, a pioneer Boston settlement house. She began visiting Denison House regularly where she found the opportunity to explore important social problems with other like-minded women reformers.

Offering a pragmatic approach to reform, the settlement house movement gave white, middle-class, college-educated women, like Simkhovitch, a chance to bring their sociological talents to the inner city to address urban social problems. Founded in 1886, the movement was named for its workers who lived, or "settled," in the neighborhoods where they worked. Residence in settlement houses gave settlement workers the rare opportunity to gain "hands-on" knowledge about social issues in the urban industrial environment. The movement employed the "learn by doing" theory of social action developed by settlement resident John Dewey and settlement leader Jane Addams.

While at Denison House, Simkhovitch played organ at St. Augustine's Chapel, a local black congregation, and also ran the Primrose Club for young girls. There, she writes: "I was invited to visit the families and . . . I had a chance to see the inadequacies of the tenements in which they lived. They were wooden buildings, unsanitary, and often dark" (HIGP, 1949, p. 164). Discovering that many tenements she considered unfit for living were owned by "leading citizens" of the white community, Simkhovitch grew deeply concerned about the lack of social and economic opportunities available in Boston's black neighborhoods. This early "consciousness-raising" experience ignited her lifelong interest in housing reform.

The experience of seeing impoverished housing conditions left a lasting impression. It was not long before Simkhovitch developed a genuine intrigue for the settlement idea, its theory, and its method. As she writes:

Soon the drama of lives shut in by poverty, prejudice and lack of opportunity became my major interest. I must find out more, learn how these things came about and what could be done to make life more tolerable (N, 1938, p. 43).

Like Jane Addams, of Hull House in Chicago, Simkhovitch saw settlement work as a "postgraduate course in 'things as they are'" (Simkhovitch, 1947, p. 281). Returning from studying abroad in 1897, she went to live and work at the College Settlement on New York's Lower East Side, thus embarking on a settlement career that lasted until her death in 1951.

Drawn to the idea of "plunging into life where it was densest and most provocative" (N, 1938, p. 58), Simkhovitch immersed herself in the political and social life of the Lower East Side. While at the College Settlement, she became interested in the nature of working and housing conditions for Russian, Polish, and Italian immigrants, as well as the lack of suitable play environments for the children of immigrant families. She formed the Sunday Evening Economics Club at a time when "the East Side was excited about socialism" (N, 1938, p. 63), studied Marx, and learned to speak

Yiddish. These were all important aspects of understanding the community where she lived and worked. Simkhovitch also helped organize local campaigns against oppressive working conditions in the cigar-making and garment industries and against offensive over-crowding in double-decker dumbbell tenements.

When Simkhovitch arrived on the lower East Side, the neighborhood's only playground consisted of the backyard at the College Settlement, which had been converted into a small play area for children. The obvious need for children's play space in isolated New York City neighborhoods spurred the formation of the Outdoor Recreation League (ORL). Along with Lillian Wald and Elizabeth Williams, two prominent New York settlement workers, Simkhovitch helped found the ORL in 1898, with its first priority to create a park for the children of the Lower East Side. Successful toward that end, Seward Park opened in 1900.

Through her work at the College Settlement, Simkhovitch found herself quickly moving into the forefront of progressive reform in New York City. Late in 1898, she left the College Settlement to act as head resident of the Friendly Aid House (FAH). With a "determination to understand and serve the new neighborhood" (N, 1938, p. 80), Simkhovitch met her challenge at the FAH with enthusiasm. The FAH was operated by the Friendly Aid Society (FAS) which was, in turn, supported by the All Souls Unitarian Church. From the beginning, she disagreed with the moralistic mode of reform upon which the FAS was based. She soon realized that the directors of the Society viewed the settlement purely in terms of a philanthropic venture rather than a social movement. They saw the House "as a mode of altruism for the church members, rather than an attempt at social understanding and a cooperative effort for social betterment" (N, 1938, p. 88). Simkhovitch, like many other radical settlement workers, felt there was nothing more contrary to the settlement idea than conventional charity.

The social welfare pioneer challenged the charity approach to reform for treating the symptoms and not the causes of poverty and for treating poverty as an individual, rather than a societal, problem. She was not alone in this regard; together with a supportive group of ten other settlement workers, Simkhovitch organized the New York Association of Neighborhood Workers (ANW) to explore these and other questions about settlement method and philosophy. As one of the earliest efforts to unite settlement workers in a citywide federation, the ANW's purpose was to "effect cooperation among those neighborhood workers who are working for neighborhood and civic improvement and to promote movements for social progress" (United Neighborhood Houses, n.d., p. 1).

Through the ANW, Simkhovitch further developed her belief that settlement workers must be free to create settlement programs based on their experiences with the surrounding neighborhood. Her negative experience with the FAS convinced her of the absolute necessity to separate settlement work from sectarian affiliations. She resigned from the FAH in 1901 with the intention of forming a nondenominational settlement house. Along with some of her comrades from the ANW, Simkhovitch formed the Cooperative Social Settlement Society (CSSS) of the City of New York in 1901. The CSSS was founded on her belief that every neighborhood could act on its own political behalf; the settlement's role, then, was to facilitate and protect the interests of the neighborhood. A strong settlement program was essential toward that end. However, she also felt that:

> The activities settlements conduct are wholly secondary, no matter how useful or fascinating, to their primary purpose of energizing their neighborhoods to develop a common consciousness of need and a common effort to meet those needs, in other words, as we say nowadays, a plan (Simkhovitch, n.d. p. 3).

In fact, Simkhovitch came to see the work of settlements and the idea of planning as one and the same endeavor.

Simkhovitch perceived settlements to be natural vehicles for neighborhood planning—to articulate neighborhood residents' need for shelter, food, and access to resources. Her overriding goal was to see that every city resident could attain the basic necessities of life; the place to begin that quest was the neighborhood. To Simkhovitch, the neighborhood was a "manageable microcosm" of the larger world upon which the city was dependent for the articulation of local needs. If settlements could act as conduits for the articulation of local needs, they could play an active role in the development of the neighborhood as the social unit of urban life. Toward this end, Simkhovitch founded Greenwich House, the first cooperative social settlement in New York City, in 1902.

Simkhovitch believed every city neighborhood had three basic needs: 1) social services, 2) a center to provide such services, and 3) local community involvement. She directed Greenwich House to fulfill these for the Greenwich Village neighborhood. On a practical level, the settlement was the primary social service provider to neighborhood residents. In essence, Greenwich House functioned as a social planning agency as it coordinated the provision of child care, health care, and recreational and educational services to the surrounding neighborhood. As was common with other settlement houses, Greenwich House was actively involved in laying the groundwork for what would become a primary methodological tool in planning: the social survey to determine neighborhood conditions and needs based on sociological and economic research. Greenwich House conducted a series of ground-breaking social investigations that sought to understand the exact nature of turn-of-the-century urban industrial conditions. Toward that end, Greenwich House sponsored a number of permanent committees and published numerous studies on education, health, and other urban social issues.

Through her work in the New York settlement house movement, Simkhovitch worked closely with both Florence Kelley, Secretary of the National Consumers' League, and Lillian Wald, head of the Henry Street Settlement. These three women were among the first members of the Committee on Congestion of Population (CCP) in New York City, organized in 1907, with Simkhovitch as the chair. The CCP, with its emphasis on housing reform as part of the solution to overcrowded urban conditions, provided a forum for discussing this country's need for city planning. Through the auspices of the CCP, Simkhovitch, Kelley, and Wald helped organize the first National Conference on City Planning (NCCP) held in 1909. They played an important role in articulating the agenda and goals of that initial conference. Simkhovitch was also the only woman to address the conferees. In her address, she argued for links between housing and neighborhood planning and advocated a notion of planning based not only on a civic but a social point of view.

In her chapter on housing from *Here Is God's Plenty,* Simkhovitch reminds us through the words of author James Ford that "'virtually all leaders in housing reform in the 1890's and early 1900's were persons with a settlement background'" (HIGP, 1949, p. 30). She exemplifies this phenomenon when discussing the realities and problems of housing as she grew to understand them through her settlement experience. She writes about grateful immigrants "so happy to be in America that their dwellings were accepted without protest" (HIGP, 1949, p. 27), as well as the burgeoning garment industry's sweatshop era and its concomitant practice of tenement piecework—the problem of "homework." "The tenements buzzed with the song of the sewing machines," remembers Simkhovitch (HIGP, 1949, pp. 27–28). She traces the history of housing on New York's Lower East Side from the yellow fever epidemic of 1795, to the great fire of 1835, to the introduction of water closets in 1879, to the construction of multiple dwellings shortly after 1850, and to the prominence of railroad flats before that.

Simkhovitch also writes about how, despite the passage of the Tenement House Act of 1901, she saw no basic improvements in older dumbbell tenement dwellings. She discusses how the indiscriminate, generalized use of the word "slum" to mean "poverty, disease, and crime" (HIGP, 1949, p. 30) was not only inaccurate but misleading. She details her efforts at understanding the complexity of the urban environment through her work at Greenwich House and her chief interest "in the development of the neighborhood as the social unit of our urban life" (HIGP, 1949, p. 31). As just one aspect of the neighborhood, Simkhovitch felt that housing should be seen as a public health issue. She also believed that housing needed to be linked to other social services: "From housing to neighborhood planning was the necessary next step!" (HIGP, 1949, p. 31). She goes on to describe, in detail, housing conditions between the two world wars and talks about her "conversion to the necessity of government housing for persons unable to pay commercial rents" (HIGP, 1949, p. 39).

As an "American Planner," perhaps Simkhovitch's most important historical contribution was her persistence on linking settlement work and planning. Settlements were at the center of her idea of planning because they were the one institution most involved in the development of local neighborhoods at the turn of the century. She felt strongly that, in both philosophy and methodology, the settlement was well equipped for the "mission of neighborhood planning" (Simkhovitch, 1943, p. 174). Through Greenwich House, in particular, she realized that planning *was* the process by which to articulate and provide for the various needs of the neighborhood. In her understanding of the relationship between planning and settlements, Mary Kingsbury Simkhovitch contributed a unique perspective to both the settlement house movement and to planning.

HOUSING

NOBODY TALKED ABOUT HOUSING when I was a child. Building houses, yes, and having attractive homes. But Housing with a capital H was unknown. Everyone hoped for a good home and a garden whether in or out of the city. Our suburb, Chestnut Hill, was a part of Newton and only seven miles from Boston. Every house in Chestnut Hill had its own attraction, from the houses on the hill where the Lees and Saltonstalls lived, to my grandfather's old farmhouse with its low ceilings, ample rooms, and fireplaces. Especially pleasing to a child was the "clock room" where my great grandfather, before my time, had lived, and after twenty years of tuberculosis with closed windows, finally died. Back of the clock room was the roomy dining room with its old brick oven in which four kinds of pie—apple, mince, squash, and custard—were baked for Thanksgiving dinner; and at the other side of the porched front door, flanked by lilac bushes, were two parlors where my Aunt Hattie was married, slightly late as usual, but beautiful, and creating quite a sensation in her organdy dress trimmed with little ruffles edged with lace. And to that same room, so soon after, her body returned in a leaden casket from the South, where she had died, stricken by typhoid on her honeymoon.

There are plenty of houses that I remember, but one struck a startling note and made a scar not ever to be forgotten. That was an old tenement on Kneeland Street in Boston. My Sunday School teacher had gathered her little students together on a cold Thanksgiving morning to visit a poor old woman, without turkey or coals for a fire, who sat in the icy place alone and helpless. In later years this scene struck one as staged for the occasion where a happy outcome was doubtless in view. However, this dreary, dark place made a dent in one's mind, and the fact that not everyone lived in a warm, pretty, comfortable house sank in.

The uncluttered mind of a child is more impressionable than in later life, and often the memory of that visit would appear like a jack-in-the-box with the unspoken inquiry, "How can such things be?" But it was not till college days when I used to drop in to old St. John's on Bowdoin Street that I began to see many such homes. I had promised to make visits for the clergy there. In the old shacks of the West End lived many low-income families—both white and Negro. No matter how clean the tenants or how self-respecting were the majority of them, the old houses themselves were hopeless from the point of view of sanitation, light, and air. Here was a whole district marked by neglect and decay. "Housing" became a reality and a "problem." Yet it seemed to be not something to be tackled, but rather a devastating fact one encountered as a natural phenomenon.

I got to know many of the young people living in these houses and they seemed to take their disadvantages rather lightly. They had not known a more commodious life. Still it was these houses that drove me to try to understand something more of their meaning. And it was this rather than any academic consideration that led me to study economic history with Ashley at Radcliffe in graduate days and urged me on to Berlin. It was not till I went to Rivington Street to work at the College Settlement in 1898 that I came face to face with a whole great area in New York where housing was a major factor in the teeming life of the East Side. In and out of the tenements day by day, one gradually got the feeling of the significance of these dwellings, their congestion, their inconveniences, their darkness, their noise, their smells, and their lack of privacy. No matter how clean the individual family, there was no way to keep bugs from crawling in from the airshaft. And one family I knew well had to close the airshaft windows, thereby increasing the summer's heat, to avoid this plague. This family, whose sons and daughters fought their way through college to lives of comfort and wide influence in ample and beautiful surroundings, was an example of the drama of the East Side.

In my day the East Side was a picture of its old Irish and German period in the midst of an overwhelming Jewish stream that had its origin in persecution and pogrom. The East Side was a haven to this group who were so happy to be in America that their dwellings were accepted without protest. From the outside this new population looked compact and like-minded. But in fact it represented the most heterogeneous backgrounds, occupations, and interests. There were craftsmen, poets, actors, and theologians. There were ignorant and learned, many whose speech was Yiddish, but also many who were deeply acquainted with European languages—especially German, as well as Polish and Russian. Good talkers and interested in history, philosophy, economics, and theology, they were always centers for the ferment of thought and its expression in cafés or theater, which made an interesting and exciting life. However, the political activities of an older New York soon permeated the region and the growing clothing industry became the dominant daily occupation of the majority of newcomers. It was the era of the sweatshop. It was an easy and handy matter to take home clothing to sew and return to the shops. The tenements buzzed with the song of the sewing machines. An immigrant poet, Morris Rosenfeld, immortalized this song. At the College Settlement, where I lived, this poet read his verses on a memorable occasion. They summarized the life about us—the life of change, of American promise, of intellectual ferment and economic opportunity.

These immigrants brought with them the economic ideas that their oppression in their homelands had produced. The varieties of imported socialist dogma were many—and many were the battles between them. Many religious attitudes—ranging from traditional orthodoxy to a purely racial bond—existed side by side. Cultural interests grew rapidly in this hotbed of energy, intelligence, and freedom. The Yiddish Theater attracted many from other parts of New York as well as from the local population. Music, drama, and poetry flowered in this scene of poverty and squalor. It was a boiling mass whose most striking note was congestion.

The housing of the old East Side has an interesting history. The yellow fever epidemic of 1795 drove people away from the crowded streets at the foot of the Island of Manhattan, to seek the countryside of Greenwich or even Yorkville. Between 1840 and 1855, with steam navigation established, the population rose rapidly. Emigration from Ireland, England, Germany, Russia, and Italy crowded lower New York. The Irish population doubled in that period due to the famine in Ireland. Pogroms in Russia caused a rapid increase of Jewish immigrants. Each national group crowded out its predecessor. To escape either oppression or poverty, Europeans came to this land of promise. What they found was an opportunity for work and freedom to express their opinions, but under the most deplorable living conditions.

The great fire of 1835 had wiped out many dilapidated buildings. Croton water was not introduced until 1842 and water closets were available in 1879, though the Association for the Improvement of the Conditions of the Poor had put them into houses two decades earlier. Indeed they existed here and there in the late 1700's.

It was shortly after 1850 that multiple dwellings were constructed. Prior to that date, tenants lived in houses built for one or sometimes two families. These early tenement houses were called

FIGURE 4.2   *Probably a picture postcard of Minetta Street; probably by*
photographer Jessie Tarbox Beals.

COURTESY TAMIMENT INSTITUTE LIBRARY, NEW YORK UNIVERSITY, GREENWICH HOUSE PAPERS

railroad flats. Light and air came only from the front and rear of these houses—the intermediate space being dark and divided into many rooms. The original 25' x 100' lot had been used for single families with provision for ample garden space in the rear. The tendency, of course, with the pressure for homes was to build on this garden space also, either by the erection of rear houses or by extending the house through the lot. Attempts to improve the situation were made, and as time went on private persons or companies for the purpose of alleviating the evils occasioned by overcrowding, entered the field of model housing.

Pioneers and leaders were Alfred White of Brooklyn and, somewhat later, Elgin Gould of the City and Suburban Homes Company. Various legislative committees brought home to New York from time to time the gravity of the situation. The competition and exhibit of the Charity Organization Society in 1900 brought this interest to a head. The nineties was a period of gradual awakening and action on the part of the public. In 1895 an act was passed providing for two small parks on the lower East Side. The opening of Seward Park is still fresh in my mind. This was the time when pioneering went on for school playgrounds and recreation piers. Hearings held by the Legislative Commission were dramatic indeed. Leaders of this period were Dr. Felix Adler, Professor E. R. A.

Seligman, Stanton Coit, and Charles B. Stover. The publicity given to the whole movement by Jacob Riis in his famous book *How the Other Half Lives* greatly added to the growth of the social conscience of the community.

As James Ford[2] tells us, "virtually all leaders in housing reform in the 1890's and early 1900's were persons with a settlement background." All this ferment came to a head with the passage of the Tenement House Act of 1901, the landmark of emergence from the chaos of private effort and occasional legal requirement into the basic structure of law.

At the College Settlement on Rivington Street, where I went to live after my university work in Berlin, housing was naturally a main interest. It was there that Lawrence Veiller started his long career. His intimacy with tenement house life and problems, and his position as secretary—with Robert W. DeForest as chairman—of the first tenement house commission, ushered in a new era for housing in New York. After the passage of the 1901 law it was impossible to erect a "dumbbell tenement," the type which had won the prize in a competition in 1879 and which turned out to be the curse of many generations. The law provided specifications for new buildings with roomier courts and good lighting. The old buildings remained, however, and notwithstanding subsequent legislative enactments on all multiple dwellings, no basic improvements in the old houses took place or could take place. On the 25-foot lot no significant changes for tenants were possible.

I spent 1898 at the College Settlement visiting these tenements and getting acquainted with the life of the East Side. What a deep chasm exists between publicity and facts! The word "slum" is used indiscriminately for poverty, disease, and crime. These generalizations are not only inaccurate but misleading. For life in the tenement can and often does exhibit the loftiest character and the finest human relationships. But it is against great odds. The slum is most of all a menace to health, and it is for this reason that housing in England and other countries is placed under the direction of public health authorities. Yet the death rate in cities is steadily declining even where housing is at a standstill or even deteriorating. The fact is that science in the field of health has advanced far more rapidly than has city planning and its concomitant arts. For architecture, zoning, parks and playgrounds, and educational and health facilities all hang together.

It was no accident that in the decade following the passage of the Tenement House Act of 1901, the public conscience became aware that decent housing must be seen in its relationship to the whole social pattern. All of us who had the advantage of living in "slum" areas during the nineties and the first decade of the twentieth century, saw this whole scene as one picture—the picture of the neighborhood. The settlements were neighborhood houses to whom the neighborhood was a composite of all the elements that frame our daily life. Housing was a leading factor but it was the life of the people in the houses that was our main concern. Our burning interest was the life of families, parents and children, teachers and pupils, landlord and tenant, doctor and patient, priest, minister, or rabbi and their congregations, politicians and voters, merchants and shoppers. From housing to neighborhood planning was the necessary next step!

I went to live on Jones Street when my husband and a few friends of ours opened the doors of Greenwich House in 1902. The Tenement House Law had been passed. After my return from study abroad I had been associated both at the College Settlement and at the Friendly Aid House with all the settlement residents of that time in working for improved living conditions, but from 1902 on, my chief interest was in the development of the neighborhood as the social unit of our urban life.

The Housing of the lower West Side was a strange mixture of types; it was indeed an illustrated chronology of New York's housing. The old small three-story, or two-story and basement, house with a mansard roof or dormer window attic, was the basic type. But old barracks occupying practically the entire lot, the railroad flats open to air and light in front and rear, and also, to a limited degree, the dumbbell tenement with which I had been so familiar on the East Side, existed in our midst. Here and there were remains of the great houses of the well-to-do families who had moved up to Greenwich Village, either for health reasons after the yellow fever epidemic, or because of the desire to spread out into ampler regions where space for gardens was possible. On Laight Street or Grove Street or Thirteenth Street, or in the immediate vicinity of Washington Square, such mansions were not uncommon. Some large properties under single ownership were to be found on single streets, such as the Nicholas Low estate on Sullivan Street, where the wooden houses had gardens fronting the street, or the Rhinelander estate on

FIGURE 4.3 *Greenwich House, c. 1920s.*
COURTESY TAMIMENT INSTITUTE LIBRARY, NEW YORK UNIVERSITY,
GREENWICH HOUSE PAPERS

11th Street. Lofty tenements south of Washington Square filled several streets. At this time the small single houses were beginning to be let out in floors. In the case of occupancy by a single family, heating was provided by what was known as the Baltimore heater, which was quite efficient for two floors. Kitchen and dining room made up the basement, front parlor, back parlor or bedroom, the main floor, and above, bedrooms.

The law of 1901 classed as a tenement any building occupied by three families. One of the first duties we had to undertake in Greenwich Village was to oppose a bill introduced by our local assemblyman which would remove the three-family house from the provision of the law of 1901.

It seemed to us that our neighbors did not realize the deterioration and danger to the community a nearby group of buildings exhibited. With some Columbia friends as guides for study, we published a pamphlet entitled "A West Side Rookery," edited by Elsa Herzfeld. In this nest of buildings lived a hard-working washerwoman who was bringing up her family in the best traditions of behavior and character. She was one of our staunch friends in the development of our work. The apartments were without toilets, which were in the yard. Our friend's husband had been killed while working on a scaffolding. Left alone with a large family, she took in washing. I can see her now, bent over the old wooden tubs (for there were no stationary tubs in the flat) keeping one eye on the yard below where her youngest child was playing. She was an expert laundress, and she applied the same skill and efficiency in bringing up her children, all of whom have lived and looked after her well in her old age.

But she was an exception in that old Rookery. Opposite her was a family of five with three men lodgers. There was one single bed in the back room. The others lived in the front. One man slept on a chair at night. In this house, during the winter of 1904–5, there were eleven people in two rooms, four of them adults. At night there were often fifteen men making flowers in the room, some of whom were members of a famous gang of thieves and criminals. In the same room was a woman with a baby.

We felt that the tenants of our neighborhood did not know how to gain redress when laws and ordinances were being violated, and so under the editorship of Emily W. Dinwiddie, we published a *Tenants' Manual* which circulated among our neighbors, enlightened them as to the content of the law and how to get it enforced.

It was one more step in social education. We realized that research, publicity, and education were not enough, and that underlying causes must be brought to light. One of our residents, Paul Kennaday, a young man of fastidious tastes but great moral passion, had become interested in the campaign against tuberculosis that was under way. He arranged an excellent exhibit in a neighboring library auditorium, and when he asserted that the spread of tuberculosis was furthered, if not directly caused, by the bad housing in which these afflicted people lived, quite a sensation was kindled. The exceptionally high death rate of our district from tuberculosis, the highest in the city at that time as a matter of fact, substantiated his assertion.

The question of housing in our area was still further a matter of local interest when Mr. Vincent Pepe, one of our most enterprising realtors, who loved our neighborhood and who was active in the neighborhood civic association we had formed in 1901, began his career of remodeling the old dwellings of the Village. People, as they grew older, were glad to let out floors in their houses. This meant organization and enterprise. But it meant a great neighborhood change, for new people came in with different points of view.

These outsiders who were enabled to get apartments in the remodeled old buildings, were regarded as "bohemians" by the old neighbors, and the neighborhood became divided into many groups— the old Irish population, the more recent Italian neighborhood, the well-to-do American group of older stocks, and the new artist, pseudo artist and others who enjoyed the charm and informality of the remodeled houses with their fireplaces and spacious rooms, but who knew little of the mores of the old neighborhood. These groups were largely self-contained, each carrying on its own customs and attitudes. The latest comers in the 1920's created a sensation that became country-wide. The old Ninth Ward became the Village with a vengeance.

The changed physical aspect of the neighborhood, with the wide swath made by new traffic highways, cut up the staid village streets, making new boundaries, destroying the compactness and enclosure of the old district. Such changes take a long while to effect social adjustment. Many newcomers of a later period take little notice of local happenings. Like other New Yorkers they live in the Village, but their associations are largely outside of it. People look in general for three things—good housing, good schools and libraries, and easy access to recreational and shopping facilities. Young people make their friendships largely with fellow students, wherever they live. Older people find their associates in churches, clubs, or special interest groups. But still the neighborhood itself in its interrelationships plays an important part. Centrifugal and centripetal forces compete. People move out of town for many reasons—to avoid noise, congestion, and uncongenial contacts. But others stay in town because of schools, shopping conveniences, good transportation, and associations they do not wish to break.

As the Village idea took root, rehabilitation rather than new building became the dominant factor in housing. From the Greenwich House roof today can be seen the whole drama of New York's housing: the little old houses occupied sometimes by the owner or rented with two or three or four apartments, the old railroad flats with enough changes to conform to the multiple dwelling law, but still basically unfit, an occasional dumbbell tenement, and a few modern high apartments, looking a little strange in the old Village landscape. Gradually the old buildings give way to modern buildings, though there is room for a widespread development of rehabilitation. With all these improvements, rents advance. And there still exists the unspoken hostility of tenement dwellers and the higher rental groups.

BETWEEN THE FIRST and second World Wars these changes were taking place. Incidentally, with the depression and its unemployment a type of housing sprang up in our neighborhood—repeated in other communities—presenting an unforgettable picture of collapse.

In the autumn of 1931 unemployment among homeless men became visible to even the most indifferent New Yorker. In various parts of the city where there were open spaces and vacant lots, "jungles" appeared. These villages of the unemployed built by them for shelter were as creditable to ingenuity as they were pitiful exhibits of the failure of organized society.

Our own local jungle[3] was located on West Street at the corner of Charlton Street. It occupied one of the blocks cleared by the New York Central Railroad for its tracks. The adjacent blocks were surrounded by high board fences.

On the side toward West Street were located the shacks of the white settlers. The Negroes were on the Washington Street side. The white and Negro communities kept separate from each other socially, although they were physically near. One or two of the Negroes, however, fraternized with the whites. There was also a group of Mexicans, Central Americans, and South Americans, with whom the whites had little or nothing to do.

The houses were in large measure below the ground. Since the lot was originally covered with houses, the cellar excavations formed a good base for construction. Many of the houses were at least three-quarters under ground, with only enough above the surface to permit a window and roof. Some of the houses located in the original cellars were not dugouts, their walls being entirely of board and a space existing outside of the walls. The shacks varied greatly in quality. Some of the dugouts and the shacks which were above ground were well built and snug, as well as fairly roomy. Others were merely thrown together or scooped out; they were dark, cold, and cramped. The best house built above the ground was a two-room bungalow with well-matched boards, good flooring, true beams and doorjamb, good roofing, and a good window. Inside the wall was wainscoted halfway up. The wood used for this purpose consisted of narrow laths carefully cut and fitted together and stained green. The upper part of the walls was lined with cardboard and papered with white wallpaper, as was the low ceiling. The main room contained substantial shelves, the bedroom firm bunks. An old coal range, secured in return for assistance to a man who was moving, had been installed in one corner. A piece of linoleum covered the floor. At the windows, over the shelves, and over the door to the second room were curtains. The walls were decorated with pictures drawn by one of the neighboring shack-dwellers. This shack was shared by three men, and others came in to do their baking in the stove, as it was the only oven in this part of the jungle. It took one man about three days to build the main room, and when his friends joined him, they built the addition.

The best dugout was constructed by three sailors. They lined the walls with stone chinked with clay, whitewashed over the stone, constructed firm shelves and three bunks, carpeted the floor, installed a skylight in the roof and a window on one side, wallpapered the ceiling and one part of one wall, and curtained the window and bunks. For heat this house used a tin oil barrel laid on its side, with a piece of tin over the hole at one end; the top side was flattened so that a frying pan might be rested on it. A smokestack at the opposite end went out through the roof.

Furniture for these and other shacks had been secured from the city marshal. When furniture belonging to persons who have been dispossessed is not claimed within a certain period, the city marshal has to get rid of it. From this source the shacks were well furnished with tables, chairs, and so forth, and also with dishes (from this or some other source). In some cases open fireplaces with a piece of tin over the top were used for heat, but most of the shacks used a tin barrel and stovepipe. Light was furnished by candles or lanterns in most shacks. One or two were dark, though at least one had an excellent kerosene lamp donated to it. In contrast to the shacks which were comparatively well built, there were a few miserable hovels without heat, air, or light. One of these looked like an overgrown coffin on stilts. It was raised about a foot off the ground, was hardly high enough for a man to sit up in, and was perhaps four or five feet wide and ten feet long. It had neither heat nor light. Another had only a hole through a flap of canvas for an entrance. Its owner crawled in with his coat off and then dragged his coat in after him. It had neither heat nor light. Another consisted of an over-turned Ford with a fireplace where the engine was and a couple of packing boxes out behind. The occupant slept with his feet in the fireplace.

Food was secured by periodic trips to the downtown market when produce was coming in. Here it is always possible to pick up supplies. The rest of the food was purchased. Since wood for heat can be picked up in plentiful quantities and building materials also requisitioned, only food and candles or kerosene had to be purchased. Water was carried in pails or milk cans from a gas station nearby. Most of the white occupants were permitted by the gas station people to use the toilet facilities there.

The men went looking for work nearly every day. Someone stayed behind in each shack to see that it was not rifled while the other occupants hunted for an hour or two of work on the docks, helped load trucks, or did other odd jobs. Some brought in funds by panhandling, but the "better element" did not approve of this. Panhandling was common among both Negroes and whites. The publicity given to the settlement brought a number of sightseers, who left a contribution for food or cigarettes in the houses which they visited. A few of these men worked regularly. Possessions were shared, according to one man on the assumption that "everything I have is yours and everything you have is yours also." This he says, "worked fine." It did not work well enough, however, to make it unnecessary to guard the shacks.

The men who lived in this town were estimated, in the fall of 1931, at approximately fifty whites and three hundred blacks and Central Americans. New men came in every day, although it was difficult to see from the crowding of shacks just where newcomers would be able to stake their claims. Many of the whites came in from the sea, being sailors, stokers, firemen, engineers, and so forth, on the ships which docked nearby. Others were longshoremen. Among them, in numbers estimated by the "better element" as constituting a majority, were steady workingmen. The white group included mostly Americans, with a few miscellaneous characters described as "Polacks" and an occasional Italian. The blacks and mestizos included American Negroes, West Indian "spics," "Cubans," and Central Americans. Many of them came in on the boats. Among the West Indians there were many who habitually took ship at the end of the coffee season, to return in the spring.

There were only men in the jungle. Some had sent wife and children home to the wife's parents and had dug themselves in to take their chances on finding work. One engineer from one of the coastwise steamship lines took his wife and children home to New England (from Fourteenth Street where they had been residing) and hitch-hiked all the way to Texas looking for work along the way. When he got back he decided that the chances were better as a squatter in New York than working for six dollars a week in the New Bedford mills. He said that he thought the best thing to do if they got chased off this lot was to find another place where it was possible to squat in the same way. The men who occupied the better shacks kept their places clean and maintained their own personal appearance, being well washed and shaved and altogether upstanding in appearance and manner. One man was said to have his sons with him.

It was in 1931 that the cumulative impressions of the housing picture I had witnessed since childhood resulted in my conversion to the necessity of government housing for persons unable to pay commercial rents. I had been asked by the Riverside Church in New York to give a talk at one of their forum meetings on life in the tenements. I had given many a talk on this subject for which my wide acquaintance with tenement dwellers had prepared me. I had lectured on the subject both at Barnard and at Teachers College, but in preparing for this address, I was anxious to bring together this material more cogently. It was with dismay that I realized how little progress had been made and how slow it was likely to be. For the great mass of tenement dwellings in New York remained in their old congested squalor. There were still the old airshafts unopened at the base and filled with refuse. There were the toilets in the basement or the halls for common use. There were the dark interior rooms, for which the design of the buildings did not allow of radical improvement. In other words, the slums were there as they had been for many decades. The new buildings after the passage of the 1901 legislation to be sure were a real improvement, but they did not alter the basic picture for the mass of low-income families. Was there no answer? Surely the people as a whole, that is, government, must make this a major concern. It was then that I became convinced that the answer lay in this direction.

The Public Affairs Committee in New York had published material bearing on the subject and I therefore joined this group to learn and to act. My address at the Riverside Church focused on this conclusion. And my work in the public housing field dates from that meeting. The Public Housing Conference was formed through the energetic leadership of Helen Alfred. It became a national group of which I was president until 1943.

These years were lived in close contact with two other women—the tireless, provocative organizer Helen Alfred to whom this work was a mission and a passion, and Edith Elmer Wood, scholar and leader in the understanding—both philosophical and practical—of the place of housing in the economy of our country and indeed of the world.

This was a period of conflict, development, and public education. Public housing is a controversial subject, for private interests are fearful of public measures they regard as competitive. But from the beginning it was made plain by advocates of public housing that two basic ideas were to be observed—one, that decent shelter and the abolition of slums are essentials for the maintenance of the American standard of living; and two, that public housing is not intended to compete with private enterprise wherever and whenever it can produce shelter within the means of low-income families.

Today too, it is essential to repeat this statement over and over until people understand it. Again and again, private interests oppose public housing as if it were a competitor. Opposition has decreased as public housing has become a reality and demonstrates its efficient meeting of this vast need.

This whole theme brings to light the various current attitudes toward the nature and function of government. The first comers to our shores had good cause to be suspicious of governments as they had known them. They came here for freedom and independence and opportunity. Town meeting was government by the people. The Constitution we adopted preserved this fundamental idea of local self-government, but rightly recognized functions that were statewide or that related to the country as a whole. Under the general welfare clause of the Constitution, the Supreme Court has upheld legislation which inures to the benefit of all the people. Congress is made up of representatives of the people. If they misrepresent the people, redress is obtainable through ballot. However, forces of self-interest often elect persons who cater to these interests, and the public welfare is disregarded. How can this be remedied? It is easy to say that the public should be more interested in political and social matters and should see to it that disinterested candidates should be endorsed and elected. But the machinery of election is a complicated affair. It is dependent upon those who work constantly for party control. This means a devotion which often interferes with home life, business and professional engagements, and cultural pursuits. By and large, only those who feel it will be to their advantage frequent political clubs or associations with the assiduity it takes to become effective in the choice of candidates and in their election to public office. Local government, newspapers, and radio are not immune from the pressure of powerful interests. Private enterprise does not always have the public welfare as its goal. These simple and basic facts are highlighted in the consideration of housing policies. Regard for the public welfare demands that America should, in the interests of health and decent living, abolish slums and provide good housing. This should be correlated with income capacity. Government should aid where private enterprise fails to supply the need, preferably by grants to local communities, or, where state legislation exists, to states for use by localities.

Opportunities for graft or political favor are so vast that the establishment of nonpolitical administrative entities is desirable to ensure continuance of good service. The "Authority" is such a device which has as its purpose the removal of a great public enterprise from political control. Within the framework of democratic administrative practice, the Authority is a variant that has proved most useful for the working out of adopted social policies. It is a body which is given "the right to determine, adjudicate or otherwise settle issues or disputes; the right to control, commend or determine."[4] The powers of an Authority have been sustained by the courts. Through housing authorities federal, state, and local support have operated in the production of public housing.

As a matter of fact, however, government housing was initiated as a measure for employment. Only public works could relieve unemployment when the great depression of 1929 and the years thereafter struck us. The obvious field of construction was indicated as a major factor in employment. The act of 1933 provided for government construction of housing for low-income families on two counts—the need for such housing, and the immediate necessity for employment.

It was in the little Georgian house in Washington occupied by Mary Harriman Rumsey, who was especially interested in consumers' problems and in the part the consumer should play in our economy, and by Frances Perkins, Secretary of Labor, that I met Hugh Johnson, director of the N.R.A. [National Recovery Administration]. My mission was to urge the inclusion of low-rental housing in the program to meet unemployment. It was a time of excitement and creative activity. I can never forget the telephone message from Johnson, assuring me of the inclusion in the legislation of this housing provision. Public Works was in the hands of Secretary [Harold] Ickes of the Interior, and it was in the Public Works Administration that housing made its debut. Ickes appointed an advisory committee on which the late Edith Elmer Wood and I served, as the only women members.

Previous to this time, limited-dividend housing had been the most forward step in creating a supply of reasonably priced housing rentals, though not reaching low-income families. Practically all of the advisory committee had come from this level of experience and were loath to recommend public housing as we know it today. Mrs. Wood and I were indeed the only two members of the group who stood our ground as public housing adherents. We were not architects or builders or technicians of any kind. But Mrs. Wood had vast knowledge of the history of housing in all countries, was a social economist of wide experience, and I agreed with her that the slums which infested our country could not be abolished without subsidy. Ickes, a forthright man, went ahead, and construction began.

In New York the Slum Clearance Committee was the precursor to state legislation creating housing authorities in the cities of New York State. And it was in 1934 that this act was passed and the first New York City Housing Authority was appointed by Mayor La Guardia. Other authorities have come into being subsequently, until now in New York State there are forty-one authorities, and in the country as a whole almost five hundred.

NEW YORK HAS HAD THE ADVANTAGE of a long-time active interest in housing. (Other states have followed in creating a State Division of Housing.) The New York State Housing Board had been established in 1926; under Governor Alfred Smith's leadership, the development of limited-dividend housing had taken place. Undoubtedly more would have been accomplished had the feature of a state bank in the original draft been accepted. This, however, was deleted and it was not until the Municipal Housing Law of 1934 was passed to follow up the N.R.A. Act, that power of financing and assistance to local housing authorities was effected. In 1938 the Constitution of New York State was amended so that the state could make loans for public housing to local authorities. This pioneer legislation would have worked more successfully than it has and conflicts between state and local authority arising under the implementing legislation would not have taken place, had the whole financing procedure been well defined.

Housing is now of such vast importance that it is bound to be a field of country-wide interest. It is obvious that rehousing America must include provision for all income groups which of necessity brings government into the picture. Relief to individuals advocated by some can never be the answer, for relief to individuals will never provide for new buildings, new neighborhoods, and a change in the face of the city.

Public housing like private housing employs architects, engineers, and labor of many categories. It acquires land, develops sites, and is financed by bond issues guaranteed by government. It differs from the housing of higher income groups only in that it is empowered by law, in the interest of the public welfare, to own and manage projects, to abolish slums, and to build new neighborhoods within the reach of low-income families. It is also available without cash subsidy for that part of the middle-income group that cannot afford to meet commercial rentals.

Public housing is still too recent a development to show statistically its relation to increased public health and reduction in delinquency. But it is already a matter of common knowledge that the greatly improved living conditions afforded by better housing and the concomitant development of neighborhoods furnished with schools, parks, shopping centers, and good transportation make for better family life. After all housing is for people.

In my fifteen years of experience as a member of the New York City Housing Authority—a longer continuous service than that of any other member—I have had an unusual opportunity to observe the workings of the housing authority law, to face the problems that have arisen, and to have participated in the growth and development of public opinion in this whole field. It has been my good fortune to have had friends with divergent points of view in regard to various aspects of housing, and to have had the blueprint of their thought and study to guide my work, both as a private citizen and a public official. Housing indeed is almost another name for the social situation as a whole, involving as it does the questions of land use, of planning, of technical skills, of public policies on segregation, of tax exemption, of concern for all income levels, of administrative policy, and of management.

To allow this national need to drift along without regulation or with outmoded social attitudes is to exhibit irresponsibility at its worst. Democracy is known by its fruits. This tree has been tossed about in the wind, not mulched or fertilized, and has been too bereft of rain and sun to bear rich fruit.

Defects that have naturally developed in the course of the brief time that public housing has been a part of our national structure are receiving careful attention and valuable criticism. It is important to secure greater variety in architectural design, to reduce as far as possible the volume of project population, to promote a greater degree of self-management, and to foster a greater amalgamation of tenant participation in neighborhood life. In other words the whole business should be regarded as a normal development of sound family life.

Especially is it desirable that families of different income levels should share the same areas. Solid blocks of one racial, religious, or income group are questionable for good democratic practice, though preferences for living patterns must also be respected.

The damage to home life occasioned by housing shortages is perhaps the most obvious defect in our economy today. With husband and wife often separated, with the doubling up of families and the consequent tensions and unhappiness, no one can be unfamiliar with the incompetence, ingratitude, and neglect with which the country has greeted its returning veterans. Nor should the misfortunes of countless families unable to meet commercial rents deprive them of decent homes.

A countrywide policy envisions of course not only public housing features, but the whole housing scene of which public housing, though of great importance, is a minor part. Occupational groups have shown initiative and resourcefulness as in the case of the Amalgamated Clothing Workers. Life Insurance companies and banks are using their vast funds for housing developments. Cooperative housing is taking on new aspects. The day of the independent individual owner is limited by zoning and by area planning.

In our part of New York the waterfront is a dominant factor. The housing of waterfront workers has always been of special concern to Greenwich House. We were enabled through the interest and help of the Pierce Foundation to make a study of longshoremen's homes which was published in 1939.[5] Today, when the rehabilitation of New York's waterfront is recognized as a major problem, the housing needs of waterfront families may well be restudied.

Indeed housing is an integral part of our whole life pattern. Hopeful signs surround us of a deeper recognition of the key place that housing occupies. But not until home life is buttressed by a substantial and responsible national policy shall we begin to meet this outstanding economic and social need. To recognize a problem is not to solve it. Private enterprise and government are not to be envisioned as enemies in mortal combat. They are the two aspects of democratic society which, finding it difficult to live together, yet cannot live apart. Out of this fruitful conflict between the individual and the community sparks are struck which light our path to new levels. This constant rebirth is the essence of a democratic society. But there is no assurance of the outcome. This depends on the effective purposes of a developing society.

Notes

1. Simkhovitch, 1949, preface. For the sake of brevity, further citation of this work, *Here Is God's Plenty*, will refer to "HIGP." Similarly, citations in the text of her 1938 book, *Neighborhood: My Story of Greenwich House*, will refer to "N."
2. James Ford (1936) *Slums and Housing*, Cambridge, Massachusetts, Harvard University Press, p. 123, with special reference to New York City. I am indebted to this author for a description of this early development.
3. I am indebted to a group of my associates, Mildred Oliver, Helen Johnson Small, and Murray Sachs, for the detailed accuracy of this description.
4. *American College Dictionary*, New York, Random House, 1948.
5. Elizabeth Ogg (1939) *Longshoremen and Their Homes*, New York, Greenwich House.

References

Simkhovitch, Mary Kingsbury (1938). *Neighborhood: my story of Greenwich House*. New York: W.W. Norton and Company.

——— (1943). "Neighborhood planning and the settlements," *Survey Midmonthly: Journal of Social Work* (June), p. 174.

——— (1947). "In our part of town," *Survey Midmonthly: Journal of Social Work* 83 (October), p. 281.

——— (1949). *Here Is God's Plenty: Reflections on American Social Advance*. New York, Harper and Brothers.

——— (n.d.) "The neighborhood looks at planning," Simkhovitch Papers, p. 3, Schlesinger Library, Radcliffe College, Cambridge, Massachusetts.

United Neighborhood Houses (n.d.) "New York," SWD5, p. 1, Social Welfare History Archives, University of Minnesota, Minneapolis.

5

Benjamin C. Marsh
and the Fight over
Population Congestion

HARVEY A. KANTOR

In the early years of the twentieth century, city planning existed less as a profession than as a mélange of experiments and untested ideas. Engineers, housing reformers, municipal officials, and journalists all claimed solutions to the disorders of unrestrained urban growth. Throughout this embryonic stage speculative thinking flourished. The success of a particular scheme usually depended upon the passion of its promoters; and unsupported proposals were quickly dropped and replaced by new ones.

One of the most radical of these programs struck at the heart of urban dynamics. Known as the "congestion movement" and headed by an energetic reformer named Benjamin C. Marsh, it attacked the overcrowding of population as the single most important cause of big city ills. Focusing on real estate speculation and unplanned development, Marsh and other leaders of the congestion movement fought for land and tax reform, public control of undeveloped real estate, and planned communities to decentralize inner-city population. These programs for guiding future urban growth were the most original and far-reaching programs of the time and helped to catalyze the disparate planning movement into a national organization.

Reprinted with permission from Harvey A. Kantor (1974) "Benjamin C. Marsh and the Fight Over Population Congestion," *Journal of the American Institute of Planners* 40, no. 6 (1974): 422–429.

The anticongestion campaign began in the nation's largest urban center, New York City, under the leadership of that city's active social settlement workers. Wrestling with the day-to-day problems of aiding the poor of the slums, social workers astutely analyzed the problems of urban poverty. So forceful were they in their pursuit of remedies that they constituted one of the most vital elements in the national progressive drive for reform (Davis, 1967; Kraus, 1970). In searching for ways to ease the burdens of the poor, the settlement workers recognized that alleviation of the crowded conditions of the slums had to be a major goal.

CCP Established

In early winter 1907, Florence Kelley, an influential social worker and secretary of the National Consumers' League, became convinced that congestion of population, so apparent on the Lower East Side of New York, stood as the chief affliction of thousands of poor people in large cities throughout the United States. "Instead of assenting to the belief that people who are poor must be crowded," Kelley argued, "why did we not see years ago that people who are crowded must remain poor?" (Davis, 1967, p. 70). In discussing her views on this problem, she found that others had come to the same conclusion. She then joined with Mary Simkhovitch, director of Greenwich House; Lillian D. Wald, head of the Nurses Settlement; the Reverend Gaylord S. White of Union Theological Seminary and Union Settlement; Dr. Herman C. Bumpus, director of the American Museum of Natural History; and others, in 1907, to form in New York an organization called the Committee on Congestion of Population (CCP).[1] The Committee's purpose was to collect data on the population question and to present it to the public in hopes of arousing concern (Lubove, 1960, pp. 231–8; Toll, 1969, pp. 122–4; Scott, 1969, pp. 84–8).

Marsh Joins Committee

In February 1907, the CCP retained Benjamin C. Marsh as its first executive secretary. Marsh was a wiry young man with a tremendous capacity for work. Associated with a variety of reform issues during his lifetime, he gained a reputation as one of the nation's most effective lobbyists for reform causes. A combination of I. F. Stone and Ralph Nader, Marsh brought an equal degree of ardor to each of his projects and infused all of his activities with a missionary zeal. He was a feisty infighter; a bantam rooster who poked at the shibboleths of the establishment with obvious relish. Described as a "character," a "charlatan," and a "radical," Marsh cluttered numerous offices throughout his Washington, D.C., career with propaganda supporting his causes of peace, consumer protection, and trust-busting (Marsh, 1953, pp. vii–xii).

When he came to the Congestion Committee in 1907, Marsh was only a budding, young "people's lobbyist." Yet his alertness, his restless energy, and the originality of his ideas impressed his colleagues. So brash was the young Marsh, however, that his early rantings quickly drew the warning from patrician reformer Robert W. DeForest that "if you touch the land problem in New York, you probably won't last here two years" (Marsh, 1953, p. 35).

Marsh's iconoclastic ways were molded both by his parents and by his teachers and stayed with him throughout his long life from 1879 to 1953. The son of New England Congregational missionaries, he spent much of his youth in Bulgaria observing his parents' methods in spreading the gospel. Back in the States he graduated Phi Beta Kappa from Grinnell College, a small liberal arts school in Iowa, attended the University of Chicago, took a job with the YMCA, and became a fundraiser for overseas church missions. In 1902 he won a fellowship to the University of Pennsylvania which enabled him to refine his social philosophy (New York Times, 1953).

As an undergraduate Marsh had absorbed some of the doctrines of Fabian socialism and also became enamored of the single-tax thinking of Henry George. Now in graduate school at Penn he naturally gravitated toward the progressive economist Simon Patten. Patten, a captivating professor, stressed the notion that industrialism had rendered scarcity obsolete and that abundance, the new order of the day, wiped out the necessity of poverty. Patten infused Marsh with the ideal of a society that could provide for the basic needs of its citizens. Fresh from these heady theories, Marsh tried out his ideas in his position as secretary of the Pennsylvania Society to Protect Children from Cruelty. Advocating better housing, Marsh offended some of the slumlord members of the Society's board and his tenure came to an abrupt end. It was with this intellectual baggage and experience that Marsh came to New York in 1907 to tackle the problems of population overcrowding.

To prepare for his work, Marsh spent the summer of 1907 in Britain, France, and Germany collecting material on housing and city planning for the CCP. His visits to Europe's major cities impressed him, but the highlight of the trip occurred at the International Housing Congress in London. Here the major question of congestion drew a great deal of attention and the conferees concluded that "the creation of new congested districts without the necessaries of healthy life now going on in large cities, can only be prevented by obtaining power to forbid the erection of any new buildings except in accordance with a general plan for developing all uncovered land within the city boundaries." The emphasis on state planning laced neatly with Marsh's own notions of social responsibility (Marsh, 1908a, p. 1515).

THE CONGESTION EXHIBITION

Marsh and his colleagues in the CCP launched their anticongestion campaign with an exhibition held from March 9 to March 28, 1908, at the American Museum of Natural History. Governor Charles Evans Hughes opened the show and generated much publicity with a speech expressing his basic sympathy with the aims of the Congestion Committee (Simkhovitch, 1938, pp. 160–61; "Congestion," 1908, pp. 1730–40). According to the catalogue, the show aimed to "depict some of the causes, the conditions and the evils of the massing of people in New York and in limited areas; and present methods of dealing with the problems involved and the methods, legislative and others, which should be adopted to remedy such congestion" (*Catalogue*, 1908). Maps, diagrams, charts (one of which read, "The population of the world could be contained in Delaware if they were as congested as the people in eleven New York City blocks, at the rate of twelve hundred per acre"), statistics, models, photographs, and pictures all presented the image of congestion as New York's most urgent social problem ("Problems," 1908; "Main," 1908).

Various civic and social agencies in the city—such as the Charity Organization Society, Tenement House Department, and the National Consumers' League—sponsored booths at the exhibition to display graphically contemporary living conditions in New York City. The show emphasized the vast increase in the numbers of people that crowded all aspects of New York's life and maintained that if anything were to be done about substandard housing, spreading tuberculosis, poverty, and crime, the crowding would have to cease.

The displays reflected the general philosophy of the CCP. They showed that concentration of land ownership, high rents, and an imperfect system of taxation aggravated the evils already caused by economic growth and immigration. Oppressive rents charged by owners who made huge profits from skyrocketing land values were the crux of the issue. Tenement house reform and tax adjustments seemed logical, though conservative, cures. But the Congestion Exhibition offered far more creative solutions, in the most original discussion of land use to which New Yorkers had ever been exposed.

SUGGESTED SOLUTIONS TO OVERCROWDING

The first of these solutions recognized that expansion of the transportation network could not relieve congestion. More subways only caused more concentration of tenements, and the original purpose of the track extension inevitably became subverted. Instead, factories needed to be evenly distributed with a zone of working-class housing near each new industrial site. Workers could then walk to work and to the park and recreational facilities also provided nearby. The scheme, originally proposed by the City Club of New York, ranked as one of the first that understood the limited value of subway extension as a means of easing congestion and offered an alternative.

A second more drastic solution suggested bodily removal of individuals and families to less densely populated areas of the country. Citing the work of the Industrial Removal Office, the Jewish Agricultural and Industrial Aid Society, and the Children's Aid Society, the exhibition hailed the benefits of a back-to-the-land movement. The New York State Department of Agriculture featured its own program which attempted to convince recent immigrants of the value of fresh air in a rural locale.

A model village plan suggested a third possible solution. Unsettled parts of the city, with cheap land still available, could be chosen as sites for new communities. A plan was shown by which nine hundred persons could live in individual houses with plenty of open spaces and pay only $2.00 to $2.25 a month rent. Private developers could still make a profit, and the slums could be somewhat eased by allowing workers to move out of the city into these prototype communities.

Besides these innovative suggestions of factory distribution, removal to the farm, and model villages, the exhibition stressed planning within the city itself as an urgent necessity. The Cologne, Germany, example of zones set up for specific land uses was displayed. And Charles Robinson, a leading author on city planning, speaking during the exhibition, made the point that "deliberate planning secures an enlargement of the habitable area available for the least paid workers by improving the means of circulation and the removal of factories to the suburbs" (Martin, 1908, pp. 29–38).

But perhaps the Congestion Exhibition was too successful in drawing public attention to the problems of urban overcrowding. According to Mary Simkhovitch, reflecting several years later on the effects of the presentation, "many superficial observers horrified at the evils of overcrowding felt that the problem was of such magnitude that it was hardly worthwhile to have brought the public to a realization of evils which in the nature of the case could be remedied or prevented only in the course of years and after a prolonged struggle" (Simkhovitch, 1910). Marsh, in his usual direct manner, maintained that the exhibit "was a distinct success from every point of view—except producing action to remedy the condition shown!" (Marsh, 1953, p. 18).

Nevertheless, after the exhibition, the CCP continued its work, beginning further investigations and accumulating more data to aid its cause. Several smaller exhibits were held in Brooklyn (Marsh, 1908b) and at the National Conference of Charities and Correction; speech-making continued at a furious pace; and then Marsh took off to spend his second consecutive summer in Europe. This 1908 trip motivated him to collect his New York and European experience into a small book which became the first volume published by an American dealing exclusively with city planning.

MARSH'S BOOK

Supremely confident in his cause, Marsh published privately in 1909 his *An Introduction to City Planning: Democracy's Challenge and the American City.* This 158-page paperback attempted to catalogue the achievements of foreign cities and to review the status of planning in America. But Marsh, of course, was no simple list-maker. The main purpose of the work prompted action. "A city without a plan is like a ship without a rudder" blared the opening headline, and

Marsh intended civic activists to heed his pleas for planning to "prevent the direful conditions of congestion, maladjustment and pre-eminently land speculation which have reached their horrible limit in Manhattan." For guidance he included a chapter on the "Methods of securing a city plan in some cities," model statutes for planning commissions in Hartford and cities in Wisconsin, a list of steps to follow in establishing a city plan, and a bibliography of "some good books on city planning."

Marsh ranked Frankfurt, Germany, as the ideal model and concluded from his observations there that "the most important part of City Planning, as far as the future health of the city is concerned, is the districting of the city into zones" (Marsh, 1909, p. 28). Frankfurt's additional policies of taxing the increased land values after each title change and purchasing land on its own for future development greatly appealed to Marsh. In comparison, he found American cities woefully lacking and a public that "has not been trained to demand such a farseeing outlook and plan for the city as a whole" (Marsh, 1909, p. 98).

Marsh's little book provides an interesting glimpse not only of his own thinking but of the state of city planning in general in 1909. The first manual on the subject came from a social worker, a supporter of reform causes. The technical aspects of the field were only touched upon briefly in a separate chapter by Marsh's architect friend George B. Ford. The primary examples of good planning drew on European, particularly German, models. Reflecting Marsh's own proclivities, the work emphasized zoning, land taxes, and municipal control of undeveloped property. *An Introduction to City Planning,* activist in overtone, strongly carried the message of the city's responsibilities in land development, and Marsh clearly challenged the dominant urban trend of unrestricted growth.

Having pioneered in the textbook field, Marsh moved to present the first City Planning Exhibition ever held in the United States. In early 1909, the CCP joined with the Municipal Art Society in providing an exhibition stressing the need for planning. The joint sponsorship of the program signified that these two private groups, one concerned with social problems and the other primarily with aesthetic ones, had come to the same conclusion—planning could solve the major questions with which each was concerned. Charles Robinson, describing the value of the exhibition, said, "No loyal New Yorker, or, indeed, American, could leave the hall with a smug and comfortable feeling as to the future of urban life under the conditions now usual" (Robinson, 1909).

CITY COMMISSION ESTABLISHED

The agitation by the Congestion Committee finally caused city officials to act (Kelley, 1909; Goodnow, 1910). On April 12, 1910, the Board of Aldermen authorized the appointment of a commission to investigate the issue of population congestion and to make recommendations. From the start, however, skepticism greeted the city's efforts. CCP members Gaylord White and Edward T. Devine wrote to the president of the Board beseeching him to set up immediately a city planning body within the government rather than merely appointing an investigative group (Board of Aldermen, 1910a). The New York City chapter of the American Institute of Architects also thought that nothing would happen if a temporary commission were established. The group maintained that "the history of every such commission in the past is the production of many schemes, beautiful to look at and admirable in themselves were they possible of execution, but the actual result of the work of these previous commissions has been almost nil" (Board of Aldermen, 1910b). Brushing aside such pleas, the Board of Aldermen created in May the City Commission on Congestion of Population to investigate the problem of overcrowding.

The *New York Times* endorsed the new group but urged the Aldermen to stay off the Commission and appoint only qualified experts (*New York Times,* 1910). This advice, too, was rejected, and when, on May 17, 1910, the nineteen members of the Commission were appointed, ten of them were Aldermen. Chosen to head the Congestion Commission, however, was Jacob Cantor, the former Manhattan Borough President and early advocate of city planning. Cantor had retained his political connections and was a close associate of the new Tammany mayor, William J. Gaynor (*New York Times,* 1912). Frank J. Goodnow, of Columbia University, sat as the resident municipal expert on the staff; and Benjamin Marsh, because of his knowledge of overcrowding, was appointed secretary. The remaining places on the Commission were filled primarily by real estate men. After eleven months of investigation and public hearings, the group presented its extensive report to its fellow Aldermen and Mayor Gaynor on February 28, 1911 (*Report,* 1911).

CITY COMMISSION'S REPORT

The most significant finding of these investigations held that the congestion situation now appeared worse than it had been when the issue was first raised (McAneny, 1910). Density figures in Manhattan had jumped 15 percent, from 131.8 persons per acre in 1900 to 166.1 in 1910, and the Commission concurred with housing expert Lawrence Veiller's appraisal that "the limits [of congestion] have not only been reached but have long been past" (*Report*, 1911, p. 1830). The Committee attributed the congestion to a variety of causes: poverty, concentration of factories and offices, consolidation of the Greater City, intensive use and high cost of land, lack of control over aliens and immigration, long hours of work, cost of transit and general transportation conditions, lack of a definite city plan, inadequate taxation, failure to prepare land for housing purposes, methods of administering charity, and failure of the city to adopt a policy that would attract people to outlying boroughs. All aspects of these causes and their effects were exhaustively treated in the final 270-page report.

On the subject of city planning, the Commission believed that "the failure to provide a City plan determining the way in which various sections of the City are to be developed is also largely responsible for the congestion through intensive use of land. . . . Intensive congestion has been perfectly natural," the Commission felt, because "private interest" rather than "the public welfare" had been "permitted to control the development not only of Manhattan but of the other Boroughs" (*Report*, 1911, pp. 1830–34).

The findings were a severe indictment of the city's role in dealing with the physical well-being of its citizens. The various subcommittees of the Commission made remedial suggestions, but none of the recommendations was drastic enough to counteract the impressive physical forces and the governmental inertia responsible for the condition. The most controversial of the proposals, however, dealt with the question of taxation of land.

Not surprisingly, Marsh pushed land tax issues to the forefront of the report. Some members of the Commission agreed with the more doctrinaire single-taxer, Frederic C. Howe, that "the housing question is the land question" and that "an ounce of land taxation will do more than a pound of regulation" (Howe, 1911, p. 1067). Therefore the Commission, although it did not directly advocate a land tax, strongly urged that the municipal government seriously study the possibility of its enactment. Also the Commission recommended that land be taxed at a higher rate than the structure built upon it. Thus taxes on buildings would be halved while taxes on land would be doubled (*Report*, 1911, p. 979).

Another even more innovative proposal in the Congestion Commission's Report dealt with public incentives for improvement of private land. This scheme would have changed the manner of apportioning tax on real property. Instead of taxing at an equal rate the value of improvement and land, the rate for improvements would be only half the rate on unimproved land. The landholder would therefore be given a tax break if he did something constructive with his property. Although the idea did not gain acceptance at the time, it stands as one of the earliest expressions of municipalities giving tax incentives to property owners for improvements carried out at their own expense.

REACTION TO THE REPORT

The New York Commission's Report was on the whole a valuable document—hailed by some as "epoch-making" ("Overcrowding," 1911). Unfortunately it went the way of so many city reports, to obscurity in a file cabinet. Although it contained nothing extreme, even the mere use of phrases like "land tax" and "keeping land cheap" scared people. Its mere implications for restructuring the tax system on property infuriated its critics more than the actual measures it proposed. For instance, Grosvenor Atterbury, an architect and original member of the Committee on Congestion of Population, latched onto the ideal stated in the report for keeping land cheap. Although nothing specific was advocated to accomplish this goal, Atterbury attacked the report for merely alluding to the proposition. In reviewing the final Congestion Commission's Report, Atterbury stated that making land cheap enough for anyone was not "true economics" and was therefore inappropriate. He wrote:

> The Report recommends "keep land cheap." This, of course, can be done only by limiting its usefulness. Is it certain that we want that? Cheap land, like labor, may be the most expensive from the point of view of true economy. Would the effect of the restriction of the price of land (even if feasible) be true econ-

omy? What we want in this matter is the most economical use of land compatible with hygienic and social standards, a situation not necessarily synonymous with "cheap" or low price land (Atterbury, 1911, p. 1070).

Thus even though the Commission only talked about the ideal of keeping land cheap, and stopped short of making concrete recommendations, still it drew heavy attack. Even though it never definitely advocated a single tax, but only requested a study of its effects, it was attacked as radical. The Board of Aldermen refused to allocate funds to press for enactment of any of the proposals, and with this lack of official support for the Congestion Commission's proposals, the entire effort failed. Governor Hughes appointed a State Commission on the same matter with Marsh at its unpaid head, but the damage had been done on the local level (Hebbard, 1910). Municipal officials had rendered their verdict—massive urban crowding would somehow have to dissipate on its own.

Mary Simkhovitch analyzed the congestion campaign's failure on the grounds of the public's reluctance to act. "It needs far more than five years work to effect so radical a change" (Simkhovitch, 1910). But fundamentally it was a question of more than time. For beneath all the agitation dealing with problems of congestion lay a basic need to reorder the prevailing economic structure. In Marsh's words, congestion resulted primarily from "protected privilege and exploitation" and "with expensive land no remedy for congestion among unskilled workers can permanently be found" (*The True Story*, 1910, p. 14). The high cost of land, low rate of wages, congestion of factories, and speculation in real estate sales all had to be drastically rectified. Such conditions, he thought, were "largely the outcome of a system of laissez-faire . . . and the police power of the state must be extended and enlarged to deal with it" (Marsh, 1910a). Marsh clearly believed something more than time was necessary for change to take place. He vociferously attacked land owners who benefited from increased value of unimproved land, and his views painted the congestion movement with a hue of radicalism which retarded immediate action.

MARSH AND THE SINGLE TAX

Marsh's brand of Henry George single taxation clearly unnerved people. He advocated a sharp departure from traditional tax systems called the differential or graded tax. Besides the regular tax on land, a progressive levy would be charged on increases in land values. This differential tax would tax land at a much higher rate than buildings, and the "unearned increment" derived from merely holding property while it rose in value would be partially returned to the community. Such a tax therefore would make it far less profitable for the speculator to hoard unimproved land (Lubove, 1960, p. 236).

In true Henry George fashion Marsh argued that no individual should benefit merely from the increased value of his land when that increase usually stemmed from improvements in the community as a whole. High land values inevitably led to landholders making the most use of their property and congestion always resulted. The differential tax promised to keep land cheap and therefore lower building costs as well as rents. In addition, the increased tax revenues could fill the growing "social needs" of the city.

MARSH'S CRITICS

Such a dramatic shift in taxation, of course, did not sit well with the financial community. An example of the hostility Marsh engendered was the reaction of Charles Pratt, the treasurer of Standard Oil, who declined an invitation of Frank Goodnow to appear before the Congestion Commission. He wrote: "I don't believe you know how radical that man Marsh is, or you wouldn't have anything to do with him." Goodnow, in turn, remarked to Marsh: "I'm backing you, but I suppose we can't expect people to contribute to the cutting of their financial throats" (Marsh, 1953, p. 24).

Marsh's views also ran against the grain of the professional economic thinking of the day. When he wrote to the Department of Economics at Harvard University, hoping to obtain expert opinion on the reasons behind congestion, he received the following caustic reply: "We must reckon with the fact that people flock to the congested districts because they want to be there; just as, for instance, single taxers flock to membership in congestion committees because they want to be there" (Bullock, 1913).

However, irritating established financial or educational interests was perhaps not as significant as dividing the small band of planning supporters themselves. This apparently is what Marsh also had done. The breach is evident in a confidential letter from Robert

DeForest to Jacob Riis. DeForest, president of the Metropolitan Museum of Art and a member since 1906 of the Municipal Art Commission, was one of the leading planning spokesmen in New York ("DeForest," 1967, p. 61). He was perhaps the prototype of the cultivated supporter of City Beautiful programs and, according to some, let his upper-class background keep him "a little distant with commonplace people and affairs" (Reynolds, n.d.). Yet DeForest did advocate city planning, and his support for the Congestion Commission could have been crucial. On this occasion his support was not forthcoming, as he wrote to Riis: "The leader of this movement [Congestion] is I think Mr Benjamin C. Marsh, who has lots of enthusiasm, lots of go, lots of good intentions, but as to whose practical judgment I have serious doubts. Some of my friends who have been more or less associated with him have found it desirable to withdraw and I should not look for practical results from a Commission, the leadership of which rested in some of our Aldermen and Mr Marsh" (DeForest, 1910).

Even Charles Mulford Robinson, publicist of civic improvement and enthusiast of almost everything having to do with planning, criticized Marsh and his methods. Robinson believed it "a questionable policy for city planners to appeal as yet—though one may eventually come to it—for a radical change in methods of taxation" (Robinson, 1909).

Although obviously not seeing eye to eye with everyone who supported planning in general, Marsh worked to coalesce the fledgling profession into a single national organization in hopes of enlarging the forum for his views and advancing the cause of city planning in general. His efforts in early 1909 to form such a group were further evidence of his capacity for work. For while involved in the establishment of the national organization, Marsh still retained his position with the New York CCP, served as the unpaid secretary of a new Society to Lower Rents and Reduce Taxes on Homes in New York, lobbied for the creation of the City Commission on Congestion of Population, delivered numerous speeches and wrote many articles as well as his *An Introduction to City Planning,* and coordinated the city planning exhibition with the Municipal Art Society. As the author of the first text, designer for the first exhibition, and founder of the first national organization of city planning in 1909, Marsh clearly ranked as a prime mover in the evolution of this young field.

The First National Conference on Planning

Henry Morgenthau, the chairman of the New York CCP, worked closest with Marsh in setting up the national conference. A director of several banks and real estate firms and owner of large amounts of undeveloped New York property, Morgenthau was a curious champion of anticongestion. Nonetheless, eager for civic responsibility, he pledged $1,500 to the CCP, donated office space for its use, and served as its chairman. Morgenthau and Marsh formed that special kind of partnership (similar to Robert DeForest and Lawrence Veiller in the housing field) that existed in many reform causes, that of the well-bred civic promoter listed on the organization's masthead allied with the energetic social reformer who did most of the work. During the period of American progressivism this union usually resulted in the conservative tempering the reformer's ardor. No one could do this to Marsh and this alliance soon withered. But not until it bore the fruit of the first National Conference on City Planning and Congestion.

Morgenthau and Marsh approached President William Howard Taft to preside at a national meeting on city planning. Taft, fearing reprimand from the Congress for usurping initiative, begged off but suggested Secretary of the Interior Richard A. Ballinger as an appropriate alternative. With Ballinger, Speaker Joseph Cannon, and Senator Francis Newlands in attendance, the National Conference on City Planning and Congestion met in Washington, D.C., on May 21 and 22, 1909, to discuss the multifaceted problems of housing, transportation, recreation, and planning in the cities (U.S. Congress, 1910).

The forty-three conferees met in an air of excitement and hope. Many of the nation's leaders in urban affairs attended, including Frederic Howe, Jane Addams, Mary Simkhovitch, George Ford, John Nolen, Frederick Law Olmsted, Jr., and Herbert Croly, the editor of the *Architectural Record* and author of the recently completed *The Promise of American Life*. Representatives of municipal art, social work, architectural, civil engineering, and conservationist groups also attended. The meeting vividly reflected the many interest groups concerned with city planning at the time.

Henry Morgenthau displayed his upper-class social morality and Darwinistic economics in his address before the group on the evening of May 21 at the Masonic Temple in Washington, D.C. "We are all proud of our country, its achievements, and the opportunities it has offered us and is offering others," the financier pronounced. But, he warned,

we will not permit anything to mar its onward and upward progress, if we can help it. There is an evil [congestion] which is gnawing at the vitals of the country, to remedy which we have come together—an evil that breeds physical disease, moral depravity, discontent, and socialism—and all these must be cured and eradicated or else our great body politic will be weakened. This Community can only hold its pre-eminence if the masses that compose it are given a chance to be healthy, moral and self-respecting. If they are forced to live like swine they will lose their vigor (U.S. Congress, 1910, p. 59).

Marsh, on the other hand, struck a more pragmatic chord in his remarks before the conference. Taking the themes developed in his book, Marsh outlined the steps necessary to advance a meaningful city plan—a survey, publicity, and legislation allowing cities to plan. This outline fit squarely with Marsh's modus operandi of gathering "facts" to be used as weapons "against which corporate interests cannot contend" and publicity, similar to the Congestion Exhibition, "to make possible the awakening of the public interest" (U.S. Congress, 1910, p. 61). Marsh's speech bristled with his own personal vigor, and Mel Scott observed: "If some delegates had the impression that city planning was for Marsh a holy war against predatory forces, especially real estate speculators, they were perhaps not mistaken" (Scott, 1969, p. 99).

As one of the principal organizers of the group Marsh stayed on in Washington, D.C., after the two-day meeting ended and testified before the Committee on the District of Columbia. The Conference proceedings and Marsh's testimony were then published by the federal government. The history of the first National Conference on City Planning is therefore recorded as a Senate Document.

The 1909 meeting in Washington, D.C., began a long and fruitful existence for the city planning profession as a national movement. It remains, however, the only significant juncture where Marsh and the national urban planning drive stood together. The reasons for the subsequent division are as varied as Marsh's personality and interests and as discordant as the numerous elements of early city planning.

Division in the Planning Movement

After the national conference Marsh returned to New York to continue his anticongestion campaign on the local level. The City Commission began its work and it was then that Marsh began engendering the opposition of powerful financial groups against his single tax schemes. The fire got hot and even housing reformer Robert DeForest attacked him. Worse still, the financial support and backing of the CCP by Henry Morgenthau ended. Morgenthau, worried that adoption of the single tax would hurt his investments, could not convince Marsh to drop the proposal from the CCP's platform. He therefore resigned his chairmanship, reneged on his financial pledge, and kicked the group out of the office he had been providing. Marsh's uncompromising advocacy of taxing land higher than buildings struck the majority of New Yorkers of the day as radical. He could not budge the powerful financial interests arrayed against him and even his potential allies dropped support (Marsh, 1953, pp. 27-9).

The national picture appeared equally dismal. Marsh's hopes for a single national organization devoted to city planning shattered in 1910 when Robert DeForest and Lawrence Veiller formed the National Housing Association (NHA). Although the NHA worked closely with the National Conference on City Planning and speakers at each group's conventions frequently overlapped, the division remained essentially damaging. Housing and planning were inextricably bound and a national organization for each served neither's best interests. Also, since DeForest served as president of the National Housing Association, Marsh could hardly expect a sympathetic forum within that group (Walker, 1950, p. 12).

The winds rapidly changed within the national planning conference also and worked against Marsh's prime interests. At the second meeting in Rochester, New York, in 1910, the group dropped "Congestion" from its title and became the National Conference on City Planning (NCCP). The name change was significant. The NCCP, beginning in 1910, concerned itself far more with the techniques of professionalism than with broad social problems. Fewer social workers and civic reformers attended, and increasingly the NCCP revealed itself as a "professional" organization concerned with data, statistics, techniques, management, standards, efficiency, and evaluation.

One of the principal movers in this regard, George B. Ford, had written the technical chapter in Marsh's textbook. In part reacting to the overly aesthetic City Beautiful mode of planning, Ford stressed "scientific management" applied to urban planning. Planning must become systematized, Ford and others argued, in order to develop as a meaningful profession and gain the support of the businessman "who has to pay the bills." Obviously, Marsh fumed at planners' desires to dovetail with business interests (Hancock, 1967).

Zoning emerged as the tool the scientific planners latched onto, and increasingly zoning became the major preoccupation of the planning profession. Supported by Marsh, zoning initially had the same radical connotations that Marsh's land tax proposals had. But when the first comprehensive zoning law was passed by New York City in 1916, real estate men supported it. That city's large business-men realized that zoning could stabilize the uncertain real estate market while placating those concerned with overcrowding. Zoning therefore outflanked its radical predecessor, the anticongestion fight, because it bolstered the real estate market while purporting to do something about easing congestion. Zoning became the conserva-tive's tool to temper the reformer's ardor—something that Marsh's single tax would never have done (Kantor, 1971, pp. 165–229).

Marsh Abandons Planning

Marsh continued his lonely advocacy for his differential tax and appeared briefly before the zoning commission's hearing (Marsh, 1910b, 1914). But by 1917 his isolation from the new mainstream of city planning was complete. In that year the American Institute of Planners formed to serve even more closely defined professional interests than the NCCP. Two years' experience in city planning activities were required for membership. Benjamin Marsh, although meeting the requirements easily, failed to appear on the list of charter members (Scott, 1969, p. 164).

The absence signified as much an interest in new fields as an isolation from professional planning. The Balkan War had taken Marsh away from New York as early as 1912 and he served as a correspondent there for two years. Upon his return he worked with the Farmer's National Council and beginning in 1918 with the People's Reconstruction League. Marsh became a familiar figure in Washington, D.C., during the Hoover administration and led his

People's Lobby of over a thousand members in numerous reform causes. He constantly appeared before Congressional committees and orchestrated press releases on depression relief, social control of industries, and a myriad of other popular causes. Under a new law in 1946 Marsh became the first lobbyist to register with the federal government. Characteristically, when sent the form to register income and expenditures, Marsh replied on his own stationery and not on the newly printed government form (*New York Times*, 1953).

Marsh himself did not slow up at all on his exit from the planning field he had so visibly affected. One wonders, however, if his absence did not reduce the vitality of his jilted profession. To be sure, his restless energy could never have been restrained by the confines of a single interest. But the growing professionalism of city planning which offended Marsh the reformer and the propagandist could surely have used a bit of his iconoclastic verve in its efforts to guide the future of the metropolitan leviathan.

NOTE

1. Other original members in the Committee on Congestion of Population included Grosvenor Atterbury, Edward T. Devine, Charles Ingersoll, Paul V. Kellogg, John Martin, and Carola Woerishoffer.

REFERENCES

Atterbury, Grosvenor (1911) "City planning and congestion," *Survey*, 25 (March 25), pp. 1069–70.

Board of Aldermen (1910a) *Proceedings* (April 12), pp. 135–7.

——— (1910b) *Proceedings* (February 4), p. 3.

Bullock, C. J. (1913) Bullock to Marsh, March 27, Benjamin C. Marsh Papers, Library of Congress.

Catalogue of Exhibit of Congestion of Population in New York (1908).

"Congestion and its relief" (1910) *American City*, 3 (December), pp. 285–8.

"Congestion of population" (1908) *Charities and the Commons*, 19 (March 21), pp. 1739–40.

Davis, Allen F. (1967) *Spearheads for Reform*, New York, Oxford University Press.

DeForest, Robert W. (1910) DeForest to Riis, April 5, 1910, Jacob Riis Papers, New York Public Library.

"DeForest, Robert W." (1967), in *National Cyclopaedia of American Biography*, vol. XLII, Ann Arbor, Michigan, University Microfilms, p. 15.

Goodnow, Frank J. (1910) "Reasons for a Commission on Congestion," *Survey*, 24 (April), pp. 77–8.

Hancock, John L. (1967) "Planners in the changing American city, 1900–1940," *Journal of the American Institute of Planners*, 33 (September), pp. 290–304.

Hebbard, Robert W. (1910) "The work of the State Commission on Distribution of Population," in New York State Board of Charities, *Report*, 1, pp. 907–15.

Howe, Frederic C. (1911) "Land values and congestion," *Survey*, 25 (March), p. 1067.

Kantor, Harvey A. (1971) "Modern urban planning: origins and evolution in New York City, 1890–1933," Ph.D. dissertation, New York University.

Kelley, Florence (1909) Kelley to George McClellan, June 22, Mayoral Papers, New York City Municipal Archives.

Kraus, Harry P. (1970) "The Settlement House movement in New York City, 1806–1914," Ph.D. dissertation, New York University.

Lubove, Roy (1960) *The Progressives and the Slums: Tenement House Reform in New York City, 1890–1917*, Pittsburgh, University of Pittsburgh Press.

"Main charts contributed to the Congestion Exhibit" (1908) *Federation*, 5 (May), pp. 19–48.

Marsh, Benjamin C. (1908a) "City planning in justice to the working population," *Charities and the Commons*, 19 (February), pp. 1514–18.

——— (1908b) "Congestion Exhibit in Brooklyn," *Charities and the Commons*, 20 (May), pp. 209–11.

——— (1909) *An Introduction to City Planning: Democracy's Challenge and the American City*, New York, privately published.

——— (1910a) "Causes of congestion of population," Second National Conference on City Planning, *Proceedings* (1910), pp. 35–9.

——— (1910b) "Taxation and the improvement of living conditions in American cities," *Survey*, 24 (July), pp. 605–9.

——— (1914) "Can land be overloaded?," *Annals*, 51 (January), pp. 54–8.

——— (1953) *Lobbyist for the People*, Washington, D.C., Public Affairs Press.

Martin, John (1908) "The Exhibit of Congestion interpreted," *Charities and the Commons*, 20 (April), pp. 27–39.

McAneny, George (1910) "Bulletin for press release on congestion, February 26, 1910," George McAneny Papers, Princeton University.

New York Times, April 13, 1910.

———, January 20, 1912.

———, January 1, 1953.

"Overcrowding must stop" (1911) *Survey,* 25 (March), p. 989.

"Problems of overcrowding" (1908) *Outlook,* 88 (March), p. 615.

Report: New York City Congestion Commission (1911) in *The City Record,* 40 (March 7), pp. 1830–1903.

"Report of New York Congestion Commission" (1911) *Survey,* 25 (March), pp. 977–9.

Reynolds, Jackson (n.d.) "Reminiscences," Columbia Oral History Project, Columbia University.

Robinson, Charles M. (1909) "The City Plan Exhibition," *Survey,* 22 (July), p. 317.

Scott, Mel (1969) *American City Planning since 1890,* Berkeley and Los Angeles, University of California Press.

Simkhovitch, Mary (1910) "Speech of November 16, 1910," Mary Simkhovitch Papers, Schlesinger Library, Radcliffe Library.

——— (1938) *Neighborhood: My Story of Greenwich House,* New York, W. W. Norton.

Toll, Seymour I. (1969) *Zoned American,* New York, Grossman.

The True Story of the Worst Congestion in any Civilized City (1910).

U.S. Congress (1910) "City planning," 61st Congress, 2nd Session, 422 Senate Documents, LIX, pp. 57–105.

Walker, Robert A. (1950) *The Planning Function in Urban Government,* Chicago, University of Chicago Press.

6

BURNHAM'S *PLAN* AND
MOODY'S *MANUAL*

CITY PLANNING AS
PROGRESSIVE REFORM

THOMAS J. SCHLERETH

To CHICAGOAN WALTER DWIGHT MOODY, "the completion of the *Plan of Chicago* was the most important civic event in the history of the city." Moody maintained that if implemented, the 1909 metropolitan plan prepared by Daniel H. Burnham and Edward H. Bennett[1] would enable Chicago to become nothing less than "the center of the modern world." No small claim for a city hardly seven decades old, but not atypical braggadocio for a midwestern metropolis already notorious for its special brand of civic and architectural boosterism.

Moody, a former general manager of the Chicago Association of Commerce and the first managing director of the Chicago Plan Commission (CPC), made his boast in a strangely titled, now largely unread work called *Wacker's Manual of the Plan of Chicago: Municipal Economy*.[2] First published in 1911, this curious volume in the history of American city planning literature went through several editions during the decade (1911-21) that Moody superintended the promotion of the Burnham/Bennett *Plan*. The book's misleading

Reprinted with permission from Thomas J. Schlereth, "Burnham's *Plan* and Moody's *Manual:* City Planning as Progressive Reform," *Journal of the American Planning Association* 47, no. 1 (1981): 70–82.

title prompted contemporaries as well as a few modern scholars mistakenly to attribute the work's authorship to Charles H. Wacker, prominent Chicago brewer turned real estate developer, financier, civic leader, and first chairman of the CPC. Moody's middle and surname also occasionally prompted confusion with that of the popular Chicago evangelist Dwight L. Moody, whose tabernacle and ancillary structures (bible college and institute, bookstore, radio station, etc.) still dot Chicago's near northside cityscape.[3]

THE *MANUAL*'S AUTHOR

Who was Walter Dwight Moody? Why did he write a best-seller and ascribe it to another man? What were the work's principal ideas? What might such ideas reveal about the philosophy and the practice of turn-of-the-century urban planning in Chicago and the nation? What might the intellectual history of this segment of the American city planning movement add to our understanding of the main currents of American intellectual history?

This chapter attempts to explore these questions through a textual analysis of Moody's widely promulgated book as an early classic in city planning promotional literature. While other historical data (e.g. correspondence, municipal archives, CPC minutes) have also been consulted, the *Manual* itself stands as the principal documentation that informs this study. Thus the *Manual*'s ideas—belief in mass education, progressivism, the efficiency movement, and environmentalism—are the focus of the analysis that follows. Concentrating primarily on Moody's text rather than his context, on what he wrote rather than what he did, this study interprets the *Manual* as an important document both in the intellectual history of the American city planning movement and in the history of the many-faceted reform movement known as progressivism.

The occasional mistaken identity of Walter Dwight Moody with Dwight Lyman Moody contains one clue to the former's character. In his efforts in "putting the *Plan* across," W. D. Moody openly acknowledged that he did so with all the zealotry of "the clergyman and the pedagogue."[4] In an era when many reformers had clerical backgrounds (e.g., Richard Ely or Graham Taylor) or personal religious motivations (e.g., John Bates Clark or Charles H. Cooley) behind their attempts to bring about social and political change,[5] his evangelical fervor to promote urban planning as the redemption of

American cities seems to put Moody perfectly in step with many of his fellow progressives.

Moody's career began, however, not in salvation but in sales. The title of one of his early publications can serve as a capsule biography. On a 1907 book cover, he proudly proclaimed himself as one of those "men who sell things," the book being the *Observations and Experiences of Over Twenty Years as a Travelling Salesman, European Buyer, Sales Manager, Employer.*[6] Drummer, promoter, adman, business college teacher, showman, Moody personified the late-nineteenth-century American whom Daniel Boorstin has symbolized as "the go-getter" and whom both Burnham and Wacker saw as "a hustler, a man who knows how to do things and to get the greatest amount of publicity out of a movement."[7]

To such a man the CPC entrusted the monumental task of making every Chicagoan fully plan conscious. The objective was to reach the one and one-half million citizens who could not afford the prohibitively expensive ($25), lavish, limited first edition of two thousand copies of the *Plan* published by the Commercial Club.[8] Handsome though it was, filled with evocative sketches in both color and black and white by Jules Guerin and Jules Janin, Burnham and his Commercial Club associates recognized that the *Plan of Chicago* was little more than sagacious advice from people with no official power. In accepting one of the limited edition copies, Mayor Fred Busse, who would later create the CPC, was careful to note that the *Plan*'s proposals were not "hard and fast" and would not necessarily result in immediate changes.[9] The unofficial nature of the venture, however, inspired Charles Eliot, the retired president of Harvard, to write:

> That a club of businessmen should have engaged in such an undertaking, and have brought it successfully to its present stage, affords a favorable illustration of the workings of American democracy. The democracy is not going to be dependent on the rare appearance of a Pericles, an Augustus, a Colbert, or a Christopher Wren. It will be able to work toward the best ideals through the agency of groups of intelligent and public spirited citizens who know how to employ experts to advantage.[10]

To promote the *Plan* that they had had experts produce, the Commercial Club members, through their control of the CPC,[11] employed another expert. Walter Moody, a professional organizer

and one of the new breed of public executives who made careers out
of managing civic organizations, assumed this responsibility. As
early as 1909 Moody had been approached by Charles D. Norton
(later Assistant Secretary of the Treasury under President William
Howard Taft) to publicize the *Plan* as the exclusive promotional
property of the Commercial Club. When the *Plan* was presented to
the city, and the Chicago Plan Commission, a public agency, was
created by municipal ordinance, Moody's talent was again solicited—this time by the CPC's first chairman, Charles H. Wacker.
Moody accepted the task of mobilizing a comprehensive promotional campaign to match the sweeping metropolitan scope of the *Plan*
itself.[12]

Although he never pretended to be a practicing planner like
Burnham or Bennett, Moody considered his task of "the scientific
promotion of scientific planning" to be equal in importance to
whatever was accomplished on the drafting table or in the architectural office. He defined city planning as "the science of planning the
development of cities in a systematic and orderly way." Furthermore, he divided city planning into

> two distinct and widely separate scientific branches. The first,
> or technical branch, embraces architecture and engineering.
> The second, which is promotive, is likewise scientifically pro-
> fessional and could be truthfully termed the dynamic power
> behind the throne of accomplishment.[13]

The term "scientifically professional" indicated another characteristic that Moody shared with many other thinkers of his era. As
David Noble, Richard Hofstadter, and Charles Forcey have argued,
many progressives believed strongly in the efficacy of the scientific
method, guided by professional expertise, to achieve social change.[14]
Walter Moody shared this assumption, not only in his promulgation
of the Chicago plan but also in his promotion of city planning as a
profession. The special identity that Herbert Croly claimed for
architects, that Frederick Winslow Taylor coveted for industrial
engineers, and that Louis Brandeis wished firmly established for
lawyers and businessmen, Moody sought for city planners.[15] Like
Charles Mulford Robinson and John Nolen, his contemporary colleagues in city planning, he endeavored to contribute to what has
been called the late-nineteenth- and early-twentieth-century "culture of professionalism." Moody's decade of work with the CPC, his

FIGURE 6.1   *McCutcheon, a friend of Moody, drew this cartoon for Moody's use in widening the exposure and appeal of the 1909* Plan of Chicago.

numerous magazine and newspaper articles, and his two major books all were methods by which he sought to make the profession of city planning a vehicle of urban reform.[16]

The key to Moody's reformism was publicity. In debt to the social scientific advertising techniques he borrowed from the pioneering social psychologist Walter Dill Scott (a fellow Chicagoan who later became president of Northwestern University), Moody made his appeal for implementation of the 1909 *Plan* to each of the assorted interest groups and power blocs in Chicago.

Of the multiple constituencies to be persuaded of the necessity of the *Plan,* Moody felt most confident of the city's capitalists. After all, had it not been an informal competition as to who would actually sponsor a city plan that encouraged the merger of Chicago's Merchants and Commercial Clubs? By the time the Commercial Club produced the Burnham plan, its members had also invested over a half million dollars in the enterprise.[17] Moody was less sure of the general electorate. His first major publication as managing director of the CPC, therefore, sought to reach this citywide, adult audience. A ninety-page, hardbound reference work titled *Chicago's Greatest Issue: An Official Plan* was distributed to over 165,000 Chicago residents; these were property owners and tenants who paid $25 or more per month in rent. The booklet is usually credited with countering the initial critiques of the *Plan* (such as George Eddy Newcomb's caustic *Chicago Replanned* [Chicago, privately printed, 1911] and the protests of the Twelfth Street Property Owners Association) and with securing support for the passage of the first plan bond issue (the widening of Twelfth Street) proposed to the Chicago voters in 1912.[18]

THE *MANUAL*'S ORIGINS

Within the first six months of administering the CPC, Moody moved to institute a city planning study program in the Chicago schools. Daniel Burnham had suggested this move, believing that for comprehensive urban planning to succeed "children must grow up dreaming of a beautiful city." Burnham, who had been extremely disappointed when his 1905 *Plan for San Francisco* failed to be implemented because of inadequate promotion and subsequent citizen apathy, hoped to achieve this educational objective by lectures and the distribution of literature in the city schools.[19] Moody had bigger plans. Believing that "the ultimate solution of all the major problems of American cities lies in the education of our children to their responsibilities as future owners of our municipalities and arbiters of their governmental destiny," he proposed introducing an accredited course on the Chicago plan into the city's public school curriculum. The course would be a part of Moody's program for "scientific citizen making."[20]

To assist in such civic nurture, Moody wrote the first city planning textbook to be used in American schools. He named the text *Wacker's Manual* because he believed that the people "should come to know intimately the individual who to a large extent held the destiny of the city in his hands." He felt it imperative for the populace to have the same confidence and knowledge about their plan leader, Charles Wacker (chairman of the CPC), as in their plan.

Influenced by the work of German educators who had been instructing children in urban planning since the 1880s, he designed his text and its accompanying teacher's handbook for use in the second semester of a civics course already operating in the final term of Chicago's public grammar schools. The eighth grade was selected because many contemporary educational psychologists contended that at that stage of growth children were most impressionable. Also, after grammar school many would drop out of the system. While writing the *Manual,* Moody sought help from the University of Chicago faculty, the staff at the Chicago Historical Society, and the Art Institute. He persuaded Ella Flagg Young, city superintendent of schools, to have the Board of Education officially adopt and purchase (at thirty-four cents a hardbound copy) the 1911 first edition for use in the spring of 1912. Eventually over fifty thousand copies of *Wacker's Manual* were printed. They were read not only by Chicago schoolchildren but also by their parents.

While by no means as stunning as the *Plan* in terms of diversity of pictorial media or aesthetic quality, the *Manual* aspired to make as powerful a visual impact. The *Manual* included over 150 charts, maps, and pictures—many reproduced from the *Plan*. (The *Plan* had 142 illustrations.) Similar to the parent *Plan,* nearly a third of the *Manual*'s graphics were of foreign urban design. Color renderings in both Burnham's treatise (where they were largely the work of Jules Guerin)[21] and Moody's textbook were hazy, subdued pastels, connoting a tranquil, sunlit environment for Chicago which corresponds with an equally unreal absence of automobiles, pollution, and congestion in these visual utopias of Chicago's future.

Moody further modeled his 137-page primer along organizational lines roughly parallel to the 164-page, octavo-size *Plan*. He divided the textbook into four major topics: (1) general urban planning philosophy and nomenclature (chapters 1–3); (2) a historical survey of city planning since antiquity (chapters 4–7); (3) Chicago's historical, geographic, economic, and civic development, including the origins of the 1909 *Plan* (chapters 8–10); and, (4) a detailed exegesis of the plan's main components—transportation network, street system, Michigan Avenue redevelopment, park system, and civic center (chapters 11–16).[22]

Of the four media he produced in advancing the *Plan of Chicago*,[23] Moody considered the *Manual* to have the most long-range influence. Like previous American educational reformers Benjamin Rush, Horace Mann, Henry Barnard, and Francis Parker, he believed that the promise of a more enlightened, public-minded citizenry rested with the current school-age generation. Moody had been an educator for several years in Chicago's LaSalle Extension University, and he felt that his text "recognized the need for bringing out in the children of our cities a sharp, clear, vivid interest in those cities, in their history, their growth, in their present and their future."[24] As a consequence, the *Manual* can be considered one of the earliest urban histories for use in the secondary schools. Moreover, given its visual and verbal coverage of the American and European urban built environment, the *Manual* also introduced eighth graders to civic art and public architecture—areas of the fine arts that progressive educators usually found sorely neglected in most American classrooms.

Through his *Manual,* Moody shared with fellow Chicagoans Francis Parker and John Dewey the desire to create a larger classroom by relating school and society. Like Parker and Dewey, Moody sought to adjust education, through the discipline of city planning, to the interests of young people and to tie what he called "civic learning" to the real world outside the classroom.[25] The *Manual*'s injunctions to use the city itself as a part of the curriculum were perfectly consonant with Dewey's principles of integrating *The School and Society*. Although in actual practice he exhibited none of the innovative pedagogical techniques that Dewey and his followers advocated,[26] Moody completely agreed in theory with progressive education's concern to adapt schooling to fit the needs of the child rather than to the demands of tradition.

Perhaps the greatest common ground shared by Moody (as a promoter of planning education) and Dewey (as a proponent of progressive education) was the assumption regarding the correlation between education and politics. Just as Dewey in *Education and Democracy* (1916)—a major educational manifesto of progressivism—wrote: "we may produce in the schools a projection in the type of society we should like to realize and by forming minds in accord with it generally modify the larger and more recalcitrant features of adult society," likewise, Moody, in *Wacker's Manual* (1911) proposed to "prepare the minds of our children to grasp and lay fast hold upon the science of city planning for the future glory of Chicago and the prosperity and happiness of all her people."[27]

THE *MANUAL*'S IDEAS

Along with providing a pioneering pedagogy for disseminating "the principles and practices of scientific planning," Moody also wrote his primer, quite unabashedly, in order to inculcate what he variously termed "community patriotism," "united civic interest," "civic patriotism," and "community virtue." In the *Manual* building citizens and planning cities were synonymous since Moody saw the *Plan* and its implementation across the cityscape as the artifactual evidence that "gave the people of Chicago a way to express in solid form their progressive spirit."[28]

In an article in *Century Magazine,* "White City and Capital City," Daniel Burnham specifically identified himself and his city planning with the progressive movement.[29] Architectural historian Thomas S. Hines has pointed out the ramifications of Burnham's reformist liberal Republicanism, particularly its influence on the shape and substance of the 1909 *Plan*.[30] Such progressivism became further pronounced when Moody translated the plan into a manual.

By progressivism, Moody and Burnham meant something more than the Progressive (or Bull Moose) party formed in Chicago by the Republican insurgents who supported Theodore Roosevelt for the presidency in 1912. As contemporaries such as B. P. DeWitt (*The*

Progressive Movement, New York, Macmillan, 1915) almost universally recognized, progressivism was a pervasive, many-sided crusade of uplift and reform, often inconsistent, often naive, and sometimes palpably conservative. This broad impulse toward criticism and change was increasingly conspicuous after 1900 and had quite dissipated by the mid-1920s; as Richard Hofstadter states, progressivism was not so much the movement of any one social class, or coalition of classes, against a particular class or group as it was a rather widespread and remarkably good-natured effort of a significant segment of the urban middle class to achieve within their areas of expertise (e.g., law, academe, politics, social work) a societal self-reformation.[31] Accepting industrialization and urbanization as facts of twentieth-century American life, never seriously doubting the continued possibility of progress and prosperity, the majority of progressives sought the restoration of a type of modified economic individualism within a collective political democracy that was widely believed to have existed earlier in America and to have become threatened by greedy corporations, corrupt political machines, and apathetic citizens.

As representatives of what might be called "mainline progressivism" Moody and Burnham shared this political and social temper that was, paradoxically, innovative and reforming as well as traditional and conserving. Given this brand of progressivism, they understandably had an affinity with local Chicago reformers such as Charles Merriam (political scientist at the University of Chicago) or Mayor Tom L. Johnson (who first enlisted Burnham in comprehensive planning for the city of Cleveland). With moderate social progressives such as George E. Hooker and Jane Addams, Moody and Burnham's cautious reformism had only partial acceptance. More radical social progressives like Graham Taylor or Florence Kelley questioned Moody and Burnham's lack of concern in both the *Plan* and the *Manual* for adequate neighborhood housing and social welfare. Chicago labor progressives like John Fitzgerald and militant socialists like Lucy Parsons considered almost all progressive reforms, including proposals such as the *Plan* and the *Manual,* as but "band-aid" remedies designed to bolster the city's corporate capitalist interests.[32]

Moody, while basically a supporter of capitalistic individualism (he had been the executive director of the Chicago Association of Commerce before joining the CPC), also saw the need—perhaps in

the interest of preserving capitalism—for greater social collectiviza-
tion and municipal cooperation among individual citizens. Long-
range, large-scale city planning would, he admitted, proscribe certain
rights and prerogatives of the city dweller. Moody worried, however,
that in early-twentieth-century American cities such as Chicago,
rampant individualism perhaps had gone too far and that the system's
inherent atomism was rapidly destroying communal urban life.[33]

To meet this dilemma, Moody advocated major environmental
and architectural change as a method by which to infuse his form of
progressivism into the American city. Calling for planners to design
a "New Metropolis"—an image bearing a striking resemblance to
other "new" reform manifestos being issued by fellow progressive
publicists (e.g., Walter Lippmann's *New Republic* or Walter Weyl's
New Democracy)—Moody espoused a politics that wished to con-
serve what was valuable from the past and also remain cognizant of
the new challenges brought on by economic and urban concentration. In short, he argued in both the *Manual* and in his later writings
for a greater combination of central planning and voluntary individual cooperation. As his friend Bernard W. Snow summarized it in an
address honoring the CPC in 1910: "Every generation has its burdens. To this is given the duty of curbing the individualism and
establishing the collectivism of Democracy."[34]

Walter Moody promulgated a political progressivism that historian Stow Persons has labeled neodemocracy.[35] Nonpartisan, believing in the political role of public opinion, anxious to separate
electoral politics from public administration, Moody's writings are
a perfect case study of an early-twentieth-century neodemocrat in
action. With his fellow progressives, Moody was willing to revise his
original ideal of social progress as achievable solely in individualistic
terms and to concede to the state (particularly via a strong executive
and numerous public commissions) the rapid expansion of its functions and powers. Moody saw in neodemocracy a political philosophy which did not threaten the prerogatives of the expert. Like
Walter Lippmann, he did not fear either a big leader (especially if the
leader were a Burnham) or bigness in business, labor, or government. The public relations man who translated the philosophy of a
business client such as Burnham (who always insisted "Make no
little plans") could hardly see bigness as a bogey.[36] Nor could he deny
the power of the *word,* especially the printed word, in shaping
democratic political thought and action. A reformer who had writ-

ten a half dozen books, over forty pamphlets, position papers, reports, and newspaper and magazine articles would not think otherwise.[37] Finally, insistent that change would come about by working through the established political system, Moody concurred in the direct democracy principles of reformer Frank Parsons and maintained "that the ballot box always precedes the city planners."[38]

Since the ultimate implementation of the Burnham *Plan* depended upon widespread voter acceptance of each of its specific proposals, Moody saw his task as identical to that of Frederic C. Howe who in *The City, The Hope of Democracy* (New York, Charles Scribner's, 1905) had argued the necessity of linking all city planning reform with an extensive information and publicity program for adults and a comprehensive educational component for children.[39] Moody's *Wacker's Manual* and his adult primer *What of the City?* served these purposes. They also contain evidence of at least two other important intellectual currents of late-nineteenth- and early-twentieth-century America: a quest for efficiency and order in personal, commercial, industrial, and political activity and the belief in the physical environment as a primary determinant of human behavior.

In a work subtitled *Municipal Economy,* it comes as no surprise to find repeated pleas for greater centralization, the absolute necessity of eliminating all waste, the commercial value of beauty, and the civic efficacy of "good order, cleanliness, and economy."[40] In fact, many sections of Moody's tract could have been written by any number of Chicagoans—George Pullman, Marshall Field, Gustavus Swift—each of whom sought to impose an entrepreneurial system on the industrial and commercial landscape. This "search for order," as historian Robert H. Wiebe labels late-nineteenth-century American history,[41] pervades the *Manual,* a work that anticipates Walter Lippmann's *Drift and Mastery* in its demand for a "community patriotism to substitute order for disorder; and reason, common sense and action for negligence, indifference and inertia."[42] Moreover, Moody's incessant arguments for the efficient use of public space strongly parallel Frederick W. Taylor's similar claims (published in the same year as the *Manual*) for *The Scientific Principles of Management* in the organization of industrial space.

Moody took the making of Chicago into a centralized city rather than a group of overcrowded villages to be a basic premise of the Burnham *Plan.* Chicago's street and highway pattern, railroad network, and cultural and civic activities would each have a center and, in turn, be a component of a new central city. The linchpin on this new urban core was a monumental civic center that would be to Chicago what the Acropolis was to Athens, the Forum to Rome, and St. Mark's Square to Venice—the very embodiment of the reformed civic life that Burnham and Moody hoped to see come to pass in Chicago. Although we have understandably lost sympathy for neoclassical expressions of institutionalized political power, the progressives felt that neoclassicism's unity, permanence, balance, order, and symmetry best proclaimed both the symbolic role and the functional role of public buildings and communal spaces. A civic center, a unified cluster of "vast civic temples," as Moody called Burnham's proposed building group dominated by a colossal municipal administration building,[43] would typify the permanence of the city, record its history, and express its aspiration for reform. In Moody's estimate, the civic center would "give life to the spirit of unity in the city."[44]

Congestion and waste would be eradicated in the process of centralization. In his *Manual,* Moody warned his young readers that "the *elimination of waste is the World's Greatest Scientific Problem*" (emphasis original); and in his manifesto for adults he suggested various ways by which scientific planning would solve this international dilemma: zoning controls, public health regulations, uniform building codes, and standardized construction materials and designs.[45] A pet Moody project was a proposal he outlined in a pamphlet titled *Fifty Million Dollars for Nothing!* where he discussed how the people of Chicago could obtain thirteen hundred acres of lakefront parks, playgrounds, and watercourses by recycling the city's garbage and waste material—old bricks and mortar, excavation soil, street sweepings, cinders, and ashes. In twelve years, estimated Moody, Chicago taxpayers would have new parklands along the lakefront worth $50 million, at no cost whatsoever.[46]

As both Samuel Haber and Samuel P. Hays demonstrate in their investigations[47] of the scientific management and conservation movements, progressives like Moody, Burnham, and their associates became enthralled with the principles of rationalization, standardization, and centralization in civic life because they had already attempted to implement such principles in business life. Although they looked to Europe for their aesthetic inspiration—particularly to that of Baron Georges-Eugène Haussmann and the French École *five feet above the surface in water fifteen feet deep?*

25. *What is it evident that the city furnishes?*

26. *How do city officials, Sanitary District engineers, manufacturers and building contractors all agree they will save money?*

27. *How is the total waste of the city divided?*

28. *What is the number of cubic yards of cinders and ashes produced each year by the city's consumption of coal?*

29. *How is this moved?*

30. *What will be the value of the land Chicago can create upon the lake front in five years?*

31. *What do expert engineers say can be created from the city's waste within thirty years?*

32. *What did the architects take into account in planning the lake front parks?*

33. *How did they answer this demand in the plans?*

34. *Where do the plans provide for the filling in first of a wide strip of shore land facing the open lake?*

35. *What will run along this shore?*

36. *What will be built beyond the water course to protect it and provide safety and shelter forever to pleasure craft?*

37. *What will be located at the northern terminus of the long park at the foot of Twelfth Street?*

38. *What is to be located on the main shore in the mile of park land between Twenty-second and Twelfth Streets?*

39. *What will extend northward from the athletic field on the main shore?*

40. *What will be situated at the northern extremity of the main harbor?*

41. *Where are the piers to be built, and how will they be reached?*

42. *What is to be provided off Jackson Park where the water is quite shallow?*

43. *How is the lake front to be improved in the district from the mouth of the river north to Chicago Avenue?*

44. *What steamers will dock at the wharves in the harbor between the Chicago River and Chicago Avenue?*

45. *How do the lake front plans vary in detail from the south shore plans to the northward of Chicago Avenue?*

46. *How will the people benefit from the parks along the lake shore?*

47. *What does the second element in park development for the future Chicago aim to create?*

48. *What was decided in the plans after con-*

sidering the shape of the city, location of its great body of citizens, direction of future growth and all other conditions?

49. *Where are the three large new parks to be located and how connected?*

50. *Why was it decided to give the west side the largest single park in Chicago and make that park the center of the future city's park system?*

51. *What relation does the park system as planned bear to the rest of the future city?*

52. *Why is the great west side park planned to be located on Congress Street?*

53. *Describe the proposed Congress Street Park.*

54. *Describe the south side park as proposed.*

55. *Describe the north side park as proposed.*

56. *What have the architects projected to connect the three parks?*

57. *Describe the curving connecting boulevard, beginning with the great south side park.*

58. *What is the relation of Western Avenue to this sweeping bow-shaped boulevard?*

59. *What would the acquisition of these three parks and the bow boulevard add to Chicago's park area and where would it place Chicago in relation to the park area of other cities?*

60. *What have modern cities learned that they must do to provide recreation areas for their people?*

61. *What does every European capital have within easy reach of its people but outside of its limits?*

62. *What do the people of London, Paris, Berlin and Vienna do on Sundays in Summer?*

63. *Where is New York acquiring outer territory for park purposes?*

64. *Describe the territory surrounding Chicago procurable for forest parks.*

65. *Describe the sort of spaces that should be acquired for forest reserve purposes.*

66. *What has provisional search resulted in?*

67. *Describe the five proposed forest reserves, in their order.*

68. *What has modern man learned of city life in a period of less than a century?*

69. *How is city life different from country life?*

70. *What is the only way known by which a city may lessen these ills or do away with them?*

71. *What is necessary to upbuild Chicago and enable her to keep her place in commerce and to grow in power in the modern stressful warfare of trade?*

72. *State the only way for Chicago to increase and maintain the vigor of her people.*

FIGURE 6.2   *Catechetical questions at the end of each chapter illustrate the "primer" nature of Moody's* Manual.

des Beaux Arts[48]—their planning ideas reflected primarily the order and systematization they prized in their own businesses. For example, Frederic Delano, a Commercial Club Plan Committee member who had made his way up to the presidency of the Wabash Railroad at age twenty-two, maintained that, in his mind, "a comprehensive city plan represented a natural progression from his own idea of centralization of the Chicago passenger railroads."[49]

CHAPTER XVI

CREATING A CIVIC CENTER

In becoming the second city of the United States in population, Chicago has not until now taken any account of unity, or of centralizing its governmental activities. First there was the settlement about Fort Dearborn, then the extension of the village to cover a square mile or so. While this was in progress at the heart of affairs nearby farm centers grew into little settlements. Township governments were established, and in each township a village came into being. Chicago grew toward these villages in all directions, and the villages extended their streets and settlements toward Chicago. Finally Chicago spread out until these villages were swallowed up within the city, giving up their little local governments and becoming districts of Chicago itself.

In this process by which Chicago absorbed its neighboring towns and villages there was no planning for the creation of a center. Instead of creating a great unified city, therefore, we built up one by grouping together numerous adjoining towns. By good fortune, these towns and villages were so laid out that for the most part their streets blended well with the street system of Chicago, and so we do not notice, in going about the city, that Chicago is really the result of patching several towns together.

CHICAGO. View, looking west, of the proposed civic center, plaza and buildings, showing it as the center of the system of arteries of circulation and of the surrounding country.
[Copyrighted by the Commercial Club.]

Lavish graphics at the chapter beginnings were intended to catch the reader's eye and attention.

During a decade that produced studies on waste and scientific management in education, churches, and private homes,[50] it is hardly surprising that Moody should refer to the Chicago *Plan* as an instrument of "the City Practical" as opposed to the City Beautiful with which it was often confused.[51] A rational, unified, efficient, scientific, practical plan, he insisted, was the sole way to order the chaos attendant to rapid urban growth.

To the elements of education and efficiency that have been suggested thus far as crucial to Moody's strategy for civic reform must be added a third feature: environmentalism. Like many of his generation, Walter Moody believed in a modified ecological determinism. He was taken with the emergence of American social science in the latter half of the nineteenth century and was confident of its beneficial application to city planning. Thus he maintained that the "physical conditions which make for good health, good order and good citizenship must be made clear to our children." Moody stated the conviction that "splendid material upbuilding" of the metropolis would yield "a social, intellectual and moral upbuilding of its people" as a simple environmental equation: "city building means man building."[52] Following an evolutionary analogue used earlier by Chicago novelist Henry Blake Fuller to explain the progressive development of "a higher type of Chicagoan" in cultural achievements, Moody predicted a parallel social evolution to follow upon the advent of social scientific urban planning in the "prairie city."[53]

Such city planning could not come too soon in Moody's judgment. "The physical condition of people in the cities as compared with the people of the open country is deteriorating," he warned his young readers, because "city life is an intense life, many times more wearing upon the nerves than country life." Quoting various social scientists, he also proposed that the unplanned and unkempt city "saps the energy of men and makes them less efficient in the work of life." Moreover, it was "this strain of city life which increases insanity and brings weaknesses of many kinds to shorten life and deprive people of their vigor."[54] Heady stuff for mere fourteen-year-olds but only one example of the *Manual*'s argument that the physical environment conditions public behavior.

Several of the *Manual*'s proposals to correct physical deterioration of urban dwellers bear a striking resemblance to the theories of American psychiatrist George M. Beard, discoverer of neurasthenia, or "nervous weakness." Beard believed that environmental tensions, particularly when exacerbated by the stress of urbanization, modernization, and technological innovation, were the chief causal factors in the etiology of mental illness. In his most famous book, *American Nervousness,* Beard claimed that the incidence of mental disorders was unusually high (and growing even more so) in late-nineteenth-century urban America. There had been no nervous exhaustion or physical deterioration, for example, in those cities of ancient Greece or Rome that Burnham and Moody held up as exemplary of ordered, planned, urban design. These ancient civilizations, Beard contended, lacked five characteristics peculiar to nineteenth-century civilization: steam power, the telegraph, the periodical press, the sciences, and the mental activity of women.[55] Beard felt America was a quarter century more advanced than any European country in each of these aspects of modernity.

Since at least the time of Benjamin Rush, American physicians had almost as a matter of course acknowledged that the unique pace of American life (e.g., its competitiveness, its religious pluralism, its lack of stability in social status) was somehow related to America's higher rate of mental illness. After the Civil War, two other ideas— the concept of evolution and the increase in the population and number of American cities—had been added to this traditional belief in the relationship between American civilization and psychological and physical health. Beard accepted and amalgamated both evolution and urbanization into his interpretation of American nervousness. He maintained that the conquest of neurasthenia need involve no change in man himself, just in his environment. The technology which had produced the telegraph, the railroad, and the factory had already begun to provide other technological innovations which helped to reduce the tensions of American experience. Beard cites as specific examples the elevator, the sewing machine, and the Pullman palace car.[56]

Although there is no evidence that he ever met or read Beard, Moody shared Beard's belief in evolution and in urban neurasthenia. Like Beard, he looked to the continued advance of material and technological progress to offset evils of the American urban environment. City planning, in Moody's view, naturally provided one panacea whereby urbanites could overcome, or at least mitigate, ecological determinism. In the school text that he also called "a physical geography," Moody (with an analogy he borrowed from Frederick Law Olmsted) made a special case for how urban parks and forest preserves could be "compared with the lungs of a person, as the means by which the city and its people get the stimulus of fresh air so necessary to normal well-being."[57] Much like Olmsted, who argued for orderly park design as a method of social control and urban reform, Moody envisioned the parks of the 1909 *Plan* as crucial components in alleviating stress, overcrowding, and congestion. In the Chicago city parks, the masses supposedly would find an environment conducive both to activity and to contemplation.[58]

THE *MANUAL*'S DEFICIENCIES

Critics of Burnham's *Plan* and Moody's *Manual* complained, however, that the *Plan* did not do enough to alleviate the social evils that afflicted numerous Chicagoans: lack of housing, schools, or adequate sanitation. Charges of elitism and lack of concern for public improvements at the neighborhood level were directed at a plan that, admittedly, dealt primarily with elaborate transportation systems, monumental aesthetic centerpieces, and symmetrical street façades. In several respects the Chicago that Burnham had planned and that Moody promoted was a metropolis for businessmen where, ironically, with the exception of the central business district, there were no carefully designated areas for commercial expansion throughout the rest of the city. Nor were there any model tenements for workers, much less model neighborhoods.

Not that Moody was oblivious to Chicago's housing or social problems. Slums were mentioned in both the *Manual* and the *Plan* but only briefly. Once in the *Plan,* for example, it was suggested that "it is no attack on private property to argue that society has the inherent right to protect itself [against] gross evils and known perils" by imposing restrictions on overcrowding, enforcing sanitary regulations, and limiting lot coverage.[59] As Mel Scott has discovered, there is even assertion in the *Plan* that if private enterprise cannot rehouse persons forced out of congested quarters, the city itself may have to do so "in common justice to men and women so degraded by long lives in the slums that they have lost all power of caring for themselves."[60] But this daring idea only appears as an afterthought in the Burnham/Moody philosophy of the city, tucked away surreptitiously, at best a very minor chord in a grand symphony of magnificent boulevards, imposing structures, and splendid parks. The housing concerns of other progressives in other cities (e.g., Lawrence Veiller and Jacob Riis in New York) did not exist in most of their counterparts of the Burnham/Moody persuasion in Chicago.[61]

Moody, as his writings reveal, had many of the myopias of the contemporary neo-democratic mind. He had little notion of the racial changes that were going to sweep over neighborhoods in a city such as Chicago. He was far too sanguine about the coexistence of the city and the automobile. Furthermore, he tended to exaggerate the beliefs that the conservation of wasted energy and resources alone would solve urban problems or that ordered civic spaces, efficient circulatory systems, and grandiose natural landscapes would yield contented, prosperous, virtuous citizens. Had social problems been stressed more directly in Moody's translation of Burnham's *Plan,* however, as they were in the St. Louis *City Plan* of 1907,[62] perhaps nothing of the Chicago 1909 *Plan* would have been implemented. So argues historian Robert Akeley, who is persuaded that if Moody had not played down the social reform dimension of what would have eventually had to accompany any genuine municipal rejuvenation, the success of the physical proposals and the image of the *Plan* as a comprehensive program of civic renaissance would have been seriously jeopardized. Akeley also feels that "Chicago planning salesmanship was based upon enthusiasm and commitment, rather than on calculated exploitation."[63]

THE *MANUAL*'S LEGACY

Moody assuredly was an enthusiast. "No one has ever equaled him in promoting city planning, convincing an entire metropolis of its value, and winning support of a particular plan from voters and public officials alike."[64] An ingenious and skillful propagandist, he promulgated the necessity of scientific city planning in ways other than through *Wacker's Manual.* Thousands of pamphlets, mailings, and circulars with titles like "Chicago can get fifty million dollars for nothing!," "Reclaim South Water Street for all the people," "Pull Chicago out of the hole—united action will do it!," and "Economic readjustment from a war to a peace basis" were his work.

As adroit with other communications media as he was with publications, he developed an extensive stereopticon slide library illustrating all aspects of the Burnham *Plan* and many examples of city planning throughout the world. Over the ten years that he gave slide lectures on planning all over Chicago and around the country, he estimated he had talked to approximately 175,000 people. Under his direction, the CPC even made its own movie, *A Tale of One City,* a two-reeler contrasting the existing conditions of Chicago with the 1909 *Plan* proposals. The first documentary film on city planning ever produced, it opened in Chicago (a city that in 1915 still hoped to become the movie capital of the country) to a sellout crowd at the

Majestic Theater. Shown in fifty theaters in the Chicago metropolitan area and then in other U.S. cities, over 150,000 people saw the film during its premier year of 1915.[65]

Finally, in 1919 Moody wrote a 440-page treatise titled *What of the City?* where much of the history of the CPC as well as his own history in the planning movement was recounted. Probably his most sophisticated analysis of Chicago city planning within the context of the national urban planning movement, the book's highly autobiographical content also reveals much about Moody the plan promoter; along with the *Manual* it summarizes his main political and planning ideas. Whereas the *Manual* had proselytized on the local level, *What of the City?* sought converts throughout the nation. Moody designed the former publication to reach the generation of the future, still occupying Chicago's classrooms; he prepared the latter book for the continuing adult education of his own generation throughout the country's cities.

To talk of converts and proselytizing recalls an initial characterization of Walter Moody made earlier in this chapter. W. D. Moody, it will be remembered, was occasionally confused with fellow Chicagoan D. L. Moody. A later historian of American city planning, while not mistaking the two men, aptly calls Moody an "evangelist of planning" whose "bible" was the 1909 *Plan* and who sought to spread that gospel of municipal reform "with the aggressiveness of a salesman and the fervor of a religious zealot."[66]

Within this context Moody might also be compared to William Thomas Stead, editor of the Anglo-American *Review of Reviews,* who a decade earlier had written another municipal reform tract, *If Christ Came to Chicago!* Stead's best-selling exposé of municipal corruption and his program for urban reform included in a final chapter a comprehensive city plan to implement comprehensive civic reform.[67] A detailed comparison of Moody's primer and Stead's intriguing city plan for making Chicago "the ideal city of the world," while pertinent to this discussion, will not be done here; mention is made merely to suggest that Moody's techniques were by no means novel to the Chicago reform effort that sought to improve the city by altering the cityscape.

Moreover, W. T. Stead, a Congregational minister who preached civic and social reform at rallies in the city's Central Music Hall in the wake of the World's Columbian Exposition,[68] could only have smiled with approval at one of Moody's last official acts to promote

FIGURE 6.3   *In his last planning treatise,* What of the City?, *Moody included a photograph of Charles H. Wacker, for whom the* Manual *had been named.*

the Burnham *Plan.* In early 1919, Moody wrote *Seed Thoughts for Sermons,* a seven-page appeal to the city's clergymen to recognize the humanitarian and social value of the *Plan of Chicago* that had been written a decade earlier. Numerous clergy followed Moody's injunction to preach the value of comprehensive planning to their congregations on January 19, 1919, the date chosen as *"Plan of Chicago* Sunday" throughout the city. Later that day was alluded to as "Nehemiah Sunday" because so many ministers had used Nehemiah's description of the rebuilding of Jerusalem and the temple as their text; many congregations also displayed the Chicago flag on their churches while others sang hymns such as "Work, for the night is coming!"[69] W. T. Stead would have loved it.

The British reformer would also have endorsed Moody's career as a propagandist, particularly Moody's crucial role in effecting the transition whereby a private plan drawn up by a private club became a public ordinance to be implemented by a public commission which, in turn, hired as its managing director a former publicist for private enterprise who became a public civil servant who wrote a public school textbook. Stead, had he lived to see a copy,[70] would have also approved of Moody's *Manual,* a book that can serve the historian as a tracer element in order to reveal some of the less familiar intellectual history of the vast effort surrounding the 1909 *Plan.*

Thus the legacy of the Burnham *Plan* and Moody's promotion of it is assuredly multiple. Simply in terms of actual alteration of Chicago's cityscape, it has been estimated that over $3 million in public construction can be directly attributed to the inspiration of the *Plan* and its purpose.[71] Every major subsequent planning enterprise in the city of Chicago has had to react to its premises and its presence. For example, in the struggle to keep the city's lakefront "forever open, clear and free," historian Lois Willie credits Burnham, Wacker, and especially Moody with launching "the most energetic public information effort in the city's history."[72]

While Moody's enthusiastic promotion of the changing, building, regrouping, and restructuring of the face of America's urban landscape on the Chicago model did assume the dimensions of a real reform movement (or at least a significant planning and architectural arm of that movement), his progressivism in planning was not without its inadequacies. For instance, his own myopias (e.g., his overreliance on the premise that structured, orderly, public buildings, circulatory systems, and civic landscapes would result in an enlightened citizenry) and his unquestioned support of Burnham's retreat to the safety of the neoclassical womb as the recommended style for the new urban America remind us of the strong conservative strain in his progressivism and the high degree of caution in that reform movement generally. This inconsistency, ambiguity, and paradox were also bequeathed to posterity via the 1909 *Plan* and the 1911 *Manual.*

On balance, however, Moody's numerous publications contributed positively to the early literature of the city planning profession. His prolific corpus, but especially the *Manual* and his most mature work, *What of the City?,* sought consciously to provide the professional city planner with personal inspiration for the work in the decades ahead.[73] The *Manual* also prompted an increased demand for the services of city planners in cities all over the nation thereby giving the emerging profession even greater visibility through the actual practice of its craft.[74]

Finally, because of Moody's salesmanship of Burnham's idea, the Burnham *Plan* became the paradigm for the American city planning movement for the next generation, the model of the City Practical that future planners and politicians in Chicago[75] and elsewhere built on, adapted, or rebelled against in their collective task of what Moody called the science of city planning and citizen building.[76]

NOTES

1. Daniel H. Burnham and Edward H. Bennett (1909) *Plan of Chicago Prepared Under the Direction of the Commercial Club During the Years 1906, 1907, 1908*, edited by Charles Moore, Chicago, Commercial Club of Chicago; hereafter cited as *Plan of Chicago*. A modern edition (1970), with an introduction by W. R. Hasbrouck, has been issued in the DaCapo Press Series in *Architecture and Decorative Arts*, 29, New York, DaCapo Press.

2. Walter D. Moody (1911) *Wacker's Manual of the Plan of Chicago: Municipal Economy*, Chicago, Chicago Plan Commission, p. 3; hereafter cited as *Wacker's Manual*. As an example of a full-blown instance of Moody's proposed economic and cultural hegemony for Chicago, see his essay (1912) "Chicago destined to be the center of the modern world," *Municipal Engineering*, 43 (3), 49–61, and also (1912) in *The Bank Man*, 7, 307–24.

3. See James Findlay (1969) *Dwight Moody*, Chicago, University of Chicago Press.

4. Walter D. Moody (1919) *What of the City? America's Greatest Issue—City Planning, What It Is and How to Go About It to Achieve Success*, Chicago, A. C. McClurg, p. 3; hereafter cited as Moody, *What of the City?*

5. Henry May (1949) *The Protestant Churches and Industrial America*, New York, Harper & Row, pp. 182–234.

6. Chicago, A. C. McClurg, 1907. This handbook of "modern salesmanship" went through seventeen editions.

7. Daniel Boorstin (1973) *The Americans: The Democratic Experience*, New York, Random House, pp. 5–88. Chicago Plan *Proceedings*, p. 86. When Moody accepted the position of managing director with the CPC, R. W. Butler, a member of the CPC, wrote Daniel Burnham that "from this time forward the work will be pushed by the 'Chief of all Pushers'—Mr. Moody." Butler to D. H. Burnham, January 20, 1911, Burnham Papers, Art Institute of Chicago.

8. The origins, underwriting, and unveiling of the *Plan* have been copiously documented; see Ira Bach (1973) "A reconsideration of the 1909 'Plan of Chicago,'" *Chicago History*, 2, 132–41; Françoise Choay (1969) *The Modern City, Planning in the 19th Century*, London, Studio Vista; Patrick Geddes (1915) *Cities in Evolution*, London, Williams & Norgate; Werner Hegemann and Elbert Peets (1922) *The American Vitruvius: An Architect's Handbook of Civic Art*, New York, Architectural Book Publishing; Vilas Johnson (1977) *A History of the Commercial Club of Chicago including the First History of the Club by John J. Glessner*, Chicago, Commercial Club of Chicago; Lewis Mumford (1961) *The City in History: Its Origins, Its Transformations, and Its Prospects*, New York, Harcourt, Brace & World; John Reps (1965) *The*

Making of Urban America, Princeton, Princeton University Press; and Lois Willie (1991) *Forever Open, Clear and Free: The Struggle for Chicago's Lakefront*, Chicago, University of Chicago Press.

9. Helen Whitehead (1960) *The Chicago Plan Commission, A Historical Sketch, 1909–1960*, Chicago, Chicago Plan Commission, pp. 3–9.

10. Charles W. Eliot (January 1910) "A study of the New Plan of Chicago," *Century Magazine*, 79, 418; see also Perry Duis (1976) *Chicago: Creating New Traditions*, Chicago, Chicago Historical Society, p. 49.

11. On the complicated machination whereby "an alliance of businessmen, planners and politicians, by persuasion, pressure and politics" set the 1909 *Plan* in motion, consult Michael P. McCarthy (1979) "Chicago businessmen and the Burnham Plan," *Journal of the Illinois State Historical Society*, 63 (3), 228–56.

12. Moody, *What of the City?*, pp. 329–32; *Chicago Tribune*, July 7, 1909, p. 3; *Chicago Record-Herald*, November 2, 1909, p. 2.

13. Moody, *What of the City?*, pp. 21–2.

14. David Noble (1958) *The Paradox of Progressive Thought*, Minneapolis, University of Minnesota; Richard Hofstadter, ed. (1963) *The Progressive Movement 1900–1915*, Englewood Cliffs, New Jersey, Prentice-Hall; Charles Forcey (1961) *The Crossroads of Liberalism: Croly, Weyl, Lippmann and the Progressive Era, 1900–1925*, New York, Oxford University Press, 1961.

15. Chapter II, "The new profession—city planning," *What of the City?*, pp. 18–27.

16. Robinson (1869–1917) and John Nolen (1869–1935) also contributed to the literature of American city planning and the city planning profession. Robinson, who wrote three important books—*The Improvement of Towns and Cities*, New York and London, G. P. Putnam's Sons, 1901; *Modern Civic Art*, New York and London, G. P. Putnam's Sons, 1903; and *City Planning*, New York and London, G. P. Putnam's Sons, 1916—was the first appointee to the first university chair of civic design (Illinois) in the United States. Nolen, a founder and later president of the American Institute of Planners, wrote *Replanning Small Cities*, New York, American City Bureau, 1912; *City Planning*, New York and London, D. Appleton, 1916; and *New Ideals in the Planning of Cities, Towns and Villages*, New York, American City Bureau, 1919. On the quest for professionalism, see Burton J. Bledstein (1976) *The Culture of Professionalism: The Middle Class and the Development of Higher Education in America*, New York, W. W. Norton, pp. 80–128, 287–332.

17. The most comprehensive assessment of the business community's involvement in the Chicago *Plan* is chronicled in Neil Harris (1979) *The Planning of the Plan*, Chicago, Commercial Club of Chicago, and Michael P. McCarthy's previously cited "Chicago businessmen and the Burnham Plan," pp. 228–56.

18. W. D. Moody (1911) *Chicago's Greatest Issue: An Official Plan*, Chicago, Chicago Plan Commission (CPC); Executive Committee, CPC, *Proceedings* (June 19, 1911), p. 237. Robert Akeley (1973) "Implementing the 1909 Plan of Chicago: an historical account of planning salesmanship," unpublished master's thesis, University of Texas, calculates (pp. 185–7) that there

were eighty-six separate bond issues totaling $233,985,000 falling within the recommendations of the plan.

19. *Chicago Daily News*, October 26, 1910, p. 1; on Burnham's disappointment with the inadequate promotion of the San Francisco Plan, see D. H. Burnham to Willis Polk, April 22, 1909, Burnham Papers, Art Institute of Chicago.

20. W. D. Moody (1912) *The Work of the Chicago Plan Commission during 1911*, Chicago, Address to the Commercial Club of Chicago, p. 10; *What of the City?*, p. 50; "City planning and the public schools," *American City*, 6 (May 1912), 720.

21. On the visual pedagogy of the *Plan's* illustrations, see Robert Bruegmann (1979) "Burnham, Guerin, and the city as image," in *The Plan of Chicago, 1909–1979*, edited by John Zukowsky, Chicago, Art Institute of Chicago, pp. 16–28.

22. Historians of American city planning have traditionally interpreted the 1909 Burnham *Plan* to have had six basic objectives: (1) improvement of the Chicago lakefront from Winnetka on the north to the Indiana state line on the south; (2) creation of a beltway/highway system on the rim of the city; (3) relocation of railway terminals and development of a complete freight and passenger traction system; (4) acquisition of an outer park system and of parkway transport circuits; (5) systematic arrangement of streets within the city to facilitate movement to and from the central business district; and (6) promotion of centers of intellectual life and civic administration so related as to provide coherence and unity for the metropolis. Carl Condit (1973) "The Chicago Plan," in his *Chicago, 1910–29; Building, Planning, and Urban Technology*, Chicago, University of Chicago Press, pp. 59–88.

23. In his highly autobiographical *What of the City?* (pp. 107–8), Moody listed his major educational achievements in advancing the plan as his work with the daily and the periodical press, his book on *Chicago's Greatest Issue*, the various lecture series he coordinated, and, of course, the *Wacker's Manual*.

24. *Wacker's Manual*, pp. 3–4. One product of Moody's teaching efforts was his ten-volume research series (1910–11) on *Business Administration: Theory, Practice and Application*, Chicago, LaSalle Extension University.

25. On Parker's progressive pedagogy see Jack K. Campbell's well-researched life (1967) *Colonel Francis W. Parker, The Children's Crusader*, New York, Teachers College Press, and Merle Curti's assessment (1965, pp. 374–95) in his *The Social Ideas of American Educators*, Paterson, New Jersey, Littlefield Adams; for Dewey's impact in Chicago, see consultant Katherine Mayhew (1966) *The Dewey School: The Laboratory School of the University of Chicago, 1896–1903*, New York, Oxford University Press.

26. Moody's inclusion of study questions (as many as sixty-seven in chapter 4), at the conclusion of each of the seventeen chapters, gave his text a highly catechetical tone reminiscent of the predetermined memorization, disciplined recitation, and rote learning that the progressive educators wished to eradicate.

27. John Dewey, *Education and Democracy*, pp. 100–102; *Wacker's Manual*, p.

10. Another example of the progressives' interest in education and city planning reform can be seen in Randolph Bourne's discussion (1916) of the curriculum unit, "The city: a healthful place to live," in *The Gary Schools*, Boston, Houghton Mifflin, pp. 117–19.

28. *Wacker's Manual*, pp. 4, 8, 97.

29. D. H. Burnham (1902) "White city and capital city," *Century Magazine*, 63, 619–20; see also Burnham's speech (1910) "A city of the future under a democratic government," *Transactions of the Town-Planning Conference, Royal Institute of British Architects*, pp. 368–78.

30. Thomas S. Hines (1973) "The paradox of progressive architecture," *American Quarterly*, 25, 427–48. For Hines's extended treatment of this facet of Burnham see his biography (1974) *Burnham of Chicago: Architect and Planner*, New York, Oxford University Press, chapters 8 and 14.

31. Richard Hofstadter (1955) *The Age of Reform, From Bryan to F.D.R.*, New York, Vintage, pp. 5–6.

32. William J. Adelman (1980) "Robber barons and social reformers," *Inland Architect*, 24 (3), 12–15.

33. *Wacker's Manual*, pp. 140–5; *What of the City?*, pp. 412–30; see also McCarthy, "Chicago businessmen and the Burnham Plan," p. 233.

34. Commercial Club of Chicago (1910) *The Presentation of the Plan of Chicago*, Chicago, Chicago Plan Commission, p. 29.

35. Stow Persons (1958) *American Minds, A History of Ideas*, New York, H. Holt, pp. 349–52.

36. Burnham's famous credo—"Make no little plans, they have no magic to stir men's blood and probably themselves will not be realized. Make big plans; aim high in hope and work, remembering that a noble, logical diagram once recorded will never die"—is but another example of what David Burg (1978) calls "The aesthetics of bigness in late nineteenth century American architecture" in *Popular Architecture*, edited by Marshall Fishwick and J. Meredith Neil, Bowling Green, Ohio, Bowling Green University Popular Press, pp. 108–14.

37. Consult Hofstadter, *The Age of Reform*, on the role of print in progressivism, pp. 186–97.

38. *What of the City?*, pp. xi, 4; on Parsons, see Persons, *American Minds*, pp. 366-8. Other theorists of public opinion discussed in this context include A. Lawrence Lowell (1913) *Public Opinion and Popular Government*, New York, Longmans, Green; Walter Lippmann (1922) *Public Opinion*, London, Allen & Unwin; and Edward L. Bernays (1923) *Crystallizing Public Opinion*, New York, Boni & Liveright.

39. *Wacker's Manual*, p. 45. Moody was particularly taken with Howe's critical study on Düsseldorf, Germany, because in addition to insisting on constant publicity of plan purposes and educational programs, the Düsseldorf plan (like the Burnham *Plan*) planned for city life a half century in the future and, perhaps best of all, it was a plan originally sponsored by the city's businessmen.

40. *Wacker's Manual*, p. 4.

41. Robert H. Wiebe (1967) *The Search for Order, 1877–1920*, New York, Hill

and Wang; an earlier study that buttresses the Wiebe thesis is Samuel P. Hayes (1957) *The Response to Industrialism*, Chicago, University of Chicago Press.

42. *Wacker's Manual*, pp. 4, 17, 104–8.

43. Burnham's proposed municipal building (see *Plan*, pp. 115–18) was modeled, in part, after Richard Morris Hunt's administration building at the 1893 World's Fair and the building that prompted Henry Adams to muse:

    One sat down to ponder on the steps beneath Richard Hunt's dome almost as deeply as on the steps of Ara Coeli, and much to the same purpose. Here was a breach of continuity—a rupture in historical sequence! Was it real, or only apparent? One's personal universe hung on the answer, for, if the rupture was real and the new American world would take this sharp and conscious twist towards ideals, one's personal friends would come in, at last, as the winners in the great American chariot race for fame (*The Education of Henry Adams*, New York, Modern Library, 1931, pp. 340–41).

44. *Wacker's Manual*, pp. 135–7.

45. Ibid., pp. 13, 66–70; *What of the City?*, pp. 38–60. Moody was also something of a historic preservationist in that he opposed the destruction of old structures having aesthetic, historic, and functional utility. He always argued for "the value of permanency in city building," especially since there were "many sites within Chicago that, within the space of seventy years, have been occupied by three, four, or five different buildings." *Wacker's Manual*, p. 69.

46. *Fifty Million Dollars for Nothing!*, Chicago, Chicago Plan Commission, 1916.

47. Samuel Haber (1964) *Efficiency and Uplift: Scientific Management in the Progressive Era, 1980–1920*, Chicago, University of Chicago Press; Samuel P. Hayes (1959) *Conservation and the Gospel of Efficiency*, Cambridge, Massachusetts, Harvard University Press.

48. On Haussmann see Howard Saalman (1971) *Haussmann: Paris Transformed*, New York, G. Braziller.

49. Michael P. McCarthy (1970) "Businessmen and professionals in municipal reform: the Chicago experience, 1887–1920," unpublished Ph.D. dissertation, Northwestern University, p. 106; McCarthy, "Chicago businessmen and the Burnham Plan," p. 231.

50. John Dewey, "Waste in education," in *The School and Society*, edited by Jo Ann Boydston (1976) in *John Dewey: The Middle Works*, vol. I: 1889–1924, Carbondale, Southern Illinois University Press, pp. 39–56; Shailer Mathews (1912) *Scientific Management in the Churches*, Chicago, University of Chicago Press; Charlotte Perkins Gilman (1913) "The waste of private housekeeping," *Annals of the American Academy of Political and Social Science*, 48, 91–5.

51. On the differences between these two modes of planning see John W. Reps (1965) *The Making of Urban America: A History of City Planning in the United States*, Princeton, Princeton University Press, pp. 331–9, and Will-

iam H. Wilson (1964) *The City Beautiful Movement in Kansas City*, Columbia, University of Missouri Press, pp. 40–54; Moody's argument for the Burnham *Plan* as primarily one of the "City Practical" can be found in *What of the City?*, pp. 15, 93.

52. *Wacker's Manual*, pp. 4, 145, 80–81.
53. Henry Blake Fuller (1897) "The upward movement in Chicago," *Atlantic Monthly*, 80, p. 534; "Chicago's higher evolution," *The Dial* (October 1, 1892), pp. 205–6; *Wacker's Manual*, pp. 80–81.
54. *Wacker's Manual*, p. 133.
55. *American Nervousness*, New York, G. P. Putnam's Sons, 1881, p. 96; see also George M. Beard (1884) *Sexual Neurasthenia (Nervous Exhaustion): Its Hygiene, Causes, Symptoms, and Treatment, With a Chapter on Diet for the Nervous*, edited by A. D. Rockwell, New York, E. B. Treat, p. 238n.
56. Charles E. Rosenberg (1976) *No Other Gods: On Science and American Social Thought*, Baltimore, Johns Hopkins University Press, p. 107.
57. *Wacker's Manual*, p. 97.
58. Geoffrey Blodgett (1976) "Frederick Law Olmsted: landscape architecture of conservative reform," *Journal on American History*, 62 (4), 869–89; Michael McCarthy (1972) "Politics and the parks: Chicago businessmen and the recreation movement," *Journal of the Illinois State Historical Society*, 65 (2), 158–72; Peter J. Schmitt (1969) *Back to Nature: The Arcadian Myth in Urban America*, New York, Oxford University Press.
59. *Plan of Chicago*, p. 105.
60. Mel Scott (1969) *American City Planning since 1890*, Berkeley and Los Angeles, University of California Press, p. 108; *Plan of Chicago*, p. 109.
61. Roy Lubove (1962) *The Progressives and the Slums: Tenement House Reform in New York City, 1980–1917*, Pittsburgh, University of Pittsburgh Press, pp. 217–56.
62. Civic League of St. Louis (1907) *A City Plan for St. Louis*, St. Louis, Civic League.
63. Akeley, "Implementing the 1909 Plan," pp. iii, 52.
64. Scott, *American City Planning*, p. 139.
65. *What of the City?*, p. 108.
66. Scott, *American City Planning*, p. 140.
67. William T. Stead (1894) *If Christ Came to Chicago!*, Chicago, Laird & Lee, pp. 421–2. Akeley, "Implementing the 1909 Plan" (p. 31), recognizes one similarity between the two reformers in noting that both saw the Chicago citizenry as "full of a boundless élan and full of faith in the destiny of their city."
68. On Stead in Chicago, see Joseph O. Baylen (December 1964) "A Victorian's 'crusade' in Chicago, 1893–1894," *Journal of American History*, 51 (3), 418–34; also "Stead in the slums," *Chicago Sunday Tribune*, November 12, 1893, p. 1.
69. *Chicago Tribune*, January 19, 1919, p. 1.
70. Stead perished aboard the *Titanic* when it sank on its maiden voyage in 1912.
71. Robert L. Wrigley, Jr. (1960) "The Plan of Chicago: its fiftieth anniversa-

ry," *Journal of the American Institute of Planners*, 26, 37.

72. Lois Willie (1991) *Forever Open, Clear and Free: The Struggle for Chicago's Lakefront*, Chicago, University of Chicago Press, p. 88.

73. Moody, *What of the City?*, p. x.

74. Sally Anderson Chappell, "Chicago issues: the enduring power of a plan," in *The Plan of Chicago: 1909–1979*, ed. Sally Anderson Chappell, John Zukowsky, and Robert Bruegmann, Chicago, Art Institute of Chicago, p. 14; Scott, *American City Planning*, p. 139.

75. In Chicago, some of the most important progenies that have followed in the wake of the 1909 Burnham *Plan* are: *Harbor Plan of Chicago* (1927); *The Outer Drive Along the Lake* (1929); *The Axis of Chicago* (1929); *Building New Neighborhoods: Subdivision Design and Standards* (1943); *Master Plan of Residential Land Use of Chicago* (1943); *Planning the Region of Chicago* (1956); *Development Plan for the Central Area of Chicago* (1958); the *Comprehensive Plan* (1966); *Chicago 21* (1973); and *Riveredge Plan* (1974). A summary of several of the post-1909 plans is also found in a report written by J. T. Fink (1979) entitled *Grant Park Tomorrow*. (All works listed here were published by the Chicago Plan Commission.)

76. *Wacker's Manual*, p. 8.

FIGURE 7.1 *Charles Dyer Norton.*

7

CHARLES DYER NORTON AND THE ORIGINS OF THE REGIONAL PLAN OF NEW YORK

HARVEY A. KANTOR

THE PASSAGE OF THE NATION'S first comprehensive zoning law in 1916 brought a great deal of attention to the urban planners of New York City. The "promising start" that zoning represented vaulted New York to the forefront of the national planning movement.[1] The next step to be taken would be important in setting a trend for the planning profession in general.

The New York planners did not abdicate their leadership role. The route chosen after 1916 was a broadened concern for regional rather than mere city planning. The scientific techniques of surveying and data gathering employed during the zoning campaign would now be applied to the entire metropolitan area. The result of these expanded efforts—*The Regional Plan and Survey of New York and Its Environs*—would again be a model of comprehensive achievement.[2]

The man who single-handedly inspired the New York Regional Plan was Charles Dyer Norton. Through influential connections in the community and a personal dynamism, Norton was successful in overcoming the timidity of his contemporaries and in converting his vision into concrete proposals. The New York Regional Plan was the

Reprinted with permission from Harvey A. Kantor, "Charles Dyer Norton and the origins of the Regional Plan of New York," *Journal of the American Institute of Planners*, 39, no. 1 (1973): 35–44.

boldest effort at mastering a metropolitan area yet attempted by urban planners of the day.

NORTON'S BACKGROUND

Charles Norton was not a planner himself, but he had a reputation for interest in urban planning activities. Born a clergyman's son in Oshkosh, Wisconsin, in 1871, Norton worked hard to save enough money to attend Amherst College. After graduation, he returned to the Midwest to work for Northwestern Mutual Life Insurance in Chicago.[3] In 1897, tall, handsome Norton married Katherine McKim Garrison, niece of Charles Follen McKim, the architect. It was this contact with McKim which stirred his interest in planning.[4]

While working in Chicago, Norton was active in the Commercial Club and helped to obtain Daniel Burnham as head of the Chicago Plan project. Indeed, the inauguration of this plan, so influential in the planning movement, may be credited largely to Norton.[5] He became imbued with Burnham's enthusiasm and vision and for the remainder of his life followed Burnham's dictum— "make no little plans."

Norton left Chicago in 1909, the year in which the Chicago Plan was published and turned over to city officers. He went to Washington, D.C., as an assistant secretary in charge of the fiscal bureau in the U.S. Treasury Department. There he caught the eye of the president, and from 1910 to 1911 he served in the White House as personal secretary to William H. Taft. In his capacity, Norton worked on planning in another sense. He was a guiding figure in the efficiency drive in the government, and Taft credited him with designing the new system of budgeting ultimately adopted by the federal government. He also promoted establishment of a bureau of research as a permanent center for efficiency studies.

Norton's work in the White House points up the close connection between the joint interests of city planning and budget management. In many ways, the impulses toward greater efficiency and management are the same in both of these areas, and they tend to complement each other. Locally, for instance, New York City established a Bureau of Municipal Research in 1906 and soon after began working on zoning as a means of efficient land use control.[6] Thus Norton's experience as a presidential secretary was valuable for his interest in planning; and he earned the complete respect of the president as well. Taft later wrote of Norton, "his interest was catholic, his mind constructive, his energy intense, and his vision broad and confident."[7]

Norton left Washington, D.C., to become vice president of the First National Bank of New York. Once in the city, he immediately became engaged in a number of financial, social, and civic activities.[8] George McAneny, the Manhattan Borough president who was interested in planning, quickly realized the value of someone like Norton; and when he attempted to bolster public support for his new City Planning Committee in 1914, he asked Norton to head the Advisory Commission.

Norton accepted McAneny's offer because he had become completely fascinated by the planning possibilities in New York. He found the streets, squares, and towers of the city magnificent and took long walks around New York to acquaint himself with the charms of its neighborhoods.[9] His experience as head of the City Planning Advisory Commission was unproductive, however, as that group which McAneny had worked so hard to create never really got off the ground. As Norton stated, "our Advisory Committee met in a beautiful room in the City Hall once or twice and wisely resolved to give our advice only when asked for, which was never."[10]

A Vision Too Big to Be Believed

The experience was valuable in one respect, though. It led Norton to think about having a private group support the kind of planning he wished to promote for New York. On November 27, 1915, he drew up a memorandum that became the basis for extended discussions on future planning in the city. In the memorandum, Norton maintained that before a plan would succeed in New York, it had to encompass all the areas in which New Yorkers earned their living and made their home. Thus, "from City Hall a circle must be swung which will include the Atlantic Highlands and Princeton; the lovely Jersey hills back of Morristown and Tuxedo; the incomparable Hudson as far as Newburg; the Westchester lakes and ridges of Bridgeport and beyond, and all of Long Island."[11] Clearly, Norton was indulging a Burnhamesque vision in calling for a community plan that would take in all of New York City and its environs. But he believed firmly in the concept and wanted to test his ideas on his New York contemporaries.

After meeting several times with friends, Norton found their reaction sympathetic but noncommittal. McAneny was too concerned with current zoning problems, and Frederic Pratt was too involved in his own Brooklyn planning projects. John Pine, a lawyer friend who had been a member of the city's Municipal Art Commission, probably expressed the sentiment of all when he wrote to Norton: "It does not seem to me wise to include so wide an area in your City plan. I do not myself see the connection between Princeton, Tuxedo, and Stamford, and our immediate problems, and I think that the issue will be greatly confused if so much is attempted."[12] Norton's vision seemed too advanced for his associates in 1915.

The skepticism of his contemporaries, as well as the demands of his own work, caused Norton to shelve his idea of a regional plan for the moment. President Woodrow Wilson had appointed him to the Red Cross War Council, and this demanded a great deal of his attention. But in 1918, Norton was named to the Board of Trustees of the Russell Sage Foundation, and he saw renewed hope there for advancing his ideas.

The Russell Sage Foundation Backs the Plan

The Russell Sage Foundation had already shown its interest in urban planning by sponsoring the Forest Hills Gardens project in 1911. Since that time, the Foundation had not engaged in further planning endeavors, but its personnel had changed little. Robert W. DeForest, active in a broad range of civic enterprises, was still influential as president of the Foundation's Board of Trustees; and John M. Glenn was the organization's secretary. Glenn had experience in public charity work, primarily in Baltimore, and he was an able fiscal administrator.[13] Also serving on the Board of Trustees was Alfred T. White, a Brooklyn philanthropist who had sponsored model tenement projects in Brooklyn in the 1880s and 1890s and who was closely associated with the Brooklyn planning movement.[14]

When Norton assumed his new position as trustee, DeForest asked him to give thought to projects the Foundation might undertake, and Norton proposed his scheme for a regional plan. He discussed the project with DeForest, Glenn, and White several times late in 1919 but again met the response that the idea was too grandiose.[15]

Gradually, Alfred White was converted to Norton's way of

thinking, and in December 1920, he supported him at a meeting with Glenn, DeForest, and Nelson Lewis, who had recently retired from his position as chief engineer of the city of New York. DeForest was still appalled at the enormous amount of territory Norton wanted to survey but ultimately agreed to employ Lewis for a preliminary investigation of the area.[16]

Alfred White's Death a Setback

Norton finally had a foot in the door. He suffered a setback, however, when his main supporter, Alfred White, drowned on January 29, 1921, just before the two were to present their plan formally to the entire Board of Trustees of the Foundation.[17] Norton carried on, nonetheless, working with Lewis and McAneny on a draft of the proposal, which he presented at the Trustees' meeting on February 7, 1921.[18] Happily, the Russell Sage Foundation now viewed his ideas with sympathy. They established a committee to prepare a new city plan for the New York region and authorized $25,000 for the services of specialists to work on it. Several months later, the Foundation made a larger commitment in the form of an additional $25,000 for immediate use as well as an authorization to spend up to $300,000 over the next several years.[19]

Once he had received formal permission, Norton began to organize the work. On February 11, 1921, he called a confidential meeting in his apartment at 4 East 66th Street for some of the city's and the nation's leading figures in urban planning. Present at that historic first working session of the Regional Plan group were Norton, Glenn, and DeForest of the Russell Sage Foundation; Frederick Law Olmsted, Jr., a leading American planner; George McAneny, Lawrence Veiller, and Edward Bassett, leaders in the New York housing and planning movements; Frederic B. Pratt of the Brooklyn planning movement; Lawson Purdy, the former vice chairman of the Zoning Commission; E. P. Goodrich, a civil engineer who had been on the technical staff of the Zoning Commission; and Shelby Harrison, a social worker and member of the Sage Foundation staff.[20]

At this meeting, Norton read aloud his draft of a proposal of a new plan for New York. Citing the Sage Foundation's sponsorship of Forest Hills Gardens as precedent for involvement in planning, Norton tried to stir the imagination of his listeners with a call for boldness and vision in planning endeavors. He then carefully laid out his tentative scheme for the preliminary survey of a regional plan.

This outline called for Nelson Lewis to visit personally every municipality in the plan area and to map and record local conditions. Shelby Harrison would study and report on the social aspects of the area; E. P. Goodrich would study transportation facilities; Edward Bassett would relate problems of zoning to general planning considerations; Lawrence Veiller would study housing, Lawson Purdy the tax structure, and Frederick Olmsted, Jr., the parks; Frank Williams would be called upon for legal counsel; and other advisers would be asked to consult their respective professions and to submit recommendations to the general group. These advisers would include Herbert Hoover for engineers, Burt Fenner for architects, James Greenleaf for landscape architects, Daniel French for sculptors, Francis Jones for painters, Arnold Brunner for the Fine Arts Federation, and Eugenius H. Outerbridge for business interests.[21]

Norton had devised one of the most comprehensive ventures in the history of American city planning. The area he sought to encompass in planning was the largest yet attempted for this purpose and contained more people than any area of similar size in the United States. In addition, the personnel he proposed were the finest and most experienced in the nation. Norton was truly a giant among promoters of greater planning for the New York area.

After the February 11 meeting, Norton continued working behind the scenes to modify and refine his suggestions. He felt it was necessary to avoid publicity until a definite proposal could be announced to the general public.[22] And he worked closely with all members of the group that he had called together in order to get a wide range of opinion.[23]

NORTON'S ASSOCIATION WITH FREDERIC A. DELANO

During this period before the Regional Plan was announced publicly, the individual upon whom Norton relied most was his very close friend Frederic A. Delano. Delano had worked with Norton in Chicago as vice chairman of the Chicago Plan and had since moved to New York. Norton was eager to get Delano involved in his new project and had proposed his election as a Trustee of the Sage Foundation at the meeting of the Board on February 7, 1921.[24] Once this was accomplished, the two Chicago friends renewed their close relationship and talked almost daily on matters concerning the new planning endeavor.[25] From their activities sprung the statement that "the leadership in New York planning has been borrowed from Chicago."[26]

Delano, a Harvard-trained engineer, had worked his way up the ranks of railroading, beginning as an apprentice machinist. Eventually he became president of the Gould railroads, the Wabash-Pittsburgh Terminal, and the Wheeling and Lake Erie, which were in financial difficulty. In 1904, Delano proposed the consolidation of all but one of Chicago's railway terminals into one central spot. This idea spurred his interest in more general planning, and his railroad scheme was later incorporated into the Chicago Plan. After he left Chicago, Delano was appointed by President Wilson to the Federal Reserve Board on which he served until the First World War, during which he was Major of Engineers for the American Expeditionary Force. When he returned to the United States, he resumed directorship of several railroads; and it was then that Norton sought him out to work on the Russell Sage designs for a New York Regional Plan.[27] Norton intended that Delano initially be in charge of collecting data on harbor and railroad terminal problems for the area.[28]

Delano was extremely enthusiastic about the possibilities New York offered to planners to test some of their methods, and he wrote to Norton about his ideas for double-decking arteries of traffic in order to accommodate greater volume.[29] But Delano insisted that any new suggestions for planning in New York be approached with caution and urged Norton to make a careful study of each suggestion and to build public opinion step by step to gain maximum support for an overall scheme.[30]

Thomas Adams Inspects the Working Model

Throughout 1921, Norton continued to seek advice from the men he had originally called together, and on November 3 he prepared a memorandum for the Sage Foundation's planning committee which reflected these deliberations. The report reiterated Norton's beliefs that a man of Burnham's stature should lead the project and also that a series of preliminary inquiries should be made before the actual plan was developed. Unlike his February 11 announcement, the memorandum of November 3 grouped the subjects to be treated under four major headings—headings which would eventually form the framework for the actual survey of the regional plans. These broad categories were: (1) physical, which included railway and water transportation, highways, parks, buildings, and density and distribution of population; (2) economic; (3) legal, inquiring into various statutes on zoning, excess condemnation, and stabilization of official city maps; and (4) social and living conditions.[31]

Norton was almost ready now to make his plans public and to begin the project. Characteristically, however, he decided to seek one more opinion on his working model, that of Thomas Adams of the Town Planning Commission of London. Adams, a Scot, had had extensive experience in city planning in England. He was a founder and secretary of the Garden City Association, which in 1900 established Letchworth, the first garden city in England, inspired by the writings of Ebenezer Howard. He was also an early mover and first president of the Town Planning Institute of Great Britain in 1904. From 1913 to 1921, as advisor on town planning to the Canadian government, he received much praise for his work on connecting urban centers with agricultural districts, as well as for his advice on controlling the use of natural resources. While in Canada, Adams also took part in early planning conferences in the United States; he had even testified before the 1916 New York City Zoning Commission. In 1921, however, he returned to England to set up his own firm and made plans for several towns in Great Britain. The following year he came to America as a visiting lecturer on town planning at Massachusetts Institute of Technology.[32]

The views Adams held regarding regional planning are perhaps best expressed in his address to the National Conference on City Planning in 1919. Here he contended that "the real controlling factors" determining industrial growth are "physical and natural to a greater extent than they are administrative and artificial." He saw the regional survey as "the investigation and mapping of the existing physical, industrial and residential features of a region that has interests and problems in common, which need comprehensive and coordinated treatment without regard to arbitrary administrative boundaries." A regional plan, he said, involved the general planning of the area included in a regional survey. "It is a skeleton and tentative plan of a region within which there is comprised a series of municipal units in juxtaposition to one another and having overlapping and interrelated problems."[33]

Clearly, Adams had anticipated the kind of surveying techniques that Norton was proposing. He was frank with Norton and made constructive comments on every point in his outline. In the first place, he disagreed that the project should be led by a strong figure in the tradition of L'Enfant, Haussmann, or Burnham. Adams felt this approach invited charges of "singlehandedness" and that "it would create dissatisfaction among the staff, who were bound to feel that they were doing the work and only one person was getting the credit." He thought that a group of specialists was far preferable to a single planner with a famous reputation.[34] Adams endorsed the suggestion for a series of preliminary investigations and suggested that the men who were ultimately to carry out the plan also should be involved in the early studies. He further cautioned against expending too much energy and too many resources on the preliminary efforts, lest everything be dissipated before the actual planning took place.[35]

Adams approved the four categories of subject matter that Norton had set up for the survey, but he made valuable suggestions under each. His most important suggestions dealt with the economic study. Here he stressed that all aspects of the value, method of development, and uses of land had to be carefully analyzed. He also pointed out that in the occupational surveys distinctions should be made between those pursuits that created populated districts and those that followed population. This difference between manufacturing and retail concerns was vital in understanding the relationship of business to population; and Adams felt that it would not show up if all businesses were studied the same way.[36]

Public Approval of the Plan

Adams's comments in hand, Norton was at last convinced that he had done enough homework on his plan and that it was time to begin the actual surveys. On the evening of May 10, 1922, Norton's dream of a regional plan for New York and its environs was announced to the public. A special meeting was held in the auditorium of the Engineering Societies Building. Present were about six hundred prominent citizens from the New York metropolitan region. Robert W. DeForest, president of the Board of Trustees of the Russell Sage Foundation, opened the meeting and introduced Norton. Norton explained the project and set out the four fields of inquiry—physical, economic, legal, and social—that the Regional Plan Committee would tackle. He took obvious pleasure in outlining the project and chided the commissioners of 1811 for fearing that the amount of territory they had chosen to plot might be so large that it would become "a subject of merriment."[37] For now, just a little over a century since the first New York plan, Norton was proposing surveys of an area embracing three states, three hundred municipalities, and nearly ten million people.[38]

Speaking immediately after Norton, Herbert Hoover, then Secretary of Commerce as well as a noted engineer, praised the Sage Foundation for its foresight in sponsoring the plan and asserted that the lack of planning not only was wasteful but prevented cities from making the contribution they should to the national life:

> The enormous losses in human happiness and in money which have resulted from lack of city plans which take into account the conditions of modern life, need little proof. The lack of adequate open spaces, of playgrounds and parks, the congestion of streets, and misery of tenement life and its repercussions upon each new generation, are an untold charge against our American life. Our cities do not produce the full contribution to the sinews of American life and national character. The moral and social issues can only be solved by a new conception of city building.[39]

Other speakers were Lillian Wald, John J. Carty, Elihu Root, Charles Dana Gibson, and Mrs. August Belmont; and each lauded the vision of the men working toward the Regional Plan.

The press reacted enthusiastically to the proposal for a regional plan.[40] The *New York Times* gave ample news coverage to the speeches of all the participants. It also published an editorial entitled "City conservation," which interpreted planning of the metropolitan area as "the application of those principles which have long been approved in regard to forests and mines."[41] The planning movement had always drawn on the methods used by the conservation movement, but never before had this relationship been made explicit for the citizens of New York.[42] Now, the *Times* believed, an end to wasted natural resources could come about, not only by traditional conservation means but also by regional planning, which could develop New York into "an economically ordered, a healthful and a beautiful metropolis."[43]

Endorsement by the press was followed by that of the New York

Architectural League, the New York Section of the Society of Civil Engineers, and the National Conference on City Planning.[44] Such application was heartening to the men working on the plan, and they needed all the encouragement they could get, for before their project was finished, seven years of hard work would pass.

The sheer size of the territory their plan was to encompass and the comprehensive manner in which they proposed to treat the subject were the primary reasons the task was to take so long to complete. The region contained 5,528 square miles, roughly the commuting radius of New York City, and represented the greatest aggregation of population and industry in any comparable area in the world. The 1920 census recorded the area's population at 8,979,055 and projected continued growth. The number of manufacturing plants had increased from 19,416 to 57,753 between 1900 and 1920, and the number of employees from 655,170 to 1,209,447. The Port of New York, which was primarily responsible for this tremendous industrial expansion, comprised 125 miles of waterfront, accommodating 868 piers. Thirteen railroads served the region, with annual freight tonnage of 88,000,000 tons. It was estimated that more than 2,800,000 commuters and visitors entered and left Manhattan below 59th Street every day. A total of 858,000 cars were registered in the area.[45]

In attempting to deal with a problem of this magnitude, the Regional Plan Committee formulated a body of doctrine containing the principles upon which their work would be based. Their central purpose was to promote better living conditions for all people in the New York region. A second major premise was the desirability of a more balanced pattern of growth for the region. For example, standards for open spaces had to be maintained, business areas needed to be more concentrated for efficient functioning, and better transportation links were necessary to promote growth of satellite and neighborhood communities, thereby relieving core-city congestion. The third goal, closely related to the second, was the maintenance of certain major activities in central areas, particularly the financial center in Lower Manhattan and the trade activity of the port. A fourth assumption was that all transit and transportation facilities had to be expanded; new highway construction was crucial. Fifth, all public expenditures had to be confined to essential social needs—such as government, public health, education, and recreation. And sixth, the highest standards of architectural design were to be applied to all projects undertaken within the jurisdiction of the master plan.[46]

Thus, at the outset, the Regional Plan Committee viewed its task as one of blending the logic of the lawyer, the technique of the artist and engineer, and the idealism of the prophet. This sensitive balance was needed in planning and preserving land and water areas for the best functioning of the region and for determining what areas were best suited for business, industry, residence, and recreation.[47]

Work Begins with Expertise and Controversy

With public enthusiasm attending their initial announcement and their task clearly outlined before them, the Regional Plan Committee vigorously embarked upon its activities in 1922. Serving on the committee at this time were Charles Dyer Norton, chairman; Robert W. DeForest, John M. Glenn, and Frederic A. Delano; Dwight W. Morrow, a Trustee of the Sage Foundation and a partner of J. P. Morgan and Company; and Frank L. Polk, lawyer and former acting Secretary of State under Woodrow Wilson. Added to this group at various times during the 1920s were John H. Finley, an associate editor of the *New York Times* and former editor of *Harper's Weekly*, as well as professor of politics at Princeton; Frederic B. Pratt, president of the Pratt Institute; Lawson Purdy, then active in the Charity Organization Society; George McAneny, then executive editor of the *Times* and also chairman of the New York State Transit Commission; and Harry James, lawyer and Trustee of both the Rockefeller Institute for Medical Research and the Carnegie Corporation. These men comprised the overall Regional Plan Committee.[48]

Norton naturally carried out most of the early organizational work. He asked Nelson Lewis to continue his studies of the region's physical outline and called in as economic consultants Columbia University professors Robert M. Haig and Roswell C. McCrea. Shelby Harrison, who had edited the important *Pittsburgh Survey*, agreed to head the social division and Edward Bassett the legal division. Frederick P. Keppel, secretary of the International Chamber of Commerce, was persuaded to leave Paris to become executive secretary of the group. These individuals and their assistants formed the working staff of the Regional Plan at its inception.

Norton, in his restless search to recruit the best talent and advice

available, turned to Raymond Unwin, chief architect for the British
Government on Housing and Town Planning. The internationally
known planner agreed to come to New York to advise Norton.[49]
After studying Norton's scheme, Unwin expressed his belief—ex-
pertly stated in his famous essay "Nothing gained by overcrowding"—that decentralization ought to be the regional planners' guiding
hypothesis. He warned against reliance on increased transportation
facilities as a means of curing congestion, reminding his host that,
in fact, the opposite might result. He argued against the promotion
of travel by private automobile and stressed the need for dispersal of
industry away from the city's central core. He also encouraged the
development of new suburbs or garden cities.[50]

Unwin's admonitions were not endorsed wholeheartedly by the
staff of the Regional Plan Committee. Haig and McCrea, who were
working on the economic survey, felt transportation was essential to
the region's continued economic growth. Their response to Unwin's
criticism of multiplying traffic facilities was that transportation
must be developed in any way "suited to the topography and suited
to the type of economic activity for which the Region is best
adapted."[51] This disagreement over the relation of traffic facilities to
decentralization of population, while only a minor argument in the
early stages of the Regional Plan, exploded into the major controversy when the plan was finally completed.

Because he was genuinely seeking advice and not just looking
for support, Norton continued his search for objective opinions
from outside experts. In 1923, he requested that a group of architects
suggest aesthetic improvements for the area's physical appearance,
particularly Manhattan. Cooperating with Norton on his project
were famous New York architects Cass Gilbert, D. Everett Waid,
William A. Delano, Harvey Corbett, Thomas Hastings, John Russell Pope, and Hugh Ferriss. Before their deaths, Arnold Brunner
and Burt L. Fenner also worked briefly on the Regional Plan.[52]

Besides the architects, Norton solicited a group of city planners
to aid the preliminary studies. Meeting for the first time on February
22, 1923, at the committee's headquarters at 130 East 22nd Street
were six leaders of the urban planning profession—Thomas Adams,
Harland Bartholomew, Edward H. Bennett, George B. Ford, John
Nolen, and Frederick Law Olmsted, Jr.[53] Each planner agreed to take
an area of the region and to survey its needs by mid-September.[54]

THE PLAN LOSES NORTON

Norton had assembled a spectacular group of individuals to work on the initial stages of the Regional Plan. By the middle of 1923, he had not only a competent professional staff working full-time but the benefit of expert opinion from those working on an advisory basis. Everything was moving along smoothly; then tragedy struck.

Norton had been ill on several occasions during 1922. Late in the year, he came down with a "tremendous cold" which put him to bed for most of December.[55] His cold worsened, and complications set in. For two months he survived, but then on March 6, 1923, he died at the age of fifty-three.[56] The man who single-handedly had launched the great project of the Regional Plan was sorely missed. William Howard Taft, his former boss and now Chief Justice of the U.S. Supreme Court, glowingly praised him in a long letter to the *New York Times*.[57] The paper itself extolled Norton's virtues and praised him for "dreaming Burnham's dream for New York."[58] The work of the Regional Plan continued, and throughout the process there seemed almost a hallowed reverence for the memory of Charles Dyer Norton. When the project was finally completed, it was dedicated to him.

One year later, Nelson Lewis passed away also, and the Regional Plan lost a second major figure. Lewis had been a pioneer in all the work that had been done in modern city planning in New York. He had taken part in virtually every effort for greater planning. In 1920, with Lewis's completion of a twenty-one-year tenure as the city's chief engineer, Mayor John Hylan justly claimed that he could "rightly take unto himself much credit for the advancement which the city has made to its present stage of municipal preeminence."[59]

But even though he had ended a career that would have filled most men's life, Lewis had been receptive to Norton's overtures for working on the huge Regional Plan. Although somewhat tired (he confessed to George McAneny in 1923 that "after a month or more spent in some of the unspoiled places I am more and more convinced of the foolishness of living in the city unless one has to"), he endeavored to survey all of the New York region, and his studies were the basis for all the planning done by the group.[60] Upon his death in March 1924, Herbert Hoover, speaking as one engineer about another, said that Nelson Lewis had rendered "a public service of a most enduring type."[61]

With the death of Norton and Lewis and the loss of Keppel to the presidency of the Carnegie Corporation, major restructuring of the Regional Plan Committee had to take place. Robert DeForest was anxious that replacements be named as soon as possible and that he not be one of them. DeForest himself was getting old; and although he had gone along with Norton's original plans, his heart did not seem to be in the Regional Plan project. For one thing, DeForest never really seemed to grasp the significance of what was being done. In January 1922, he made the unbelievable statement that the Regional Plan was starting at a particularly fitting time because "the factors which might have changed radically a City Plan are no longer liquid, or uncertain. The Erie Canal is located. There will probably be no more trunk railroad lines terminating in New York."[62] DeForest's lack of recognition of what the automobile might have in store for the New York region was revealing, even for a statement made in 1922. Besides his failure to grasp the significance of the Regional Plan for New York, DeForest was anxious not to spend too much of the Russell Sage money. He was constantly pressing for the group to finish its work, present it to the public, and then let some other civic-minded body be formed to promote its implementation.[63] Clearly, DeForest was not the man to take Norton's place.

The man selected by the Regional Plan Committee was Frederic A. Delano, an excellent choice. Probably Norton's closest associate, Delano knew more than anyone else the possibilities the Regional Plan had for the future. While Delano assumed the leadership of the committee on the Regional Plan, Thomas Adams was named director of the general staff in 1923. Adams, too, was a fine selection, and together Frederic Delano and Thomas Adams saw the work through and completed the project initiated by Norton.

THE SIGNIFICANCE OF THE PLAN

Eight volumes of survey material were published at various times during the 1920s, and the two volumes of the completed Regional Plan were presented in 1929 and 1931.[64] Containing 470 proposals for the 5,528 square miles, 10 million people, and 421 communities in the region, the final product was a monument to the organization and foresight of its staff. The Regional Plan represented the most extensive survey and plan of a metropolitan area yet attempted in the

United States. But apart from the sheer size of the project, its significance for urban planning history can be seen in several other important ways. First, by accepting the prospect of continued growth for the New York area, the Regional Plan identified itself as the helpmate of further urban congestion. The project in effect planned *for* growth rather than attempting to *direct* it in any way. By adopting this strategy, the Regional Plan lost a golden opportunity to become an instrument for the "balanced growth" it advocated and won the everlasting antipathy of such critics as Lewis Mumford.[65] Second, by placing primary emphasis upon the private automobile as the major means of transportation for the area, mass transit was relegated to a secondary role. Highway plans were always foremost in the minds of the men working on the project, and the precedent they set in this regard had enormous consequences for the development of the New York area. Third, by concentrating on such a large geographical area, the plan was an early promoter of the concept of regionalism, and its impact was felt nationwide. Upon receiving his copy of the published document, President Franklin Delano Roosevelt said, "now we are really getting somewhere, and all of the fine work which your Association did is bearing fruit. I hope, of course, that all new projects will be studied in light of regional planning."[66] Roosevelt, a man the planners felt could be "counted upon as a lifelong friend," did not forget the Regional Plan.[67] He appointed its head, Frederic Delano (also his uncle), to his newly created National Planning Board to try to apply the New York planning techniques on the federal level.[68] Finally, the plan spurred the organization of a private group, the Regional Plan Association, to work for implementation of the projects.[69] This important group still exists as one of the most active promoters of urban research and design.

On balance then, the Regional Plan of New York has a mixed record. Although it aided the further agglomeration of people in the metropolitan area and increased dependency upon the automobile, it nonetheless heightened an awareness for the larger urban region and created a commitment in the private sector to the ongoing examination of that region. It is this commitment which is the legacy of the promotional skill and imagination of Charles Dyer Norton.

Notes

1. George McAneny to Flavel Shurtleff, September 26, 1916, George McAneny Papers, Princeton University. For a convenient summary of the status of American city planning immediately after the passage of the 1916 Ordinance see George B. Ford, ed. (1917) *City Planning Progress in the United States, 1917*, Washington, D.C., American Institute of Architects.

2. Brief accounts of the Regional Plan appear in Mel Scott (1969) *American City Planning since 1890*, Berkeley and Los Angeles, University of California Press, pp. 199–204; Roy Lubove (1963) *Community Planning in the 1920's: The Contribution of the Regional Planning Association of America*, Pittsburgh, University of Pittsburgh Press, pp. 115–27.

3. "Biographical sketch of Charles Dyer Norton," Russell Sage Foundation Papers, Russell Sage Foundation, New York City, and *National Cyclopaedia of American Biography*, VI, 489–90.

4. Christopher Tunnard (1968) *The Modern American City*, Princeton, Van Nostrand, p. 77.

5. Charles Moore (1921) *Daniel H. Burnham, Architect, Planner of Cities*, Boston and New York, Houghton Mifflin, pp. ii, 11, 14, 45.

6. See Jane S. Dahlberg (1966) *The New York Bureau of Municipal Research*, New York, New York University Press, especially pp. 81–92.

7. *New York Times*, March 10, 1923.

8. "Biographical sketch of Charles Dyer Norton," Russell Sage Foundation Papers, Russell Sage Foundation, New York City.

9. The major source of information on Norton's interest in planning and his activities in setting up the Regional Plan Committee of New York is an extended letter he wrote to Frederic A. Delano on November 24, 1921. The letter was updated and privately published in 1923 under the title, *The Plan of New York with References to the Chicago Plan*, New York. The original letter is in the files of the Regional Plan Association in New York City. Future references will be from the original, "Norton Letter of 1921."

10. Ibid., p. 4.

11. Ibid., p. 7.

12. Ibid., p. 9.

13. "Biographical sketch of John M. Glenn," Russell Sage Foundation Papers, Russell Sage Foundation, New York City.

14. Robert H. Bremner (1967) *From the Depths: The Discovery of Poverty in the United States*, New York, New York University Press, p. 207.

15. "Norton Letter of 1921," p. 14.

16. Ibid., p. 16.

17. Ibid., p. 17.

18. "Norton Memorandum," January 31, 1921, George McAneny Papers, Princeton University.

19. "Norton Letter of 1921," p. 18.

20. Ibid.
21. Ibid., pp. 20–22.
22. Charles Norton to George McAneny, May 10, 1921, George McAneny Papers, Princeton University.
23. Ibid., February 5, 1921.
24. "Norton Letter of 1921," p. 17.
25. Charles Norton to Frederic A. Delano, November 8, 1922, Regional Plan Association Papers, Regional Plan Association, New York City.
26. Thomas Adams (1929) "Regional planning in the United States," *American Civic Association Pamphlet*, 4, 3.
27. David C. Coyle (1946) "Frederic A. Delano: catalyst," *Survey Graphic*, 45 (July), pp. 250–69; and *National Cyclopaedia of American Biography*, Supplement A, pp. 410–11.
28. "Norton Letter of 1921," p. 20.
29. Frederic A. Delano to Charles D. Norton, April 27, 1921, Regional Plan Association Papers, Cornell University.
30. Ibid., April 4, 1921.
31. Charles D. Norton, "Memorandum for City Plan Committee," November 3, 1921, Regional Plan Association Papers, Cornell University.
32. John M. Glenn, Lillian Brandt, and F. Emerson Andrews (1947) *Russell Sage Foundation 1907–1946*, New York, Russell Sage Foundation, pp. II, 442–3.
33. Thomas Adams (1919) "Regional and town planning," *Eleventh National Conference on City Planning, Proceedings*, pp. 77–88.
34. Thomas Adams to Charles D. Norton, April 14, 1922, Regional Plan Association Papers, Cornell University.
35. Ibid.
36. Ibid.
37. "Program of meeting of May 10, 1922," Regional Plan Association Papers, Regional Plan Association, New York City.
38. "Planning for an urban population of thirty-seven million," *American City*, 26 (1922), 533.
39. "Program of meeting of May 10, 1922," p. 11.
40. *New York Tribune*, May 14, 1922.
41. Ibid., May 11, 1922.
42. Roy Lubove (1967) *The Urban Community: Housing and Planning in the Progressive Era*, Englewood Cliffs, New Jersey, Prentice-Hall, pp. 2–6.
43. *New York Times*, May 11, 1922.
44. Ibid., May 13 and 18, 1922; *Fourteenth National Conference on City Planning, Proceedings* (1922), 198.
45. Thomas Adams (1927) *Planning the New York Region*, New York, Committee of the Regional Plan of New York and Its Environs, pp. 17–22.
46. Ibid., pp. 23–30.
47. Regional Plan Committee (1923) *Report of Progress*, New York, Regional Plan Committee.
48. Forbes Hays (1965) *Community Leadership*, New York, Columbia University Press, pp. 15–16.

49. *New York Times*, October 15, 1922.
50. Raymond Unwin, "New York and its environs as a regional planning problem from a European point of view," summarized in Adams, *Planning the New York Region*, pp. 42–3. A good account of Unwin's general planning views may be found in Walter Creese (1967) *The Legacy of Raymond Unwin*, Cambridge, Massachusetts, MIT Press.
51. Adams, *Planning the New York Region*, p. 44.
52. Ibid., p. 10.
53. *New York Times*, February 23, 1923.
54. Ibid., February 25, 1923.
55. Charles D. Norton to Eleanor Robson Belmont, December 2, 1922, Eleanor Belmont Papers, Columbia University.
56. *New York Times*, March 7, 1923.
57. Ibid., March 10, 1923.
58. Ibid., March 11, 1923.
59. John Hylan to Josiah Fitch, December 7, 1920, Nelson P. Lewis Papers, Cornell University.
60. Nelson Lewis to George McAneny, September 8, 1923, George McAneny Papers, Princeton University.
61. Herbert Hoover to Mrs. Nelson P. Lewis, April 1, 1924, Nelson P. Lewis Papers, Cornell University.
62. Conference on Fundamental Considerations in City Planning, "Report," January 4, 1922, Regional Plan Association Papers, Regional Plan Association, New York City.
63. Robert DeForest to Frederic A. Delano, January 22, 1926, and Delano to DeForest, February 5, 1926, Russell Sage Foundation Papers, Russell Sage Foundation, New York City.
64. Committee on the Regional Plan of New York and Its Environs (1929) *The Graphic Regional Plan*, vol. I, New York; Thomas Adams, assisted by Harold M. Lewis and Lawrence M. Orton (1931) *The Building of the City*, vol. II, New York. An explanatory volume published under the auspices of the Regional Plan Committee is R. L. Duffus (1930) *Mastering a Metropolis*, New York, and a condensed version of the entire plan may be found in a brief descriptive brochure also published by the Regional Plan group (1929) *A Close-Up of the Regional Plan of New York and Its Environs*, New York.
65. The Mumford attack may be found in Lewis Mumford (1932) "The Plan of New York," *New Republic*, 71, 121–6, and "The Plan of New York, II," *New Republic*, 71, 146–53. A rebuttal appears in Thomas Adams (1932) "In defense of the Regional Plan," *New Republic*, 71, 267–70.
66. Franklin D. Roosevelt to George McAneny, August 7, 1933, George McAneny Papers, Princeton University.
67. Frederic Delano to Lawrence Orton, December 7, 1931, Regional Plan Association Papers, Cornell University.
68. Scott, *American City Planning*, pp. 300–311. Also see John L. Hancock (1967) "Planners in the changing American city, 1900–1940," *Journal of the American Institute of Planners*, 33, 299–300.
69. Regional Plan Association (1931) *Annual Report, 1930*, New York, pp. 1–10.

8

BETTMAN OF CINCINNATI

LAURENCE C. GERCKENS

THE OLD FIFTH STREET MARKET WAS demolished in Cincinnati on February 24, 1870, clearing the site for the Tyler Davidson Fountain that would become the symbol of the city and the focal point of a future Fountain Square.[1] The refreshing murmur of falling water was still new to the hot streets of the riverboat-dominated Queen City of the Ohio River West on August 26, 1873, when the former Rebecca Bloom[2] presented her husband, Louis Bettman, a German immigrant and a clothing manufacturer, with their first son— Alfred. Raised in an environment of bold municipal creativity and individual opportunity, of mob violence and political corruption, Alfred developed both a sincere enthusiasm for his city and a deep concern for its future.

George B. Cox, a local barkeep soon to become the Republican "boss" of Cincinnati whose political "machine" would dominate Cincinnati politics for more than a quarter of a century (1886–1912), began his nefarious career in 1880 (Vexler, 1975, p. 38). His political activity would lead the city to financial disaster and shape young Alfred's future in reform. Cincinnati in the 1880s was a city in which both beer and blood flowed freely and frequently. On March 28, 1884, a race riot filled the streets with barricades and soldiers; the courthouse was burned.[3] To man's mayhem, Nature added its own that year, sending one of many periodic floods to devastate the lower central business district.

The coming of the railroads threatened Cincinnati's riverboat-based prosperity. To assure continuation of the city's role in provid-

183

ing stockyard, machine-shop, and agricultural products to the American inland South, the city of Cincinnati built the Cincinnati Southern Railroad, the only municipally owned railroad in the United States. In 1869 the city raised $10,000,000 through the sale of bonds to finance the Cincinnati Southern. Completed in 1880, running from Cincinnati to Chattanooga on 339 miles of city-owned right-of-way, the Cincinnati Southern, a bold expression of municipal creativity (Condit, 1967, pp. 61–71), saved the economy of the city upon the demise of the riverboat era. Another such expression was the Centennial Exposition of 1888 that celebrated the founding of the city and extolled its civic virtues just four years after the Courthouse Riot. The exposition featured an exhibition hall that straddled the Hamilton Canal, providing taxi service by gondola inside the building! And in sharp contrast to the civic background of corruption, riot, and debauchery, Isaac Mayer Wise, the most prominent American Jew of his time, made Cincinnati the center of a progressive reform Judaism movement in the 1890s that would shape the futures of young Alfred, Cincinnati, and America.[4]

Gilbert Bettman, one of Alfred's three brothers, was born in 1881. Both Alfred and Gilbert would follow careers in law and become deeply involved in political processes in Cincinnati, in Ohio, and in the federal government, but through divergent careers: Alfred joined Rabbi Wise in following the route of progressive reform; Gilbert followed the route of Boss Cox in machine politics.

As with most sons of successful midwestern merchants, Alfred traveled East to complete his education following graduation from Cincinnati's old Hughes High School in 1890. He earned a B.A. degree at Harvard in 1894 and completed both an M.A. and a law degree there in 1898. When he returned to Cincinnati in 1898, the city's per capita debts were among the highest in the nation while its urban services were among the worst, thanks to the irresponsibilities and political corruption of the Boss Cox machine, earning for Cincinnati its undisputed title as "the worst governed city in America" (Bent, 1926, pp. 308–9).

Families such as the Bettmans were referred to in the Cincinnati press of the 1890s as "German Jews," a term viewed solely as descriptive and in no way anti-Semitic. There was little such prejudice in Cincinnati at that time because their German-Jewish ways did not identify them for prejudicial action in a city that was commonly more German than American (Miller, 1968, p. 129).

Reform Judaism, as developed by Rabbi Wise in Cincinnati during the last two decades of the nineteenth century, became a new "urban gospel" in which service to mankind was a medium of religion intended to "change the mode of life in the immigrant sectors, transform the appearance of the city, broaden the activities of municipal and state governments, and rescue politics from the sordid abyss into which it had fallen" (Miller, 1968, p. 132). Wise's "urban gospel" became a foundation for the Social Gospel Movement in the United States and for twentieth-century American liberalism.[5] When the German Jews began to arrive in the wealthier suburbs of Cincinnati during the early years of this century they brought with them a new commitment to the city, to government, and to reform. They eagerly participated in, and initiated, local actions to increase the effectiveness and justice of American democracy (Miller, 1968, p. 135). When Alfred Bettman returned from Harvard in 1898 to practice law in Cincinnati, he joined this community of reform-minded Jews to participate in a movement in social and political reform that reached its early maturity (1910–15) simultaneous with his first direct involvement with city politics. Alfred's new activities in municipal reform met the community service obligations of a rising, financially successful professional who was an Eastern-educated son of a wealthy clothing manufacturer and a socially conscious Cincinnati German Jew of the turn of the century.

Alfred married Lillian Wyler on June 20, 1904. They would be childless. Alfred devoted his time away from his law practice to Lillian and to his avocations, among which he would count reform of a city very much in need of reformation. Appalled by the corruption and economic waste of government under the political machine,[6] Alfred found himself drifting toward Democratic, anti-Cox, reform politics. His brother, Gilbert, who also went to Harvard, earning an A.B. (bachelor of arts) in 1903, an A.M. (master of arts) in 1904, and his law degree cum laude in 1907, was admitted to the Ohio Bar in that year. He took advantage of the opportunities of the machine to begin his rise in Ohio Republican politics.

The modern urban planning movement in Cincinnati began in 1906 when a Parks Commission was appointed and $15,000 was appropriated for the development of a parks system plan (Vexler, 1975, p. 47). In 1907, George E. Kessler of Kansas City was hired to execute the parks plan, which was completed and adopted in 1908,

FIGURE 8.1   *Caricature of lawyer Alfred Bettman, c. 1905.*

NEWSPAPER CARTOONIST ASSOCIATION OF CINCINNATI. FROM *A GALLERY OF PEN SKETCHES IN BLACK AND WHITE OF "CINCINNATIANS AS WE SEE 'EM,"* CINCINNATI, OHIO, THE ASSOCIATION, © ANGUS MCNEILL, TREASURER, P. 29, "ALFRED BETTMAN, ATTORNEY AT LAW," BY "J.A.W."

becoming the official guide to the development of the Cincinnati parks system (Hebble and Goodwin, 1916, pp. 150-6).

Alfred entered the political arena in 1909, at the age of thirty-six, when he began a two-year term as an assistant county prosecutor for Hamilton County (Cincinnati). He came to the attention of Henry T. Hunt, a Democrat, who sought his support in opposing the Republican machine. In an astounding political upset in November 1911, the voters of Cincinnati rejected Louis Schwab, the machine candidate for mayor, electing Democrat Hunt as mayor (1912–13) and Alfred Bettman as city solicitor. Hunt was fiscal reform personified. He held that city spending had to be based on concepts of municipal efficiency and not on the political spoils system; he believed in government by experts, with experts in charge of each municipal department. Mayor Hunt undertook a comprehensive topographic survey of the city to serve as the basis for future capital investment decisions and authorized a national expert, Bion Arnold, to produce a plan for integrating the interurban railways into a rapid transit system (Hebble and Goodwin, 1916, p. 237). He introduced scientific budget-making. Under Hunt, each department would itemize expenses and their purposes. These lists would then be reviewed by citizen advisory groups and would be debated in lengthy public hearings before final budget decisions were made. Mayor Hunt operated the city of Cincinnati in 1913 on a budget that was a quarter of a million dollars less than in 1912 yet covered the cost of several new projects (Miller, 1968, pp. 214–15).

In his capacity as city solicitor, Bettman became involved with the liquidation of turnpikes, toll roads, and interurban railroads, becoming intimately aware of issues of public finance, capital construction, and the influence of land development patterns (American Planning Association [APA], 1980, Segoe Tape 1, p. 22). Alfred Bettman gained his first direct exposure to rational budget-making, to municipal public works planning, and to the virtues of citizen participation in policy-making through his day-to-day involvement with this revolutionary, but short-lived, Democratic reform administration. These Hunt administration innovations became the cornerstones for a lifetime of contributions to municipal reform and to American city planning (Simpson, 1969, p. 83). During 1912–13 Bettman also served as an attorney for the Trustees of the municipally owned Cincinnati Southern Railroad.

The Republican machine regained City Hall in 1913 following a series of destructive ice plant and street railway strikes.[7] Mayor Hunt was defeated; Alfred Bettman lost his position as city solicitor; their reform efforts were aborted. But this brief exposure to machine politics, to municipal potential, and to the corruption that surfaced in virtually every investigation into the affairs of previous administrations was sufficient to motivate Bettman to declare war on the political machine and on the fiscal mismanagement it represented. In 1913, when Alfred Bettman was forty, he returned from the fifth National Conference on City Planning, his first, as a true believer in urban planning as a vehicle for needed reform, particularly in the

area of public capital investments.[8] He saw city planning as a means
by which the citizen, through policy participation in what he called
"the art and science of both the placing and timing of the use of
land" (O'Brian, 1945, p. 2), could check the power of corrupt
politicians and create rational, public-interest-founded policies on
capital construction that could achieve Hunt's ends of municipal
honesty and economy. Bettman's enthusiasm, intellect, and immediate political experience commended him to this young organization.
He was appointed to the National General Committee of the Conference in 1914 and served on the Executive Committee the following year.

A new charter proposal for Cincinnati that included a department of city planning as an integral part of city government, headed
by a citizen commission, was defeated at the polls in 1914 (Charter
Commission, 1914, pp. 50–3). On January 4, 1914, Alfred Bettman
assisted in the founding of a group that in 1915 would become the
United City Planning Committee. This group of reform-minded
businessmen included representatives of the city planning committees of various civic organizations, among which were the City Club
and the Chamber of Commerce (Ford, 1917, p. 37). The United City
Planning Committee, primarily antimachine Republicans among
whom Democrat Bettman was in the minority, was dedicated to the
goal of starting a city planning movement in Cincinnati and creating
a rational, public-interest-focused "master plan" for the future
development of the city to stop the seemingly endless series of
capital investment disasters that had plagued the city under the
pork-barrel politics of the Republican machine[9] (National Conference on City Planning [NCCP], 1924, pp. 35–6). The constitution of
this group specified its purposes as those of conducting an educational campaign, raising funds, and serving as an organizational
contact between the people of the city and its government relative to
the proposed master plan (NCCP, 1924, p. 36).

The United City Planning Committee took its first major action
when it turned its attention to the Statehouse in Columbus. What
Ohio's cities needed, according to the committee, was a state act
authorizing creation of municipal planning commissions that gave
such citizen groups the authority to create a master plan for the city
as a guide to capital construction and to enforce it over the objections of a machine-corrupted city council. Without such authority,
the committee reasoned, no plan could be effective in channeling

capital funds to their most cost-effective and community-interest-determined use. Alfred drafted such a bill, requiring a two-thirds vote of the city council to overrule a decision of the planning commission concerning public construction "whenever the commission shall have made a plan of the municipality, or any portion thereof" ("State of Ohio," 1916, p. 145). The United City Planning Committee experienced its first victory on May 27, 1915, when this bill was unanimously approved in both houses and was enacted by the Ohio legislature to be effective January 1, 1916 (International City and Regional Planning Conference [ICRPC], 1925, p. 325).[10] With passage of this act, Alfred Bettman's capabilities in urban planning legislation came to national attention, initiating a lifelong career as the primary author of planning enabling legislation in the United States. In 1915 Alfred also served as attorney and Trustee for the municipally owned Cincinnati Southern Railroad.

For the next thirty years virtually all of the planning enabling legislation adopted by the state of Ohio would be drafted by Alfred Bettman (Simpson, 1969, p. 51). Although enacted, this enabling legislation, being permissive and not mandatory, was not implemented in Cincinnati where the machine politicians feared the power of the city planning commission to override the city council once a master plan was prepared. Instead, an unofficial "advisory" commission was created that was completely under the control of the political machine (Vitz, 1964, p. 5; *Official City Plan*, 1925, p. 26).

In 1917, George B. Ford, in a national survey of planning progress in the United States, recognized Alfred Bettman as a leading figure in support of city planning in Cincinnati (Ford, 1917, p. 38) while faulting the machine government for not implementing the "enabled" official city planning commission: "Of the leading cities in America, in point of size and population, Cincinnati (410,476) is one of the few that has been tardy in giving official recognition to city planning" (Ford, 1917, p. 37).

The ninth National Conference on City Planning was held at the Muehlebach Hotel in Kansas City in May 1917. Twenty-three persons who attended this meeting elected to create the American City Planning Institute (ACPI), the first professional organization for city planners in the United States.[11] Alfred Bettman was among the fifty-two persons invited during the course of the following months to become charter members of the new institute. The ACPI was officially organized on November 24, 1917, in New York City

(Black, 1967, p. 29). Alfred became a member of the Board of Directors. Among the first actions of the new institute, upon conception in Kansas City, was an offer of its services to President Woodrow Wilson. It was 1917 and the United States was at war. Active promotion of the Plan of Cincinnati was deferred, and the United City Planning Committee went inactive for the duration of the First World War (NCCP, 1924, p. 36).

President Wilson appointed Alfred Bettman as a special assistant to A. Mitchell Palmer, Attorney General of the United States. He was assigned to the War Emergency Division of the U.S. Department of Justice and put in charge of Espionage Act cases. Together with John Lord O'Brian, Bettman took the major responsibility for prosecuting hundreds of Americans for violation of wartime Sedition and Espionage Acts. Bettman did most of the legal drafting on the sedition cases himself, including *Schenck* v. *U.S.* and *Debs* v. *U.S.*, which resulted in the imprisonment of Eugene Victor Debs, the Socialist party candidate for president of the United States in 1912, for making an antiwar speech in Canton, Ohio, in the spring of 1918.

At the end of the war, upon the recommendation of both Bettman and Palmer, President Wilson granted clemency to over one hundred of the 239 persons still in prison for violations of the Espionage Act, most of whom were put there by the successful prosecutions of Bettman and O'Brian (Coben, 1963, pp. 200–201). Bettman and O'Brian recommended pardons or commutations of sentences in 109 cases involving Espionage Act convictions (Sterling, 1969, p. 151). However, in March of 1919 Bettman advised against the pardoning of Debs (Coben, 1963, p. 201). As a result of these war-related activities, Bettman had created, in less than two years, a national reputation for effective criminal prosecution. In conservative circles he became known as "the man who jailed Socialist Debs." The war being over, and the national-defense-in-wartime logic of the Espionage and Sedition Acts no longer being applicable, Bettman and O'Brian resigned their positions with the Department of Justice in May 1919.

Responding to local public pressures, the Republican-machine-dominated city council of Cincinnati created an official city planning commission, consistent with the Bettman-drafted enabling act of 1915, that began to function on January 1, 1918 (ICRPC, 1925, p. 324). This commission, headed by the machine mayor, was in no hurry whatsoever to create the master plan that would limit the machine's political power! The commission contracted with the Technical Advisory Corporation of New York City to execute a preliminary survey of Cincinnati to highlight the city's problems and potentials (APA, 1980, Segoe Tape 1, pp. 21–3).

On June 2, 1919, less than one month after Bettman's resignation from the Department of Justice, Attorney General Palmer's house was bombed by radicals. Shaken by the experience, Palmer, a former progressive Democrat and a liberal, turned away from liberal clemency. Following the lead of a Red-scared, archconservative Republican Congress, Palmer carried out what may well have been the greatest executive restriction on personal freedom in the history of the country (Coben, 1963, p. v). During the era of the Palmer Raids (1919–20), simple suspicion of un-Americanism was sufficient to warrant a jail sentence or deportation for sedition; approximately 1,400 Americans were arrested under the state antisedition laws (Sterling, 1969, p. 95). Bettman and O'Brian were angered by this wholesale violation of civil liberties (Coben, 1963, p. 208). Bettman opposed Palmer and the new rash of peacetime sedition laws at every opportunity. And he had ample opportunity! In reaction to labor strikes and rumors of an imminent "Red Revolution," the Ohio legislature passed the Criminal Syndicalism Act on May 7, 1919. This act, passed without a dissenting vote in both houses of the legislature (105–0 in the house; 30–0 in the senate), penalized the mere advocacy of insurrection in any form. Bettman traveled repeatedly to Washington, D.C., after the war, at his own expense, to appear before congressional committees in opposition to such repressive legislation (O'Brian, 1945, p. 5), and particularly to oppose peacetime antisedition laws (Coben, 1963, pp. 241–2). Bettman testified to the Committee on Rules of the U.S. House of Representatives on January 23, 1920, against the Graham Bill. This proposed federal peacetime antisedition bill imputed criminality from mere membership in an organization, irrespective of personal guilt in an illegal act undertaken by other members. Bettman fought this "guilt-by-association," arguing that conspiracy was covered under existing laws once two or more people act illegally and that to advocate change is not to advocate violence against the United States unless and until that violence actually occurs. Under the Graham Bill, *talk* of violence would be illegal. Bettman held that this act cut at the very foundations of Anglo-Saxon law and American democracy (Bettman

1920). His reputation as "the man who put Debs behind bars" rapidly changed to that of being the most outspoken legal advocate for free speech and association in America.

Alfred returned to Cincinnati in 1919 where, as president of a revitalized United City Planning Committee, he set out to raise $100,000 in private donations, an amount determined by the committee to be the minimum required for the preparation of a comprehensive plan for the future growth of the city that could serve as a rational guide to capital investment in community facilities (Vitz, 1964, p. 6). He also collaborated with Robert H. Whitten, planning consultant to Cleveland,[12] and with a group of Clevelanders in founding the Ohio State Conference on City Planning, now known as the Ohio Planning Conference (OPC), the first statewide citizen's organization in support of planning in the United States, which would become the model for the future American Society of Planning Officials (ASPO). Bettman became the first Ohio Conference vice president in 1919 and its president in 1920–21 and 1922–3. From the beginning, because of his success in drafting the 1915 Ohio enabling act, he chaired the Ohio Conference Committee on Legislation (Simpson, 1969, p. 5). His new activities in support of the United City Planning Committee and the Ohio Conference did not diminish his commitment to earlier associations, however. He remained active in the National Conference on City Planning, serving on its Board of Directors for ten of the next seventeen years (1919–36). Primarily due to Bettman's leadership, the twelfth annual meeting of the conference was held in Cincinnati, April 19–22, 1920.

All of Bettman's efforts in support of city planning through conferences, the drafting of legislation, and creating the framework for the emerging Plan of Cincinnati, as well as his work in support of civil liberties, was avocational. His vocation was corporate law; everything else was done in his spare time. In his own words, "An ordinary but continuous law practice has served to finance a nonlucrative activity in the legal, legislative and administrative phases of urban planning" (O'Brian, 1945, p. 3). His financially rewarding employment in 1921 was as a partner in the law firm of Moulinier, Bettman, and Hunt and as director general and counsel for the Title Guarantee and Trust Company of Cincinnati.

Alfred's national reputation in criminal prosecution was recognized in 1921 by appointment as an adviser to the National Conference on Law Observance and Enforcement while his brother, Gilbert, rising in those Republican machine politics to which Alfred was so constitutionally opposed, was elected vice mayor of Cincinnati. On November 8, 1921, the voters of Cincinnati supported a referendum creating a city manager form of government in an effort to replace machine politics with good government. Although supported, it would not be implemented for four years (Vexler, 1975, p. 51).

Among Alfred Bettman's greatest contributions to American law were his "mortality tables" for criminal cases, tracing the progress of each case from arrest to prosecution and conviction. First undertaken for the Cleveland Foundation Crime Survey in 1921, they indicated frequent failure of prosecution at the pretrial stages, exposing the lax and often corrupt nature of criminal law enforcement in the United States (Bettman and Burns 1922). In recognition of his emerging reputation in criminal law reform, Bettman was appointed in 1923 to membership on the Judicial Council of Ohio where he would serve for sixteen years, recommending improvements and reform of the judicial system.

By 1922 the United City Planning Committee had succeeded in raising $105,000 from 5,000 donors in support of its master plan for the city (Vitz, 1964, p. 41). The largest donation was $15,000; the smallest $1. The Plan of Cincinnati was included in annual Cincinnati Community Chest (United Way) fund drives for contributions "specially designated." Virtually all collections were made this way. The original idea was that the United City Planning Committee would raise $70,000 and the city would contribute $30,000. The city, in fact, contributed nothing (NCCP, 1924, pp. 36–7).

With these funds committed, Bettman and a committee of four appointed by him drafted a contract with the Technical Advisory Corporation (TAC), then at work on its survey of the city for the city planning commission, authorizing the corporation to prepare a general plan for the city (Vitz, 1964, pp. 6–7). The plan was projected to cover a period of fifty years (ICRPC, 1925, p. 326). Funds raised by the United City Planning Committee were turned over to the official Cincinnati City Planning Commission, which worked with TAC to produce the plan (NCCP, 1924, p. 36; ICRPC, 1925, p. 324).

TAC, the first private urban planning consulting firm in the United States, was founded by George B. Ford and Ernest P. Goodrich in 1912. Ford and Goodrich visited Cincinnati frequently during the preparation of the plan and assigned Ladislas Segoe, a twenty-eight-year-old recent arrival from Hungary, to be their full-time on-site project supervisor. Segoe was so new to America that he had to ask an uncle to help him look in a Rand-McNally atlas to see where it was! (APA, 1980, Segoe Tape 1, p. 24). Segoe, paid $37.50 a week by TAC to be the on-site producer of the Cincinnati Plan (APA, 1980, Segoe Tape 1, p. 31), thus began an intimate day-to-day working relationship with the president of the United City Planning Committee, Alfred Bettman, "a very close, almost a father and son, relationship" (Segoe Tape 1, p. 51), that resulted in the mutual evolution of both the concepts and details of the Plan of Cincinnati.[13] The plan, begun in 1922, was timely, founded as it was in the imperative to realize municipal economy and rationality in the expenditure of public funds: Cincinnati was virtually bankrupt. In an effort to defuse a politically explosive situation, the Republican members of the city council voted to reduce their own salaries to aid in solving the financial crisis (Vexler, 1975, p. 51). But the "last straw," in terms of both machine politics and civic economics, was the Cincinnati subway.

Mayor John Galvin (1909–10, 1918–21), a machine Republican, inaugurated the construction of the Cincinnati Rapid Transit System in 1920. This scheme was based on Hunt's survey executed by Bion Arnold, funds from a pre–First World War bond issue, and the building of an extensive subway section under the now derelict Hamilton Canal in the downtown area (Condit, 1967, pp. 165–73). This expensive program, originally instituted by Mayor Hunt and City Solicitor Bettman but undertaken by the political machine with out-of-date financial data and little concern for its overall effect on the postwar finances of the city, had a profound effect on Cincinnati's future. Imposed on a city already suffering from the highest public debts in America, this project severely strained both the economy and the political credibility of the city. Two years after construction began, the city stood on the brink of bankruptcy, and the economic precariousness of the still unfinished and soon-to-be-abandoned subway was publicly revealed. The subway was about half complete when studies made in support of the emerging Plan of Cincinnati determined that the system would not be cost-effective (Upson, 1924, pp. 311–13). Construction was "temporarily" halted in 1923, never to be resumed, and $6,000,000 worth of tunnels, stations, and graded rights-of-way were abandoned (Condit, 1967, p. 173).

By 1923 political and financial conditions in Cincinnati were simply intolerable. Under Republican Mayor George P. Carrel (1922–5) streets were impassable and the police and fire departments were undermanned. There was so little faith in government that essential tax levies consistently failed at the polls in spite of political machine support (Bentley, 1934, p. 5).

Continuing his work with Ohio planning enabling legislation, Alfred Bettman drafted a bill, adopted in 1923, that gave cities with adopted master plans the right to regulate subdivisions within three miles of their boundaries. Bettman believed that without such "extra-territorial" controls, developers wishing to avoid development restrictions would simply build just outside the municipal boundaries.

While incompetence, corruption, and lack of rational public planning for municipal expenditures were leading Cincinnati to disaster, Alfred Bettman's capabilities in drafting planning-related legislation and his more recent activities in support of state and national planning organizations brought him to national attention for his contribution to city planning, complementing his national recognition for criminal prosecution and for the defense of civil liberties. In 1924 he was appointed to Secretary of Commerce Herbert Hoover's Advisory Committee on Housing and Zoning for which he drafted a Standard State Zoning Enabling Act that was published by the federal government and used throughout the country, encouraging the establishment of numerous zoning commissions.

Conditions in Cincinnati were deteriorating to the point of absolute frustration. Perhaps seeing "the handwriting on the wall," the Cincinnati City Council unanimously passed the first element of the Plan of Cincinnati, the zoning ordinance, on April 1, 1924 (ICRPC, 1925, p. 324) in an effort to identify municipal fiscal economy and rationality with the machine-dominated administration. Bettman could announce the following year that the "city officials are quite committed to the idea" of planning (ICRPC, 1925, p. 325). Nevertheless, a group of reform-minded Cincinnati businessmen under the leadership of the Cincinnatus Association and Murray Seasongood met on June 15, 1924, to create a "Charter Party" dedicated to revision of the city charter as a means toward permanent removal of the machine from City Hall (Bentley, 1934, p. 6). Most were nonmachine Republicans. Thanks to Alfred Bettman's leadership of the United City Planning Committee, which had a city plan nearing completion and which had pushed the official city planning commission to a position in support of planning, planning for municipal economy became a basic plank of Charterite politics and now had *both* machine and reformer political support. In the municipal elections of November 1924 the people of Cincinnati voted overwhelmingly in support of the new city charter (92,511 for, 41,105 against), a victory gained by the active participation of a massive number of citizen volunteers. The City Charter Committee was created at a dinner celebrating this bold political upset in order to assure continued political success (Bentley, 1934, pp. 6-7).

The Plan of Cincinnati, sponsored by the United City Planning Committee, paid for by public donations, and created between 1922 and 1924 primarily by Alfred Bettman and Ladislas Segoe, under the guidance of George B. Ford and Ernest P. Goodrich of TAC, was presented to Mayor George P. Carrel's official Cincinnati City Planning Commission as a gift of the people of Cincinnati. The plan was completed in the middle of 1924, primarily through the day-to-day efforts of Segoe and Bettman, with either Goodrich or Ford coming out to Cincinnati from New York one week each month to monitor the progress and to provide guidance. The final plan document, involving the synthesis of the local studies, was primarily the work of George B. Ford (APA, 1980, Segoe Tape 1, pp. 30-31). The Plan of Cincinnati was officially adopted by the commission, with machine mayor Carrel as its chairman, in the spring of 1925 (ICRPC, 1925, p. 324), becoming the first such long-range master plan for community development to be officially adopted by the planning commission of a major American city. Segoe observed, "How Alfred managed to engineer that I do not know, . . . He wasn't even on the commission" (APA, 1980, Segoe Tape 1, pp. 24-5). Having completed the plan in mid-1924, Segoe returned to Hungary, where he was seeking a place to open an office when he received a telegram from TAC offering him a junior partnership in the firm if he would return to America to do an industrial survey for Cincinnati and a master plan for Dayton. He returned to Ohio (APA, 1980, Segoe Tape 1, pp. 31-2).

It should be noted that the Plan of Cincinnati, in its two parts, the zoning element (1924) and the capital improvements component (1925), was adopted by the city of Cincinnati *before* the political revolution that brought reform government to Cincinnati and that both a strong planning commission, operating under Bettman's 1915 guidelines, and the Plan of Cincinnati were in place prior to the election of 1925.

The revised charter, authorized in the election of 1924 and completed in 1925, declared comprehensive planning to be a necessary and permanent part of Cincinnati city government (Bentley, 1934, p. 5; Upson, 1926, pp. 399–401). In the 1925 elections, the first under the new charter, the Charterites under the leadership of the Cincinnatus Association and Murray Seasongood elected six council members, four nonmachine Republicans and two Democrats, against three for the Republican machine (Bentley, 1934, p. 7). The machine was defeated! On December 30, 1925, the new Charterite-dominated city council elected Murray Seasongood mayor and appointed Colonel Clarence O. Sherrill as Cincinnati's first city manager, charging Sherrill with bringing businesslike objectivity and economy to the operation of municipal affairs (Vexler, 1975, p. 51). It also reaffirmed the powers of the official city planning commission and its commission-adopted plan. The Cincinnati City Planning Commission, the first in the nation to be specifically empowered to establish and officially adopt a comprehensive plan (Kent, 1964, p. 200), was now assured political support for the implementation of the Plan of Cincinnati.

Although the Republican machine suffered a fatal setback in Cincinnati, Gilbert Bettman continued his career in party politics when the Ohio Republican organization appointed him chairman of the Republican State Convention in 1924, permitting him to rise in Republican state politics where prospects for future success were much brighter.

Murray Seasongood, the first Charterite mayor of Cincinnati (1926–9), became chairman of the city planning commission in 1926, assuring political implementation and enthusiastic promotion of the plan. In May 1926, Alfred Bettman was appointed to the city planning commission that his efforts had created.

Insofar as the primary purpose of the Plan of Cincinnati was that of acting as a guide to rational public investment in capital projects, Bettman suggested shortly after taking his seat on the commission that a capital budget be prepared based on the plan. This concept, developed jointly by Bettman, Segoe, and John B. Blanford, Jr. of the Bureau of Government Research (APA, 1980, Segoe Tape 1, pp. 56–7), was rapidly adopted in various forms throughout the United States, usually under the title of a Capital Improvement Program (CIP). But for many years this was simply referred to as "The Cincinnati Plan," a plan for municipal financial efficiency through long-range capital investment planning based on a comprehensive plan (Scott, 1969, pp. 253–4). That is what the comprehensive plan, and the city planning revolution in Cincinnati, was all about.

By 1926 Cincinnati had an operating official city planning commission with strong local support and implementation powers, a master-plan-based capital improvements planning system, and a commission-adopted master plan that was to become the foundation for the evolution of the comprehensive plan idea in America. In two short years, from 1924 to 1926, but based on a decade of preparation, Cincinnati was changed from "the worst governed city in America" to "the best governed city," thanks to Alfred Bettman's concepts of city planning as reform and municipal economy, his implementation of Hunt's concepts of participatory democracy and capital planning, and the Charterite political revolution.

In the 1920s American city planning commissions were generally volunteer committees of laymen who were almost totally lacking in in-house expertise. They were virtually always either grossly underfunded by public sources, or totally dependent on charitable contributions for the continuation of their work. In 1926, when Bettman took his seat on the Cincinnati City Planning Commission, he immediately addressed these two issues; he initiated actions to assure the continuing financial support of the planning function in Cincinnati with public funds (Vitz, 1964, p. 9) and arranged for Ladislas Segoe to be employed by the city as a "planning engineer." Segoe thus became a full-time municipally employed professional planner charged with continuing studies and with formulating the implementation actions needed to fulfill the promise of the adopted master plan.

Segoe, who was employed at that time by TAC, was at Dayton, Ohio, where he was working on a Dayton version of the Plan of Cincinnati. He left Goodrich and Ford to accept Cincinnati's offer of $6,000 per year and the directorship of a city planning department that consisted of himself, a draftsman, a secretary, and a total annual budget of about $14,000 (APA, 1980, Segoe Tape 1, pp. 32–3). This made Segoe the head of one of the best-funded municipal planning agencies in the United States.

On January 27, 1926, oral arguments were conducted before eight members of the U.S. Supreme Court in the case of *Village of Euclid et al. v. Ambler Realty Company,* the first such constitutional test of comprehensive zoning. Bettman viewed land use zoning as the most direct tool for guiding private development toward fulfilling the objectives of the comprehensive planning program. Two years earlier, as an appointed member of Secretary of Commerce Herbert Hoover's Advisory Committee on Housing and Zoning, he had drafted a Standard State Zoning Enabling Act that was published by the federal government and was used throughout the country. By this means, Bettman became the primary author of those state enabling acts that supported the zoning actions that were now being contested as unconstitutional. He not only viewed the zoning power as critical to the success of the comprehensive planning idea, he also viewed zoning and the comprehensive plan as an integral unit. He told the attendees of the 1924 meeting of the Ohio State Planning Conference, "Cincinnati . . . started from the beginning upon the principles of a comprehensive city plan, the zoning ordinance being conceived simply as a part of this plan" (Simpson, 1969, p. 12). Through *Euclid,* a primary component of his comprehensive plan idea, a component for which he had been the primary legal author, was under attack as unconstitutional.

The Village of Euclid, Ohio, adopted a zoning ordinance on November 13, 1922. This ordinance, for all intents and purposes, was the New York City Zoning Code of 1916, the first comprehensive zoning code to be adopted by an American city, with the names and locations changed to fit this tiny village located a short distance to the east of Cleveland (Toll, 1969, p. 231). The Ambler Realty Company had sixty-eight acres in Euclid that were not zoned to its liking. It instituted legal action. The ordinance being upheld in the Ohio courts, Ambler claimed violation of the "due process" clause of the U.S. Constitution and entered the federal courts. James F. Metzenbaum, noted Cleveland attorney and advocate of planning control actions, the attorney who had amended the New York City Zoning Code to fit Euclid (Toll, 1969, p. 229), represented the village. Newton D. Baker, former reform mayor of Cleveland and President Wilson's Secretary of War, represented Ambler. Judge D. C. Westenhaver of the U.S. District Court for the Northern District of Ohio found for Ambler. Metzenbaum took the case directly to the U.S. Supreme Court (Metzenbaum, 1955, 1:57).

Chief Justice William Howard Taft, a Cincinnatian and personal friend of Alfred Bettman, presided over the oral arguments in
Euclid v. *Ambler.* At the end of the day, Metzenbaum realized that he
had failed to convince the court and filed a request for permission
to file a reply brief. Chief Justice Taft concurred, taking this opportunity to correct a critical oversight. Alfred Bettman had been
promised the opportunity to file a brief in support of the zoning
power which, due to the forgetfulness of a court clerk, had not been
requested and thus had not been heard (Scott, 1969, pp. 238–9).
Reopening the case permitted Taft to fulfill the obligation to Bettman.
While the case was being reopened to argument, Judge George
Sutherland, the one justice absent during the earlier oral arguments,
began to draft the majority opinion of the court in support of
Ambler, holding that comprehensive zoning is unconstitutional!

Taft's friendship with Bettman and, one may suppose, his long-
term support of planning[14] led him to schedule reargument of the
case, permitting Metzenbaum to sharpen his arguments and Bettman
to present his promised brief in support of the zoning power. It has
also been reported that Justice Sutherland's convictions became
clouded while he was developing the majority opinion against
zoning, contributing to Chief Justice Taft's decision to rehear the
case (McCormack, 1946, p. 712). Such reargument was a Supreme
Court rarity. Bettman's amicus curiae brief changed the course of
American urban history.[15] Bettman's brief, a brilliant defense of the
zoning power, is credited with swaying the court toward support of
Euclid's position. On November 26, 1926, the Supreme Court issued
its opinion: a 6:3 vote for Euclid, with Justice Sutherland writing the
majority opinion *in support* of the zoning power! (Metzenbaum,
1955, 3:1904). *Euclid* is the constitutional foundation for all current
American zoning. Before *Euclid,* although eleven states had upheld
the zoning power in state courts, more states had decided against
zoning than had decided for it. Bettman, through his *Euclid* brief,
reversed the tide, thus saving the day for both zoning and comprehensive planning in America.

In mid-1928 Ladislas Segoe left the employ of the city of Cincinnati in favor of a locally based private consulting practice (APA,
1980, Segoe Tape 1, p. 36). Myron D. Downs replaced Segoe as the
director of planning for Cincinnati.

Bettman's views on the integration of zoning and comprehensive planning, "The Building Zone Ordinance printed herein . . . is

an integral part of the City Plan" (*Official City Plan,* 1925, fore-word), were to be forcefully expressed again when *A Standard City Planning Enabling Act* was published by Secretary Hoover's Depart-ment of Commerce in 1928. The result of a three-year effort by a nine-person committee, this proposed state enabling act was prima-rily based on Alfred Bettman's legal draftsmanship. The Standard Act accepted zoning, the immediate control of private property rights, as a part of the comprehensive plan. It permitted piece-at-a-time adoption of components of the comprehensive plan, and it stated that zoning, to be legal and to be effective, had to be based on and intended to fulfill the purposes and objectives of a comprehen-sive plan. As Kent observes (1964, p. 33), this uncharacteristically confused work, although totally supported by all of Bettman's earlier work at Cincinnati, where these conditions had been fulfilled with positive results, created a plethora of state enabling acts that in fact permitted, and fostered, the adoption of zoning ordinances that were not based on comprehensive planning at all. Under the terms of this Standard Act, any zoning, once adopted, could be claimed to be "part one" of a comprehensive plan and therefore always based *on* a comprehensive plan (itself!), even when executed totally out of context of a comprehensive planning process. Instead of creating the legal foundations for a system assuring that local land use control is predicated on long-range comprehensive community development objectives and capital investment implications, as was clearly in-tended, this "model," widely adopted in the United States, had the reverse effect. It discouraged comprehensive planning and confused public understanding of it by making the act of zoning, by defini-tion, synonymous with comprehensive planning. This legal confu-sion still characterizes planning and zoning in vast areas of the United States today, a half century after this strange lapse in Bettman's usually clear thought and normal careful channeling of legal efforts to assure the desired results. Bettman later realized the error of including zoning in the comprehensive plan. When the next Plan of Cincinnati was being prepared under his direction, in the 1940s, a careful distinction was made between long-range land use planning in the comprehensive plan and immediate land use control through zoning (APA, 1980, Segoe Tape 1, p. 60).

ALFRED BETTMAN'S NATIONAL REPUTATION for effective criminal prosecution kept pace in the late 1920s with his growing national impact on American urban planning. In 1929 Alfred began a four-year term as a member of President Herbert Hoover's Commission on Criminal Prosecution Procedure, the "Wickersham Commission." In that same year his brother, Gilbert, still rising in Ohio Republican machine politics, began a two-term, four-year period in office as Attorney General of the state of Ohio, sworn to uphold all of Ohio's laws, including those antisedition laws to which his brother, Alfred, was so strongly opposed.

The Ohio Criminal Syndicalism Act of 1919, an antisedition act that had seen many arrests but no convictions in its ten-year history, was applied on July 12, 1929, when two members of the Communist party were arrested for the crime of distributing leaflets outside a steel plant in Martins Ferry. In reaction, on "International Red Day," August 1, 1929, three members of the party from Cleveland came to Martins Ferry to pass out handbills that threatened "revolutionary mass action" and predicted "the overthrow of capitalism." They were arrested, found guilty, and sentenced to five years in prison, although they had not distributed a single leaflet, having been arrested before the meeting began. The International Labor Defense (ILD), a clear adjunct of the American Communist party, established an appeal. Being underfunded, the ILD asked the American Civil Liberties Union (ACLU) for help. The ACLU, in turn, asked one of the leading American spokesman for civil liberties, Alfred Bettman, to defend the Communists. The case, *Johnson et al. v. State of Ohio* (Gilbert Bettman, Attorney General), was heard under appeal in the Seventh District Court of Appeals for Belmont County, St. Clairsville, Ohio (Sterling, 1969, pp. 94–7).

The Communist party wanted to use the trial as a propaganda device, preferring to *lose* the case after maximum publicity in order to create class martyrs and to stimulate increased labor agitation. Alfred Bettman refused the Communist party the help of the ACLU unless the case was fought solely on legal and constitutional ground and was fought to win. Being without funds, the party had no choice but to agree. The case was heard against the background of the financial "Crash" of October 1929.

Bettman prepared a careful brief, focusing on the fact that since none of the handbills had been distributed prior to the arrest, the State of Ohio was using this act to prevent an opinion from being heard. He argued that this was a clear violation of the U.S. Constitution's guarantee of free speech. On May 24, 1930, the court upheld

Bettman's views, adding that even if the handbills had been distributed they did not incite an unlawful act. The Communist party lost
both its propaganda and its martyrs (Sterling, 1969, p. 150). Seven
months later, Bettman won a similar case at Cadiz, Ohio.[16] In both
cases he donated his services in defense of civil liberties against his
brother's sworn duty to uphold the laws of Ohio.

Murray Seasongood, the first Charterite mayor of Cincinnati,
resigned the chairmanship of the Cincinnati City Planning Commission in 1930. Alfred Bettman was appointed to replace him. He
would serve as chairman of the Commission until his death in 1945.
As chairman, Bettman kept the City Planning Commission together
during the darkest days of the Great Depression, from 1930 to 1933,
when planning commissions throughout the country lost their
meager funding and their staff positions to municipal economy
drives generated by the deepening economic crisis (Simpson, 1969,
p. 29). The major capital construction projects projected in the 1925
Plan of Cincinnati, such as the Western Hills Viaduct (1930–32) and
the immense Cincinnati Union Terminal passenger railroad complex (1929–33), became the vehicles for depression-era unemployment relief. The Union Terminal complex, consisting of twenty-four
buildings, was financed by a city-backed $42 million bond issue that
was floated just one month before the Crash of 1929, giving the city
cash-in-hand for unemployment relief construction at the very
beginning of the economic catastrophe. It also permitted construction with predepression dollars at depression wages and prices,
resulting in an even more grand facility than originally contemplated (see Condit, 1967, pp. 215–73, for a superb account of these
projects). In 1931, as the Great Depression deepened, Alfred Bettman
again answered Herbert Hoover's call, this time to serve as a member
of the City Planning Committee of President Hoover's Conference
on Home Building and Home Ownership. This conference revealed
the true extent of the national economic problem and the total
collapse of the American home-building industry.

In 1932, in the depths of the depression, Alfred Bettman, the
chairman of the Cincinnati City Planning Commission, served once
again as the president of the Ohio State Conference on Planning
(now known as the Ohio Planning Conference), and championed
concepts being propounded by his friend Ernest J. Bohn, a member
of the Cleveland City Council (1930–40) and future chairman of the
Cleveland City Planning Commission, that called for the public

construction of low-cost housing and a 50 percent federal subsidy for such housing (Simpson, 1969, pp. 36–7). These concepts, formulated and propounded in the more liberal environment of Cleveland and Cincinnati, were decidedly unpopular with the dominant conservative Republicans at the Statehouse in Columbus and with the Hoover administration in Washington, D.C. But the Columbus Republicans were out of step with emerging public values. In the election of November 1932, Gilbert Bettman, running as a Republican candidate for the U.S. Senate from Ohio, was swept aside, his national political aspirations crushed by the anti-Republican, anticonservative, and anti-Hoover Democratic landslide that brought Franklin Delano Roosevelt and the New Deal to Washington, D.C.

Alfred Bettman's long-term high national repute in such areas as planning and zoning, criminal prosecution, and the defense of civil liberties, combined with the fact that in 1932 he was serving as president of both the Ohio Planning Conference and the National Conference on City Planning, being the visible head of the planning movement in both Ohio and the nation as a whole, brought him to the attention of the New Deal. Thanks to Alfred Bettman's maintenance of the City Planning Commission during the "dark days" of the early 1930s, Cincinnati was among the few American cities that were adequately staffed with planners and ready to take advantage of New Deal programs when they began to flow in 1933 (Simpson, 1969, p. 29). Cincinnati became a New Deal showcase for federal new town construction (Greenhills)[17] and for the implementation of Ernie Bohn's public housing concepts.

Bettman, a Democrat, a legal expert, and an experienced public planner, was particularly valuable to the Roosevelt administration. In 1933 he was appointed legal consultant to a federal commission charged with the development of the Tennessee River. His work led directly to the creation of the Tennessee Valley Authority ("Chairman," 1945, p. 19). From 1933 to 1941, he promoted state planning. This concept was eagerly supported by the Secretary of the Interior, Harold Ickes, and was implemented throughout the country at that time, creating the foundation for most current state planning activity in America—but not in Bettman's own Ohio, where Statehouse Republicans consistently defeated every attempt to create a state planning board. In 1934 Bettman accepted the chairmanship of the Fourth Region of the new National Planning Board, consisting of the states of Ohio, West Virginia, Tennessee, and Indiana, and

FIGURE 8.2
Alfred Bettman,
c. 1930.
DEPARTMENT OF
MANUSCRIPTS AND
UNIVERSITY ARCHIVES,
OLIN LIBRARY, CORNELL
UNIVERSITY.

served the newly created American Society of Planning Officials, now the American Planning Association, as its first president (1934-8). The last half of the 1930s were fruitful years for the indefatigable corporate lawyer chairman of the Cincinnati City Planning Commission. In 1935, in *U.S. v. Certain Lands in Louisville*, Bettman produced legal arguments in support of Ernie Bohn's housing concepts that were then being implemented by the Roosevelt administration through the Public Works Administration. These arguments, published at the time in an article entitled "Is housing a public use?" (Bettman, 1935), would later be accepted by the U.S. Supreme Court, creating the legal foundations for all future public housing programs in America. Bettman also began to write a section of the *ASPO Newsletter* in 1935 called "Planning law and legislation," that came to be a separate publication called *Zoning Digest* (Vitz, 1964, p. 40), and the only book ever written by Alfred Bettman, *Model Laws for Planning Cities, Counties and States* (Bassett et al., 1935), coauthored with Edward Murray Bassett, Frank B. Williams, and Robert Whitten, was published by the Harvard University Press. From 1935 to 1938 he served one of many three-year terms as a member of the Board of Directors of the American City Planning Institute. In 1936 he became the chairman of the Ohio Valley Regional Planning Commission. His national visibility in leadership roles in planning associations, his clear support for public housing, and his legal contributions to the public housing issue in *U.S. v. Certain Lands in Louisville* led, in 1936, to his chairmanship of the ASPO committee on the federal Wagner Housing Bill. This bill became the U.S. Housing Act of 1937, the first major federal legislative commitment to public housing in America. The 1937 act implemented Ernie Bohn's concepts on a national scale. Bettman's committee became ASPO's permanent Committee on Planning Legislation, which he would chair until 1942 (Vitz, 1964, p. 43).

Alfred Bettman's planning-related activities in the 1930s were not limited to the United States. In 1937 he represented the United States on the Executive Committee of the International Congress for Housing and Town Planning. A member of the British Town Planning Institute, he spent many summers in attendance at town planning courses in the United Kingdom. But war clouds were gathering in Europe and Asia. As America walked to the brink of the Second World War, Alfred Bettman served as a member of the Board of Governors of ASPO (1938-40) and saw the American City Planning Institute, that he helped to found in 1917 and which he served as a member of the Board of Governors from 1935 to 1938, become the American Institute of Planners in 1939.[18]

In 1941 Bettman was serving as a consultant to the National Resources Planning Board, drafting the planning statutes for Puerto Rico. These statutes are commonly recognized as the most advanced planning enabling legislation ever enacted in America; 1941 also saw his brother, Gilbert, still involved in Ohio Republican politics, elected as a justice of the Ohio Supreme Court, the position he held when stricken, at the age of sixty, by a fatal heart attack on July 17 of the following year.

As with the early depression years, the early years of the Second World War devastated local planning departments: staff positions were abolished and budgets were cut to support programs more directly related to the war efforts and to reflect grossly diminished available manpower. Most American cities did little during the war years with regard to long-range urban planning, permitting their planning processes, staff, and local support to atrophy and exhibiting little concern for the future postwar era. But at Cincinnati things were different. Again, as in the Great Depression, Alfred Bettman held the planning commission together during trying times and made positive progress toward planning for the future. While other planning agencies slowed their nonwar-related activities to a crawl, the Cincinnati City Planning Commission continued its technical studies. Realizing the need for a total reevaluation and expansion of the comprehensive plan for the city that had been originally adopted more than fifteen years earlier, Bettman used the war years to execute new long-range planning studies of the Cincinnati region toward the end of the adoption of a new master plan for the city as soon as possible following the end of the war. An appropriation to the City Planning Commission to prepare the revised master plan was provided by an ordinance passed by the city council on February 16, 1944 (*The Cincinnati Metropolitan Master Plan and the Official City Plan,* 1948, foreword). But preliminary studies had been begun much earlier. In the course of these studies, Bettman concluded that control of perimeter development, the key issue in planning during the 1920s, would have to be complemented in the new plan with new devices for the reconstruction of the older deteriorating core areas of the central city. The years 1941 to 1943 "were the formative years for his pioneering work in urban redevelopment enabling legislation"

(Vitz, 1964, p. 41), when he served as chairman of the ASPO Urban Redevelopment Committee (Bettman, 1943). Bettman built the legislative bases for the area redevelopment program, now commonly referred to as the "urban renewal" clearance program, to fulfill the postwar need for rebuilding the deteriorated areas of the city of Cincinnati and to fulfill the promise of the new comprehensive plan that was taking shape under his leadership and that of Myron Downs and Sherwood Reeder, director of Master Plan Studies for the City of Cincinnati. As chairman of the Legislative Committee of the American Institute of Planners, he drafted model state legislation to support such central city redevelopment, including an Ohio Urban Redevelopment Act, in which reconstruction was to be primarily undertaken by private enterprise with local project control. But he argued that the financing of such large-scale undertakings was beyond the capacities of a local municipal government and had to be carried by either state or federal government. "He was utterly devoted to the cause of urban redevelopment" (Hansen, 1945, p. 38).

Alfred Bettman's wartime vision resulted in Cincinnati's being virtually the only American city that was ready to meet the challenge and promise of the postwar era. Thanks to his efforts, the new Cincinnati Master Plan, adopted on November 22, 1948, a decade in advance of most other American cities and the first to be adopted by a major American city following the end of the war, coordinated postwar construction and reconstruction activities in Cincinnati in an unprecedented manner, permitting the careful targeting of capital projects and redevelopment activities in the context of a coherent overall program of public policies. This master plan was primarily the work of Bettman, Myron Downs, Sherwood Reeder, Malcomb Dill, and consultants Ladislas Segoe and Tracy Augur. The plan's adoption was dedicated to the memory of Alfred Bettman (*The Cincinnati Metropolitan Master Plan and the Official City Plan*, 1948, introduction), who did not live to see this fruit of his efforts.

Robert A. Taft, U.S. senator from Ohio, known throughout the nation during the mid to late 1940s as "Mr. Republican," was a friend of Alfred Bettman, a fellow Cincinnatian, and the son of Chief Justice William Howard Taft, who had manipulated the outcome of the *Euclid* decision. Robert A. Taft, while a member of the Ohio legislature, had introduced rural zoning bills for Alfred Bettman although he was politically lukewarm to these ideas, being by nature a staunch conservative (Simpson, 1969, p. 38). Alfred solicited Taft's support for federally funded urban redevelopment legislation that he drafted to permit America's postwar cities to undertake the large-scale urban reconstruction that his ongoing studies toward a new comprehensive plan for Cincinnati indicated as essential. He also solicited his support for "test case" legislation to be introduced in Congress establishing such a redevelopment program for the District of Columbia as a model for the rest of the country. Most significantly, Bettman, the Democrat, convinced "Mr. Republican" Taft of the need for a new postwar federal public housing program to replace the now financially depleted U.S. Housing Act of 1937 that had resulted from the Wagner Housing Bill. He further convinced Taft that this new U.S. Housing Act should be a vehicle for fulfilling public housing and area redevelopment purposes and for encouraging overall comprehensive planning. Conservative Republican Taft, convinced that such a program was essential by Bettman's wartime studies of the postwar needs of his own hometown, Cincinnati, was no longer a lukewarm friend to such planning ideas and introduced this legislation in Congress with the support of Senator Allen J. Ellender and liberal Democrat Robert F. Wagner of New York. This legislation, debated during the end-of-the-war years, became the U.S. Housing Act of 1949, the foundation for American postwar central city reconstruction and public housing activities and for the future "701" comprehensive planning assistance provision of the U.S. Housing Act of 1954. Taft's support of these programs, embodied in a bill cosponsored with archliberal Wagner, probably cost him his presidential aspirations as such "Rooseveltian" approaches were anathema to most conservative Republicans.

Because of Alfred Bettman's wartime activities, Cincinnati was ready in 1949, upon passage of the new U.S. Housing Act including both area redevelopment and public housing programs, to utilize immediately these programs in the context of the new master plan Cincinnati had adopted the year before, fulfilling those specific and local needs in Cincinnati *that they were created to address.*

During the first week of January 1945, while the U.S. Supreme Court, in *Cleveland* v. *U.S.,* supported the constitutionality of public housing programs based on the legal logic that had been developed by Bettman in *U.S.* v. *Certain Lands in Louisville* ten years earlier, Alfred Bettman traveled to Washington, D.C., with his wife, Lillian, to testify to Senator Taft's Subcommittee on Housing and

Urban Redevelopment of the Senate Special Committee on Postwar Economic Policy and Planning (Bassett, 1945). He testified as chairman of the American Bar Association Committee on Planning Law and Legislation and as a representative of the American Institute of Planners,[19] specifically as chairman of the Institute's Committee on Federal Activities (Scott, 1969, p. 418). He spoke in support of postwar redevelopment legislation, urging the federal government to adopt a program, such as that which he had drafted for Ohio, permitting cities to demolish deteriorated central city areas and to lease or sell these areas to private enterprise for proper guided reconstruction ("Alfred Bettman," 1945, pp. 1, 6; Hansen, 1945, p. 38). He argued the need for federal finance of such projects (Evans, 1945, p. 4). Following his testimony on behalf of the American Institute of Planners, he appeared again as legal counsel to the National Capital Park and Planning Commission to promote these concepts further (O'Brian, 1945, p. 3). While in Washington, D.C., he attended a meeting of the Board of Directors of the American Planning and Civic Association (Bassett, 1945) and then proceeded to New York City, where he attended a meeting of the American Institute of Planners.

> Alfred Bettman passed away yesterday en route home from New York. *(Telegram from Sherwood Reeder to Ernest Bohn, January 22, 1945)*

In the early morning hours of January 21, 1945, while returning to Cincinnati with Lillian, Alfred Bettman suffered a fatal heart attack aboard a Pennsylvania Railroad train as it passed through Altoona, Pennsylvania. He was seventy-one. His remains were returned to his beloved Cincinnati, where they were buried in the United Jewish Cemetery.[20]

In all probability, no single person contributed more to the development of American city and regional planning between 1920 and 1945 than Alfred Bettman of Cincinnati. He published about eighty-five works on planning and housing during his lifetime (Bettman, 1946, p. 41). "In fact, a full list of his planning activities would parallel the historical evolution of the American movement for municipal, state, and national planning in all of its aspects" (Bettman, 1946, p. xvi). Cincinnati, the state of Ohio, and the federal government became his laboratories for experimental statutes, ordinances, bills, and planning methods intended to "make planning not merely to fit into, but actually preserve and strengthen democracy" in America (Vitz, 1964, p. 46). He did all of this as an avocation, as a hobby, as a self-fulfilling uncompensated service adjunct to his vocation of corporate law. When asked how he could afford to donate so much of his time and effort to his planning interests,[21] Bettman said, "Well, when I come to the end, I would like to feel that I have been a part of the life of my time" (O'Brian, 1945, p. 6). Alfred Bettman was not only "a part of the life" of his time but also a primary shaper of modern American urban planning practices and, through them, a primary shaper of the modern American city . . . and he did it all in his spare time.

NOTES

Portions of this chapter were presented at a session of the Annual Conference of the Association of Collegiate Schools of Planning held at Howard University, Washington, D.C., on Friday, October 23, 1981.

The author wishes to recognize the contributions of Luis Roberto Martinez, graduate student in the City and Regional Planning Department at Ohio State University, who assisted in the basic research upon which this paper is based. The cooperation of Ohio Historical Society, in locating historic views of Cincinnati that helped the author to comprehend the physical realities of the city over time, is also most sincerely appreciated.

1. The Tyler Davidson Fountain, a gift to the people of Cincinnati from Henry Probasco in honor of his late brother-in-law, Tyler Davidson, was dedicated on October 6, 1871. Designed by August von Kreling, the forty-three-foot-high fountain is topped by a figure of the "genius of waters," "beckoning" to the city of Cincinnati.

2. Alfred's mother, Rebecca, was born in Cincinnati of immigrant parents from Alsace.

3. The 1884 riot resulted from a protest over the results of a trial in which two men, one white and one a mulatto, were convicted of murdering their employer. The white man received a lighter sentence than the mulatto, precipitating a violent outburst of mob action (Vexler, 1975, p. 41).

4. Isaac Mayer Wise founded Hebrew Union University in Cincinnati in 1875. He died March 26, 1900.

5. Among the more prominent Christian proponents of the Social Gospel was Washington Gladden (Solomon Washington Gladden), who directed the First Congregational Church in Columbus, Ohio, from 1882 to 1914. He preached that religious principles must be applied to current social problems. Among his more influential works were *Social Salvation* (1902) and *Where Does the Sky Begin?* (1904). He died July 2, 1918.

6. In 1906 George B. Cox and others were brought to trial for taking money from the city treasury. The court ruled that taking the money, under the circumstances, was not a criminal act! Cox was tried again in 1914 for the

misapplication of state funds. The case was dismissed (Vexler, 1975, pp. 47, 50).

7. Street railway strikers broke into violence on May 19, 1913. The city seized six strike-closed ice plants on the advice of the Board of Health, ice being essential then for the safe preservation of food.

8. The first National Conference on City Planning was held four years earlier, in Washington, D.C., in 1909.

9. The entry in the *Dictionary of American Biography,* Supplement Issue: *1941–1945,* would appear to be in error when it reports relative to Bettman that "in 1917 [*sic*] he joined the United City Planning Committee."

10. The entry in the *Dictionary of American Biography* (see note 9, above) would also appear to be in error in stating that in "that year (1917) the committee successfully lobbied for an enabling act, drafted by Bettman, which allowed cities in Ohio to create planning boards."

11. The American City Planning Institute was created under the initiative of Flavel Shurtleff, an attorney from Boston, and Frederick Law Olmsted, Jr., a landscape architect from Cambridge. They developed the idea of a professional institute for planners at an earlier Boston meeting and during the train ride to Kansas City (Scott, 1969, p. 163).

12. Robert H. Whitten had previously been secretary to the New York City Commission on Building Districts and Restrictions, receiving national recognition when the report of this group became the New York Zoning Code of 1916, the first comprehensive zoning code to be enacted in the United States.

13. "We spent some weekends picnicking together, we went to the conferences, traveled together, we spent summer vacations on Georgian Bay fishing, feeding worms [*sic*], and gathering berries together, and canoeing together and we were together much of the time we were talking about planning" (APA, 1980, Segoe Tape 1, pp. 51–2).

14. William Howard Taft, former dean of the University of Cincinnati Law School, received Daniel Burnham's Plan of Manila when he was Secretary of War, called the first National Conference on City Planning in 1909, and signed into law, as president, the federal act creating the National Commission of Fine Arts that acted to implement the McMillan Plan for Washington, D.C.

15. The Ohio State Planning Conference provided Bettman with the sum of $382 in support of his amicus curiae brief in the *Euclid* case and his travel to Washington, D.C. (Simpson, 1969, p. 14).

16. *Gannet and Yoki v. State of Ohio.*

17. The federally built new town of Greenhills was located at Cincinnati because of the city's history of good planning during the previous decade (Scott, 1969, p. 337).

18. The American Institute of Planners (AIP) is now known as the American Institute of Certified Planners (AICP).

19. Alfred Bettman served as a member of the Board of Governors of the American Institute of Planners from 1941 to 1944.

20. Lillian passed away three years later, on July 19, 1948.

21. The donation of so much of his time to public service projects resulted, for a corporate lawyer, in a rather frugal and modest life-style.

REFERENCES

"Alfred Bettman dies suddenly when returning aboard train from business trip to East," *Cincinnati Enquirer*, January 22, 1945, pp. 1, 6.

American Planning Association (1980) *The Ladislas Segoe Tapes*, transcript of an interview with Ladislas Segoe conducted May 22–24, 1978, in Cincinnati, Ohio, by Sydney H. Williams, AICP, Washington, D.C., and Chicago, American Planning Association.

Bassett, Edward M. (1945) "In memoriam, Alfred Bettman 1873–1945," *Planning and Civic Comment*, 11, 65.

Bassett, Edward M., Williams, Frank B., Bettman, Alfred, and Whitten, Robert (1935) *Model Laws for Planning Cities, Counties and States*, Cambridge, Massachusetts, Harvard University Press.

Bent, Silas (1926) "Liberating a city," *Century Magazine*, pp. 304–11.

Bentley, Henry, chairman, Committee on Citizen's Charter Organization (September 1934) *The Cincinnati Plan of Citizen Organization for Political Activity*, New York, National Municipal League.

Bettman, Alfred (1920) *Do We Need More Sedition Laws?*, Testimony before the Committee on Rules of the House of Representatives, National Popular Government League Pamphlet no. 20, New York, Graphic Press.

——— (October 1928) "The Paris International Housing and Town Planning Congress," *City Planning*, 4, 261–8.

——— (1935) "Is housing a public use?," *Proceedings of the Joint Conference on City, Regional, State and National Planning*, Chicago, National Association of Housing Officials, pp. 63–8.

——— (1943) "Federal and state urban redevelopment bills," *American Planning and Civic Annual*, pp. 166–71.

——— (1946) *City and Regional Planning Papers*, Arthur C. Comey, ed., Cambridge, Massachusetts, Harvard University Press.

Bettman, Alfred, and Burns, Howard (1922) *Prosecution: Criminal Justice in Ohio, Part II*, Cleveland, Cleveland Foundation.

Black, Russell VanNest (1967) *Planning and the Planning Profession: The Past 50 Years, 1917–1967*, Washington, D.C., American Institute of Planners.

"Chairman of Cincinnati Planning Board dies on train," *New York Times*, January 23, 1945, obituaries, p. 19.

Charter Commission of the City of Cincinnati (1914) *The Charter of the City of Cincinnati*, Cincinnati.

The Cincinnati Metropolitan Master Plan and the Official City Plan of the City of Cincinnati (1948) Cincinnati, City Planning Commission.

Coben, Stanley (1963) *A. Mitchell Palmer: Politician*, New York, Columbia University Press.

Condit, Carl W. (1967) *The Railroad and the City: A Technological and Urbanistic History of Cincinnati*, Columbus, Ohio, Ohio State University Press.

Dictionary of American Biography, Supplement Issue: *1941–1945*, s.v. "Bettman, Alfred."

Evans, Lee (1945) "Boon to cities envisioned in plan to reclaim slums," *Cincinnati Enquirer* January 22, p. 4.

Ford, George B., ed. (1917) *City Planning Progress in the United States, 1917*, Washington, D.C., Journal of the American Institute of Architects.

Hansen, Alvin H. (1945) "Institute affairs: Alfred Bettman," *Journal of the American Institute of Planners*, 11, 38–9.

Hebble, Charles R., and Goodwin, Frank P., eds. (1916) *The Citizens Book*, Cincinnati, Stewart & Kidd.

International City and Regional Planning Conference (1925) *Planning Problems of Town, City and Region, Papers and Discussions at the International City and Regional Planning Conference* held in New York City, April 20–25, Baltimore, Norman, Remington.

Kent, T. J., Jr. (1964) *The Urban General Plan*, San Francisco, Chandler Publishing.

McCormack, Alfred (1946) "A law clerk's recollections," *Columbia Law Review*, 45, 710–12.

Metzenbaum, James F. (1955) *The Law of Zoning*, 2d ed., 3 vols., New York, Baker Voorhis.

Miller, Zane L. (1968) *Boss Cox's Cincinnati*, New York, Oxford University Press.

National Conference on City Planning (1924) *Planning Problems of Town, City and Region, Papers and Discussions at the Sixteenth National Conference on City Planning* held in Los Angeles, California, April 7–10, Baltimore, Norman, Remington.

O'Brian, John Lord (1945) "Alfred Bettman, 1873–1945," *Journal of the American Institute of Planners*, 11, 1–6.

The Official City Plan of Cincinnati, Ohio (1925) Cincinnati, City Planning Commission.

Scott, Mel (1969) *American City Planning since 1890*, Berkeley and Los Angeles, University of California Press.

Simpson, Michael (1969) *People and Planning: History of the Ohio Planning Conference*, Bay Village, Ohio, Ohio Planning Conference.

"State of Ohio: an act to provide for a city planning commission in municipalities" (1916) *Proceedings of the Eighth National Conference on City Planning*, Boston, University Press, Appendix III, pp. 144–6.

Sterling, David L. (1969) "The 'naive liberal', the 'devious Communist' and the Johnson case," *Ohio History*, 78, 94–103.

Toll, Seymour I. (1969) *Zoned American*, New York, Grossman Publishers.

Upson, Lent D., ed. (1924) *The Government of Cincinnati and Hamilton County*, Cincinnati, City Survey Committee.

Vexler, Robert I. (1975) *Cincinnati: A Chronological and Documentary History 1676–1970*, Dobbs Ferry, New York, Oceana Publications.

Vitz, Martin H. (1964) "The contribution of Alfred Bettman to city and regional planning," master's thesis (typewritten), Ohio State University.

OTHER SOURCES

"Alfred Bettman 1873–1945" (1945) *American Society of Planning Officials Newsletter*, p. 14.

Bettman, Alfred (1931a) "Master plans and official maps," *Planning Problems of Town, City and Region, Papers and Discussions at the Twenty-Third National Conference on City Planning* held in Rochester, New York, June 22–24, Philadelphia, William F. Fell.

——— (1931b) *Report on Prosecution: National Commission on Law Observance and Enforcement*, Washington, D.C., U.S. Government Printing Office.

"Bettman's work draws praise; mayor lauds fame as planner," *Cincinnati Enquirer*, January 22, 1945, p. 6.

Cincinnati Facts and Figures (1918) Cincinnati, Times-Star.

"An expression of our appreciation," a tribute to Frederic A. Delano and Alfred Bettman (1943) *American Society of Planning Officials Newsletter*, p. 74.

"Gilbert Bettman, Ohio jurist, dead," *New York Times*, July 18, 1942, obituaries, p. 13.

Goss, Charles F. (1912) *Cincinnati: The Queen City 1788–1912*, 4 vols., Chicago, Clarke Publishing.

"Mrs. A. Bettman, 71, clubwoman in Ohio," *New York Times*, July 20, 1948, obituaries, p. 23.

National Municipal League (1934) *The Cincinnati Plan of Citizen Organization for Political Activity*, New York.

Nolen, John, ed. (1929) *City Planning*, New York, D. Appleton.

"Planning metropolitan Cincinnati" (1947) *Planning 1947: Proceedings of the Annual Meeting of the American Society of Planning Officials* held in Cincinnati, Ohio, May 5–9, 1947, Chicago, American Society of Planning Officials.

U.S. Congress, Senate (1945) Special Committee on Postwar Economic Policy and Planning, *Hearings before the Sub-Committee on Housing and Urban Redevelopment* on S.B. 102, part 9. 79th Congress, 1st Session.

Walker, Robert A. (1941) *The Planning Function in Urban Government*, Chicago, University of Chicago Press.

Who Was Who in America, 1943–1950, vol. 2, 1950 edition, s.v. "Alfred Bettman."

FIGURE 9.1   *Harland Bartholomew.*

9

HARLAND BARTHOLOMEW
PRECEDENT FOR THE PROFESSION

NORMAN J. JOHNSTON

WHEN SEVERAL YEARS AGO it came time for the American Institute of
Planners (AIP) to seek an appropriate chairman for its approaching
fiftieth anniversary celebration it turned felicitously to Harland
Bartholomew, and he in turn, in spite of the pleasures of semiretirement,
characteristically added this important responsibility to the long
record of his services to the profession. It was ground, in fact, that
he had already personally been over: his own fiftieth anniversary as
a planning professional had been passed in 1962.[1] Now, five years
later, it was appropriate that he would be chairing for the Institute
the occasion of its first half century of service to planning.

Bartholomew's origins are Yankee: born near Boston in 1889,
raised on a New Hampshire farm, late teens and early twenties in
Massachusetts and New York, he graduated from a Brooklyn high
school with the expectation of accepting the offer of work as a bank
clerk. But other events intervened. At the urging of one of his high
school teachers, he made inquiries at Rutgers. Some scholarship help
and part-time work gave him the necessary boost, and he began his
studies for a civil engineering degree.

Those studies were not to continue beyond the sophomore level.
Economics, work load, and academic regulations discouraged him

Reprinted with permission from Norman J. Johnston, "Harland Bartholomew:
Precedent for the Profession," *Journal of the American Institute of Planners*, 39,
no. 2 (1973): 115–124.

beyond that point, and so he chose to serve engineering by a more direct route, accepting a job with E. P. Goodrich, a New York City civil engineer. (Nevertheless he was to receive degrees from Rutgers: an honorary civil engineering degree in 1921 and in 1952 their Doctor of Science for leadership in his profession.)

Again there were to be outside influences at work. In 1912, Goodrich together with George B. Ford, a New York architect, signed a contract with the city of Newark, New Jersey, for preparation of what was then a quite unorthodox document—a city comprehensive plan—and Bartholomew was chosen to be the firm's representative. Thus his anticipations of working with bridges, dams, and harbor works (the sorts of commissions for which Goodrich had a considerable reputation) were suddenly and unceremoniously channeled into the legwork of a planning contract. Nevertheless, in spite of his initial disappointments, the switch proved unexpectedly permanent.

CITY BEAUTIFUL/CITY EFFICIENT

By 1912, the planning profession had passed through its earliest formative years, loosely grouped into an era known as City Beautiful. The leaders of the City Beautiful were likely to have been from the design professions or men allied with them: architects like Daniel Burnham and Arnold W. Brunner, landscape architects Frederick Law Olmsted, Jr., and John Nolen, and journalist-turned-planner Charles Mulford Robinson. Indeed, of a listing of forty-two comprehensive plans issued prior to 1912, only eleven had not been the product of one or the other of these men (Nolen, 1927, pp. 21–5). They dominated planning practices of the day.

Yet the visual civic art biases of that period, propagandized so effectively by the environmental imperialism of the 1893 Columbian Exposition in Chicago, had in the decade or so that followed come to be found wanting. Not that goals of urban monumentality and beautification were being dismissed out of hand, but there was a discernible shift away from their elusive promise toward what were seen as harder, more practical, and measurable objectives. Here was a different set of values whose focus was functional and social, comprising a program designed to create the City Efficient.

For these newcomers, the primacy of the visual city was displaced by a different set of priorities. Theirs too was a program for building, but its center of gravity had shifted away from civic centers, parks, and boulevards and over to sanitation, housing, transportation, and municipal efficiency. The shift was of course paralleled by shifts in the predispositions of its leaders. Political reformers, lawyers, housing officials, social workers, and engineers were more likely to be the protagonists of the new faith: Lawrence Veiller, Robert DeForest, Benjamin C. Marsh, Virgil Bogue, as well as John Nolen (who was successfully able to make the transposition). This was the context that included engineer Goodrich who in turn enlisted architect George B. Ford. And this is the partnership with its recently awarded planning contract for Newark that, in its assembling of resources in March 1912, assigned engineering aspirant Harland Bartholomew to the task.

The circumstances out of which the partnership was formed and Bartholomew's sudden involvement in its contract were characteristic of the professional informality of the day. These were formative years for planning in which somewhat spontaneous arrangements and methods arose in the absence of more structured and established procedures and precedents. Planning as a profession was still undefined, and in the relatively uncharted field the expert came with no set pattern of credentials. Professional training was nonexistent. Harvard had begun some instruction in city planning in 1910 in its School of Landscape Design, but it was still alone in the field in 1912. Nor were its ambitions at that stage to educate planners but rather to enrich the breadth of its landscape program.

A similar kind of spontaneity marked the nature of the planning process. Though there might be efforts among some to clarify its functions and give structure to its service, wide variety marked the tone and detail of what the client bought from his planning expert. What data were needed? What measurements used? What values applied? What objectives sought? How to compose the parts into some structured and convincing whole? To answer such questions and others like them, one plan report could be almost entirely preoccupied with beauty, parks, and streets (Brunner and Olmsted's *Rochester Plan*), another contrastingly biased toward arterial highways, harbor improvements, and transportation (Bogue's *Seattle Plan*), and both be products of the year 1911. What was this process of planning? There were those who by 1912 might be seeking the rationale and the format, but the returns were still not yet in.

PROFESSIONAL BEGINNING

When Bartholomew arrived in Newark to take up his assignment it had been the result of what was, for then, rather unique civic initiative. By 1912, there were only some thirteen cities in the United States with official planning commissions; Newark had joined their number in 1911 in response to an act the New Jersey legislature had passed in the spring of that year authorizing appointment of a nine-man city planning commission "to prepare a plan for the systematic and future development of said city" (Newark City Plan Commission, 1911, p. 3). The authorization also granted commissions power to employ "experts," and Messrs. Goodrich and Ford were their choice. It was the partners' first such contract, individually or as a team; as Bartholomew has written, "Neither Mr. Ford nor Mr. Goodrich had prepared a comprehensive city plan, it was new to everyone, and we were groping."[2]

Groping or not, the work progressed, and by the end of 1913 the commission had before it the partners' summary report, *City Planning for Newark,* comprising two principal steps: data collecting and, after their initial analysis, a roughing out of immediate proposals. But the third and most uncharted of the steps, the development of a comprehensive plan for Newark's future, remained only a sketch as to how it was to be transposed into specific rationale and planning practice.

Bartholomew's responsibilities in subsequent work expanded abruptly when the partners' contract was not renewed, Bartholomew instead being appointed in March 1914 as the commission's "engineer" and its secretary on a salaried basis. He thus became one of the nation's first full-time professional employees of a planning commission. The earlier tentative framework of the plan was now Bartholomew's charge to complete. He had arrived at his own independent course, and though he did not realize it at the time, he was to spend the rest of his professional life giving substance to step three.

By 1916, he had moved on to St. Louis as that city's planning engineer, where he followed a general planning process begun in Newark. This was the beginning of an association with St. Louis that would continue to the present day: its planning engineer until 1950, the home office of the private consulting firm that carries his name,[3] and still his place of residence. But his professional reputation was founded more on his work as a private planner rather than as civil servant. By 1919, he had laid out the basic planning program for St. Louis and had seen it through the preliminary effort toward the 1923 passage of a comprehensive bonding program for plan implementation. Now was the time to open his private office as a planner,[4] the professional format that was very much the rule rather than the exception in those days.

PRIVATE PRACTICE

To understand the impact that Bartholomew was to have on these developmental years of the profession, there are certain things about his office and his methods that need to be realized. Almost immediately after his debut as a private consultant, he came to occupy a special place in the hierarchy of American planners and, apparently, in the affections of the nation's cities seeking solutions through planning for their problems of urbanism. The mode of expression for this has been by volume: the size of the Bartholomew operation quickly outranked those of his professional colleagues in numbers of contracts and populations served.

His move was made into an area already occupied by some prestigious planning personalities: John Nolen, credited with some twenty comprehensive plan reports between 1906 (date of his first, for Savannah, Georgia) and 1919; Edward H. Bennett, Daniel Burnham's associate on the Chicago Plan of 1909, whose comprehensive plans had been completed for such major cities as Portland, Oregon (1912) and Minneapolis (1917); two generations of Olmsteds with their coast-to-coast practice; and even his former employers, Goodrich and Ford (later to become the Technical Advisory Corporation—TAC) who had completed their work on the Newark Plan in 1913, prepared for Omaha, Nebraska, in 1917, and were moving on toward expanded planning services. Exact figures scaling the relative level of activities of the private planners of that time (or our own) are elusive, but some idea can be gained from the appendix John Nolen attached to his president's address to the nineteenth National Conference of City Planning in Washington, D.C., May 1927 (Nolen, 1927). Here Nolen listed cities having comprehensive plans from 1905 through 1926 together with the date of the reports and their planners; an examination of this list indicates some interesting evidence of the nature of the services of the planning profession during those years. Of the 201 planning reports listed, only seven were not the product of a planner or planning firm brought in by the city to provide this special contract service. The days of the permanent municipal planning staff were still well ahead of the events Nolen was reporting. Bartholomew became a part of them as a consulting planner in 1919 with a report for Omaha (chiefly streets and parks). In 1920, however, his specialty in the preparation of comprehensive plans was under way, and the balance of the Nolen appendix scales his volume of work in this activity (see Fig. 9.2). The years from 1920 through 1926 include eighty-seven comprehensive plan reports by all planners (not included in this figure are fourteen reports indicated as something less than a comprehensive plan, e.g., "partial," "streets and parks," "streets"). These plans were the product of twenty-three different consulting firms, the total number of plans for each firm ranging from one to twenty. Of the twenty-three, only six consultants had prepared three or more plans during the seven-year period:

TABLE 9.1

PLANNER	NUMBER OF COMPREHENSIVE PLANS
Lawrence V. Sheridan	3
Arthur A. Shurtleff	4
TAC (Goodrich and Ford)	9 (3 "preliminary")
M. H. West	10
John Nolen	12
Harland Bartholomew	20

It is also of some interest to rank the consultants by the numbers of people whom their planning recommendations were presumably to affect, the total populations whose municipal leaders had turned to the planner for assistance.[5]

TABLE 9.2

PLANNER	POPULATION SERVED
Lawrence V. Sheridan	74,618
M. H. West	356,886
Arthur A. Shurtleff	364,519
John Nolen	511,022
TAC	1,281,106
Harland Bartholomew	1,779,508[6]

FIGURE 9.2   *Map of geographical spread of some Bartholomew comprehensive plans and zoning ordinances, 1920–48.*

In either case, Bartholomew's services are shown to have picked up remarkably quick professional momentum, and the size of his operations has since never been seriously challenged. All this had obvious contributions to make toward familiarizing the planning profession and American cities with the Bartholomew approach to the planning process. The distribution of its services has been at the broadest level, so that some portion of most of the nation's major population areas has been the subject at one time or another of Bartholomew's studied dismembering and diagnosis and his equally studied proposals for their assembly. The fact also that these services were being provided at a time when few permanent municipal planning staffs were organized helped to fill an important functional vacuum—and with the Bartholomew image. Under these circumstances, one begins to understand the dissemination of the firm's influences by means of its reports for cities distributed throughout the nation.

PERSONNEL COLONIZATION

There are other significant policies and practices of the firm and of its founder that deserve acknowledging in sensing the forces that contributed to the popularity among American cities of Bartholomew's

services. One such policy was, in effect, that of personnel colonization. From the beginning of his consulting activities, Bartholomew
determined upon a relationship between the consultant and his
contract city differing from the usual practice. He always committed
himself to the goal of plan realization and saw an opportunity for
organizing his work toward this end. Noting the usual practice of the
"expert" who arrives in town for a survey visit, does a certain amount
of legwork, basic data gathering, and public appearing, and then
disappears in the direction of his home office, to return some time
later with a completed report, Bartholomew decided to establish a
quite different footing on which to base his services in the city which
had contracted for them.

How to enlist at the local level the interest and support of the
people for whom the planning process was being pursued? Part of
Bartholomew's answer (to this question still plaguing any planner
today) was by means of his office personnel policy: his people did
not just visit a city; they were assigned to and lived in it. A key man
from the St. Louis office would be selected to supervise the field-
work and take up residence in the contract city for a period that
usually ran about three years, the normal amount of time required
for completing its comprehensive plan. As part of the contract,
office space would be arranged for directly under the noses of the
local administration, in the city hall itself if possible; and out of this
office the gathering of the necessary basic data, preparation of
statistics, field mapping, and so on would proceed.

Every effort was made to provide for this field operation the
reality as well as the sense of decision-making at the local level. An
advisory committee of perhaps one hundred of the city's citizens was
organized into various working committees to assist the technical
staff in gathering and interpreting basic data about the community
and in clarifying the goals toward which it appeared suitable to go.
As with today's municipal advisory planning commissions, this
citizens' committee would have responsibility for reviewing the
reports as they developed, reviewing the final comprehensive plan,
and acting as the local vanguard for providing support and leadership for its adoption. Basic policies, key planning decisions, and
final plan drafting were still the responsibility of Bartholomew in his
St. Louis office; but within this framework the maximum degree of
autonomy was encouraged for the field man and the city to which he
had been assigned. It was as close an approximation as possible—

FIGURE 9.3   *Map of geographical spread of some of the personnel formerly associated with the Bartholomew firm.*

given the reality of a temporary contract relationship—of a permanent advisory city planning commission and its technical staff as parts of the municipal administration.

There is an additional policy practice here, and one that again was accepted from the founding as a result of Bartholomew's concern for plan realization. Extending the idea of colonization a step further, Bartholomew realized that the plan would more likely be implemented if his field man were to become a permanent local fixture. Therefore his training policy and practice encouraged such a development, and although obviously expensive in terms of personnel costs for his office, if it was the wish of the contract city to retain its Bartholomew representative on a permanent basis (as it often was) and the latter was agreeable, Bartholomew acted as a kind of sponsor for the union and gave it his blessing. In terms of sustained planning momentum at the local level, this had obvious advantages. But there was another consequence of such a colonization: another area of the country was provided permanent personnel trained in the philosophy and techniques of Harland Bartholomew (see Fig. 9.3). And this same person would possibly return to Bartholomew for consulting services when circumstances at either his original city or another one to which he had moved suggested the need for aid in plan updating or an initial comprehensive plan study.

PERSONNEL MOVEMENT

The Bartholomew expertise was of course to be disseminated through more obvious channels than the above. One such means was through the normal come-and-go of employees through the office; and when that office has been a focal point in a profession for the number of years that Bartholomew's can claim, the ranks of employees, past and present, assume impressive proportions. Harry W. Alexander, one of the firm's retired partners, once listed names of planners he recalled who at one time or another had been associated with the firm; their distribution became nationwide. Another point of interest is the pivotal place that most of these former Bartholomew associates hold in the profession's hierarchy: most can claim rank among the leaders of planning, including retired partner Earl O. Mills, AIP's president in 1946–7.

EMPLOYEE TRAINING

Training: this was actually the role the firm was providing in the pre–Second World War period. Following Harvard's 1912 initiative in offering city planning course work, similar service-course ambitions followed at the University of Illinois in 1913. These beginnings were later expanded by more extensive professional planning programs; but although some eighty colleges and universities were offering planning courses by 1929, the courses were still primarily designed to serve students enrolled in architecture, landscape architecture, or engineering degree work rather than as professional majors in planning (T. Adams, 1936, pp. 249–50). Even by 1940 there were only four universities in the United States granting professional planning degrees: Harvard, the Massachusetts Institute of Technology, Cornell, and Columbia (F. J. Adams, 1954, p. 17).

Given the prevailing thinness of the professional curriculums of the period, Bartholomew turned to the resource from which he got his own training—experience—combining this with his developing methodology as he proceeded to organize his interpretations of the professional role into what he would call a systematized "science." Personnel would be drawn from various disciplines, especially from among engineering graduates and landscape architects, but they all then participated in a shared experience of the Bartholomew interpretation of the planning function. This was to be no intuitive process but a kind of professional module within which each planner and planning contract found a basic order. It was out of this training experience that Bartholomew employees would come and go, some released to other positions by what was in effect the firm's colonization policy, others simply going on to new opportunities after they had served their professional apprenticeship. Although no diploma changed hands, in the scarcity of university curriculums in the field the new profession was being served by the firm's function as a training ground for new personnel.

A FACULTY ROLE

Bartholomew was directly involved in planning education in the more common understanding of the phrase, for it was just before his emergence as a consultant that he accepted a university post as associate professor of civic design. This was at the University of Illinois. The original occupant of the position there had been Charles Mulford Robinson, who initiated the Illinois program in 1913 as a part of the College of Agriculture's Department of Landscape Gardening and who became its (and the nation's) first professor of civic design. He gave lectures to the students on city planning and would also periodically organize a field trip that would bring them to St. Louis to see the planning work there under Bartholomew's direction, incidentally introducing Bartholomew and Illinois to each other. Therefore, after the death of Robinson in the winter of 1917, the University turned to Bartholomew in the following year with a request that he assume the vacated post. He reacted to the suggestion with some misgivings, feeling that his obvious professional role was that of a practitioner rather than academician; but this entirely suited what Illinois's department head had in mind, and so Bartholomew agreed to teach the course on a nonresidence basis for one year, beginning in the fall of 1919. The "one-year" experiment lasted until 1956.

The arrangement apparently suited the University, and it obviously suited Bartholomew. He enjoyed student contacts and stimulation, requiring as they did a constant examination of purposes and processes "from population to capital budgets" that he found provided a valuable kind of perspective not inherently available within the confines of a growing practice. Later more full-time personnel were added to the landscape faculty, combining both landscape and planning people, including Karl B. Lohmann, and he and Bartholomew came to share the planning seminar for many years. The course was called "Planning of towns and cities" and was required for landscape architecture majors, certain majors in civil engineering, and, Lohmann recalled, possibly majors in municipal administration. It was also available as an elective for others who cared to choose it.[7]

Lohmann was, of course, the professor-in-residence while Bartholomew, on his more or less once-a-month schedule of visits during the academic year, would come in "to explain what planning was and what we [his firm] were doing. I would take plans up with me, showing how principles applied in actual practice."[8] The two men thus shared a relationship and responsibility that they both recalled with warmth. Bartholomew would come up from St. Louis by train the night before, arriving the next morning on campus always some thirty minutes ahead of the ten o'clock class time. Choice of subjects was left up to him, and these he would change from year to year, reviewing Lohmann's course outline and selecting those items on which he felt he had something to say and demonstrate; Lohmann carried the balance. From talking with either Lohmann or students who took the course one gets a sense of Bartholomew as a teacher. Calm, serious, "practical," he used few notes, relying more on his experiences, an excellent memory, and a general depth of information, including planning's prevailing legal and legislative atmosphere; these he supported with maps and reports from his current studies. Presentation was marked by its sense of clarity and, as Lohmann mentioned, his "emphasis on the positive. . . . Bartholomew was very positive in his expectations."[9] On one occasion, Lohmann scanned the 1960–61 roster of the AIP for names of former students who had been in the class, and he recalled forty-one who occupied various roles in the profession after having been prepared under the Lohmann-Bartholomew tutelage (see Fig. 9.4). Understandably, many of these students worked at one time or another for Bartholomew; one of them, Eldridge Lovelace, is now a principal partner in the firm.

If Bartholomew was then to be a participant in the educational experience of generations of students, his academic influence can also be marked in another way, although its outline is less clearly defined: this is on Lohmann himself. A graduate of the landscape architecture program at Harvard and then on the staff of the Bureau of Municipalities of the Pennsylvania Department of Internal Af-

FIGURE 9.4   *Map of geographical spread of some of the personnel who were in the Lohmann-Bartholomew planning class at the University of Illinois.*

fairs, he joined the landscape architecture faculty at Illinois in 1921. Someone was needed to work with Bartholomew in the planning course; Lohmann expressed an interest and was chosen. So at the same time when he was sharing a teaching responsibility with Bartholomew he was also sharing a learning one, for he sat in on all of the sessions that Bartholomew conducted.

In 1931, Lohmann published what Henry Vincent Hubbard at Harvard called the first textbook on planning, certainly the first introduction to planning for many people who subsequently moved into the profession as a career. This was his *Principles of City Planning,* a textbook used by the planning classes at Illinois as well as various other universities in the country, attaining a respectable circulation for its day. Lohmann has acknowledged that the chances are the book was "influenced a lot" by the Bartholomew lectures. Scanning the book, one senses this pattern of relationship: the subject matter and its treatment (for instance, the comprehensive plan, its preparation, role of the consultant, and so on; street and recreation planning; and housing) are both approached in terms reminiscent of Bartholomew practice, although specific details sometimes vary (Bartholomew and Lohmann differ somewhat as to organizational elements categorized as making up the comprehensive plan, a difference, however, more of nomenclature than spirit). Lohmann's book, then, became a primer for the professionals of that decade and the one that followed. And directly or indirectly, the

Bartholomew viewpoint had been established in this prewar academic atmosphere out of which the American planning world sought a portion of its new professionals.

PROFESSIONAL LEADERSHIP

In one final way, the impact of Harland Bartholomew on American planning has been reinforced, and this is through his role as a leader and spokesman for his profession. The American City Planning Institute (AIP's predecessor) had been founded in 1917 with Frederick Law Olmsted, Jr., as its president. Bartholomew was one of its original members and the Institute's sixth president (1927–9), his predecessors having included one of his former employers, George B. Ford, and John Nolen, whom he followed in office. One is struck again by a certain career precociousness; the average age of his predecessors was fifty-three, ranging from forty-four to sixty-three; Bartholomew ascended to the presidency at thirty-eight, the youngest ever to hold the office, then or since.

His role as spokesman for the developing science of planning is preserved in part by the proceedings of the National Conference on City Planning. His first appearance before that group and in the pages of its proceedings is his report on Newark progress in 1915, and this is followed with a 1918 report on the St. Louis plan, in 1919 by one on residential zoning, and in 1921 by an updating of the St. Louis report. All through the 1920s and into the 1930s, he continued to provide for the delegates a sequence of analyses and recommendations on aspects of the problems professionals were being asked to face, ranging from distributing the cost of street widening (1924) to St. Louis metropolitan planning (1934).

These papers are paralleled and extended by those prepared for other forums, such as articles for the *American Civic Annual* (now the *American Planning and Civic Annual*), as well as appearances and addresses before a wide spectrum of groups that called upon him as an after-dinner and convention speaker. Bartholomew has interpreted his responsibility as one calling not only for the development of a planning technology for the needs of his own practice but also for contributing that knowledge to the profession at large and for strengthening the general public's awareness of the planner's availability for using that knowledge in the search for solutions to the urban problems that all were finding increasingly about them. The combination of circumstances surrounding his practice and his supporting activities gave an unusually nationwide cast to his efforts.

Thus when one reviews Bartholomew's career and examines certain of its innovative characteristics, doing so provides not only details and dimensions to his record but to a remarkable extent similarly explains a whole milieu of the profession itself in the years before and, for a time, following the Second World War. Bartholomew would willingly acknowledge that he was not alone in developing certain characteristic ideas and practices, that others assisted him or worked independently along similar lines. Yet the ubiquity of his practice, the particularity of his means, and the personal stature which he came to realize in the profession gave his precedent special impact, a kind of semiofficial cachet which both the literature and practice acknowledged and made their own.

After the how of the matter, what of the substance? Bartholomew's career covered the full range of the planning consultant's services of the times, ranging from complete comprehensive city plans through zoning ordinances to more specialized facets of service: traffic engineering studies, site plans, economic studies, various types of engineering reports, and so on. There were, however, certain themes which ranked high in his goals and, through the nature of his position in the profession, were by his examples to represent influences on contemporary practices or portend those just ahead.

Bartholomew and the Comprehensive Plan

Though the concept of the comprehensive plan was by 1912 no longer an innovation in the thinking or vocabulary of planners of that date, it was one whose specifics were by no means clarified; and this search was to be a central theme in Bartholomew's career:

My interest in city planning beginning with the Newark work was to produce for every city a true comprehensive plan. This feeling has so dominated my thinking that my family have jokingly remarked on numerous occasions that I should have a middle name, i.e. "C" for Comprehensive. This has seemed to me to be the basic essential in this field and my work was always oriented in this direction. . . . I still feel very strongly on this point. I feel that cities are woefully lacking in comprehensive city plans. . . .

I am as keenly interested as most people in many of the

planning studies that are being produced today for unit areas, for cluster development, and for neighborhoods and such. I am far more interested, however, in whether there is a basic comprehensive plan which furnishes the framework and substance within which these individual designs can be made.[10]

The principles he was examining in the Newark Plan of 1915 continued to occupy him, in which any decision affecting the growth and development of the city—annexations, subdivisions, location and design of public buildings, street extensions, rapid transit, and other franchises were to be guided by the comprehensive plan. In the 1920s, he would arrive at a formula for his "science of planning" which, with variations through time, established the parameters that comprehensive planning had previously missed, aided by burgeoning opportunities as a planning consultant for him to pursue his search.

The prefatory and shakedown phases of the practice came to an end with a series of reports in the 1920s. Out of this emerged a prototype report which in program and content would continue to be the measure of the firm's service to a city in preparing its comprehensive plan.[11] After the report's acknowledging preliminaries, it would present a several-page introduction on the "Principles of city planning," in effect a kind of goals statement which guided the planner in his work and the reader in understanding it. He had written similarly in previous reports, but in these later reports it stands more independently as a general statement of principles, a central rationale in the development of Bartholomew's interpretation of his work.

In contrast to the planning preoccupations of the 1970s, the span backward of fifty years permitted a more simplistic orientation: "City Planning is essentially concerned with the *physical* development of cities" (Bartholomew, 1924, p. 11). The "Principles" then list physical elements which "properly constitute the city plan," six in number: streets, transit, transportation (rail and water), public recreation, zoning, and civic art. (Housing had in earlier reports been included as an integral element, but in his consulting practice Bartholomew was finding that his clients would refuse to spend money for a housing survey.) "These are the physical elements which, when properly planned and correlated, make possible the creation of an attractive and orderly working organism out of the heterogeneous mass we now call the city" (Bartholomew, 1924).

The explanations follow lines already established by earlier work. Streets are main arterial thoroughfares "like the spokes of a wheel" with at least 100-foot rights-of-way, secondary (crosstown) thoroughfares (80- to 100-foot rights-of-way) spaced approximately one-half mile apart, and minor streets, chiefly for residential districts (50-foot rights-of-way). Supplementing these could be special service streets such as those serving industrial districts. Transit confines itself to route coordination with the street plan and population patterns. Under transportation the aim is to plan for rail terminal and route locations to expedite movements and serve industry with minimum friction between them and the other functions of the city. The section on recreation is also a restatement of ideas clarified in his earlier reports, a hierarchy of facilities using school plans where their location and offerings fit in with the comprehensive plan. Zoning follows in the planning, the ordinances based on typical use, height, area, and yard standards, all as part of the comprehensive city plan.

Closing with some rather elliptical attention to civic art, the "Principles" in their range and sequence established what the report would then examine in specific detail. Hence the methodology of the science was established, and the planner could now apply it step-by-step leading to planning proposals for the ultimate betterment of the community. Although an analytical framework, it was not a static one; without doing violence to the rationale, as the impact of changing forces such as the automobile and suburbanization became increasingly apparent, the "Principles" found their proper place within the science. Thus the firm became known for a reassuringly clear program of service—thorough, sound, and businesslike.

From scanning of contemporary evidence, whether the reports of other planners or the professional literature, while Bartholomew's comprehensive planning may not appear to be unique in its ideas and methods, it brought to the profession a refining of standards and a special sense of system and cohesiveness in which each step in the planning process assumed its logical place. In the Hubbards' national survey on planning and zoning (Hubbard and Hubbard, 1929), there is an implication that the systematism of Bartholomew's planning practice was if not the universal prescription of the profession then an admirable and respected criterion. The antecedents of his interest had emerged prior to his planning debut, but it was Bartholomew who was to formulate most rigorously the "capricious procedure" of planning into a "science." In the 1920s his work assumed a form and content which became recognizably his with its sense of professionalism and technical competence, a knowledgeability and clarified sequence of steps through which the planner took the commissioners in their search for an orderly and prosperous future of middle-class values as appropriate reflections of the type of clients and their ambitions. This was the portfolio of talents and techniques which, through the effectiveness of its methods and policies and its coast-to-coast applications, came to assume a kind of semiofficial stature within the practice.

URBAN LAND USE DATA

The 1920s may have been formative in shaping professional methodology, but the research base on which the work was constructed was notably insecure. In the 1930s, Bartholomew was to be central in developments leading to some repair of this weakness in his science. The firm's work had resulted in the accumulation of a considerable body of material on land uses in its contract cities, and Bartholomew realized that this represented a valuable resource from which to draw. Here were the means to make certain inferences of scale and ratio between the community and its areal needs for the various land use types, particularly helpful in zoning studies, and to bring a certain realism to the enthusiasm of planning commissions in their manipulation of local zoning ordinances. Bartholomew had discovered an interestingly constant ratio between amounts of developed land uses among cities of differing character, size, and location and mentioned this to Henry Hubbard. Hubbard saw that this material was sufficiently significant to call for its more general availability and suggested its preparation for publication as one of the Harvard City Planning Studies.[12] This resulted the following year in Bartholomew's *Urban Land Uses* (1932), a study of the actual amounts of land given over to the several land uses within the city limits of some twenty-two different cities of varying sizes and types, based on surveys the firm had made in them at various times.

The objectives of the book as stated in the preface (by the editors of the Harvard City Planning Series, Theodora K. Hubbard and Henry V. Hubbard), were to make generally available

a method for estimating the total area required for each particular urban use for any given future population of between

5,000 and 300,000 persons. In addition, it should aid municipalities confronted with the problem of determining the desirable extent of city area and the location of future boundaries, since the aggregation of amounts of land needed for each particular use will naturally determine how much peripheral land can economically be absorbed (Bartholomew, 1932 p. v).

This may sound oversimplified in light of present practices, but the place this book occupies in the development of the science of planning must be scaled against the vacuum of urban research then prevailing. By this contribution, Bartholomew was pioneering in a field untouched by any other such ventures, public or private, and the material he here presented would be a standard reference work, still cited as a source on the subject of land use areal ratios a decade later in *Local Planning Administration* (Segoe, 1941)—although by then with some reservations. Not until the latter part of the 1930s with the figures coming out of the Real Property Inventories of 1934–6 would there be any comparable additions to the body of research on the urban characteristics of American cities. The first census to include questions on housing on a nationwide scale was that of 1940. Thus urban research which had evolved out of the experience of Bartholomew's own practice and had come to serve him in it was made generally available to the profession and the public.

URBAN LAND POLICY AND RENEWAL

The opportunity that the 1930s presented Bartholomew "to consider and study fundamental problems" was uniquely met in his work on *Urban Land Policy* for the City Plan Commission of St. Louis. It was by this effort that research techniques were extended and major planning directions anticipated. It came about by the nature of the period: the Depression-induced lethargy of professional activities, assistance from federal work programs, a background of years of planning activities in St. Louis, the city's need for area redevelopment, and the typical Bartholomew pragmatism which recognized that he could make his program against slums and blight more meaningful to the community and its leaders if he could give it a dollars-and-cents dimension. What were "the true costs to the community of slum areas?" The group he assembled consisted of St. Louis Plan Commission staff, some of the "married employees of the largest St. Louis architectural offices with little other active work," and a number of technicians whose employment was supported by the Works Progress Administration (WPA). The results were summarized in the publication of *Urban Land Policy* (City Plan Commission of St. Louis, 1936).

Bartholomew examined land use and population shifts in St. Louis from 1910 to 1935 and revealed the scale of some disturbing forces at work; he and his commission saw in its message the relationship of urban land policy to the city's social and economic future and hoped to convince the city administration of the situation's seriousness and the wisdom of their proposed policy. For the first time St. Louis measured urban trends, and it found to what an extent it was headed toward economic and social collapse as the center city lost population and property values, deterioration at the center moved farther and farther out, and population abandoned the city's congestion for the suburbs.

The study also examined the record in terms of measured economics, an effort to determine the extent to which slums were costing the city money in dollar terms. It was a comparative analysis for 1930 through 1935 of municipal service costs against income for twenty different representative districts among the city's typical land use areas—downtown residential, midtown residential, newer residential, downtown business, industrial, and so on. From these figures, calculations were made which in summary demonstrated that St. Louis "slums" paid to the city only about 40 percent of what they received in costs of services, that "higher value residential districts" paid twice as much to the city as they received from it, the central business district two and a half times as much, and that the city as a whole annually was subsidizing its slum districts by $5,500,000.

The causes for this were in part planning's: excessive commercial and industrial zoning, declared the report. The ordinance had been designed when there had been no "scientific data" on actual area needs for land use types, but recent years had brought more knowledge of this relationship, including such a study for St. Louis (more WPA-financed urban research) comparing actual land uses against amounts of land zoned for those uses. Excessive areas zoned for commerce and industry not only often faced unlikely development as such but discouraged appropriate residential use and thereby drove additional population to the suburbs. Similar overzoning for apartments (Bartholomew states by 149 percent) encouraged speculative property development while single-family residential areas were insufficiently safeguarded by the existing ordinance. Such policies added up to speculative exploitation, gradual neglect, and eventual abandonment.

The urban land policy proposed in their place was multifaceted:

1. Revised zoning ordinance scaled to "known laws of supply and demand" with more protection to residential uses.
2. Enforcement of sanitation and fire laws.
3. Elimination of smoke nuisance.
4. Enactment of a minimum housing standards ordinance.
5. Rehabilitation of structures where advisable.
6. Removal of unsafe, obsolete, and unfit structures.
7. Development of neighborhood units embracing all residential areas in the city for the improvement of the environment and elimination of nonconforming uses.
8. Construction of low-cost housing "in the older sections of the city."
9. Enforcement of building codes (City Plan Commission of St. Louis, 1936, pp. 21, 23).

Also proposed was action toward encouraging rehabilitation and conservation programs in residential neighborhoods not yet requiring more drastic measures: rezoning as necessary; home maintenance; surveys for park, playground, and other community needs; code enforcement; deed restrictions; and the power to organize protective and improvement associations. This section was accompanied by a map organizing the city into "suggested neighborhood district boundaries." The policy statement closed by advocating passage of enabling legislation for the formation of a local housing authority to undertake reconstruction in neighborhoods requiring large-scale renewal and to accept federal grants for construction of low-cost housing for those income groups whose housing needs could not otherwise be provided.

What one reads in this report is an anticipation of the urban renewal program of the 1950s and 1960s. With other cities working along similar lines, this research work of Bartholomew and his St. Louis staff would help move public opinion and national legislation toward placing federal and local governments in a new relationship with the forces responsible for urban environment. The subsequent U.S. Housing Act of 1937 with its commitment of federal money to the support of improved housing opportunities testified to the effectiveness of their message and is of course the antecedent of present-day federal involvement in urban concerns.

Housing Policy

The matter of housing and responsibility for providing it in reasonable amounts based on decent standards had been an early area of Bartholomew's concerns, and one that in the 1930s was to resume its position in his priorities. The spirit of the 1930s was conducive to the social implications of a positive housing policy, and its possibilities for both work-producing activity and the satisfaction of human needs were obvious to the Roosevelt administration. The previous administration had also made some effort to stimulate housing construction through the Reconstruction Finance Corporation. Even by 1933, however, a pattern was emerging with which Bartholomew could not agree. This was what appeared to him to be housing officials' disinclination to think in terms broader than the immediate project instead of "comprehensively."

At the twenty-fifth National Conference on City Planning in Baltimore in October 1933, he read a paper which he hoped would bring housing into the larger planning scene. Entitled "Technical problems in slum clearance" (Bartholomew, 1933, pp. 121–30), he sought to tie together the rebuilding and preservation of the city and discourage decentralization with housing as one phase of the total urban plan of action: reconstruction of slums would be meaningless unless linked with a broader plan of action getting at the heart of urban decay. Thus he indicated that the nation's housing program could not be separate from the larger planning scheme but must be intimately associated with it to succeed, reaffirming again his anticipation of the present-day renewal program. Coupled with limitations imposed on city size and standards of design excellence for the new residential environments, housing could hope to become meaningfully comprehensive for its own sake and that of the city and the public as investor. Bartholomew subsequently observed that his paper was not a critical success among the new housing officialdom, but eventually, through his membership on the national Slum Clearance Advisory Committee, his ideas helped shape the original Housing Act of 1937 and later that of 1949.[13]

OTHER CONTRIBUTIONS

Other facets of precedent for the profession come to mind: the approach of the firm's design team to its office and work production (as early as 1919); capital improvement programming backed by passage of successive supporting bond issues (St. Louis beginning in 1923); and the incorporation of planned unit developments as standard zoning recommendations (from 1939). In all this Harland Bartholomew was central, and "while he would be the first to share any credit with people that worked with him, he is the one that was responsible."[14] Reviewing the output of that responsibility and noting the ranking of the firm in these formative years for planning, one comes to understand something of the nature of American planning policy through the years between the two world wars and even into the 1950s.

Since then, quite different forces have been at work, revolutionizing in their effects on our cities and on the profession so directly charged with working with them. Seen from our present kaleidoscopic urban scene, this look backward may have a deceptively simplistic projection. Suitable, then, is a reminder that the crises of those days—expansionism, depression, experimentation, and initial postwar fragmentation—and Bartholomew's participation in them had their own sense of immediacy and urgency. When practitioners and precedents were few and techniques were largely intuitive, his work helped to define and clarify the planning process; when most universities failed to include planning education among their curriculums, his firm not only acted as a training center but encouraged the placing of its "graduates" throughout the country; when the basis of planning decision was made on the sketchiest of researched understanding, his investigations helped bring dimension to and clarify the American urban phenomenon; when legal concepts and tools were still rudimentary, his concerns and discoveries helped evolve them. These were no doubt some of the thoughts of the Board of Governors of the AIP when in 1955 they awarded to Harland Bartholomew the Institute's Distinguished Service Award with the following citation:

Pioneer in the science and art of city planning, educator, public servant; through the practice of his profession he brought his skills and his understanding to the service of the people of our cities from coast to coast; his contributions in teaching and research, as well as in his practice, have helped to form standards of the profession of city planning.

NOTES

1. See "An appreciation," *AIP Newsletter* (August 1962), pp. 9–11.
2. Letter from Harland Bartholomew to the author, April 9, 1952.
3. His firm, Harland Bartholomew and Associates, continues, currently with seven offices, a staff of 150, and a wide variety of planning and engineering activities. Bartholomew retired from active participation in the firm in the 1960s, though remaining in an advisory and consulting capacity.
4. He remained on a half-time basis as the city planning engineer until 1950 and as a consultant for four more years.
5. U.S. census figures nearest to report date.
6. If one adds the 1917 *Problems of St. Louis*, a comprehensive plan report for that city published under Bartholomew's direction by the St. Louis Plan Commission, this population figure increases to 2,601,468.
7. Interview with Karl B. Lohmann, August 19, 1961.
8. Interview with Harland Bartholomew, April 23, 1960.
9. Interview with Karl B. Lohmann, August 19, 1961.
10. Letter from Harland Bartholomew, November 30, 1961.
11. His reports for Memphis (1924), Kenosha (1925), and Des Moines (1928) are typical.
12. Letter from Harland Bartholomew, July 15, 1963.
13. Interviews with Harland Bartholomew, June 14, 1960, and July 13, 1961, and with Eldridge Lovelace, July 25, 1961.
14. Letter from Eldridge Lovelace, February 22, 1971.

REFERENCES

Adams, Frederick J. (1954) *Urban Planning Education in the United States*, Cincinnati, Ohio, Alfred Bettman Foundation.

Adams, Thomas (1936) *Outline of Town and City Planning*, New York, Russell Sage Foundation.

Bartholomew, Harland (1924) *Memphis Plan.*

———— (1932) *Urban Land Uses*, Cambridge, Massachusetts, Harvard University Press. This book has been revised and reissued under his authorship in 1955 as *Land Uses in American Cities*, Cambridge, Massachusetts, Harvard University Press.

———— (1933) "Technical problems in slum clearance," *Planning and National Recovery: Planning Problems Presented at the 25th National Conference on City Planning*, Philadelphia, Pennsylvania, William F. Fell.

City Plan Commission of St. Louis (1936) *Urban Land Policy* (October).

Hubbard, Henry V., and Hubbard, Theodora K. (1929) *Our Cities To-Day and To-Morrow*, Cambridge, Massachusetts, Harvard University Press.

Lohmann, Karl B. (1931) *Principles of City Planning*, New York and London, McGraw-Hill.

Newark City Plan Commission (1911) *The City Plan Commission*, Newark.

Nolen, John (1927) "Twenty years of city planning progress in the United States," in *Planning Problems in Town, City and Region*, Philadelphia, National Conference on City Planning.

Segoe, Ladislas, ed. (June 1941) *Local Planning Administration*, Chicago, International City Managers' Association.

10

Henry Wright
1878–1936

HENRY CHURCHILL

HE WAS A NICE MAN TO KNOW. He knew what he knew, but he would take great pains to tell it to you. If, as sometimes happened, you knew something too, he would listen; and if, as sometimes happened, what he learned from you upset something he had thought before he learned it, he did not get mad. He would revise what he had thought he knew to what he now knew.

It was this spirit of inquiry, this lack of dogma, that gave Henry Wright his place of importance among the pioneer "planners." There was no arrogance about him, but he could be obstinate. His continual search for something better, his refusal to compromise, made it difficult for him to work with clients. He worked best in a group, and he was fortunate in that the group into which he was drawn was composed of similar talents, eager for the catalyzing properties of the minds of others.

Wright came from St. Louis. He was by training and practice a landscape architect, which meant that he planned subdivisions and did the grading, drainage, and road design as well as specified "plant materials." He later became an architect and a Fellow of the American Institute of Architects (AIA) although he did not "build" or practice in the accepted use of the term. I do not know when he got his degree, but Frederick Bigger, to whom Pittsburgh is so much

Reprinted with permission from Henry Churchill, "Henry Wright: 1878–1936," *Journal of the American Institute of Planners* 26, no. 4 (1960): 293–301.

The most valuable agricultural section of the state has been found in practice to be the area bounding the southern shores of lakes Ontario and Erie.

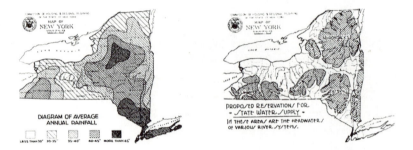

Restoration of forests throughout the headwaters of the rivers would cause a less rapid flow off of rain and melting snows, and thus a greater regularity in the volume of stream flow.

FIGURE 10.1   *A portfolio of maps by Henry Wright, selected from the* Report of the Commission of Housing and Regional Planning to Governor Alfred E. Smith, *May 7, 1926.*

indebted, thinks that he and Wright were at Penn at about the same time.

Frederick Bigger also recalls that Wright for a time was chairman of the AIA Committee on Community Planning. This committee was very active in stimulating the architects to an interest in community planning instead of brooding about the City Beautiful and great, big but no-little-plan Uncle Dan [Burnham]. Bigger followed Wright as chairman; Clarence Stein had also been chairman some time before. During the First World War Wright worked on war housing, and it was Robert D. Kohn of New York, who was in charge of the program, who induced him to come East and who introduced him to Clarence Stein.

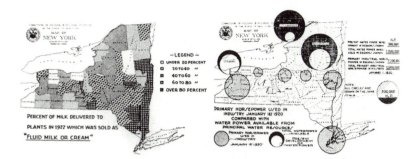

Surplus milk produced near New York City is sold as fluid milk; the surplus produced far from New York City is made into cheese.

This map shows a composite of areas that are generally favorable for more intensive agricultural development.

This map shows a composite of areas more suited for reforestation.

Stein was the main driving force of a group of men of diverse technical training and interests, whose common focal point of interest was the use of land. They called themselves the Regional Planning Association of America (RPAA). It had nothing to do with the Regional Plan Association of New York, a rich outfit that was (and still is) doing a splendid job of an entirely different kind. Several of the members of the RPAA were deeply immersed in the nascent Housing Movement; all stimulated and influenced each other's ideas. There was, for instance, Frederick L. Ackerman, who was associated as architect with Stein and Wright on Radburn and other jobs. He was a technocrat and a disciple of Thorstein Veblen, who was then teaching at the old New School for Social Research.

EPOCH I: Rapid development of natural resources; small towns economically independent; industry served by local water wheels and canal system; all widely distributed over state. Toward end of period drift to new rail lines had set in.

EPOCH II: Development of central rail routes, change of industry to steam power, and competition in agriculture of fertile west combine to concentrate growth in central valley belt and undermine the industrial prosperity of towns off main-line transportation.

EPOCH III: Comparable in importance with the railroad and the steam engine in determining the character of development in the second industrial epoch are the modern factors of the automobile, good road, and electric transmission line. These modern forces do not portend a return to the widely distributed development of the first epoch. Rather they will lend themselves to a more effective utilization of all the economic resources of the state and to the most favorable development of areas especially adapted to industry, agriculture, recreation, water supply, and forest reserve.

FIGURE 10.2.   *These three maps with the accompanying captions concluded the* Report of the Commission of Housing and Regional Planning to Governor Alfred E. Smith. *Chairman of the Commission was Clarence S. Stein. Maps were drawn by Henry Wright.*

Later he was a powerful force in shaping the policies of the New York City Housing Authority. There was Lewis Mumford, and there were others, economists and administrators. There was Benton MacKaye, who almost single-handed created the Appalachian Trail and who was a great assistance to Stein and Wright when they were developing the really remarkable first "comprehensive" study for a region— New York State—for the New York State Commission for Housing and Regional Planning under Governor Alfred E. Smith in 1926.[1] Stein was chairman.

This was the first study in the United States that took into account all the resources of a region: the agricultural land of varying kinds, the forests and wild areas, the watersheds and the grand drainage basins, the minerals and the power potentials, industry and the transportation and trade routes, the cities and the eventual distribution of people in the light of the rising new technical developments—electricity and the automobile. It is broad, it is beautifully presented as analysis, clear and simple as synthesis. This simplicity and clarity is perhaps its greatest virtue, the distillation of essentials from what must have been, as always, a vast amount of data. It is very short, only eighty-two pages octavo, but it says all that needs to be said to comprehend the basic resources and potentials of the state. The maps, which were Wright's particular contribution, tell the whole story: there are no tables, for none are needed. The succinct summation of what it is all about, with brilliant suggestions for the future, takes eleven pages of text and seven pages of maps. It is too bad that New York State never did anything constructive about it.

Stein and Wright were the perfect team, and they worked together so well that in the design aspects of their collaboration it is not possible to separate their work. Besides the State Regional Plan, Sunnyside, Radburn, and Chatham Village are their joint efforts. They would not have come into existence without Stein and his organizing ability, but development of the concepts and their physical form was due to collaboration. There were, of course, many others who shared in the work. It is all set down in meticulous detail and with due credit in Stein's *Toward New Towns for America*.[2]

What, then, was Wright's particular contribution to planning? There were several. Perhaps the most important was demonstrating that site planning, town planning, is a socioeconomic function which, in spite of—or because of—its multiple effects on what is now called the "structure" of a community, could not be considered as a mere mechanical process of laying out lots. That this idea had a long history in the Garden City and in Patrick Geddes and informed the teaching of Lewis Mumford is obvious; it goes back to Robert Owen and the Fourierists. But as practical and applied planning it was ignored in this country, and any reference to its sources was considered not even "socialism"—which would have been to take it seriously—but as just plain crackpot. What Henry did was to evolve a qualitative as well as quantitative analysis of land planning and house planning, considered as an unitary and indivisible process. He developed economic analysis to match, and to justify, social reform. Thus, by a process of indirection, he gave respectable status to "social values." All costs were included in his method: pavement, sidewalks, curbs, drains, water mains, sewers, laterals, grading, party versus nonparty walls, and the cost of corners, of maintenance, and of operation. Previously all costs had been gross, cubic-foot costs, and a breakdown of site costs was unknown. Money was lent solely on cubic content: the greater the cube the greater the loan—larger cubage meant more materials. Maintenance costs, except for heating, were not even considered.

He demonstrated not only that proper site layout combined with the proper type of house (or apartment) design could squeeze the waste out of the speculator's routine plats, but that at the same time the saved land could increase the value of the investment by increasing amenities—common open space, more pleasant gardens, safer and more accessible play space. This combination was consequently not only saving immediate dollars but also was an insurance against obsolescence.

This has now become so commonplace that it is taken for granted; indeed the statistical analysis is often so overdone by unimaginative bureaucrats as to be obstructive to new proposals. Yet there was a time when the only acceptable method of subdividing was to cut up the surveyor's standard block into standard lots for standard freestanding houses eight feet apart. That, said the developers, was what people wanted. (There were exceptions—there always are—but most of the exceptions were for high-priced dwellings in "restricted" subdivisions.) It was official doctrine, too, which then as now is automatically against innovation. Stein notes that at Sunnyside they had to fit the housing to the blocks because it was officially "impossible" to close a mapped street even if it dead-ended against a railroad. And it was only because Sunnyside was zoned "industrial" that it was possible to build it at all.

Wright helped the spread of the superblock idea by pointing out the economic absurdities of conventional zoning which prevented rational development of large-scale integrally designed projects by the insistence on platting "lots." (This absurdity still persists as a legal requirement for "for-sale" projects.) Tied up with superblock design were two other ideas which he considered essential: the row house as the most desirable as well as the most economic type of dwelling; and the facing of living rooms to the garden side of the block, with the service on the street. This latter twist too was stubbornly resisted; it was "not acceptable" to the consumer, according to real estate wisdom. This fight still goes on, even though it is now known how pleasant and private it is to live on the garden side, even though it saves money by eliminating the alley, even though the car is an added argument in favor of it.

These ideas were tried out over a period of years. Sunnyside was the first on any large scale. It was a rowhouse rental development on city land within the city pattern. Apartments followed, located in the same general area of the city, and other investors and archi-

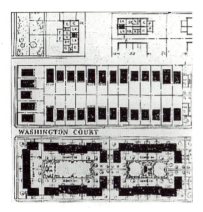

BELOW: Sunnyside plan utilizing shallow, attached, two-room-deep dwellings in both houses and flats. ABOVE: same building space as is usually wastefully arranged in free-standing, individual buildings. Typical building plans for each type also shown at top. The center park play space is about equal to the narrow side yards in upper plan.

FIGURE 10.3 *Contrasting Sunnyside with normal block plan.*

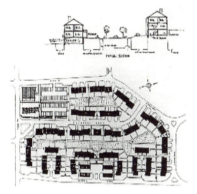

ABOVE: Shows how on upper side of streets, houses appear three-stories high with basement garages, while on opposite side, houses apparently two-stories high have basement sun rooms on rear, or garden, side. BELOW: Shows the general plan of unit of Chatham Village completed. Note interior park and walk system and streets with parking bays. Hatched portion shows late additions.

FIGURE 10.4 *Final Chatham Village plan; and cross section through hillside block at Chatham Village.*

tects—notably the Metropolitan Life Insurance Company—took up the basic formula also, thus gradually forcing acceptance by the official city departments and initiating changes in the zoning resolution.

Radburn followed. The story of the Town for the Motor Age has been well told too often to bear repeating. I want only to point out that Stein and Wright continually revisited what they had designed and from management and occupants learned what mistakes they had made and profited by what they learned.

Chatham Village, just outside of Pittsburgh, on a very difficult site, is perhaps the most distinguished of all Wright's designs. It still repays careful study for the way in which the adjustments of levels are handled, the parking and garaging provided for, the treatment of the open spaces, and the architectural embellishments. Ingham and Boyd, the architects, were sensitive and appreciative collaborators,

First unit (750 dwellings)
shaded.

FIGURE 10.5
Greenbrook,
"ultimate" plan.

not only in the landscape features but in the handling of rooflines and entrances.

During the Great Depression, Wright, Albert Mayer, and I were the team in charge of Greenbrook, the "Suburban Resettlement" town which was to have been built near New Brunswick, New Jersey. For various political reasons it was dropped from the program, just as plans were completed. What was interesting about it was that Wright did not repeat the Radburn plan. He used superblocks and carefully separated main traffic streets from secondaries, but there were fewer culs-de-sac, and the large interior block parks and particularly the walkways which, he felt, invaded privacy at Radburn were more carefully located. The overpasses and underpasses were omitted, too; schools and neighborhood shopping were accessible without crossing major streets. Yet the town was not "conventional"; there was great care to develop pedestrian courts, variety of grouping, arrangements of charm, and changes of pace.

Wright and Stein took infinite pains with the design of their

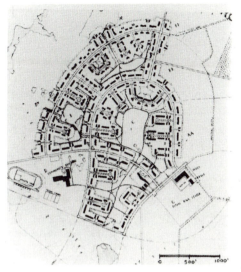

SITE PLANNER: Henry Wright.
ARCHITECTS: Henry S. Churchill
and Albert Mayer.

FIGURE 10.6   *Greenbrook,
first unit.*

sites. Henry had the most delicate feeling for contours; he could walk over a fifty-acre tract and go home and sketch its contours with uncanny accuracy. His objective was always to fit the houses and the roads to the land, to save trees, to achieve beauty and variety by the arrangement of buildings, by walls, steps, adjustments of the man-made elements to the land. He really loved it. He was fortunate in having Ralph Eberlin[3] as civil engineer for much of his (and Stein's) work. He was that rare anomaly, an engineer with a sensitive regard for land, trees, meadows, and even human beings.

In Wright's time "town planning" was recovering from the opprobrium of "the City Beautiful" but had not yet swung into the stultification of the City Statistical. It was a rather simple time, and the statistical approach used by Wright and others for proving something was also simple, limited to the direct use of verifiable data. *City* planning, as it is known today, was just starting to roll. There were not many planning commissions, and almost all of them were moribund. The Housing Movement had not yet become a Planning Movement, in fact "planning" was still a word of reproach. The speculative possibilities of zoning and eminent domain for the creation of unearned increment were not then understood by real estate manipulators. They were all too inclined to take such things at the face value virtuous planners innocently ascribed to them and to scream "socialism." Nor had the fantastic profits to be derived from borrowing-out—a practice in bad odor since the collapse of such institutions as S. W. Straus and Company during the Great Depression—which were latent in the Federal Housing Administration (FHA), been more than tentatively explored. The heat for guaranteed, effortless profits was not yet on, and the analytical theories of Henry Wright, and their resultant application to good subdivision design, were built into the manuals of FHA in its early days by such men as Miles Colean and E. Henry Klaber. No matter how low FHA has sunk since then, those basic principles left ineradicable traces.

As has been implied, Henry was a good teacher. For some years he had an informal summer school at his home in Mount Olive, New Jersey. This, unlike the school of the Greater Wright, was not exploitative. It was explorative, learnful, and his methods and ideas were spread by men and women who absorbed a method and later, almost unwittingly, applied it as their own. His "Town-planning Studio" at Columbia was a first step toward formal teaching of the subject, perhaps the first in a major university.

Another of his activities during the Depression was as a director, guide, and mentor of the Housing Study Guild. This had been started, almost informally, in the first days of unemployment, with the aid of private funds, by Albert Mayer, Lewis Mumford, Frederick L. Ackerman, and others. It was set up to do research in the field of housing. As the Great Depression deepened, it was taken over by the Works Progress Administration, and a considerable staff was assembled. Henry, as usual, provided not only guidance but inspiration.

When Henry died he was only fifty-eight, which is not old, but I always thought he was younger. The bibliography which accompanies these comments was put together for the U.S. Resettlement Administration by Benjamin M. Gruzen. His library, pamphlets, and notes were given to the Avery Memorial Architectural Library of Columbia University.

Wright's book, *Re-Housing Urban America*,[4] has fallen into unbecoming disuse, for it is one of the few primary textbooks we have on site and town design along with Stein's *Toward New Towns for America*, Frederick Gibberd's *Town Design*,[5] and E. Henry Klaber's *Housing Design*.[6] They are all by architects. The Wright and the Stein books must be taken together, the Then and the Now, for now, as then, the two men are necessary to each other.

Perhaps this may serve as a summary of Henry Wright's contribution to planning and its importance: "His contribution was pervasive and consequently cannot be measured; its importance is that of a quiet stream that makes a land rich."

A Chronological List of References Written by, in Collaboration with, or about Henry Wright, Compiled by Benjamin M. Gruzen

This list of references was prepared in the Library of the Division of Suburban Resettlement, U.S. Resettlement Administration, December 31, 1936.

1913

"Co-operative group planning; suburban development work of Henry Wright, architect and landscape architect," by David E. Tarn. (In the *Architectural Record*, New York City, vol. XXXIV, no. 5, November, pp. 467–75, photographs, plans, plats.) "It is with the hope of suggesting some basic principles that a most interesting study has been made by Henry Wright of St. Louis in his treatment of a new residential subdivision known as Brentmoor Park, St. Louis, Mo."

1915

"The economic side of city planning," by Henry Wright, landscape architect. Read before the Engineer's Club of St. Louis, January 6. (In the *Journal of the Association of Engineering Societies*, vol. 54, February, pp. 79–93, maps of St. Louis.)

1920

"Allotment and community planning," by Henry Wright, St. Louis. (In the *National Real Estate Journal*, Chicago, Illinois, vol. XXI, no. 2, January 19, pp. 15–20, photographs, plans, elevations.)

"Platting city areas for small homes," by Henry Wright, advisor in allotment and community planning, member of the Committee on Community Planning, AIA, assistant town planner in the housing developments of the Emergency Fleet Corporation during 1918–19.

Foreword by John Irwin Bright, chairman of the AIA's Committee on Community Planning. (In the Supplement to the *Journal of the American Institute of Architects*, August, 16 pp., floor and site plans.)

1921

"Architect's ideal home," by Henry Wright. (In *Good Housekeeping*, New York, vol. 72, June, pp. 64–5.)

"Shall we community plan?" by Henry Wright. (In the *Journal of the American Institute of Architects*, vol. IX, no. 10, October, pp. 320–24, site plans and elevations.)

1923

"Site planning practice," a review by Henry Wright of the book by F. Longstreth Thompson. (In the *Journal of the American Institute of Architects*, vol. XI, no. 10, October, pp. 405–7, illustrations from Thompson's book.)

"Preliminary study of a proposed garden community in the New York City region," by Alexander M. Bing, Henry Wright, and Clarence S. Stein, New York, n.p., 38 pp., typewritten, plans, charts.

1924

In "Testimony of Mr. Henry Wright." (In the New York Commission of Housing and Regional Planning. Tax exemption hearing; minutes. Wednesday, February 20, pp. 137–48, typewritten.)

"Town planning in England," a review by Henry Wright of *Town Planning and Town Development* by S. D. Adshead. (In the *Journal of the American Institute of Architects*, May, pp. 222–4, illustrations)

1925

"The road to good houses," by Henry Wright. (In the *Survey Graphic*, vol. 54, May, pp. 165–8, 189.)

"Testimony of Mr. Henry Wright." (In the New York State Department of Architecture, Commission of Housing and Regional Planning. Emergency rent law hearings; minutes. Friday, November 13, vol. 2, pp. 605–17, mimeographed.)

1926

"Vicious 'own-your-home' propaganda," an abstract of the report of the AIA's Committee on Community Planning, by Henry Wright, chairman of the committee. (In the *Journal of the American Institute of Architects*, vol. XIV, no. 1, January, pp. 35–6.) Acceptance of this report by the AIA Board of Directors is printed on page 134 of the March 1926 issue of the *Journal*.

"Home ideal versus reality," by Henry Wright. (In the *American Federationist*, vol. 33, January, pp. 65–9.)

"Lo! the poor one-family house," by Henry Wright. (In the *Journal of the American Institute of Architects*, vol. XIV, no. 3, March, pp. 118–21, diagrams.) This is found in a section called "Community planning," which also contains two short articles signed: Henry Wright, chairman.

"Housing: how much for how much?," by Henry Wright. (In the *Survey Midmonthly*, vol. 55, March 15, pp. 673–7.)

"The six-cylinder house with streamline body," by Henry Wright. (In the *Journal of the American Institute of Architects*, vol. XIV, no. 4, April, pp. 175–8, floor plans.)

"Studies of forces which have shaped the economic history of New York State." (In the New York Commission of Housing and Regional Planning; Clarence S. Stein, chairman. *Report to Governor Alfred E. Smith*, Albany, J. B. Lyon, May 7, 82 pp., charts and diagrams.) Henry Wright, active Planning Adviser.

"Regional planning in East Kent," a review by Henry Wright of the *East Kent Regional Planning Scheme* by Patrick Abercrombie and John Archibald. (In the *Journal of the American Institute of Architects*, vol. XIV, no. 5, May, pp. 224–6, 2 maps.)

"Cottage and tenement in the USA; some determining factors," by Henry Wright. (In the *International Housing and Town Planning Congress*, Vienna, 1926, Part One, pp. 261–73.)

"Report on the 1926 conference of the International federation for town and country planning and garden cities, Vienna," by Henry Wright, chairman of the AIA's Committee on Community Planning. (In the *Journal of the American Institute of Architects*, vol. XIV, no. 11, November, pp. 499–500.)

"Report of the committee on community planning," by Henry Wright, chairman. (In the *Journal of the American Institute of Architects*, vol. XIV, no. 12, December, p. 550.)

1927

"Primer of housing," by Arthur C. Holden in collaboration with Henry Wright and Clarence S. Stein, with a preface by William J. Tracy, New York, Workers Education Bureau Press, 48 pp., illustrations, charts. (Workers Education Bureau of America, Workers' Education Pamphlet Series no. 11.)

"Exploiting the land," by Henry Wright, chairman of the AIA's Committee on Community Planning. (In the *Journal of the American Institute of Architects*, vol. XV, no. 10, October, pp. 305–6.) This article tells a little of what was before the committee as a result of the resolution passed at the 60th Convention of the AIA and recorded on page 227 of the June 1927 (vol. XV, no. 6) issue of the *Journal*. The resolution ends as follows: "Resolved that the Institute, through its Committee on Community Planning, make special study of the problems of land development and regulation, and report its findings to the next convention."

1928

"For block playgrounds," by Henry Wright. (In *Playground*, vol. 21, January, p. 540.)

"Is the low cost house a myth?," by Henry Wright. (In the *National Conference of Social Work, Proceedings*, 1928, pp. 161–5.)

"Costs of utilities; basis of estimates for land studies at the Garden Suburb," 1928 data, one sheet, typewritten.

"Cul-de-sac streets effect marked economies," by Henry Wright.

1929

"The modern apartment house," by Henry Wright. (In the *Architectural Record*, March, pp. 213–45, illustrations.) Important article extending from pages 212 to 288.

"Planning a town for wholesale living," by Henry Wright. (In *Playground*, vol. 22, March, pp. 682–4.)

"Inner block playgrounds," by Henry Wright. (In *Playground*, vol. 23, July, pp. 257–9.)

"How to plan and build group housing," by Henry Wright. (In the *Building Developer*, vol. IV, no. 5, August, pp. 28–31, 58–62, plans, diagrams, charts.) Note: The text was delivered in the form of an address before the Subdividers' Division of the recent convention of the National Association of Real Estate Boards in Boston.

"Application of apartment house data to an actual layout," by Henry Wright. (In the *Architectural Record*, vol. 66, August, pp. 187–9, plans.)

"How to reduce the cost of land development," by Henry Wright. (In the *National Real Estate Journal*, Chicago, Illinois, vol. XXX, no. 18, September 2, pp. 17–22.) Second article appears in the September 30 issue.

"The Radburn plan; illustrating the public and private advantages of group building and planning," by Henry Wright, consulting architect, New York. (In the *National Real Estate Journal*, vol. XXX, no. 20, September 30, pp. 74–6, illustrations of a plan of Radburn, a cul-de-sac plan, and two house drawings.) Editor's Note: This is the second article to appear in the *Journal* based upon Wright's address before the Homebuilders' and Subdividers' Division of the National Association of Real Estate Boards at the Boston Convention. Wright was associated with Clarence S. Stein as a town planner for Radburn, New Jersey. (The first article appeared in the September 2 issue.)

"Wastefulness of gridiron street plan," by Henry Wright. (In the *National Real Estate Journal*, vol. XXX, no. 21, October 14, p. 24.) "Before" and "after" street plan and a paragraph of explanation.

"Some principles relating to the economics of land subdivision," a paper delivered at the November 1, 1929, meeting of the American City Planning Institute, by Henry Wright. (In the *American City Planning Institute, Paper*, New York, 1930, Series 1930, no. 1, pp. 1–20, plans.)

1930

"Picturesque architecture," by Henry Wright. (In the *Architectural Record*, vol. 67, no. 2, February, pp. 172–3.) Contains a photograph of Ruislip, England, housing.

"Place of the apartment in the modern community," by Henry Wright. (In the *Architectural Record*, vol. 67, March, pp. 207–38, illustrations.)

"Wanted: a substitute for the gridiron street system," by Henry Wright. (In the *American City*, vol. XLII, no. 3, March, pp. 87–9, street layouts, tables.) (Also May 1930, p. 100.)

"Autobiography of another idea," by Henry Wright. (Reprint from the *Western Architect*, September, 7 pp.)

"Can the architect promote more business?," by Henry Wright. (In the *Architectural Record*, vol. 68, October, pp. 288–90.)

1931

"The architect, the plan and the city," by Henry Wright. (Reprint from the *Architectural Forum*, February, pp. 217–23.)

"The apartment house—a review and a forecast," by Henry Wright. (In the *Architectural Record*, vol. 69, March, pp. 187–95.)

"Machine-made house," by Henry Wright. (In the *New Republic*, vol. 68, September 2, p. 76.)

"Summary and further development of 'A housing research' for the consideration of the Temporary Housing Commission of Illinois," by Henry Wright. No place of publication given, December 11, variously paged, typewritten.

"What does the architect know about small house costs?," by Henry Wright. (In the *Architectural Record*, vol. 70, December, pp. 431–4, tables, illustrations.)

1932

"Large-scale operations," by the Committee on Large-Scale Operations; Henry Wright, research secretary. (In the *President's Conference on Home Building and Home Ownership*, vol. III, Slums, large-scale housing and decentralization, pp. 66–142, illustrations.)

"Costs of housing," by Henry Wright. (In the *Architectural Forum*, March, pp. 299–305, tables.)

"How can apartment facilities be provided for the lower income groups?," by Henry Wright. (In the *Architectural Record*, vol. 71, March, pp. 147–56.) Portrait (Supplement 38).

"Comparative cost studies of new group dwellings," by Henry Wright. (In the *Architectural Record*, vol. 71, March, pp. 213–16, 44.)

"Re-search versus research," by Henry Wright. (In *Shelter*, May, p. 50.)

"Was weiss der Architekt von den Kosten des Kleinwohnhaus?," by Henry Wright. (In *Moderne Bauformen*, June, pp. 309–12.) This article was taken from the *Architectural Record* of December 1931, "What does the architect know about small house costs?," by Henry Wright. The American currency costs were changed into deutsche marks and the measurements into the metric system.

"The in-betweens of community planning," by Henry Wright. Mimeographed statement used for university students, 1932.

"Economics of site-planning and housing," prepared by the AIA Committee on Economics of Site-Planning and Housing; Frederick Bigger, chairman; F. L. Ackerman, G. F. Cordner, G. H. Gray, P. J. Horner, E. H. Klaber, C. W. Stedman, C. S. Stein, and Henry Wright. (In the *Architectural Record*, June, pp. 369–75.)

"A self-starter for the building industry; a search for a national housing type which will meet the average income and replace blighted areas. . . . A search for the simplest way to start profitable, non-competitive building activity," by Henry Wright. First article. (In *Building Investment*, vol. VII, no. 12, August, pp. 12–16, plans, photos.)

"To plan or not to plan," by Henry Wright. (In the *Survey Graphic*, vol. 68, October 1, pp. 468–9.)

"Hillside group housing," by Henry Wright and his Summer School students. (In the *Architectural Record*, October, pp. 221–2.)

"City planning in relation to the housing problem," by Henry Wright, architect and city planner, New York City. (In the *National Conference on City Planning. Planning Problems of Town, City and Region*, twenty-fourth conference, Pittsburgh, Pennsylvania, November 14–16, 1932, pp. 17–22.)

"The architect and small house costs," by Henry Wright. (In the *Architectural Record*, vol. 72, December, pp. 389–94, illustrations.)

"To plan or not to plan," by Henry Wright. (In *Die Neue Stadt*, Frankfurt am Main, Germany, December, pp. 194–5.) Reprinted in German from the *Survey Graphic* of October 1, 1932, with an English summary.

1933

"Servicing apartments for lower rentals," by Henry Wright. (In the *Architectural Record*, vol. 73, March, pp. 223–9, illustrations, plates.)

"The sad story of American housing," by Henry Wright. (Reprinted from *Architecture*, March, pp. 123–30, illustrations.)

"Are we ready for an American housing advance?," by Henry Wright. (Reprint from *Architecture*, June, pp. 309–16, illustrations.)

"A national housing and rehabilitation policy," preliminary report of the AIA's Committee on Economics of Site-Planning and Housing. (In the *Octagon*, vol. 5, no. 7, July, pp. 8–10.) Committee signed as follows: F. L. Ackerman, G. F. Cordner, Detroit; G. H. Gray, New Haven; P. J. Hoener, St. Louis; R. D. Kohn, New York; E. F. Lawrence, Portland, Oregon; W. S. Parker, Boston; C. W. Stedman, Cleveland; C. S. Stein, New York; Henry Wright, New York; E. H. Klaber, chairman, Chicago.

"Remarks by Mr. Henry Wright." (In the National Conference on Slum Clearance, *Proceedings*, Cleveland, Ohio, July 6 and 7, pp. 105-7.)

"Housing—Where, when, and how?," by Henry Wright. Part I. (In *Architecture*, July, pp. 1-32, illustrations.)

"Housing—Why, when and how?," by Henry Wright. Part II. (In *Architecture*, August, pp. 79-110, illustrations.)

"Sinking slums," by Henry Wright. (In the *Survey Graphic*, vol. 22, August, pp. 417-19.)

"Planning and financing of low cost housing," by Henry Wright. (In the National Conference on Low Cost Housing, Proceedings of October 25, 26, and 27, pp. 3-7.

"Cost analyses of Cleveland and Indianapolis plans," by Henry Wright and his Housing Laboratory group. New York City, n. pub., 1933, unpaged, manuscript report, blueprints, and schedules.

1934

"New homes for a new deal." "I. Slum clearance—but how?," by Albert Mayer. "II. Abolishing slums forever," by Henry Wright. "III. The shortage of dwellings and direction," by Lewis Mumford. "IV. A concrete program," by Albert Mayer, Henry Wright, and Lewis Mumford. (Reprinted from the *New Republic*, vol. 78, February 14, 21, and 28 and March 7.)

"A study of a regional area comprising 488 acres in Astoria-Queens, New York City," by Carol Aronovici, Henry S. Churchill, William E. Lescaze, Albert Mayer, Henry Wright, and associates. Drawings by Charles K. Agle. March-April 1934, 27 pp., plates. The plates and a short article were also printed in the *Architectural Forum*, July, pp. 49-55, under the title of "Realistic replanning."

"The New Housing problem in the large city," by Henry Wright. (In *America Can't Have Housing*, Carol Aronovici, editor, New York, published for the committee on the housing exhibition by the Museum of Modern Art, c. 1934, pp 63-5.

"Housing conditions in relation to scientific machine production," by Henry Wright. (Reprint from the *Journal of the Franklin Institute*, October, pp. 485–98.)

"A housing problem for the United States," a report prepared for the National Association of Housing Officials by Sir Raymond Unwin, Ernst Kahn, Alice M. Samuel, Henry Wright, Ernest J. Bohn, and Coleman Woodbury. Chicago, Public Administration Service, 1935, 42 pp. (Public Administration Service Publication no. 48.) The "Summary of a housing program for the United States"— herein printed as an appendix—was also printed earlier (November 1934) as a twenty-two-page pamphlet.

1935

"Housing and education," by Henry Wright. (In the *Housing Study Bulletin No. 6*, March, pp. 1–2.)

"Housing and the FHA," by Henry Wright. (In the *Housing Study Bulletin No. 7*, May, pp. 4–6.)

"Preliminary report on Hamilton Heights," by the Town Planning Studio, School of Architecture, Columbia University. Henry Wright in charge. Henry S. Churchill, Assistant. (In the *Studio*, New York City, May, 24 pp., charts, tables, maps, plans.)

Rehousing Urban America, by Henry Wright, New York, Columbia University Press, 173 pp. (including plans). Two representative reviews of the above book follow: "No mere facial uplift can cure the wrinkles of our cities," by Henry S. Churchill. (In the *American City*, June, pp. 55–6.) "Rehousing urban America," by Albert Mayer. (In *Architecture*, July, pp. 29–32.)

1936

"Henry Wright," by Coleman Woodbury. (In *National Association of Housing Officials Bulletin No. 93*, 850 East 58th Street, Chicago, Illinois, July 17, 2 pp., mimeographed.)

"The passing of Henry Wright," an editorial. (In *The Nation*, 20 Vesey Street, New York City, vol. 143, July 18, p. 59).

"An editorial on the death of Henry Wright." (In the *New Republic*, 40 East 49th Street, New York City, vol. 87, July 22, pp. 308–9.)

"Henry Wright," by Lewis Mumford. (In the *New Republic*, vol. 87, July 29, pp. 348–50.)

"Necrology—Henry Wright." (In the *American Society of Planning Officials News Letter*, vol. 2, no. 7, July, p. 51.)

"Deaths . . . Henry Wright." (In the *Architectural Forum*, August, p. 56, p. 58 photograph). "A challenge to the younger men in the planning profession," by Flavel Shurtleff. (In the *American City*, August, p. 64.) "The roll [of those who have died] is too long for the comparatively short span of the planning movement, and the death of these leaders has placed a heavy responsibility on the profession at a critical time when there is a great need for counsel."

"Henry Wright, town-planner, dies suddenly." (In the *Architectural Record*, vol. 80, August, p. 83, photograph.)

"Obituary." (In the *American Magazine of Art*, vol. 29, August, p. 540.)

"Henry Wright . . . 1878–1936," by Clarence S. Stein. (In the *American Architect and Architecture*, August, pp. 23–4, photograph.)

"Site planning and sunlight as developed by Henry Wright." (In the *American Architect and Architecture*, August, pp. 19–22, illustrations.) Sunlight control on a scientific basis now affects both site planning and architectural form according to studies carried on in the late Henry Wright's Town Planning Studio at Columbia University. This article is illustrated with the work of two of Wright's students. Photographs by Henry Niccolls Wright.

"Henry Wright, site planner of Village, is taken by death; outstanding career as pioneer in housing and town planning left rich heritage." (In the *Chatham Village News*, Pittsburgh, Pennsylvania, vol. V, no. 3, August 29, p. 2.)

"Henry Wright: creative planner," by Albert Mayer. (In the *Survey Graphic*, vol. 25, September, p. 530, portrait.)

NOTES

1. *Report of the Commission of Housing and Regional Planning to Governor Alfred E. Smith*, Albany, J. B. Lyon, 1926. "The Committee on the Plan of New York and Its Environs" was established by the Russell Sage Foundation in 1922 with Frederick A. Delano as chairman. The "environs" were a fifty-mile radius from New York City. "The Niagara Frontier Planning Board," covering some 1,550 square miles, turned in a report in 1925.
2. New York, Reinhold Publishing, 1957.
3. Ralph Eberlin once said in a conference to another engineer who purportedly was saving money by redesigning something: "If you'd designed it right in the first place there wouldn't be anything to save." As Colonel

Eberlin he had a very large part in the building of the Burma Road. This note is just to point out a characteristic of this group of collaborators—they were *really* tough but they were not ashamed to be sensitive and they strove for perfection.

4. New York, Columbia University Press, 1935.
5. London, Architectural Press, 1953.
6. New York, Reinhold Publishing, 1954.

11

Lewis Mumford, Benton MacKaye, and the Regional Vision

JOHN L. THOMAS

I

In May 1925 the International Town, City, Regional Planning and Garden Cities Congress met in the ballroom of the Hotel Pennsylvania at the corner of 32nd Street and Seventh Avenue in New York City. The selection of the site in midtown Manhattan was a fitting symbol of the mood of the dominant American wing of the postwar urban planning movement, confident of success and eager to present the preliminary findings of their already well-publicized report. The "Regional Plan of New York and Its Environs," financed by the Russell Sage Foundation and compiled under the scrutiny of the internationally recognized urban planner, Thomas Adams, would eventually be published in two volumes— *The Graphic Regional Plan* in 1929 and *The Building of the City* two years later—but already the New York group hoped to impress their colleagues from abroad as well as at home with their new model of what Adams called the "city efficient." Adams, who had been appointed General Director of Plans and Surveys three years earlier, was a highly respected veteran

From *Lewis Mumford: Public Intellectual*, ed. Thomas P. Hughes and Agatha C. Hughes (New York: Oxford University Press, 1990). Copyright © 1990 by Oxford University Press, Inc. Reprinted by permission.

of British and Canadian urban planning who brought to the New York project a hard-headed Scotch utilitarianism summarized in his promise, worthy of Bentham himself, "to so direct urban growth in the future that the greatest practicable measure of health, safety, convenience and general welfare will be secured for the inhabitants."[1] For New York City that promise meant, first of all, acceptance of a projected population of twenty-one million by 1965 and of the resultant need for some plan of "recentralization" to secure "the benefits of concentration without congestion." It also spelled more skyscrapers and highways.

The progressive regional planning movement in the United States dated from the turn of the century, and after a brief interruption during the First World War, had acquired renewed momentum by the mid-1920s. Signs of revived interest in managing metropolitan growth could be seen in Philadelphia's new Tri-State District, Chicago's Regional Planning Association, and stirrings in Los Angeles as well as in Thomas Adams's massive planning project for New York City and environs. Progressive planning rested on the twin assumptions of irreversible urban concentration and the urgent need for citizen enlightenment in the hope of fostering "a passion for improvement," as Adams himself explained. Yet improvement frequently deduced to accommodation to rapid growth of the central city and schemes for zoning reform and projects for slum clearance undertaken for reasons of profit as well as philanthropy. Such genuine decentralization as Adams and his planning staff were willing to consider involved make-shift attempts to relieve congestion in the center city by suburbanizing its surrounding areas and linking them to Manhattan with a modernized system of transportation. The vision of New York City as organically linked to a larger regional social and economic context somehow eluded them.

The Adams group's vision of a metropolis renovated along purely pragmatic lines could be read clearly in their Diagrammatic Scheme for Regional Highway Routes, a series of concentric arcs rippling from an inner beltway around the five boroughs out to the periphery running from Bridgeport to Newburgh to Far Hills to Asbury Park. The philosophy underlying their visualization the New York planners stated with disarming candor: admitting that "we cannot overcome the economic forces that make cities as large as New York," they recognized no danger lurking in megalopolis and believed devoutly in their ability "to plan for that which is good and sound and practical." "There is nothing to be gained by conceiving the impossible," Adams warned as though anticipating an attack on his pragmatic achievements.

That assault had already been mounted by the vanguard of a Spenglerian "Barbarian Invasion" from up the Hudson comprised of Lewis Mumford, Benton MacKaye, Clarence Stein, Henry Wright, and a handful of followers recruited from the ranks of the Regional Planning Association of America and presently encamped across the lobby of the Hotel Pennsylvania with their own battle plans and maps. The Regional Planning Association of America had been formed two years earlier at a gathering of friends at Hudson Guild Farm in Mount Olive, New Jersey, in the foothills of the Poconos. The group of some ten or a dozen architects and planners had acquired experience during the war in planning demonstration garden cities modeled on Ebenezer Howard's alternative to the "dinosaur cities" to which Thomas Adams and his metropolitanists had seemingly become captive. Mumford and MacKaye, who headed the regionalist forces, had prepared their own strategic campaign in advance in a special edition for May 1925 of the *Survey Graphic* calling for a "fourth migration" out of the city and into its regional surroundings. They were also ready to denounce the Adams plan as "nothing bolder . . . than an orderly dilution of New York over a fifty mile circle." Even the title of their official report was a misnomer. True regional planning, Mumford scoffed, was not "just a technique" or the concern of a single profession but "a mode of thinking and a method of procedure." To attack the problem as primarily a matter of housing was to begin at the wrong end. The inevitable results of such faulty logic would be an increase in real estate speculation, a massing of outsized Manhattan towers, overcrowding, and impenetrable commercial zones. Adams and his staff, Mumford complained, had surrendered to the very forces that had produced the urban chaos they now sought to remedy. Their plan was being drafted simply to meet the needs and prejudices of America's corporate rulers, and "its aim from the beginning was as much welfare and amenity as could be obtained without altering any of the political or business institutions which have made the city precisely what it is." A genuine regional plan pointed toward

> the reinvigoration and rehabilitation of whole regions so that the products of culture and civilization, instead of being

confined to a prosperous minority in the congested centers shall be available to everyone at every point in a region where the physical basis for the cultivated life can be laid down.[2]

To illustrate their alternative proposal the regionalists countered with a "visualization" of their own—a simple map of the entire state of New York divided into three areas: *Plains* stretching up the Hudson and out into the Mohawk Valley and filled with market gardens and orchards, small factories and medium-sized cities; *Plateau* as table-land for dairy and subsistence farming; and *Highlands* with their forest and water reserves. Together these natural features comprised a relief model of the "valley section" defined by the Scotch urban planner Patrick Geddes—a topographical dish rising from regional cities and rich staple-crop bottomlands up the sides to small farms and diversified agriculture through pastoral slopes to wilderness along the rim. With the valley section as his organizing concept, Mumford proposed the regional dispersal of people and their economy in a planned migration out of New York. "For a hundred years in America," he explained, "business has been concentrating financial resources, concentrating factories and urban districts, attempting to create material prosperity by producing goods which could be quickly 'turned over.'" Now a new industrial revolution was in the process of spreading real income by decentralizing industry and propelling people out of the city and into its supporting environs. This dispersal was Mumford's version of the "fourth migration": an exodus from the metropolis.

In fashioning his own indictment of the Adams plan Mumford's new friend MacKaye agreed that the metropolis "brings its own chaos" from which Americans must escape in a "new exploration" of the valley section from the river's mouth back through the flow to the source. Only by surveying the entire configuration from a vantage-point high on the wilderness ridges, MacKaye insisted, could the planner discern the natural framework in which cities like New York must take their subordinate place. In summing up for his colleagues at the convention his charges against the metropolitanists, Mumford began at the other end of the valley section, in the city itself and the need to lift from it "some of the burden of the business overhead and sales-promotion, ground rents in congested districts and so forth."[3] The appearance of the forty-six-year-old MacKaye and of Mumford sixteen years his junior marching at the head of their self-styled "Barbarian Invasion" marked the convergence of careers but also of vantage-points. Their differing perspectives on the city and the region reduced ultimately to Mumford's view of Manhattan from the massive piers of Brooklyn Bridge and MacKaye's outlook from Hunting Hill across the watershed of the Nashua River in Shirley Center, Massachusetts.

II

MacKaye's outlook in 1925, as it had been in childhood over three decades earlier, was Hunting Hill, a rock cropping only 542 feet high but affording a full sweep of the surrounding countryside. To the southeast flowed Mulpus Brook to join the Nashua River. Beyond the ridge and above its hardwoods rose a white spire identifying Shirley Center and the three-cornered green hard by the MacKaye farmhouse. North lay the Whitman River, along its banks the railroad bringing lumber and staples east to Boston and carrying manufactures back to the Berkshires and beyond. From this familiar elevation, which an adolescent MacKaye properly termed a "drum-lin," he could watch what he came to define as two types of "flow"— the natural downstream pitch of the water course to Boston Harbor and the Gulf of Maine and the man-made "molten framework of industry" pouring westward along the railroad in finger-like projections up the same rivers back to the source.

MacKaye had come to Shirley Center as a boy of nine in 1888 from the frenzied theatrical world of Broadway, where his father, Steele MacKaye, the well-known actor, playwright, and producer, staged great "dramas" for his audiences on "the meaning of their country."[4] After a chaotic early childhood in a crowded New York apartment, the farmhouse in Shirley Center offered the young MacKaye feelings of continuity and deep contentment. "MacKaye Cottage," as the neighbors always called it, was a small white clapboard house set in the middle of a shaded yard which looked out on hay meadows and hardwood groves. The center of the village was the nearby common, a triangular green dominated by the meeting-house and belfry which the boy saw as the sun in the center of his universe. Across the river through thick growths of alder ran the Nashua River in a setting which Thoreau had revealed half-a-century earlier.[5]

Mumford once described the mature MacKaye as "a man built

to the measure of a Natty Bumppo, or an Emerson, or Uncle Sam without whiskers, with a touch of the Indian, or more likely the Highland Scot in his saturnine features." The man whom Mumford met and befriended in the 1920s was big-boned, hard-muscled, trim and compact with a prominent Roman nose set between high cheekbones beneath overarching brow and high forehead rising to a shock of coarse black hair. MacKaye claimed to have received two quite different educations. "I graduated from Longley's barnyard in 1893 and from Harvard in 1900," he explained in memorializing his next-door neighbor, Melvin Longley, dairyman, surrogate father, town selectman and state legislator—altogether the embodiment of "a culture and a mode of government." This rural New England culture became MacKaye's ideal, a way of life still buffered by the woods and fields west of Concord from metropolitan Boston which was already spilling across nineteenth-century suburban dikes. "The basic geographic unit of organic human society," MacKaye later argued, "is the single town of definite physical limits," a way-station between Boston and the wilderness at the end of the state.

The seventeen-year-old MacKaye entered Harvard in 1896 and quickly turned to geology and geography as the academic equivalent of a perch on the top of Hunting Hill. These two fields in the golden years of academic reform under President Charles Eliot were the domains of Nathaniel Southgate Shaler, an immensely popular teacher and author of numerous works on geology and topics of general social interest, and William Morris Davis. MacKaye vividly remembered his first day in Davis's *Geography A* which he gave in a packed lecture-hall in the Agassiz Museum. Standing immobile on the platform, his hands behind him, Morris suddenly produced a six-inch globe, gave it a spin, and held it aloft as he intoned: "Gentlemen, here is the subject of our study—this planet, its lands, waters, atmosphere, and life; the abode of plant, animal, and man— *the earth as a habitable globe.*" Shaler and Morris helped focus MacKaye's attention on the idea of *process,* both natural and conceptual, as a *drama* of man's interaction with nature in a reflexive relationship which their student would come to call "flow"—the making of patterns on the land through the transit of people and their goods across it.[6]

The idea for a long-distance trail running the length of the Appalachian chain which MacKaye spent a lifetime realizing came out of early first-hand contact with wilderness, beginning with hikes with an older brother "when he a Big Boy and I a little returned home fishless or gameless but having 'bagged' the one thing—a pursuit at nature's sources—that we were really after." In the summer of 1897 together with three companions he spent six gruelling weeks backpacking in New Hampshire on the "toughest and greatest trip" of his life. Here in dense forests or mountainous terrain was the evening campfire that he would turn into an emblem of wilderness complete with story-telling and harmonica-playing, at both of which he excelled. Again six years later in the deep woods above Keene, having graduated from Harvard but still searching for a vocation, he met naturalist and conservation pioneer Raphael Zon—"friend, philosopher, and patron saint"—who urged him to find himself by becoming a forester. MacKaye received a master's degree in forestry from Harvard in 1905, the year in which the feisty Gifford Pinchot took command of the United States Forest Service. Admitted to the "Chief's" domain, MacKaye was dispatched to New Hampshire, where he surveyed and mapped the forest cover of the White Mountains in relating it to the flow of the rivers of northern New England in a pioneer report which provided the technical data for establishing the White Mountain National Forest.

In 1913, MacKaye returned to Washington. Woodrow Wilson's Washington in the years before the outbreak of World War I was a clearinghouse for new reform proposals and a collecting-point for bright young bureaucrats and publicists intent on implementing them. Not until two decades later did the city attract similar talent and dedication to reform. If the symbolic center of the New Deal was a plan for economic recovery, the yardstick of progressive Washington was *conservation* initiated and even managed by a partnership between government and big business, but ramifying through a growing public awareness everywhere in the country. MacKaye took a strong hand in drafting a series of legislative proposals for achieving conservationist goals, the first of them a bill, never passed, to develop and control timber, mining, and transportation in Alaska through the establishment of balanced "primary resource communities" planned, like the original models of John Wesley Powell for the Arid Region, as an alternative to the unregulated and destructive practices of the nineteenth century. Three years later a second of MacKaye's proposals—his National Colonization Bill—met a similar fate, and his vision of redeemed land in the Lake States focusing on the small community modeled on his own Shirley Center went glimmering.[7]

Gradually MacKaye began adding a cultural dimension to his conservationist work. Forestry and watersheds concerned people's relations with primal nature. From then on he began to concentrate increasingly on the kind of community life and culture available to Americans on their land, concerns lying beyond questions of watercourses, cut-capacities, and timber-yields, and involving communal activity as well as individual "self-organization."

By 1920 it was clear that progressivism had stalled and that the regulatory and planning machinery of the war state was being dismantled rapidly. "Washington went down like a circus tent," MacKaye recalled. "Everything dropped. That was the beginning of normalcy right there."[8] There would be no conservation program forthcoming from the new Harding administration or from a suddenly laggard Congress. With little concrete to show for his ten-year education in conservation politics, MacKaye retreated to Shirley Center undismayed by the fact that he now had no job and few prospects of finding one. MacKaye was a man of extreme spartan habits who, like Thoreau, had pared his wants to the bone. Now he was free, after a decade of government service, to develop two ideas he had been holding in reserve for some time: a plan for a regional "folkland" of unspoiled nature along the ridges of the Appalachians; and looming behind it "a new social order the keynote of whose productive system shall be service—not profits."

Then suddenly, in 1921, MacKaye was struck by personal tragedy: his wife died. Shattered and depressed, he retreated on the invitation of the kindly Charles Whitaker, editor of the *Journal of the American Institute of Architects,* to his farm in Mount Olive in northwestern New Jersey to recover. There he made new friends who helped him regain his health and his equilibrium—the architect Clarence Stein, the landscape architect Henry Wright, and, most important, the young cultural critic and publicist Lewis Mumford. These colleagues formed the nucleus of the American Institute of Architects' recently formed Committee on Community Planning. Within two years all of them, together with a dozen or so other activists, would break off and form their own splinter organization, the Regional Planning Association of America. Whitaker promptly introduced MacKaye to his new circle, and in long weekend walks through the countryside or lively evening discussions around the fire they listened as the newcomer expounded his plan for a "folkland," a wilderness trail running the Appalachian ridge from Maine to Georgia. Mumford and his friends quickly realized that here was a man whose "visualizations," as he called them, embraced more than housing and urban planning, city parks, and slum clearance. MacKaye, they soon understood, was proposing to build a conceptual bridge between the conservation movement in which he had been trained and community planning with which they themselves had been almost exclusively concerned. Here, in short, was a highly original exploratory mind equipped with a forceful if somewhat wooden expository style which mixed Yankee colloquialisms and philosophical meditations in equal proportion but whose sense of regional planning as "a single thing" transcended their own.

MacKaye envisioned his trail as a network of interrelated systems—"a thing to grow and be developed apart from our more *commercial* development." He proposed the establishment of a connected series of wilderness "neutral zones" offering all citizens "equal opportunity for real life." In "An Appalachian Trail: A Project in Regional Planning," which appeared in the October 1921 issue of Whitaker's journal, MacKaye also conceived of the trail as a school— a place where "you look *at* in order to look *through,* where you look at a forest in order to perceive its pyramid and food cycle; where you view a landscape in order to perceive its water cycle." For such "visualizing" the vantage-point is all-important, just as his own had been as a young boy on the top of Hunting Hill. "Let us assume the existence of a giant standing high on the skyline along these mountain ridges, his head just scraping the floating clouds. What would he see from this skyline as he strode along its length from north to south?" Beginning at the summit of Mount Washington, MacKaye as explorer-guide in a "new exploration" points his pupils north to survey the heavily forested hunting-ground of the Indian; then west to the Berkshires and the Adirondacks; next to the "crowded east— a chain of smoky bee-hive cities extending from Boston to Washington, home to a third of the nation's population"; and finally south, down to the Southern Appalachians, the primal environment unchanged since the time of Daniel Boone and climaxing on the summit of Mount Mitchell.

Here stood revealed a "broad gauged enlightening approach" to the problems presented by industrial and commercial life: a way to

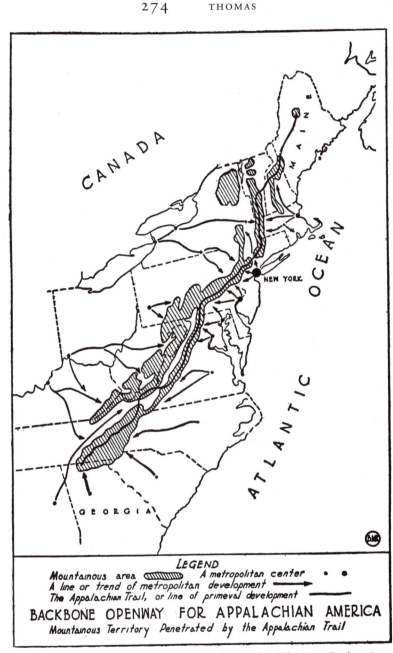

LEGEND

Mountainous area ⟨▨▨▨⟩   A metropolitan center • •
A line or trend of metropolitan development ➤
The Appalachian Trail, or line of primeval development ▬

BACKBONE OPENWAY FOR APPALACHIAN AMERICA
Mountainous Territory Penetrated by the Appalachian Trail

FIGURE II.I   *Benton MacKaye's directional lines: from* The New Exploration,
1962 edition.   His sketch of the Appalachian Trail.

FROM BENTON MACKAY, *THE NEW EXPLORATION: A PHILOSOPHY OF REGIONAL PLANNING.*
URBANA–CHAMPAIGN, IL: UNIVERSITY OF ILLINOIS PRESS. © 1928 BY HARCOURT, BRACE
AND COMPANY, INC. © 1956 BY BENTON MACKAY. © 1962 BY THE BOARD OF TRUSTEES OF
THE UNIVERSITY OF ILLINOIS. © 1990 BY CHRISTY MACKAY BARNES.

preserve "habitability" as a counter to the "grinding-down process of our modern life." Begin, MacKaye advised Mumford and his friends, by building a solid regional base for "a more extensive and systematic development of outdoor community life." Beneath the Appalachian ridge running like a backbone down the Atlantic littoral lay footlands ready for communal farms and recreation camps, the building of which would call forth "the primal instincts of a fighting heroism, of volunteer service, and of working in a common cause." Above these base-camp communities, in MacKaye's "vision," looms the Trail itself, "a path of exploration . . . leading to the physical mysteries of the land and sky inhabited by a primal life dating from the verdant slime on the first pools of water." Just here, he announced, was "something to be dramatized . . . the primal story of Planet Earth—its life, its structure, and its oneness." Then suddenly, as though catching himself before he soared off into mystical realms, he returned to the practical world of the architect and planner. "It is a project in housing and community architecture," he reminded his readers.[9]

MacKaye's vision also proved to him the indispensability of local initiative and popular participation in building the Trail in the spirit of old-time barn-raisings and corn-huskings. He called for government to provide the land and for people to repossess and reclaim it in a new collaboration.

> We should survey and chart our *areas* of highland wilderness as well as cut our *lines* of trail. We should plot the boundaries of our realm. We should find and know what lies within—what forests, actual or potential; what upland range lands; what cabin sites; what vistas to unfold. And on this basis we should visualize a plan of occupation: that is, we should *reveal* the hidden plan of nature to this end.[10]

These were MacKaye's orders to architects and city planners: join forces with conservationists like himself and launch an educative Barbarian Invasion of the metropolis. One of his listeners, first at Whitaker's farmhouse and then at Hudson Guild Farm, the rural retreat of social workers from the West Side, was Mumford who recognized in his new friend with his "eaglelike profile, his black hair, his gift for picturesque epithets and oaths, his campfire stories," the archetypal Yankee—"almost the stage Yankee." Mumford immediately warmed to the lean, laconic MacKaye who seemed a spiritual son of Thoreau, "tart as a wild apple, sweet as a hickory nut," though to more prosaic minds, perhaps, "in Benton's own lingo, 'as wild as a wolf, as crazy as a loon.'"[11]

Mumford had just published his first book, *The Story of Utopias* in which, having surveyed utopian literature from Plato to Bellamy and rejected industrial capitalism and the war state, he called on Americans "to develop an art of regional planning, an art which will relate city and countryside in a new pattern from that which was the blind creation of the industrial and territorial planner." If MacKaye's vantage point was the wilderness view from the top of Mount Washington, Mumford's was the outlook high on the piers of Brooklyn Bridge out across his own New York City, "immense, overpowering, flooded with energy and light."

In the immediate postwar years, however, Mumford's estimate of the possibilities of reconstructing either the city or the nation was not a sanguine one. It was absurd, he had argued in an article for *The Nation* in 1919, to leave corrective measures to the uncertain charitable instincts of those private interests responsible for the problems in the first place.

> The housing problem, the industries problem, the transportation problem, and the land problem cannot be solved one at a time by isolated experts thinking and acting in a civic vacuum. They are mutually interacting elements, and they can be effectively dealt with only by bearing constantly in mind the general situation from which they have been abstracted.[12]

That general context, Mumford was already convinced, was the region itself, visualized from his own urban perspective as well as from Benton MacKaye's mountain-top. Bounding the region, the two men agreed as they began to share ideas and plans, was wilderness at one end of the valley section and the metropolis at the other. Here was the dual focus of the genuine regional planner, one that defined a lifetime challenge for the two new friends.

III

If the young MacKaye graduated from Melvin Longley's barnyard, Lewis Mumford, by his own account, was a child of the city. He was born in Flushing, Queens, in 1895, the illegitimate son of Elvina Conradina Baron Mumford whose marriage years earlier to John

Mumford, an Englishman twice her age, was never consummated but whose liaison with the nephew of the well-to-do bachelor for whom she kept house was. The first of the boy's surrogate fathers was his grandfather, Charles Graessel, the retired headwaiter at Delmonico's, now a gentleman of leisure living carefully but well on his "competence," a highly knowledgeable guide to the walking city which was New York at the turn of the century. Lewis accompanied his grandfather on daily jaunts through Central Park to the mansions along Fifth Avenue and back again to stop at the west carriage gate and watch the afternoon procession of broughams and victorias "in a sort of parkwide carousel" that formed the boy's aesthetic background. As he grew older, the journeys became longer—to Canal Street for his grandfather's custom-made shoes and the East Fifties for an occasional box of hand-rolled Cuban cigars. "These excursions," Mumford would recall, "gave me my first impression of the city that lay beyond my neighborhood; and if my grandfather introduced me to a whole variety of strange streets and occupations, he also made me at home in the Metropolitan Museum of Art and the American Museum of Natural History."

The young Mumford's Upper West Side neighborhood was the grid of gray streets running from Central Park West to Riverside Drive that in the 1880s had acquired architectural definition and a class structure of "diagrammatic neatness"—with the working classes confined to cheap tenements along Amsterdam and Columbus Avenues; the costly townhouses of the city's wealthy classes at the extremities facing the Park or the Hudson; and in between the middle classes solidly entrenched in uniform row houses. Mumford's recollection of various uptown interiors was as strong as his sense of the street: dark narrow hallways, their walls lined with lithographs of "The Stolen Kiss" and "Moonlight in Venice," dusty dens stuffed with bric-a-brac and missionary furniture, windows overwhelmed with wooden shutters, roller shades, lace curtains, and velvet drapes. "Visually my domestic memories are mostly bleak and stuffy," an octogenarian Mumford recalled, "and I hate to think how depressing the total effect would have been had not Central Park and Riverside Drive always been there to gladden my eyes and beckon my legs to a ramble."[13]

Like the Upper West Side the great city below it had also acquired temporary shape in the 1880s and 1890s as a walking city reachable through wide tree-lined avenues pointing the pedestrian

downtown, a scaled city still wearing a Richardsonian air of permanence even as the boy's world was changing irrevocably. The railroad
bridge over Hellgate suddenly spanned the East River. Saint John's
Cathedral was approaching medium magnificence next door to
Columbia. The Flatiron Building now pointed north like the prow
of a ship toward new commercial development, and the New York
Public Library seemed to the adolescent Mumford both awesome
and unnerving. The "colorful, still selective, middle-class world" of
uptown, where growing consumerism had not yet prevented New
Yorkers from registering a "variety of little changes, little differences," would be gone by 1920—the mature Mumford's lost city—but
two decades earlier, when goats still roamed pastures beyond 180th
Street and trolleys carried passengers out from dingy tenements to
"wide meadows and farms" on route to Belmont Park or Sheepshead
Bay, this middle-class lifestyle seemed indestructible. Here was the
urban equivalent of Benton MacKaye's "flow" in a metropolis seen
in reciprocating motion—the city as regional fact and the core of an
intricate ecological complex.

As soon as he was old enough to appropriate a tradition and play
the role it assigned, the young Mumford looked to Walt Whitman,
whose Manhattan still seemed a "simple, compact, well-join'd scheme"
with its solitary observer "disintegrated" yet part of the scheme.
Whereas the adolescent Benton MacKaye positioned himself on the
crest of Hunting Hill, itself precisely "situated," he noted in his
journal, "at the southeast point of a plateau on the North side of
Mulpus Brook," a somewhat older Mumford, standing in Brooklyn's
Atlantic Avenue neighborhood, stopped to take his urban bearings:
"Furman Street has on the West warehouses, refrigerating establishments, the marginal ways and docks: on the East a wall of some
twenty feet high under which are occasional saloons, shacks, and
hovels, and above which are the gardens and backyards of the old
aristocratic district. . . ."[14] MacKaye's visualizations disclosed patterns hidden in nature; Mumford's came as epiphanies like the one
on Brooklyn Bridge on a spring day when, with the wind coursing
through him, he looked out on what he suddenly recognized as his
own city.

Mumford's deepening encounters with New York left a lifelong
conviction that the ultimate meaning of the city was *education* as a
wholly self-directed process of absorption and reflection. "We must
conceive of the city," Mumford would write in 1968 in recalling his

own boyhood, "not primarily as a place of business or government but as an essential organ for expressing and actualizing a new personality."[15] His own discovery of a Whitmanic persona was not an accident but a conscious attempt through his city to make connections with the nineteenth century which would figure so prominently in his early excursions into cultural criticism.

Following graduation from Stuyvesant High School on New York's East Side in 1912 Mumford drifted in and out of night classes at City College of New York where there was no required curriculum at the Evening Session, and for the next two years—"the best two years of my college life"—walked often through the deepening twilight up Amsterdam Avenue past the Hebrew Orphan Asylum to the college buildings "in their dark stone masses and white terra cotta quoins and moldings, rising like a collection of crystals above the formless rocks of the hill." But two years of sampling a widening variety of subjects did not qualify him for full-time work in the Day Session, and his formal education—a smoldering rebellion against academic requirements and routine—was cut short by the discovery in 1915 of a lesion on his lung necessitating a withdrawal from college in favor of the seashore in Ogunquit, Maine, where he read Plato and declaimed Whitman, "reciting verses at the top of my voice, or racing along the hard sand for the pure joy of motion."[16]

In his enforced moratorium Mumford made a key intellectual contact which strengthened his preference for amateurism and helped define his career as a generalist. Patrick Geddes, whose writing Mumford stumbled across, was a Scotch biologist-turned-regional planner whose prescription for cities proceeded from a sense of ecological wholeness rooted in his initial discipline. Reading Geddes's *City Development*, his massive report to the Carnegie Dumferline Trust published in 1904, as well as the more recent *Cities in Evolution*, Mumford recognized an organic "three-dimensional" way of conceptualizing the city which provided a focal point for his own scattered impressions.[17] Geddes's survey method which correlated the city with surrounding countryside in the heuristic device of the "valley section" appeared to offer a total clinical picture of the region as the fundamental unit in any future "science of cities."

To teach this new integrated science Geddes had invented a multisyllabic glossary of terms, some of which found their way directly into Mumford's vocabulary—"megalopolis," "conurbation," "geotechnics"—while other undecipherable neologisms—"poliography," "politogenics," "eu-politogenics"—simply attested to the master's delight in coupling and mating sciences. Geddes's most useful intellectual bequest for his American student was a nineteenth-century universalistic history neatly divided into a "paleotechnic" age of mining civilizations based on coal, iron, steam, and capitalist profit, and an emergent "neotechnic" era resting on electricity, improved alloys, increased socialization, and civic efficiency. Geddes's Outlook Tower, his regional "index-museum" at the end of Edinburgh's Royal Mile, that served as the center for the visual exploration of the surrounding valley section, was only one of his innumerable projects for revitalizing the city and the region. Geddes, his young convert realized, had also pioneered with university hostels, urban restoration, mixed housing, folk festivals, educational extension experiments, utopian communities, international expositions—projects taken up not sequentially but simultaneously, and not as a simple instrumentalist "learning by doing" but as a total immersion in an idealist "learning by living."

In 1917 Mumford's draft number came up, and when, despite his brush with tuberculosis, he was pronounced fit for duty he hurried instead to enlist in the navy. Despite an admitted "inner resistance" to routine and the "insistent discipline" imposed by navy regulations, military life toughened him up while access to a life at sea brought him his first sustained contact with New England. Ordered from Newport to Harvard for a course in radio, he spent his first night in Winthrop House which convinced him that he had arrived in heaven. Boston, he discovered, was still the "genuine metropolis in the literal sense of the word: a true 'Mother City,' the attractive nucleus of a whole ring of communities, more nearly country towns than suburbs, which reached out as far as Concord. . . ."[18] Here, approached from the other end of the regional territory, was Benton MacKaye's middle rural ground as it appeared from Beacon Hill and Boston Common, a buffer zone in need of protection and preservation. The wartime Cambridge interlude also introduced him to the architecture of Henry Hobson Richardson—Austin and Seaver Halls and the shingled Stoughton house—and the exciting mixture of housing converging on Harvard Square "from dingy workmen's quarters on Mount Auburn Street to the palatial dwellings of Brattle Street." Across the Charles he strolled along Frederick Law Olmsted's strip of park through the fens and out to the staid suburb of Longwood, gathering impressions of a nineteenth-century New

England cultural landscape that would presently acquire precise definition in *The Golden Day.*

Mumford returned in the spring of 1919 to a New York jammed with veterans and a Greenwich Village teeming with young artistic and literary talent. He accounted himself a member of the Younger Generation, "rebellious, defiant of conventions, but not yet wholly disillusioned." He had already made two decisions, more by default than intent. The first was to remain a generalist, ready to undertake any intellectual assignment he fancied and to discover something to say which a literate public would find significant and provocative. His second decision followed from the first: he would support himself by the craft of writing rather than formal university teaching of a single discipline. By the time he returned to New York in search of an editorial position he had committed himself to a journeyman's life of "dabbling here and there, often floundering in water beyond my depth" and constantly subject to the "nagging need" from week to week to cash in quickly on an article or review. Out of these early determinations came a set of lifetime literary habits: maintaining a writing schedule crammed with a variety of assignments; constant oversight of his literary capital and retention of every scrap for reinvestment; and a tendency to reissue, as the market allowed, usually without revising.

In the four years between his return to New York City and his meeting with MacKaye at Hudson Guild Farm, Mumford worked briefly on *The Dial* and wrote for *The Freeman* while contributing an essay on "The City" to Harold Stearns's *Civilization in the United States,* and placing a number of pieces in magazines ranging from *Scientific Monthly* to *The Nation* and *The New Republic.* In the spring of 1920 he sailed to London hoping to make contact with Geddes who in turn sought to enlist him in his planning project for the university in Jerusalem. But a five-month stay at LePlay House in Pimlico persuaded him that intellectual debts to Geddes and his colleagues notwithstanding, he himself was a distinctly American product and that "any further time spent in work extraneous to my own vocation as a writer would be time lost for my essential work." By October 1920 he was back in Greenwich Village bent on the "reconstruction" of postwar American society and an early marriage.[19]

Mumford's first book, *The Story of Utopias,* appeared in 1922. For an advance of $300 he researched, wrote, edited, and saw the book through press in six months, a record he would occasionally approach but never break. In *The Story of Utopias* the interpretive lines lead out of the city and up the valley section through clustered communities along its sides to mountain wilderness against the horizon. The lines sketch a plan for the regional reconstruction of the United States which Mumford would develop, expand, modify, elaborate but never essentially change. Ostensibly a quick survey of utopian literature from Plato to Bellamy, the book finds its conceptual center along that strip of landscape depicted in Patrick Geddes's representation of the valley section. "Geographically speaking," Mumford observes in introducing his discussion of Plato's *polis*, "the ideal commonwealth was a city-region; that is, a city was surrounded by enough land to supply the greater part of the food needed by the inhabitants; and placed convenient to the sea." Then Mumford makes the telling comparison that reveals his own present intentions:

> It is a mountainous region, this Greece, and within a short distance from mountain top to sea there was compressed as many different kinds of agricultural and industrial life as one could single out in going down the Hudson Valley from the Adirondack Mountains to New York Harbor. As the basis for his ideal city, whether Plato knew it or not, he had an "ideal" section of land in his mind—what the geographer calls the "valley section."[20]

Mumford's "story" tells of the search for the ultimately good society which lies beyond fictional utopias of "escape" and "reconstruction," beyond such pastoral fantasies as William Morris's *News from Nowhere,* on the one hand, and repressive bureaucracies like Bellamy's *Looking Backward,* on the other. The story is one of declension from Plato's noble Republic through the late medieval artisan democracy, Christianopolis, of Johann Valentin Andreae to Campanella's coercive City in the Sun, to perversions of utopia and the dystopian realities of the Baroque Country House, the grimy industrial Coketown, and its Frankenstein creation, Megalopolis, the organizing center for the modern state. Megalopolis houses the functionaries and bureaucrats who run the National Utopia which is willed into existence as a pure abstraction "without regard to geography, topography, or regional surroundings." Megalopolis, in short, is precisely what the group of planners recently gathered around Thomas Adams had in mind for New York City.

Late in the book Mumford reaches a turning point as his indictment veers from description to prescription with a call for a Regional Survey as the means of entry into the real world of human values. "In looking at the community through the Regional Survey," he insists, "the investigator is dealing with a real thing and not with an arbitrary idolum."[21] Here Mumford's vision of "home, meeting-place, and factory; polity, culture, and art," brought together within the region, merged with MacKaye's "visualization" of an indigenous landscape filled with "hidden potentiality." It was time for the two men to join forces.

IV

The immediate result of the meeting at Hudson Guild Farm was Mumford's and MacKaye's decision to mount an attack on Thomas Adams and the Metropolitanists in a special issue of the *Survey Graphic*. Mumford agreed to undertake the job of editing the various contributions and supplying an interpretive framework. Soon he began to have doubts. "The damned regional planning number," he complained to MacKaye in December, 1924, six months before scheduled publication, "lives up to my worst misgivings." Perhaps the two of them left to their own devices could come up with a "whopping piece," but "for the rest of the crowd the idea is a little unbaked."

> The regional planning idea exists for the present in the nega-tive state of criticism, criticism of the big city and of "city planning." It is not yet sure enough of itself to offer anything positive: or rather, we are not as a group united on a positive program; we are, in fact, still fumbling around for it.[22]

Precisely here, he continued, was where MacKaye came in, for neither Clarence Stein nor Henry Wright nor any of the other members of the recently formed Regional Planning Association was able to "visualize" their garden cities "on their social and civic side" in a regional setting. "We must start a regional movement in America before we can have regional planning." Unless and until they broke the habit of considering regional planning as a mere

technological exercise, they could not hope to advance the reconstruction of America beyond "what the Russell Sage people are
setting out to do."

The answer to the question "What is regionalism?" Mumford
had already located in the past; and the recovery of the past, in turn,
meant writing history if only as an escape from the present dismal
fact "that we live in a spiritual chaos."[23] There were a number of
intellectual forces and cultural preferences converging on Mumford
as he began to take the measure of American culture in the mid-
1920s, predispositions that would combine in a powerful indictment
of modernism. There was, first of all, his need to stake out a
philosophical middle-ground between John Dewey's instrumental-
ism and George Santayana's aesthetic idealism—to make "a living
synthesis of their philosophies" which would allow him to have the
best of both worlds of science and humanism. He confessed to
having been helped "enormously" by a reading of Santayana, and
insisted that "it's a mistake to consider the pragmatists the sole
spokesmen of the American spirit."[24] On the other hand, Dewey's
theories of education and the experiments they had engendered held
an appeal nearly as strong as that of Geddes's views. Perhaps history
could provide the clues to a middle way.

A second determinant in Mumford's rediscovery of history
proceeded directly out of first-hand contact with it. While lecturing
at Alfred Zimmern's summer institute in Geneva in 1925, he climbed
the steep streets of the old city and poked endlessly into its corners.
"Age hangs over the stones, the smells are unaltered since the
fifteenth century; there are sudden open spaces with trees and
fountains; and at the end of dank passageways the blackness heaves
abruptly against a garden. . . ."[25] Long ago he had learned how to
appropriate a city by walking through it, but now he was acquiring
a felt sense of the past and its uses. He knew exactly what he was
seeking in history—"a vision to live by again."[26]

Mumford's search for a usable past led him to undertake two
books in quick succession—first, *Sticks and Stones: A Study of
American Architecture and Civilization* (1924), a thumbnail architectural history of the rise of the modern world out of the collapse of
the medieval and its culmination in American building; and scarcely
two years later, *The Golden Day* (1926). Both find their center in the
culture of nineteenth-century New England which lingers as a
counterforce to the pull of the frontier and the depredations of the

pioneer. "In the villages of the New World there flickered up the last dying ember of the medieval order."[27] Utopia survives momentarily in New England seaboard towns which nucleate rather than mushroom, and retain their institutions and their identity into the nineteenth century by perpetuating what Benton MacKaye called a form of "Yankee communism." The New Englanders' rough equality and shared spiritual purpose were embodied in the towns they laid out and the homes they built which sealed a tight bargain between men and the earth in severe meetinghouses and stark mills, an absence of decoration and the persistence of the "dynamic qualities of medieval architecture" wholly different from the "prudent regularities" of the Georgian mode that replaced it.[28]

To make his reader see, Mumford conducts a tour of the John Ward House (1684) in Salem, as he would do with countless other buildings and communities in all of his subsequent histories, pointing to the unpainted, weathered oaken masses and taking the measure of their solidity. "Every step that brings one nearer to the house alters the relations of the planes formed by the gable ends. . . ." The Ward House, like the village to which it is fitted, "seems in motion as well as the spectator; and this quality delights the eye."[29] Mumford then leads an excursion out into the village itself, a living core much like Benton MacKaye's Shirley Center with the common as its focal point, a meetinghouse to one side, an adjacent grammar school across the way, and along the converging roads, set at regular intervals, clapboard houses, their dark green shutters visible through the spreading arc of great elms. Here in an infinitely extendable pattern stands MacKaye's "basic geographic unit of organic human society" in "the single town of definite physical limits and integrity." Unlike his friend's insistent Shirley Center, Mumford's townscape is a cultural artifact, a model in the mind signifying community, permanence, and continuity—a benchmark for measuring subsequent backslidings.

The story of the New England village is one of slow decline in the nineteenth century as an industrial revolution destroys the artisanal self-sufficiency of the small town and dissolves the unity of the original community by dangling the promise of unlimited wealth before its pioneering sons. As country village becomes commercial town after the American Revolution, there arrive new invidious distinctions between rich and poor, craftsmen and merchants, "better" and "meaner" sorts. The vaunted Age of the Common Man

simply puts its imprimatur on decisions of rich merchants to hire a
Samuel McIntire or one of his fellow-practitioners of the vernacular
to convert the traditional low-lying New England farmhouse into a
"bulky square house with its hipped roof, its classical pilasters, its
frequently ill-proportioned cupola, its 'captain's walk' or 'widow's
walk.'" Recalling falsely for Americans "a thin and watered Greece,"
such neo-classical structures marked the victory of the merchant
"with his eye for magnitude" over the sturdy yeoman farmer "with
his homely interest in the wind and the weather." The transit from
outlying hill village to bustling mercantile city can be measured in
the piles of conspicuous waste that spread from country manor to
city mansion.[30]

Both the vernacular tradition and the neo-classical revival are
overrun by the eclecticism of the pioneer, Mumford's nemesis, who
makes the first of his many appearances as villain in *Sticks and Stones*.
The pioneer is the purveyor of an extractive and exploitative "mining" civilization and appears in two roles: as "land" pioneer following his Manifest Destiny into the abyss; and as "industrial" pioneer
propelled by a misplaced faith in material progress. With their
partnership these entrepreneurs preside over "a century of disintegration" that is clearly reflected in profit-skimming land deals and
jerry-built urban development.[31] Architecture is reduced to a symp-
tom of social and spiritual dislocation and a way of life that becomes
"sullen, grim, gauche, unstable." Only the lone Henry Hobson
Richardson kept the New England builder tradition alive in shingle-
style adaptations of an earlier regional tradition. All else after the
Civil War was either a desperate retreat to an imaginary medieval
serenity or a masking of the commercial spirit with an imperial
façade as architecture abandoned producing towns for spending
cities and "came to dwell in the stock exchanges, the banks, the
shops, and the clubs of the metropolis."[32]

The decline of American architecture from the original achievements of New England vernacular defined for Mumford the regional
planner's present task—establishing contact once more with that
cultural totality lost in the moment when the American forest
became "an enemy to be conquered" and "the obliteration of the
natural landscape became a great national sport."[33] Knitting home,
meeting-place, and factory back together again, uniting polity,
economy, and art, he was convinced, could only be accomplished in
a community "limited in numbers, and in area, and formed, not

merely by the agglomeration of people but by their relation to definite social and economic institutions."[34] To express these relations clearly was the aim of the genuine community planner.

In supplying his fellow "Barbarian Invaders" of New York City in 1925 with a philosophy of regionalism and a thumbnail history of architecture and city-planning Mumford anticipated a division of labor with MacKaye. He, as editor and contributor, would provide a historical sketch of three American "migrations" and the imminence of a fourth, while MacKaye, with a bit of editorial prodding and pruning, would describe and map the regional terrain over which these migrations had traveled. Mumford was fully aware of his friend's conceptual strengths as well as stylistic shortcomings, both traceable to his isolation in the family cottage in Shirley Center. In returning to the family homestead, MacKaye had settled into quarters which Mumford once said that "for sheer seediness would make most monastic cells look palatial."[35] MacKaye Cottage was a plain, uninsulated clapboard house, built in 1837, that sat unevenly on its tumbling stone foundation. Since it lacked electricity and running water, all the cooking and household chores were performed with hand pump, coal stove, fireplaces, and kerosene lamps. MacKaye had set up his study in "Sky Parlor," as the family called it, an upstairs room over the kitchen detached from the rest of the house and reached by a narrow stairway. Sky Parlor, with large windows facing north, west, and south, and a smaller one looking east, afforded an interior version of the view from Hunting Hill. Here in a bare workroom whose unpainted walls were lined with bookcases and maps of southern New England, MacKaye retired to do his "digging into the realm of the *living*."

For MacKaye, despite a penchant for dreaming and visualizing, no idea was ever abstract. As a self-defined "hermit," having, like Thoreau, taken a vow of poverty, he was firmly grounded in "the territory around about Shirley Center" and had taken his stance there, and with it a point of view from which to examine the ecological structure of that territory. MacKaye, as Mumford realized, salted and spiced his prose with colloquialisms, folk-language, and regional slang which gave it a conversational directness and earthiness, but he lacked the larger shaping-power of language needed to convey the reality of his vision. On the other hand, as Mumford also sensed, MacKaye's very rootedness in the hill village made him a keen if apprehensive witness to the onrushing metropolitan flood pouring out of Boston into the suburbs and beyond. MacKaye felt an immediacy and an urgency—a need to act quickly—while Mumford as an urbanite still seemed content to educate people as publicist and critic. MacKaye's need for action was fed, not simply by his practical training as a forester, but also by his conviction that the best way, as he explained, to "put across" his plan was "to develop a single idea—to meet the metropolitan challenge by the development of the indigenous environment as a synthetic art." For such a project, as he was frank to admit, he would need his friend's help and advice.

With this unspoken recognition of mutual need and divided responsibilities, the two men undertook their contributions to the special issue of *Survey Graphic* designed by Mumford as an alternative to the emerging Russell Sage plan of Thomas Adams. Mumford intended his essay "The Fourth Migration" as the framing device both for the volume and for his larger history of two Americas: "the America of the settlement" consisting of seventeenth-century communities planted along the Atlantic seaboard and its river valleys; and the "America of the migrations" of which there have been three in the course of two centuries. The first migration cleared the land west of the Alleghenies and opened up half a continent to exploration and exploitation by the "land pioneer" in his covered wagon. Despite its romantic mythology, the first migration is the simple history of "restless men who burned the forests of the Mohawk Valley in order to plant farms, who sifted into the soft glacial deposits of Ohio to cleave their plows through its rich soil; men who grabbed wheat land and skinned it, who grabbed urban sites and 'turned them over'; who staked out railway lines, sometimes strategically . . . sometimes stupidly . . . in a mad scramble to cover the continent." The price of such progress?—"Butchered forest; farms gone to ruin or into a ruinous system of tenantry; villages so sterile that they drive all their ambitious or sensitive young people to the big towns."[36]

This uprooting becomes the second migration—from countryside to factory town—on the iron horse this time rather than the Conestoga wagon: to Cleveland and Columbus in the 1840s, Chicago in the 1850s, and to Milwaukee on the eve of the Civil War. The motive behind this second migration, Mumford argues, was "narrowly industrial," its results a series of "depletions" measured in "homes blocked and crowded by factories; rivers polluted; factories and railroad yards seizing sites that should have been preserved for recreation; inadequate homes thrown together anyhow, for sale anyhow, inhabited anyhow."[37]

The magnet of the metropolis as financial center presently draws Americans out of their small towns and provincial cities in a third migration that begins with the Civil War and culminates in World War I. This time urban concentration exacts as its toll the subjection of industry to finance, advertising, insurance, marketing, and all the other "paper-making" enterprises of consolidated capitalism.[38] Although Mumford was quick to point out that these migrations came in successive if overlapping waves, cumulatively if unintentionally their effect, he insisted, has been to open the way for a fourth migration out of the city as Americans come to realize that the automobile, the airplane, the radio, and the telephone have made concentration of people in mass cities "obsolete" and that twentieth-century technology thus offers "a new opportunity and a new task."[39]

The actual job of engineering the fourth migration MacKaye considered even more urgent than Mumford, and to the application of his friend's general principles he brought a home-grown ecological history of his own. Choosing the word "empire"—a misnomer, Mumford thought—to describe his system of natural and man-made "flows," MacKaye begins his essay "The New Exploration: Charting the Industrial Wilderness" with a search for the "most efficient framework" for containing and managing the movement of resources, goods, people and culture across his home state of Massachusetts from Boston to the Berkshires.[40] Clues lie ready at hand in three types of topography comprising MacKaye's cross-section: the Appalachian barrier at the western end of the state in the Berkshire–Green Mountains chain; the Threshold Plain or the New England Plateau covering three-quarters of the state; and the Seaboard, consisting of the Boston Basin.

The first section of this industrial web is the barrier itself, a "source region with its ample water power and forest growths." Two hundred miles eastward lies the "mouth region," the most densely woven part of the web with its factories, railroads, wharves, and stores serving at once as a mouth ingesting natural resources and as an original source of manufactured goods for the hinterland. In between these two poles lies "a country of fields and woodlots" with

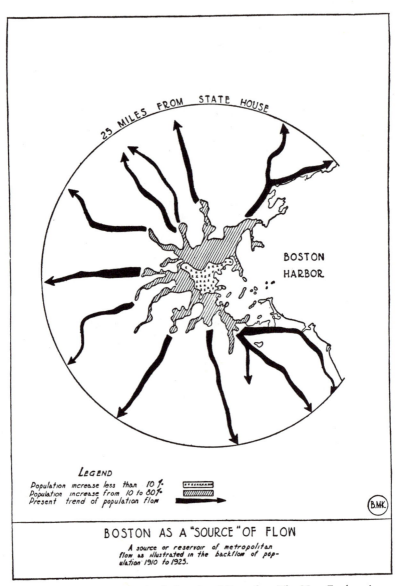

FIGURE II.2   *Benton MacKaye's directional lines: from* The New Exploration, *1962 edition. A map of Boston's "Backflow."*

FROM BENTON MACKAY, *THE NEW EXPLORATION: A PHILOSOPHY OF REGIONAL PLANNING.*
URBANA–CHAMPAIGN, IL: UNIVERSITY OF ILLINOIS PRESS. © 1928 BY HARCOURT, BRACE
AND COMPANY, INC. © 1956 BY BENTON MACKAY. © 1962 BY THE BOARD OF TRUSTEES OF
THE UNIVERSITY OF ILLINOIS. © 1990 BY CHRISTY MACKAY BARNES.

a village producerist economy which is more complex than wilderness but less so than the industrial segment in Boston and its environs. Where then, MacKaye asks, do "we of the new exploration" begin our survey? In the Berkshires as the "sphere of origin" and more particularly with Somerset Valley, a miniature "empire" seventeen miles long and eight miles wide comprising the drainage basin of the Upper Deerfield River northwest of Greenfield. The first settlers in Somerset Valley arrived in 1776, and the subsequent history of the region concerns the rise and fall of successive lumber empires that mined the forests and stripped the watershed, only to move on. It is just these ruins left by the timber-mining empire that MacKaye takes as his framework for regional reconstruction. Old railroad grades and rights of way can be remade into good roads for new settlers; abandoned logging camps will serve as refurbished stable communities; timber harvesting will replace the old practice of clear-cutting.

MacKaye's plan for his home region was a conceptual halfway house between his earlier proposals for resource communitarian experiments harking back to nineteenth-century alternatives and an updated version of regional planning aimed at checking the urban outflow and preserving wilderness at the top of the valley section. In his contribution to the *Survey Graphic* issue he encapsulates Mumford's successive migrations and the whole historical process of former explorations. The original explorers, according to MacKaye, charted the wilderness of nature in order to exploit it; the new explorers must chart the wilderness made by people in order to escape it.[41]

Neither of the two friends' hopes for immediate results from their manifesto in the *Survey Graphic* were particularly high, and their skepticism proved warranted. As members of a commission appointed by Governor Alfred E. Smith they joined with other RPAA [Regional Planning Association of America] members to issue *The Regional Report of the New York State Commission on Housing and Regional Planning* published in May 1926. Their report called for a co-ordinated system of rail and motor transportation for the entire Hudson Valley, stringent controls on bulk, height, and use of buildings in Manhattan, a low ceiling on urban property values, and subsidized decentralization of industry, all of which required intervention by state and local government on a monumental scale. Only one thousand copies of their report were published, and most of these mouldered in state archives until they were exhumed fifty years later.

Nor did Thomas Adams's publication in two volumes (1929, 1931) of the "Regional Plan of New York and Its Environs" succeed in attracting much more public attention. Mumford leveled two blasts at it in the pages of *The New Republic* in 1932, accusing Adams of being "willfully obtuse" and dismissing his report as a huge pudding, "indigestible and tasteless." Adams fired back by denouncing Mumford as a hopeless visionary, an apostle of massive economic change that would require "the combined power of the President, Congress and state legislature to bring about."[42] The task of implementing the Adams report fell to the Regional Plan Association, a voluntary clearing-house which could do little more than encourage co-operation among the region's 400 public and private sponsoring organizations. New York City waited until 1937 to establish a modestly financed and empowered planning commission, by which time Robert Moses, another Mumford nemesis, was firmly ensconced in the metropolitan driver's seat. Serious regional planning on a nationwide scale awaited the initiative of a President and Congress confronting a massive collapse of the American economy, catastrophic unemployment, and the appearance of a host of young regional planners. But in 1925, at the beginning of a frenzied financial boom, neither a philosophy of regional reconstruction nor specific schemes for implementing it held any appeal for the politicians.

The significance of the *Survey Graphic* episode and the skirmish with the metropolitanists in 1925 lay elsewhere—in a deepening friendship which lasted until MacKaye's death in 1975, and, of more immediate importance, in sharpening each man's understanding of the meaning of their joint regionalist enterprise and of the resources available for undertaking it. Those resources, spiritual and material, they now knew lay, not in New York City but in New England, and each determined to make use of them. Out of their mutual recognition came two assessments: *The Golden Day* (1926), Mumford's account of the New England renaissance as a legacy for twentieth-century planners; and *The New Exploration* (1928), MacKaye's survey of the available means for putting that inheritance to work.

V

In 1925, driven out of Greenwich Village and then Brooklyn Heights by high rents, Mumford and his wife Sophia moved to Sunnyside Gardens in Long Island City, the RPAA's experimental garden-city

project sandwiched in between the railroad tracks and the goat
pastures girdling the factory district of this ugly industrial suburb.
At first the Mumfords found their surroundings so depressing that
they were driven on Sundays to seek respite in the nearest cemetery
for a glimpse of nature. "But as this new housing grew under our
friends' [Clarence Stein's and Henry Wright's] direction," Mumford
recalled, "it created its own environment; and if you knew your way
about, you might follow a footpath through a network of rear
gardens and green lawns for almost half a mile, with all sorts of
charming vistas."[43] Mumford remembered Sunnyside Gardens as a
vital community of intellectuals and professionals mixing freely
with all classes though not races. For the rest of his life he would
associate the garden city experiment on Long Island with the potential for co-operative communal reconstruction of urban life, not as
suburbia with its single-family isolation and false self-sufficiency,
but as *satellite settlement* on the perimeter of the regional city,
maintaining an intense and varied participatory culture. Sunnyside
convinced Mumford once and for all that "with a little leeway for
experiment, the democratic process would still function provided
the social unit allowed a mixture of political, religious, and social
beliefs—and of occupations, too."[44]

Mumford's uncertain income and modest lifestyle seemed to
him opulent compared with MacKaye's "hermit" existence in Shirley
Center, where he and his sister Hazel managed a hand-to-mouth
existence. He was so poor, MacKaye admitted with wry satisfaction,
that on his tax form he listed his chief asset as "not having children."
His "cave man" life was intellectually isolated, and his letters to his
friend, as he worked in Sky Parlor on the manuscript of *The New
Exploration,* were filled with plaintive requests to "send us a wee line
sometime" giving the particulars on what "the crowd" was "up to"
in his absence.[45] And when Mumford invariably obliged him with a
full account of his own life in New York, MacKaye would reply in
kind, prefacing his own report with an amiable apology for its
length. "There are some souls with whom there is so much in
common that a mere pull at their shirt means the unearthing of an
avalanche."[46] If Mumford would only agree to come and "do the
hermit act" with him, they could have their long "jaw," and "the face
of the future earth would be the different for it."

MacKaye combined writing, which came slowly and painfully,
with household chores and handyman repairs on "cisterns, roofs,

and such" in a heroic effort to keep his cottage livable. He explained his intent to Mumford repeatedly as he groped his way toward an ultimate philosophical statement. "In reading these chapters," he warned Mumford in sending him a batch of manuscript, "you may find them somewhat muddy. Don't fail to tell me if you think so. I have the stuff so firmly in my own head that I am a poor critic of myself (a truism). But I think that I can lighten them, upon revision, and air them out as we can do with soggy hay."[47] There was, in fact, no middle distance in MacKaye's prose written from the perspective of Hunting Hill or Sky Parlor. Ready at hand lay the colloquialisms, the slang and salty sayings that served admirably as the primary vernacular language of the Yankee storyteller who described a spring day in Shirley as "tempestuously glorious" or told of his longing "for a pow-wow with that soul of yours" or admitted going to church now and again "just for the hell of it." This was the straight-faced comic Yankee who insisted on giving "old Lewis" the "latest dope" or admitted to "bellyaching and belching" and then apologized for running off at the mouth in "a long drool." But words to explain the spiritual pull of the primeval wilderness or his need to study the mysteries of nature came only haltingly and with great difficulty. As he struggled to find his expository voice, he found in his friend's writing useful hints. He heard the "voice of an artist" in *The Golden Day*, a copy of which Mumford sent him, and in the words themselves "certainly an urge to the engineer; but Oh, for more of the artist in me to comprehend, and for more of the engineer to carry forth."[48]

Interspersed with inquiries about the Mumfords and reports of domestic routines at MacKaye Cottage in letters explaining "in a few swift words" what "to hell I've been up to," came increasingly detailed accounts of "digging in the realm of the living" as MacKaye began organizing the concepts underlying *The New Exploration*.

> I have carved out a little region in that realm. It consists of the territory around about Shirley Center. This little region embraces the fundamental environments (as I conceive of them) which are necessary for man's full development. These are the primeval, the rural, (the "colonial" in New England), and the urban. The primeval is represented by a little range of mountains—the Wapack Range. The colonial is presented by several little "hill villages," among which is Shirley Center. The urban is represented by Fitchburg (of 40,000), and Boston is near by.

Each environment, I point out, should be kept intact, and developed as a basic human resource in itself. But each one is threatened (and the urban already immersed) by a fourth environment (a diseased environment we might call it) called the "metropolitan." And the job of planning a region for play, as I see it, consists in repelling the "invasion" of this metropolitan influence and of developing as assets in themselves, the other three basic environments. This splits itself into three parts: the *preservation* of the primeval; the *restoration* of the colonial; and the salvaging (some day) of the true urban. The immediate tasks seem to the first two just named—the problems of the primeval and the colonial environments.[49]

Mumford responded to these progress reports with an enthusiasm and encouragement that came easily to him. Always there was his ready response to "old Benton's" ideas and plans although such attention competed with an even stronger concern with the present state of his own particular project which he was eager to describe. Now, on reading MacKaye's prospectus, he offered immediate support. "The work that you are doing seems a real crystallization of everything you've been thinking this last six years. Haven't you got the stuff of a book there? As soon as you have it in any sort of shape I'd like to see it; I'll engage to peddle it around this spring, with a high and enthusiastic recommendation."[50]

In a letter of December 1926 offering encouragement to his friend, Mumford reported that his own book, *The Golden Day,* had sold a thousand copies in the first month which "has made my stock rise with the publisher almost as fast as U.S. Steel."[51] *The Golden Day* was intended as a pioneer work in American Civilization and at the same time a piece of regional history unearthing the "cultural motive" he had been seeking for the last six years. Regionalism, Mumford now understood clearly, involved first and foremost the recovery of a specific past.

The creation of an American culture, Mumford announces on the opening page of *The Golden Day,* began with "the unsettlement of Europe," and in the beginning the American Adam was merely "a stripped European" who colonized a continent with other people similarly "incapable of sharing or continuing its past."[52] Mumford traces this European "delocalized man" to the New World where he becomes the "composite American" furnished with a Protestant theology, a capitalistic appetite, and a new abstract politics of possessive individualism. Having emerged from the deep shadows of his ancestral home, the pioneer appears as a silhouette—"a man without a background"—highlighted against the wilderness by his illusions that time is money and opportunity there for the taking. The pioneer's inexorable march across the continent from the seventeenth century through the nineteenth, laying waste to nature as he goes and making the path of progress "smooth as a concrete road," signified the triumph of sheer motion over reflection, of romantic restlessness over steady cultural habit, an incorrigible present-mindedness over values inherited from the past. "The truth is that the life of the pioneer was bare and insufficient: he did not really face Nature, he merely avoided society."[53] The American pioneer could never create a community or establish an identity with the land because he never stopped long enough to reflect on their meaning. Searching for sublimity, he achieved only a self-induced oblivion.

The Golden Day of mid-nineteenth-century America dawned only on those with sense enough to stay at home in New England, where they continued to live "between two worlds" at the precise moment when an inherited social and cultural order fractured. Europe's final disintegration comes in America, but its collapse precipitates a brief but powerful renaissance in the region where its culture was first planted and briefly flourished. "Regionalism" as a cultural motive, for Mumford, was both a *specific time* and a *definite place,* the precise point at which past and present intersect and in so doing inform and determine the future. The regional moment is quite literally a day in the life of a culture. Despite critics who objected to his title as arcane, Mumford knew precisely what he wanted his extended metaphor to say. Emerson is the "morning star" of New England's renaissance, a figure rising on the horizon of a recovered past who portends new cultural achievement. Emerson, more clearly than any of his fellow New Englanders, understood the workings and thus the meaning of history even as he sought to transcend it. It is Emerson's persona even more than his ideas that attracts Mumford, particularly his notion of himself as interpreter or what Benton MacKaye called "visualizer." "The preacher, the farmer, the scholar, the sturdy New England freeholder, yes, and the shrewd Yankee peddler or mechanic were all encompassed by him." But comprehended as promise rather than accomplishment: "what they meant in actual life had fallen away from him: he represented what they stood for in eternity."[54]

What Emerson promises in a dim pre-dawn, Thoreau fulfills at sunrise and Whitman celebrates at high noon. Emerson's thought occasionally abandoned experience and transcended regional realities in its bookishness, "its impatience to assume too quickly an upright position, its too tidy moral housekeeping." Thoreau, on the contrary, showed exactly what the pioneer might have achieved had he honored the surveyor's bounds rather than extending himself in illimitable space. Together Emerson and Thoreau point the way out of a spiritual wilderness to those who seek to be saved from the pioneer's misplaced confidence in "calculating," "reckoning," and "figuring." If Emerson foreshadows, Thoreau bodies forth the "poised and finely balanced personality." Emerson surveys a symbolic New England landscape, but Thoreau inhabits a real one, studying it and learning from it.

> As for his country, he loved the land too well to confuse it with the shifting territorial boundaries of the National State. In this he had that vital regional consciousness which every New Englander shared. What he loved was the landscape, his friends, and his companions in spirit: when the Political State presumed to exercise a brass counterclaim on these loyalties, it might go to the devil.[55]

Noon of the Golden Day arrives with Whitman who gives to American poetry the power of the Veads, the Nackas, the Talmud, and the Old Testament by crystallizing experience and infusing spirituality into everyday life. Following Emerson's example, he absorbs in himself the Quaker, the Puritan, the cosmopolitan, pioneer, and republican, "and what came out in his poems was none of these things; it was a new essence; none of the ordinary labels described it."[56] Whitman visualized—even in the midst of a fratricidal war—a renewed America emerging from the war, a vision quickly demolished by Gilded Age hucksters, yet one leaving a legacy of idealism to be repossessed by a modern world. "What is valid in idealism," Mumford insists, "is the belief in the possibility of re-molding, reforming, recreating cultural life."

Hawthorne, whose art is suffused with the shadows of an autumnal New England afternoon, realized keenly what the pioneer failed to credit—the persistence of evil and thus the inevitability of tragedy. Hawthorne too turned to the past in a spirit which Mumford could only approve: "with a consciousness that remained outwardly

Puritan, he projected the figures of his day," animating them with his sense of history. Finally, Melville plunges the Golden Day into dark metaphysical night with his saga of the white whale which "threatens man and calls forth all his heroic power, and in the end defeats him with a final lash of his tail." The early Emersonian promise of endless renewal is baffled and ultimately betrayed by Melville's destructive element. The Golden Day is ended.

The culture of New England's Golden Day rested on a specific political economy of small property—which, as Emerson explained, is "always moral"—and diffused wealth, which ensures respect for the terms dictated by the land, a guaranteed "competence" for industrious farmers and artisans alike, self-government and sturdy independence. This free labor economy, in turn, ensured the survival of necessary cultural traits and personal values: steadiness of habit and sureness of self, industriousness and invention, the willing embrace of hard work and cultivation of civic spirit. "Manual labor," Emerson reminded Mumford, "is the study of the external world." And the *social form* revealed by Mumford's own study of that world was the New England village whose very locus and structure embodied the values of its builders and sustaining members. For a brief moment, Mumford insists, mid-nineteenth-century New England remained in perfect equilibrium poised between past and future. Its regional culture was *old* in its inherited awareness of wholesome tradition but also *new* in its assumption of the historical mission to make a fresh integration of culture that would carry America into the modern age.

The accomplishment of the New England renaissance, Mumford concluded, was the work of cultural counter-revolutionaries who at the same time were precursors of the twentieth-century regionalists, inveighing against the rapacity of the pioneers in industry and on the frontier who had destroyed the American land and impoverished the spirit. Their lives stood for and their work celebrated "an older but more youthful America, part achieved reality, part hopeful ideal, which we have lost." Their example now calls a postwar generation of Americans to an act of recovery by acknowledging themselves the spiritual children of those representative men who "people the landscape with their own shapes" as discoverers of "a new hemisphere in the geography of the mind."[57]

In *The Golden Day* Mumford succeeded in defining with precision the regional "cultural motive" he had been seeking. This he did in a series of linked propositions. "Human culture is a continuous process of choosing, selecting, nurturing, a process also of cutting down and exterminating those merely hardy and fecund weeds which have no value except their own rank life."[58] This process of weeding involves the selective assimilation of the past, transforming it into new cultural growths. A genuine and vital culture is tended and managed by a constituent people; and it roots and flourishes in their locale, for only there are they able to take from their cultural inheritance needful and life-sustaining elements. When such a culture as that produced by the New England renaissance breaks with the past, having acquired the essential elements from it, it then becomes *indigenous* to a *place*. In this sense all vital cultures grow in regional soils. Independence comes in a break from tradition but also in the recognition of what is usable in the past. No previous culture can ever be recovered, nor would it be desirable to attempt to do so. "But the principal writers of that time [of the Golden Day] are essential links between our own lives and that earlier, that *basic America*. In their work, we can see in a *pristine* state the *essential characteristics* that still lie *under the surface:* and from their example we can more readily find our own foundations, and make our own particular point of departure."[59] Whether in the center of Concord village or on the shoreline of Walden Pond, in the Manse at Salem or on unfathomed oceans beyond Nantucket, or starting from Paumanok where I was born, the classical writers of the New England renaissance bore the mark of their region even as they embarked on their interior explorations which even now can be repeated. "Culture," Mumford explains finally, ". . . implies the possibilities of repetition."[60] And repetition means renewal.

Mumford sent a copy of *The Golden Day* to MacKaye, who blamed his slowness in reading it on the "cave man" standard of living he had been reduced to in Shirley Center "with wood and water and light and every other primal element to be extracted from its source" with the result that "time for reading is almost nil."[61] Still, he had managed to dip into the book here and there, and marvelled at "your keen powers of expression" which reminded him to get busy and start building his own regionalist structure from indigenous New England materials. Mumford proved a loyal friend, helpful critic, and at times virtual collaborator, urging MacKaye toward ever more concrete formulations of his ideas. Sometimes help came in the form of pointed reminders to use words accurately. Sometimes he made major objections argued at length, as he did in demanding sharper discrimination between hiking trails which were entirely suited to colonial and wilderness environments and costumed masquerades which were not. "It is not merely a digging up of the past, or even a re-living of it," he warned MacKaye, "it is a fresh mode of living." The fate of regionalism in Europe, where it had stalled at the stage of simple cultural recovery, should serve Americans as a warning of the dangers of mere "piety to the past, as if life could or should get stuck in one particular mold and stay there."[62]

MacKaye needed all the editorial help he could get, for he admitted to great difficulty in "getting round" his ideas and putting them "across." *The New Exploration* takes the reader on a New England journey across uneven and occasionally uncertain terrain on a path strewn with stylistic boulders, cluttered with verbal underbrush, and filled with metaphorical potholes. But MacKaye's "war map," as he called it, indicates a clear understanding of his developmentalist enemy and presents a defensive strategy for repelling the metropolitan invaders and saving Thoreau's indigenous world.

The argument of *The New Exploration* is deceptively simple: the old explorers were lone freebooters and adventurers; the new ones are engineers, economists, landscape designers, and—the synthesizer of their findings—the regional planner who serves as a "composite mind." In giving shape to his "visualization," the regional planner discerns three worlds from his mountain height in New England— the indigenous world of the *primeval,* the *rural* world of the hill village, and the *cosmopolitan* world of the big city. Each is a genuine and vital community, and each is now threatened by the spread of a standardized, mass-produced *metropolitan* "slum" oozing out across suburbia. From the top of Mount Monadnock, MacKaye surveys these various environments, the primeval world at his feet, the rural lying in the middle distance, and against the far horizon the city with its cancerous metropolitan growth.[63]

Primeval America of the pre-Columbian epoch still lies within reach of the American imagination, and in places in western and northern New England it is still there to preserve. Monadnock, Aroostook, Katahdin—"we spell these names and place them on our maps. We cleave to them as symbols. . . . We visualize the *name.* Our job now, in the new exploration, is to visualize the *thing.*" To look out across New England is to see remote stands of fir and spruce sliding down into high pastures and rocky upland slopes of hill villages, and rising again to unbroken forest just below the skyline, images reminding modern man of an "indefinite past" imaged in the *campfire*.

The emblematic as well as the functional center of the rural or, in New England, the "Colonial" environment is the village common, serving as a nucleus of the community which is arranged "in all the structural symmetry of a starfish" with its five points representing religion, politics, education, commerce, home:

> There is the church (with its steeple); there is the town hall (with its stately Doric columns); and the little red brick school house; and the general store; and the thirty or so dwelling-houses, these last being placed around the Common and along the radiating roads.

Packed around this structural core of the hill village are fields of corn and hay, sheep and cattle pastures, gardens and woodlots, and at the bottom of the hills in the valley stream, grist mills and saw mills. This rural world is the stage for a vital participatory culture that in following the seasons maintains "a primal natural balance" between outdoors and indoors, daytime and night, summer and winter. The colonial village culture, even in 1929, is no mere exercise in nostalgia or figment of the antiquarian imagination but a living fact with "deeply embedded roots" reaching down into "the indefinite past."[64]

The urban environment—the *cosmopolitan* as distinguished from the bastard *metropolitan*—is no less real or necessary to modern life. The true city is a "village grown up," its various institutions expanded, heightened, intensified. The meetinghouse becomes the cathedral; the town hall a golden-domed State House; the red brick schoolhouse a university; the country store the huge urban mart. In the genuine urban environment the geographical definition of identity and place gives way to new group activities and cultural sectioning into different worlds of drama, music, sport, religion, technology, and statesmanship, each with its own "station."[65]

All three of these structured communities—the primeval, the rural, and the urban—are threatened by a spreading pseudo-environment, a metropolitan massing, and flooding, which has already swamped the center city and now is seeping like back-flowing sewage across suburbia and the surrounding countryside. Ironically, the city itself has become the first victim of the metropolitan flood in which it is now fairly submerged. But the towns and villages in the broad band of rural New England—from river towns along Maine's Kennebec to pastoral enclaves at the mouth of the Connecticut—are beginning to go the way of Goldsmith's Deserted Village. "A rootless, aimless, profoundly disharmonious environment has replaced the indigenous one." The ultimate objective of the invading metropolitan developers is wilderness itself—the whole primeval world of the Appalachian chain:

> The invasion would take its start from the central community. Its movements here as elsewhere we may liken to a glacier. It is spreading, unthinking, ruthless. Its substance consists of tenements, bungalows, stores, factories, billboards, filling-stations, eating-stands, and other structures whose individual hideousness and collective haphazardness present that unmistakable environment which we class the "slum." Not the slum of poverty, but the slum of commerce.

When the invading forces finally triumph, New England will have become "a world without a country."[66]

What, then, does the regional planner propose as a strategy for checking, reversing, and hopefully mopping up the metropolitan flow at its source? Since metropolitanism advances along the highways radiating out of the city, it is precisely here on its outskirts that it must be checked by the "intertown" (or, as he would presently call it, the "townless highway") banding the city as a major throughroute that connects the arteries running out of it but—even more important—serving as a barrier, "dike," or "levee" to hold back the spillage from suburbia. MacKaye's was literally a containment strategy for damming metropolitanism, plugging the "thousand ruptured reservoirs" of suburbia, and turning the flood of people back into the center city where a genuine cosmopolitan culture still survived. Along these "intertown" throughways, MacKaye pointed out on his map, lay wide strips of undeveloped public land to serve as free zones closed to development and reserved for parks. At intervals along these intertowns would cluster *waysides,* as MacKaye somewhat dimly envisioned them, links to the outer framework of the regional city. "This does not mean," he explained a trifle vaguely, "that it would be an urban environment; on the contrary, it would be a rural environment. By no means would it be a suburban environment."[67] Mumford, sensing a certain visual lapse on his friend's part, pointed to "one danger" in the loose concept: "The danger of forming bad little messes of 'towns' on the townless highway itself: hence the planning of certain necessary services on these roads should be an integral part of the project, or they will come in by the backdoor and create the very slum we are trying to prevent." MacKaye acknowledged the justice of Mumford's warning and accepted his suggestion.

The "open ways" and the public land that flank and cut across the intertown highways provide the dikes and levees for holding back the metropolitan flood. At these crucial points the regional planner helps nature recover its primeval territory by planting publicly owned and maintained havens from the developers:

> Mountain crestline and summits (such as the Mt. Holyoke range). Escarpment, or steep slope from a lowland to upland (as the west side of Hoosac Mountain). Canyon, or steep valley along a stream (the Deerfield River). River Bottom, or level valley along a stream (Ipswich River). Swamp (the Great Cedar Swamp and others). Beach (wherever sufficiently unsettled).[68]

In the concluding pages of *The New Exploration,* MacKaye assumes once again the role of "visualizer" and, like Mumford in *The Golden Day,* returns to mid-nineteenth-century New England to place his emblematic environments of campfire, village green, and wayside inside Thoreau's spiritual realm. Each of MacKaye's revealers—naturalist, historian, dramatist, and artist—creates images on paper or canvas, with word or brush, pictures of "the vital forces, rhythms, and aspects" of a vibrant, life-enhancing existence—*a life of living.* The challenge confronting the regional planner is to fuse their several visions "in a medium more vital and real." "It is something," Thoreau wrote in a passage which MacKaye had learned by heart, "to be able to paint a particular picture, or to carve a statue, and so to make a few objects beautiful; but it is far more glorious to carve and paint the very atmosphere and medium through which we look. . . . To affect the quality of the day, that is the highest of arts." Mumford's *The Golden Day* was the work of the transcendental word; MacKaye's visualization in *The New Exploration,* like Thoreau's original prophecy, was an act of regional spirit. "Environment," he wrote in attempting a summation of his intuited philosophy, "is the influence upon *each* inner mind of the thing shared by *every* inner mind. . . . 'Look *out* and not *in'*—we are told, for when we look *out* we thereby look *in* to our fellow souls on earth. Environment, therefore, provides a sort of *common mind*—the total life which everyday life must share: it is the least common denominator of our inner selves."[69]

VI

Mumford and MacKaye remained firm friends until the latter's death in 1975, seeing each other only intermittently over the years but keeping up an affectionate if not uninterrupted correspondence in which MacKaye continued to restate his Thoreauvian premises and Mumford to report on the many uses to which he put them in his books. *The New Exploration* would be MacKaye's only full-length work, although he continued to labor on a massive manuscript for the rest of his life only to be gently dissuaded by his friend from attempting to publish it. Mumford knew what MacKaye only sensed dimly—that he had had his say, and that his contribution henceforth lay in translating his vision into the engineer's terms which in the 1930s he tried to do by joining the Planning Division of the newly established TVA [Tennessee Valley Authority] and writing a series of position papers on preserving the ecology of the Tennessee Valley. His reports, digests of which he forwarded to Mumford, were duly acknowledged and promptly ignored by the bureaucrats. More to his liking was weekend work on sections of the Appalachian Trail and the organizational spadework done with Robert Marshall for the Wilderness Society. After a year's frustration trying to press on his superiors at TVA a preservationist rather than a developmental agenda, MacKaye retreated once more to Shirley Center and the writing of what he hoped would be his magnum opus.

As for Mumford, *The Golden Day* was only one of the first of a growing number of regional reassessments, the most important of which was the 200-page concluding essay in *The Culture of Cities* (1937). With his friendship, MacKaye supplied an experiential dimension and a planning technique for the "cultural motive" Mumford had indicated to Patrick Geddes but had not been able fully to define. The New England villages in Mumford's early *Sticks and Stones* and *The Golden Day* were symbolic landscapes—natural images remodeled and refitted to serve as emblems of a vigorous and harmonious late medieval society brought to the New World to flourish briefly and then die. His village spaces were ceremonial settings for the abstract communal dramas he would later stage in his re-creations of the medieval town, the baroque country house, and the mephitic Coketown. MacKaye, with his simpler and more direct sense of the felt history of the New England town, taught his friend to populate and animate a still vital culture with real people, their routines and ceremonies, and to devise new means of saving it from threatened extinction. Mumford would never lose interest in the city which in the mid-1920s he and his fellow barbarian invaders attacked as the key to a fundamental reorganization of American life. The metropolis would remain for him the center of a vital high culture as well as the commercial command-post of an American empire of paper. But his hopes for a fourth migration as the way to a recovery of traditional Western values remained strong. Increasingly for Mumford it was the region—reaching up the Hudson and embracing his farmhouse in Amenia—that was home to a primary indigenous culture which, with MacKaye as its exemplar, he would define as "healthy," "sane," and "normal." Regionalism, he explained in 1931, did not mean resurrecting a dead way of life or mummifying local customs or canonizing the primitive and the illiterate. Regionalism, correctly perceived, was simply "an effort which recognizes the existence of real groups and social configurations and geographical relationships that are ignored by the abstract culture of the metropolis, and which opposes to the aimless nomadism of the modern commercial enterprise the conception of a stable and settled and balanced and cultivated way of life."

To his friend's conservative cultural philosophy Benton MacKaye added an ecological supplement with his land ethic and concept of a national commons. MacKaye, moreover, put his forester's survey system to work laying out an actual route to Mumford's undiscovered country. In a letter to Van Wyck Brooks in 1934, having completed *Technics and Civilization* and now preparing to embark on *The Culture of Cities,* Mumford explained his own method of thinking and working: "In youth, the sketch: weak in detail, but with the main lines in the right place. In maturity, the main lines get slightly rectified as one alters one's position and takes a wider strip of horizon for background." Yet once the initial lines of argument have been properly aligned, he assured Brooks, "one is justified in filling every inch of canvas. . . ."[70] In helping to draw those

directional lines in his friend's early regional sketches Benton MacKaye
showed Mumford, in the authenticity of his person as well as in the
force of his ideas, the proper alignment.

In the spring of 1968, Mumford and his wife drove out from
Cambridge to Shirley Center to visit MacKaye, now nearing ninety.
They found him frail and bent, a bit unsteady on his feet, his
eyesight failing. Mumford, as was his habit, recorded his impressions of what he sensed would be their last conversation. "By now,"
he explained in a note in his journal, "Benton is concentrated on two
things: his opus and his immediate problems." Cataracts had developed on both eyes. ". . . yet when he wanted to read to us some of
the opus, on calculations of population and habitability, he managed by concentration to read it, apparently a word or two at a time."
MacKaye appeared to bear his affliction stoically with only a passing
comment that it was "a hell of a business not being able to see." He
took his guests on a tour of MacKaye Cottage, long vacant, stuffed
with dusty bric-a-brac, shabby beyond belief, and then led them to
the porch at the rear that looked out over the meadow sloping down
to a curtain of woods—the original view, he boasted, unchanged for
over a century and still screening his realm of the living from the
commercial development in Shirley Center. Both men knew without
having to acknowledge it that this was probably their last meeting.
Mumford found himself strangely moved. "We embraced awkward-
ly; and then we parted, without any overt expression of sentiments;
and that, I think, is the way he wanted it to be. . . ." Yet on his return
to Cambridge, Mumford confessed to a feeling of profound desola-
tion which memories of a lifetime's public profession of admiration
and affection for his friend could not solace. "We were never
intimate," he admitted, "in the sense that I had once been with
Harry Murray; but I realized that there was much about both our
lives that remained to be said, and would never be said."[71]

NOTES

1. Thomas Adams et al. (1929, 1931) *Regional Plan of New York and Its
   Environs*, 2 vols, New York, Regional Plan of New York, I: 131, 408; II:
   575–6.
2. Lewis Mumford (1925) "Regions—to live in," reprinted from *Survey Graphic*,
   7 (May), 151–2, in *Planning the Fourth Migration: The Neglected Vision of the
   Regional Planning Association of America*, edited by Carl Sussman, Cambridge, MIT Press, 1976, 92–3.
3. Ibid., 92.

4. Percy MacKaye (1927) *Epoch: The Life of Steele MacKaye, Genius of the Theatre, in Relation to His Times & Contemporaries*, 2 vols., New York, Boni and Liveright, 2: 319.

5. Ibid., 2: 195–289.

6. Benton MacKaye (1950) "Growth of a new science," *The Survey*, 86 (October), 439–52, reprinted in (1968) *From Geography to Geotechnics*, edited by Paul T. Bryant, Urbana, University of Illinois Press, 21–2. For an account of MacKaye's early years see Paul T. Bryant (1965) *The Quality of the Day: The Achievement of Benton MacKaye*, Ann Arbor, University Microfilms International, passim.

7. See MacKaye's account of his Washington activities in "Growth of a new science," reprinted in Bryant, *From Geography to Geotechnic*, 35–8.

8. MacKaye is quoted in an interview with Bryant, *The Quality of the Day*, 118–19.

9. Benton MacKaye (1921) "An Appalachian Trail: a project in regional planning," *Journal of the American Institute of Architects*, 9 (October), 3–8.

10. MacKaye's explanation of his "Barbarian Utopia" and the way to achieve it appears in (1927) "Outdoor culture—the philosophy of through trails," *Landscape Architecture*, 17 (April), 163–71, and is reprinted in Bryant, *From Geography to Geotechnics*, 169–79.

11. Lewis Mumford (1982) *Sketches from Life: The Autobiography of Lewis Mumford*, Boston, Beacon Press, 340.

12. Mumford's article for *The Nation* published in 1919 is quoted in Sussman, *Planning the Fourth Migration*, 13.

13. For Mumford's account of his origins, early childhood, and family life see *Sketches from Life*, chapters 2–4. The quotations in this account appear on pp. 10, 16–18, 62.

14. Lewis Mumford (1975) "Urban notes," in *Findings and Keepings: Analects for an Autobiography*, New York, Harcourt Brace Jovanovich, 25.

15. Mumford is quoted by John Fischer in (1968) "Schools for equal opportunity" in *The Schoolhouse in the City*, edited by Alvin Toffler, New York, Praeger.

16. For an account of these years see *Sketches from Life*, 100–156, and in particular 100–101, 133, 140–41, 151, 156.

17. Sir William Holford cites Mumford in his foreword to Philip Mairet (1957) *Pioneer of Sociology: The Life and Letters of Patrick Geddes*, London, Lund Humphries, xi–xii, xvi.

18. For Mumford's account of Cambridge and Boston in 1918, see *Sketches from Life*, 201–10.

19. Ibid., 202, 215, 218, 222, 276.

20. Lewis Mumford (1950) *The Story of Utopias*, Compass edition, New York, Viking, 33–4. First published in 1922.

21. Ibid., 280.

22. Lewis Mumford to Benton MacKaye, December 18, 1924, MacKaye Papers, Baker Library, Dartmouth College, Hanover, New Hampshire. Selections from the Mumford–MacKaye correspondence are quoted with the permission of the Baker Library.

23. "Random notes and letters," *Findings and Keepings*, 161.

24. "Geneva adventure," ibid., 94.
25. "Notes on Geneva," ibid., 96.
26. Lewis Mumford to Dorothy Cecilia Loch, December 8, 1925, ibid., 98–99.
27. Lewis Mumford (1955) *Sticks and Stones: A Study of American Architecture and Civilization*, 2d rev. ed., New York, Dover, 14. First published in 1924.
28. Ibid., 28.
29. Ibid., 27.
30. Ibid., 60–61.
31. Ibid., 96.
32. Ibid., 125.
33. Ibid., 201.
34. Ibid., 230.
35. Lewis Mumford (1928) "Introduction" in Benton MacKaye, *The New Exploration: A Philosophy of Regional Planning*, New York, Harcourt Brace, xvi.
36. Lewis Mumford, "The fourth migration," in Sussman, *Planning the Fourth Migration*, 57.
37. Ibid., 58.
38. Ibid., 60.
39. Ibid., 62.
40. Benton MacKaye, "The new exploration: charting the industrial wilderness," in Sussman, *Planning the Fourth Migration*, 98.
41. Ibid., 106–10.
42. The exchange between Mumford and Adams, which originally appeared in *The New Republic*, 15 (June 22, July 6, 1932), is reprinted in Sussman, *Planning the Fourth Migration*, 224–67.
43. Mumford, *Sketches from Life*, 411.
44. For Mumford's account of his life in Sunnyside Gardens see ibid., 410–21.
45. Benton MacKaye to Lewis Mumford, December 3, 1926, MacKaye Papers.
46. Ibid.
47. Benton MacKaye to Lewis Mumford, May 21, 1927, MacKaye Papers.
48. Benton MacKaye to Lewis Mumford, March 9, 1927, MacKaye Papers.
49. Benton MacKaye to Lewis Mumford, December 3, 1926, MacKaye Papers.
50. Lewis Mumford to Benton MacKaye, December 22, 1926, MacKaye Papers.
51. Ibid.
52. Lewis Mumford (1926) *The Golden Day: A Study in American Experience and Culture*, New York, Boni and Liveright, 1.
53. Ibid., 41.
54. Ibid.
55. Ibid., 34, 37, 41–2.
56. Ibid., 62–3.
57. Ibid., 34, 37, 40–1.
58. Ibid., 89–90.
59. Ibid., 142. Italics added.
60. Ibid., 130.
61. Benton MacKaye to Lewis Mumford, December 3, 1926, MacKaye Papers.

62. Lewis Mumford to Benton MacKaye, July 25, 1927, MacKaye Papers.
63. Benton MacKaye, *The New Exploration*, 50.
64. Ibid., 60–61.
65. Ibid., 63.
66. Ibid, 71–2ff.
67. MacKaye discusses the controls and their effects on metropolitanism in chapter XII, "Controlling the metropolitan invasion," ibid., 168–200.
68. Ibid., 195.
69. Thoreau is quoted in ibid., 212. MacKaye's comment follows directly.
70. Lewis Mumford to Van Wyck Brooks, July 30, 1934; Robert E. Spiller, ed. (1970) *The Van Wyck Brooks–Lewis Mumford Letters: The Record of a Literary Friendship, 1921–1963*, New York, E. P. Dutton, 107.
71. Lewis Mumford (1960s) "Random notes and personalia, 1960s," Lewis Mumford Papers, Special Collections, Van Pelt Library, University of Pennsylvania, Philadelphia. Quoted with permission.

FIGURE 12.1   *Catherine Bauer would have a lifelong interest in housing and planning issues.*

I 2

An Urban View
CATHERINE BAUER'S FIVE QUESTIONS

EUGENIE LADNER BIRCH

SOME FIELDS HAVE AN IMMENSE dynamism and vibrancy because an exceptional person comes along who asks the right questions, incisively criticizes current conditions, and accurately foresees future trends. This critical capacity endows the individual with the directive power to actually shape a profession and its paradigms for a generation. Catherine Bauer Wurster was such a person, a fact confirmed yet again by the American Institute of Certified Planners, which has named her a "planning pioneer" joining Harland Bartholomew, Tracy Augur, and Clarence Stein. Bauer's influence rests on a variety of positions that she took in her writing during a thirty-year span from 1934 to 1964, a critical period in the life of the nation as well as in the history of American city planning.

Clearly, other factors have to be in place for such leadership to emerge and to capture interests and concerns in a singular fashion. Catherine Bauer Wurster was active during a time when the United States experienced enormous socioeconomic changes. The nation's

I would like to thank Roger Montgomery who inspired me to write this essay, Deborah Gardner who served as an incisive critic, Molly Vaux who lent a sharp eye and pencil to the final version, and three anonymous reviewers who offered advice.

Reprinted with permission from Eugenie Ladner Birch, "An Urban View: Catherine Bauer's Five Questions," *Journal of Planning Literature*, 4, no. 3 (Summer 1989): 239–258. Copyright © 1989 by the Ohio State University Press. All rights reserved.

population, which grew from 123 million in 1930 to 179 million in 1960, was becoming increasingly more urban. In 1930 more than half of all Americans lived in urban areas: by 1960 almost three-quarters would dwell in them. In these three decades metropolitan districts gained 55 million people—more than 70 percent (or 38 million) of whom settled in the suburbs.[1] Reeling from an era that had progressed from depression and massive relief through a world war to a time of unparalleled prosperity, this mobile population would create a new metropolitan pattern across the nation in the postwar period. As in the thirties, urban areas of the sixties featured a business core and its surrounding residential rings. But unlike the earlier model, the center was a desolate and obsolete central business district just experiencing the beginning of the migration of retail and office trade to the outlying areas. Next came surrounding blighted areas filled with poor newcomers—southern blacks, Puerto Ricans, and Appalachian whites—living in worn-out housing in deteriorated neighborhoods. This ring blended into the so-called gray areas of older but solid housing mixed with stores and small factories. Finally came the suburbs, the prewar railroad commuter towns and the new ones made accessible by mass car ownership, all raw with newly developed subdivisions leapfrogging across the landscape. These changes seemed to be out of control and to threaten past economic and political security.

Throughout these volatile years, the nation redefined the roles of federal, state, and local governments, particularly with regard to metropolitan concerns. For example, during this thirty-year period, the nation slowly accepted the provision of low-cost housing and the sponsorship of urban renewal as public responsibilities to be addressed at local and federal levels. It also struggled to respond to suburban expansion by supporting the construction of the federal highway system and the propagation of local zoning and master plans. Planners, though few in number, were immersed in these activities, acting as lobbyists for urban-oriented policy, interpreters of newly passed legislation, and administrators of proliferating metropolitan programs.

Just as the nation was restructuring its intergovernmental posture toward cities, planners were redefining their profession to encompass a larger number of efforts. In fact, in 1938 they had even changed the name of the American City Planning Institute to the

American Institute of Planners to reflect their participation in activities not exclusively focused on the city. For during the New Deal era they had helped design greenbelt towns, they had become state planners for the National Resources Planning Board, and they had run the technical division of the Federal Housing Administration. After World War II they oversaw urban renewal programs and wrote the comprehensive plans so eagerly demanded by cities and suburbs alike in the fifties and sixties. Numbering under three hundred in the thirties, the planners were almost three thousand strong in the sixties.[2] It was in this environment that Catherine Bauer Wurster developed her philosophy and assumed a leadership role.

For over three decades Catherine Bauer Wurster was the conscience for urban America. She was always present, commenting, reminding, cajoling, and highlighting those critical issues that were at the center of America's metropolitan transformation and its attempts to redefine public responsibility and restructure intergovernmental relations. Combining activism with reflection, she focused on five key issues: low-cost housing, its design and delivery; urban renewal, its content and placement; suburbanization, its nature and form; social planning, its definition and integration with public policy; and urbanization in the developing world, its problems and possible solutions. Together, her positions on each of these topics form an integrated view of a desired urban world.

Catherine Bauer Wurster based her vision on a firm, individualistic philosophy that combined tenets of regional planning with her own brand of architectural criticism and plain common sense. As the years wore on she never shrank from admitting mistakes, and revised her thinking accordingly. Thus her views evolved, but addressed the full dimensions of metropolitan concerns as they emerged over time. At all times, she was ahead of the urban professionals. While they tended to be absorbed in narrow solutions to specific problems, she added a broad perspective as she framed answers to the same questions. She did this as a self-taught observer of public life who was particularly sensitive to metropolitan conditions and trends. By 1959 even those whom she criticized most harshly, the planners, recognized her contributions. That year, the American Institute of Planners named her an honorary member, noting her influence as a writer, lecturer, housing lobbyist and administrator, and teacher of planning.

A Brief Biography

Investigating the nature of Catherine Bauer's vision must begin with a look at her life. This will place her work in context and help explain the origin of some of her beliefs. Additionally, it will demonstrate that, despite the limitations on women's career choices during much of her lifetime, Bauer's expertise won her achievement.

Born in 1905 in Elizabeth, New Jersey, to upper middle-class parents, Bauer had a thoroughly conventional upbringing. Her early appreciation of the physical environment may have come from her father, Jacob L. Bauer. He was a highway engineer who oversaw the construction of the Pulaski Skyway linking New Jersey and New York, experimented with early cloverleaf intersection designs and advocated superhighway city bypasses. Her later concern for land conservation may have been stimulated by her mother, Alberta Krouse Bauer, who imbued her three children with a love of nature.[3]

Catherine, the oldest child, was an excellent student and exhibited an independent streak that bordered on rebellion when confronted with unwanted restrictions. She had a rigorous education for her day. She attended the exclusive Vail Deane School for Girls before enrolling at Vassar College, where she majored in literature and art. In her junior year, she transferred to Cornell to study architecture but returned to Vassar to graduate with her class in 1926.[4]

For the next few years, she openly rejected the conventions of her background as she blossomed intellectually. A daughter of the "Roaring Twenties," she lived fully, taking a post-graduate year in Paris and then a few more in Greenwich Village. In this period, she acquired a broad knowledge of modern architecture—she sought out Le Corbusier's workers' flats outside Paris and sold an article about them to the *New York Times Magazine* when she was only twenty-three. During a short-lived job as advertising manager of Harcourt Brace, she met Lewis Mumford. He was ten years older and already an established writer. Joined by a common interest in architecture—and in each other—Bauer and Mumford were lovers between 1930 and 1934. On the intellectual level, they had an uncommon equality in their relationship. In this period and in the ensuing thirty years, they would discuss and critique each other's work. They were united by their shared belief in regional planning based on garden city principles.[5]

FIGURE 12.2   *Lewis Mumford was intellectually united with Catherine Bauer by their shared interest in architecture and regional planning.*

During these years, Bauer immersed herself in the study of architecture and urban design. On two European trips—one by herself and one with Mumford—she visited Sweden, Austria, England, Holland, France, and Germany where she focused on residential construction. She even enrolled as the sole American out of 150 participants in a new buildings course held in Frankfurt in 1930. She soon concluded that modern architecture was more than just an aesthetic statement. Believing its best expression was found in low-cost housing in large-scale developments employing mass production techniques, she assumed a lifelong interest in what was known in Europe as "social housing."[6]

Returning to New York, Bauer eked out a living as writer and researcher. After making her mark by winning a *Fortune Magazine* contest with an article on German housing, she became an architectural critic for *Arts Weekly*, a freelance contributor to the *New Republic* and the *Nation*, and an assistant to Mumford's friend, Clarence Stein. Stein, the architect of Sunnyside (Long Island City, N.Y.) and Radburn (N.J.), commissioned Bauer to study shopping centers and community facilities for large-scale residential developments. This work gave her firsthand experience in analyzing the social and economic intricacies of integrating community facilities with housing.[7] Following the 1932 European trip with Lewis Mumford, she tired of her scrambling existence and decided to write a book on housing using the material she had gathered. The result, *Modern Housing*, published in 1934, was a critical success.[8] Appearing in the depths of the Depression, her defense of publicly financed new construction appealed to many Americans. Her call to organize labor to gain political support for that goal seemed logical to others.

Although these varied experiences established Bauer as a "public housing expert," the field offered her few employment opportunities. In the early days of the New Deal, the only housing activity was the temporary relief operation of the fledgling Public Works Administration (PWA) created by the National Industrial Recovery Act of 1932.[9] The PWA Housing Division, under the leadership of New York architect Robert D. Kohn, was just getting organized. It had granted its first loan to a Philadelphia labor union to build a limited dividend project, the Carl Mackley Houses.[10] Secured by Russian émigré architect Oscar Stonorov and Quaker hosiery-worker organizer John Edelman, the project received enormous publicity, and its sponsors numerous requests for information and technical aid. They hired Bauer to assist them in dealing with these demands. After moving to Philadelphia, she not only immersed herself in these aspects but also jumped into organizing the Labor Housing Conference, a group formed to lobby for federally supported low-cost shelter.[11]

As the tireless executive secretary of this organization—which was always on the brink of bankruptcy—she would spend the next four years fighting for a permanent housing program, a campaign that culminated successfully in the passage of the Wagner–Steagall Act in the summer of 1937. Dubbed "a little blonde girl with big brunette economic ideas," by a mocking *Chicago Daily News* reporter covering her activities, she first convinced the American Federation of Labor to recognize the Labor Housing Conference and to make her the A.F. of L. official housing lobbyist—no mean feat for a Vassar graduate.[12] Thirty years old, savvy and full of energy, she was so diligent that Harold Ickes, Secretary of the U.S. Department of the Interior, which housed the PWA program, regarded her with suspicion and labeled her a "wild eyed female" in his *Secret Diary.*[13] Undeterred, Bauer galvanized critical labor support, assisted in drafting public housing legislation, and later became Director of Information and Research in the United States Housing Authority (USHA), the agency created to administer the new program. Her government career lasted less than a year, for she quickly tired of bureaucratic detail. While at the Authority, however, she orchestrated a public relations campaign, wrote prodigiously, and most important, helped draw up the working regulations to implement the legislation.[14] The latter included setting minimum physical standards, tenant selection policies, and rent schedules.

In the forties, Bauer would have a different and almost conventional life. Resigning from the USHA in 1939, she returned to Europe to complete a postponed Guggenheim Fellowship—the first awarded, by the way, for the study of architecture and housing—but aborted her plans with the onset of the Second World War. Returning to America, she accepted an invitation to be the Rosenberg Professor of Public Social Services at the University of California at Berkeley.[15] There she met and married William Wilson Wurster in August 1940. Ten years her senior, Wurster had a broad San Francisco architecture practice that included commissions for residences, college dormitories, war housing, office buildings, and recreational facilities, all of which earned him the high regard of his peers.[16]

FIGURE 12.3   *William W. Wurster and Catherine Bauer were a forceful team in planning and architecture.*

Settling in California, Bauer taught, wrote, consulted, and was active in local housing and planning affairs.

In 1942, Bauer and Wurster moved to Cambridge, Massachusetts. Seeking a respite from his sixteen years of practice, Wurster retired temporarily and became a student again, enrolling at Harvard and MIT. In 1944, he was named the dean of MIT's School of Architecture, a position he would hold for the next six years.[17] During this time, Bauer followed a typically frenetic schedule: she taught a housing seminar at Harvard, helped reorganize the failing lobbying group, the National Housing Conference, and in 1945 at the age of forty bore a child, Sarah Louise Wurster.[18]

Bauer continued to focus on the fate of public housing. The 1937 authorizations under the Wagner–Steagall Act had run out and the legislative struggle for the Housing and Slum Clearance Act of 1949 was even more bitter than the earlier fight. In this context she was, however, opposed to the brand of slum clearance—advocated by real estate interests—that focused on land acquisition and ignored low-cost housing. She considered this tactic a bailout and spoke against it at every opportunity.[19]

In 1950, when the Wursters returned to the University of California at Berkeley—William as dean of the School of Architecture and Catherine as a lecturer in city and regional planning—Bauer's career took a new turn. While continuing to monitor the federal housing program and even revising her views on how the program should be carried out, she began to call more forcefully for what would become the concerns of social planning—increased citizen participation and inclusionary zoning. Further, clearly influenced by California's accelerating postwar growth, she turned her attention to suburbanization. When treating contemporary urban spatial development, she of course integrated her outspoken views on housing and redevelopment. Finally, she enlarged her concerns to include urbanization in developing countries. Consulting assignments to India in the fifties and a later Ford Foundation project there led to an enduring interest that she translated into several notable publications.

By the fifties, through her clear articulation of metropolitan growth issues and her advocacy of long range planning, Bauer emerged as a principal theorist recognized by policymakers regardless of political affiliation. In 1960 she wrote "Framework for an Urban Society," a chapter in the final report of President Dwight D. Eisenhower's Commission on National Goals.[20] Four years later, President Lyndon B. Johnson included her among a small group of experts on his Task Force on Urban and Metropolitan Problems.[21]

In November 1964, Catherine Bauer's career was cut short when she died in a hiking accident. Only fifty-nine years old, she left many mourners. Coleman Woodbury, a long-time associate who had worked with her in the 1937 legislative campaign, wrote in an obituary that

[a]mong her contemporaries she was unique: the career of none of them paralleled or matched hers and no one on the scene today seems likely to take her place. Her career, of course, covered years of drastic and far reaching changes in urban life. . . . Two principal features of the period have been the vastly enlarging role of governmental . . . programs and more recently, the outpouring of scholarly . . . writing about urban affairs. . . . Yet somewhat paradoxically Catherine's unchallenged position was attained despite the fact that, with the exception of a few months in the early days of the United States Housing Authority, she never held a significant government job and, although she taught part time over many years, she [was not] essentially an academic. . . . .She had a first-rate

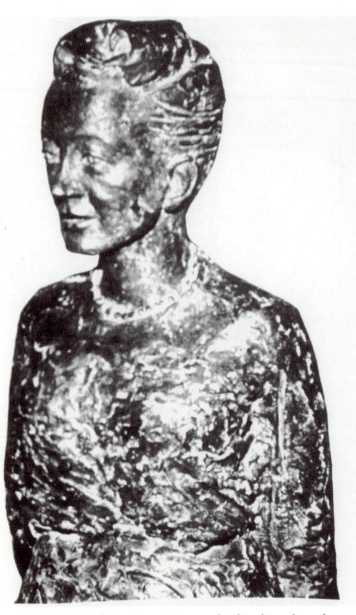

FIGURE 12.4   *Catherine Bauer is immortalized in this sculpture by Oscar Stonorov.*

intellect and knew how to use it. . . . Her conversation, speeches, and writing revealed a clear perspective on the urban scene, a sense of priorities, an almost unerring feel for what was central and essential in all the complexity of modern urbanism.[22]

At the time of Bauer's death, the federal government was still deeply engaged in urban programs, some of which had more political clout than others. Public housing slowly plugged along while redevelopment activities blazed ahead. In the twenty-six years since the passage of the first housing legislation, the government had built about 350,000 units at a total development cost of over $5 billion. In contrast, under the newer Housing and Slum Clearance Act of 1949, the Urban Renewal Administration secured authorizations for $8.3 billion for its projects.[23]

In 1967, three years after Bauer died, Robert C. Weaver, Secretary of the recently formed Department of Housing and Urban Development (HUD), would dedicate its new ten-story office building—a far cry from the makeshift quarters that the USHA occupied when Bauer was Director of Information and Research. At the same time, he would unveil a rough-hewn statue of a small woman. Her hair brushed back, her mouth half-smiling and her eyes intent upon an unseen goal, Catherine Bauer lives on at HUD, commemorated in Oscar Stonorov's sculpture and in Weaver's words: "Few individuals have left more of a mark on public policy in the area of urban and metropolitan problems."[24]

A VISION OF BALANCE

Bauer's mark was a consistent and logical urban vision based on the acceptance of an amended American capitalistic system, an understanding of modern economics and sociology as directed to the metropolis, an appreciation of the use of technological advances in architecture in helping to solve human problems, and a sensitivity to social indicators pointing to impending changes in urban life. This vision called for the deployment of public resources to promote the balanced development of neighborhoods, cities, and metropolitan regions.

In developing her scheme, she began from the smaller unit, the house, and worked toward the larger, the region. America, she believed, should provide low-cost housing for all workers. These units should be designed to enhance human interchange and strengthen social bonds in impersonal urban environments. Cities should never grow too large nor cater to only one sector of the population. Regions should contain well-planned areas for living, working, and playing. Government, assisted by appropriately trained professionals, should oversee equitable, orderly, and efficient urban development. They should take local customs and values into account when planning neighborhoods, cities, and regions. The key word in all her work was balance. Life in the American metropolis would be in equilibrium when every working citizen had a decent home, every city had a mixed population and rational land-use arrangement, and every region had a series of self-contained cities and ample recreation space. The details of Bauer's view are best understood by examining her positions in her five areas of interest (low-cost housing, urban renewal and slum clearance, suburban development, social planning, and urbanization of the third world). Posing the following questions about these topics assists in comprehending Bauer's prescriptions and, more important, in appreciating her mark on urban policy:

1. How can we produce abundant, low-cost housing satisfying to its inhabitants?
2. Do we really want to support slum clearance and urban renewal?
3. What should the postwar metropolitan region look like?
4. How can planners incorporate social questions into their approaches—and why should they?
5. How should we regard urbanization in the third world?

QUESTION ONE: *How can we produce abundant low-cost housing satisfying to its inhabitants?*

In Bauer's view, increasing the supply of inexpensive yet satisfying housing could occur only one way: under public sponsorship, using modern architectural techniques, and employing contemporary economic knowledge for site location. Like most reformers of her time, Bauer believed that America owed its workers decent, affordable dwellings. Further, she argued that such housing had to be regarded as a public utility because the private sector clearly could not produce sufficient inexpensive, safe, and sanitary shelter. Therefore, the government had the responsibility to do so.[25]

In the beginning of her career, Bauer had more faith in exclusive public landlordship of low-cost housing than at the end. In *Modern Housing* she insisted that "only governments can make the decisive steps and set up the new method of house production as social investment."[26] By the late fifties, she reversed herself admitting that dependence on public housing had been a strategic mistake from the point of view of both political support and production.[27] Earlier she had envisioned the growth of massive union support but this did not materialize. After the war, fully employed organized labor would fight for wage increases and not look to public housing programs for jobs and cheap shelter. Other political support for public housing was either too weak or too disorganized. Consequently, government did not initiate any more than a minimal amount. Further, after witnessing more than twenty years of centralized control in the American program, Bauer called for a more decentralized approach. Localities needed to create individual solutions, she argued. She called for community-level comprehensive housing plans, generated in conjunction with a master plan.[28] Studying a locality's shelter needs would also identify the financial arrangements—mortgage insurance, loans and grants to support rehabilitation or construction of private and public housing and community facilities, and funds for land acquisition—necessary to make the plans a reality. Flexibility would be the guiding principle directing all manner of forces to alleviate the shortage of low-cost housing. Bauer made the latter suggestion in 1953, well before federal legislation mandated housing assistance plans as a prerequisite for community block grant funds. Both in the thirties and later in her revisionary period, Bauer was well in advance of her contemporaries in her prescriptions for the delivery of low-cost housing.

Bauer believed that masses of inexpensive housing could be produced by employing modern architectural techniques. She was especially attracted to the modernists' functionalism or "full use of technology in design" to "improve the human environment in modern industrial society." She singled out the work of J. J. P. Oud in Rotterdam, Walter Gropius in Berlin, and others who fashioned cheap, durable industrial products—cement slabs, glass, and iron—into low-cost shelter.[29] Their unornamented, flat-roofed, box-like dwellings displayed not only their real use but also declared that mass production in architecture could be aesthetic as well.[30] In Bauer's opinion, modern architects made their projects economical and efficient through extensive use of the principles of large-scale development, an approach elaborated and demonstrated by the British and American architects Raymond Unwin and Henry Wright. This concept required planning multiple-acre sites as whole entities and allowed for significant savings in infrastructure investment and upkeep. Fewer streets and more carefully plotted sewerage and water lines left more land for amenities and, in fact, led to lower densities. Such layouts also had value because the sizable sites gave more opportunity for imaginative massing of buildings and creative landscaping.[31]

For Bauer, a student of land economics, the most logical way of siting the housing designed according to modernist principles was to place new units on cheap land that would most likely be found at the perimeter of the city.[32] In all her years of observation, she never wavered in this belief despite the disagreement of many of her peers, who adhered instead to replacement housing on slum clearance sites.[33] Originally, Bauer believed that slum clearance and the delivery of housing were incompatible, citing European experience that indicated that more dwellings would be produced when the delivery of shelter, not the destruction of deteriorated areas, was the priority. After the passage of the 1949 Housing and Slum Clearance Act, however, Bauer called for using the legislated write-down process, that is, government condemnation and later resale of land at a bargain price to reduce costs and to ensure the construction of inexpensive housing. In fact, she added, these smaller units might even be palatable in suburban communities.[34] Her optimism seems unwarranted today, in light of the continuing resistance to subsidized housing in the suburbs. In Yonkers, New York, for example, opponents of public housing have spent millions of dollars in legal fees fighting a court order to provide a few hundred units throughout the town.

Not only did Bauer advocate the use of modern architectural techniques to produce abundant low-cost housing but she also believed that these techniques could be helpful in producing shelter that was satisfying to its inhabitants. Satisfaction could be achieved by copying the modernists' "scientific approach to human needs and uses in programming, planning and design."[35] They studied local conditions and customs to adapt designs to social, economic and environmental needs. Bauer extolled German site planning, which consciously maximized sun exposure, a quality that distinguished the twentieth-century dwelling from the dreary, dark tenement of the past.[36] But she strongly decried the mindless choice of inappropriate materials, observing, "Maximum glass may have been desirable in Northern Germany but hardly in South America."[37]

A more important application of her maxim of rational analysis pertained to density in postwar public housing. Fully cognizant of existing economic constraints, she nonetheless condemned the local authorities' sponsorship of skyscraper-dominated projects. American families did not want to live in high-rise buildings, she declared in her famous article, "The Dreary Deadlock of Public Housing," which appeared in the *Architectural Forum* in May 1957.[38] In her mind, multistory apartments not only were deficient in both interior and exterior space, but also lacked true residential character. Architects who studied American tastes, customs, and habits, rather than duplicating the Corbusien aesthetic, should know that skyscrapers were the antithesis of the American Dream, the single-family house with its own backyard. Although they probably could not design individual dwellings within government economic restrictions, she continued, they could design other forms, such as the row house, to provide the desired qualities of privacy, independence and affordability.[39]

Finally, Bauer's concept of an architecture based on a "scientific approach" incorporated more than physical principles. She envisioned the use of social science analysis that could inform designers about social organization. "The modern planner does not only provide shelter for that statistical 'average' family composed (so it is rumored) of 4.5 persons," she wrote in 1934. "He realizes that there is no such thing as an average person and that even a small housing development will include" large families, the elderly, and single women who should be accommodated in dwellings designed to meet their special requirements.[40]

Bauer also recognized that superblocks, which were the basic building block in the modern architects' schemes, could support "indoor [and outdoor] social space," thus enhancing opportunities for community life within the settlement.[41] Originally, Bauer believed that a major benefit of large-scale developments was their transfer of individualized household functions to more efficient group services such as communal laundries and child care. Like many women of the thirties, she hoped that these amenities would enhance the modern family by encouraging a more satisfying collective life. By the fifties she revised this view, bowing to contemporary psychological theories that avowed the primacy of the child-mother relationship and called for housing that would bolster this concept by providing individual backyards and parental child care. While not recommending the total deletion of parks, playgrounds, and community space, she cautioned designers to be wary of losing sight of the need to allow for privacy and independence. Of course, her revision came at the height of suburban expansion. This form of domestic life was centered ideally around the single-family house and depended on a working father and a homebound mother catering to the needs of two or three children. Dad performed the weekly lawnmowing with ceremony and Mom would no more have left her babies in a community playground than have gone to the moon! Or so it was believed. Betty Friedan's *Feminine Mystique*, published twenty-five years ago, revealed the dismal underpinning of this model for middle-class women.[42]

QUESTION TWO: *Do we really want to support slum clearance and urban redevelopment?*

Bauer supported slum clearance and urban redevelopment but conditioned her support on quite specific beliefs. Her formula was simple and sequential: link redevelopment with provision of low-cost housing. Build inexpensive dwellings on cheap peripheral land obtained through eminent domain for a population to be displaced by center city slum clearance or rehabilitation. Rebuild cities according to sound economic principles, knowing that land in downtowns—whether or not a write-down procedure is used—is expensive. It should be used for and by those who can pay for it. Timing is important. Slum clearance should occur only after the construction of replacement shelter. In her prescription, she would differ with both the housers and the redevelopment officials of the times. The former wanted slum site replacement shelter, the latter did not want to bother with relocation.[43]

Before and after the passage of the 1949 Housing and Slum Clearance Act, Bauer persistently challenged those urban redevelopment advocates whose ideas differed from hers. In particular, she rejected their vision of using slum clearance solely to rescue declining central city real estate values, their strongly held belief in the town-by-town approach, and their narrow focus on blighted areas. Instead, she called for redevelopment policy based on regional population movements, metropolitan economic conditions, the improvement of race relations and the comprehensive analyses of larger-than-city-based housing needs. "What we need," she insisted, "is representative regional government with a unified and effective land use policy. It's too late for that in this boom but surely this is the time . . . to take some step in that direction."[44]

When Bauer reported on one of the earliest redevelopment trials, New York City's Stuyvesant Town, which was built under state enabling legislation in 1947, she labeled it a prime example of a misguided scheme. Not only did this slum clearance project double the population of an already congested area but its tenant selection policies precluded residence by ninety-three percent of the neighborhood's inhabitants and sanctioned racial discrimination. Outraged at the use of public subsidy—tax abatement—to accomplish these ends, she condemned all programs that did not address the problems of low-cost housing. In particular, she berated planners for ignoring this essential fact in an address to their annual meeting: "One great central illusion of the redevelopment movement has been the notion that urban redevelopment could be successfully promoted and achieved quite apart from housing."[45]

Over the years, Bauer was profoundly disappointed by the lack of support for her vision among redevelopment leaders, despite being fully cognizant of the tenuous nature of the coalition of public housing, planning, and real estate lobbies that had joined forces to secure passage of the 1949 Housing and Slum Clearance Act. "Seldom has such a variegated crew of would-be angels tried to sit on the same pin at the same time," she observed in a 1953 essay, "Redevelopment: A Misfit in the Fifties." Further, she recognized that everyone involved substantially underestimated the complexity and responsibilities of the program.[46] Nonetheless, she puzzled at why a situation so clear to her seemed to evade the government administrators charged with implementing the policy. What she lacked, perhaps, was a more hardened understanding of what compromises were required to achieve her design. Or perhaps she knew all too well, but felt that someone—she, herself—had to keep reminding the public about what kind of slum clearance and urban redevelopment would best serve its collective interests.

QUESTION THREE: *What should the postwar metropolitan region look like?*

Bauer derived her clear vision for metropolitan development

FIGURE 12.5   *Bauer decried post-war urban renewal programs featuring extensive clearance and high-rise construction as a perversion of the original housing precepts she had fought for earlier.*

from the tenets of the Regional Planning Association of America (RPAA), which promoted British garden city principles in the 1920s. She called for "balanced, reasonably self-sufficient communities with open space between." Her metropolitan network, however, differed in scale from the parent paradigm. Cities of half a million— not the English town of thirty thousand to sixty thousand—were the aim. Interdependence and integration among cities—not total self-sufficiency—were desirable. And above all, Americans needed to create communities that they themselves really *liked*.[47]

Not a pure decentrist, as were Lewis Mumford and others of the RPAA, Bauer was a conservationist, primarily concerned about the ill effects of suburban sprawl (or "scatteration" as she first called it). In *Modern Housing*, in 1934, and again in several wartime articles, she had correctly warned about the impending disaster.[48] To Californians (and by implication to all Americans) she wrote:

If the trends of the 30's were simply picked up and continued after the war, metropolitan areas such as Los Angeles County would simply find themselves with wider and wider circles of blight at the center (and in outlying shantytowns) alleviated only partly by oases of public housing and more strings of speculative development farther and farther out until the whole county would be gray and formless with buildings everywhere, no community integration anywhere and hopeless problems of transportation utilities and service and general amenity.[49]

Bauer had a particular talent for describing current trends. During the 1950s and 1960s she relentlessly pounded in her message, becoming especially strident as she unhappily surveyed the course of contemporary urban policy. Stealing from Gertrude Stein, she reported of suburbs: "There is no there out there."[50] She lamented the brutality, overstandardization, and loss of local history in redeveloped central cities.[51] She decried public housing's institutional character and uninspired design.[52]

As she sought to convince America to recast its programs in accord with her vision, she used every journalistic trick she could muster: shock, enchantment, reason, and anger. In a tightly argued 1956 article in the *Architectural Forum*, "First Job: Control New City Sprawl," she worked with what would be a rather accurate projection. Predicting a thirty-five percent increase in population by 1975 (there was, in fact, such an increase) she envisioned "a staggering prospect. . . . The overwhelming majority of the newcomers—at least 46 million of them and probably more will veer from the central city to the fringe."[53] Further, she argued, if this flow were undirected, the fate of the suburbs would be traffic congestion, expensive infrastructure installation, leapfrog development, and designed monotony. In her usual blunt language she would point out what, lamentably, has also become a fact of life in today's world: "[T]he greatest threat to old cities . . . is the trend toward increasing domination of the disadvantaged, low income and minority families who have no other choice in the current housing market."[54] In fact, as early as 1952 she had already accurately foreseen what today has become an unpleasant and problematic reality:

To some future historian, the most significant fact about housing and city planning policy in the United States in our time may be the extent to which it promoted racial integration or conversely strengthened the pattern of discrimination and segregation.[55]

Reasonably, she analyzed American choices. We could, she speculated, look to visionary models—Ebenezer Howard's Garden Cities, Stein's Radburn, Frank Lloyd Wright's Broadacre City, or Le Corbusier's Ville Radieuse. But she quickly rejected these as being, respectively, too simplistic, too indefensible, too wasteful, and too contrary to American values. We need to understand, she urged, the reasons for the popularity of the suburbs and the lack of appeal of the cities.[56] In "Can Cities Compete with Suburbia for Family Living?," a 1964 article in the *Architectural Record,* she isolated five desirable qualities found in outlying areas: automobile mobility; moderately priced, acceptable homes; good schools; accessibility to nature; and exclusive communities (meaning homogeneity in population).[57]

She angrily attacked current urban policies that threatened or discouraged the promotion of the five desirable features. Urban programs would work, she argued, only if employed on a regional basis. What we need, she insisted, is a "consistent framework for the social, economic and physical organization of metropolitan communities [for] at this level . . . we have a tremendous opportunity to

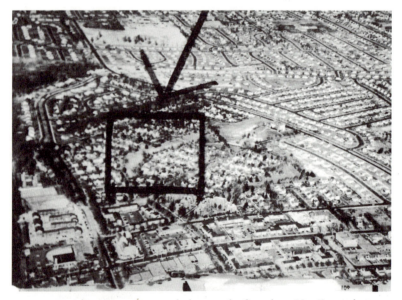

FIGURE 12.6   *A post-war areal photograph of northern New Jersey shows Radburn (boxed area) engulfed by suburban sprawl.*

shape the . . . environment."[58] The suggested framework's elements
included:

- Suburbs with residential choice open to all economic and
  racial groups;
- Cities with a selection of homes suitable for families;
- Superior urban schools;
- Downtowns offering distinct and exciting features;
- Suburbs with organized urban elements;
- Transportation networks co-ordinated between city and
  suburb;
- Leisure-time facilities on an urban and regional basis;
- Controlled suburban growth planned to minimize envi-
  ronmental pollution.[59]

In sum, what was needed, she insisted, was balanced growth
with compact, better-organized hinterlands and redefined, less dense
cities. She envisioned this new type of organization because, in her
words, "modern metropolitan trends have destroyed the traditional
concept of urban structure, and there is no image to take its place."[60]
It would be fair to say that more than twenty-five years after she
made this observation in her sole theoretical article, "The Form and
Structure of the Future Urban Complex," no one has developed a
new model of contemporary urban development.

QUESTION FOUR: *How can planners incorporate social questions into
their approaches—and why should they?*

In her writing, Bauer put her finger on an enduring professional
dilemma: the definition of the planner's role. Ideally, she noted, a
planner is a technical analyst and a reformer. Yet these two positions
are basically incompatible. The technical analyst's scientific base
tends to explain current conditions and usually concludes that the
observed phenomena are inevitable. In contrast, the reformer who
calls for bold change looks at but does not undertake rigorous
scientific study to come to his or her conclusion. By nature, the
cautious analyst hates to look foolish while the brash reformer likes
to take chances. Finding these qualities in a single practitioner is
unlikely.[61]

Nowhere was this dilemma more obvious than in the postwar
housing and urban redevelopment movement. Party to a small
conference organized to deal with these topics that was held in
Cambridge in 1949, Bauer reported a series of policy questions

emanating from these concerns. The concerns ranged from the most elemental to the most technical and were first published in an essay appearing in the *Journal of Social Issues* and later reprinted extensively.[62] While the technical questions are interesting and illustrate the need to find precise answers, the more probing issues raised in the essay address the technician-reformer conflict.

The essay, titled "Social Questions in Housing and Community Planning," was a group effort and benefited from an incipient postwar interest in urban sociology. It laid out the foundation for what would be recognized more formally fifteen years later as social planning. Written in the form of a series of questions, the text addressed five areas within the context of housing and urban redevelopment: "How does the decision-making process occur? Who should make value judgments about individual needs, preferences, family and community functions, group relations and the whole pattern of civic life? Who are the 'experts'? How do you transfer decision-making responsibility to citizens? How do you get people to consider the full range of possibilities available to them?" On the surface these questions appear routine, but, in reality, they formed the basis of a deep challenge to the way in which power was distributed and decisions made in the implementation of the housing and urban redevelopment programs.

In addition to raising these conceptual questions, Bauer always kept issues of social justice in the forefront of her work. In particular, she decried racial discrimination and urged its elimination at all levels. She objected to any federal housing or redevelopment policy that promoted racial segregation. She also spoke out against economic segregation. By the mid-fifties, in a major revision of her earlier stance she questioned the usefulness of the large-scale development that, ironically, through her (and others') efforts had become elementary planning dogma. Her early advocacy of public housing's economic and aesthetic benefits in her 1941 *Architectural Record* article, "A Balance Sheet of Progress," had originally blinded her to its greatest problem: ghettoization.[63] Sixteen years later in "The Dreary Deadlock of Public Housing," she admitted, "The public housing project . . . laid out as a 'community unit' as large as possible and entirely divorced from its neighborhood surroundings . . . only dramatizes the segregation of charity-case families."[64]

Bauer and her colleagues wanted social issues resolved for one important reason. In their view, planners and housers could make no progress unless they confronted and resolved these questions of equity, power, and planning. They had to investigate the fundamental values and implications of their recommendations and policies. Otherwise, all that they did would be for nought.

Bauer was clearly a pioneer in her effort to make the planning profession more conscious of power and citizen needs. Unfortunately, the majority of planners then did not listen to these questions. Perhaps they were too involved with the details of the burgeoning redevelopment program. Perhaps their professional training, largely in design, did not equip them to respond. Further, the American public neither paid attention to these issues nor forced the planners to do so. The times were relatively passive. None of the great social crises that dominated the sixties had even appeared on the horizon. The major civil rights battles had yet to be fought. The ignominy of a disastrous foreign war was unknown. The disappointment with urban schemes as expressed by the intellectuals, the activists, and the poor was not yet felt. In general, enfranchised Americans were satisfied and self-assured. They were not receptive to Bauer's disquieting questions.

QUESTION FIVE: *How should we regard urbanization in the third world?*

Although Bauer's experience in the developing world was limited—her total involvement spanned only about a decade—she nonetheless applied her analytical abilities to the emerging problems of these nations with her usual clarity and common sense. Population distribution and economic development had to be considered together, she maintained. National plans that disregarded the physical implications of economic development, as did the plans of India that she studied, were worthless.

Bemoaning the "lack of systematic coordination or contact between the economic planners . . . and city planners" in the developing world, Bauer argued that a country could not make substantial investments in its industrial and agricultural sectors without affecting land uses. Waiting until after urban problems occurred to act, as some experts recommended, was not only wasteful but foolish. What was needed was "a unified policy with respect to the location of basic economic activities and desirable patterns of urban growth."[65]

For Bauer, the guiding feature in development planning was the

FIGURE 12.7   *European housing architecture, driven by modernist principles, inspired Bauer's advocacy of similar designs in the United States.*

effort to derive maximum benefit from the allocation of limited resources. Thus, investing in smaller cities made more sense than pouring money into larger ones. She believed that land would be cheaper, infrastructure costs lower, and the promotion of self-help housing more likely in these areas than in the metropolises.[66]

Bauer had no time for the thoughtless imposition of European planning and architectural schemes in developing countries. New towns, for example, simply could not handle the expected one hundred million population growth in India and therefore would have "little meaning except as showpieces for tourists, Sunday supplements or political propaganda."[67] Urban redevelopment schemes and high-rise public housing were equally inappropriate because they were too expensive and socially unsuitable. She urged planners and architects to forget the supposed cultural superiority of the West and seek solutions sensitive to local conditions.[68]

CATHERINE BAUER'S LEGACY

These five questions form a full circle. At the center is Catherine Bauer with a simple, straightforward, logical, and consistent message that is at the same time elemental, incisive, and critical.

Much of the message seems commonplace today. Most planners have adopted as dogma what Bauer offered as vision. Although we may not be satisfied with today's answers, we can say that we have moved towards her urban view. Of course, the design of low-cost shelter should more closely reflect American residential norms. Today we are destroying high-rise postwar housing and replacing some of it with row houses or other units of more suitable residential character for families. Clearly, public sponsorship of affordable dwellings is necessary to ensure a proper supply. We recently passed a new housing act and are ever more insistent on government programs for the homeless. Certainly, urban redevelopment should incorporate economically based land uses. Downtown office construction on centrally located sites dominates our economic development schemes. Obviously, cities must be exciting and hospitable. Festival malls, aquariums, domed stadiums, gentrified neighborhoods, and historically preserved districts bear witness to this truth. Naturally, we believe in balanced and managed growth. Many communities are sponsoring land-use plans and wrestling with creative environmental controls in the face of challenging Supreme Court decisions like the *Nollan* and *First English* cases. Concentration of the disadvantaged in the inner city? Yes, it happened just as Bauer predicted. But inclusionary zoning is at the forefront of many planners' agendas. And the urbanization of other countries? New towns are largely dead, and self-help housing is standard procedure.

Bauer was not infallible. She made some errors; she misjudged the use of the large-scale development; she accepted the fifties nuclear family as status quo; and she exclusively relied on the concept of public landlordship of low-cost housing. Yet she did supply something that is clearly lacking in today's world: a broad vision. That vision shaped all her work. She did this despite her very narrow expertise in housing. She could easily have disappeared among the legions of shelter specialists who emerged in the postwar period. But she did not. Why not? Because she understood that no single functional element of the urban world—housing, transportation, infrastructure, employment programs, or environmental concerns—stands alone. Her deep appreciation of the interrelationship between architecture, urban design and land use, economic development, political power, and citizen participation allowed her to structure her thought and view her surroundings with an uncommon acuity. Few people today have taken as their life's work the ongoing observation and assessment of the urban world around them as did Catherine Bauer.

Perhaps someone will inherit Catherine Bauer's legacy and provide a vision to guide us into the twenty-first century. What will this new vision encompass? Following Bauer's model, it might treat:

1. Broad specifications for appropriate shelter for today's households—designs that incorporate an appreciation of our changing demography.

2. A prescription for sufficient, affordable housing.

3. A map for metropolitan organization—making sense of current urban dispersion and redefined downtowns as well as dealing with growth management issues.

4. A plan for democratic planning balancing citizen participation with centralized decision-making where the public interest would not be hostage to the NIMBY (not-in-my-back-yard) syndrome.

5. A sensitive view of world urbanization processes.

May this visionary of the future receive the same tributes as were accorded to Catherine Bauer in 1964:

> Among her contemporaries, she was unique. She had a first rate intellect and knew how to use it. [She had] an almost unerring feel for what was central and essential in all the complexity of modern urbanism.[69]

NOTES

1. Carl Abbott (1987) *Urban America in the Modern Age: 1920 to the Present*, Arlington Heights, Illinois, Harlan Davidson, 1–7.

2. Eugenie Ladner Birch (1980) "Advancing the art and science of planning, planners and their organizations," *Journal of the American Planning Association*, 76, 1 (January): 22–49.

3. Mary Susan Cole (1975) "Catherine Bauer and the public housing movement, 1926–1937," Ph.D. dissertation, George Washington University, 1975, 87–90.

4. "We Present . . . Catherine Bauer in her own words," *Journal of Housing*, 1 (November 1944), 27.

5. Catherine Bauer (1928) "Machine-age mansions for ultra-moderns: French builders apply ideas of the steel and concrete era in domestic architecture," *New York Times Magazine* (April 15), 10, 22; Lewis Mumford (1979) *My Works and Days: A Personal Chronicle*, New York, Harcourt, Brace, Jovanovich, 302–16.

6. "We present . . .," 27.
7. Catherine Bauer (1931) "Prize essay: art in industry," *Fortune*, 3 (May), 94–110; Catherine Bauer (1931) "Who cares about architecture?," *New Republic*, 66 (May 6), 326–7; Catherine Bauer (1931) "The Americanization of Europe: three leaves from a notebook," *New Republic*, 66 (June 24), 153–4; Catherine Bauer (1931) "Goût Américain, Demi Sec," *New Republic*, 69 (November 25), 45–6; Catherine Bauer (1932) "Exhibition of modern architecture, Museum of Modern Art," *Creative Art*, 10 (March), 201–6; Catherine Bauer (1932) "Architecture in Philadelphia," *Arts Weekly* (March 18), 151, 154; Catherine Bauer (1932) "Existenzminimum: apartments at $400 to $10,000 per year," *Arts Weekly* (April 2), 74–5; Catherine Bauer (1932) "More apartments," *Arts Weekly* (April 23), 124–5; Catherine Bauer (1932) "The palace of the popes," *Arts Weekly* (April 30), 177–8; Catherine Bauer (1933) "The Swiss family Borsodi," *Nation*, 137 (October 25), 489–91; "'Slum Clearance' or 'Housing'?," *Nation*, 137 (December 27), 730–31; Clarence Stein and Catherine Bauer (1934) "Store buildings and neighborhood centers," *Architectural Record*, 75, 2 (February), 174–87.
8. Catherine Bauer (1934) *Modern Housing*, Boston, Houghton Mifflin.
9. Eugenie Ladner Birch (1975) "Edith Elmer Wood and the rise of liberal housing," Ph.D. dissertation, Columbia University.
10. John F. Bauman (1987) *Public Housing, Race and Renewal: Urban Planning in Philadelphia, 1920–1974*, Philadelphia, Temple University Press, 22–56.
11. Cole, "Catherine Bauer," 208–371 passim.
12. "We Present . . .," 27.
13. Harold Ickes (1953) *The Secret Diary of Harold L. Ickes, the First Thousand Days, 1933–1936*, New York, Simon and Schuster, 218.
14. Catherine Bauer (1938) *Facts for a Housing Program*, Washington, D.C., U.S. Department of the Interior; Catherine Bauer (1938) *Housing progress and the Southeast*, Washington, D.C., U.S. Department of the Interior; Catherine Bauer (1938) "A year of the low rent housing program," *Shelter*, 3, 4 (November), 4–6; Catherine Bauer (1938) *Labor and the Housing Program*, Washington, D.C., U.S. Department of the Interior; Catherine Bauer (1939) *Local Housing Authorities and Their Public*, Washington, D.C., U.S. Department of the Interior; Catherine Bauer (1939) "Low rent housing and home economics," *Journal of Home Economics*, 31, 1 (January), 1–5; Catherine Bauer with Jacob Crane (1940) "What every family should have: two federal experts tally up the standards from cellar to garret, from neighborhood to community," *Survey Graphic*, 29, 2 (February), 64–5, 136–9; Catherine Bauer (1940) *A Citizen's Guide to Public Housing*, Poughkeepsie, New York, Vassar College.
15. "Housing's white knight," *Architectural Forum*, 84 (March 1946), 116–19, 146–52.
16. "William Wilson Wurster," *Architectural Forum*, 81 (July 1943), 45–65.
17. Eugenie L. Birch (1982) "William Wilson Wurster," in *Macmillan Encyclopedia of Architects*, New York, Macmillan, 50.
18. "Housing's white knight," 146–52.
19. See for example, Catherine Bauer (1943) "Urban redevelopment: crisis in land economics produces Hansen Greer plan and others," *Public Housing*

Progress, 9, 1 (January), 2, 5; Catherine Bauer (1946) "Is urban redevelopment possible under existing legislation?," in *Planning, 1946,* Chicago, American Society of Planning Officials; Catherine Bauer (1953) "The homebuilders take a 'new look' at slums—and raise some questions," *Journal of Housing,* 10, 10 (November), 371–3, 389.

20. Catherine Bauer (1960) "Framework for an urban society," in *Goals for Americans,* U.S. President's Commission on National Goals, New York, Prentice Hall, 223–47.

21. Coleman Woodbury, Weaver, Robert C., Shiskin, Boris, and Abrams, Charles (1964) "Catherine Bauer Wurster dies," *Journal of Housing,* 21 (December) 570–73.

22. Ibid., 570.

23. Warren Jay Vinton (1964) "The vital statistics of housing and community development," in *Housing Yearbook,* Washington, D.C., National Housing Conference.

24. "Bust of late Catherine Bauer Wurster placed in HUD building," *Journal of Housing,* 25, 8 (August 1968), 406–9.

25. Bauer, *Modern Housing,* 129.

26. Ibid., 242.

27. Catherine Bauer (1957) "The dreary deadlock of public housing," *Architectural Forum,* 106, 5 (May), 222.

28. Bauer, "The home builders," 372.

29. Catherine Bauer (1965) "The social front of modern architecture in the 1930's," *Journal of the Society of Architectural Historians,* 24, 1 (March), 48–52; Catherine Bauer (1961) "Architecture and the cityscape," *Journal of the American Institute of Architects,* 27 (March), 36–9.

30. Bauer, "The social front," 50.

31. Bauer, "The dreary deadlock," 221; Bauer, "Exhibition of modern architecture," 201–6.

32. Catherine Bauer (1941) "A balance sheet of progress," *Architectural Record,* 89, 5 (May), 89–105 passim.

33. Birch, "Edith Elmer Wood," chapter 6.

34. Catherine Bauer (1951) "Redevelopment and public housing," in *Planning, 1950,* Chicago, American Society of Planning Officials, 39–44; Catherine Bauer (1944) "Planning is politics . . . but are planners politicians?," *Pencil Points,* 25, 3 (March), 67.

35. Bauer, "The social front," 48.

36. Bauer, *Modern Housing,* 162, 178–82.

37. Bauer, "The social front," 49.

38. Bauer, "The dreary deadlock," 140–42, 219, 221–2.

39. Catherine Bauer (1939) "Clients for housing: the low income tenant: does he want supertenements?," *Progressive Architecture,* 33, 5 (January), 62–4. Catherine Bauer (1939) "Architectural opportunities in public housing," *Architectural Record,* 85, 1 (January), 65–8.

40. Bauer, *Modern Housing,* 204.

41. Bauer, "A balance sheet," 100.

42. Bauer, "The dreary deadlock," 221.

43. Bauer, "Clients for housing," 61.

44. Bauer, "Is urban redevelopment possible?," 70.
45. Ibid., 64.
46. Catherine Bauer (1953) "Redevelopment: a misfit in the fifties," in *The Future of Cities and Redevelopment*, edited by Coleman Woodbury, Chicago, University of Chicago Press, 9.
47. Bauer, "Planning is politics," 67; Catherine Bauer (1944) "Towards a green and pleasant England? A critical review of English publications in postwar planning," *Pencil Points*, 25, 4 (April), 78, 94, 100, 102, 104 passim; Catherine Bauer (1956) "Do Americans hate cities?," *Journal of the American Institute of Planners*, 23, 1 (Winter), 3.
48. Bauer, *Modern Housing*, 186; Catherine Bauer (1943) "Cities in flux, a challenge to the postwar planners," *American Scholar*, 13, 1 (Winter), 70–84; Catherine Bauer (1942) "War-time housing in defense areas," *Architect and Engineer*, 150, 2 (August), 33–5.
49. Catherine Bauer (1943) "Housing: a memorandum," *California Arts and Architecture*, 60 (February), 18–19.
50. Bauer, "Architecture and the cityscape," 36.
51. Ibid., 38.
52. Catherine Bauer (1952) "Low buildings? Catherine Bauer questions Mr. Yamasaki's arguments," *Journal of Housing*, 9, 9 (September), 322.
53. Catherine Bauer (1956) "First job: control new city sprawl," *Architectural Forum*, 105, 3 (September), 105.
54. Catherine Bauer (1964) "Can cities compete with suburbia for family living?," *Architectural Record*, 136, 6 (December), 155.
55. Bauer, "Redevelopment: A misfit," 22.
56. Bauer, "Can cities compete," 149.
57. Ibid., 152–5.
58. Bauer, "Framework," 228.
59. Ibid., 232–41.
60. Catherine Bauer (1963) "The form and structure of the future urban complex," in *Cities and Space*, edited by Lowden Wingo, Jr., Baltimore, Johns Hopkins University Press, 73.
61. Catherine Bauer (1964) "Introduction," in *Exploration into Urban Structure*, edited by Mel Webber, Philadelphia, University of Pennsylvania Press, 10–11.
62. Catherine Bauer (1951) "Social questions in housing and community planning," *Journal of Social Issues*, 7, 1/2, 1–34; reprinted as Catherine Bauer (1952) *Social Questions in Housing and Town Planning*, London, University of London Press; and under its original title in *Urban Housing*, edited by William L. C. Wheaton, Grace Milgram, and Margy Ellin Meyerson, New York, Free Press.
63. Bauer, "A balance sheet," 89–105 passim.
64. Bauer, "The dreary deadlock," 221.
65. Catherine Bauer (1956) *Economic Development and Urban Living Conditions: An Argument for Regional Planning to Guide Community Growth*, New York, Housing, Building and Planning Branch, United Nations Bureau of Social Affairs, May, ii.
66. Catherine Bauer (1961) "Urban living conditions, overhead costs and the

development pattern," in *Seminar on Urbanization in India: India's Urban Future*, edited by Roy Turner, Berkeley, University of California Press, 2.
67. Catherine Bauer (1957) Review of Lloyd Rodwin's *The British New Towns Policy: Problems and Implications*, in *Journal of the American Institute of Planners*, 23, 1 (Winter), 45.
68. Catherine Bauer, with William W. Wurster (1959) "Indian vernacular architecture: Wai and Cochin," *Perspectiva*, 5, 36–48.
69. Woodbury et al., "Catherine Bauer Wurster dies," 570.

REFERENCES

Abbott, Carl (1987) *Urban America in the Modern Age, 1920 to the Present*, Arlington Heights, Illinois, Harlan Davidson.

Bauer, Catherine (1928). "Machine-age mansions for ultra-moderns: French builders apply ideas of the steel and concrete era in domestic architecture," *New York Times Magazine* (April 15), 10, 22.

—— (1931a) "The Americanization of Europe: three leaves from a notebook," *New Republic*, 66 (June 24) 153–4.

—— (1931b) "Goût Américain, Demi Sec," *New Republic*, 69 (November 25), 45–6.

—— (1931c) "Prize essay: art in industry," *Fortune*, 3 (May), 94–110.

—— (1931d) "Who cares about architecture?," *New Republic*, 66 (May 6), 326–7.

—— (1932a) "Architecture in Philadelphia," *Arts Weekly* (March 18), 151, 154.

—— (1932b) "Exhibition of modern architecture, Museum of Modern Art," *Creative Art*, 10 (March), 201–6.

—— (1932c) "Existenzminimum: apartments at $400 to $10,000 per year," *Arts Weekly* (April 2), 74–5.

—— (1932d) "More apartments," *Arts Weekly* (April 23), 124–5.

—— (1932e) "The palace of the popes," *Arts Weekly* (April 30), 177–8.

—— (1933a) "'Slum clearance'" or "'housing'?," *Nation*, 137 (December 27), 730–31.

—— (1933b) "The Swiss family Borsodi," *Nation*, 137 (October 25), 489–91.

—— (1934) *Modern Housing*, Boston, Houghton Mifflin.

—— (1938a) *Facts for a Housing Program*, Washington, D.C., U.S. Department of the Interior.

—— (1938b) *Housing Progress and the Southeast*, Washington, D.C., U.S. Department of the Interior.

—— (1938c) *Labor and the housing program*, Washington, D.C., U.S. Department of the Interior.

—— (1938d) "A year of the low rent housing program," *Shelter*, 3, 4 (November), 4–6.

—— (1939a) "Architectural opportunities in public housing," *Architectural Record*, 85, 1 (January), 65–8.

—— (1939b) "Clients for housing: the low income tenant: does he want supertenements?," *Progressive Architecture*, 33, 5 (January), 62–4.

—— (1939c) *Local Housing Authorities and Their Public*, Washington, D.C., U.S. Department of the Interior.

—— (1939d) "Low rent housing and home economics," *Journal of Home Economics*, 31, 1 (January) 1–5.

—— (1940) *A Citizen's Guide to Public Housing*, Poughkeepsie, New York, Vassar College.

—— (1941) "A balance sheet of progress," *Architectural Record*, 89, 5 (May), 89–105.

—— (1942) "War-time housing in defense areas," *Architect and Engineer*, 150, 2 (August), 33–5.

—— (1943a) "Cities in flux, a challenge to the postwar planners," *American Scholar*, 13, 1 (Winter), 70–84.

—— (1943b) "Housing: a memorandum," *California Arts and Architecture*, 60 (February), 18–19.

—— (1943c) "Urban redevelopment: crisis in land economics produces Hansen Green plan and others," *Public Housing Progress*, 9, 1 (January), 2, 5.

—— (1944a) "Planning is politics . . . but are planners politicians?," *Pencil Points*, 25, 3 (March), 67.

—— (1944b) "Towards a green and pleasant England? A critical review of English publications in postwar planning," *Pencil Points*, 25, 4 (April), 78, 94, 100, 102, 104.

—— (1946) "Is urban redevelopment possible under existing legislation?," in *Planning, 1946*, Chicago, American Society of Planning Officials.

—— (1951a) "Redevelopment and public housing," in *Planning, 1950*, Chicago, American Society of Planning Officials.

—— (1951b) "Social questions in housing and community planning," *Journal of Social Issues*, 7, 1/2, 1–34; reprinted as *Social Questions in Housing and Town Planning*, London, University of London Press, 1952; also reprinted under its original title in (1966) *Urban Housing*, edited by William L. C. Wheaton, Grace Milgram, and Margy Ellin Meyerson, New York, Free Press.

—— (1952) "Low buildings? Catherine Bauer questions Mr. Yamasaki's arguments," *Journal of Housing*, 9, 9 (September), 322.

—— (1953a) "The homebuilders take a 'new look' at slums—and raise some questions," *Journal of Housing*, 10, 10 (November), 371–3, 389.

—— (1953b) "Redevelopment: a misfit in the fifties," in *The Future of Cities and Redevelopment*, edited by Coleman Woodbury, Chicago, University of Chicago Press.

—— (1956a) "Do Americans hate cities?," *Journal of the American Institute of Planners*, 23, 1 (Winter), 3.

—— (1956b) *Economic Development and Urban Living Conditions: An Argument for Regional Planning to Guide Community Growth*, New York, Housing, Building and Planning Branch, United Nations Bureau of Social Affairs, May.

—— (1956c) "First job: control new city sprawl," *Architectural Forum*, 105, 3 (September), 105.

—— (1957a) "The dreary deadlock of public housing," *Architectural Forum*, 106, 5 (May), 222.

—— (1957b) Review of Lloyd Rodwin's *The British New Towns Policy: Problems and Implications*, in *Journal of the American Institute of Planners*, 23, 1 (Winter), 45.

—— (1960) "Framework for an urban society," in *Goals for Americans*, U.S. President's Commission on National Goals, New York, Prentice Hall.

—— (1961a) "Architecture and the cityscape," *Journal of the American Institute of Architects*, 27 (March), 36–9.

—— (1961b) "Urban living conditions, overhead costs and the development pattern," in *Seminar on Urbanization in India: India's Urban Future*, edited by Roy Turner, Berkeley, University of California Press.

—— (1963) "The form and structure of the future urban complex," in *Cities and Space*, edited by Lowden Wingo, Jr., Baltimore, Johns Hopkins University Press.

—— (1964a) "Can cities compete with suburbia for family living?," *Architectural Record*, 136, 6 (December), 155.

—— (1964b) "Introduction," in *Exploration into Urban Structure*, edited by Mel Webber, Philadelphia, University of Pennsylvania Press.

—— (1965) "The social front of modern architecture in the 1930's," *Journal of the Society of Architectural Historians*, 24, 1 (March), 48–52.

Bauer, Catherine, with Jacob Crane (1940) "What every family should have: two federal experts tally up the standards from cellar to garret, from neighborhood to community," *Survey Graphic*, 29, 2 (February), 64–5, 136–9.

Bauer, Catherine, with William W. Wurster (1959) "Indian vernacular architecture: Wai and Cochin," *Perspectiva*, 5, 36–48.

Bauman, John F. (1987) *Public Housing, Race and Renewal: Urban Planning in Philadelphia, 1920–1974*, Philadelphia, Temple University Press.

Birch, Eugenie L. (1975) "Edith Elmer Wood and the rise of liberal housing," Ph.D. dissertation, Columbia University.

—— (1980) "Advancing the art and science of planning, planners and their organizations," *Journal of the American Planning Association*, 76, 1, 22–49.

—— (1982) "William Wilson Wurster," in *Macmillan Encyclopedia of Architects*, New York, Macmillan.

"Bust of late Catherine Bauer Wurster placed in HUD building," *Journal of Housing*, 25, 8 (1968), 406–9.

Cole, Mary Susan (1975) "Catherine Bauer and the public housing movement, 1926–1937," Ph.D. dissertation, George Washington University.

"Housing's white knight," *Architectural Forum*, 84 (March 1946), 116–19, 146–52.

Ickes, Harold (1953) *The Secret Diary of Harold L. Ickes, the First Thousand Days, 1933–1936*, New York, Simon and Schuster.

Mumford, Lewis (1979) *My Works and Days: A Personal Chronicle*, New York, Harcourt, Brace, Jovanovich.

Stein, Clarence, and Bauer, Catherine (1934) "Store buildings and neighborhood centers," *Architectural Record*, 75, 2 (February), 174–87.

Vinton, Warren Jay (1964) "The vital statistics of housing and community development," in *Housing Yearbook*, Washington, D.C., National Housing Conference.

"We present . . . Catherine Bauer in her own words," *Journal of Housing*, 1 (November 1944), 27.

"William Wilson Wurster," *Architectural Forum* 81 (July 1943), 45–65.

Woodbury, Coleman, Weaver, Robert C., Shiskin, Boris, and Abrams, Charles (1964) "Catherine Bauer Wurster dies," *Journal of Housing*, 21 (December), 570–73.

FIGURE 13.1   *Rexford Tugwell.*

COURTESY FRANKLIN D. ROOSEVELT LIBRARY.

13

TUGWELL IN NEW YORK

THE PERILS OF LIBERAL PLANNING

GEORGE C. HEMMENS

REXFORD GUY TUGWELL IS A NAME to be reckoned with in planning history. Perhaps best known for the new towns program of the Resettlement Administration he directed during the 1930s, he was also a significant contributor to other New Deal planning experiments, including the National Recovery Administration and the agriculture subsidy program. Tugwell was the first permanent director of the innovative planning program created in New York City under the reform charter of 1936, and in that role he was a pioneer in the attempt to systematically integrate capital budgeting and long-range planning in a large city. While governor of Puerto Rico, he designed and established a planning program that has served as a model for regional economic development planning for much of the world. Later he organized one of the first truly modern planning education programs at the University of Chicago, which subsequently had a major influence on planning education through the work of its faculty and students. Tugwell's many writings on planning have left a legacy of permanent additions to the planning vocabulary.

This is a substantially revised version of a paper originally prepared for the Association of Collegiate Schools of Planning Conference in November 1990. Grateful acknowledgment for support of this research is given to the National Endowment for the Humanities and the University of Illinois at Chicago Campus Research Board.

Yet he is not well remembered or honored by the planning profession. I suspect that most planners under the age of forty have only a vague and confused notion of Tugwell's ideas and planning work and of the debates about planning that he was part of from the 1930s through the 1950s. If asked about him, they may at best be able to conjure up the phrase "the fourth power." In his survey of planning theory, John Friedmann has given an appreciative account of Tugwell's contribution, presenting both strengths and weaknesses (Friedmann, 1987). This is, I think, a useful corrective and valuable service to people entering the field who encounter Friedmann's text because it connects them fairly with our intellectual history. The more common treatment presents Tugwell as a failure and something of an embarrassment. He was made the goat during the 1980s when planners, suffering under the decline of the field, looked around for someone to blame. As much as any single individual in planning, Tugwell has been picked out as an example, safely distant, of what is wrong with planning and, by inference, what would be better.

In an important article, Mark I. Gelfand (1985) reviewed planning in New York City during Tugwell's tenure and concluded that he was responsible in part for the perceived failure of that experiment. In a basic text on planning published by the American Planning Association, Melvin R. Levin (1987), drawing heavily on Gelfand's analysis, has characterized Tugwell as a model of planning ineptitude and failure; from his analysis of the New York experience, he inferred a preferred model in the person of Tugwell's presumed nemesis, Robert Moses. While the author is solely responsible for the book's content, the fact that the book bears the imprimatur of the profession and is the only book of its kind published by the professional association gives it privileged status.

In this chapter, I tell the story of Rexford Guy Tugwell in New York with two objectives. The first is to review the record of how and why planning in New York faltered, and why what appeared to be an opportunity to create a national model of advanced practice was not realized. There is no question that the planning experiment failed. I will argue that recent readings of that experience, such as Levin's, are one-sided and perhaps misguided. The second objective is to examine the moral of the story. Levin titles his story of Tugwell and Moses as the minnow and the shark. The message is to despise the minnow and emulate the shark. I will argue that this is not the correct moral for planning in the story but that there is a very important lesson to be learned. First, I will review the charge against Tugwell. Next, I will retell the story and draw out the morals of this version.

THE PLANNER AS MINNOW

"The besetting sin that played so important a role among planning giants such as Rexford Tugwell was pride, laced by conceit, arrogance, rigidity and self-righteousness and underpinned with contempt for one's opponents" (Levin, 1987, p. 11). Thus the first and basic charge is laid against Tugwell specifically and against past planning leadership generally.

Discussing Tugwell's approach to the planning commission in New York, Levin accepts Gelfand's conclusion, "Between 1938 and 1941 Rexford Tugwell attempted to make the planning commission a virtually autonomous fourth power of New York government with the capacity to force its rational decisions upon the city's elected officials" (Gelfand quoted in Levin, 1987, p. 26). Levin ties this assessment to his view of Tugwell's work in the New Deal, where he terms his advocacy of ideas as "dropping intellectual hand grenades" (Levin, 1987, p. 12). He suggests that Tugwell was unrelentingly antibusiness, as suggested by some of his professorial writings in the 1920s and early 1930s, to the extent that he would have opposed public-private cooperation on the greenbelt towns (Levin, 1987, p. 22). This results in two additional charges. "In short, he acted as an ideologue, not as practical reformer" (Levin, 1987, p. 22), and following the historian Arthur Schlesinger, he accuses Tugwell of "persistent gullibility and endless reserve of naïveté" (Levin, 1987, p. 34).

Focusing on the interactions of Tugwell and Robert Moses, Levin accepts Robert M. Caro's conclusion that Moses "drove Tugwell out of his City Planning Commission Chairmanship—out of New York" (Caro, 1974, quoted in Levin, 1987, p. 30). He agrees with Gelfand that Tugwell's error was confronting Moses. "Rexford Tugwell must bear some of the responsibility for this lost opportunity. Fitting this new agency into the traditional government structure demanded immense political skill and tact—qualities he lacked. . . . By pushing ahead on the master plan and being drawn into a fight with Moses that he could not win, Tugwell dealt the idea of comprehensive planning a blow from which it never recovered" (Gelfand quoted in Levin, 1987, p. 33). "One of Tugwell's failings was his unfailing taste for confrontation" (Levin, 1987, p. 34).

Conversely, "Tugwell's foe, Robert Moses, was and remains one of the most productive and formidable master builders that the U.S. or any other country has ever known" (Levin, 1987, p. 28). Levin reviews Caro's criticisms of Moses—his McCarthy-type smear tactics, ruthlessness, arrogance, and racial and class prejudice—and concludes that "it is unfair to judge Moses's [*sic*] *ex post facto* for projects that were broadly supported in their day. . . . Moses was very much a creature of his time." (Levin, 1987, p. 31). So Tugwell, standing in for the "planning giants," is charged with pride, evidenced in arrogance and rigidity, being an ideologue, gullibility and naïveté, ineptitude, and confrontational behavior. Levin draws a moral for contemporary planning practice from this story, but before we get to that, I will tell the story.

COMING TO NEW YORK

Tugwell came to the New York City Planning Commission from an executive position with the American Molasses Company. That job had been created for him by Charles Taussig, president of the company and a colleague of Tugwell's from the New Deal, after Tugwell resigned from the Roosevelt administration. Taussig had been a late addition to Franklin Delano Roosevelt's advisers who worked with the Brain Trust, where Tugwell held a central position, and continued as an adviser to Roosevelt and a liaison to the liberal business community during the administration.

Tugwell had gone to work in business because he lacked other opportunities. He left his position as Undersecretary of Agriculture after the 1936 election and before the second inaugural. He had offered to resign early in the 1936 election campaign and Roosevelt accepted. The immediate issue forcing his resignation was the proposed food and drug bill that Tugwell championed. This was not a priority issue for Roosevelt or for Tugwell, who had championed it in support of the Agriculture Department staff, who had developed the bill and urged it on him. Roosevelt had agreed to the bill's introduction but made it clear that he would not put his influence behind its passage (Tugwell Papers, 1977, B30 Diary Notes; B refers to box number). Tugwell became the target for opponents of the

FIGURE 13.2   *Senate hearing—June 11, 1934, Rexford Tugwell at microphone.*
COURTESY FRANKLIN D. ROOSEVELT LIBRARY. REPRINTED WITH PERMISSION OF
AP/WIDE WORLD PHOTOS.

bill—the food, drug, and cosmetic industries and the local news-papers that depended on their advertising—and was attacked for being a radical—Rex the Red (Tugwell Papers, B76, F8; B refers to box number and F refers to file number).

The fight over the food and drug bill was only the most recent controversy involving Tugwell's activities in the New Deal. He was widely recognized as the most liberal of Roosevelt's close advisers and was outspoken on issues within Agriculture and throughout the administration, irritating both friends and foes of the New Deal. As Roosevelt faced reelection, he reluctantly agreed to accept Tugwell's offer to resign (Tugwell Papers, B5, F7).

Tugwell believed that he could not return to university life. He had been a tenured professor of economics at Columbia when he entered the Roosevelt administration. His advocacy of national economic planning and his association with New Deal social legislation made him unwelcome among that university's conservative faculty and trustees. However, Tugwell was also disillusioned with the life of an academic economist. He did not agree with either the orthodox liberal or conservative versions of economic theory. His own version, institutional economics, was completely out of favor. Besides, he wanted to lead an active professional life involved with issues of public policy.

Although disillusioned by his New Deal experience and discouraged about the possibility of significant social and economic change through federal government action, he retained a commitment to Roosevelt and continued to advise him. Tugwell was not particularly interested in state and local government. He was not interested in seeking public office. He had to earn a living. So he accepted the position of vice president of the American Molasses Company.

The job was a disappointment. The position was not essential to the operation of the company, and Tugwell was not brought into company operations. Instead, he spent his time helping Taussig maintain Roosevelt's relations with liberal businessmen in New York, doing occasional odd jobs for Roosevelt (including developing a requested plan for revamping the Supreme Court), and writing on national policy issues for liberal journals. Although the job gave him ample opportunity to pursue his policy interests, he was desperate for a new challenge and to resume a meaningful career.

During this time, Tugwell's former Brain Trust colleague, A. A. Berle, was serving as New York City Mayor Fiorello La Guardia's principal aide and as temporary chairman of the New York City Planning Commission. Berle was given the task of finding a permanent director for the commission. He did not recommend Tugwell. Berle was no longer close to Tugwell, and there was some competition between them for Roosevelt's ear as both were still advising him. Berle did work closely with Taussig and tried in December 1937 to cut Tugwell out from a private meeting of business, labor, and financial leaders called by Taussig to advise Roosevelt. He failed, and Tugwell ended up being the person to take the results of the meeting to the president. Berle recommended Samuel Ordway for chairman of the planning commission in February 1938 and believed he had accepted (Berle Papers, B210). Meanwhile, Tugwell was exploring the possibilities of returning to the New Deal administration. Roosevelt continued to be personally friendly, but he did not offer him a place in the administration and discouraged those, such as Harold Ickes, who were willing to welcome him back.

Roosevelt was responsible for Tugwell going to the New York City Planning Commission. He recommended Tugwell to La Guardia. For Roosevelt, it was a typical, personally useful solution to a problem of how to help a friend and supporter. Tugwell was, after all, a planner. More important, he was a Progressive, as was La Guardia. While Tugwell was serving in the Department of Agriculture, one of his informal jobs for Roosevelt was to serve as liaison to the Progressives in Congress and to the remnants of the Progressive movement in the nation. Tugwell had worked with La Guardia in carrying out that assignment. So Roosevelt expected Tugwell to serve as his personal ambassador to La Guardia while he was at the planning commission.

This arrangement suited La Guardia for the same reasons. He had his own eye on Washington, D.C., and was looking for a way to return to the national scene. His ambition was to be named Secretary of War. Helping Roosevelt place a friend in New York strengthened Roosevelt's obligation to him and gave La Guardia a direct line to the president.

For Tugwell, this had to be a very imperfect solution to his own problem. His personal life and his professional interests were still based in Washington, D.C. He had divorced and then married his former assistant in the Department of Agriculture, Grace Falke, who remained in Washington, D.C., working for the New Deal. Tugwell had never expressed much interest in city planning. When Roosevelt tried to get him to take charge of the urban slum clearance and housing programs of the New Deal, he begged off. As he recorded in his diary, "FDR let me off city housing, though he laughed at me for not wanting to do it" (Tugwell Papers B32, Diary Notes). In fact, he proposed the greenbelt towns program to Roosevelt as an alternative to taking over the city housing program. However, the New York planning position paid well, Tugwell would be in charge, and he would be helping Roosevelt. So he accepted and moved to the planning commission in the spring of 1938.

TUGWELL'S NEW YORK PROGRAM

In Washington, D.C., Tugwell proposed innovative programs, promoted reorganization in the Department of Agriculture and throughout the administration, and argued for major structural changes in society and in the economy. His reputation as a radical among the enemies and as a troublemaker among the friends of the New Deal was based on this constant criticism of present practices and advocacy of change. In New York, Tugwell did none of these things.

Instead of criticizing the existing government structure and proposing major innovations, he set about the task of developing an effective planning program. That task was, however, a very innovative one. The reform charter gave the planning commission a central role in decisions about major public investments, as well as significant influence over private development. Responding to past excesses of the city government's mismanagement of the public investment process, especially decisions about the type and location of new public facilities, the charter gave the planning commission the task of developing the annual and the long-term capital budget for the city. The Board of Estimate could change the commission's recommendations only with a three-fourths vote. To give more public control over private development, the charter mandated the creation and adoption of a comprehensive plan and revision of the zoning ordinance and other development regulations in accord with the plan. The Board of Estimate was required to act on planning department recommendations within thirty days and needed a three-fourths vote to overturn the planners' recommendations.

The assignment given to the planning commission was as close to the ideal form of planning practice promoted at that time by leaders of the field as they could expect to achieve. The New York City planners were in a position to become exemplars for the emerging profession. Whether this was enough challenge to satisfy Tugwell or whether he was still weary and wary from the responses to his New Deal innovations or if he just did not have any strong ideas about city planning is unclear, but the approach he chose was to stick close to the assigned program. He focused on developing a competent professional planning staff and carrying out the mandated planning activities.

Probably this was an easy choice for Tugwell. The planning commission appeared to meet two fundamental requirements for effective planning that he had become convinced were necessary during his New Deal days. Planning had to have autonomy and planning had to have implementation powers. Autonomy was provided by the planning commission's appointment structure, Tugwell's joint occupancy of the commission chairmanship and staff directorship, the commission's established budget, and the extraordinary vote required to override the commission's recommendations. Implementation powers came through the capital budget and the master plan and related regulations and approvals.

In organizing the planning staff and directing its work, Tugwell followed his earlier practice in the Resettlement Administration. He tried to get the best staff he could and then delegated the technical work to them. He gave them considerable latitude so that they could significantly influence the policy positions the commission would be asked to advocate. Tugwell assigned himself the role of presenter and presider.

What Happened

Although Tugwell would later look back approvingly on the accomplishments of the planning commission during his tenure, the actual experience was not smooth and his contemporary accounts of it reveal considerable frustration and disappointment. I will briefly review that experience with respect to some of the major issues.

Staff Development

Securing an adequate budget and staff was essential to competently satisfy the charter mandate and meet Tugwell's expectations. Unfortunately, Tugwell quickly learned that he would have a very limited staff. Many of the staff were loaned or transferred from other departments and did not have the skills or attitudes desired for the work. Initially, the planning commission was given a budget of $140,000 and the promise of one hundred transfer appointments. Tugwell immediately asked for an additional $100,000 for specialized personnel and $40,000 for nonpersonnel expenses (Tugwell Papers, 1977, B46). La Guardia resisted Tugwell's requests for more positions and a larger budget. Tugwell did attempt one government reorganization. He asked La Guardia to consolidate all the research activities of the city departments under the planning department. La Guardia refused.

After two years of repeated funding requests, La Guardia, exasperated, finally wrote to Tugwell on February 14, 1940, "Your request to pile up an enormous personnel is exactly the argument used against the establishment of a City Planning Commission. . . . If more personnel is needed then we had better abolish the entire City Planning Commission. . . . Its purpose was to reduce the personnel in the various Borough Offices" (Tugwell Papers, B5, F7). Tugwell never gained the material support he believed was needed to do the job.

PROGRAM ISSUES

Despite the budget problems, Tugwell pushed ahead with the full program assigned to the planning commission by the charter. He achieved some successes but more failures. Often the successes were undercut. For example, Tugwell succeeded in changing New York's practice of locating public housing on poorly located peripheral sites but had to accept much higher densities than he proposed in order to meet the federal government's housing cost limits. Most of the defeats and most of the undercutting of the planning commission's efforts came from within New York City government and politics, however.

The charter required planning department review and recommendation on all assessable improvements more than $10,000. This placed a considerable administrative burden on the department and placed it squarely in the path of all significant development decisions. The planners were given six weeks to respond. To prepare their response, the planners investigated, held hearings, and deliberated, so they were easily perceived as an impediment to progress.

The annual capital budget and five-year capital program that the planners were required to prepare meant that the planners had to review all the capital projects proposed by other city departments and by borough politicians. This placed the bureaucrats and politicians in the position of supplicants to an authority they had no reason to recognize and respect. It was particularly unnerving because the planners' recommendations could be overridden only by a three-fourths vote of the Board of Estimate. The capital budget planning process was intended to stop logrolling and pork-barrel decision-making and clearly had that potential. To implement capital planning and budget-making, the planners held more hearings.

The politicians and bureaucrats were annoyed with the planners' scrutiny. They complained to La Guardia, suggesting that Tugwell was high-handed. La Guardia wrote to Tugwell:

> It is my desire that hereafter all hearings of the Planning Commission be held in your own offices and also that these hearings follow the procedures of conferences rather than inquiries or judicial proceedings. By that I mean that the members should sit around a table on the same level with officials who appear before them to "confer on the Capital

Outlay Budget." I have already detected the psychological effect on your Commission of being elevated and assuming a judicial as well as an inquisitorial attitude. Please cut it out. I don't know exactly what it is, but just a few feet of elevation brings an individual or group of individuals into what they seem to think is a loftier atmosphere. They get a "bench" psychosis, a superiority complex, which always affects judgment in the reverse ratio of the degree of such complex. This has been disappointingly noticeable in your commission of late. Please acknowledge receipt and complete understanding of this request. (Tugwell Papers, B5, F7).

A mystified Tugwell replied that

. . . the Capital Budget hearings of this year were all conducted in the offices of the commission with the exception of one— that on Schools, which was held in the Committee of the Whole Room at City Hall because of the large attendance. At no time, however, did the Commission sit on any other elevation than that of those who were appearing.

This mistake in facts however apparently does not affect your judgment that you are, as you say, disappointed in the Commission. I hope that we shall be able to do something to change your disappointment into approval. I am somewhat at a loss to know what it might be, but I feel very keenly the implied criticism of my management (Tugwell Papers, B5, F7).

In fact, there probably was nothing Tugwell could do to get La Guardia's approval of the planning commission short of not following and fulfilling the mandate given it in the charter. La Guardia did not particularly want a powerful, independent planning commission and, as Berle noted in his diary, was uncertain how to deal with it (Berle Papers, B210). He often held it back when he could.

Tugwell became especially frustrated with La Guardia's foot-dragging on zoning revision. This, too, was mandated in the charter, and Tugwell directed his staff to pursue it aggressively. La Guardia delayed zoning hearings regularly and put various impediments in Tugwell's path but never directly told him to leave things be. Instead, La Guardia became increasingly peevish, complaining to Tugwell about the planners' behavior, perhaps without merit, as in the case of the hearings, and nit-picking. For example, La Guardia wrote the following memo to Tugwell: "I was grieved and hurt that you were not in your office when I wanted to get in touch with you Monday. It sets a very bad example to the force" (Tugwell Papers, B5).

La Guardia could not bring himself to directly oppose the planning commission. He also could not bring himself to directly oppose Tugwell because the other half of Tugwell's job—the political connection to Roosevelt—was too important. The split affected Tugwell as well and was always present. The letter in which Tugwell responded to La Guardia's criticism of the planning com- mission hearings ended with, "I am leaving for the West tomorrow night and will talk with a number of people along the lines suggested in our conversation the other day. Your message has already been conveyed to Ed O'Neal." In the West, Tugwell would talk national politics with La Guardia's fellow progressives, at La Guardia's behest. Whether unconsciously or with considerable subtlety, Tugwell was reminding La Guardia of the basis of their relationship, and so, because of the tie of the conflict at home with the national alliance, tensions developed between them that could not be cleanly resolved. La Guardia and Tugwell became peevish and whiny with and about each other. Tugwell confided his complaints to his diary and, occa- sionally, to Roosevelt, who was amused. La Guardia, caught in the political crossfire of New York and jealous of his political power as mayor, was more public.

DEALING WITH MOSES

Tugwell's best-known problem at the New York City Planning Commission was the fight with Robert Moses over the master plan. Tugwell was totally committed to the preparation and formal adop- tion of a master plan for the city for many reasons. For one, the master plan was mandated in the reform charter. Tugwell, accepting the city planning ideas of the time, intended the master plan to be the underpinning and justification for the principal development control activities of the commission—the official map, zoning, and the capital budget. Also, Tugwell's personal philosophy of planning strongly favored the preparation and adoption of a master plan. He considered the technical tasks of forecasting the future and pointing out the implications of the likely future for current public action to be the central skills and contribution of the planner. He was a true follower of John Dewey in his reliance on experts to translate the public interest into treatable problems and propose solutions. Further, Tugwell saw the public hearing part of the plan-making process as the primary means of securing public participation in planning and realizing his commitment to democratic planning in the public interest.

In one of his first publications on planning in New York, Tugwell argued the importance of public participation in plan making and called for mandatory public hearings on master plans (Tugwell, 1940). He presented his argument for the technician role of the planner and for rational planning to planning conferences during the period. To the members of the American Society of Planning Officials (ASPO), he said, "I think that the function of planning, at least as I see it, is to determine action on a rational basis. The rational basis is pretty much a matter of research, and is pretty much a matter of facts. Any form that will permit this rational basis to come through and determine action is alright with me" ASPO, 1940). To the Fifth Annual Southeastern Planning Conference he said, "The people who created the charter of New York City . . . had in mind something more than an advisory body and a group of technicians who would say 'Yes, sir and No, sir.'" He said that the master plan and capital budget could be done "provided a capable staff is in charge," and "I think we are making some real progress. But we are not doing it by timidity and withdrawal." He told the planners he expected to get the new zoning resolution passed because the Board of Estimate had only thirty days to act on it and needed a three-fourths majority to reject any part of it. "This," he told the planners, "is the kind of implementation I feel planning ought to have in more places than it does and in more ways than it does" (Tugwell Papers, B59).

On the zoning resolution, Tugwell underestimated La Guardia's intent and ability to undercut him by failing to call hearings. On the master plan, he underestimated the commitment of New York politicians, dealmakers, and bureaucrats to business as usual and their resistance to the voice of sweet reason. Robert Moses is generally given credit for derailing the master plan. He certainly opposed it very effectively, but he was speaking for many others, including La Guardia, who were very nervous about the plan's possible intrusion on their freedom of action.

The proposed plan for New York was conventional in its content and followed closely the charter mandate, which called for it to treat streets and highways, mass transportation, parks and recreation, and public buildings and services, as well as land use. The conflict with Moses came over the land use plan, which included general proposals for expressways and parks. The land use plan was based on 1938 data and projected development to 1965, twenty-five years in advance of the plan's presentation in 1940.

Although the plan was conventional, Tugwell's thinking about its purposes was not, and he made his views public:

> I am perfectly sure that the planning body of New York should do absolutely no planning at all as planning is usually meant. We should confine ourselves to what are usually called—well, in foreign parts, at least—conjunctural questions; that is, questions having to do with the city at large, with the complicated impact of many forces on each other. I realize that the only way we can have any real influence on the future of the city is by approaching everything from this conjunctural point of view; that is from the point of view of the welfare of all, not some, of the people in New York City. We cannot think of a neighborhood, we cannot think of an individual, we cannot think of a department. If we do, we are sunk. We have to approach everything from the center out, and not from the outside in or from the bottom up.
>
> I sit and shudder sometimes when I hear planners talk about democracy in planning and about building from the ground up and about talking the language of ordinary legislators and so on, because I know that would be ruinous. If you try to do that in New York, you do nothing but what the city engineer is now doing and what he is properly doing, because planning in a city like New York, accepting the conjunctural function as somebody's responsibility, and presumably that of the planning commission, is a matter you cannot approach with ordinary language and ordinary tools. It cannot be done with ordinary mathematics, nor with ordinary approaches to government. It is an extremely technical matter; and if we can not be trusted to approach it with an extremely complex, complicated technique which is unique in itself and not the same as is used for anything else, then we had better stop and let the city engineer do his job" (ASPO, 1940).

This manifesto was bound to engender fear, distrust, and confusion in those uncertain about planning. It undoubtedly caused confusion in the planning department as well. The planning work in New York was not unusually technical, complex, or innovative. Tugwell did not give the staff direction on technique; he delegated the choice to them. The limited, overworked staff had no time for fundamental research or method development. Outside the staff, Tugwell's pronouncements could be interpreted in various ways, none of them reassuring. Tugwell did not explain clearly or in detail what he meant by the conjunctural task of planning. The call for planning from the center out was bound to appear as an attempt to take over the planning and decision functions of other government agencies. So many who might have supported Tugwell on the master plan were put off by his claims and his attitude. For his part, Tugwell had difficulty understanding why others would disagree with him. He believed his planning conception to be only a rational response to a reasoned analysis of the situation and exactly what the reform charter mandated.

Robert Moses would have none of it. If he could identify with anything in Tugwell's manifesto it was Tugwell's recognition that the city engineer was doing his job well, and if the planner could not do something different and better, the planner should retire from the field in favor of the engineer. Moses was virtually the city engineer without portfolio on all major public works that interested him. He wanted nothing more than to go on doing what he had been doing. Moses had worked comfortably with Tugwell and the planning commission from 1938 until the first informal presentations on the master plan in the summer of 1939. Of course, there had been differences. Moses, as commissioner of the Department of Parks, resisted Tugwell's attempts to centralize research and planning in the city, as did other department representatives. Generally, though, Tugwell experienced cooperation and support from Moses. In retrospect, it would be clear that Moses supported the information and routine management activities of the planners, exactly the functions Tugwell believed were useless unless they were conducted within an overarching conjunctural planning framework.

The planners showed a preliminary proposal for future expressways and parkways to the Parks Department in June 1939. Moses responded strongly. He asked and Tugwell agreed to postpone hearings on the issue. Then he wrote to Tugwell, with a copy to La Guardia, a three-page letter full of biting criticism of the plan's general and specific recommendations with the obvious intent of trying to discredit the planning staff's technical ability. Moses' real concern and agenda were revealed in this sentence: "You will recall that I suggested that if your staff had preliminary ideas about these matters they should be kept in the form of memoranda for your files, and should not be scheduled as part of the official master plan" (Tugwell Papers, B5, F7). Put simply, Moses told Tugwell to stay out of the highway planning business. He even added a warning: "As the matter stands you are putting those of us who have worked for many years on this arterial problem and who are with you in principle, in the position of opposing you."

Tugwell, of course, could not accept Moses' request. So when elements of the plan began to be finalized and hearings were scheduled, Moses attacked. In a letter on May 23, 1940, he wrote to Tugwell:

In the first place, we all know quite well that there are plenty of things in the Charter, the Code, and other laws which are postponed, modified in practice, ignored or honored in the breach. A good deal of the new Charter is meaningless, wholly unworkable, vague and hopelessly confusing. Every public official admits this. There is no compulsion upon you or your associates to prepare a comprehensive far-reaching long range plan. Nobody can make you do it and my hunch is that there are plenty of people who will stop you if you try it, and that in the process you will wreck the Planning Commission and a lot of constructive work which might otherwise be done.

All that is necessary—and this will consume fully your talent, time and energy at your command—is put on your map what is now in existence, what is underway, what is actually pending, and what there is a reasonable expectation of accomplishing in a comparatively short time.

If you attempt to go beyond these boundaries and seriously consider distant objectives, you will bring your Commission and the administration which it must serve into disrepute, and what's more you won't get away with it (Tugwell Papers, B5, F8).

Tugwell responded with soothing words about his acceptance of "your judgment about most planning issues in the city" but went on to say:

> There cannot, I think, be any question that I have a mandate to make a master plan. On nothing else is the charter so specific. . . . I do not want to work up a grievance. I merely want to ask you again if you will not give up your attacks on all master plan work and tell me clearly what it is you do not like in our proposals. They have been put forward modestly. They were submitted to you even in advance of hearings. None of us here thinks our judgment is better than yours. On the contrary we want to embody yours in the plan. The hearings are still some time ahead (Tugwell Papers, B5, F8).

Since Moses did not want any plan, even one based on his own proposals, there was no possibility of accommodation between the two men. Moses continued to be supportive, as he had promised, on other activities of the planning commission, such as the new zoning resolution, but he was determined to fight against any long-range plan.

Tugwell continued with the plan-making and in December 1940 presented the land use element of the proposed master plan at public hearings. Moses predictably attacked. The wrangle continued without resolution, since completion and adoption of the master plan was a lengthy process, until after Tugwell had left the planning commission for Puerto Rico in September 1941. Moses was appointed to the planning commission in November 1941 and stayed on it until 1960. The planning commission scrapped the master plan and killed all work on comprehensive planning shortly after Moses' appointment. No master plan was produced during Moses' long tenure on the commission.

Leaving New York

Rexford Guy Tugwell did not leave New York because he was running from a fight or because he thought he would lose the fight. Although he confided to his diary that he thought he had accomplished as much as he probably could in New York, he left because he had been trying to leave from the beginning and finally found an acceptable position. Tugwell believed he had done a good job under the constraints, that the planning commission was well established, the department well staffed, and that both would go on well without him.

Tugwell's aim was to return to the national level in the New Deal administration. He continued to write on national issues for journals and the popular press while at the planning commission. He continued to take on informal assignments for Roosevelt, in addition to the liaison with La Guardia. He continued to inquire about possibilities of coming back to the Roosevelt administration. Harold Ickes was the person most sympathetic to his request. In November 1939, he, with Roosevelt's consent, offered Tugwell the post of Administrator of the Division of Territories and Overseas Possessions. Tugwell was asking for the then vacant position of Undersecretary of Interior. Ickes was interested, and had previously tried to draw Tugwell to that post away from the Department of Agriculture, but Roosevelt was not willing to have Tugwell in such a high-profile position. Tugwell was tempted by the administrator position but felt he could not take it for financial reasons. It paid considerably less than his New York job, and, as he wrote in his diary, "I should want to be in a 'conjunctural' position" (Tugwell Papers, B32).

A year later, Tugwell asked Ickes for the then vacant position of head of the Forest Service. Ickes did not offer it, but he did ask Tugwell to consult for the administration on the implementation of the land reform law in Puerto Rico. Tugwell was familiar with Puerto Rican agriculture problems from his days in the Department of Agriculture, and at the American Molasses Company he was further exposed to sugarcane agriculture throughout the Caribbean. La Guardia agreed to give Tugwell a leave of absence from New York so that he could do this work for Roosevelt; thus, Tugwell went to Puerto Rico. This offer came in December 1940, a week after Moses had denounced the proposed land use plan and the press had given it a hostile reception. A disgruntled Tugwell confided to his diary, "The Press is useless as a civic aid." About the same time, La Guardia turned down his latest request for an increase in the planning department budget. Tugwell groused in his diary, "It is one more in a long series of attempts to scuttle the whole capital budget procedure as set up in the charter."

While working in Puerto Rico in early 1941, Tugwell met Luis

Munoz-Marin, who was influential in Tugwell's being offered the chancellorship of the University of Puerto Rico later that year. While the university position was being negotiated, Ickes proposed appointing Tugwell to the newly vacant governorship of Puerto Rico. Roosevelt agreed. The nomination caused considerable controversy and was delayed, so Tugwell accepted the university position and was sworn in as chancellor on August 1, 1941. He was appointed governor shortly thereafter.

Tugwell did not get the national position he hoped for but was very enthusiastic about the opportunity to work in Puerto Rico and had a successful and, as usual, controversial tenure as governor. Back in the States, La Guardia was not successful in his quest to become Secretary of War. Roosevelt eventually appointed him to administer civil defense.

Morals of the Story

Why did planning under the reform charter not live up to its promise? In retrospect, it is easy to explain. The prospects for effective planning were very poor. While the charter set up a structure that appeared to give planning considerable autonomy and influence, it was very dependent on the support of the mayor. The mayor appointed six of the eight planning commission members. Tugwell would later complain about the poor quality of many of his commissioners and that La Guardia left positions vacant. Three members of the Board of Estimate—the mayor, the comptroller, and the president of the City Council—controlled a majority of the vote, and in La Guardia's time, the three usually voted together. In effect, the charter increased the power of the mayor and the Board of Estimate relative to the City Council. The planning commission was to represent the general public and be a check on the increased power of the executive. The system might have worked if the mayor supported an independent planning commission and was relatively weak. Since neither was the case, planning would not do well.

The master plan was not the main issue and Moses was not solely responsible for the failure of planning. The long-term and annual capital budgets, planning approval of all significant expenditures, and zoning revision worried business leaders, politicians, and especially La Guardia. He stalled and blocked the planning commission on those actions as much as he could without outright opposition to planning. Planning, after all, was dear to the liberal voters who were critical to his electoral success. La Guardia probably did not team up with Moses to gut planning; rather, it was like throwing him a bone. La Guardia was concerned about Moses' ambition and needed to keep him reasonably content. As Berle noted in his diary early in 1937, "The evidence seems to be accumulating that Robert Moses decided to betray the Mayor if he could" (Berle Papers, B21).

After reviewing this story, Levin says, "Tugwell's experience suggests a moral: Without a political constituency or some other independent source of strength, the planner is always a kind of courtier serving at the pleasure of the chief executive or the clique that runs the planning board" (Levin, 1987, p. 25); and, "Like Tugwell, the planner who proceeds to undertake a task on the basis of what he regards as logic, intellectual honesty and faithful adherence to professional standards may unwittingly raise storms all around him" (Levin, 1987, p. 48). The moral gets spelled out in ten principles that refer back to the original charges placed against Tugwell. Some of these include, in paraphrases: don't get out ahead of the crowd; don't rock the boat; communicate; be flexible; and be "guileful, worldly or sophisticated in the ways of power and politics" (Levin, 1987, p. 41). The list goes on in this tone.

If we examine one by one the specific charges against Tugwell, I think their validity is questionable. Starting at the top of the list, Tugwell's communication with Moses does not suggest arrogance or rigidity. It is a plea for participation and the only claim made is that the job has to be done—the plan is required. Similarly, he does not seem an ideologue in sticking to the charter tasks. He did not naively believe that La Guardia or Moses wanted planning. He knew that planning as designed in the charter was a deliberate impediment to business as usual. He may have been inept in his personal relations with La Guardia and Moses, and it was perhaps impolitic for him to discuss his ideas about planning in the professional community. He did not seek confrontation with Moses or the Board of Estimate. Doing his assigned job created conflict. In sum, it seems that the charges are more dramatic than the reality. What is being attacked is the prevailing conception of planning practice—and Tugwell is the scapegoat.

Scapegoats are chosen to bear the blame when there is disappointment with and rejection of formerly approved practices. Usually, the scapegoat is one who has performed the rejected practice well rather than poorly. I think that is the case here. We are being asked to reject the role of planning that Tugwell tried to embody.

PUBLIC VIRTUE

Tugwell could have chosen one of several roles. In the New Deal, he had played the young turk—aggressive reformer, intellectual gadfly. A pragmatic role of loyal lieutenant to La Guardia was also possible, the role Berle had played with La Guardia. Tugwell opted for another role and a new one for him. I call it the role of public virtue.

The ordinary definition of virtue is moral excellence. Common synonyms are integrity and righteousness. The concept of civic or public virtue goes back to the classic Greek philosophy of Plato and Aristotle and focuses on the general, shared, common moral excellence of good citizenship. Historically, it represents the general against the specific, the common against the particular, the public against the private. In taking on the role of a representative of public virtue, Tugwell struck out for the high road, the very highest.

What that role meant practically is clear from his interaction with Moses over the master plan. Tugwell wanted Moses to place his ideas in the public discourse. As an honest broker of ideas, Tugwell thought the planner should shine the light of open discourse in the dark corners of political decision. He was willing to cater to Moses' significant ego to get him into the process but was unwilling to compromise the process. He treated La Guardia similarly. Tugwell saw himself as an advocate of planning process—a process that was open, rational, and technical.

Tugwell did not invent the role. He was not a self-appointed guardian of public virtue. The liberal political community in New York created the role in its design of the planning commission as a check on the increased power of the executive, and the general public validated the role through charter adoption. The charter in effect said that certain decisions affecting the well-being of the whole community had to be made through a new political process. These were the development and quality-of-life issues treated in the master plan and capital budget. The charter solved the perennial question of who is to plan the planners by the ability of the Board of Estimate to override planning recommendations with a three-fourths vote. Thus, politics could have the final say, but it would have to be consensus politics. The charter also said that these public interest decisions should be made on the basis of technical expertise and representative citizen choice. The unusual single-headed, double-bodied planning commission and staff were meant to effect that partnership. The organization for planning in New York followed the general pattern proposed by government reformers and planners at the time, but went farther than existing practice in trying to implement that ideal.

Levin's complaint against Tugwell is characteristic of much of the backlash within planning during the 1980s. The general complaint has been: Planners are not appreciated; they lack power and influence. The backlash was a response to the decline in the profession's prestige and federal government support during the decade. Scapegoating is an outlet for self-hatred. It turns the unacceptable feelings of failure away from oneself and into aggression. Someone else can be blamed and then we feel better. Tugwell is an ideal candidate to carry this burden. He failed, and it is his fault. He could have done differently, so it is not a problem with planning and definitely not with us.

The proposed remedy is also to be found in the story of the scapegoat's disgrace. In this case, two general remedies for planning are suggested. Planners should trade in their ideals for deals. Tugwell is the idealist, Moses the dealer. Moses becomes the model. Some caution is raised about his excesses, but his strategy of developing special constituencies and a bargaining model of decision-making is to be emulated. This was the primary prescription for planning to survive in the 1980s, and anyone familiar with trends in planning practice and education knows how far it has penetrated the field. The second remedy is to revive a popular planning critique of the 1950s—Robert Walkers' proposal to place planning in the mainstream of municipal administration, and abandon its hybrid arrangement as citizen commission and municipal administrator. That these prescriptions may be practically mutually exclusive is not addressed, but that does not matter. The real point of the critique is to discredit inherited traditions of the profession and offer some basis for recovering a sense of efficacy.

The difficulty with this critique is that it misses the point. The fault is not simply Tugwell's or other planners'. It is in the planning role, and the role is based on the model of planning adopted in progressive reform. The attack, or questioning, ought to be about the pragmatic philosophy and the liberal model on which modern planning is based, and which continues to dominate the profession. Despite changes in practice during the 1980s, when planners have become economic developers and "done deals" rather than made plans, they continue to aspire to the traditional liberal aim that Charles Hoch has so aptly called "doing good and being right" (Hoch, 1984). The result is more confusion rather than a solution to the profession's problems.

The New York City Planning Commission is an exemplar of the liberal model of urban planning on which all U.S. urban planning is based. There are two basic elements to the model. One is confidence in and commitment to technical expertise as the means to explore public decisions. The other is a preference for apolitical decision-making on key public issues affecting the general interest. The model is based loosely on the various government reform programs, especially the Progressive movement, of the early twentieth century, and on the empirical, pragmatic tradition of American philosophy and applied science of the same period.

Tugwell is a good practitioner exemplar of the model. In his early education at the University of Pennsylvania, he was strongly influenced by Scott Nearing and Simon Nelson Patten. Through them, he absorbed the basic ideas of scientific management, social responsibility, and an organic conception of society. Later, at Columbia University, he learned directly from John Dewey and Wesley Mitchell the application of pragmatic philosophy and the usefulness of forecasting. Professionally, he was an institutional economist. Politically, he was a Progressive, not a Democrat or a Republican. He was an heir and advocate of the Progressive reform tradition. His approach to planning was a precursor of the rational model or rational action model of planning practice, which is a natural outgrowth of the liberal ideal.

To evaluate the criticism of Tugwell, it is useful to keep in mind this distinction between the liberal model that underlies American planning and the rational planning model that dominates our conception of professional practice. The latter is built on and is consistent with the former but is much narrower. It focuses on the technical expertise component of the liberal model and largely finesses the apolitical decision-making, public interest element. The rational model can be tied indirectly to Tugwell. The standard source for the rational model in the professional literature is the middle section of Edward C. Banfield's appendix to the book he and Martin Meyerson wrote about public housing site selection in Chicago (Meyerson and Banfield, 1955). The book is a product of the Chicago planning program that Tugwell founded and influenced, and there is a close fit between the liberal model Tugwell was struggling to implement and the practice protocol implicit in Banfield's analysis. However, in the appendix to the Chicago book, Banfield was simply explaining the analytic framework they used to study planning. He was not intending to establish a professional practice protocol. The analytical framework drew on prevailing concepts of planning and naturally reflects liberal thinking.

The fundamental problem of liberal planning is that it is a radical political act that is to be carried out under the banner of apolitical expertise. The inherent contradictions in this formula prevent effective planning. Tugwell was aware of the structural contradictions in the liberal prescription and his best-known contribution to the planning literature directly addresses the problem. Drawing directly on the New York reform structure for planning, and indirectly on his disillusionment with legislative decision-making in the New Deal and executive decision-making in New York, he formalized a solution to the problem of liberal planning in his famous paper on planning as a fourth power of government (Tugwell, 1939). Subsequently, he created a facsimile of the model in the Puerto Rico Planning Board and later influenced the Program in Planning Education and Research at the University of Chicago to pursue operationalizing the model.

Tugwell's conception of planning as the fourth power of government would give planning the independence it appeared to have in New York City and, in addition, give it position and status in the government structure. Planning would be "ruled by necessity," that is, be objective, factual and technical, and conjunctural. By conjunctural, he meant that planning should be synoptic, spanning public and private, executive, and legislative and judicial, with respect to those issues that were "longer-run, wider-minded and differently allied" than the existing branches of government were capable of dealing with. As in New York, the legislature could override the planners, in this case with a two-thirds vote (Tugwell, 1939).

Tugwell's fourth power has been largely discredited, primarily on the grounds that it is unrealistic. It is an extreme model in many ways, and the prospect of implementing it as schematized is small. However, that is not the point. The model is an honest exploration of the implications of taking seriously the task of democratic planning in the public interest in the American political and intellectual context of the first half of the twentieth century. Its conclusions are unpalatable because they suggest that the liberal planning ideal is not achievable. This certainly was Tugwell's conclusion, and he became increasingly discouraged about the possibility of democratic planning to the extent that he essentially abandoned the Chicago planning program even before the university did.

In addition to the contradictions in the liberal model, there are serious personal or performance problems. The liberal planning model is an open invitation to hubris. Here, too, we can learn from Tugwell's experience because he clearly did not escape the trap of presumption and personal resentment that awaits the liberal planner. The presumption, a major source of hubris, is that the technical expertise of the planner, mastery of facts and forecasts, gives him or her a privileged position in the plan-making process. Planners acting on this presumption are quickly corrected. Further, there are few things more repulsive to the informed citizen than to observe a person claiming to be acting for the public but perceived as acting for himself or herself. Then righteousness becomes self-righteousness and integrity is seen as hypocrisy.

I think that neither Tugwell nor those he worked with could always separate the public and the private in his performance. Despite the sincere humility he demonstrated in formal aspects of the role, as shown in the letters to Moses and La Guardia, his appearance, personality, and fondness for elaborate rhetoric made him appear egocentric, judgmental, self-satisfied, superior, and a host of other unpleasant attributes. It is one of the interesting contradictions in Tugwell's public life that all firsthand accounts of his behavior stress his kindness, openness, humility, and helpfulness; yet most secondhand reports describe him as arrogant. John Friedmann has described Tugwell as having the bearing of a Roman senator (Friedmann, 1987). This image of an authoritarian, patrician, aloof didact is unfortunately the perception others probably had of him. His self-image, the role he tried to enact, was a humble Greek philosopher—a Diogenes shining a lantern into the dark corners of public decision, a Plato trying to create Socratic dialogue.

Whether the confusion between the private man and his public role was entirely Tugwell's doing or was projected on him, the problem was real and negatively affected his ability to represent public virtue. Perhaps the lesson of Tugwell's personal story is that it is not humanly possible to play well this role as scripted in the liberal model of planning.

Tugwell read the role correctly from the script of the reform charter. Whether it was sensible to act out the role is debatable. For Tugwell, I think there was no choice. His personality, experience, ideas, and beliefs were all congruent with the role. He fell into it. The alternatives of being the good bureaucrat, the loyal political aid, like Berle, or the political operator, like Moses, were not conceivable. In effect, he embodied the role model of the self-conscious, liberal, pragmatic planner.

The morals of the story as I read it are many. First, nothing is gained by blaming the victim. Planners are the victims in this situation. The balm gained from scapegoating is temporary, and it introduces mischievous remedies and obscures the fundamental problems. Second, the liberal planning model is the culprit. However, that is the only accepted model of democratic planning we have, although it is accepted more in rhetoric than in reality. This suggests that the reactionary strategies of the 1980s—developing special constituencies, acting like a deal maker, strategically narrowing planning's scope—are bound to fail. We fool no one but ourselves.

Instead, we could learn from Tugwell's story that so long as we work within the framework of liberal planning at least two corrective changes would be helpful. A different emphasis in training is needed that better prepares planners for the normative aspects of public planning, for working with values formulation and conflict, and for an appreciation that planning is a practical art and not a technical or disciplinary skill. While certain technical skills are necessary to planning practice, Tugwell's story shows clearly how the presumption of technical expertise is the major source of planners' hubris. Since his time, following the dictates of the rational planning model, we have become more one-sided.

The second change needed concerns public participation in planning. The planning process in New York completely failed to meet the citizen participation expectations of the liberal ideal. Our failure to achieve broad-based public involvement in planning since the 1930s is testimony to the difficulty of the task. However, we have not worked at it very hard. Like Tugwell, we approach the public in a technocratic mode, now with computer graphics in hand, strategic models in mind, and negotiation on our lips. If the planning profession took community building seriously, we would do it differently. It is a commonplace criticism that the liberal planning model is, or at least is prone to, becoming, elitist. Tugwell's practice was, despite his rhetoric, and we have followed the same model.

These practical changes would improve planning's functioning under the liberal model. However, the fundamental moral of the story is that the pragmatic liberal model does not work and changing the personal characteristics of planners will not make it work. A more careful reading of the situation would suggest that the text Tugwell took for guidance, the reform charter, was not meant literally. It warned against the resumption of what had been as much or more than it pointed to what was wanted. Tugwell, like other planners before and since, was captured by a public rhetoric and overestimated the commitment to it because it matched the planner's own rhetoric. Individual planners like Tugwell, or all planners together, cannot make it work so long as it is rhetorical. Working toward a different model seems like the only solution. This, though, opens us to greater hubris, as Tugwell's story also teaches. He worked for many years on a model constitution that featured planning as a central component of democratic government. As John Friedmann dryly notes, "It was an undertaking that brought him few admirers" (Friedmann, 1987, p. 108).

To Robert Moses, planning was only window dressing to pacify a troublesome but gullible public. He could not understand Tugwell's taking it seriously and so found him "a Don Quixote, absurd, brave, pathetic, weighed down with armor, and tilting at fantastic enemies" (Moses, 1970, p. 418). By siding with Moses in our planning psyche and against Tugwell in response to the planning crisis of the 1980s, we have avoided coming to grips with the fundamental dilemma of democratic planning that made Tugwell a tragic figure in planning history. The final moral of the story is not that we should do as Rexford Guy Tugwell did or that we should do the opposite but that we should try again to learn to do what he was trying to learn to do.

References

American Society of Planning Officials (1940) *Conference Proceedings*, Chicago, American Society of Planning Officials.

Berle Papers, Franklin Delano Roosevelt Library. References are to box and file numbers.

Caro, Robert M. (1974) *The Power Broker*, New York, Alfred A. Knopf.

Friedmann, John (1987) *Planning in the Public Domain*, Princeton, Princeton University Press.

Gelfand, Mark I. (1985) "Rexford G. Tugwell and the frustration of planning in New York City," *Journal of the American Planning Association*, 51, 2.

Heckscher, August (1978) *When La Guardia Was Mayor*, New York, W. W. Norton.

Hoch, Charles (1984) "Doing good and being right," *Journal of the American Planning Association*, 50, 3.

Kessner, Thomas (1989) *Fiorello H. La Guardia*, New York, McGraw Hill.

Levin, Melvin R. (1987) *Planning in Government*, Chicago, APA Planners Press.

Meyerson, Martin and Banfield, Edward C. (1955) *Politics, Planning and the Public Interest*, Glencoe, Illinois, Free Press.

Moses, Robert M. (1970) *Public Works*, New York, McGraw-Hill.

Tugwell, Rexford G. (1939) "The fourth power," *Planning and Civic Comment*, 5.

——— (1940) "Planning in New York City," *The Planners' Journal*, 6, 2.

——— (1977) *Roosevelt's Revolution*, New York, Macmillan.

Tugwell Papers, Franklin Delano Roosevelt Library. References are to box and file numbers.

14

THE U.S.A.
1938–1955

HANS BLUMENFELD

INTRODUCTION
BY DONALD A. KRUECKEBERG

HANS BLUMENFELD WAS RAISED IN Hamburg, Germany, but was not
born there. In 1892, a cholera epidemic plagued the city of Hamburg, claiming eight thousand souls. The Blumenfelds escaped for
the time to Osnabrück where Hans was born in the same house as his
father and grandfather, a fact he found to be "a source of silly but
persistent pride" (*Life Begins at 65*, p. 23; hereafter, only page
numbers will be cited). His family was well to do, with his father a
corporate lawyer, and his mother's family prominent in banking.
They always expected he would come back to these family businesses. He did not, but he explains this. After the cholera epidemic
abated, his brother Franz caught the whooping cough and his
mother took his brother to the North Sea to recuperate. Hans was

Hans Blumenfeld's principal papers in the city and regional planning field have
been collected and published in two books: *The Modern Metropolis* and *Metropolis . . . and Beyond.* The first was published in Boston by MIT Press in 1967 and
simultaneously by Harvest House in Montreal; the second volume was published by John Wiley & Sons of New York in 1979.
    Reprinted with permission from Hans Blumenfeld, "The USA: 1938–1955,"
in *Life Begins at 65: The Not Entirely Candid Autobiography of a Drifter* (Montreal:
Harvest House, 1987), 185–89, 190–93, 197–208, 220–22, 231–35.

FIGURE 14.1   *Hans Blumenfeld.*
COURTESY CORPORATION PROFESSIONELLE DES URBANISTES DU QUEBEC

sent to his father's office in Hamburg and was quartered there with a wet nurse. "Unfortunately," he observes, "this early association with the legal profession has instilled in me neither legal skills nor a profound respect for the law" (p. 23).

His father died when Hans was sixteen. Hans was always close to his older brother Franz. They did everything together: "When he started school and learned to read, I immediately used his schoolbook to teach myself to read. I shared his buddies, though he did not share mine" (p. 18). Yet they were very different. Hans was difficult, temperamental, stubborn, a lover of sports but good at none, a dreamer, the "silent one." Franz was the opposite personality: a good child, not interested in sports, the one who later studied law, political science, and philosophy at Lausanne, Switzerland, and Cambridge, England, as a protégé of Charles Kay Ogden, a founder of the study of semantics. Hans likened his relationship to his brother as the classical one between commander in chief and chief of staff. "Much later in life I discovered, by analyzing my dreams, that this relation to my brother had irrevocably prefigured my relations to anyone with whom I collaborated in professional or voluntary work. I did not, and do not, shrink from developing policies and advocating them firmly, but I need an elder-brother surrogate to make the ultimate decision" (pp. 19–20). He attributed his ability to work happily and successfully later in life with bosses half his age, such as Edmund N. Bacon in Philadelphia and Murray Jones in Toronto, to this "prefigured attitude."

In 1913, Germany was swept up in enthusiasms for war. Torn between an urge to protest for peace and the conscience to duty, the brothers volunteered during the First World War for field artillery regiments. Franz was sent to the front in 1914. He wrote back, "I am afraid of losing my faith in human beings, in myself, in everything good in the world. What does it signify if all bullets and shells spare me, but I suffer damage to my soul? . . . You know that I have always been opposed to war, but now that I have experienced it, I have decided to devote all my life to work for peace, if I ever come back" (p. 46).

He did not come back. "Toward the end of the war," Hans tells us, "a professor of literature at Freiburg published a collection of letters from students killed in the war. In the 1920s the *Nouvelle revue francaise* reprinted some of them, including all those written by Franz. The French novelist, critic, and essayist André Gide added a comment, dealing almost exclusively with my brother's words, which had profoundly moved him. 'War swallows the best,' Aby Warburg, the art historian, wrote to my mother. 'We are stoking the furnace with pianos'" (pp. 46–7).

After another year of war, twice at the front, Hans adopted the bitterness of his colleagues: "Nobody hated 'the enemy'; our enemies were our officers; even more hated were the rear-echelon swine and the war profiteers at home; most hated of all were the journalists and clergymen who continued to glorify the war. To us it was anything but glorious. Nobody ever talked of 'this war'; it was always 'this shit-war'" (p. 49).

Blumenfeld's stories of the war are chilling, of a comrade dying in his arms, of hospitals, of prison, of a growing inner resistance to "the utter criminality of war" (p. 50). After the war he returned to school, became active in peace and communist youth movements, and fell deeply in love with Gertel Stamm, a painter who was already married to another man. In the short run, the love did not work out. In the long run, the peace and communism did not either.

Between 1924 and 1926, Blumenfeld kicked around the United States: in Gimbel's basement in New York, wrapping packages; as a draftsman in Baltimore; and as an apprentice architect in Los Angeles. Then he did more of the same around Europe. Finally from 1930 to 1937 he settled in Russia, working as a planner. He recalls, warmly, a horse-and-buggy conversation with a friend named Rosenberg. The two were working on a site plan for a branch of the Soviet Academy of Agriculture near Moscow:

> I said to Rosenberg, "We really have picked a nice profession." "Yes," he said. "You know back in the States people always asked me, 'What is this town planning you are doing; is there a lot of money in it?'—'No, you never know if and when you may get your next commission!'—'Does it give you standing in the community?'—'No, nobody respects a town planner.'— 'Then, why the hell are you doing it?'—'I'll tell you why; you can do what you darn please and call it work!'" I do not know of a better recipe for a happy life. I consider myself highly privileged to be one of the fortunate few able to follow it (p. 131).

Blumenfeld left the Soviet Union with extreme reluctance. He was, however, caught up in the Great Purge, as it came to be called. He was a foreigner. He could not get his residency permit renewed. He tried everything. Finally, he went to the Soviet Bureau of Complaint and asked to see Marya Ilyitchnaya:

> The people at the desk refused to call her, stating that she could do nothing in my case. I wrote a note to her: "I appeal to you, not as the head of this office, but as a human being, a Communist, and the sister of Lenin: help me." She came out of her office and, with an old woman's helpless gesture, said in a barely audible voice, "I cannot help you," and turned back. At that moment, I realized that it was over, definitely and irrevocably. For the first and only time in my adult life I broke into tears (p. 170).

Where to go? Blumenfeld considered Sweden, Turkey, Mexico, Canada (thought of by Europeans as a paperback edition of the United States), and the United States. He applied for admission to the United States, but was not surprised that the consulate "did not look with favor on a fellow who had lived seven years in the Soviet Union." Nonetheless, with the aid of his sister and brother-in-law in

New York, the Jewish Agency, and the fact that he could show that he "had lived three years in God's Own Country without shooting the president," he was accepted (p. 180). The story of his experience here is told in the excerpts from his autobiography that follow. They omit nearly one-half of his chapter on these years from 1938 to 1955. The omitted portions are his running observations on world affairs, including the Second World War, the cold war, and his foreign travel.

Blumenfeld was offered a job in Toronto in 1955; by that time, under the cloud of McCarthyism, he had decided that he preferred Canada. "For one thing, not being big—except in territory—it is free from the temptation to play 'Big Brother' to the rest of the world. . . . At the time I came to Canada, it did not even have a national flag. Considering all the crimes committed in the name of national flags, I found this an attractive distinction."

His final chapter sums up eloquently Blumenfeld's philosophy of life, which is his philosophy of planning, too, on communism versus capitalism and socialism; on Marx and Kant; on materialism, reason, ethics, and free will. The movement in his writing, shuttling back and forth, from world to local view, weaves a story of restless and intense effort to portray the world as it is and to see things in synopsis:

Why do so few people take a synoptic view? Noticing the many stupid things that people say, write, and do, I had concluded that they had no brains. That conclusion was wrong; they do have brains, as is evidenced by the many clever little things they do. They do have brains; they just don't have the guts to use them. They do not dare to use them where it really matters, on the basic questions of human life in society and nature (p. 119).

Hans Blumenfeld had the guts. In recognition of this, he was awarded the Order of Canada, two honorary doctorates, the distinguished Service Award of the American Institute of Planners, the Medal Award of the American Society of Planning Officials, and the Patrick Abercrombie Prize for Town Planning from the International Union of Architects. In 1984, at the age of ninety-two, he was appointed honorary vice president of the World Peace Council.

The U.S.A.: 1938–1955
In Greater New York

At the end of the same month of October which had seen the Munich betrayal I finally received my U.S. visa. After a visit with my cousin Elsbeth and her husband, Fritz Oppenheimer, in London, I embarked for New York. During the passage we received the news of the "Crystal Night," the start of the final destruction of the Jews of Germany. I arrived on the evening of the sixteenth of November, the last day of validity of my French residence permit. My brother-in-law, Alfred Plaut, was at the pier and drove me to his home in New Rochelle, over the just-completed Westside Highway. I was happy to see my sister and my nephews, who had grown from babies to teenagers. Olga Solmitz was also there. She had finally left Germany, just in time to be still permitted to take some of her possessions with her. She had included part of my library which had been stored in the farmhouse on the common Solmitz–Blumenfeld property in Gross-Borstel near Hamburg. The balance went up in flames a few years later, ignited by bombs dropped by the Royal Air Force.

There were other relatives and friends whom I met again in America after many years. A cousin remarked that I had not changed at all in ten years; I countered that this was an obvious sign of complete sclerosis. In my first week in my sister's home, at a party at the house of neighbors, a lady told me that she had just met another German refugee architect by the name of Konrad Wittmann. Wittmann had been the only friend whom I had found among my follow students in Munich, in 1911 and 1912; I had last seen him in 1913. We renewed our friendship. He was an excellent architect and an outstanding human being. After some difficult early years he became a teacher at the Pratt Institute, greatly loved and admired by his students.

America had changed in the twelve years since I had left it. In the twenties, in the days of Calvin Coolidge, the Americans whom I met had talked only about jobs, money, spectator sports, cars, and girls. As to more important subjects, this "New World" seemed satisfied in theology with the concepts of the seventeen[th] century, in politics with those of the eighteenth, and in economics with those of the nineteenth. The depression had shocked Americans out of that kind of complacency; they had begun to question and to think. Also, the arts—in the twenties regarded as a ladies' parlor game, unworthy of the attention of respectable men—were now taken seriously. America had become a much more interesting country.

The negative side of the depression was also apparent. I was shocked to see the many gray, tired, worn faces in the subway. I never had that depressing experience in the subways of Paris or of Moscow.

Lucky as I was to have the support of my relatives, I still needed a job. Would I be able to find one in the depressed economy of 1938? Would I be able to hold one? I had been out of regular work for three years, and out of competition in the Western world for more than eight. At the age of 46 I had to start from scratch.

Again I was lucky. A German colleague in Paris had given me the address of his friend in New York. From him I learned about the recently established trade union of architects and engineers, the FAECT. I went to their headquarters and was well received. They directed me to an office which was designing a big model for General Motors to be shown at the New York World's Fair. To my pleasant surprise, they regarded my Soviet experience as an asset and took me on. It was a huge project employing several hundred architects and designers under the direction of Norman Bel Geddes. My immediate boss was Melville Branch, who has remained a friend. There I also found Albert Löcher, a talented collaborator of Ernst May, whom I had met in Moscow and subsequently in Paris.

I designed the harbor and the central park of the big city which was the core of the model, generating freeways which spread all over the landscape. It was fun, but it lasted only three weeks; I had come in at the tail end of the design stage.

What next? I figured that there were three ways for an unknown architect to establish himself. First, win a competition. But I was a very poor draftsman, so that was out for me. Second, find a job in an office and gain appreciation for my work, possibly to the point of becoming indispensable and being taken in as a partner. This could happen but was a matter of luck. Third, write and publish. This seemed the most promising way in my case.

I had been interested for years in the question of sunshine in housing. I found that the existing literature was limited, dealing only with one or two aspects of planning for—or against—sunshine. I wrote a study with a number of illustrations which explored orientation and distance from other structures, together with shape of rooms, as well as location, size, and shape of windows. Overlays were developed to indicate the floor area covered by sunshine in any room at various latitudes and seasons.

I presented copies to several persons. They found the study interesting but hard to publish—too short for a book, too long for an article. However, James Marston Fitch, then editor of the *Architectural Record*, liked it enough to invite me for a talk. He commissioned me to write an article on "the coordination of natural and artificial light." I plunged into the subject, found it fascinating, and produced a lengthy article which actually dealt primarily with the relation of lighting and seeing. It was published in two sections in the *A.R.* in 1940 and 1941 and received favorable comment.

At that time the USA had just embarked on its program of "Public Housing." The FAECT strongly supported it, and I went out to meetings of other CIO [Congress of Industrial Organizations] unions to "sell" it. I got a lukewarm reception. "We are not eligible because our wages are above the specified maximum," was the reaction. I concluded that the program could only be a success if it was broadened. I had learnt that at that time the U.S. Housing Authority raised money on short term at extremely low interest rates and lent it to the local agencies on considerably higher long-term rates. I estimated that rents could be reduced, without direct subsidies, to a level accessible to most workers if the local agencies received loans from the Federal Authority at the rates which it paid to its short-term creditors, and if the projects remained exempt from local taxes. I developed a proposal for such a program in a short pamphlet entitled *Housing Union Labor.* It was published, in mimeographed form, by the FAECT and subsequently also by the New York CIO. The New York architect-planner Albert Mayer, to whom I had given a copy, expressed satisfaction that a refugee architect, rather than talking about his achievements in his old country, had tackled a problem of his new one.

In Paris, Max Raphael and André Lurçat had given me letters to the art critic Meyer Shapiro, whom I found very interesting, and to the architect Simon Breines. Breines took me to a meeting at the Metropolitan Museum where Robert Moses presented his program of "urban redevelopment." We both were shocked by this ruthless proposal for wholesale demolition. Subsequently I joined a study group of the New York Citizens Housing and Planning Council which attempted to prepare redevelopment legislation. It was a very interesting group; its members included Clarence Stein, Henry

Churchill, Fred Ackermann, Clarence Perry, Bill Vladeck and Carl Feiss. I did not share their enthusiasm; I warned, "Whatever good urban development may do, it will certainly worsen the housing situation of low-income groups." I insisted that it should be recommended only if accompanied, or better preceded, by rent control and by a large-scale program of subsidized housing.

It has always been a puzzle to me how persons of eminent good will and high intelligence could favor "slum clearance." At a later date I put it this way: "If you want to help a fellow who has worn out his pants, you buy him a pair of new ones or repair the old ones; you don't just tear off his pants." It is really as simple as that.

Breines hired me for a week to help with working drawings for the installation of the Soviet pavilion for the New York World's Fair, but otherwise I was unemployed during the first several months of 1939.

In the spring the FAECT directed me to the firm of Kelly & Gruzen in Jersey City, which wanted a site planner for a small public housing project in Harrison, NJ. I developed the site plan, which later received official praise from the New York chapter of the AIA [American Institute of Architects]. More important, when I later asked the opinion of a tenant, he said, "It is nice; every court is different." That is exactly what I had tried to achieve.

Gruzen kept me on for other work, first on details of this project and later on other commissions. When work ran out in the fall, he promised to call me back as soon as a commission came in.

I had moved to Jersey City. First I rented a furnished room, but the landlady threw me out because I made her house look disreputable by pulling down one shade, which was hit by the afternoon sun, and not the other, which was shadowed by the next house. I then rented a furnished cold-water flat. By every definition it was a slum dwelling. The bedroom was windowless, but I used it only for storage, sleeping in the "living room." The bathroom was shared with another apartment, but nobody lived there. So it was really quite adequate. Its great attraction was the view from the bay window: from the edge of the Palisades, it swept across the flats to the Hudson River, the bay, and the Manhattan skyline. I stayed until the end of the year, when the winter cold drove me out.

I REMEMBER THE START of the Second World War; from my window I saw the *Bremen* sail out of New York Harbor. It was the second piece of deadly news in a few months; four months earlier Gertel had passed away. A period of my life had come to an end.

There was no dramatic change; the U.S. was still neutral. I rented a furnished room at the corner of Riverside Drive and 142nd Street, with a view over the Hudson River. Once more I returned to my old love, the history of cities. I spent my days at the marvelous Avery Library, the architectural library of Columbia University. Through Carl Feiss I had joined the newly founded Society of Architectural Historians. When I discovered in my studies at Avery a peculiar feature of the ancient Indian city of Mohenjo-Daro, I published it in their journal in January 1942. It was my second publication in an American professional journal. It was followed by an article on "Regional and City Planning in the Soviet Union," published in the third issue of *Task*, a journal founded by young teachers and students at Harvard and MIT. I learned that this article had been discussed at a meeting of the American Institute of Planners. I was beginning to get a reputation—but not a job. During the entire year of 1940 I had only four weeks of paid work, at Albert Mayer's office.

Given the insouciance and insolence of my unshakable self-confidence, this did not bother me too much. I lived frugally but happily on borrowed money, digging into the treasures of Avery Library. In studying the beautiful publication by Hulot and Fougères on the ancient Greek city of Selinus, I got caught up again by that question which had arisen in my mind in the spring of 1927 when I contemplated the Temple of Concordia in Agrigento, Sicily: was this a synthesis of two independently existing building types, the "naos" (cella) and a ring of sacred columns on their stylobate, the latter symbolizing the trees of a sacred grove on a mountain?

I have spent more time on this question of the origin of the Doric peripteros than on any other problem which I have ever researched. Several times in 1940 and 1941 I felt close to writing down my tentative conclusions, but I always deferred it. I finally wrote a fragmentary summary in 1985 which is still unpublished.

In the fall of 1940 I participated in a seminar on planning given by Carl Feiss and Raymond Unwin at Columbia University. I had admired Unwin's book since 1912 and his work at Hampstead since 1924; his person fully lived up to my expectations.

PHILADELPHIA

It was also on Carl Feiss' recommendation that the Philadelphia Housing Association asked me to present myself for a job as a research assistant. After a talk with the director, Edmund N. Bacon, I was hired to start in February of 1941. For reasons still obscure to me, Ed insisted on reducing my modest demand for $200 a month to $2000 a year, after three trial months at $150.

I have often thought that I have cheated educators of a model deterrent by not dying at that time. Just imagine: here was a man with many gifts by nature and education, with all conditions for a brilliant career, but he always refused to listen to his betters and pigheadedly went his own way; where did it lead him? To end up in his fiftieth year as a research assistant at $2000 a year in an obscure little organization. Let this be a warning to you, young man.

I had been just two weeks in Philadelphia when I got a call from Sumner Gruzen asking me to come back to work on the site plan for an army camp. I decided to stay with the Housing Association, but did come over some evenings to help in developing the site plan. I recommended Albert Löcher to Gruzen; it worked out very well. Löcher stayed with Gruzen as chief designer for several decades until his premature death; during this time the firm became one of the well-known architectural offices of New York.

I found the work with the Housing Association interesting. I extended our annual survey of housing construction, conversion, and demolition from the city to the entire metropolitan area. I found many previously overlooked aspects and correlations significant for housing; some results of my research were published in the association's annual reports or in special pamphlets. I found that the city could be analyzed in terms of concentric zones, characterized by predominance of demolitions, conversions, no change, and new housing construction, respectively. In analyzing the census of 1940, I found that racial segregation had actually increased. I wrote up my findings at the request of a black student activist—he later became one of the leading reporters of *The Baltimore Afro-American*—and he included them, with reference to their source, in a militant pamphlet which he wrote. When Ed Bacon saw it and called me in, he was livid, fearing some backlash which actually never occurred.

One of our board members, Scholz, a professor of economics, questioned the qualification of an architect for a job of socioeconomic research. So I took a course in statistics, during which I learned a lot, and Scholz' seminar on economic planning. He was very interested in what I had to say about Soviet planning and became one of my strongest backers.

I also met the architect Oscar Stonorov and his then practically unknown partner, Lou Kahn, who became and remained a close friend. They were among the members of an organization of reform-minded Young Turks which had been formed to bring about the adoption of a city charter for Philadelphia. The charter was backed by a majority of Philadelphia voters but rejected by the Pennsylvania legislature. After this defeat the group decided to pursue the more limited goal of establishing an active city planning program in Philadelphia. A City Planning Commission had been appointed many years ago, but it existed only on paper, without funding and without a staff.

Ed Bacon and the Housing Association were deeply involved in this campaign. The focus was to be the annual meeting of the American Society of Planning Officials to be held in Philadelphia. The key speaker on Philadelphia's needs was Hugh Pomeroy; I was charged with supplying him the relevant information on the city's housing conditions.

Hugh, who had started as a Baptist preacher and had subsequently been a member of the California legislature, gave a true fire-and-brimstone speech. Using my material, he thundered that Philadelphia had the worst slums in the nation. The mayor, who had been scheduled to follow Hugh on the platform, got redder and redder in the face and left without giving his speech.

Ed Bacon was desperate, but I told him that the cause was by no means lost. The mayor was to receive a citizen's delegation on the following day which would submit a detailed proposal for a well-staffed planning commission. I recalled my trade union experience in Hamburg. I anticipated that, after the rantings of that "wild radical" Pomeroy, the proposals of the delegation would sound most moderate and reasonable. It worked like a charm. There was support from the banks which handled the city's bonds and were disturbed about the way in which contracts for public works were handed out to friends of the political machine, and also from the city's chief engineer, an able and dedicated technocrat.

A new City Planning Commission was established. Its chairman was Edward Hopkinson, head of the bank of Drexel, Biddle, & Co., the city's main creditors. He handled his task very well. Robert B. Mitchell was appointed director and began to lay out a program and assemble a staff. He had the benefit of the advice of Professor Sweeney, the wizened and experienced head of the Institute for Local and State Government. He gave Bob Mitchell two tips on how to ward off attempts to cut his staff. First, do not ask for research; there was, instead, a division for "Planning Analysis"—evidently an indispensable activity. Second, never give the same title to more than one staff person; when the cutting starts, you can always counter, "This is the only man I have who can do this job."

THE WAR [THE SECOND WORLD WAR] made me technically an "enemy alien." But the controlling office in Philadelphia, in contrast to that in New York, was very liberal and gave me unlimited permission to visit both New York and the Atlantic Seashore. I also visited Princeton, where both Ervin Panofsky, the art historian from Hamburg, and the philosopher and historian Erich Kahler, whom I had known in Munich and Vienna, had settled.

The war also created new housing problems in the USA which modified the work of the Housing Association. Rent control was introduced, but sales were not controlled. The consequence was that the owners of rented row houses, the predominant type of workers' housing in Philadelphia, sold their houses and evicted their tenants. This set off a chain reaction: the evicted tenant, unable to find a row house for rent, bought one and in turn evicted its tenant. I argued that it was absurd to attempt to control the cost of housing in one form, rent, but not in the other, sale, and proposed a moratorium on evictions. The proposal got nowhere; nor did another proposal to ease the housing shortage: a progressive tax on "surplus" rooms, defined as exceeding $n + 2$, n being the number of occupants. The tax would be moderate on the first surplus room, but increase steeply for each successive one. The occupants affected by the tax, owners or renters, would have three ways to avoid it: move to smaller quarters, share their dwelling with friends or relatives, or sublet rooms. All three ways would help to relieve the housing shortage. I still think it is a good idea. But my trade union contact on housing problems did not like it; he lived with wife and child in a six-room house.

I was a member of the office workers' union and one of their alternate delegates to the CIO Council. At one session the question of the liquidation of the *Record* came up, the only one of the three Philadelphia newspapers which favored the Democrats and the New Deal. The discussion turned exclusively on the question of the jobs of the *Record* employees after its takeover by the *Bulletin*. I proposed that the CIO and the AFL [American Federation of Labor], who worked closely together in Philadelphia, buy the *Record* and continue it as a prolabor and pro–New Deal paper. I was laughed out of court; labor could not dream of raising the money. This stunned me; in Germany the labor movement, Social Democrat or Communist, had been able to support its own press. In the Philadelphia area there were over half-a-million union members. Because of the wartime no-strike policy, huge sums had accumulated in the union treasuries; individual workers also had bigger savings than ever. Yet they could not afford to publish a newspaper; the workers, the vast majority of the population, were excluded from any control of the press. What kind of democracy was this?

Ed Bacon joined the navy and Dorothy Schoell–Montgomery succeeded him as director of the Housing Association. She was a long-time housing activist whom I admired greatly. I used to say that there were only three red-blooded he-men in the somewhat wishy-washy North American housing movement: Elizabeth Wood, Catherine Bauer, and Dorothy Schoell.

Bob Mitchell wanted to have me on his staff at the Planning Commission, but for this I had to be a U.S. citizen. I had taken out my "First Papers" on my arrival in late 1938, so I was eligible after five years of residence. I had not been sure that I wanted to take that step. I thought of returning to Germany after the defeat of Hitler, anticipating the formation of a broadly based Popular Front government. But now it looked doubtful whether there would be a German government; and I was offered the kind of work in the States which I had wanted to do all my life. So I applied; I knew I might be rejected if I were asked if I had been a member of the Communist party, as I would have to answer in the affirmative. But the question was not asked and I became a U.S. citizen in 1944.

As the war drew to a close, the Pennsylvania legislature established a Postwar Planning Commission to prepare urban redevelopment legislation. It was headed by Abraham Freedman, legal counsel to the Housing Association. I became his associate; my assistant was Margy Ellin, a young sociologist from New York. When I explained to Freedman my misgivings about the negative effects of urban redevelopment, he asked, "Should we recommend against it?" I said, "No, some such legislation will be enacted in any case; we better frame it so as to minimize the damage." We devised a two-step process: first an "area" had to be defined and its intended future use confirmed by the City Planning Commission; and second, specific projects within such areas, again subject to approval by the Planning Commission, had to be submitted.

I also devised a clause stipulating that occupants could be displaced only on condition that the Housing Authority certified that safe and sanitary housing was available to them at the same rent and with equal accessibility. Evidently, if such housing had been available, the slum dwellers would already have moved into it. So it meant that slums could only be "cleared" if an equal amount of subsidized public housing were built for all displaced persons; but, in practice, the Housing Authorities were not that scrupulous in giving their certification.

I broadened the definition of "blight" to also cover vacant and nonresidential areas and wanted to divorce "redevelopment" from "slum clearance." But Abe Freedman objected that slum clearance had been recognized by the Supreme Court as a "public purpose" and was the only legal basis for expropriation for redevelopment. The legislation was enacted pretty much as we had drafted it.

I was first in the civil examination for senior planner in the Land Use Division of the City Planning Commission and started work early in 1945. The division was headed by Ray Leonard, a most lovable man. My responsibility was to develop the general plan of land use distribution and major transportation facilities. We agreed that the plan had to cover not only the territory of the City of Philadelphia, to which our jurisdiction was limited, but the much larger Metropolitan District, hoping that the logic of our proposals would persuade other jurisdictions to adopt and implement them.

I remember discussing the question of the basic form and structure of our metropolis with Bob Mitchell. I felt that it was far too large to allow for the traditional approach as a system of streets and squares. It had to be organized as an urban landscape of districts of different character, built up or open. I did not believe in the then predominant preference for "decentralization" into satellite towns, nor in the "linear city" propagated by others, but felt the best general solution was a star-shaped pattern, with development radiating from the existing core along main transportation lines, and "wedges" of green open land between the radiating districts approaching as close as possible to the core. Such a scheme had just been adopted for Copenhagen under the name of a "Finger Plan." Of course, it would have to be substantially modified for our jurisdiction, as for any urban area, to fit the existing natural and man-made topography.

In 1947 a meeting of the American Society of Planning Officials celebrated the fiftieth anniversary of Ebenezer Howard's book *To-Morrow*, in which he had developed his proposals for new "garden cities." The notion of channeling urban growth into new towns of predetermined size, designed once and for all to be neatly balanced, was hailed as the answer to the vexing problems of the unpredictable "chaotic" big city. I was the only doubting Thomas. After asking my audience to ponder why in half a century "To-morrow" had failed to become "Today," I noted that, difficult as it had proved to initiate the growth of a New Town, it would be far more difficult to stop it. If successful, the New Towns would soon grow beyond their pre-planned size, reproducing all the problems from which the planners hoped to escape. I concluded by sketching alternative forms of metropolitan growth. My presentation, subsequently published, was the first in a series of essays devoted to understanding the metropolis as a new form of human settlement, radically different from the big city which had given it birth [see the footnote at the opening of this chapter].

Ray Leonard gave priority to the planning of a comprehensive system of freeways. I agreed, but insisted that we also develop plans for the extension and improvement of rapid rail transit, by both subways and suburban railroad service. Some of our proposals, adopted at the time, have not yet been carried out. On the other hand, my proposal to connect the suburban terminals of the Pennsylvania and Reading railroads, rejected at the time as completely unfeasible, is now being realized.

Public opinion favored redevelopment, in particular of the badly decayed oldest section of Philadelphia next to the Delaware River. I wrote a short article entitled "The Waterfront, Key to Redevelopment," stating that redevelopment could succeed only if the commercial piers as well as the wholesale food market, both generators of heavy truck traffic, were relocated. Everyone thought this was a quite impractical "far-out" idea, but several years later it was done. I had encountered the problem once before. When, shortly after my arrival in New York, I talked to Robert Weinberg, an excellent architect then working with the City Planning Commission, I told him that I considered it urgent to eliminate from Lower Manhattan the obsolete piers which obstructed access to and enjoyment of the waterfront to over a million downtown workers and residents. He was shocked by such a radical proposal; it has now been carried out.

Later, I went through the same experience with the "Old City" waterfront in Montreal. I have come to realize that it is a worldwide problem, resulting from the historical fact that so many cities originated as harbors. As they grow, both city and harbor must expand and, inevitably, collide. The city center can be relocated only at tremendous cost, if at all. Relocation of the harbor is a great gain in terms of land incidentally made available for loading, storage, and transportation. Harbor relocation is occurring in city after city, but usually only after long and costly delays.

Because of the complexities of the situation, redevelopment of the central waterfront had to be deferred, but applications for many other areas came in. I was now stuck with administering the law which I had drafted; I had to make recommendations concerning the establishment of "redevelopment areas." I soon realized, as did others, that designating an area for redevelopment caused its further decay because it discouraged investment. I could think of no other remedy than to declare the entire city, except its newest areas, a "redevelopment area." This was not accepted at the time, but by now practically all old sections of Philadelphia have been so certified.

I did succeed in turning attention to the redevelopment of two nonresidential areas. One, the largest ever tackled in America, was an area at a level too low to be served by sewers. Despite this fact it had been subdivided, on paper, and many lots had been sold; most of these had reverted to the city for unpaid taxes during the depression. Redevelopment involved raising the level of the entire area by landfill and replanning it, primarily for residential development; the residential area was to be separated from a major trucking highway, rail line, and airport by a belt reserved for industry. The development has had a checkered history but has in the main followed the original concept.

Another smaller industrial area contained a number of soap and rendering plants whose penetrating stench was felt as a severe nuisance. As the chemical composition of the gases and the nature of the processes producing them were not known, we contracted with the Franklin Institute, a prestigious research establishment, to investigate this problem. The discussions which the institute's scientists had with the engineers and managers of the plants prompted them into action in order to avoid expropriation, which could be undertaken since their sites had been declared part of a redevelopment area. A few small plants moved out; most corrected the nuisances. As a result, the area, without further government action, "redeveloped" into a sound industrial area which attracted other plants, in particular truck terminals.

As far as existing poor residential areas, officially called "blighted" or "slums," were concerned, I stuck to my view that it was better to rehabilitate them than to tear them down. The question had come up earlier, while I was still with the Housing Association. One day Ed Bacon asked me to select an area of Philadelphia suitable for clearance and redevelopment. I objected for two reasons: first, wholesale clearance was socially destructive, and second, a project built on a man-made desert would look the same everywhere, regardless of the site or city. I suggested instead a project for rehabilitating an existing area in South Philadelphia. Ed had been somewhat secretive about the reason for his request; it turned out that it was destined for the city planning exhibition which he and Oscar Stonorov were planning and which was successfully implemented in Philadelphia after the war. Lou Kahn, at the time still associated with Stonorov, took up with enthusiasm the idea of rehabilitating the area in which he had grown up, and his proposals, presented at the exhibition, attracted nationwide attention.

Significant experience in rehabilitation was gained in a small project initiated by the Quakers, who operated a community center in a large designated "redevelopment area" inhabited mainly by blacks. During the depression the Quakers had successfully organized several self-help cooperative housing projects. They now suggested clearing the block around their community center and rebuilding it by a similar project. I noted that it was not economically feasible to replace four-story buildings by self-built cottages, but that it might be possible to organize a cooperative for rehabilitating the block. They took up the idea and started to enlist members for a racially mixed housing cooperative.

Several unanticipated things happened. The Quakers had been worried that they might have to evict the present tenants. That did not happen; by the time the cooperative took over, the landlords had relocated their tenants into other slum dwellings which they also owned. Another worry arose when the organizers scrutinized the names of the white applicants for membership in the racially mixed housing cooperative; they found that most of them were known for Communist sympathies. Later, when the members got together for their first meetings, the white intellectuals dominated the discussion, and the blacks observed an embarrassed silence; when it came to work with tools, the roles were reversed. The rehabilitated apartments, designed by Oscar Stonorov, were attractive; but very few of the previous occupants could afford the cost.

One day an unexpected request came from City Hall: the city invited the United Nations to establish themselves in Philadelphia, and we were to propose a suitable site, immediately. I suggested a large plateau in Fairmount Park which overlooked the city, and my suggestion was accepted. The commission charged by the U.N. with recommending the most suitable city and site came to Philadelphia. Le Corbusier made a presentation followed by a discussion.

The staff of the Planning Commission drove the visitors around to show them the site and the Philadelphia area generally. As I spoke some Russian, I was charged with taking care of the two Soviet delegates, together with the Polish delegate, who rode in the same car. He was Mathew Novitzki, a highly creative and cultivated architect of outstanding sensitivity and intelligence.

After completion of the U.N. project Novitzki stayed in America, and I saw him several times in New York. Subsequently, he went to Raleigh, North Carolina. On the occasion of a visit to Chapel Hill, friends drove me to Raleigh to see him. Mathew showed me his project for the "Cow Palace." I did not immediately grasp the novel concept. While he was trying to explain it to me, my friends came to drive me back. So Novitzki said, "I will explain it to you the next time." There was to be no next time. On his return flight from Chandigarh [in India] he perished in a plane accident. It was an irreplaceable loss.

At the Planning Commission there were personnel changes. My assistant was Martin Meyerson. When he told me that he had become engaged to my former assistant Margy Ellin, I asked, "Am

I responsible?" He answered, "Oh no, I met her years ago in New York—and I did not like her at all." It has become a very happy marriage.

After the end of the war Ed Bacon, who had served in the navy, returned and became my colleague as senior land planner. Soon after, Robert Mitchell resigned and Ray Leonard became director. An internal competition was arranged for the vacant position of chief of the Division of Land Planning, in which Ed Bacon came first, I second, and Paul Croley, a very capable administrator, third. A few months later the unexpected and tragic death of Ray Leonard again orphaned us. Ed Bacon succeeded him. I was temporarily put in charge of the Division of Land Planning. Shortly before, Harold M. Mayer, who had headed the Division of Planning Analysis, had left for the University of Chicago. I had worked closely with Harold in preparing the general plan, and he told me that he would like me to take over as his successor. However, the division was temporarily headed by its senior staff member, Harlan Loomer, an able sociologist and demographer.

I felt entitled to succeed Ed Bacon as head of the Division of Land Planning, but he did not want me to occupy that position. When, in the course of our discussion, I mentioned Harold Mayer's wish that I should succeed him, Ed thought that was an excellent idea. I objected that I did not want to push aside Harlan Loomer. When I talked to Harlan—who did not get along too well with Ed— he said that he realized that he had no chance to be appointed as chief and would rather work under me than under someone else. So I accepted the position as chief of the Division of Planning Analysis with the condition that the work on the general plan which I had started would be transferred with me.

I was, however, still interested in the Division of Land Planning. So, when a nation-wide competition for chief was opened, I applied. Out of about two dozen applicants, fourteen were admitted to the second stage, the design of residential development for an existing, still rural, area of Philadelphia. Only two competitors survived, I and Thomas Schocken. Curiously, both of us were German architects of Jewish descent, and both of us had worked in the Soviet Union. Moreover, while I had intended to fight in Spain, Tom had actually done so, as one of a few Social Democrats who had joined the International Brigade. Even more curiously, our two projects were so similar that some people suspected us of collusion. At the final stage, the oral interview by a committee of three, Tom was nervous, while I felt very much at ease. So I won the competition.

This put Ed in a bit of a quandary. He did not want to appoint me, and he could not appoint anyone else. The only way out was to cancel the competition and call a new one six months later. This time one had to design a project in a closed one-day session. Given my poor draftmanship, I knew that I could not win that one, but I still participated. The winner was Willo von Moltke. He did a good job as chief of the Division of Land Planning. We worked together well and became good friends.

Ed Bacon was primarily interested in urban design and specific projects and left the development of the general plan pretty much to me. When the board at one meeting asked him to present a progress report on the general plan, he was surprised that I produced it in time for the next board meeting. Subsequently, several aspects of the plan—on population, industry, housing, etc.—were published.

One of the important aspects of the plan was, of course, a study of the economic base. Right at the beginning, after extended discussion by the senior staff, we had decided not to use the then fashionable approach of starting with the so-called "basic" industries, i.e. those producing for export, and derive from the employment in these the employment in the so-called "nonbasic" or "service" industries, and finally the total population. After our report, written by our staff economist, Maxine Woolston, was published, I was asked frequently by colleagues why we had not used the standard approach. I felt that my answers were inadequate and tried to clarify my thoughts. The result, almost ten years later, was an article entitled "The Economic Base of the Metropolis." It was the longest article I have published and probably the one that touched off the greatest amount of discussion among economists as well as planners.

Increased income and the end of wartime restrictions led to some changes in my personal life. When I first came to Philadelphia, I had rented a garret in an old rooming house within walking distance of the office of the Housing Association. One of the association's main activities was to put the heat on the city's Building Inspection Department to enforce the Housing Code. The code outlawed occupancy of rooms above the third floor without a fire escape. One day officers of the department appeared and closed the one in which I lived. Fortunately, I got help from Karoline Solmitz, the widow of my murdered friend Fritz. She had come to America with her four children and had established a boardinghouse, with the aid of the Quakers, in Bryn Mawr. A friend of Karoline's, a professor of German at Bryn Mawr College, had a room to rent in her house on the campus. The first night I slept there I was enchanted by the cool evening breeze which came into my room, in contrast to the stifling heat of my old abode. I realized how great the climatic differences can be within an urban area.

It is really absurd to call the climate of the northeastern United States "temperate." It is intemperate in both directions. For a while an Indian engineer worked at our Planning Office. He complained about the heat; it was never that hot in Bombay, he asserted.

I bought a bicycle and rode the country roads. People laughed at me; I may well have been the only adult in Philadelphia who rode a bicycle at the time. I discovered a beautiful swimming hole in an old millpond and struck up an acquaintance with some local fellows. When I asked a young lad who had just finished school where he worked, he answered, "In a drugstore in Wayne." That gave me a shock. In my studies of the region I had divided it into a number of areas and identified for each of them the ratio of jobs to resident labor force. My young friend lived in the Schuylkill Valley, where there was a great excess of jobs; he worked on the Main Line, where there was an even greater deficit! The following year I asked him whether he was still working in the drugstore. No, he was now working in a factory. Ah, I thought, finally economic rationality has prevailed. Where was the factory? In Bryn Mawr, one of the very few small factories to be found on the Main Line.

It dawned on me that shortening the journey to work may not be the determining factor in the choice of location of work and residence which planning theory assumes. This was later confirmed by an experience at the Planning Commission. During the war a settlement of about 600 houses had been built for workers of the Budd plant, about thirteen miles from the center of Philadelphia, surrounded by open fields. We wanted to learn something about life in such an isolated community. One group of questions covered the journey to work. Only three men worked close by, at the Budd plant. Two of them, who did not have a car, complained, "It is a long walk, and there are no sidewalks." There were few complaints among the others. One answered as follows: "Where do you work?"—"At the Navy Yard." (18 miles away)—"How do you get there?"—"I take a bus, the subway, another bus."— "How long does it take?"—"About two hours."—"Is it inconvenient?"—"Yes, I have to walk so far to the bus!"

When I became a municipal civil servant, I had to live within the city limits. I was fortunate in finding furnished accommodation, consisting of a living room, a small bedroom, and a bathroom, as big as both of them combined, on the second floor of the house of a retired businessman. Their maid kept my rooms and bed neat and clean, and I had my meals in a drugstore nearby. The house was located in a large garden at the edge of the Wissahickon Park. I often walked or bicycled in the beautiful, deep, and heavily treed ravine of the Wissahickon Creek. When my host died and I had to move, I found a furnished room in the neighborhood.

Philadelphia was at that time run by a Republican political machine; the boss of my ward prided himself on running a tight ship. His colleagues hit back by pointing out that a well-paid city employee in his ward had registered as a Democrat. Some well-meaning colleagues of mine who had heard of this advised me to change my registration if I wanted to keep my job. I refused; nothing happened.

THE COLD WAR GREW more intense. I resisted as best I could. I continued to publish articles on housing and urban reconstruction in the Soviet Union. I joined the International Federation of Scientific Workers. I participated in the debates between adherents and opponents of the cold war in my trade union. I worked with the Progressive party for Henry Wallace in the presidential election of 1948, and I supported the struggle for housing, social security, racial equality, and civil rights and against the increasing persecution of real and alleged Communists. Of course, I was regarded as a "fellow traveler." I received repeated appeals in the mail for financial and moral support from the Civil Rights Congress, which was generally regarded as a "Communist front." As I disagreed with the failure of the American Communist party to admit the evil of Stalin's terror, and as I already supported the Civil Liberties Union, I at first ignored these appeals. But as the Congress had taken up several cases which I considered just and which the Union had not been willing to handle, I sent them some money. When they approached me asking me to sign petitions, and subsequently to join their Pennsylvania board, I had to admit to myself that my hesitation was merely the result of cowardice, and I agreed to serve.

I was never called before the McCarthy or any of the other "un-American" committees, but of course I asked myself how I would best deal with the infamous "trilemma" with which they faced their victims by their standard opening question: "Are you or have you ever been a member of the Communist party?" There were three possible answers. First, take the Fifth Amendment; this would be taken as admission that one was a "Fifth Amendment Communist." Second, refuse to seek the protection of the Fifth Amendment and testify frankly about oneself. But once you waived that protection, refusal to testify about your friends was "contempt of court," punishable by imprisonment for a legally unlimited period. I certainly would not take the third option of delivering innocent friends to persecution. But I also decided against taking the Fifth Amendment. I was fortunate in not having to face an actual prison term, which might have been the result of that decision if some committee had thought to call me.

A few people engaged in housing and planning in Philadelphia had formed an informal group to discuss questions of common concern. When the Korean War broke out and the government initiated a war housing program, one participant suggested that we help in that endeavor. I objected that we should ask ourselves whether this war was worthy of support in any form. After a searching discussion I drafted a statement calling on planners to assume social responsibility for the "know why," rather than only for the "know how" of their work. With the signatures of a few other members of the American Institute of Planners, I took this resolution to their annual meeting in Chicago.

At Chicago Ed Bacon told me that the Philadelphia Planning Commission would dismiss me if I moved that resolution and asked me to promise not to introduce it. I refused. However, when the Chairman of the AIP, Paul Oppermann, whom I respected highly, implored me not to bring the resolution to the floor but to submit it to the board of the AIP, I agreed.

The board was receptive to my concern and proceeded to draft a statement on the social responsibility of planners which in some respects went further than my proposal. It was widely and seriously discussed by the local chapters of the institute, thus largely fulfilling my intention, even though it was not adopted.

In 1951 several members of the Pennsylvania State Legislature, anxious to get on the bandwagon of anticommunist hysteria, introduced legislation requiring a "loyalty oath" from all civil servants. This aroused strong protest from many persons, including myself. The legislation went through a long process of committee deliberation, and it must be said to the credit of members of both parties that what finally came out was fairly harmless. My original reaction had been to refuse to take the oath. But as it contained nothing but what I had already sworn to when becoming first a citizen and later a civil servant, I decided on a different tactic: I signed the oath but resigned from my job, protesting that I refused to be made a second-class citizen. I sent a declaration explaining my stand to the newspapers.

After my resignation I went to New York and stayed with Olga Solmitz. After a few days, coming home from an errand, I was greeted by Olga with great alarm: a letter had arrived from the Philadelphia district attorney. He was Richard Dilworth, who had strongly opposed the law and refused to take the oath. As an elected official he was not obliged to take the oath, but most of his colleagues had volunteered to do so. Now he congratulated me on my courage, as did many others.

I did not really deserve that praise; the motives for my resignation were mixed. After seven years with the City Planning Commission I felt the seven-year itch; the old wanderlust was stirring. The State Department had started to refuse passports to people regarded as "fellow travelers," and I suspected that mine would not be renewed. So this might be my last chance to fulfill my long-deferred dreams to see Greece and Egypt. When a colleague celebrating his sixtieth birthday was referred to by his staff as "the old man," it gave me quite a shock; I was in my sixtieth year; there was no time to lose.

Before leaving, I attended a conference at Yale University, on the invitation of Christopher Tunnard. I gave a talk on "Scale in Civic Design," a subject which had interested me ever since A. E. Brinckmann had discussed it during my student days at Karlsruhe. It was subsequently published in England by the *Town Planning Review.* In later years my ego was flattered when colleagues in Budapest and in Peking told me that they had it translated into their respective languages as required reading for their students.

LAST YEAR IN THE USA

In the fall I returned to the United States to a somewhat uncertain future. I visited Topeka first, where my brother-in-law, Alfred Plaut, had become chief pathologist of a big veterans' hospital, while [my sister] Margaret was teaching Freudian German to the psychologists of the Menninger Clinic.

When I returned to Philadelphia, I learned that Franklin C. Wood, who had worked with me at the Philadelphia Planning Commission and was now the planning director in neighboring Bucks County, had been looking for me to head a special study of Lower Bucks County. Having failed to locate me, he had engaged Carl W. Wild as consultant for this task. I now became Carl's associate and we worked together very well.

The special study had become necessary because U.S. Steel had built a huge new plant in Lower Bucks County, which had been followed by a very large new residential development, Levittown, and a somewhat smaller one, Fairless Hills.

Our office was in Doylestown, the county seat, a very pleasant small town in a beautiful landscape to which I commuted from Philadelphia by train.

Bob Mitchell wanted me to join his department at the University of Pennsylvania to do planning research. As there was an interregnum between two university presidents, the appointment had to be decided by the university senate; after several hours of debate, during which both Bob Mitchell and the dean of architecture, Holmes Perkins, strongly advocated my appointment, the senate turned it down for political reasons.

The first task for which Bob Mitchell had wanted me was a study of Levittown. The federal government had encountered several social problems in the "New Town" of Oakridge and wanted to know if similar problems had been found in Levittown, and how they had been dealt with.

The appointment went to Gerald Breese, who immediately hired me as his associate. "There is more than one way to skin a cat," said Bob Mitchell in making this arrangement. We found that most of the Levittown residents were not steelworkers, but worked in Philadelphia or Trenton, where, in turn, most of the steelworkers lived. Problems in Levittown were only those found in any new suburb, primarily a highly abnormal age distribution: young couples with small children, practically no old people and no teen-agers—consequently no baby-sitters.

When my passport expired, I applied for an extension, which was refused. I protested to the State Department, stating that I had no need for a passport right then, but that I reserved my right to appeal. Somewhat later I was notified by the Technion in Haifa [in Israel] that the senate had appointed me head of the Planning School. I asked for an appointment at the State Department, to which I went accompanied by my lawyer. Two gentlemen received us very politely, and then questioned me about membership in a number of organizations on the Attorney General's list as allegedly "subversive." In some cases my answer was "yes"; in some I said, "I do not know if I am a member, but if not, it is an oversight." After a fairly lengthy hearing they thanked me for my frankness. I did not get a passport. The Israelis advised me to go to Canada and board a ship for Israel; but I did not want to become an Israeli citizen, so I refused.

There was a great deal of planning work going on at the time in America. Charles Blessing, who was planning director in Detroit, wanted me to head the work on urban renewal. I warned him that he would run into political difficulties, but he felt confident that he could overcome them. A lady from the Detroit Civil Service Commission came to Philadelphia to give me a daylong written examination. Not long thereafter Charlie asked me to come to Detroit. On my arrival I asked about the political aspect; he said I had to see someone from the Civil Service Commission later in the day; but he was sure that there would be no difficulty and introduced me to his staff. When I came to the interview, the official questioned me about the Korean War, which was still going on, and a fairly heated exchange ensued. My appointment was rejected. I was not surprised, but Charlie was stunned. While we were still discussing the situation, standing in the waiting room, the official called me back in. He was now alone; a lady who had been sitting silently in a corner, and whom I suspected to have been from the FBI, had left. He said, "I cannot tell you how badly I feel about this, but I have a wife and children."

All too many Americans took that stand during the McCarthy period. They included liberals who had been full of contempt for the Germans for not daring to speak up against Hitler. In comparison to the torture and death that threatened those Germans, the risks faced by Americans were minor; perhaps loss of a good job which, in rich America, would not mean starvation.

Many of my left-wing friends—who did stand up—thought the U.S. was already or was rapidly becoming fascist. I doubted their pessimistic assessment. In fact, McCarthyism went out surprisingly fast; the underlying belief of Americans in free speech reasserted itself.

In Philadelphia I had no difficulties. I worked on a large regional transportation study, in close association with Dr. Ernest Jurkat, a very able economist, to predict future distribution of population. He had been in charge of research for the Berlin Merchants' Association. After Hitler came to power, he had headed the underground organization of the Social Democratic party in Berlin. He happened to live across the street from me, and we became fairly close friends.

Thanks to Henry Churchill, the New York chapter of the American Institute of Architects commissioned me to make a study of "Riverside," the area of Manhattan between Central Park and Riverside Park, from 58th to 110th Street. I found several interesting facts. Because the area had largely lost its former high social status with the conversion of practically all single-family houses into small apartment or rooming houses, it had been assumed that crowding had greatly increased. While there were a number of severely over-crowded dwellings, the average amount of floor space per person was practically the same as at the beginning of the century. I also found the same close correlation between altitude and level of rent which I had identified in Philadelphia—surprising in an area in which the difference in altitude between ground and top floor is much greater than the difference of altitude at ground level. Equally surprising was the finding that the tenants who had moved into new luxury multistory apartment houses, assumed to be highly mobile cosmo-politan people, had overwhelmingly come from the immediate neighborhood.

My general conclusion was that the area needed improved private and municipal maintenance and housekeeping, but that wholesale clearance and redevelopment was neither feasible nor desirable. This was probably not what the architects had hoped for; the study was never published.

While working on this project, I stayed with Olga in New York. At that time the Regional Plan Association had inaugurated a monumental study of the New York region, and I had interesting discussions with the Association's director, Henry Fagin, and with Raymond Vernon, a brilliant Harvard economist who headed the study.

Having lived in New York in 1924 and again in 1939/40, I was of course aware of the social deterioration. However, I was shocked by an accidental occurrence. I was waiting for the light to cross 96th Street at Lexington Avenue, when I noted what I assumed to be a fight between two teen-agers on the opposite side of the street, with a large crowd watching. When I crossed, I saw that it was a fight between two heavyset adult men. One had sunk to the ground, bleeding and semiconscious, but held on to the trouser leg of his opponent, who kept on beating him. I first detached the hand from the trousers, then pulled at the other man's sleeve, shouting, "Stop it; you are killing him." A boy pulled his other sleeve, saying, "Come on, dad, let's get out of here." The man started to leave, but then turned around to threaten me; fortunately, the boy pulled him away. I asked someone to call an ambulance; nobody moved. I went to a drugstore across the street and called the police. An ambulance took the unconscious man to a hospital; whether he arrived dead or alive, I do not know.

Here were about a hundred grown men, about half black, half white, and not one had felt the slightest responsibility for what was going on before their eyes, in their city. What kind of a society was this? It could never have happened in Moscow; there people did consider themselves their brother's keeper—maybe sometimes more than the brother would have liked.

FIGURE 15.1   *Charles Abrams.*

15

CHARLES ABRAMS

A LOVER OF CITIES

BERNARD TAPER

PREFACE [1983]

CHARLES ABRAMS ONCE SAID THAT any housing expert worth his salt should have a thorough grasp of economics, law, urban land policies, real estate practices, architecture, construction methods, sociology, politics, administration, and public relations. Upon being apprised of this definition, his friend and colleague Lloyd Rodwin, then chairman of the Faculty Committee of the MIT–Harvard Joint Center for Urban Studies, observed, "Wouldn't you know it? Abrams has come up with a definition that fits only himself. No housing expert in the world that I know of besides him comes even close to possessing all those qualifications."

How Abrams developed his range of expertise remains a wonder. He was very much a self-made man. Just as he made his own considerable fortune, so he made his own education. Though, at one time or other, he was on the faculty of MIT (Massachusetts Institute of Technology), the University of Pennsylvania, City College, the New School, and ultimately Columbia University, where he headed the Division of Urban Planning, he himself never went to college. His only degree was one in law, which he earned at night school

Reprinted with permission from Bernard Taper, "Charles Abrams: a Lover of Cities—II," *The New Yorker*, February 11, 1967, 45ff.

while working days. When, toward the end of his life, he was asked how he acquired the background to become a professor, he would reply in a matter-of-fact way, "By teaching courses and writing books."

The account of Charles Abrams's life and career published in this volume is a slightly abridged version of the second part of a two-part *New Yorker* profile that originally appeared under the title of "A Lover of Cities" on February 4 and 11, 1967, three years before Abrams's death at the age of sixty-eight. The first part of the profile dealt in considerable measure with Abrams's career as a United Nations (U.N.) adviser on housing problems of developing countries and with his articulation of issues involved in the unprecedented urbanization taking place throughout the Third World. Space does not permit inclusion of that part of the profile in this volume; therefore, some summary acknowledgment needs to be made here of this phase of his life since it was of special importance and satisfaction to Abrams and produced noteworthy achievements.

Beginning in 1952, Abrams participated in U.N. missions to over a score of countries, leaving his recognizable impact on many of them through the quality of his personality as well as his insights. Ernest Weissman, who headed the U.N. housing branch, commented at the time:

> The impact that Abrams's missions make has amazed us. . . . Twenty-four hours after he arrives in a country, housing suddenly becomes a front-page topic. Somehow he makes the leaders aware of the importance of problems they had been taking for granted or else had considered hopeless. He shows them possible solutions that are right under their noses, and he convinces them that they have to drop everything else and get going on the solution right then and there. Wherever he goes, he foments reform.

Barbara Ward summed up this aspect of Abrams's career well in a tribute she wrote for *Habitat*'s special Abrams *Festschrift* issue in 1980:

> Drawing on his profound knowledge of urban problems in America and seeking to apply this experience to the emerging cities of the Third World, he was a pioneer in bringing to governments and ministries and to the new professional groups

some sense of the scale of urban disorder and deprivation they would have to confront and some outlines of the strategies they would need for effective action. He could advise all the more early and successfully because he combined a very wide range of experience with great humour, immense good will and no trace of that "white man's arrogance" which, as the activity of giving advice on development grew on an ever greater scale, became all too often a source of extreme annoyance and even a block to otherwise useful plans and ideas. But Charles Abrams saw everyone as an equal and honourable member of the human family. No one could mistake his basic common sense and humility. He gave counsel. He received in return not only a ready hearing but lasting friendship as well.

Charles Abrams: A Lover of Cities

Three years ago [in 1964] a high-level team of French officials, architects, and city planners, charged with drawing up France's Fifth National Plan on Urbanism, made a month-long tour of the United States to see how we were handling our urban problems. During their stay here, they conferred with numerous American authorities and were shown significant projects and developments—Lincoln Center, various high-rise housing projects, the gleaming new business center of New Haven, the urban-renewal transformations in Philadelphia, the San Francisco slum-clearance projects, the Los Angeles freeways. Returning to New York, just before their departure for France, they met with Charles Abrams, the chairman of the Division of Urban Planning of Columbia University and one of the world's leading consultants on housing and city planning, and spent a Sunday morning taking a guided tour with him. Abrams, who is in his sixties, has a round, usually amiable face and a leisurely, rather shambling gait, which scarcely suggests that he is a person of remarkable drive and energy. As experts in his field go, Abrams is an unconventional figure, with a personality pungently compounded of zeal, shrewdness, ingenuity, and ebullient humor. His guided tour that Sunday was not a conventional one either. He did not take the French planners to view a single new project or even the site of a future development. Instead, he took them on one of his favorite walks—a walk with which many of his planning students at Colum-

bia had become familiar. It was a perambulation through the Lower
East Side: through the noisy, crooked, narrow streets of Chinatown;
along the Bowery, past a group of jewelry shops that Abrams
characterized as "the Off Broadway diamond center"; down Grand
Street, with its cluster of bridal gown shops, for a pause at an
aromatic bakery, where Abrams bought some pumpernickel and
from which the wife of one of the French officials emerged with a
string of bagels around her neck like a lei; up teeming Orchard
Street, past pushcarts heaped with bargain wearing apparel, where
one of the French planners, on an unplanned impulse, bought a
trunk, which he then had to lug along with him; on to East Houston
Street, for a stop at the delicatessen of Russ and Daughters, whose
proprietors greeted Abrams heartily, asked after his family, and
boned a whitefish for him; then across the street, where the party
paused again, this time to watch a game of boccie; up Second
Avenue, where the Yiddish theatre once flourished, and past McSorley's
Old Ale House, regrettably closed at that hour; on to visit a Ukrai-
nian shop on Seventh Street to buy some honey; south from Astor
Place, past a nondescript building that Abrams identified, with a
wave of his hand, as the largest birdseed factory in the United States,
to Waverly Place, with elegant, ornamented lofts that have so far
escaped the wrecking ball; across Washington Square; and, at last,
after a brief pause to savor Washington Mews, on to Abrams's
residence, a spacious house on Tenth Street, just off Fifth Avenue,
where they lunched on the whitefish, pastrami, lox, pumpernickel,
pickles, bagels, honey, and candies they had garnered along the
route, feeling as pleased about this as do fishermen when they make
a meal from their catch.

Abrams's purpose in taking the French group on this walk was
partly admonitory. The chaotic, crowded, vivid neighborhoods they
had toured with such fascination were not the design of any planner.
No planner could ever have created a scene so varied, so full of
enterprise and vitality. Yet planners are perfectly capable of destroying or homogenizing such a scene—and all too often do so. Instead
of identifying and appreciating the innate values that have spontaneously grown up in a neighborhood, and attempting to reinforce
and build on these values, the planner's approach is apt to be one of
distaste for all the messiness that life has generated without his
assistance; he tends to want to raze neighborhoods like these and
replace them with large, costly, sterile projects. Abrams was warning

the French planners that they had to be on their guard against forming such a mistaken conception of their role, and urging them to make plans that would cherish and foster spontaneity and diversity—even, to use a phrase he is fond of, "a diversity of diversities." It was a message whose cogency the French planners were well prepared to acknowledge by the end of their walk.[1]

Most of the world's housing and planning experts and reformers, it happens, have been people of middle-class or wealthy backgrounds; to learn about slums, they have had to make field trips and pore over surveys. Abrams acquired his knowledge of what life in a slum is like by being brought up in one. Born in Poland, he arrived in this country at the age of two, when his family immigrated and settled in the Williamsburg district of Brooklyn, which was, in those days before the First World War, more or less an extension of the Lower East Side—a polyglot neighborhood of cobblestone streets that were never cleaned and that teemed day and night with people and pushcarts and of rat-infested, highly combustible wooden tenements, which were scientifically designed to compress the greatest number of human beings into the smallest tolerable living space. The Abramses' apartment was a three-room flat in a six-story walk-up. There were four children in the family—three sons, of whom Charles was the youngest, and a daughter—which meant that six people lived in the apartment's three small rooms. Charles and his brother Ralph slept in a windowless cubicle, not much bigger than a respectable closet, the two of them sharing a bed so narrow that, no matter what furious quarrels they may have had during the day, they always had to sleep with their arms wrapped around each other to keep from falling to the floor. The apartment had no hot water and no heat, except what was given off by a coal-burning cookstove in the kitchen; on each floor of the building was a single toilet, for the use of all the families; there wasn't a bathtub in the building— or, for that matter, in the entire neighborhood, except those at a public bathhouse a few blocks away. Today, Abrams jestingly gives credit for the resilient health that permits him to take the tropics in stride on his overseas missions to his boyhood patronage of the neighborhood public bathhouse; he surmises that there are probably very few pestilences lurking in the tropics that he did not encounter, and develop an immunity to, during those weekly immersions at Bershadsky's Baths.

In Poland, Abrams's father had worked on a communal farm. In

Brooklyn, he set himself up as a sidewalk vender of herrings and pickles—a precarious business from which he was barely able to squeeze out a living, though he worked punishing hours. Some days, there wasn't enough money for a proper meal, but Charles's mother never dreamed of admitting this to anybody outside the family. On those days, she used to keep covered pots of water boiling on the stove so that neighbors who dropped in would not guess the family's desperate situation. Mrs. Abrams, the daughter of a Vilna bookkeeper, was a delicate-featured woman whose entire life was centered on her children and her concern that they must "make something of themselves." Her husband was a figure whose prototype one often encounters in stories of Jewish slums and ghettos—a man who, despite the squalor around him, managed to convey an impression of dignity, grave humor, and even wisdom. Today, Abrams says of his father, "There was something noble about everything he did. The way he comported himself, even the sale of a miserable pickled herring became somehow a courtly and humane transaction." Abrams's father had his sidewalk stand across the street from their tenement. Above Mr. Abrams's head hung a large sign belonging to the store from which he rented his few feet of space; in stormy weather, the sign used to swing and creak perilously, and the family feared that at any moment it might crash down on Mr. Abrams's head—a worry that Abrams remembers as being for some reason one of the abiding anxieties of his childhood. Yet none of the family seems to have considered it possible to cope with the problem in any way—to move the stand elsewhere or persuade the storekeeper to take down or repair the sign. It was simply fate, and when fate hung over one's head, there was nothing that an ordinary mortal could do about it, except perhaps wear a hat, and this Mr. Abrams always did anyway, being an Orthodox Jew. Young Charles was very close to his father. From the time he was seven or eight years old, it was his habit to wake up when his father returned home for the night, sometimes as late as one o'clock. Charles would put on his bathrobe and make a pot of tea, and then he and his father would sit together at the kitchen table, sipping their tea and discussing all sorts of things. Abrams says he got the greater part of his education during those sessions.

Those who don't know Abrams might picture the future reformer as a sensitive boy who vowed that when he grew up he would dedicate himself to the task of wiping out the slums that had blighted his childhood. Actually, Abrams remembers his childhood as quite happy, on the whole. If the slums were damaging him, he wasn't aware of it at the time. He simply accepted his environment as the conditions that prevailed, being unaware that it was possible for people to live in any other way. He was ultimately moved to work for better housing not so much by a feeling of personal grievance as by intellectual exasperation at what he considered the utter illogicality of the nation's housing situation. He says that when he first became active in the field, in the early 1930s, it never occurred to him to think of his own old neighborhood as an example of the slums he was inveighing against or to think of his childhood neighbors and friends as the miserable wretches evoked by the phrase "slum dwellers." Not until one day in 1933 did these words take on reality for him. As one of three lawyers drafting the basic state housing legislation under which the New York City Housing Authority was established, he was called upon to draw up a legal definition of a slum area, and as he was working on this, it dawned on him that the definition fitted his own old home and neighborhood perfectly. Abrams was almost as surprised by this discovery as Molière's M. Jourdain was to learn that he had been talking prose all his life.

Abrams may have had a happy enough childhood, but it was hardly a carefree one. He has only a dim memory of a time in his life when he did not work. "My first job was as lookout man for a gang of herring bootleggers," he recalls, half seriously. As a tot in short pants, he was given the assignment of standing watch at the front of the tenement house on Sundays while other members of his family wrapped herrings, kosher dill pickles, pickled onions, and other such snacks in a back hallway and smuggled them to customers throughout the building, in violation ("fragrant violation," Abrams, a pun fancier, now calls it) of the Sunday work laws. To be caught at these activities meant a fine of as much as $10—a punishment that the Abrams family could ill afford but that they suffered more often than the former lookout man cares to remember. By the time Abrams was nine, he was taking on outside jobs to supplement the family income. While he was in high school, he worked as a lamplighter, tending the streetlights on Lafayette Avenue. He was a very small lamplighter, being the shortest boy in his class. Every evening he strapped on a pair of roller skates and went rolling along Lafayette over to Myrtle Avenue and down to Fort Greene Park, lighting up the neighborhood, pole by pole, as he went; every morning he skated off at dawn and turned the lamps out. As he rolled along, he could be heard declaiming resonantly into the Brooklyn twilight, "If you have tears, prepare to shed them now." He was possessed of a wonderfully loud voice, and by then he had achieved some fame in school as an orator; whenever the superintendent or some other dignitary visited his school, Abrams was called on to get up in front of the assembly and tear Mark Antony's funeral oration to tatters. For his lamplighting, he was paid $4 a week by the Brooklyn Edison Company. After a year or so, however, he began to feel that he was something of a slacker, having what amounted to only a half-time job outside of school, so he quit his work for Brooklyn Edison to become a message clerk at the main office of Western Union in Manhattan. At this job, which paid $12 a week, he worked a full eight-hour shift after high school, starting at 5 P.M. By the time he got back home to Brooklyn, it would be nearly 2 A.M., and then, after a cup of tea with his father, he would settle down to his homework. He was fourteen at the time and had attained a lifelong ambition— to be completely self-supporting.

When he finished high school, he chose to study law, mainly because that seemed to him the profession that could be most easily learned at night school. He signed up for evening classes at Brooklyn Law School, and by day he worked—first as an office boy and later as a clerk—for a succession of law firms. The first of these was McLaughlin and Stern, which had offices on William Street, and his first day with them remains memorable because he was sent uptown to pick up a payment in settlement of a case and found himself being handed $60,000 in $500 and $1,000 bills. He had never before even seen anything larger than a ten. Rising to the occasion, young Abrams behaved in the way he assumed was expected of him as the sophisticated representative of a great law firm. He signed the receipt coolly, giving no indication that to be handed such a sum of money was in any way unusual, or even interesting, and, stuffing the money casually into his pockets, rode the subway back downtown. When he walked into the office and began counting out the $60,000, the office manager who had sent him on the errand appeared about to faint; she had taken it for granted that the settlement would be made in the customary form of a certified check. The event created quite a stir at McLaughlin and Stern, none of the partners responding at all coolly or casually to the idea of their new teenage office boy riding the subway with $60,000 in his pockets.

Abrams learned less law from his classes than he did from his clerkships—by far the most important of which was a three-year stint in the law offices of Arthur Garfield Hays. The apprenticeship he served under Hays not only educated but inspired him and probably did as much to determine the direction of his life as anything else that happened to him. Hays was general counsel for the recently formed American Civil Liberties Union, was associated with Clarence Darrow in the famous Scopes evolution trial in Tennessee, and was involved in a number of significant civil liberties campaigns. In the course of one such campaign (to establish constitutional freedoms and individual rights in the tough coal-mining company town of Vintondale, Pennsylvania), Hays—much to his young law clerk's admiration—succeeded in establishing his inalienable right as a citizen to get himself arrested and thrown in jail. (The right to be arrested, Abrams remembers Hays explaining shortly before he set off for Vintondale, should be valued as one of the most important of all civil rights, for if a man can't get himself officially taken into custody—and instead is, say, simply hustled out of town—he has no way of legally challenging a despotic situation.) Such battles, as Hays waged them, were undertaken not in a stodgily righteous spirit but with considerable verve and drama, and Abrams recalls the atmosphere in Hays's office when civil liberties cases were being worked on as a rousing one of derring-do in the quest for social justice—something that the youthful Abrams found both stimulating to his conscience and congenial to his temperament.

In addition to his work for the Civil Liberties Union, Hays carried on an extraordinary diverse private practice; he had labor unions, huge corporations, and foreign governments among his clients, and he did not hesitate to accept spectacular criminal and divorce cases. It was a highly lucrative practice (Hays once got a fee in excess of $200,000 for a single case), and this was a circumstance that young Abrams—who had never equated poverty with virtue— also found inspirational. For Abrams, Hays was a model as well as a mentor. He held Hays in such fervent esteem that for a while he even walked with a limp because Hays had a game leg, and he also took to smoking a pipe in what he hoped was a convincing imitation of Hays's profound, brooding manner. It was during this period that Abrams began to form some idea of what he wanted to make of his life. Like Hays, he wanted to be a fighter for unpopular social causes and, also like Hays, not an impecunious one.

While Abrams was in Hays's office, he was given ample opportunity, though a mere clerk, to poke his nose into a variety of legal
matters. He worked, for example, on the briefs of an important free
speech case, preparing all the necessary papers as it went up through
the courts to the United States Supreme Court, and, at the other end
of the scale of social significance, he did the law research on one
aspect of Hays's vain defense of a couple of crooked stockbrokers in
the lurid Fuller–McGee bucket-shop case, coming up with a bright
idea about the strategy Hays might follow in developing that aspect.
The idea caught Hays's fancy, and, in general, Hays seems to have
taken a special liking to Abrams; later they became close friends and
ardent chess adversaries. Abrams kept a big meerschaum pipe handy
for these chess encounters. As his own reputation grew, he gradually
learned to puff on it with an authoritative profundity that fully
matched Hays's; the only trouble was that the more solemn his pipe
smoking became, the harder he found it to keep from laughing at
himself.

Shortly after being admitted to the bar, in 1923, Abrams, with
$600 he had borrowed from Hays, set up a law office of his own on
lower Broadway, in partnership with another young lawyer fresh
from the slums, Bernard Botein (who has since gone on to become
Presiding Justice of the Appellate Division for the First
Department—New York and Bronx Counties—of the New York
State Supreme Court). Their practice flourished, and by 1928 Abrams
was earning $25,000 a year in fees—a sum that is considered fairly
good going for a fledgling lawyer even now. In that year, he married
Ruth Davidson, whom he had met through an improbable chain of
circumstances. A friend of his, who did not know Miss Davidson,
was arranging a blind date for Abrams, but the girl he had in mind
did not answer when he telephoned her. Something seemed to be
wrong with her phone, but just as the friend was about to hang up,
he heard a puzzled voice saying, "Hello? Hello?" It was Miss Davidson,
who at that moment happened to be phoning the same girl and
whose line the telephone company had somehow connected with
that of Abrams's friend. They got to talking. The friend was a
persuasive man, and Miss Davidson was of an impetuous nature.
Before they hung up, she had agreed to go out with Abrams that
evening. The two hit it off right away.

The Abramses began their married life in an apartment in
Greenwich Village, and they have lived in that part of town ever

since. The heterogeneity of the Village, and its constant ferment, proved to be perfectly suited to Abrams's restless, adventurous spirit. He soon became a member of a circle of radical intellectuals, social critics, and literati who used to gather every Wednesday evening at the Morton Street apartment of V. F. Calverton, the editor of the *Modern Monthly,* to discuss social and literary issues. At the same time, he became a member of a wisecracking theatre and Tin Pan Alley crowd. He was stagestruck in those days, as he still is; he and his wife used to attend nearly every opening night and were often included in the party that the show's writers or producers gave afterward. Sometimes, while still mulling over the lofty statements he had heard at Calverton's a couple of evenings before, he would drop in at the Ira Gershwins' apartment on Riverside Drive for the Friday night poker game there. Before the game got started, some of those who had shown up—among them such songwriters as B. G. De Silva, Oscar Levant, and E. Y. ("Yip") Harburg—would gather around the piano and try out their latest tunes on each other. Abrams, listening, was stirred to emulation. High on a list of secret ambitions that he drew up in 1929 appeared the exhortation "Write a great song hit!"

When Abrams had known the Gershwins for several years, Ira Gershwin phoned him one day at his law office and said mysteriously, "Charlie, it appears that a President of the United States is going to have to be impeached. Do you think you could draw up a bill of impeachment?" Startled, Abrams began to question him. Gershwin said, "Never mind why, or anything else, Charlie—just go ahead and impeach the rascal." So Abrams looked up the proceedings against President Andrew Johnson, drafted a bill modeled on them, and sent it off to Ira Gershwin. In due course, Gershwin responded with a check for $100 as a fee for his effort. Not until he went to the opening of the Gershwins' *Of Thee I Sing* and heard the chorus launched into the "Whereas" song did he discover the use that had been made of his legal work; the President he had helped impeach was that jilter of the illegitimate daughter of an illegitimate son of an illegitimate nephew of Napoleon—John P. Wintergreen. Though there wasn't much left of the tedious legal paragraphs he had sent Gershwin— little but the "whereas"es and the "hereby"s—Abrams sat back in his seat glowing with the pride of authorship. So far, this is the closest Abrams has come to realizing his ambition of writing a song hit.

Some of Abrams's clients in those days were making mortgage

loans on Greenwich Village property, and soon he began to follow their example. Then he grew restless at remaining on the sidelines and, while still keeping up his law practice, threw himself headlong into real estate—not as a broker but as an entrepreneur, a sort of freelance capitalist without any capital to speak of, embarking on shoestring operations of a wildly speculative character. Before long, he was up to his ears in deals and was becoming known among real estate men as a shrewd operator and a formidable negotiator. "Those Indians who sold Manhattan were lucky they didn't have to negotiate with Abrams," one real estate man remarked after a bargaining session with him. "I'll bet they'd never have got *him* to go as high as twenty-four dollars." Nowadays, Greenwich Village, having become one of the city's high-rent districts, is considered a prime investment area, but in the 1920s banks and other financial institutions looked down their noses at it as a shabby and disreputable bohemian quarter and, not perceiving that quaintness could be turned into a capital asset, were reluctant to put mortgage money into Village property. In order to raise funds for his dealings, Abrams had to scurry around to loan sharks and shady mortgage discount operators and to engage in complicated and ingenious transactions, piling one mortgage on top of another—occasionally as high as a fourth mortgage—and ending up with fantastic financial structures as precarious as a child's tower of blocks. He repeatedly got himself into tight and potentially ruinous situations, but he usually managed to devise some profitable way out. More than thirty years later, Abrams can still recall in detail, and recount with zest, the improbable details of some of those transactions. It was during that period, he says, that he lost most of his hair.

During the six or seven years of his speculative heyday, he acquired, all told, perhaps seventy or eighty pieces of Village property. Some he refinanced and sold. Others he remodeled and rented, turning stables into studios, transforming loft buildings into avant-garde shops, and making many of the other ingenious conversions that eventually helped bring Greenwich Village to its present curious state. He had a hand in making Eighth Street the Village's main drag, by tearing down a number of old shacks and erecting in their places shops, a nightclub, and a motion picture theatre—the last designed by the unorthodox Viennese architect Frederick Kiesler and heralded at the time as a great advance in movie house design. The tenant for whom Abrams built this was Symon Gould, who was later to be a candidate for president of the United States on the Vegetarian ticket. Gould was certain that talkies were just a passing fad (like meat eating), and he called his cinema the House of Shadowed Silence. Gould was to have bad luck all around. He lost his lease on the movie house, giving way to a more practical entrepreneur, and his political party, up against such slogans as "A Chicken in Every Pot," has never carried a single precinct. The building that contains the movie house, now called the Eighth Street Playhouse, at street level and the Village Barn in the basement is one of the properties from Abrams's early real estate days that he has held on to. In partnership with his brother Ralph, he has since invested in some other movie houses, including Cinema I and Cinema II, on Third Avenue. The theatres not only bring him in a good return but give him the privilege, any time he likes, of strolling in to see a movie without paying, which he does with the conspicuously nonchalant air of a small boy who half expects to be picked up by the scruff of the neck and tossed out.

All this real estate speculation may have been an unlikely form of preparation for a career as a reformer, but Abrams values it as having been fundamental to his education, as well as to his financial security. His real estate transactions gave him a worm's-eye view of the housing picture and an intimate acquaintance with what are generally called practical affairs—two credentials that few of his colleagues in the reform camp possess—and thus made it possible for him to move on to the activity he likes to call "finagling for society." His first opportunity for this sort of finagling came in 1933. As that rarity, a lawyer who combined a detailed knowledge of real estate with a liberal social outlook, he was named by Mayor Fiorello La Guardia as one of a team of three lawyers who were to draft a new state housing bill. This bill, which ultimately became known as the Municipal Housing Authorities Law, was the basic legislation under which the New York City Housing Authority was established, and it became the model enabling act for the country as a whole, on the basis of which a total of more than two thousand local housing authorities have since been formed. It was a piece of legislation asserting a social principle that was new to the United States—that since private enterprise manifestly could not clear slums and provide decent housing for people of low incomes, some government agency would have to do it if it was to be done at all. Nowadays, Abrams, after more than thirty years of worldwide experience, can bat out a complicated housing or city-planning law in short order; a lengthy, detailed bill that he and Dr. Otto Koenigsberger, a tropical-housing expert, prepared for Pakistan in 1957 while on a U.N. mission to that country took them only ten days to draft. But it took Abrams and his two colleagues on the 1933 committee—Carl Stern and Ira Robbins— nearly three months to draw up the much shorter Municipal Housing Authorities Law. They were aware that although the concept of public housing had been accepted in Europe for thirty or forty years, its introduction into the United States was bound to be attacked as a dangerous heresy, a forerunner of Socialism, a threat to the American Home and the American Way of Life. Inevitably, they knew, the law's constitutionality would be challenged, and they were determined that there should be no technical flaws in it. "We agonized over every comma of that law," Abrams recalls.

The housing problem as we know it is a product of the industrial revolution and the complex cities that it required and engendered. Almost everywhere, as industrialization has progressed, the state has felt compelled, for the sake of the public welfare, to show an increasing concern and assume an increasing responsibility for the habitations of its populace. This change in governmental attitude constitutes one of the dramatic historical changes of our era, Abrams notes in a volume called *Urban Land Problems and Policies.* He wrote:

> In the eighteenth century the elder Pitt, Earl of Chatham, could declaim that "the poorest man in his cottage could defy the King—the storms may enter; the rain may enter—but the King of England cannot enter; all his forces dare not cross the threshold of the ruined tenement." But in the twentieth century, the king (or his counterpart, the state) may enter for the very purpose of keeping the wind and rain from entering. The "ruined tenement" has become a matter of state concern.[2]

The most important housing legislation in the United States prior to the Municipal Housing Authorities Law had been the Tenement House Act of 1901, brought into being by disclosures of slum life horrors by such crusading humanitarians as Jacob Riis and Felix Adler. Humane and enlightened as the 1901 regulations and restrictions were, the Act itself brought no new housing into being. The slums continued to grow, and the need for decent new housing increased. By 1933, therefore, when Abrams, Stern, and Robbins sat down to draft the Municipal Housing Authorities Law, reformers were ready to turn from restrictive to constructive legislation. It was time, they felt, for the city itself, or some other agency, to build the housing that private enterprise could not supply. And because this moment—the first year of the New Deal after three years of depression—was a time of social experimentation, the new doctrine stood a good chance of acceptance. To many New Dealers, public housing was an appealing idea not only on humanitarian grounds but as a means of pumping life back into the economy. The very inefficiency of the home-construction industry, the country's most backward in its methods, appeared a virtue in the eyes of some Brain Trusters; a public housing program, they believed, would be a dandy way of creating a lot of jobs and spending a lot of public money. In retrospect, Abrams thinks that the public housing program has suffered from this initial confusion of purposes; it still operates under fossilized principles that were well suited to a time of depression but are not at all appropriate in today's inflationary, expansionist economy. "There are Newtonian laws in politics as well as in physics," he says. "A reform set in motion continues in motion long beyond the time when the reform itself needs reforming."

Early in 1934, shortly after the bill that Abrams worked on had been passed and the New York City Housing Authority had officially come into being, the Authority's chairman, Langdon Post, asked Abrams to serve as legal counsel in getting the agency started on its program. In that capacity, he devoted himself ardently to the work of the Housing Authority during its first three years—years that he recalls as in some ways the most exciting period of his life. Age-old prejudices were dissolving, injustices were being corrected, and a better, fairer, more humane world was in the making—or so, at any rate, it seemed to him and to many another idealistic young man inspired by the New Deal. There were innumerable things, large and small, to be done in getting the Housing Authority under way, and Abrams was involved in most of them. There were hearings to be held, surveys to be made, policies to be determined, contracts to be negotiated, opponents to be debated, impatient tenants' groups to be placated or exhorted, budgets to be drawn up, and interminable conferences with governmental officials to be attended. There were hasty trips to Washington for sessions with Senator Robert F. Wagner, with Harry Hopkins (who was to become Works Progress Administrator), with Secretary of the Treasury Henry Morgenthau, and with Secretary of the Interior Harold Ickes, among others—sometimes to solve New York City problems and sometimes to discuss the content and strategy of the national public housing bill that Senator Wagner was introducing and plan strategy for getting it through Congress.

Throughout the New York City Housing Authority's early days, millions of dollars were allocated to it on paper, but it had no cash to speak of. Early in January 1934, Secretary Ickes, who was in charge of the Public Works Administration, sent a telegram to Mayor La Guardia saying that he had earmarked $25 million for the New York City Housing Authority; unfortunately, it took two and a half years to extract these funds from him. If ever a man was out of place as head of an emergency agency whose job was to pour out money like water in order to prime the economic pump, it was Ickes. An honest and fearless tightwad, Ickes had risen to prominence battling the graft and corruption of the Chicago city machine, and now that power had been put in his hands, he trusted nobody in the world except himself, acted on the theory that all local officials were crooks, suspected the other cabinet members of plotting against him, and tapped the telephone wires of his subordinates. Abrams and Post battled Ickes desperately for the funds the New York City Housing Authority had been promised, but Ickes, hating to part with even a penny of the tremendous amount he had been given to spend, kept setting new requirements and finding other new reasons for delay. Meanwhile, the Housing Authority, itself ill-housed in some cramped offices at 10 East 40th Street, was trying at least to draw up some grand plans on a pittance of $12,000 that the city administration had lent it.

Obviously, this sum wasn't going to go very far, even though Abrams and other officials volunteered to work without recompense until the Housing Authority became solvent. After a few months, Post and Abrams decided that the Authority had better get going somehow on its own, without waiting for Ickes's largesse. Putting their heads together, they contrived (or perhaps Abrams's word "finagled" is the perfect one here) a financing scheme as unorthodox as any public body ever employed—one that provided certain poetic satisfactions as well as badly needed cash. Post, a man of inherited wealth that derived from real estate (including, as he was regretfully aware, some slum properties), was a dashing, idealistic figure of patrician bearing. As it happened, he was Tenement House Commissioner as well as chairman of the City Housing Authority. At the time he assumed the former office, in January, the city had suffered a number of disastrous tenement fires, and he set to work to apply the provisions of the law more rigorously than previous commissioners had. The owners of many of the most dilapidated tenements thereupon chose to close up their buildings rather than go to the expense of fireproofing them and otherwise bringing them into conformity with the law, and soon nearly two thousand tenement houses, many of them on the Lower East Side, were standing boarded up and vacant. The idea that Post and Abrams conceived was to offer to tear down these buildings free of charge if the owners would let the Housing Authority have whatever proceeds could be realized from the sale of the bricks, plumbing, and other scrap that was salvaged. Most of the owners were only too glad to accept the offer, because the vacant tenements presented a serious hazard for which the landlords remained legally liable. A force of WPA workers recruited from Harry Hopkins's agency by Post, a man with a good many friends in the Roosevelt inner circle, performed the labor of demolition and salvage, tearing down well over a thousand slum tenements during the next two years. This form of slum clearance, in itself a satisfaction to housing reformers, ultimately brought the Housing Authority more than half a million dollars, and was its only source of funds, aside from the city's loan, until 1937. Not only did this money permit the Authority to go ahead and prepare the housing program it planned to put into effect when it finally received its federal allocation but it made possible the actual construction of a small housing project on the Lower East Side at Avenue A and East Third Street. Called First Houses, this group of buildings was opened with great ceremony on December 3, 1935— the first public housing project in America.

This whole financing operation was, of course, a highly irregular demonstration of public enterprise. Shortly after First Houses was opened, the City Comptroller, awakened to the situation by the fanfare, sent the Authority a letter saying that the funds from the salvaged materials should have gone to the city treasury and peremptorily demanding that the Authority make good the treasury's loss. Abrams, worried, set to work on a tortured brief, attempting to justify, with solemn citations and footnotes, the Authority's right to the money. As he was going over his arguments with the Authority's commissioners before sending off the brief, he was interrupted by one of them—B. Charney Vladeck, the general manager of the *Jewish Daily Forward* and New York's first Socialist city councilman. Vladeck, as a young man in Russia, had once been under a sentence of death for revolutionary activities, and he was not much frightened by the fulminations of the City Comptroller. "So he says we stole the money?" Vladeck asked, with a shrug. "So all right. What are you worrying about? Did we use it for ourselves? Don't you know that as long as you act in the public interest who cares which pocket the money goes into? Forget it. The public wants decent housing."

Of all the matters that Abrams was involved in during his years as counsel to the Authority, undoubtedly the most important was the Muller case, which was the major legal test of the Municipal Housing Authorities Law and the one that established beyond question the city's right to institute eminent-domain proceedings when balked by unwilling property owners in acquiring housing sites. This right is taken for granted now, but in the early days nobody was sure that the courts would uphold it. The case involved two pieces of property owned by one Andrew Muller on the run-down block selected for First Houses. The rest of the site had belonged to Vincent Astor, who had willingly sold his holdings to the Authority. Muller refused to come to terms. When it became apparent that negotiations would get nowhere, Abrams suggested to the Authority that the time had come for a test case. Some of the commissioners were dubious, fearing that loss of the case would jeopardize the whole public housing program. Mayor La Guardia flatly advised against it, thinking it was too big a gamble. Abrams nevertheless got permission to go ahead, and, having done a notable job of preparing his argument, was victorious both in the lower courts and in the appellate division. "If Abrams hadn't pressed the Muller case and won it, there would be no public housing today," Post said later. For that matter, there might be no Stuyvesant Town, no Coliseum, and no Lincoln Center, either, for all these developments involved the exercise of eminent domain to acquire property for an avowed public purpose. And whenever this purpose was challenged in the courts, lawyers defending the developments cited the Muller case as the precedent.

After First Houses, large projects were constructed in Harlem and in Abrams's own boyhood neighborhood of Williamsburg, and, as more federal funds were pried loose from Mr. Ickes, a number of other projects were started. In 1937, Congress passed the

Wagner–Steagall housing bill, and the United States Housing Administration was established, under the direction of Nathan Straus, who said that just about everything that he knew about housing at the time he had learned from Abrams. By the end of that year, when Abrams left the Housing Authority—doing so, typically, in a blaze of public fireworks as a result of a policy disagreement with La Guardia—the wild, freewheeling days were over and the form that public housing was to take from then on had been pretty well determined. Since those tentative beginnings, the New York City Housing Authority has changed the face of the city drastically, becoming in the process the nation's largest landlord, with assets of almost $2 billion, and with about half a million tenants living in the 143,000 apartments it has constructed.

Despite such statistics, it is now generally recognized that the public housing program in the United States has not fulfilled the perhaps overenthusiastic expectations of its early advocates. In terms of such amenities as yard space, sunlight, and ventilation, the public projects are undoubtedly more salubrious than the rotting tenements they replaced—indeed, as Lewis Mumford has often pointed out, they are probably superior in these respects to most Park Avenue luxury apartments—but the majority of them are stamped with a dreary, institutionalized look, and all of them are administered under a rigid code of petty regulations calculated to distress any self-respecting tenant. Furthermore, the social benefits of housing project occupancy have not been all that the reformers had hoped for; changing the physical environment of onetime slum dwellers has not reduced the incidence of crime, delinquency, and disease to the extent anticipated. Throughout the years since the program came into existence, Abrams, while devoting energy and ingenuity to furthering the cause of public housing in this country, has at the same time been one of the most persistent critics of the direction that the program has taken. He deplores the poorhouse atmosphere and stigma that have become attached to the projects. "Why do housing projects all have to look like housing projects?" he asks. If he had his way, public housing developments would not bear distinguishing names, on the order of George Washington Carver Houses, but would simply have street addresses like all other apartment buildings. They would be smaller structures, too—"vest-pocket projects"—which would not dominate their neighborhoods. A more fundamental change that Abrams would like to make would be to do away with the government's present policy of evicting tenants whose incomes rise above the modest amount that is now stipulated as the maximum income for project tenants:

> No penalty should be put upon ambition so that the moment a family improves its income, it is forced to pull the children out of school, give up neighborhood associations, and move back to a slum. If the tenant earns more money, he should be required to pay a higher rent, at which time he ceases to be subsidized. He should be looked upon as a potential prospect for a non-subsidized dwelling unit, not as a permanent charity case whose ascent from poverty is regarded as a violation of lease. Projects should be built not as almshouses but as attractive additions to the urban scene, fit for families of improved income. The misassumption of public housing has been that there will always be stratified classes in the United States and that stratified projects must be their permanent habitat.

Actually, Abrams would go beyond merely permitting tenants to keep their apartments and pay increased rent as their incomes rose. One of his more unorthodox proposals—which has nevertheless begun to win favor recently—is that tenants who improve themselves economically should be permitted to buy their apartments from the government if they wish, so that over a period of time many projects could become private cooperatives. Though Abrams believes as strongly as ever that a government concerned about the welfare of its people is duty bound to supply housing for those whom private enterprise has neglected, he sees no inherent virtue in the government's continuing to own and manage all the housing once it is built. In fact, he thinks it would be better all around if the government did not continue to play the role of landlord. "To accomplish certain ends in a complex modern civilization we have to use the methods of socialism, but we should also be continually de-socializing as we go along," he says. It is propositions like this that have given Abrams his reputation as perhaps the most flexible and original mind in his field. Catherine Bauer Wurster, one of the crew of New Dealers who conceived the first federal public housing legislation, once said of him, in a tone of exasperated admiration, "Charlie has always kept all his friends and allies off balance. He is continually questioning and rethinking the ideas and fundamental beliefs for which all of us, including him, have fought and bled."

When the United States public housing law was drawn up, one of its essential components was the slum-clearance requirement: one slum dwelling unit had to be destroyed for every public dwelling unit built. Abrams took great satisfaction in that provision at the time, but he now regrets that it has stayed on the books, virtually unchanged, ever since. He sees its persistence as another illustration of his political Newtonian law. "The slum-clearance policy made sense during the Depression, when there were many apartment vacancies, but it is unworkable in a period of housing shortage," he says. Since the Second World War, when the shortage first became acute, he has been trying with no success to get the United States to alter its policy sufficiently to build primarily on vacant or underdeveloped land. Unfortunately, he and his fellow reformers made such a powerful impression in the old days that he has found it all but impossible to change the course of the program he and they helped set in motion. He's had much more luck at getting across-the-board slum-clearance operations suspended in Africa, South America, and Asia than in the United States. The painfulness of the whole operation here at home is exacerbated for him by the fact that slum clearance has nowadays become almost synonymous with Negro clearance, since it is Negroes who currently occupy most of the urban slums.

As a matter of fact, Abrams sometimes wishes that the concept of the slum had never been formulated, for he has come to regard it as a misleading one. "I'm no longer as sure as I once was that I know what I'm talking about when I describe some district as a 'slum,'" he says. In drafting housing legislation in the New Deal era, he and his colleagues tended to define slum housing or substandard housing according to specific physical criteria—windowless rooms, inadequate toilet facilities, sagging ceilings, wooden stairways that had not been made fire-resistant, and the like—and slum-clearance agencies throughout the nation are still using these criteria, almost unchanged, in determining which houses and neighborhoods are to be demolished as slums. But Abrams, with long years of experience under his belt, now prefers to judge a housing situation according to much broader and subtler considerations. He said recently to the students in one of his Columbia seminars,

You can't necessarily tell whether a family is happily or wretchedly housed by using a standard that takes account only of the physical attributes of the building it's living in. A family may dwell in contentment in a rickety shack without plumbing if the shack happens to be in a lovely rural setting. An ex-urbanite's mansion on a five-acre plot may have all the latest conveniences and gadgets and yet be basically a miserable housing situation if the owner finds himself having to commute for an hour and a half every morning to his work through snarled-up traffic, and if his wife and children are pining for diversion and company. In the city, a banker's family may be considered ill-housed in a thousand-dollar-a month apartment if jackhammers and steam shovels are everlastingly shattering their peace or if they have disagreeable relations with their neighbors, while for the family of a [—Abrams paused and grinned—] of a pickled-herring vender in a tenement apartment on the Lower East Side amid neighbors and friends who care about them and share their troubles and triumphs, and with all sorts of shops and lively activities right at hand, such a tenement, despite the bathtub in the kitchen and the railroad layout of the place and the insufficiency of sunshine and fresh air, may be (I say, *may* be, mind you) a better, richer housing situation than anything that city planners and bureaucrats are apt to provide as a substitute.

When Abrams resigned from the New York City Housing Authority in 1937 after clashing with La Guardia, he was given a demonstration of how rough the Little Flower could play when crossed. From the start, the strong-willed Mayor had been annoyed with Abrams for daring to have a mind of his own about housing matters. They had disagreed over whether the Housing Authority should be dominated by the Mayor or should be, as Abrams advocated (and as it later became), a semiautonomous municipal corporation. And La Guardia, who had made his peace with Ickes, had been exceedingly annoyed when Abrams continued to push for a federal housing program that was independent of Ickes (a campaign that was ultimately successful). After Abrams's ouster, the Mayor got further steamed up when the press lambasted him for forcing Abrams's resignation, and his volatile temper boiled over when Abrams, defending himself during a radio interview against disparaging comments by the Mayor, pointed out that the Housing

Authority had been forced to resort to all sorts of expedients during most of its existence because its only support from the La Guardia administration had been a measly $12,000 loan. No reactionary can aggravate a reformer more than can a fellow reformer who is accusing him of being less than wholehearted about his reform efforts; no battles in public life are apt to be more sanguinary than those between two fervent liberals, differing over aspects of policy and tactics that to the public appear trivial but that to those concerned loom as irreconcilable. Vowing that he would teach Abrams a lesson, the Mayor had his subordinates draw up a list of the buildings that Abrams owned, and he took this list over to the Buildings Department himself and ordered, "Slap these places with every violation you can find!" The man who was then Deputy Buildings Commissioner, Harry Prince, has said that this was the only time he ever saw La Guardia use this particular kind of roughhouse tactics against a political foe. Over the next few days, inspectors swarmed through Abrams's buildings, listing one transgression after another. Some of the buildings had been given routine inspections just a short while before and had been declared satisfactory, but the New York City building code is such a hodgepodge that an inspector who puts his mind to it can find violations in any building. This was comically illustrated during the La Guardia blitz of Abrams's properties. By mistake, La Guardia's avenging inspectors had 29 Washington Square West, an imposing, deluxe apartment house, listed as belonging to Abrams, so they descended upon it. The actual owner was flabbergasted when the inspectors began combing it as if it were a festering menace to the city's health and welfare. It was then virtually a new building, had passed a complete inspection not long before, and subsequently became the New York address of Mrs. Franklin Delano Roosevelt.

This experience cost Abrams several thousand dollars and some of his idealism—or, at any rate, his political innocence. For all his disagreements with La Guardia, he had admired the Mayor immensely as a fighter for human rights, and had not been in the least prepared for such a demonstration of political ruthlessness. In his distress, Abrams decided to wash his hands of public affairs forever and concentrate on the private practice of law. This resolve lasted for four days—until the first private client came into his office. As the client began detailing his petty grievances, Abrams's heart sank. He realized at that moment that, having been stirred by great public issues and having known the satisfaction of helping to determine public policy and thus affect the lives of great numbers of people, he could never be content to serve only narrow private interests. But since he also realized that his high-spirited nature was ill suited to the routines of bureaucracy, he decided that he would have to serve the public privately—that is, in his own way. He thereupon began carving out his special niche as a freelance, freewheeling combination of reformer and expert. He started writing his first book, *Revolution in Land,* which, on its publication in 1939, Lewis Mumford described as the first really important word on the subject of the social occupancy and control of land since the writings of Henry George, and which sold 1,009 copies. He began teaching courses in housing and land economics at the New School for Social Research, and later at other institutions, including MIT. He turned out pamphlets, made speeches, wrote articles for the *Nation* and the *New Leader,* appeared as an expert witness before congressional committees, showered advice on government agencies that would have been just as happy without it, criticized most of what was being done about housing in this country, and, upon being challenged to make constructive proposals instead of merely sniping from the sidelines, went ahead and, to the annoyance of his challengers, drew up detailed plans for what he believed should be done.

In 1942, Local 32-B of the Building Service Employees Union sought a wage increase, and when the members of the New York Real Estate Board pleaded that they couldn't afford to grant it, the union got Abrams to testify before an arbitration board, as an expert real estate operator, that real estate management was making ample profits. The Real Estate Board countered with a surprise witness— Abrams's own business manager, who testified that Abrams's buildings were losing money. It was a blow aimed at discrediting both Abrams's acumen as an operator and his repute as an expert. Abrams sought and got permission to cross-examine his manager, and by the time he had finished, he had elicited information that showed his buildings to be, in fact, making a handsome profit of 30 percent. The building employees got their raise.

Through the years, whenever housing, racial discrimination, or a similar cause has been at issue, and a worthy organization concerned with such matters has needed someone to address a meeting, the organization has been able to count on Abrams no matter how short the notice or how far away he might be:

The only problem is that you can never count on him to say just what you want him to [the director of one such organization says]. Most of the time he's magnificent—rousing, informed, warm, humorous, challenging, constructive. But every once in a while he'll come up with some odd idea out of nowhere—something he is probably mulling over tentatively. He'll present it as if it were gospel and derail everything. That's the chance you take, but it's worth it.

An architect who has known Abrams for a long time has found that whenever he runs into Abrams, the effect on him is always unsettling. "Charlie is always doing something new," the architect said. "He's always blithely taking on some huge new project or campaign, or decrying some new outrage. And as he goes off, at that ambling gait of his, I just stand there, saying to myself, 'Brother, I'm sure in a rut.'" In whatever Abrams has undertaken, he has seldom been content to play just one role. More often, like a gabby Marcel Marceau, he has played all, or nearly all, the parts there were. For instance, in 1949, when a major federal housing bill—what became the Taft–Ellender–Wagner Act—was being considered, Abrams played the parts of the sober expert, giving legal and technical advice to the framers of the legislation; of the passionate agitator, delivering speeches and writing articles in support of the bill; and then, after it was passed by Congress, he played the part of minstrel. He wrote songs, skits, and lampoons for a victory celebration that was held at the Mayflower Hotel in Washington, and himself gleefully breezed out on the ballroom floor and performed them for his audience. One of his comic songs caused the usually dour Senator Robert Taft to roar with laughter, and Abrams still cherishes that moment. "I'll bet there aren't many people who can say they made Senator Taft laugh," he likes to boast.

Shortly after the Second World War, Abrams embarked on a new enterprise, becoming a special reporter and housing expert for the *New York Post*. Having been given a free hand by the paper, he was able to keep City Hall in a gratifying turmoil with his denunciations of slums and segregation, and he had a fine time thinking up vast city housing programs, providing handy instructions for financing, legislating, and administering them, and then agitating for their adoption in article after article exhorting the public, badgering Mayor William O'Dwyer, and lambasting that grand panjandrum, Robert Moses, who was then the city's housing coordinator, for being picayune. ("Moses—Or Houses?" was the title of one article.) His campaigns succeeded surprisingly often, ending sometimes with Mayor O'Dwyer telephoning the *Post*'s publisher and saying wearily, "Tell Charlie he can lay off now—we're going to come through on that idea of his." In 1948, he pushed through in this way a public housing scheme for middle-income families, under which about thirty thousand apartments, with a total value of $500 million, have been built so far; the scheme, which is self-supporting and requires no cash subsidies, is nowadays regarded as one of the more successful elements of the city's housing program. After his middle-income housing campaign was put across, Abrams started in on a campaign to get the city to put up $100,000 for rat control in the tenement districts. Around this time, O'Dwyer, fed up with Abrams's articles, offered to create a cushy position for him as special housing consult-ant to the Mayor; all Abrams would be expected to do would be to drop in at Gracie Mansion now and then and give the Mayor the benefit of his advice in a friendly chat instead of splashing it before the public. "Would I be expected to give up my column?" Abrams asked O'Dwyer suspiciously. "Well, that goes without saying," O'Dwyer replied. Abrams declined, with thanks, and went back to writing for the *Post,* which he continued to do for another year, leaving after the paper's ownership changed hands.

Yet another of Abrams's activities, utilizing yet another of his talents, was, from time to time, to take on socially significant court cases without fee. Unquestionably the most significant of these was the one known as *Dorsey* v. *Stuyvesant Town,* which was initiated in 1947. At issue was a decision by the Metropolitan Life Insurance Company to rent apartments in its Stuyvesant Town development only to whites. Abrams, representing three Negroes who had been turned down as tenants, argued that this was unconstitutional. To encourage the construction of Stuyvesant Town, the city had granted Metropolitan Life tax concessions worth an estimated $75 million and had also used its condemnation and eviction powers to help the corporation acquire the site. While the case was being argued, the insurance company's attorney, Samuel Seabury, con-fronted Abrams with the precedent of Abrams's own Muller case, saying that it provided the legal basis for Metropolitan's development of Stuyvesant Town, and that he was therefore nonplussed to find Abrams challenging the project. Abrams replied that he was challenging the project's policy of selecting tenants, not its policy of acquiring land. Since the corporation had accepted extraordinary public assistance, Abrams argued, it had no right to describe itself as just an ordinary landlord, whose tenant-selection policy was a private matter. He took the position that a landlord who availed himself of government powers and government financial assistance was under the same constitutional obligation as the government itself not to discriminate against citizens because of their race. This case, as Abrams has pointed out in *Forbidden Neighbors,* an impassioned book he wrote eight years afterward on housing discrimination in America, clearly stated for the first time the constitutional dilemma posed by a partnership between government and private enterprise—a kind of partnership that was being entered into increasingly often for urban development projects of various kinds. The legal issue, he has written, was whether "what the government itself could not do constitutionally it *could* do through an agent using its power and aid," and the moral issue was which ethics would prevail in this partnership—the higher public ethics of the government or the private ethics of the marketplace. Abrams lost his case in the Court of Appeals by a four-to-three decision, but the litigation excited much public concern, and in 1950 the New York State Legislature passed a law applying the principles he had laid down to all projects built with government aid. (A few years later, Abrams found himself administering and enforcing this law as chairman of the New York State Commission Against Discrimination.) Since then, of course, the City Council and the New York State Legislature have gone even further, and it is now against the law here to discriminate against a tenant on racial or religious grounds in any apartment house or development, private or public.

Before Abrams became chairman of the State Commission Against Discrimination in December 1955, he served Governor Averell Harriman's administration for a year as the State Rent Administrator. Here, he headed a chaotic organization whose function was to deal with about a half-million complaints a year. These came from tenants who were angry about their landlords, their rents, their services, or about rat and insect infestations of their buildings, and from landlords claiming financial losses, demanding rent increases, and vituperating against the behavior and base character of tenants.

Emotions ran high. Occasionally, Abrams's morning mail would include a whopping cockroach that an irate tenant had captured and sent along to dramatize his complaint. No rats were ever received, mercifully, but one of Abrams's predecessors once got slugged by a tenant just as he was stepping out of his limousine to enter the commission's offices; thereafter, rent commissioners always sneaked in and out the back way. In theory, Abrams has always disapproved of rent control, as a measure that discourages incentive to new construction and private enterprise, but during the acute housing shortage that then prevailed he felt it to be necessary. At one point, when he learned that a deal was being arranged between Democratic and Republican leaders in the legislature quietly to scuttle rent control, Abrams raised such a public furor that the deal had to be called off.

At the State Commission Against Discrimination, when Abrams took over, the tempo was very different from what it was at the Rent Control Commission. Everything went smoothly and quietly. Voices were not raised. The prevailing tone was one of tranquillity, order, conciliation, caution, gentility, respectability. Only a few hundred complaints came in each year, and they were processed with grave decorum. This was the way the agency had operated since its establishment, in 1945, as a result of the passage of the bipartisan Ives–Quinn bill prohibiting discrimination in employment. At the time, this was a legislative experiment without precedent; the New York State Commission Against Discrimination was the first agency of its kind to be established in this country. In administering the law, the emphasis was placed on doing nothing that would alarm the general public or offend powerful interests, and this was probably sound strategy at the outset, for the success of the law depended almost entirely on the degree of public cooperation it could command. Aggressive administration was not needed at the beginning anyway; the mere existence of a law stating, for the first time, that "practices of discrimination against any of its inhabitants because of race, creed, or color or national origin are a matter of state concern" and that "such discrimination not only threatens the rights and proper privileges of its inhabitants but menaces the institutions and foundation of a free democratic state" had a powerful effect. Major corporations, whose respectability was an important part of their stock in trade, had no wish to be lawbreakers, so they immediately began making significant changes in their hiring practices. One such firm was the Metropolitan Life Insurance Company. This company carried life insurance policies on two and a half million Negroes throughout the country—and up until quite recently had been one of the few major firms willing to regard Negroes as insurable human beings. But though it considered them insurable, it had never considered them employable, even in the menial capacity of janitor or charwoman. Not a single Negro employee of any sort was to be found in the home office or in any of its thirteen hundred district offices, including the ones in Harlem and other Negro areas. Nor, if the law had not been passed, would any change have been made, the company's officers have since conceded. But when the law *was* passed, the officers met and decided that it was their duty not only to comply but to do so wholeheartedly. Everybody within the organization was informed unequivocally of this decision. There would be no subterfuges, no secret marks designating race or religion on personnel cards; there would be no special considerations in hiring, assignment, or promotion. Within a decade after this decision, Metropolitan Life was employing in its home office some six hundred Negroes (exact figures were not available, since no records of the employees' race were kept) in a wide variety of positions, including some on the junior supervisory level. From all over the country, executives of other corporations came to Metropolitan Life's home offices to learn how this had been achieved and to see for themselves how it was working out. Abrams later said, "If the law had done nothing more than make it possible for Metropolitan Life to change its hiring practices, it would still have been a most important piece of legislation." The New York experiment was watched closely, and within ten years nine states and some thirty cities passed similar laws.

But by the time of Abrams's appointment to SCAD there were many who felt that New York had lost its leadership in the battle against discrimination. Even among those who had initially favored caution, the quiet, conservative approach was considered to have accomplished its purpose and to be no longer appropriate. Among civil rights organizations, New York's SCAD had fallen into some disrepute. It was said that it worked so quietly that most Negroes did not even know it existed, and so slowly that by the time it issued a ruling the victim had forgotten what it was he had complained

about. Negroes were no longer as gratified as they had been a decade
before by a company's willingness to hire a token Negro as a
stenographer, or even to promote a Negro to a junior supervisory
position. Housing segregation, with all its disagreeable consequences, had come to be recognized as a major problem, and, partly as a
result, new powers and responsibilities had been entrusted to SCAD
by the state legislature. The agency was now responsible for preventing racial discrimination in housing built with public assistance and
in all sorts of public accommodations, and also for preventing
discrimination in employment on account of age or sex. Governor
Harriman's appointment of Abrams was explicitly intended to breathe
new life into the agency. Abrams was supposed to shake things up,
and he did. In an interview shortly after taking up his new position,
he remarked, "At the Rent Control Commission, my job was to
make order out of chaos. Here, I would say, my job is to make chaos
out of order."

Abrams's appointment created a stir that his subsequent activities did little to abate. A few months after he took office, Oswald
Heck, the Republican leader who was Speaker of the Assembly,
objected that Abrams was too much of a zealot to head so sensitive
an agency. A semantic fracas ensued, with arguments over whether
Abrams was or was not a "zealot," and whether that was a good or a
bad thing to be. Fourteen civil rights organizations drafted a letter
to the press backing Abrams and demanding to know when zeal had
come to be a liability for those in public office, and Governor
Harriman startled a group of businessmen and industrialists gathered for luncheon at the Bankers' Club in order to discuss discriminatory employment practices by addressing them as "fellow-zealots."
As for Abrams, his comment on the accusation was, "Well, now I can
truly say I've been called everything from A to Z." Some months
later, on Abrams's first anniversary as head of SCAD, he received in
the mail letters of commendation from two disparate sources. One
was from the militant Negro labor leader A. Philip Randolph,
president of the Brotherhood of Sleeping Car Porters. It read, "May
I say that your leadership of this Commission represents a fine and
constructive force in the worldwide movement for human rights."
The other letter was from Thomas Jefferson Miley, executive vice
president of the Commerce and Industry Association of New York,
an organization representing possibly the greatest concentration of

wealth in the United States. Miley wrote, "If you had asked a group of businessmen ten years ago, the things that you have accomplished in the past year would have been considered impossible. You're a great leader and, to my mind, a man of great integrity. It has been a delight to work with you." Abrams read the two letters, gazed at the ceiling, blew a thoughtful cloud of cigar smoke into the air, and said to his secretary, "Take a poem, Miss Kaslow." The poem went:

> When Randolph and Jefferson Miley
> Both praise a zealot so highly,
> Then this zealot, by Heck,
> Should not his zeal check,
> But foster it ever more spryly.

Under Abrams, who served as chairman of SCAD until Nelson Rockefeller took over from Harriman in 1959, the agency's case load soon tripled. No longer did the Commission bask in quiet obscurity. The civil rights and civic organizations were pleased with the new turn of affairs, and made sure that Abrams knew it. He himself was less satisfied, and said he sometimes thought that citizens' groups ought to be goading him harder. Once, after a session with the legislature at which he felt his proposals had been less bold than they should have been, he was heard to exclaim, "How I wish I were out of office for a couple of days! Boy, would I blast me!" He sought to improve on the slow, haphazard, case-by-case approach that the Commission had theretofore relied on, and to bring about industrywide agreements affecting tens of thousands of people at a stroke. Instead of waiting to take steps after a complaint had come in, he had his Commission initiate investigations wherever they appeared to be warranted. He set up a research program to analyze in some depth the nature and causes of discrimination in the state. And he applied all his ingenuity to the thinking up of what he calls "gimmicks"— administrative devices or economic instrumentalities to effect social change. One gimmick was an arrangement he made with the New York City Department of Licenses providing for revocation of the licences of private employment agencies—some of which had been less than scrupulous—if they did not abide by the law. Another gimmick was an agreement he worked out with the Federal Housing Administration and with the Veterans Administration to bar federal assistance to any builder found violating the state antidiscrimination law. This represented the first time the federal government had agreed to act in support of a state's civil rights law. Contrasting Abrams with his predecessors, Herbert Hill, the labor relations secretary for the National Association for the Advancement of Colored People, said, "At last the agency has a real expert at its head, not just a well-meaning but cautious gentleman with his heart in the right place. The Commissioners before him would merely say, 'Bring us in your complaints, Mr. Hill, and we'll process them.'"

In 1956, an outcry arose when it was discovered that banks and insurance companies consistently refused to take the risk of making housing and improvement loans in Harlem and other ghettos, and Governor Harriman sought Abrams's advice. Abrams thought there was little to be gained either by threatening to punish these financial organizations or by appealing to their selflessness. Instead, he set about devising an instrumentality that would not only minimize the risk for them but hold out the possibility of new profits. He called it the Mortgage Facilities Corporation, and defined it as a kind of banking syndicate, or cooperative, in which all the major banks and insurance companies would participate. The scheme was endorsed by the Governor, the banks and insurance companies agreed to try it, and a revolving fund of $20 million was established by the state legislature. Governor Harriman considered the creation of the Mortgage Facilities Corporation an impressive example of Abrams's practicality on behalf of the ideal.

Harriman, though he had never met Abrams before appointing him to his cabinet, soon became fond of his company, and there was a kind of meeting of spirit between these two men of very different backgrounds. Once, after a late-afternoon session at the Governor's Mansion, Harriman invited Abrams to take a dip in the pool with him, and Abrams remembers that scene as illustrating two contrasting approaches to life. "The Governor didn't have to impress anybody, and he never had had to," Abrams says. "He just lay on his back and floated while I, the ambitious underling, raced furiously up and down the pool with the windmill stroke I had learned at Bershadsky's Baths until I was absolutely exhausted."

Despite all his work at SCAD, Abrams still found energy while there to keep an eye on the housing situation on every level, from the local to the global. Every Friday, he went to Cambridge for the day to conduct classes at MIT, and during his summer vacations he

would take on U.N. missions, leaving New York not for the cool
seashore but for the slums of some tropical country so hot, crowded,
dirty, and noisy as to make New York City in the summer seem by
comparison a paradise. One summer he went to the Philippines, and
another summer his mission took him to Pakistan, where he arrived
in the middle of a heat wave. For one steaming day after another, the
temperature hovered around 105 degrees. Swallowing salt tablets to
ward off heat prostration and handfuls of sulfa pills as a protection
against dysentery, Abrams bustled about the country, visiting almost
every city of any size and inspecting its slums, its new developments,
its refugee camps, and its flimsy shacktowns and squatters' communities. He was in Pakistan for four weeks, during which time,
teaming up with Dr. Koenigsberger, who had accompanied him on
five U.N. missions, he drafted a housing and planning law, drew up
a memorandum on financing the program, and outlined in detail a
constructive approach to coping with the squatter problem. Then,
his vacation over, he flew back to New York, looking thoroughly
refreshed. Encountering one of his staff members in the corridor as
he stepped out of the elevator on the morning he returned to work,
Abrams greeted him cheerfully with "Hi, Dick! Now, about those
airlines that are resisting hiring Negroes for flight positions," pick-
ing up—like the irrepressible Bearded Lady, in Stravinsky's *The
Rake's Progress,* who resumes in midsyllable the aria she has interrupted in the previous act—right where he had left off a month
before.

Abrams has headed Columbia University's Division of Urban
Planning only since the fall of 1965, having at that time given up his
connection with MIT. He enjoys teaching, and he is good at it. He
is easy and informal with his students, and he keeps himself readily
accessible. After class, he may linger for as long as half an hour,
surrounded by students who are eager to go on discussing the
questions he has raised. The students place particular value on his
wide range of practical experience, for very few of their professors
have been as active in the nonacademic world as Abrams. Columbia's
Urban Planning Division has never been a very strong one, and it is
Abrams's aim to strengthen it. Enrollment in the division has already
increased fourfold since his appointment. An Institute of Urban
Environment has been established, under his aegis, and, with the
help of a $400,000 grant from the Ford Foundation, he has intro-

duced several courses on housing in underdeveloped areas—the first such courses to be given in an American university—and hopes to train a crop of young experts who can be of help to the developing nations in the way that he himself has been in his missions for the U.N. When a friend asked Abrams if he could be said to be passing on the torch, he replied, with a smile, "No, just spreading the light." He deems it important to have his students come to grips with real affairs rather than devote their time merely to theoretical exercises. He arranged for them to work on a planning job for Nassau in the Bahamas and on planning new communities in Staten Island and Queens. He has not eschewed theoretical exercises completely. Two of his assignments were for the students to draw up plans for Heaven and for Hell. Predictably, Hell inspired the more interesting designs.

At sixty-five, Abrams gives no indication of having contemplated retirement, or even of having contemplated slowing down. He still regards a vacation as a fine time for a strenuous mission for the U.N. or some other agency. During his spring vacation last year, he went to Chile to make an overall evaluation of that nation's housing programs. Last summer, he traversed the Alaskan tundra to advise the state government on what ought to be done about the Eskimos' housing, and a few weeks ago he was in Calcutta for the Ford Foundation to give his opinions on the shelter problems of India. In between, he managed to draw up a seventy-thousand-word report for Philadelphia, in which he offered the novel proposal—immensely simple in its conception though highly sophisticated in its financial and procedural details—that the best and cheapest way for Philadelphia to provide additional housing for the poor would be for the city to buy up habitable existing houses, of which many are available at prices between $2,000 and $5,000, and then simply resell them to impoverished families at minimal mortgage rates. Abrams calculates that this would bring home ownership within the reach of families with incomes as low as $3,150 a year.

In his rare gloomy moments, Abrams is given to citing what he calls his Reforms Perversion Theory, which is simply that all reforms are sooner or later perverted. "Slum clearance gets perverted into Negro clearance," he says. "Urban renewal becomes a device for profiteering without risk. Zoning becomes racial zoning. What's the use?" As he goes on in this fashion, a discouraged look comes to his face, and his eyes cloud. This transformation lasts for perhaps thirty seconds. Then Abrams remembers an idea for some new reform, and he begins passionately expounding it.

NOTES

1. A portion of the original article has been omitted here that dealt with Abrams's 1965 book, *The City Is the Frontier*, and his suggestions for improving New York City.
2. A brief portion of the original article has been omitted here that dealt with housing reform in New York City prior to 1901.

16

Kevin Lynch

HIS LIFE AND WORK

TRIDIB BANERJEE AND
MICHAEL SOUTHWORTH

KEVIN LYNCH (1918–1984) WAS ARGUABLY the leading environmental design theorist of our time whose productive career was devoted to research, writing, and teaching, as well as to consulting in city design and planning. He has left behind a rich legacy of ideas and insights about human purposes and values in built form, and possibilities for designing humane environments. Kevin Lynch's published work includes seven books (eight, including a posthumous volume) and some twenty-five journal articles and essays written for various anthologies edited by others.

To understand the contributions of Kevin Lynch we must look at his work in the context of the planning practices of earlier decades. It takes some effort to remember today, in the waning years of the twentieth century, that city planning in America at the turn of the century was rooted in the grand traditions of civic, landscape,

Reprinted, with changes by the authors, from Tridib Banerjee and Michael Southworth (1990) "Kevin Lynch: His Life and Work," in *City Sense and City Design: Writings and Projects of Kevin Lynch*, ed. Tridib Banerjee and Michael Southworth (Cambridge, Mass.: MIT Press), by permission. Copyright © 1990 by Catherine, David, Laura, and Peter Lynch.

Articles by Kevin Lynch cited in the text are included in Tridib Banerjee and Michael Southworth, eds., *City Sense and City Design: Writings and Projects of Kevin Lynch* (Cambridge, Mass.: MIT Press, 1990).

and garden city design set forth by such stalwarts as Daniel Burnham, Ebenezer Howard, Raymond Unwin, and Frederick Law Olmsted. Not only could cities be designed; the belief was that they should be designed, because aesthetic and orderly environments were essential for the health and well-being of the people. A good and beautiful city was believed to mirror—in fact, to shape—a good society; it instilled civic pride and responsibility in its citizens, and promoted their moral and social development.

This turn-of-the-century design philosophy was influenced by the thinking of anti-urbanist social reformers who were worried that the individual and the family were likely to be lost in the incipient urban transition, and that the wholesomeness of rural community life and values would be replaced by an anomic urban social order. The proliferation of smokestack industries and the attendant urban sprawl along the Eastern Seaboard further reinforced the anxieties and anti-city biases of the reformists.[1] Restoring family, neighborhood, and community values was seen as crucial to countering the impersonal tendencies of urban life. Such important social thinkers of the time as the psychologist William James, the philosopher and educator John Dewey, the sociologist Robert Park, and the social worker Jane Addams all spoke of establishing local communities, neighborhoods, and a sense of place so that the individual and the family would not get lost in the great emerging urban agglomerations. Clarence Perry's "neighborhood unit" formula, although a physical planning principle, grew out of this movement. Across the Atlantic came Ebenezer Howard's "garden city" idea, formulated to create healthy communities in industrial Britain. Clarence Stein's "superblock" concept, which was meant to create large, safe pedestrian domains free from auto traffic, was another design idea that came out of similar reactions to the expanding metropolis. Together these ideas gave legitimacy to the notion that physical planning could indeed create safe, decent, and wholesome community environments, even within seemingly faceless urban regions.[2]

In the 1950s and the 1960s, this view faced a serious challenge from social scientists who openly questioned what they called the "physical determinism" of design. They argued, sometimes convincingly, that the physical form had very little to do with the social form of our environments, and they exhorted designers to understand how social forces actually influence the physical city. They further argued that designers' sense of physical order had nothing to do with the social or the moral order of society, pointing to debacles such as Boston's West End and St. Louis's Pruitt-Igoe and to the social "blues" of the British (and, later, the American) new towns. The role of urban design was seen essentially as a matter of aesthetics. In the long list of social and economic priorities, design values were relegated to the status of window dressing—something frivolous and worth attending to only after the "real" problems were solved.

Cities were seen essentially as an outcome of the locational organization of market demand for urban space, mediated by local politics. Beyond that, the city was recognized to be a highly complex phenomenon. And since this complex entity was yet to be fully fathomed by the social sciences, any proposition that cities could be shaped by deliberate design appeared too perverse an idea. To the strong systems orientation of the social sciences, which was shaping the direction of city planning, the idea of city design was seen as anachronistic, impudent, and megalomaniacal. Yet by the early 1960s the impact of the federal urban renewal program was beginning to be felt across the country. Entire urban districts were being leveled with little concern for the social life and roots of places, to be replaced with anonymous forms on a new scale. These changes in the urban physical environment continued to have major impacts on people's life experiences.

It was against this background that Kevin Lynch began his early research on city form and city design as a young instructor at MIT. He was intrigued by the physical city and the urban experience generally, and by the interaction between physical space and its human use. He quickly became engrossed in describing and understanding the form of the modern metropolis. Between the mid-1950s and the mid-1960s he wrote a set of articles on this subject in rather quick succession: "The Form of Cities" (1954), "A Theory of Urban Form" (with Lloyd Rodwin, 1958), "The Pattern of the Metropolis" (1961), and "The City As Environment" (1965). In these articles Lynch was beginning to chart a whole new way of looking at the large-scale built environment and was searching for a taxonomy to describe the physical city.

He was also curious to know how the public, not the trained designer, saw and understood the everyday environment, what they valued in it, how it shaped their lives and activities, and how they in turn shaped the urban form. After a year of travel and research in Europe, a major grant from the Rockefeller Foundation allowed him to continue his research on how people perceive and organize their environment. Gyorgy Kepes, a well-known Bauhaus-trained painter and professor of design at MIT whom Kevin considered a great man and a great teacher, had in part inspired the research and worked with Lynch on the project. The study, conducted in three cities—Boston, Jersey City, and Los Angeles—culminated in the all-time classic of the planning literature, *The Image of the City* (1960). This book earned Lynch national and international renown. No other book in this field has touched so many, or sparked so much interest both inside and outside the field. Although considered a seminal work, it was an early venture and represented only one particular aspect of his ideas on planning and urban design. Lynch himself had considerable ambivalence about this work. When Florence C. Ladd (1985) asked Lynch about revising *The Image of the City* in a 1976 interview (published posthumously in 1985) he made clear that his thinking had progressed beyond that early work: "No, I would never go back to it. I was asked that the other day. The MIT Press wanted me to revise it and I said it is not really a matter of the work; I really don't want to do it. I feel it is some of my past, by and gone and, if I try to revise it, I know it would be like a can of worms. I would have to rewrite completely and rethink it and do another book and I am afraid that I really don't think that I will do it. Scared to open up that box." Yet later, when asked by Lloyd Rodwin and Robert Hollister in *Cities of the Mind* (1984) to reflect on his pioneering work and how it might have affected research and practice, Lynch spoke quite candidly of the criticisms of this book and his own disappointments with the limited application to practice. He defended his work against the usual criticisms, which typically questioned the sample size, validity of the technique, whether the methods usurped creativity in design, and the basic relevance of the inquiry. At the same time he added some additional criticisms of his own. One was the failure to consider observer variations; another was that the image that was elicited was a static one. But he was most disappointed in how the study, while becoming a "fad," failed to make much inroad into public policy or the practice of city design (Rodwin and Hollister, 1984).

In other writings, Lynch had begun to present different aspects of his research findings on the perception of environments and related discussions of users' needs: "Some Childhood Memories of the City" (with Alvin Lukashok, 1956), "Environmental Adaptability" (1958), and "A Walk Around the Block" (with Malcolm Rivkin, 1959). His interest in how people perceive and evaluate their environments remained strong. When asked by UNESCO (United Nations Educational, Scientific, and Cultural Organization) to write a paper on perception of environmental quality, he quickly produced a cross-cultural comparison of childhood environments, utilizing interviews with children and naturalistic field studies. Eventually the study was published as an edited book, *Growing Up In Cities* (1977), but before that it was reported in abbreviated form in two journal articles: "Growing Up in Cities" (1976) and "On People and Places: A Comparative Study of the Spatial Environment of Adolescence" (1976), both with Tridib Banerjee.

In the years that followed the publication of *The Image of the City*, the contributions of Kevin Lynch as a design theorist continued to become known and appreciated through his other books. *Site Planning* (1962), written as a textbook, proved to be quite popular. *The View from the Road* (1964), which Lynch wrote with Donald Appleyard and John Myer, was a study of the visual environment of the city as experienced while in motion, inspired by the massive freeway development in American cities. Another sabbatical in the late 1960s led to a revised and expanded edition of *Site Planning* that included new materials on design methods and behavioral research. Lynch also began the work on what was to become his favorite book, *What Time Is This Place?* (1972). In 1976 he published *Managing the Sense of a Region*, an exploration of how the form of a large metropolitan area might be designed and controlled.

By the mid-1960s Lynch had already begun his work on theories of city form and city design. In a way this work was the most significant of his contributions, because it attempted to integrate many previously unconnected branches of planning theory. In articles such as "Environmental Adaptability" and "A Theory of Urban Form" he had already begun to address specific requirements of "good city form" and how these requirements interacted with various elements of the physical city. In the 1960s and the 1970s Lynch devoted a major part of his writing to proposing what the goals of city design and ideal city form might be. The essays "The Openness of Open Space" (1965), "Quality in City Design" (1966), "City Design and City Appearance" (1968), and "Open Space: Freedom and Control" (with Stephen Carr, 1979) are examples of his efforts to define the qualities of a good urban environment.

Some of these papers were written in a speculative vein; others bordered on romanticism and utopian thinking. Yet these pieces were often engaging and inspiring, suggesting a completely different way of defining the scope of city design. Although the physical environment itself was very much the focus of Lynch's writing, his ideas had nothing to do with the "grand" and deterministic turn-of-the-century design traditions, which the social scientists openly scorned. What was distinctive about Lynch's philosophy was that he dealt with the immediate experiential qualities of place—which he was fond of referring to as the "sensuous qualities," or simply "sense"—and their importance in people's lives. He made his case simply and forcefully, yet in a rich and elegant way that was characteristic of his writing. Drawing liberally from the tradition of the social sciences, he convinced even the most skeptical of the contemporary social scientists and policy makers that the physical city mattered, and that it mattered in a very fundamental and important way. City design is not window dressing!

Lynch took care to differentiate what he preferred to call "city design" from "urban design." In contrast to urban design, which was more architectural and more project-oriented at that time, he felt that city design should address the quality and character of the entire public city, or at least large sectors of it. However, his term "city design" never really took hold; the profession continues to use the term "urban design," regardless of scale or focus. While reestablishing the importance of the physical environment in the context of policy, Lynch also revived the normative aspects of city design—the standards or ideals that urban form should achieve and the reasons for doing so. Here he parted company with the social sciences and drew inspiration from the humanities. He emphasized that city design is not just about the physical arrangement or rearrangement of things to satisfy today's needs, but that it also has to do with fundamental human values and rights: justice, freedom, control, learning, access, dignity, and creativity. He emphasized that city design is not the reproduction of environments in the images of the present order, but is really about what should be and what could be. During this period he wrote such memorable essays as "Where Learning Happens" (with Stephen Carr, 1968), "The Possible City" (1968), and "Grounds for Utopia" (1975). Eventually many of these ideas were abridged and incorporated in his last major book, *A Theory of Good City Form* (1981), which is in many ways the most complete treatise on his philosophy of good city form and city design. It is a culmination of many decades of research, thinking, and writing on the performance characteristics of city form that serve human purposes and values best.

By the late 1960s Lynch was considered the leading expert on city design. He was asked to write essays on design practice and education for several publications and symposia. "City and Regional Planning," written for the *Enciclopedia Italiana* (1973), and "Urban Design," written for the *Encyclopaedia Britannica* (1974), are cases in point; "City Design: What It Is and How It Might Be Taught" (1980) is another. Two interesting essays on growth management that proved to have considerable practical significance were also published in the 1970s: "Performance Zoning: The Small Town of Gay Head Tries It" (with Philip Herr, 1973) and "Controlling the Location and Timing of Development by the Distribution of Marketable Development Rights" (1975). However, only a few of Kevin Lynch's practice-oriented writings were published prior to the posthumous collection *City Sense and City Design: Writings and Projects of Kevin Lynch*, edited by Tridib Banerjee and Michael Southworth. Lynch was particularly proud of his contribution to the development of Boston's Government Center and waterfront. Although the results deviated from Lynch's plans in some ways and were not always to his liking, the basic concepts of creating a system of public open spaces, opening up public access to the waterfront, and preserving historic places have made the Government Center and Haymarket area of Boston one of the more successful urban places in the contemporary American city. Also special to Lynch was a study of the San Diego region he did with Donald Appleyard in the early 1970s under a grant from the Marston family. This study, based largely on public perceptions and community concerns about declining environmental quality, was written as a white paper for public discussion. It brought out ideas and presented scenarios for the future of the San Diego community, and it continues to serve as a rallying point for local groups. Other examples of Lynch's professional work include "Analysis of the Visual Form of Brookline, Massachusetts" (1965), "Sensuous Criteria for Highway Design" (with Donald Appleyard, 1966), "The Urban Landscape of San Salvador: Environmental Quality in an Urbanizing Region" (1968), "Looking at the Vineyard" (with Sasaki, Dawson and Demay, 1973), and "Designing and Managing the Strip" (with Michael Southworth, 1974). These works illustrate how Lynch tried to translate his ideas and his philosophy into proposals for specific settings and contexts.

Toward the end of Lynch's career it was clear to those who were close to him that he wanted to focus on applying some of his ideas to practice. Yet he continued to write, producing some moving essays in the final years of his life. "Reconsidering *The Image of the City*" (1985) is a brief but poignant essay on what Lynch himself thought of the work that had won him international recognition. He was deeply disturbed by world events, and in particular by the escalating nuclear arms race and the attendant prospects of a nuclear war. He chose to address this chilling prospect in "What Will Happen To Us?" (1983), written with Tunney Lee and Peter Droege. Asked to comment on what role planners and designers could play in the event of such a catastrophe, Lynch wrote a haunting scenario of a "cacotopia"—the word he used to describe the opposite of a utopia[3]—in which he tries to find his way home to Watertown after a nuclear explosion has leveled the entire Boston urban region ("Coming Home," 1984). These are powerful articles which most designers and planners probably have not yet read. Lynch also prepared the third edition of *Site Planning* (1984, coauthored with Gary Hack) shortly before his death.

Lynch's last book, *Wasting Away* (edited by Michael Southworth), was nearing completion at the time of his death and was published posthumously. In it he reflects on the processes of decline, decay, and renewal in our lives and environments. While it does deal with waste and the environment, the book goes beyond these boundaries to explore the subject from many points of view.

These works stand out as one of the most significant contributions to the field to date, linking theory and research with a strong philosophy of the human purposes of environmental form and of design as social action.

Although Lynch's work was praised by professionals and academics worldwide, he did have his critics. Many architects and students of design and planning, while finding his ideas stimulating, regret the lack of a clear image of what "the good city" would look like. Unlike Henry Wright, Le Corbusier, Clarence Stein, or Paolo Soleri and other theorists of urban form, Lynch never created drawings or models illustrating his utopia. This is both a strength and a weakness. Since his conceptions were expressed verbally in relatively vague and global terms, they can be applied to varied conditions and cultures and can be shaped to suit the needs of the reader. However, the lack of a clear image makes his ideas less compelling to many young students of design or to architects who seek three-dimensional images to arouse their intellectual interest. In this vein Allan Jacobs (1981), in his very enthusiastic review of *A Theory of Good City Form*, noted: "You may find that words like 'there are places . . .' do not always tell enough to allow us to conclude that his physical environment will be all that different than some good and not so good places you know already (to which Lynch might say, 'so what?'). If I get a great feeling of a utopian society but not enough of the *place* that's only because I want more."

Those looking for a single simple message were disappointed because his mind was subtle and never satisfied with the simple answer. Some readers have felt overwhelmed by the flow of ideas in his writing that are sometimes contradictory and usually complex. George Nelson (1975), in his review of *What Time Is This Place?*, began: "The title, of course, is a stopper. We see mountains of books about the objects and spaces in cities, but none about their passage through time." However, he went on to say that he "found the book uncommonly tough going. . . . The reader is confused by seemingly conflicting reports and made to feel uneasy about the whole situation. . . . As a rhetorical tactic, the author's questions are at once unanswerable and irrelevant. . . . There is a general flattening out of all images, a kind of homogenizing of information. Arguments suddenly shift in mid-stream. Furthermore, while questions are frequently asked, they are rarely answered. . . . The stream of totally uncolored and unaccented comments, digressions, pronouncements, proposals, questions, all liberally spiked with cliches, is simply too much to cope with. The whole thing is like opening a bushel of fortune cookies and reading the strips, each equal in length, depth, weight, and truth to all of the others. . . . For simple hints on just how one goes about moving the world in a life-enhancing direction, we are going to have to look elsewhere."

Similar sentiments were expressed earlier by Victor Gruen (1968) in his comments on Lynch's 1968 article entitled "The Possible City." Gruen found this speculative article on the future of cities "frivolous" and criticized Lynch's musings as being "capricious" and his writing full of "inconsistency and contradiction." Lynch's reluctance to make categorical statements and his penchant for bringing up the positive side of such unpopular issues as cars and freeways or undesirability of fine grain integration often made him appear ambivalent or, worse, an iconoclast.

Many readers have said that Lynch's books improve on subsequent readings and are continual sources of pleasure and insight. Perhaps quick first reads, especially by reviewers outside the fields of planning and urban design, explain the negative comments of some of Lynch's critics. Brian Goodey (1977) commented on this point in his review of *Managing the Sense of a Region:* "Taken with his *The Image of the City* and *What Time Is This Place?* Lynch's trilogy of studies in environmental awareness is either an abiding source of pleasure, or a constant frustration. . . . At first glance I was disappointed with this book, but a first glance is never enough where Lynch's writing is concerned: a second reading reveals a significant text in urban design deserving of attention now."

Some critics from outside the field of design arts found him too idealistic, too normative and unrealistic for society today. His conception of human nature was an optimistic one, in which individuals act benevolently and harmoniously in the public interest. This vision runs through many of his writings but is especially prominent in his "A Place Utopia" in *A Theory of Good City Form.*

Other critics, usually from the social sciences, aimed at his methodology, which they considered lacking in "scientific" rigor. Some have thought him to be too concerned with image structure rather than with meaning and value. This criticism, however, derives from a very narrow reading of *The Image of the City* and ignores his other writings, which expand the focus of his early work. Pipkin (1983, p. 53), for example, considered Lynch's proposals for designing the visual form of the city "unexceptionable" but "in the context of American urban problems . . . hardly incisive." While acknowledging that "the work of Lynch has led to a more human approach to urban design," Gottdeiner and Lagopoulos (1986, p. 7) question the value of cognitive mapping. They argue that in this approach, "the signification of the city" is obtained "through the *perception* of its inhabitants rather than their conception." It misses the aspect of denotation and the role of ideology, which are central to the "socio-semiotic" approach to understanding the city.

Although Lynch had repeatedly spoken out against inequities

and injustices of the existing social order in his writings, collectively his writings were not seen to be in line with modish Marxist criticism of planning and of built environments of capitalist economies (Banerjee, 1993). Some of the most vitriolic attacks on his work came from critics outside the field of planning. These critiques were once again about what they considered his unscholarly style and his failure to acknowledge extant literature or to pay due homage to the notables in the field, as is the custom in scholarly work. Robert F. Lucid (1973), in his review of *What Time Is This Place?*, belittled Lynch for not being able to transcend from "the technological arena" to "the long established discourse of the aesthetician." He derided the book as being "pre-elementary." Lynch, of course, never meant this or any of his books to be a contribution to the erudite domain of aesthetic discourse. He wrote primarily for practitioners in the design fields. He did not care whether his work stood up to the established standards of scholarly work. He was an academic heretic, an intellectual rebel, who had very little patience for any kind of formal decorum. Readers will recall that at a very early age he rejected the formal Beaux-Arts style of architectural education at Yale in favor of a more open-ended, unstructured mode of learning at Taliesin. In fact, he had a great deal of disdain for what he called "academic puffery." His articles were always devoid of elaborate citations of other people's works or even footnotes. Critics from traditional social science disciplines, where absence of such litany is an act of infamy, could not take this omission very kindly. In a review of *City Sense and City Design*, a posthumous publication of a collection of his works, P. L. Knox (1992) lashed out against Lynch for this very reason. He has essentially called his work arrogant, naive, and anachronistic. He has attacked Lynch's normative writings as paternalistic, "utopian, evangelical, and myopic." This is as much a critique of the field of design—a challenge of the authority of the designers that social scientists could never understand or tolerate—as that of Lynch himself. Critiques of this nature are a reflection of the fundamental difference in the epistemology of the modernist and positivist tradition of social scientists (lacking, incidentally, the intuitions of true natural scientists) and that of the intuitive and normative domain of the design profession. Lynch would have pleaded guilty for being hopelessly entrenched in that camp. He never aspired to be a social scientist.

A Biographical Sketch

Kevin Lynch was born in Chicago in 1918. His parents were second-generation Irish-Americans, his grandparents having emigrated from Ireland after the famine. They struggled at first, but by the time Kevin was born his parents were quite well-to-do. By his own account his father's side of the family had "boom" and "bust" years. At one time the family lived on South Parkway, then an upper-class neighborhood.

Kevin was the youngest of three brothers. He grew up in the Hazel Avenue neighborhood on the North Side of Chicago, near Lake Michigan. This was a mixed but stable city neighborhood of apartments and single-family homes, with tree-lined streets. Swimming, playing, and walking along the lake shore always remained among his most treasured childhood memories. In 1953 he returned to this neighborhood of his youth and noted the following impressions of what he described as a "sentimental journey":

. . . [the] Hazel Avenue neighborhood [is] surprisingly unchanged despite a few store alterations, a new house in Cummings' yard. . . . Still a little island of green and solid one family houses; the trees [are] thicker and higher, the buildings much as remembered, though the open spaces seem smaller. Here [is] an example of a stable mixed neighborhood; the apartments jostle the houses, but the latter [are] still well kept and well-to-do. . . . Remarkable that though remembered buildings were sharply remembered, yet memory (and presumably attention) operate only on a few points: our apartment, that next door that we saw in construction, the Holmeiers, the Cummings, the Walshes, the big house that once had rabbis, the drug store, the apartment hotel, the church and school, the el and the cemetery, Robbins Terrace and its big wild lot. The rest [is] just vaguely familiar, and probably [was] never experienced as much more than a collection to pass through. . . . The area is quiet and relaxed, and sometimes successful in its juxtaposition of different houses, but basically dull and often cramped and ugly. Strange to feel at home in it and to realize its ugliness or dullness. The church tower that I used to look on so long in the late sunlight is only a colorless copy. The circle by the parochial school is a dusty playground, heavily equipped and used but dirty and unsupervised . . . many of the kids play in the street by preference. . . .[4]

Young Kevin's early education began at home, with private tutors. He then attended a Catholic parish school for several years with his brothers. But his mother, who was quite free-thinking and knowledgeable about education, later sent her children to the Francis W. Parker School, one of the first progressive schools in the country. This was quite a courageous thing for an Irish Catholic mother to do at that time, since Catholic children were expected to attend parochial schools. Lynch recalled later: "Every time I went to confession I was asked why I wasn't attending Catholic school." This school, attended by Lynch all the way through his high school years, had been founded by Francis Parker, a former school superintendent from Quincy, Massachusetts, and a disciple of John Dewey. The curriculum and the instructional methods were innovative, inspired by Dewey's philosophy of learning by doing. The learning environment was enormously engaging and stimulating, and the teachers were excellent. Throughout his life Lynch treasured his education at the Parker School. There he met Anne Borders, his future wife, and they shared many of the same learning experiences. She recalls that "children loved going to that school and never forgot what they learned there."

The Parker School experience had a major effect on Kevin Lynch's early intellectual development—more than college—and shaped his future interests in human environments and social justice. His interest in architecture grew out of a course in Egyptian history taught by Hazel Cornell, his seventh-grade teacher. Another teacher, James Mitchell, interested Lynch in reading Bacon, Hobbes, Descartes, Hegel, Spinoza, Schopenhauer, Locke, and Mill. Also influential was his eighth-grade teacher, Sarah Greenbaum, who continued to be an advisor and a friend long after he left the Parker School. (She introduced Anne and Kevin to the island of Martha's Vineyard, off Cape Cod, where she had a summer cottage and where the Lynches later built a summer house of their own.)

Lynch's high school days coincided with the Great Depression, picket lines and bread lines, a general climate of political upheaval, and talk of social and political change. The Parker School, with its progressive educational philosophy, engaged its students in those larger social and political questions. But the Spanish Civil War was the "first real political influence" on Lynch's life. It stimulated his interest in questions of socialism and communism and other contemporary political matters. "It was one of the great times of my life," he commented to one interviewer.[5]

After graduation from high school in 1935, Kevin Lynch decided to study architecture. Not certain where to apply, he went to see John A. Holabird, Jr., of Chicago—the only architect he knew at the time—for advice. Holabird, who believed in the old-fashioned, conservative, Beaux-Arts tradition, as Lynch later discovered, suggested that he should go to Yale, the last bastion of that tradition in the United States. Thus, Lynch began his study of architecture at Yale, but he was disappointed and discouraged by the Beaux-Arts approach—he once described the Yale architecture program as "the most conservative and backward" of its time.

It was at this point that Lynch read about Frank Lloyd Wright and wrote to inquire about studying architecture with him[6]:

Mr. F. L. Wright,
Taliesin,
Spring Green, Wis.

Dear Mr. Wright,

I had heard of your school before, and considered it an interesting possibility for the study of architecture, but a few days ago I got hold of one of your bulletins, and was filled with enthusiasm to go to a place with such an atmosphere of freedom and creation. So I am writing you for some advice and a little information.

At present I am a student at Yale, entering my Sophomore year. Yale's school of architecture has a large reputation, but after one course in the history of architecture and a look at the work being done there, I think it is academic and stifling. Of course there are many things to be learned there such as technique in the drawing and the science of construction, but it seems a waste of time. One of my major deficiencies is lack of ability in drawing, but I am taking a course in freehand drawing, and I imagine that if it is only a technique that I can master it with hard work. But does your school give sufficient instruction in engineering and materials, which are so vital in architecture? Or would you advise me to take some engineering courses before applying for admission at Taliesin?

I have another question. I have hopes of qualifying myself not only for architecture, but for city-planning, although that is somewhat of a big order. Does Taliesin give adequate training

FIGURE 16.1   *Kevin Lynch (seated, second from left) with Frank Lloyd Wright at Taliesin.*

HEDRICH-BLESSING PHOTOGRAPH, COURTESY CHICAGO HISTORICAL SOCIETY

for work in that field, not only in its theoretical but its practical aspects? Or again would you advise me to get further training in some school of city planning (as at Harvard) before applying to work with you?

Perhaps I could finish my Sophomore year at Yale, and then enter Taliesin. Do you think that that would be advisable? I am now eighteen years old, never have had any practical architectural experience, despite attempts this summer to get such a job. I hope that I may join the fellowship soon or within a few years. I will appreciate it very much if you would advise me and send me any further information about Taliesin that you can. As your answer will not probably arrive before the end of this week, please send it to my college address below.

Sincerely yours,
Kevin Lynch
1440 Yale Station
New Haven, Conn.

Monday, Sept. 21

Wright replied as follows:

September 25, 1936
Kevin Lynch
New Haven, Conn.

My dear Kevin Lynch:
  Answering your questions about Fellowship at Taliesin—
  1. Your stay at Yale could be no possible help to your work at Taliesin.
  2. Your lack of ability to draw is soon rectified.
  3. We have no course nor any curriculum at Taliesin. Only performance under my direction and alongside other apprentices.
  4. No engineering course will help you here except as they are not anterior but posterior to experience in learning the nature of the thing to which they apply. The sense of the whole and its philosophy first. Technique first is the cart before the horse.
  5. Theory and practice are one at Taliesin.
  6. City planning is natural feature of our work at Taliesin (Broadacre City).
  7. The best time for an architect in embryo to join the Fellowship is before any time is wasted along conventional educational lines in architecture or engineering.

  We should want to see you and talk with you personally and have you see us before we agree to take you into Fellowship. And you would be welcome at any time for that interview.[7]

Even after receiving this letter from Wright which answered most of his questions and after he had visited Taliesin, Lynch had further inquiries prompted largely by questions raised by various advisors. The following letter captures some of his predicaments, yet confirms his determination to leave Yale.

Kevin Lynch - Yale University - New Haven, Conn.
1440 Yale Station
Sunday, Jan. 10

Dear Mr. Wright,
  Since I have been to see you different people have been giving me advice about my architectural education as if I had

a cold and they had an infinite number of home remedies. I went up to see Cranbrook Academy near Detroit on my way back East, since I had heard so much favorable comment about it. I found out that it was an ultragraduate school, seemingly good in certain specialized fields but definitely depending on a good deal of technical knowledge.

I also talked with several men here, and they stressed the need for a general cultural background and a college degree before going to work with you. There is something of value to be gotten out of college (I remember you asked me about that) from the group life, from the stimulation of certain people, from the mere quantity of activities and loose ideas that lie scattered about. And could not the knowledge of drafting and of construction well come after a general development in the field?

But they did bring up one rather solid objection, that it is necessary to have a degree from a school of architecture to become a registered architect, unless one goes through something like ten or twelve years of apprenticeship. Does that then make it at least legally necessary to go thru an architectural school? You said something about that; I don't remember what it was.

I am still pretty definite that I want to leave Yale at the end of this year; perhaps I can come to Taliesin sometime in the summer, if that is agreeable to you.

I hope you can answer my question about the state requirements.

> *Sincerely,*
> *Kevin Lynch*

Correspondence continued between Lynch and Taliesin. In one of the subsequent letters (dated April 12, 1937) Lynch asked Wright about fees and the appropriate time for joining the Fellowship. In this letter he also commented on an article that Wright had sent him. The following excerpt captures young Lynch's sentiments about the city and the country, an attitude that endured throughout his later work:

. . . If I have not written since I received your article about Taliesin and its cultural background, I like it very much. The realization that the country is a very vital part of our cultural tradition is a stimulating idea, although I do think that the city contributes another vital part to our culture. The real problem is to strip all that is unhealthy out of the city and the country too, and try to integrate those two traditions and give them a common basis and a common expression. . . .

The Taliesin experience came at a critical point in Lynch's professional schooling. The experience of Yale—not just the Beaux-Arts approach to architecture, but the university education as a whole—had set him against the conventional college education. Although going to Taliesin required some initial adjustment, he liked its "hands-on" approach to architectural education, which was very much like the Parker School's approach. Shortly after he started his apprenticeship with Wright in the fall of 1937, Lynch wrote a short essay for the *Capital Times*, a local newspaper published in Madison. The following excerpts, written when Lynch was 19, capture rather well his joy of being at Taliesin and his views of conventional university education.

Life for a new apprentice at Taliesin is a welter of new impressions, new stimulations, new jobs to handle, new friends who have much to teach you, new tensions to measure up to what is being done around you. The new apprentice must learn how to handle a tall bundle of corn-stalks, or how to cut a green oak plank, or how to translate a drawing for a building, or how to lay plaster, or even the most efficient method of scraping oatmeal out of the pot. There are new horizons of work, of creation, of meaning, lifting all around you. . . .

. . . while I was making up my mind to leave my course at Yale half-finished and come to Taliesin, my nebulous convictions as to the value of university training were hammered out into pretty definite shape. An initial vague dissatisfaction with college grew slowly into the disillusioning idea that something was radically wrong with the whole method of doling out education in standardized bucketfuls, five buckets per year per man. . . .

College as a preparation for creative activity later in life is only a period of "watchful waiting," and not very watchful at that. . . . It is an attempt by society to cast men into a mould leavened with inertia and lack of enthusiasm, so that they may not question the glaring flaws in the social structure. College is most logically considered from the student's point of view as four years of fun before the hard and unpleasant job of living begins. . . .

That is my conviction regarding university education. Taliesin, at first glance, was something entirely different and had a different ideal. It is the attempt to grasp the new ideal of hard work, of creative activity, of "learning by doing," of enthusiastic cooperation in solving common problems, that makes the life of the new apprentice so full and so fascinating here. I am afraid that a candid comparison of the large and famous university with five thousand students housed in expensive new Gothic buildings, with the small group studying and working with a great architect in a building nowhere adequate for their needs, but surrounded by beauty, might make old Elihu Yale wish he had given his money and his books to the Iroquois Indians.[8]

Kevin Lynch studied with Wright for a year and a half during an important time in Taliesin's history: 1937–38, when Wright was moving Taliesin from Wisconsin to Arizona, largely for personal health reasons. Lynch, a wonderful storyteller, recalled the amusing experiences of traveling for days in a caravan of cars and trucks laden with everything from drawings to frozen sides of beef. (As the caravan moved southwest to warmer temperatures, the beef began to thaw, forcing the entourage to eat steak three meals a day![9]) Construction of the new school began immediately upon arrival at the Arizona site, and according to Lynch's own account he and the other "apprentices" were all required to participate in the construction work.

Lynch considered Frank Lloyd Wright another great influence on his life. He did not agree with Wright's social philosophy, which he considered "backward looking" and of the "arts and crafts tradition" with a view of "individualistic society"; however, he respected Wright's genius for form and design, and he once said that Wright had made him "see the world for the first time."

Lynch left Taliesin after a year and a half because he felt that "one can get swallowed up" by the establishment, and he wanted to be on his own. According to Lynch, Wright did not always treat his apprentices gently. He could be quite harsh and rude in his criticisms, often devastating for young designers. This treatment must have troubled Kevin, who always believed in human potentialities and who himself became a gentle, fair, and kind teacher. Lynch felt that many of Wright's apprentices had missed the opportunity to blossom on their own. "You became only a small Mr. Wright if you stayed," he once commented. He never regretted leaving Taliesin, but Wright did not take his departure kindly: ". . . he cursed me up and down. That was the most wonderful bit of cursing I have ever received: it was really poetic."[10]

After he left Taliesin, Lynch felt that he needed some engineering background. He went to Rensselaer Polytechnic Institute to study civil and structural engineering. It turned out that engineering was not quite suited to his taste. He got bored and decided to discontinue his engineering studies. He stayed at RPI to study biology under Professor Bray (a self-taught man), who became another of Lynch's mentors. He then worked for a while as an assistant to Paul Schweicker, an architect in Chicago.

On June 7, 1941, Lynch married Anne Borders at the Chicago Commons, a settlement house where Anne's parents had been social workers. Three weeks later he was drafted into the Army. In the spring of 1944 he was sent to the South Pacific. He served in the Army Corps of Engineers in the Palau Islands, in the Philippines, and in Japan during the occupation.

After returning to the United States, Lynch went back to college under the G.I. Bill, pursuing a bachelor's degree in city planning at MIT. His interest in the field had been aroused in part by his reading of *The Culture of Cities*, by Lewis Mumford. His Bachelor of City Planning thesis (1947), "Controlling the Flow of Rebuilding and Replanning in Residential Areas," made a strong impression on MIT faculty members Lloyd Rodwin, Burnham Kelly, and John Burchard and was an important factor in his later being asked to teach at MIT. Interestingly, the thesis touched on the themes of change, decay, and renewal that Lynch developed many years later in *What Time Is This Place?* and *Wasting Away*.

After graduation Lynch went to North Carolina to work for the Greensboro Planning Commission—his first planning job. He was quite happy there, and apparently he intended to go on working as a planner. To his surprise, he got a call from MIT offering him a faculty position, even though he did not have a higher degree. At first Lynch was ambivalent about a teaching career and was quite content to stay at Greensboro. Anne Lynch, unhappy with this possibility, persuaded him to accept the MIT job. He joined the faculty in 1948 and continued teaching into the early 1980s, although he had formally retired in 1978.

Soon after he joined the planning program at MIT, Lynch

FIGURE 16.2   *Kevin Lynch, in U.S. Army uniform, with his bride Anne in the summer of 1943.*

became interested in the form and the visual environment of the city. Lloyd Rodwin recalled that Lynch was remarkably capable in every area of planning—not just one or two—and that he could have taught any course in the program. However, there was no particular focus, no passion. This changed when a Ford Foundation grant allowed him to spend a year in Europe with his family, based mainly in Florence. For Lynch this was a period of observing, questioning, discussing with friends and colleagues the essential nature of city experience, probing others about their reactions to Italian urban settings, and interpreting his own intuitions and feelings about what he saw and experienced. He kept a daily journal in which he recorded his travels, encounters, reflections, and occasional sketches. These pages are interesting reading in their own right, but they also give the reader a sense of how Lynch's early ideas were formed.[11] According to Rodwin, "Lynch came back to MIT transformed; the fire was burning and from that point on his course was set."

The MIT years were truly remarkable. With his colleagues Fred Adams, Jack Howard, and Lloyd Rodwin, Lynch helped build the planning program into one of the most distinguished in the world. The emphasis on city and metropolitan design within the field of planning was a creation of Lynch, shaped by his own evolving philosophy of city design. Bright and creative students from all over the world came to study with Lynch, who nurtured their creativity and stimulated them to branch out into new areas of inquiry. His teaching method was Socratic; he always asked the strategic question that would go to the heart of the problem. Those who came to him for design solutions or "answers" might have been disappointed, for he was more interested in teaching ways of asking the right questions. He enjoyed the company of his students and was always interested in them and their work. He respected their views, and was willing to listen to their ideas and to learn from them. He often said that his students were his best teachers and the part of his MIT experience that he valued most. Long after they left MIT, Lynch kept in touch with many of his students. Former students also kept in touch with him for their own intellectual stimulation and sustenance. In turn, he was interested in their career developments, which in many cases he himself supported and advanced. Throughout his life he received an enormous amount of correspondence and many examples of professional and scholarly work to review or comment on, from former students as well as from practitioners and scholars all over the world. He answered every letter in his colorful personal style and reviewed almost every manuscript, no matter how busy he was. His students remember him as a great teacher, a friend, a sounding board, a source of inspiration, and a great influence on their lives.

Throughout his academic career at MIT, Lynch maintained an active involvement in planning practice. In the early years he was associated with the Cambridge-based consulting firm of Adams, Howard and Greeley. In the middle years he worked largely as an independent consultant. After he retired from MIT, besides continuing his research and writing, he became more actively involved in practice as a principal partner of Carr/Lynch Associates, with a former student and colleague at MIT, Stephen Carr. Notable examples of their work are the redesign of Columbia Point (one of the worst public housing projects in the Boston area) and a plan for a linear regional park and urban development along forty miles of the Rio Salado corridor in Phoenix. He was also involved in several international projects, many in the Third World. His interest in the planning and development of cities in developing countries took him to Africa, Cuba, China, El Salvador, and Morocco. His interest in the future of human settlements was indeed global in scope.

Lynch particularly enjoyed projects in which the present or future users of the environment were directly involved. He always recommended what he felt would be best for the "substantive" clients—the actual users—even though at times they might be at odds with the desires of the "nominal" or institutional clients.[12] He felt quite strongly that ultimately it is the people who make a place successful, not the designer.

Kevin Lynch was honored by a number of professional societies. He received the American Institute of Planners' Fiftieth Anniversary Award in 1967 and the American Institute of Architects' Allied Professions Medal in 1974. He was conferred honorary doctorate degrees by Stuttgart University [in Germany] and Ball State University [in Muncie, Indiana]. In 1984, shortly before his death, he became the first recipient of the most prestigious recognition in the field of planning: the Rexford G. Tugwell Award.[13]

On the evening of April 23, 1984, at his Watertown house, Lynch was happily talking with Professor Zhu Zixuan, making plans for Lynch to teach a course at Tsinghua University, in Beijing, that November. He left the next morning for his summer home on

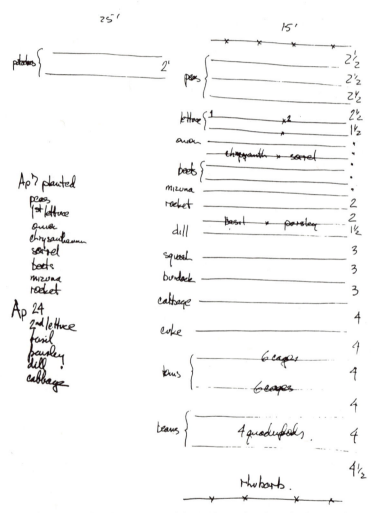

FIGURE 16.3   *The last design: a carefully laid-out plan for a kitchen garden on Martha's Vineyard.*

Martha's Vineyard. There, on April 25, 1984, he died suddenly, alone, seated before the hearth. He had spent the time immediately before his death reading, writing, and planting a garden according to his carefully drawn plan. At his side was *In My Father's Court*, by Isaac Bashevis Singer, opened to the passage where Singer describes his first visit to the country as a boy:

> I had not seen any wild cows, but what I had seen already was wonderful and strange. The sky here was not a narrow strip as on Krochmalna Street, but broad, spread out like the ocean, and it descended to the earth like a supernatural curtain. Birds flew overhead in swarms, with a twittering, a cawing, a whistling—large birds and small birds. Two storks were circling above one of the hills of the Citadel. Butterflies of all colors fluttered above the grass: white, yellow, brown, with all kinds of dots and patterns. The air smelled of earth, of grass, of the smoke of locomotives, and of something more that intoxicated me and made my head reel. There was a strange stillness here, and yet everything murmured, rustled, chirped. Blossoms fell from somewhere and settled on the lapels of my jacket. I looked up at the sky, saw the sun, the clouds, and suddenly I understood more clearly the meaning of the words of Genesis. This, then, was the world God had created: the earth, the heaven, the waters above that are separated by the firmaments from the waters below.

The works of Kevin Lynch, which have appealed to different audiences for their research, analytical, theoretical, and application values, can be seen as constituting the only extant philosophy of large-scale design. There is a need for a special group of talented designers who can conceptualize design issues at a scale larger than that of buildings or projects. "Urban design" continues to be defined as large-scale architecture, because many design practitioners—mainly architects—choose to define it that way. The architecture profession does not deal with policy; it deals with forms that can be built. Thus, any concept of large-scale design that extends beyond project-scale site plans and collections of buildings becomes too unwieldy for the vast majority of practitioners. Yet, as the quality of the urban experience continues to decline all around the world, there is a growing and urgent need for thinking about design at the city scale. Lynch not only wrote extensively in this vein but showed,

FIGURE 16.4   *Kevin Lynch, Charlotte, North Carolina, 1981.*
© MARK B. SLUDER, 1981

as in San Diego [*Temporary Paradise?*, 1974], how design guidelines can be developed for landscapes and built environments at the regional scale. His genius was many-faceted, yet our sense is that the common conception of his thoughts and works may be very limited and superficial. Many people know Lynch only as the author of *The Image of the City*. Even within the design profession, few are fully aware of his talents as a designer. And yet, in the words of his colleagues at MIT, he was "a brilliant and subtle designer, always looking for those few simple strokes which would both give form to a place and open it to the creativity of its users."[14]

Asked to talk about the failures and successes of planning on the occasion of the Tugwell Award presentation in Los Angeles in April 1984, Kevin Lynch gave a speech entitled "Localities." In this speech—

his last, as it turned out—he spoke of the need to understand the bond between place and community. He spoke of how the most successful places are those that are owned, cared for, and intensely loved by people. He felt that planning and planners had not been very effective in creating localities, and that where localities exist they have happened without much formal planning. The point, which Lynch had made in many of his writings, is that planning and design must begin with community participation, local control, and individual engagements with the immediate environment. The success of planning and design will ultimately depend on our ability to create such opportunities and environments.

NOTES

1. See, for example, Morton White and Lucia White (1962) *The Intellectual Versus the City*, New York, Mentor.
2. For a more detailed discussion of these points see Tridib Banerjee and William C. Baer (1984) *Beyond the Neighborhood Unit*, New York, Plenum, chapter 2.
3. See *A Theory of Good City Form*, Cambridge, Massachusetts, MIT Press, 1981, p. 69.
4. "Florence journals," unpublished, MIT Archives.
5. In a video interview by Ann Buttimer, then of Clark University in Worcester, Massachusetts, conducted at MIT.
6. The letters from Kevin Lynch to Frank Lloyd Wright are reprinted by courtesy of the Frank Lloyd Wright Foundation and the Archives of the History of Art at the Getty Center for the History of Art and the Humanities.
7. Frank Lloyd Wright (1982) *Letters to Apprentices/Frank Lloyd Wright; Selected and with Commentary by Bruce Brook Pfeiffer*, Fresno, California, The Press at California State University. Reprinted by permission of the publisher.
8. This essay was brought to our attention by Anne Lynch and was made available by Randolph Henning, an architect from Winston-Salem, North Carolina. Reprinted by permission of the *Capital Times*, Madison, Wisconsin.
9. From personal conversations with Tridib Banerjee.
10. Interview by Ann Buttimer.
11. For excerpts of the travel journals see *City Sense and City Design: Writings and Projects of Kevin Lynch*, edited by Tridib Banerjee and Michael Southworth, Cambridge, Massachusetts, MIT Press, 1990.
12. This distinction between substantive and nominal clients is taken from Koichi Mera (1967) "Consumer sovereignty in urban design," *Town Planning Review*, 37, 4, 305–12.

13. Established by the colleagues and students of Rexford G. Tugwell—a member of Franklin Delano Roosevelt's "brain trust" and the founder of the prestigious planning program at the University of Chicago—the award is administered by the School of Urban and Regional Planning of the University of Southern California in Los Angeles.

14. From a tribute written by MIT alumnus Stephen Carr and faculty members Lloyd Rodwin and Gary Hack for the memorial service held at Trinity Church, Copley Square, Boston, on May 14, 1984.

References

Appleyard, Donald; Lynch, Kevin; and Myer, John (1964) *The View From the Road*, Cambridge, Massachusetts, MIT Press.

Banerjee, Tridib (1993) "Anti-planning undercurrents in U. S. planning education: antithesis or ideology?" *Environment and Planning B*, 20, 519–36.

―――― and Southworth, Michael, eds. (1990) *City Sense and City Design: Writings and Projects of Kevin Lynch*, Cambridge, Massachusetts, MIT Press.

Goodey, Brian (1977) "Review of *Managing a Sense of Region*," *The Planner*, p. 121.

Gottdeiner, M., and Lagopoulos, Alexandros Ph. (1986) *The City and the Sign: An Introduction to Urban Semiotics*, New York, Columbia University Press.

Gruen, Victor (1968) "Comments on Lynch," in *Environmental Policy: The Next Fifty Years*, edited by William Ewald, Jr., Bloomington, Indiana University Press, pp. 157–61.

Jacobs, Allan (1981) "Review of *A Theory of Good City Form*," *Journal of the American Planning Association*, 47, 3, 356–7.

Knox, Paul (1992) "Review of *City Sense and City Design*," *Environment and Planning A*.

Ladd, Florence (1985) "An interview with Kevin Lynch," *Children's Environments Quarterly*, 2, 3, 4–6.

Lucid, Robert F. (1973) "Better late than never," *The American Scholar*, 42, 2, 336–8.

Lynch, Kevin (1954) "The form of cities," *Scientific American*, 190, 4, 55 ff.

―――― (1958) "Environmental adaptability," *Journal of the American Institute of Planners*, 24, 1, 16–24.

―――― (1960) *The Image of the City*, Cambridge, Massachusetts, MIT Press.

―――― (1961) "The pattern of the metropolis," *Daedalus*, 90, 1, 79–98.

―――― (1961) *Site Planning*, Cambridge, Massachusetts, MIT Press.

―――― (1965) "An analysis of the visual form of Brookline, Massachusetts," in *City Sense and City Design*, edited by Tridib Banerjee and Michael Southworth, Cambridge, Massachusetts, MIT Press, 1990, 287–315.

———— (1965) "The city as environment," *Scientific American*, 213, 3, 209–14.

———— (1966) "Quality in city design," in *Who Designs America?*, edited by Laurence Holland, New York, Doubleday.

———— (1966) "Sensuous criteria for highway design," in *City Sense and City Design*, edited by Tridib Banerjee and Michael Southworth, Cambridge, Massachusetts, MIT Press, 1990, 563–78.

———— (1968) "City design and city appearance," in *Principles and Practice of Urban Planning*, edited by William I. Goodman and Eric C. Freund, Washington, D.C., International City Management Association.

———— (1968) "The possible city," in *Environment and Policy*, edited by William R. Ewald, Jr., Bloomington, Indiana, Indiana University Press.

———— (1968) "The urban landscape of San Salvador: environmental quality in an urbanizing region," in *City Sense and City Design*, edited by Tridib Banerjee and Michael Southworth, Cambridge, Massachusetts, MIT Press, 1990, 205–25.

———— (1972) "The openness of open space," in *The Arts of Environment*, edited by Gyorgy Kepes, New York, Braziller.

———— (1972) *What Time Is This Place?* Cambridge, Massachusetts, MIT Press.

———— (1973) "City and regional planning," *Enciclopedia Italiana*.

———— (1973) *Looking At the Vineyard*, Martha's Vineyard, Massachusetts, Vineyard Open Land Foundation.

———— (1974) "Urban design," *Encyclopedia Britannica*, 15th edition.

———— (1975) "Controlling the location and timing of development," in *The Transfer of Development Rights: A New Technique of Land Use Regulation*, edited by Jerome Rose, New Brunswick, New Jersey, Center for Urban Policy Research, Rutgers University.

———— (1975) "Grounds for utopia," in *Responding to Social Change*, edited by Basil Honikman, Stroudsburg, Pennsylvania, Dowden Hutchinson and Ross.

———— (1976) *Managing the Sense of a Region*, Cambridge, Massachusetts, MIT Press.

———— (1977) *Growing Up in Cities*, Cambridge, Massachusetts, MIT Press.

———— (1980) "City design: what it is and how it might be taught," *Urban Design International*, 1, 2, 48–53.

———— (1981) *A Theory of Good City Form*, Cambridge, Massachusetts, MIT Press.

———— (1983) "What will happen to us?" *Space and Society*, 22, 87–97.

———— (1984) "Coming home: the urban environment after nuclear war," in *The Counterfeit Ark: Relocation for Nuclear War*, edited by J. Leaning and L. Keyes, New York, Ballinger.

———— (1985) "Reconsidering *The Image of the City*," in *Cities of the Mind*, edited by Lloyd Rodwin and Robert Hollister, New York, Plenum, 1984.

———— (1990) *Wasting Away*, edited by Michael Southworth, San Francisco, California, Sierra Club Books.

———— and Appleyard, Donald (1974) *Temporary Paradise? A Look at the Special Landscape of the San Diego Region*, San Diego, California, San Diego City Planning Department.

———— and Banerjee, Tridib (1975) "On people and places: a comparative study of the spatial environment of adolescence," *Town Planning Review*, 47, 105–15.

———— and Banerjee, Tridib (1976) "Growing Up in Cities," *New Society*, 37, 722, 281–4.

———— and Carr, Stephen (1968) "Where learning happens," *Daedalus*, 97, 4, 1277–91.

———— and Carr, Stephen (1979) "Open space: freedom and control," in *Urban Open Spaces*, edited by L. Taylor, New York, Cooper-Hewitt Museum.

———— and Herr, Philip (1973) "Performance zoning: the small town of Gay Head tries it," in *Performance Zoning*, edited by Lane Kendig et al., Chicago, Illinois, American Planning Association.

———— and Lukashok, Alvin K. (1956) "Some childhood memories of the city," *Journal of the American Institute of Planners*, 22, 3, 144–52.

———— and Rivkin, Malcolm (1959) "A walk around the block," *Landscape*, 8, 3, 24–34.

———— and Rodwin, Lloyd (1958) "A theory of urban form," *Journal of the American Institute of Planners*, 24, 4, 201–14.

———— and Southworth, Michael (1974) *Designing and Managing the Strip*, Cambridge, Massachusetts, Harvard-MIT Joint Center for Urban Studies.

Nelson, George (1975) "City time, city space," *Technology Review*, 78, July/August, 66–7.

Pipkin, John S. (1983) "Structuralism and the uses of cognitive images in urban planning," in *Remaking the City: Social Science Perspectives on Urban Design*, edited by J. S. Pipkin, M. E. La Gory, and J. R. Blau, Albany, New York, SUNY Press, pp. 51–76.

Rodwin, Lloyd and Hollister, Robert, eds. (1984) *Cities of the Mind*, New York, Plenum.

Singer, Isaac Bashevis (1962) *In My Father's Court*, New York, Farrar Straus & Giroux.

17

FROM CIVIC WORKER TO
CITY PLANNER
WOMEN AND PLANNING, 1890–1980

EUGENIE LADNER BIRCH

We scorn this ill-conceived conference. While the profession claims to be trying to humanize its practice, the conference panel topics and the resource people are a denial of this claim. Discussions of the inner city, of minorities in the profession of land use policies and of neighborhood planning all affect women and community people intimately. Women who are a legitimate constituency and an invaluable resource have been dealt with by the conference only as "wives" of "delegates," shunted off to . . . department stores and museums . . . (only) 15 to 20 percent of all planners and urban specialists are female. Why indeed are not all planning commissions 50 percent female to accurately represent the constituencies of the urban community? We deplore the planning that is done by men. It takes little account of the needs of women . . . (who) should be the guiding force for human communities.[1]

THIS SHARP CRITIQUE, read at the 1970 annual meeting of the American Society of Planning Officials (ASPO) by a representative of the newly formed Women's Caucus, was thoroughly predictable in its timing and content. Paralleling similar protest from women in other occupations, it reflected the impact of the mid-century feminist movement on the planning profession. Not since the presuffrage days at the turn of the century had women been so vocal about their needs and concerns.[2] Much of the action resulted from a quiet revolution in female roles, expressed by the increasing participation of women in the labor force (by 1970 43 percent of all women were working) and by a growing discontent with what some women considered the forced domesticity of the suburbs (documented so vividly by Betty Friedan in the *Feminine Mystique*).[3] The National Organization for Women (NOW), founded in 1966 and aided by the antisex discrimination clause to Title VII of the 1964 Civil Rights Act, began to press for equality in education and employment. Women defined themselves as an oppressed minority and shaped their protests on the civil rights model.[4] Part of their campaign was to publicize evidence of sexual discrimination. This tactic gained the attention of many professional groups, including the planners, whose examinations of their own field led to organized outrage. The statement of the Women's Caucus, then, grew out of this reformist urge.

Aside from professional discrimination, a second and equally significant theme in the Women's Caucus petition was the claim to gender-related expertise. Women, they stated, should be the "guiding force for human communities."[5] In the tradition of the late nineteenth century, the protesters listed activities where domestic knowledge gave women dominance. Access to work for the now heavily female labor force, for example, and questions of residential planning should be included in women's issues along with more conventional concerns: child care, community services, and employment conditions.

While these two themes, professional access and gender-related expertise, reflected the unique mid-century version of American feminism, they had not appeared independently but were the product of the previous eighty years. Furthermore, they echoed another refrain recently proclaimed in the planning profession: the need to recognize the field's pluralistic nature, a view articulated by Paul Davidoff and Thomas A. Reiner, whose 1962 essay, "A Choice Theory of Planning," was well accepted in the profession by 1970.[6]

The actions of the women planners of the 1970s reflected the larger trends of society and their profession, just as did the work of their predecessors who helped advance the cause of planning in the early twentieth century. An evaluation of female participation in planning must therefore draw both on the history of planning and on general women's history. It also requires an analysis of two phenomena in the history of planning: first, its rise as a profession encompassing an area of expertise, an educational tradition, and a self-regulating component; and second, its acceptance by the public as a legitimate exercise of government power.

In the first area, professional development, women clearly had little direct impact.[7] Through 1940 only one woman held full membership in the American Institute of Planners, the field's credentialing society.[8] (By the same token, few women participated in the growth of any of the traditional professions, including law, medicine, architecture, and engineering.[9]) However, some individual females did make important indirect contributions in shaping the field. As librarians, executive secretaries, and in other positions, they helped form the intellectual content and participated in the administrative aspects of the field. The careers of Theodora Kimball Hubbard, Charlotte Rumbold, and Elisabeth Herlihy illustrate this type of activity. In the second area, acceptance by the public, women played a far more important role, garnering community support and providing financial backing at critical points. Into this category fall club activity, philanthropy, and public relations, all open to women. The work of the General Federation of Women's Clubs, the Russell Sage Foundation and the Spelman Fund, and Harlean James of the American Civic Association exemplify this aspect. Finally, the fact that there were enough women to form a caucus in 1970 is evidence that women did enter the profession during the postwar period. They entered slowly, and despite equal training did not advance as quickly as their male counterparts. They would provide the critical mass of supporters for the call for reform.

WOMEN AND PLANNING AT THE TURN OF THE CENTURY

Planning was the product of late-nineteenth-century progressive reform efforts. Although it had many roots, one of its earliest tangible forms was the 1893 Chicago World's Fair which many regard as a visible precedent for the wave of civic improvement then sweeping the country that culminated in the planning movement in the early twentieth century. Drawing from many strands, from municipal arts to sanitation, cities of all sizes sought to create well-ordered, beautiful urban environments administered in an economic and rational manner. By the late 1920s planning which originated as a private-sector effort had become a legitimate exercise of local government power.[10]

Its primary concern was to direct the physical development of the city. Several organizations promoted its aims—the American Civic Association (ACA) founded in 1904, the National Conference on City Planning (NCCP) created in 1909, the American City Planning Institute (ACPI) formed in 1917, and subsections of the American Society of Civil Engineers (ASCE) and the American Institute of Architects (AIA).[11] The emerging field was explained to supporters and practitioners in periodicals such as *The American City* magazine, started in 1909, and *The City Plan*, originated in 1915, and its successor, *City Planning Quarterly*; and in several basic books, including Benjamin Marsh's *An Introduction to City Planning* (1909), Charles Mulford Robinson's *The Improvement of Towns and Cities* (1907), John Nolen's *Replanning Small Cities* (1912), and *Carrying Out the City Plan* (1914) by Flavel Shurtleff and Frederick Law Olmsted, Jr.[12]

At this time, the technical aspects of city planning practice were clearly in the male domain and were taught in schools of architecture or engineering. At first professionals in these areas purveyed their services to private groups, primarily chambers of commerce, the most notable example being Daniel Burnham's contract with the Commercial Club of Chicago to produce a comprehensive plan. Later, with the proliferation of planning commissions, they consulted directly with cities.

City planning spread rapidly because it was sought by urbanites, who by 1920 were the majority of the nation's population. The demand did not rise spontaneously but derived from multiple sources.

Historians have documented the role of businessmen's groups but few have outlined the quite substantial contributions of women. In the thirty-year span between 1890 and 1920, groups of women had become highly active in civic affairs. Predominantly college-educated, a rarity at the beginning of the period, they created clubs to recapture the intellectual life and companionship of their undergraduate years, to justify their education, and partly to seek the control over their environments that would ultimately lead to their enfranchisement in 1920.

The club network was vast.[13] By 1909, for example, the General

Federation of Women's Clubs claimed 800,000 members in more than 495 affiliates.[14] In addition, women belonged to other groups, such as the American Association of University Women, the Women's Division of the National Civic Federation, local municipal art societies, and general civic improvement organizations.

Despite much public skepticism, the movement of women into public affairs gained momentum. In 1912, *The American City* magazine dedicated a complete issue to the phenomenon. In a lengthy preface, entitled "The old order changeth," the editor sought to reassure his subscribers (90 percent men): "How needless was the widespread fear that woman's attempt to spell the task (of civic work) would work havoc to the social structure." In fact, he claimed, the opposite occurred because the distinctive feminine view, "often the reverse of man's," had made "the ideal city a practical reality . . . (for) we are coming to learn that the term city implies of necessity concentration of population but it does not of necessity imply ugliness, squalor or disease."[15]

At this time, a clear division existed by mutual consent between men's and women's civic activities. In the effort to gain acceptance, women had consciously claimed certain urban problems as their own. For example, likening the metropolis to "a home, clean and beautiful," Eva Perry Moore, longtime president of the General Federation of Women's Clubs, maintained that congestion and competition, two earmarks of the early-twentieth-century city, particularly affected mothers because they hindered homemaking efforts. Therefore, she argued, women should extend their domestic roles to ameliorate the municipal environment. In specific terms, they should view their urban mission as achieving the "City Cleanly, City Sanitary, and City Beautiful." Although the "vast army" of club workers whom Moore addressed were essentially elite, they, like all good progressives, believed their efforts would reach across the social structure to provide "a future gain to every class of society."[16]

One of the first national efforts to be organized by women was at the 1893 Chicago World's Fair. The planning of the Exposition had been delegated by Congress to an all-male commission headed by Daniel H. Burnham. Nevertheless, women gained a foothold by forcing Congress to appoint a 115-member Board of Lady Managers, who were to award the site and an appropriation for a women's headquarters building on the fairgrounds. The Board, headed by Bertha H. Palmer (wife of a wealthy Chicago hotelier) who had been long involved in civic work, soon expanded the women's narrow mission. With Burnham's consent they sponsored a national competition for the design of the Women's Building, as the project was bluntly called, awarding the commission to a twenty-two-year-old Massachusetts Institute of Technology (MIT) graduate, Sophia G. Hayden, who later won the Fair's Artist's Medal for her design. All the work in the building was done by women. For example, the Board commissioned Mary Cassatt, the expatriate American artist, and Mary MacMonnies, the wife of Frederick MacMonnies who sculpted the Fair's fountain, to execute two massive murals for the main gallery.

Not content merely to sponsor a resting place for female visitors, as Congress had envisioned, the Board made their building as important as the other exhibition halls. They filled it with gender-related resources, including a seven thousand–volume library, a survey of women's social and economic position in forty-seven countries, and a model kitchen filled with appliances designed to lighten domestic chores. In addition, the Board financed the nearby Children's Building for day care. Once the Exposition opened, they scheduled lectures, conferences, and demonstrations.[17]

Like their counterparts in the growing, locally based civic movement, the Lady Managers succeeded because of the personal influence of their leaders, their strong organization, and their care to frame their work in terms of women's domestic functions. Using a conservative definition of female roles, they brought their interests into the public view under the cloak of domesticity: in addition to examples of women's crafts they also provided demonstrations about women's suffrage and the entry of women into the professions.

Male observers supported the women's claim that their civic work was merely an extension of their domestic duties. While *The American City* editor writing about the 1912 "women's number" implored his readers to "examine this issue with care," he bid them to "place it within the proper context." Every woman, he reminded them, "realizes that she cannot make an ideal *home* without the right kind of house":

This much the American woman has known for generations, [he continued] but a greater vision is now being raised before her . . . she has come to realize that no home liveth unto itself alone. She has come to see that the physical things of the city affect every home in it and that to her, as the homemaker, the improving of these municipal conditions is of vital concern.[18]

Within municipal affairs club women of the time had diverse interests. The General Federation therefore devised separate departments (Civics, Health, Education). However, early on the whole Federation came to support city planning, believing that their independent efforts in sanitation, hygiene, playground construction, child welfare, and outdoor art could be accomplished only within a broader framework. By 1912, Alice Davis Moulton, chairman of the Federation's Civic Department, had articulated their position:

> To designate any one phase as the fundamental requirement in a movement so pregnant with virtual issues as the civic movement is most difficult, but authorities on civics agree that a city plan is a fundamental requirement for comprehensive civic improvement.[19]

Pledging the backing of the national Civic Department, she called for the local branches to contribute the grass-roots support necessary for the expansion of planning into municipalities. She bid her followers to "secure universal interest in city planning (and give) an impetus to civic betterment that ultimately would lay the cornerstone for the future."[20]

Although the disenfranchised women had no direct political or economic clout, they argued that their impartial views on planning and other reform issues were untainted by selfish motives and therefore more impressive. Typical was the accomplishment of Whytheville, Virginia, women who despite having "to contend with man's tendency to subvert everything to a monetary basis," had successfully campaigned for a town park. In the same mode, Mildred Chadsey, chief inspector of the Cleveland Bureau of Sanitation, claimed "women can successfully divorce work from politics," thereby making their projects respectable. Many men concurred with this assessment. George B. Dealey, vice president and general manager of the *Dallas News*, attributed women's civic achievements to their "sincerity of purpose." Furthermore, he recognized a certain rationale in their choice of projects when he reported that they "have never undertaken an enterprise that was not vital, timely, and practical (which) did not appeal to the public as sane and just."[21]

As women became increasingly secure of their place in civic affairs, they enlarged the scope of their interests and undertook increasingly sophisticated projects. Correspondingly, as their efforts grew more ambitious, their support for city planning became more significant. In the beginning, they had concentrated on high visibility and short-term, easily defined commitments. Cleanup campaigns were typical; for these efforts they organized parades, rallies, refuse collection days, and planting ceremonies for all citizens, young and old. They soon moved to more substantial endeavors, often raising funds for them. In 1914 Zona Gale reflected on the significance of this trend: "the most potent and least indirect way of cooperation at present in woman's power is actually to inaugurate and pay for the particular advances which they are advocating." Using traditional means, such as holding bazaars, serving home-cooked meals at county fairs, and performing in "ladies minstrel shows" they raised thousands of dollars in countless communities to support their chosen causes.[22]

Park projects were a frequent choice. Observing that "only too often American villages have grown up into towns and become great cities before it was remembered to set apart suitable space for a community rallying center, the real-estate excesses having swallowed up every last vacant lot," they condemned the thoughtless greed of their male counterparts and called for more open space to relieve congestion and minimize the insalubrious effects of competition. These sympathies coincided with park schemes proposed by professional planners. For example, in Dallas, Texas, the women's clubs equipped two playgrounds and paid the salaries of recreation supervisors in two problem neighborhoods. In the process they created a recreation association which soon affiliated with the city's Park Board and Board of Education to promote the park system called for by George E. Kessler in his "City Plan for Dallas." In conjunction with the early-twentieth-century parks movement, they supported "social centers"—the use of neighborhood schools for off-hour recreational and assembly purposes—long before this idea become the nucleus of the neighborhood unit concept articulated by Clarence Perry and adopted by technical city planners in the 1930s.[23]

The unity between women and professional city planners is even more closely drawn in the analysis of civic beautification schemes. From Los Angeles to Tampa to Lock Haven (Pennsylvania), city residents moved to improve their town centers. Women's clubs frequently stimulated professional efforts to replan an area, often consulting with leading designers John Nolen and Charles Mulford Robinson.[24]

In later years Ladislas Segoe, longtime Cincinnati planner, related the continuity of the tradition of women's clubs' support for planning well into the twentieth century:

> The typical start of a planning program in a community had its origin in some members of a garden club, who read something maybe in a foreign publication about something called planning and next, taking the Cincinnati newspaper, they found out that there is a guy called Segoe in Cincinnati who was a planner. Now we had to have some speaker at the garden club . . . so why not call up this Segoe guy and see whether he is willing to come . . . and talk to us about planning? Well, the date had been agreed upon, the speech was dutifully made, and then nothing happened for several months, and then you got a call from the League of Women Voters . . . and after that . . . then came a call from the members of some other . . . club. . . . Then . . . somebody . . . suggested if I come down for a day that he could introduce me to somebody in the city hall. . . . Now by that time . . . the groundwork had been laid . . . and . . . planning had managed to take root.[25]

With increasing involvement in civic affairs, women gained recognition as legitimate forces in the community and participated in the activities and boards of local and national organizations. As early as 1909, Richard B. Watrous, secretary of the ACA, ascribed "to the enthusiasm, the untiring efforts and practical suggestions" of women the "splendid headway attained by general improvement propaganda." In his opinion, their most important accomplishment was to promote the vision of a desirable urban environment. "Hundreds of cities, that have distinguished themselves for notable achievements," he claimed, "can point to some society . . . of women that have been the first inspiration to do things."[26]

Additional examples of women's participation in a sphere wider than the clubs come from many cities. For example, at St. Louis in 1912 women had prominent positions on the program of a three-day civic conference. In Los Angeles, they occupied two slots on the five-member board of the Municipal Art Commission, the body that ordered the first city plan for the West Coast metropolis. And in

Boston, they contributed a major demonstration at the famed "Boston 1915" exhibition, sponsored by leading businessmen of the city.[27]

Although the general population unquestioningly accepted women's skill in specific domestic-related areas, popular sentiment strictly circumscribed their performance in the public arena, on the basis that their primary duties were familial and their services supplementary. Consequently, while women would provide the "head and heart" in municipal affairs, men were to be the administrators and implementors of urban policy.[28] The most common view saw women contributing their leisure time to this work. In 1912, the editor of *The American City* clearly expressed this sentiment when he discussed the role of members of women's clubs. Noting that in American cities there were "thousands of women whose housework did not need all their time," he argued that such women had "time and ability for the research and experimental work which should usually precede any radical enlargement of municipal activities." When they had demonstrated "the wisdom of their pioneer work," he concluded, "they may properly turn over to the city the administration of the enterprise . . . and direct their energies to other community needs."[29]

Most women agreed with this limited role. A few, however, did not, and turned their expertise into full-time professional positions. Caroline Bartlett Crane of Kalamazoo, Michigan, for example, marketed herself as a "municipal housekeeper" and consulted on street cleaning in over fifty cities.[30] Wisconsin activist Zona Gale defined and promoted the paid position of "civic organizer" and in 1913 wrote a handbook, *Civic Improvement in the Little Towns*, for those communities unable to afford a professional.[31] Finally, by 1916 the ACA had hired an energetic young woman, Maud Van Buren, as a community organizer. In this job she traveled widely, lecturing and giving advice on organizational strategy, and wrote extensively instructing women to become informed about town ordinances and municipal budgets. She urged them to participate in city planning decisions and to question public officials about the priorities set by their expenditures. Yet even she couched her pleas in familiar terms: "The budget, the city's financial measures for each year, is surely not beyond the comprehension of the woman who conducts her own household expenses on a systemized basis."[32]

A few rare voices called for more women to join the professional ranks. In 1912 chief inspector of the Cleveland Bureau of Sanitation Mildred Chadsey observed that "town planning, transportation, street cleaning and lighting, water supply, sewage systems, and garbage disposal are all questions of 'domestic economy.'" It seemed only logical and fitting, she concluded, "to find women specialists along these lines, as well as men."[33] Yet as the second decade of the twentieth century closed, although women were beginning to make some professional inroads, they did not gain entry to city planning.[34]

By 1917, the city planning movement had divided into two wings: the citizen participants, who remained in the broad based NCCP and its affiliated group, the ACA; and the professionals—twenty-four men in all—who created the ACPI. The ACPI was consciously created to "study the science and advance the art of city planning" by means of discussions of technical subjects at meetings limited to qualified participants whose credentials had to include specified professional education, several years of paid city planning experience, and a vaguely defined "comprehensive view" of the city. Although torn by internal differences about the precise definition of these criteria, the original members were clear about one item: they were professionals, not reformers or citizen activists.[35]

Women simply did not qualify for membership in the ACPI. They had no professional education, their practical experience was volunteer, their projects tended to be narrowly focused, not comprehensive in scale, and they were avowed reformers who always left technical decisions to the experts. Thus as the movement split into the two sectors, women continued to participate in the citizen wing. In fact, the ACA would soon hire a young women, Harlean James, to head its daily administration.

As the practitioners adopted their professional stance, they tended to become more efficiency-minded and less humanistic, being concerned mainly with overall land use issues, traffic engineering, and zoning. Perhaps the diminished attention to the social welfare and aesthetic aspects of the field could be related to the lack of female participation in the ACPI. More likely, however, was the overall decline of citizen participation in the public sphere. As the general move for reform in the progressive era petered out, would-be crusaders, male and female, turned to personal self-fulfillment rather than social change. After 1920 women tended to be far less active in the civic affairs of their clubs and their communities.

In the planning field, the emerging professionals focused on differentiating between the layperson and the expert; seeking consulting jobs as well as professional standing, they identified a marketable product—the master plan and its implementing arm, the zoning ordinance—which only they could prepare. In this way they widened the gulf between the professional and the ordinary citizen, removing themselves from the arena of civic action and citizen input, and thrust themselves into the government advisory role which constituted most of their business in the 1920s.

Women and Planning in the 1920s

With the decline of interest in civic affairs in the 1920s, middle- and upper-class women devoted themselves to domestic issues, especially marriage and motherhood. A symbolic end to their earlier agitation for social reform was the achievement of female suffrage in 1920. The strategists for the enfranchisement campaign had early opted to keep their work narrowly focused on the vote, eliminating from discussion other issues relating to more basic structural reorganization of female roles, a policy wise in the short term but imprudent in the long term. Consequently, after the passage of the Nineteenth Amendment, the leaders declared victory and submerged their efforts by transforming their activist lobbying group, the National American Women's Suffrage Association (NAWSA), into the nonpartisan League of Women Voters.[36]

Concurrently, other female club and organizational networks tended to focus on domestic issues. In 1929, for example, the American Association of University Women disbanded its ten-year-old National Housing Committee, which had supported a federal workers' housing program, and replaced it with another more directly concerned with campus affairs.[37] Despite this trend, the civic clubs did not completely die out. Some of them carried on with a narrowed focus and became more institutionalized by hiring executive secretaries to oversee their daily administration. Representatives from the previous generation of well-educated, single women frequently filled these low-paying although highly responsible positions.

Despite their lack of participation in the professional side of planning, women were not totally without influence in the planning movement. A few, such as librarians and executive secretaries or clericals who advanced in rank, participated through their positions as service professionals. The careers of four are illustrative of this activity: Theodora Kimball (1897–1935), librarian of the Harvard School of Design and later wife of Henry V. Hubbard, head of the first planning degree program; Charlotte Rumbold (1865–1960), lobbyist, administrative assistant, and citizen activist in Cleveland; Harlean James (1877–1969), executive secretary of the ACA (later the American Planning and Civic Association) for almost forty years; and Elisabeth Herlihy (1880–1953), secretary of the Boston Planning Commission from its inception in 1913 until her appointment to the chair of the Massachusetts State Planning Board, a position she held until 1950.

THEODORA KIMBALL

More than a librarian, Theodora Kimball used her position as a vehicle to make major intellectual contributions to the newly emerging planning field. After education at the Girls' Latin School of Boston and graduation from Simmons College, she joined the staff of the Harvard Library in 1908. At age twenty-nine, seeking additional professional training, she returned to Simmons to earn that institution's first Master's Degree in Library Science.[38]

Although involved in her field, she was clearly more interested in academic pursuits and turned to writing until her untimely death in 1935. By 1917 she had coauthored textbooks in city planning and landscape architecture. After that she edited two volumes of the professional papers of Frederick Law Olmsted, Sr.; produced the annual survey of city and regional planning, which had first appeared in 1912 in *Landscape Architecture* and later *City Planning* journals founded by Hubbard; assembled city planning bibliographies for *The American City*, the *National Municipal Review*, the U.S. Department of Commerce Advisory Commission on Zoning and the President's Conference on Homebuilding and Homeownership; and produced numerous book reviews for *City Planning*, of which she was an editor.[39]

Kimball wrote her most significant book, *Our Cities, Today and Tomorrow*, an outgrowth of her annual surveys, in collaboration with Hubbard whom she had married in 1924.[40] Both the book and the reports synthesized city planning progress in the United States and defined the central issues of the field. Kimball wrote not as a reporter but as a critic, assigning priority to topics she considered

FIGURE 17.1   *Theodora Kimball Hubbard.*

crucial. The reports usually started with her assessment of current progress, based on the number of zoning and planning commissions founded, outstanding publications, and the status of special concerns: regional planning, transportation, parks and recreation, and civic center development. She favorably reviewed implementation schemes such as zoning and capital budgeting and provided ample illustrations of model projects. She compiled practical instruction material for practitioners and students of the new field.

Kimball established a scholarly tradition emulated by many women. Among them were Katherine McNamara, Kimball's protégé and successor at Harvard, whose career spanned several decades; Lucille Keck, librarian of the Charles E. Merriam Library at the Chicago offices of the ASPO and its sister organizations; and Mary Vance, former head of the Council of Planning Librarians who expanded the field's research potential by editing thousands of planning-related bibliographies.

CHARLOTTE RUMBOLD

A second group active in the field were executive secretaries of planning or civic organizations. While it is difficult to judge the influence of these women because of the ephemeral nature of their work, Charlotte Rumbold and Harlean James do stand out. Both had a strong commitment to citizen-based efforts, a personally based network of contacts in planning, a strong organizational legacy, and a series of legislative accomplishments. They were both unmarried college graduates who entered planning through an initial interest in housing reform.

Rumbold, born in St. Louis and educated at the University of Missouri, immersed herself in civic activities, including supervision of a pioneering housing study for St. Louis. She later became Supervisor of Recreation, a municipal position from which she resigned in 1915 after a battle with the city council who refused to pay her at an equal rate with a male counterpart.[41]

Following the unpleasantness in St. Louis, she resettled in Cleveland where she had moved to supervise a slum survey. Through this work she became interested in city planning and took an administrative position at the Chamber of Commerce, combining two functions, assistant secretary and secretary of the City Planning

Committee. In 1919, she helped found the Ohio Planning Conference (OPC), a citizen-based group dedicated to the propagation of
planning. For more than two decades, Rumbold was the OPC's
guiding light. Serving in various capacities (secretary/treasurer 1919–25,
vice president 1925–8, president 1928–30, and secretary 1938–43), her
most notable efforts were as a registered lobbyist in the 1920s.[42]
Supported by contributions from OPC's meager $500 annual bud-
get, she successfully rallied support for the basic state enabling
legislation to establish local planning commissions, comprehensive
zoning, and subdivision regulations.

Although interested in local planning through the 1930s, as
indicated by her tenure on the Cleveland Planning Commission,
Rumbold devoted much energy to housing, working for the first
laws authorizing public housing, state park development, and state
planning.[43] After her retirement in 1943 she continued to support the
citizen role in planning until her death in 1960. Early in her career,
she had made a clear distinction between citizens and technical
planners, in which she emphasized the important role of citizens
"who want to learn not to make a city plan . . . but how to put a city
plan in force."[44] It was to this constituency that Rumbold directed
her efforts.

HARLEAN JAMES

Sharing Rumbold's views was Harlean James, executive secretary of
the ACA. She too believed that public education in city planning
was crucial to the advance of the field. Many early city plans "lay
unused on the shelves of public libraries or hidden in the back of
desk drawers," she observed. Planners tended to "despise the homely, everyday knowledge of the residents in the towns and cities in
which they were working," putting forth proposals which could "be
easily challenged by ordinary everyday people with no special knowledge
and little insight into the future." She therefore urged the ACA to
create linkages between citizens and professionals.[45] Like Rumbold,
she had developed these ideas from her own experiences as a long-
time worker in civic affairs. Born in 1877, she graduated from
Stanford University in 1898 and became the executive secretary of
the Women's Civic League of Baltimore. In this position she encountered a wide range of issues, from health to housing to public art. She

FIGURE 17.2 *Harlean James.*
DEPARTMENT OF MANUSCRIPTS AND UNIVERSITY ARCHIVES,
OLIN LIBRARY, CORNELL UNIVERSITY

next served as executive secretary of the U.S. Housing Corporation, the wartime defense housing agency. After the Armistice, she took the same position with the ACA. Her interest in city planning, which had been stimulated in Baltimore and later enriched by her experience with the enlightened designs of the defense housing settlements, inspired her prior to her ACA assignment to write a popular book, *The Building of Cities*.[46]

James was an energetic woman of executive ability who made the ACA an influential force in planning. Working closely with its successive presidents, particularly Frederic A. Delano, the wealthy Chicago businessman who was among the original sponsors of the Chicago Plan of 1909 and uncle of the rising politician Franklin Delano Roosevelt, she focused ACA activities on the major issues of local comprehensive planning and protection of natural resources. In furthering these efforts, James organized nationwide support for the passage of the federal legislation creating the National Capital Park and Planning Commission (later the National Capital Planning Commission) in 1926. She also urged U.S. Secretary of Commerce Herbert Hoover to form the Division of Building and Housing which issued the exemplary state enabling legislation for planning and zoning, and she actively supported the work of the National Park Service, the U.S. Department of Interior agency that the ACA had strenuously lobbied for prior to her arrival.[47]

As executive secretary, James edited a steady stream of publications, including the monthly *Civic Comment* and the *American Planning and Civic Annual* which featured commissioned essays and an extensive annotated honor roll of civic achievers. She was a prolific author of articles, news notes, book reviews for sympathetic journals, textbooks, and other propagandistic materials. Her *Land Planning in the United States for City, State and Nation*, commissioned by noted land economist Richard T. Ely, was a factual readable book which blended the most current technical information with homely, practical advice.[48]

James's most important work, however, was the least tangible. During her thirty-seven-year tenure at the ACA, she built an extensive network of legislators, planning professionals, and civic leaders by whom the force of her opinion would be felt in planning issues, most notably in land use decisions in Washington, D.C. In 1954, her long association with the ACA gained a measure of national recognition when ASPO gave her one of its three awards for that year.[49]

ELISABETH HERLIHY

Among the other ASPO award winners in 1954 was Elisabeth Herlihy, also cited for her thirty-seven-year career as a Massachusetts planning official. Herlihy, who had the distinction of being for many years the sole woman member of the ACPI, had entered planning through an unusual route. The precocious daughter of Irish immigrant parents, she graduated as valedictorian of her high school class at age fifteen. After secretarial training in Boston she remained there to work. In her spare time she wrote short stories and essays, many of which appeared in *The Republic*, a publication owned by John F. Fitzgerald. When Fitzgerald became Mayor of Boston he hired her as his secretary. She quickly rose to chief clerk where she reigned over much of the city's administrative work. In 1913, she briefed Fitzgerald about newly passed city planning enabling legislation and persuaded him to make her secretary of the commission, a position she held until 1935 when she was appointed chair of the Massachusetts Planning Board. (She remained on the Boston City Planning Commission as a commissioner until her retirement in 1950.) In addition, in 1924 she became clerk of the Board of Zoning Appeals created to administer the city's first comprehensive zoning ordinance.[50]

Through this administrative work, attendance at American planning meetings, and frequent study trips abroad, Herlihy taught herself planning.[51] In 1927 the ACPI overlooked her lack of official credentials when it admitted her as a member, although many of her ACPI colleagues disagreed with her basic attitudes toward planning as summarized in a newspaper comment: "There's nothing sacred about planning . . . it's just common sense."[52]

Over the years, Herlihy gained the respect of her colleagues, who admired her staying power through successive mayors. They also recognized her power as the confidante of the leaders who relied on her advice for planning and zoning commission appointments and other sensitive land use decisions. "Mayors came and went," one observer noted, "but Elisabeth Herlihy was as permanent as the planning board."[53]

In addition to her administrative duties, Herlihy worked hard to publicize planning. "There is scarcely an organization in Boston nor a city or town in the metropolitan district she has not spoken to," was one contemporary description, and she was credible to realtor and women's clubber alike.[54] Her faith in citizen support, akin to the approach of Rumbold and James, led her to be a founder and

FIGURE 17.3   *Miss Elisabeth Herlihy and Mrs. Moore of Boston, 1926 National Conference on City Planning, St. Petersburg, Florida.*

OLIN LIBRARY, CORNELL UNIVERSITY

executive committee member of the Massachusetts Federation of Planning Boards, which by 1929 had a membership of 107 towns representing four million people. She also operated on the national level, serving on committees for the ACPI and as a director of the ACA and ASPO. A contributor to *City Planning* and the *American Planning and Civic Annual,* she focused her writing on administration and public relations.[55]

These three women, who based their activities on citizen organization, politics, and administration, had counterparts in many other American cities. Secretaries of city planning commissions were traditionally women. Anne Robertson of New Orleans, Edyth Howard of Des Moines, and Grace Bartlett of Honolulu are examples. Although they did not advance in rank as Elisabeth Herlihy had, they played important local roles in the functioning of the planning commissions. Executive secretaries and other civic employees were also frequently women. Edith Sampson's edition of *Municipal Facts* for Denver and the work of A. Edmere Cabana of the Buffalo City Planning Association quietly nurtured public support for planning. Finally, like Rumbold and Herlihy, women did have prominent positions on commissions or associations, as may be seen in the examples of Albion Fellows Bacon, chairman of the Evansville,

Indiana, commission, and Gertrude Bosler Biddle, a director of the Tri-State Regional Planning Federation. All in all, women participated in planning in the 1920s not as technical practitioners but as publicists, administrators, and lobbyists. Barred from professional participation by social convention, they used rather low level or unpaid jobs to advantage in establishing a presence.[56]

WOMEN AND PLANNING IN THE GREAT DEPRESSION

The 1930s saw a sharp decline in the advances made by employed women. Men were favored over women, particularly married women, for the few jobs available: the federal government refused to employ more than one wage earner in a family while twenty-six states passed legislation prohibiting the employment of married women. A 1936 Gallup Poll found that 82 percent of its respondents disapproved of spouses working when their husbands were employed. By 1940 the labor force was 25 percent female. Nonetheless, professional schools set quotas for female admissions, with medical schools, for example, restricting women to 5 percent of a class, and by 1940 women professionals fell to the 1920 level of 12 percent.[57] The planning profession reflected this trend. Until well into the 1940s, the ACPI had only one female full member (in 1932 Harlean James had joined Elisabeth Herlihy on the roster but only as an associate member).[58]

Nevertheless, some slow changes occurred in the late 1930s, related to the evolution of the planning profession itself, which was beginning to have enough adherents to merit the creation of independent degree programs. In 1929, Harvard received funds from the Rockefeller Foundation to found a school of city planning. By 1937, MIT, Cornell, and Columbia had followed suit, establishing programs within their schools of architecture. MIT was the most significant program for women because it had regularly admitted women since its inception. (Harvard, in contrast, refused to admit women to its School of Design until a later date, directing females to the Cambridge School of Architecture which drew heavily on Harvard for its faculty.) Furthermore, in 1937, the exclusively female Lothorp School of Landscape Architecture, under the direction of a recent MIT graduate, John A. Parker, directed some of its students to the Institute when it moved from its Groton campus to quarters at MIT. In 1940 MIT granted master's degrees in city planning to Flora Crockett (c. 1914–1979) and Jane S. Rodman (b. 1914), its first female planning students.[59]

Crockett and Rodman typified women planners of the period. Crockett, who had earned an architecture degree at MIT in 1937, married a Briton, Gordon Stephenson, and returned to England with him. Stephenson held a series of government positions, including chief planning officer of the Ministry of City Planning, until he became professor of planning at the University of Liverpool in 1948. Subsequently he taught in Canada and Australia. Crockett, accompanying him on these ventures, not only raised a large family but practiced planning in a variety of forms. She supervised the evacuation of British children during the Second World War, collaborated with Stephenson in his written work, and coauthored two books and several reports.[60]

A similar pattern was followed by Rodman, who had an undergraduate degree from the Lothorp School/Simmons College joint program and married Richard L. Steiner. Steiner's career took them to Washington, D.C., where he worked at the U.S. Housing Authority, while Rodman completed her master's thesis, a study of a multiracial community near Howard University. At the outbreak of the war they moved to Jacksonville, Florida, where Steiner was a housing officer in the U.S. Navy. In the five years they were there, Rodman held a variety of jobs, ranging from designing camouflage for the Corps of Army Engineers to working for a private planning consultant, George Simon. In this period the couple started a family. Following the war, they went to Baltimore where Steiner worked for the city's redevelopment agency and Rodman had her third child. Given the demands of domestic life, Rodman did not work until 1947, when she joined the Baltimore County Planning Department. She remained with the agency for fifteen years, her tenure broken for a five-year period with the birth and early childhood of her fourth child. In 1962 she retired again, deciding to spend a few years at home with her rapidly growing children, and in 1968 she and Steiner divorced. As a result of her disillusionment with planning for its failure to achieve the orderly development of the county, she did not return to work. In 1972, however, she joined the Peace Corps, which exploited her planning experience even though she did not request a professional position. Assigned to Gambia, she directed the national planning office until 1977 when she returned to the United States.[61]

A contemporary of the MIT graduates, Chloethiel Woodard Smith (b. 1910) represents a different career pattern. She trained in architecture at the University of Oregon and in 1933 earned a city planning degree at Washington University. After working in Seattle, Portland, and New York City, she became chief of research and planning for the Federal Housing Administration, a position she held for three years before entering private practice. Like many of her contemporaries, she married, bore children, and shaped her career to her husband's, but she differed in having a well-established reputation before her marriage. Resettling in Washington, D.C., in 1946, she opened her own firm, Chloethiel Woodard Smith Associates, which specialized in architecture, urban design, and planning.[62] Her work has included the award-winning designs for the Washington, D.C., South West Urban Renewal Area, new town plans for Algeria, the American Embassy in Paraguay, and the Crown Tower and Crown Court in St. Louis, Missouri.[63]

Unlike the single or childless career women of the previous generation, these women planners sought to blend marriages and children with their work. Although they often collaborated or worked in fields related to their husbands', in the interest of family solidarity they took secondary positions and compromised their employment opportunities. Their professional accomplishments, though notable, were accordingly less dramatic than they might otherwise have been.

Other well-educated but not professionally trained women continued to participate at the periphery of the profession, taking leadership positions in areas defined as female concerns, in particular aesthetics and housing. The case of aesthetics is seen most clearly in the campaign to regulate highway construction and roadside improvements in the 1930s. By the middle of the decade, when car ownership had risen to 25,000,000, middle-class Americans had become increasingly reliant upon automobiles. The rush to build a satisfactory highway network resulted in uncontrolled land development characterized by the ugly, chaotic strips bordering the roads so graphically recorded in the 1939 movie, *The City*.[64] In 1933, Mrs. John D. Rockefeller gave a grant to the ACA to support the general improvement of the highways.[65] Overseen by Harlean James, the project soon caught the interest of professional planners. The ACPI created a Committee on Roadside Improvements whose members included Alfred Bettman and Robert Whitten, noted Ohio zoning experts, and E. P. Goodrich, a principal in the Technical Advisory Corporation, a consulting firm. This group made substantive legal and design suggestions which were taken up by the ACA.[66]

Concurrently, Elizabeth B. Lawton (1873–1952), a Vassar graduate long interested in conservation, created the National Roadside Council and worked with the ACA and ACPI. She directed extensive roadside surveys to gather data for planners and legislators, edited the *Roadside Bulletin*, lectured widely, and aided lobbying efforts to restrict billboards and require landscaping.[67] Harlean James committed the ACA's resources to the cause in order to integrate the work of the professional planners, the Council, and citizens' groups. She purposely defined the issue as one where women, the backbone of the ACA membership, could claim superiority. Although clearly delineating their role, she nonetheless viewed it in essentially the same manner as had been set forth a generation earlier. "The addition of women voters should bring their influence to bear in projects involving beauty," she thought, for women "seem to observe in harmonies of color more generally than men. . . . There seems to be very good promise that we may advocate projects in city planning because they add to the beauty of a city or because they protect the natural beauty of the landscape."[68] The roadside campaign received generous attention at regular ACA meetings. In addition, Rockefeller funds supported conferences for the three special interest groups—citizen activists, lobbyists, and planners.[69] The tradition of relegating this issue to women would be continued a generation later when President Lyndon B. Johnson's wife, Lady Bird, gave strong personal support to highway beautification.

In a second area, housing reform, women had more success relating their work to the planning profession, but the linkage did not occur until the 1930s. Leaders in the field included Edith Elmer Wood (1871–1945), Mary Kingsbury Simkhovitch (1867–1951), and Catherine Bauer (1905–1964). Although they had always considered housing a major part of comprehensive planning, professional planners regarded the subject as too narrow and refused to rank it with transportation, recreation, or city center development. Thomas Adams, Director of the Regional Plan for New York and Its Environs (RPNY&E) and an active policy-making member of the ACPI, reflected this view in a letter to Wood during the late 1920s. In response to her criticism of the preliminary RPNY&E reports, which gave little attention to housing, Adams wrote that housing was regarded as inherent in the whole physical structure of the city and not a separate question.[70] Wood considered this stance absurd. "The city planning and housing movements in most European countries are so closely intertwined," she observed, "that this relationship is taken for granted. In the U.S. they have had separate origins and run generally parallel courses without making much contact."[71] This was a perceptive diagnosis. Although both the movements had their roots in the progressive era, the "housers" of the 1930s tended to be social workers associated with settlement houses who promoted general welfare issues, whereas the planners tended to be technicians associated with the design and engineering professions and were interested in urban order and efficiency.

One small segment of the professional planners, the Regional Planning Association of America (RPAA), attempted to connect the issues. Not surprisingly, the RPAA members, who included Clarence Stein, Lewis Mumford, and Robert Kohn, practiced in New York City and were more closely involved with local housing than the planning movements. Propagandists for the British garden city principles, they built two communities, Sunnyside Gardens, New York, and Radburn, New Jersey, as model residential prototypes.[72]

The wide gap between the housers and the planners, which the RPAA began to narrow, continued to close in the 1930s. The passage in 1932 of the National Industrial Recovery Act (NIRA), with its provisions for housing and slum clearance, aroused the interest of the technical planners. By 1934, they helped create the National Association of Housing Officials (NAHO), a group financed by the Spelman Fund, a Rockefeller subsidiary. At the first annual NAHO meeting old-time planners Harland Bartholomew, Jacob Crane, and Walter Blucher, pulling slum clearance and housing into their sphere of interest, sought the counsel of housers.[73] Among the experts consulted was Catherine Bauer, author of the encyclopedic *Modern Housing* and head of the Labor Housing Conference, an American Federation of Labor lobbying group.[74] Bauer was a vocal advocate for the next thirty years, as planners wrestled with the implementation of housing and renewal policy.

Untrained in planning, Bauer had come to her influential position through an unconventional route. After graduating from Vassar

College in 1926, she worked at a New York publishing house where she met Lewis Mumford. Under his tutelage she developed interests in urbanism and architecture and joined the RPAA. Later, after engineering the successful legislative campaign for the 1937 Wagner-Steagall Housing Act, she became Director of Research and Information in the newly formed U.S. Housing Authority (USHA), a position she held for two years. In 1940 she resigned from the USHA and joined the faculty at the University of California at Berkeley, where she met and married architect William Wurster who in 1943 became dean of the MIT School of Architecture. Bauer accompanied him to Cambridge, holding an appointment at the Harvard School of Design. After they returned to California in 1950, she rejoined the faculty at Berkeley. From this position she monitored the American planning and housing movements which for all intents and purposes had merged.[75] A prolific writer and harsh critic, she called for a clearer statement of national housing goals. In her view, the planners had bungled the issue by confusing slum clearance aims, city fiscal exigencies, and housing needs. Bauer indicted the planners for their heavy reliance on design approaches which she believed neglected basic human needs.[76]

Although she had a dramatic impact on the ideology of the profession and prepared the way for the redefinition of the field that occurred in the mid-1960s, Bauer remained only an honorary member of the American Institute of Planners (AIP; the ACPI had adopted this name in 1938) probably because she did not meet the organization's strict educational requirements for full membership.[77]

Women and Planning through War and Peace

The entry of the United States into the Second World War dramatically altered the condition of the working woman. New jobs were generated while the draft created vacancies in the labor force. No longer regarded as intruders in the labor market, women were called upon to join in the war effort, and Rosie the Riveter and the WAC—member of the Women's Army Corps—became familiar figures as eight million women entered the labor force. When peace came the new employees and their employers were in a quandary. On the one hand, the returning soldiers would need jobs; on the other many women wished to continue working. Although the matter was resolved with massive layoffs of the female workers, the war effort left an important legacy. Women, by demonstrating that they could be responsible, reliable workers, had begun to break down discriminatory employment barriers: by 1952 two million more women were employed than at the peak of the war. Most were relegated to low-paying, low-level jobs, however, and although in the professional arena female participation increased in some fields, the overall picture was negative. By 1960, women held only 11 percent of professional positions, and most professional schools retained some form of quota on female admissions.[78]

Opportunities in the planning field paralleled these trends. During the war women had gained some new positions. For example, with a high percentage of the AIP membership in the armed forces, Barbara Terrett, assistant to the director of the ASPO, became executive secretary of the AIP and editor of the *Planners' Journal*, a position she held for two years. Women also found jobs in planning, drafting, and survey work associated with the war-stimulated growth of urban areas, such as Hampton Roads, Virginia.[79]

Finally, with ASPO's 1946 declaration that a "desperate shortage of planners" existed and "that if all the planners still in service were released tomorrow there still wouldn't be enough of them to fill the available jobs," the number of planning schools proliferated. One consequence was that this provided additional opportunities for entry but the increase was small.

For example, from 1941 to 1960 the MIT program graduated fifteen women, 7 percent of their total, while the University of North Carolina had twelve female graduates between 1946 and 1960, 10 percent of the total.[80]

During the 1950s, the female graduates of the postwar planning programs began to show up in the AIP membership roles as women jumped from two in 1940 to seventeen in 1951. The male representation rose from 170 in 1940 to over 900 in 1951. The female growth rate was proportionately much higher, but of course their absolute numbers remained low. Furthermore, in comparison to other professionals, such as lawyers, doctors, and even engineers, women planners still constituted a much smaller percentage of the total.[81]

Although the number of women was too low to allow statistical analysis of their career patterns, the records of a few demonstrate the nature of their participation in the field. They were often encouraged to specialize in areas such as housing where they were presumed to have credibility. For example, in 1948, a U.S. Department of Labor publication, *The Outlook for Women in Architecture and Engineering*, noted that "in the field of home and apartment design . . . and in public housing, women have shown special interest and facility."[82]

The women had a mixed reaction to such career prescriptions. Being a minority, they wanted to prove themselves as professionals equally qualified as their male counterparts. Yet some were not averse to use their specialized gender-related knowledge to appear more expert in certain planning situations. Carol J. Thomas, founder of her own consulting firm, Thomas Planning Services, is representative. She entered planning by an indirect route and was an early example of a type which became increasingly important in later years, the returning housewife. A Vassar College student who majored in political science, Thomas married early, had two children, and accompanied her college professor husband on various assignments, eventually residing permanently outside Boston. In 1950 she was denied admission to graduate training in public administration at Harvard because the school was reluctant to admit an older married woman seeking a part-time program. She then took planning courses at MIT, and at joint MIT–Harvard gatherings, she met a number of prominent planners, including Arthur C. Comey, who offered her part-time work, a proposal she accepted because she had children at home (and subsequently her husband had contracted a serious illness that required her presence at home). Thomas eventually parlayed her freelance work into a steady business and she established her own firm in 1956. In forming the company, Thomas blended her technical expertise as a planner with her prior domestic experience. Capitalizing on her seventeen years as a suburban housewife—"Who knows her community better than a woman?" she claimed—she specialized in land use and environment planning.[83]

Dorothy Muncy, a Washington-based planner, represents a woman who defied the feminine stereotypes. When she graduated from high school in the midst of the Depression, she could not afford to attend college. She worked at the newly formed New Jersey Housing Authority and later at the county offices of the Works Progress Administration (WPA) until she saved enough money to attend the University of Chicago where she studied social sciences. After two

years she took a job with the national WPA Women's and Professional Division where she was exposed to planning-related projects
including the Real Property Inventory. During the war she worked
for the National Youth Administration, undertaking a study of
service needs for women in the event of their official draft into the
labor force.

After the war, Muncy married and moved with her husband to
Boston, where she completed her education. She was the first
woman admitted as a planning student at Harvard's School of
Design and subsequently earned three degrees, including a Ph.D. in
city planning. She specialized in industrial land use issues because
she believed that postwar economic growth would be tied to industrial expansion, which in turn would generate the tax revenue to
subsidize public housing. Like most married women of this period,
she shaped her career to the needs of her family. When her husband
was transferred to Philadelphia, she went to work under Edmund
Bacon in the Planning Department; when he was moved to Washington, D.C., she followed, wrote her doctoral dissertation, published articles based on her findings, and developed a consulting
practice built on her industrial location expertise.[84]

The tradition of nonprofessional women making a critical intellectual contribution to the field, in the manner of Kimball and
Bauer, was continued into the 1960s by Jane Jacobs (b. 1916), the
author of *The Death and Life of Great American Cities*.[85] An associate
editor of the *Architectural Forum* and married to an architect, Robert
H. Jacobs, Jr., she had long been an observer of planning practices
and source of community opposition to several ill-conceived Greenwich Village projects. Stimulated by a concern over what she considered the major failures of planning (slum clearance, urban renewal,
and public housing) she tried to educate the professionals in urban
dynamics. Her highly personal book defined the essence of city life
as human interaction in the haphazard, physically disordered, but
socially workable, small-scale heterogeneous neighborhood. (Much
of her evidence came from matters to which she, as a woman, was
especially sensitive: childhood development, community ties, neigh-
borliness, aesthetics, and issues of personal physical safety.) Her
vision was rapidly adopted by the profession, which integrated her
views into its own theory and promoted federal legislation favoring
neighborhood preservation.[86]

PLANNING AND WOMEN IN THE 1970S AND 1980S

A massive entry of women into the work force began during the late 1960s. Stimulated by the resurgent feminist movement and the consequent affirmative action legislation, it was bolstered by federal enforcement programs and sympathetic judicial decisions. Concurrently, the national economy had so eroded that by the mid-1970s the "second paycheck" became necessary for maintaining the expectations generated in earlier years. By 1976, 47 percent of all women and 50 percent of all mothers with minor children were in the labor force. Nevertheless, women workers did not achieve a commensurate economic advance, and their overall economic position actually declined. In 1973 women's earnings were only 57 percent of men's. This trend was repeated in the professional arena as well, where the median income for women was $9,093, compared to $14,306 for men. Professional women earned only 63.6 percent as much as men.[87]

The planning profession followed the same pattern. Women entered the field in great numbers and with relative ease. The changes in public opinion which had generated the movement of women into all areas of the labor market held for planning as well. More important, however, was a dramatic transition that had occurred in the profession: by 1976 97 percent of planners were employed in the public sector; the remainder earned their income as publicly funded consultants. This employment pattern forced the planning profession to be more responsive to governmental affirmative action pressure than others, such as medicine or law. In 1976 women earned 28 percent of all planning degrees, up from 7.5 percent in 1968.[88]

Despite their high rate of entry, female planners, like their counterparts in other professions, encountered discrimination. In 1971, ASPO reported: "At no point are female planners' median salaries equal to their male counterparts' despite equal educational background and the same amount of planning experience."[89] Three years later ASPO reported that only eight women planning directors were recorded in their survey of 670 planning agencies.[90] Although the figure reflected to some degree the small pool of female planners who had enough seniority to reach the highest executive positions, when combined with the earnings figures it demonstrated the pattern of discrimination described by the Women's Caucus whose protest was recorded at the beginning of this chapter.

On the basis of this evidence, women convinced ASPO and the AIP to endorse employment and salary guidelines designed to redress the inequalities.[91] In 1974 the U.S. Department of Housing and Urban Development (HUD) and ASPO sponsored a publication, *Planning, Women and Change*, which outlined the feminist issues that had arisen in the profession: conditions of employment and definition of specific feminine concerns to be incorporated in the planning process.[92]

By 1979 women constituted a large enough block in the AIP to create a technical department, the Planning and Women Division. This had been preceded by the formation of a Women's Rights Committee in 1971 whose members contributed to the later effort. In 1980, the Division received HUD funding to sponsor a competition entitled "Planning for the changing needs of women" and produced a book documenting demonstration projects for child care, housing design and finance, transportation access, and other issues reflecting basic female concerns.[93] This inaugurated an effort to include a new perspective in planning practice, a view that had been lost years before in the separation of the NCCP and the ACPI in 1917.

By 1980, then, women had been brought into the profession through the dissolution of educational barriers. General societal trends, not any indigenous movement from within the profession, had caused the change. When women gained access, some used their position to articulate the gender-related concerns which they had formerly voiced in other vehicles, such as civic organizations and reform associations.

WOMEN AND PLANNING: AN OVERVIEW

Clearly, women as a group had few representatives among professional planners until the postwar period. Barriers to their entry were the same as those that prevented all women from having professional careers in the first half of the twentieth century: the socially approved custom of denying or limiting admission to advanced training programs; public opinion which defined the proper female role as domestic-centered and thereby restricted employment possibilities through formal and informal mechanisms; and women's own views of their societal position as wives, mothers, and volunteer workers. The long careers of Elisabeth Herlihy, Flora Crockett, Jane

Rodman, and Chloethiel Woodard Smith were unusual.

In the nonprofessional arena, women had a much longer and more significant record of activity. Their presence as allied professionals or volunteers was in keeping with societal norms, and they used this convention to participate in planning. As librarians, writers, lobbyists, and propagandists they helped to create a receptive public opinion for planning and to define the field for the professionals. The work of Kimball, Rumbold, and James is representative of these efforts. Others built their credibility by claiming areas of presumed female expertise, such as housing reform, neighborhood design, and billboard control, to inject their perspective into segments of the field. Thus the writings of Bauer and Jacobs, based on domestic knowledge, were adopted and translated into professional concerns, particularly in the area of urban renewal.

In the postwar period, women who formerly would have supplied the armies of volunteers or allied professionals gained entry to the field. The feminist movement and federal government affirmative action policies stimulated major changes in all female employment patterns and were clearly reflected in the planning profession. In some instances, the new entrants brought a consciousness of their heritage of gender-related expertise and bid their male colleagues to integrate this perspective into planning practice.

A new era of women's history has begun, as documented in the statistical evidence of educational attainment, employment, wage scales, and professional association membership. An assessment of other impacts on professional practice will have to wait until women have been involved for a longer period.

Notes

1. "Report of the Women's Caucus" (1970) *Planning 1970*, Chicago, American Society of Planning Officials, pp. 297–8.
2. See William H. Chafe (1972) *The American Woman: Her Changing Social Economic and Political Roles, 1920–1970*, New York, Oxford University Press, for a general discussion of women's changing position in American society.
3. Chafe, *The American Woman*, p. 26; Betty Friedan (1963) *The Feminine Mystique*, New York, W. W. Norton.
4. For a discussion of the antisex discrimination provision of the 1964 Civil Rights Act see Sheila M. Rothman (1978) *Woman's Proper Place: A History*

of Changing Ideals and Practices 1870 to the Present, New York, Basic Books, pp. 231–42.

5. The full quotation in which this phrase appeared articulated the full definition of how women should contribute to planning. It read: "We deplore the planning that is done by men. It takes little account of the needs of women; of their access to employment; of their requirements for child care facilities; of the kinds of homes that would be livable for them; of the kinds of communities and usable services that would make the role of wife and mother more humane. The conference has seriously downgraded the social environment of the city as a theatre for interaction and a central focus for planning. The principal actors in the residential community are women—they should be the guiding force for human communities" (Report of the Women's Caucus, p. 298).

6. Paul Davidoff and Thomas A. Reiner (1962) "A choice theory of planning," *Journal of the American Institute of Planners*, 28, 103–15.

7. Although Mary K. Simkhovitch, head of New York City's Greenwich Street Settlement House, was a guiding light in the creation of the New York City exhibition on the problems of congestion whose success would stimulate the first meeting on the National Conference on City Planning and Problems of Congestion in Washington, D.C., in 1909, her participation is diminished in the succeeding years. No other notable women appear at this time. For details about the early planning movement, see Mel Scott (1969) *American City Planning since 1890*, Berkeley and Los Angeles, University of California Press; Jon A. Peterson (1967) "The origins of the comprehensive city planning ideal in the United States, 1840–1911," Ph.D. dissertation, Harvard University.

8. Elisabeth Herlihy was elected a full member of the ACPI in 1927. (See 1939 "Roster," *Planners' Journal*.)

9. Barbara J. Harris (1978) in *Beyond Her Sphere: Women and the Professions in American History*, Westport, Connecticut, Greenwood Press, discusses this point in chapters IV and V.

10. See John Nolen, "Twenty years of city planning progress in the United States," in National Conference on Planning, *Planning Problems of Town, City and Region*, Washington, D.C.; and Theodora Kimball Hubbard and Henry Vincent Hubbard (1929) *Our Cities, Today and Tomorrow*, Cambridge, Massachusetts, Harvard University Press, for precise data on numbers of cities having comprehensive plans, zoning ordinances, and city planning commissions.

11. See Eugenie Ladner Birch (1980) "Advancing the art and science of planning: planners and their organizations, 1909–1980, "*Journal of the American Planning Association*, 46, for details.

12. See Donald A. Krueckeberg (1980) "The story of the planner's journal 1915–1980," *Journal of the American Planning Association*, 46, for an explanation of the rise of planning literature.

13. Chafe, *The American Woman*, pp. 16–17; Rothman, *Woman's Proper Place*, pp. 63–74.

14. Mrs. Frank A. Pattison (1909) "The relation of the women's club to the American city," *The American City*, 1, 129–30.

15. "The old order changeth" (1912) *The American City*, 6, 803.

16. Eva Perry Moore (1909) "Women's interest in civic welfare," *The American City*, 1, 44; Pattison, "The relation," p. 130; Mrs. Edwin F. Moulton (1909) "Municipal housekeepers," *The American City*, 1, 123–4.

17. Susana Torre, ed. (1977) *Women in American Architecture: A Historic and Contemporary Perspective*, New York, Whitney Library of Design; Jeanne Madeline Weiman (1981) *The Fair Women: The Story of the Women's Building, World's Columbian Exhibition, Chicago, 1893*, Chicago, Academy Press.

18. "The old order," pp. 801–2.

19. Alice Davis Moulton (1912) "A city plan a fundamental requirement," *The American City*, 6, 803.

20. Ibid.

21. Mary Walton Kent (1912) "From the Southern woman's point of view," *The American City*, 6, 905; Mildred Chadsey (1912) "A woman Chief of Sanitary Police," *The American City*, 6, 873; George B. Dealey (1912) "The kind of civic work that secures newspaper cooperation," *The American City*, 6, 883.

22. Mrs. George E. Bird (1916) "The parade that inaugurated a village clean up campaign," *The American City*, 14, 162–6; "Points from the women" (1909) *The American City*, 1, 133; Zona Gale (1914) "How women's clubs can cooperate with the city officials," *The American City*, 8, 537.

23. Mrs. Edwin F. Moulton (1911) "Township parks," *The American City*, 4, 217–18; Mrs. Caroline Bayard Alexander (1912) "The children at play, effective playground work at small cost," *The American City*, 6, 848; Dealey, "The kind of civic work," 6, 883; Mrs. Amalie Hofer Jerome (1911) "The playground as a social center," *The American City*, 5, 33-5; Harriet Lusk Childs (1915) "The Rochester Social Center," *The American City*, 12, 18–22; Anna Pendleton Schnenck (1915) "The need for neighborhood centers in American cities," *The American City*, 12, 337–40; Edward J. Ward (1914) "Where suffragists and anti's unite," *The American City*, 10, 519–24.

24. Mrs. Ross W. Barrows (1912) "A women's club which raised money for a city plan," *The American City*, 6, 861–2; Mrs. Imogen B. Oakley (1912) "The more civic work, the less need of philanthropy," *The American City*, 6, 805–13; John Williams Mitchell (1916) "Los Angeles: in the making," *The American City*, 2, 149–57; Elisabeth Asker (1913) "The Tampa Civic Association—its aims and work," *The American City*, 7, 619–21; Zona Gale (1913) "The club that studied America," *The American City*, 8, 624–6; Mrs. Flora Radcliffe Harmon (1912) "Working for a permanent city plan," *The American City*, 6, 217.

25. Ladislas Segoe to Sydney H. Williams, Cincinnati, May 23, 1978 (Tape 2).

26. Richard B. Watrous (1909) "The American Civic Association," *The American City*, 1, 62.

27. "The Civic Conference in St. Louis" (1912) *The American City*, 7; Mitchell, "Los Angeles," p. 149.

28. Helen Marie Dermitt (1912) "The value of co-operation between men and women in public work," *The American City*, 6, 844; Mrs. T. J. Bowlker

(1912) "Women's home-making function applied to the municipality," *The American City,* 6, 869-70.

29. "The old order," p. 805.

30. Mrs. Caroline Bartlett Crane (1912) "Some factors of the street cleaning problem," *The American City,* 6, 895-7.

31. Gale wrote in 1911: "If our actual organization is to keep pace with our dream, then we must realize that no dream can continue indefinitely on volunteer work alone. . . . The work has grown too large for the hands of volunteers . . . if we are to get . . . a fair proportion of efficiency from the splendid, unselfish desire now awake and alive in club women who are civic workers then we must introduce into our work that to which every volunteer work should grow: the co-operation of trained and paid organizers," *The American City,* 11, 92-3; Zona Gale (1913) *Civic Improvement in the Little Towns,* Washington, D.C., American Civic Association.

32. Florence C. Floore (1916) "A state-wide civic campaign," *The American City,* 14 (3), 280; Maud Van Buren (1915) "Why women should study town ordinances and town budgets," *The American City,* 12, 411-12; Maud Van Buren (1915) "Women and town improvement," *The American City,* 12, 104.

33. Chadsey, "A woman chief," p. 872.

34. Harris, *Beyond Her Sphere,* p. 138.

35. For details see Scott, *American City Planning;* and Birch, "Advancing the art and science."

36. Chafe, *The American Woman,* p. 29; Rothman, *Woman's Proper Place,* chapter 3.

37. Edith Elmer Wood (n.d.) "Memorandum for the Committee on Housing," Edith Elmer Wood Collection, Avery Library, Columbia University.

38. "Mrs. H. V. Hubbard, landscape expert," *Boston Transcript,* November 8, 1935; "Mrs. T. K. Hubbard dead in Milton," *Boston Herald,* November 9, 1935; Henry Lefavour, "Theodora K. Hubbard," *Boston Transcript,* November 14, 1935; "Theodora Kimball Hubbard, a biographical minute" (1936) *Landscape Architecture,* XVI, 53.

39. See, for example: Theodora Kimball (1916) "What to read on city planning," *The American City,* 14, 466-7; Theodora Kimball Hubbard, "Survey of city and regional planning in the United States," *City Planning,* I (1925), 7-26; II (1926), 87-116; III (1927), 111-54; IV (1928), 89-153; V (1929), 80-96; VI (1930), 199-225; VIII (1932),113-20.

40. Hubbard and Hubbard, *Our Cities, Today and Tomorrow.*

41. Charlotte Rumbold Papers, Missouri Historical Society, St. Louis, Missouri; "Miss Charlotte Rumbold," *Cleveland Press,* July 6, 1960.

42. Michael Simpson (1969) *People and Planning: A History of the Ohio Planning Conference,* Bay Village, Ohio, Ohio Planning Conference, pp. 9-26, 57.

43. Interview with Evalina Briers, January 17, 1981; Charlotte Rumbold (1932) "Promoting planning in Cleveland," *City Planning,* VIII, 13-15; Charlotte Rumbold (1930) "The Highway Plan for the Cleveland Region," *American Civic Annual,* Washington, D.C., pp. 122-5; Charlotte Rumbold (1931) "Beyond the billboards lies America," *The Clevelander* (June), pp. 15-19.

44. Charlotte Rumbold (1926) "The Ohio State Conference on City Planning," *City Planning*, 2, 51–2.
45. Harlean James (1932) "Public education in city planning," *City Planning*, VIII, 29.
46. U.S. Housing Corporation Records, 1917–1952, the National Archives, Washington, D.C.; Harlean James (1917) *The Building of Cities*, New York, Macmillan; Harlean James (1915) "The Baltimore Flower Market," *The American City*, 8, 390–92; Harlean James (1912) "Baltimore backyards: a study of gardens and garbage," paper presented to the eighth annual meeting of the American Civic Association.
47. Harlean James (1920) "Federal City Planning Bill passed the House," *City Planning*, II, 141–2; Harlean James (1926) "National Capital Park and Planning Commission," *City Planning*, VI, 200; Harlean James (1926) *Land Planning in the United States for the City, State and Nation*, New York, Macmillan, p. 79.
48. Ibid.
49. "ASPO Award Winners Harlean James and Katherine McNamara" (1954) *Planning* (October), p. 57. (Herlihy was awarded the citation posthumously.)
50. Interview with T. E. McCormick, Boston, Massachusetts, July 18, 1980; interview with John T. Howard, July 10, 1980; Lois Kennedy, "People you ought to know," *Boston Herald*, September 13, 1929; Andrew F. Donnell, "State Planning Board puts your home on the map," *Boston Sunday Post*, October 3, 1937; "Elisabeth M. Herlihy," *New York Times*, October 29, 1953.
51. Interviews with T. E. McCormick and John T. Howard.
52. Louis M. Lyons, "Planning is just common sense says the women who heads our first State Planning Board," *Boston Globe*, May 3, 1937. In 1926 Flavel Shurtleff, executive secretary of the AICP, wrote to John Nolen reflecting upon the Herlihy membership: "I may say that the case of Miss Herlihy is the only one where the applicant has not strictly technical qualifications. However, her long experience as Secretary of the City Planning Board of Boston seems ample."
53. Lyons, "Planning is just common sense."
54. Kennedy, "People you ought to know."
55. See, for example, Elisabeth M. Herlihy (1925) "Boston zoning—its first birthday," *City Planning*, I, 81–5; Elisabeth M. Herlihy (1936) "Planning for the Commonwealth in the Massachusetts State Planning Board," *Planning Forum*, 2, 3–7; Elisabeth M. Herlihy (1931) "Boston's Master Highway Plan," *Proceedings*, National Conference on City Planning, pp. 81–4; Elisabeth M. Herlihy (1950) "Everyday planning and zoning problems," *Bulletin of the Massachusetts Federation of Planning Boards*, 10; Elisabeth M. Herlihy, chairman (1938) "The administration of a planning office," *American Planning and Civic Annual*, Washington, D.C., pp. 251–8; Elisabeth M. Herlihy (1930) "Planning for Boston—1630–1930," *City Planning*, VI, 1–13.
56. Mrs. Grace Bartlett (1925) "City planning in Honolulu," *City Planning*, I, 179–80; Raymond W. Blanchard (1932) "Ten years of city planning in

Evansville," *City Planning*, VIII, 77; A. Edmere Cabana (1936) "The Buffalo zoning campaign," *City Planning*, II, 42–7; "Who's who in civic achievement" (1929) *American Civic Annual*, Washington, D.C., pp. 245, 330.

57. Chafe, *The American Woman*.
58. "1937 Institute Roster," *Planners' Journal*, III, 26–8.
59. Interview with John T. Howard.
60. Gordon Stephenson (1979) "Class notes, 1938," *News Department of Urban Studies and Planning*, II, 19.
61. Interview with Jane Rodman, January 25, 1981.
62. Torre, *Women in American Architecture*, p. 117.
63. Chloethiel Woodard Smith and Associated Architects (n.d.) *Architecture, Urban Design, Planning*, Washington, D.C.
64. For further description, see Scott, *American City Planning*.
65. George B. Ford (1933) "A program for roadside improvement," *American Civic Annual*, Washington, D.C., pp. 184–7.
66. Committee on Roadside Improvements (1933) "Roadside improvement," *City Planning*, IX, 181–6.
67. "Our contributors" (1930) *American Civic Annual*, Washington, D.C., p. 399; interview with Mrs. Frances Utter, Vassar Alumnae Association, January 6, 1981.
68. James, "Public education in city planning," p. 31.
69. Flavel Shurtleff (1941) "Report from the American Planning and Civic Association," *Planning Broadcasts* (January), p. 120.
70. Thomas Adams to Edith Elmer Wood, December 1, 1928, Edith Elmer Wood Collection, Avery Library, Columbia University.
71. Edith Elmer Wood (1929) "Slums and the city plan," *The American City*, XLI, 93.
72. E. L. Birch (1980) "Radburn and the American Planning Movement: the persistence of an idea," *Journal of the American Planning Association*, 46, 424–39.
73. "Delegate List," National Association of Housing Officials, Baltimore, October 1934, Edith Elmer Wood Collection, Avery Library, Columbia University.
74. For an excellent discussion of Bauer's early housing career, see M. S. Cole (1975) "Catherine Bauer and the public housing movement: 1926–1937," Ph.D. dissertation, George Washington University.
75. Susan Cole (1980) "Catherine Krause Bauer," in B. Sicherman and C. H. Green, *Notable American Women*, Cambridge, Massachusetts: Harvard, pp. 66–8.
76. Sara White, "Land ownership to pose problem," *Boston Traveler*, June 17, 1943, p. 4; Catherine Bauer, "The dreary deadlock of public housing," *Architectural Forum*, 48 (May); Commission on National Goals (1960) *Goals for Americans*, Englewood Cliffs, New Jersey: Prentice-Hall; "Redevelopment: a misfit in the fifties," in Coleman Woodbury, ed. (1953) *The Future of Cities and Urban Redevelopment*, Chicago, University of Chicago Press; (1950) "The increasing social responsibilities of the city planners,"

Proceedings American Institute of Planners and (1950) *Institute of Professional Town Planners Joint Meeting*; (1961) "The belated challenge and changing role of the physical planners" (keynote address, Annual AIP Conference, 1961), *Proceedings*, Washington, D.C., 1962, pp. 2–13.

77. American Institute of Planners (1961) *Membership Roster*, Washington, D.C.

78. Harris, *Beyond Her Sphere*, pp. 150–56.

79. American Institute of Planners (1943) "Statement of the ownership," *Journal of the American Institute of Planners*, IX, inside cover; American Society of Planning Officials, "Minutes," 1943, Walter Blacher Papers, Olin Library, Cornell University.

80. "Education" (1946) *Planning*, XII, 49; John A. Parker, "Memorandum to Eugenie Birch," July 18, 1980; interview with John T. Howard.

81. American Institute of Planners (1951) *Handbook and Roster*, Washington, D.C., p. 2ff.; Epstein, *Women's Place*, pp. 200–201.

82. U.S. Department of Labor, Women's Bureau (1948) *The Outlook for Women in Architecture and Engineering*, Washington, D.C., U.S. Government Printing Office, pp. 5–1, 5–7. In 1970 the Women's Bureau published an updated brochure, *Why Not Be an Urban Planner?*, picturing female professionals participating in a wide variety of specialties.

83. Interview with Carol J. Thomas, October 17, 1980; Joan Millman, "The lady does planning," *Boston Sunday Herald Traveler*, February 6, 1972.

84. Interview with Dorothy Muncy, January 29, 1981.

85. Jane Jacobs (1961) *The Death and Life of Great American Cities*, New York, Random House.

86. Ibid; John E. Zuccotti (1974) "How does Jane Jacobs rate today?," *Planning* (June), pp. 23–7.

87. Harris, *Beyond Her Sphere*, p. 182.

88. Jacqueline Leavitt (1978) "Women in planning: do the numbers really matter?," unpublished paper, Division of Urban Planning, Columbia School of Architecture and Planning, January, p. 8.

89. Karen Hapgood (1971) *Women in Planning: A Report on Their Status in Public Planning Agencies*, Chicago, American Society of Planning Officials, p. 8.

90. Leavitt, "Women in planning," pp. 8–9.

91. Constance Lieder (1974) "Women in planning: guidelines to be monitored this year," *AIP Newsletter* (January), p. 34.

92. Karen E. Hapgood and Judith Getzels (1974) *Planning, Women and Change*, Chicago: American Society of Planning Officials.

93. Joel Werth and Mary Deal (1980) *Planning and Women: A Competition for Projects*, Chicago, American Planning Association.

INDEX